The Growth of Knowledge

The Growth of Knowledge

Readings on Organization and Retrieval of Information

Edited by Manfred Kochen

Mental Health Research Institute
University of Michigan

John Wiley & Sons, Inc.   New York · London · Sydney

Contributors

Austin, Charles J.
 Information Systems Division
 National Library of Medicine
 Bethesda, Maryland

Bush, Vannevar
 Massachusetts Institute of
 Technology
 Cambridge, Massachusetts
 Formerly:
 Office of Scientific Research
 and Development
 Washington, D.C.

Carnap, Rudolf
 Department of Philosophy
 University of California
 Los Angeles, California
 Formerly:
 Department of Philosophy
 University of Chicago
 Chicago, Illinois

Cummings, Martin M.
 National Library of Medicine
 Bethesda, Maryland

Davis, Watson
 Science Services, Inc.
 Washington, D.C.

Editorial Staff
 Scientific Research
 A McGraw-Hill Publication
 New York, New York

Flood, Merrill M.
 Mental Health Research Institute
 University of Michigan
 Ann Arbor, Michigan

Harman, R. Joyce
 Lincoln Laboratory, MIT
 Lexington, Massachusetts

Karel, Leonard
 Bibliographic Services Division
 National Library of Medicine
 Bethesda, Maryland

Kasher, Asa
 Mathematics Department
 Bar-Ilan University
 Ramat Gan, Israel

Keen, E. M.
 Department of Computer Science
 Cornell University
 Ithaca, New York
 Formerly:
 Aslib Project
 Cranfield, England

King, Gilbert W.
 Aerospace Corporation
 Los Angeles, California
 Formerly:
 IBM Research Center
 Yorktown Heights, New York

Knox, William T.
 McGraw-Hill Book Company
 New York, New York
 Formerly:
 President's Office of Science and
 Technology
 Washington, D.C.

Kochen, Manfred
Mental Health Research Institute
University of Michigan
Ann Arbor, Michigan
Formerly:
IBM Research Center
Yorktown Heights, New York

Lesk, M.
Division of Engineering
Harvard University
Cambridge, Massachusetts

Luhn, Hans P. (1896–1964)
Inventor, Pioneer in Information
Retrieval, Engineer; IBM

MacKay, D. M.
Department of Communication
University of Keele
Keele, Staffordshire, England

Maron, M. E.
School of Library Science
University of California
Berkeley, California
Formerly:
Computer Sciences Department
The RAND Corporation
Santa Monica, California

Overhage, Carl F. J.
Engineering School
Massachusetts Institute of
Technology
Cambridge, Massachusetts

Parkinson, Cyril N.
Les Caches House
St. Martin's Guernsey
Channel Islands
Formerly:
Raffles Professor of History
University of Malaya
Pantai Valley, Kuala Lumpur

Price, Derek J. de Solla
History of Science Department
Yale University
New Haven, Connecticut

Salton, G.
Department of Computer Science
Cornell University
Ithaca, New York
Formerly:
Computation Center
Harvard University
Cambridge, Massachusetts

Samuel, Arthur L.
Department of Computer Science
Stanford University
Stanford, California
Formerly:
IBM Research Center
Yorktown Heights, New York

Schmitt, Otto H.
Department of Biophysics
University of Minnesota
Minneapolis, Minnesota

Scriven, M.
Department of History and
Philosophy of Science
University of Indiana
Bloomington, Indiana

Simmons, Robert F.
Systems Development Corporation
Santa Monica, California

Swets, John A.
Bolt, Beranek and Newman, Inc.
Cambridge, Massachusetts
Formerly:
Psychology Department
Massachusetts Institute of
Technology
Cambridge, Massachusetts

Uhr, L.
Department of Computer Science
University of Wisconsin
Madison, Wisconsin
Formerly:
Mental Health Institute
University of Michigan
Ann Arbor, Michigan

Van Doren, Charles L.
*The Institute for Philosophical
Research
Chicago, Illinois*

Weinberg, Alvin M.
*Oak Ridge National Laboratory
Oak Ridge, Tennessee
Formerly:
President's Science Advisory
Committee*

Weiss, Paul A.
*Rockefeller University
Departmental Biology
New York, N.Y.*

Wells, Herbert G. (1866–1946)
*British Historian, Novelist, General
Scientist, Scholar, Innovator,
Master of Synthesis*

Preface

This book is intended for the reader who wishes to share some exciting ideas concerning the dynamics of knowledge and the development of information technologies. It differs from other books about information retrieval in that it stresses ideas rather than accomplishments. It invites the reader to pay as much attention to the goals and the choice of problems for current research and development in information technologies as has been paid to the results and claims.

Who among us has not occasionally been overwhelmed, on using a large library, by the feeling that it might contain much that could really make a difference to us, if we could only locate and absorb it conveniently? The intelligent nonspecialist may well be concerned that growing knowledge is passing him by, that he is no longer keeping pace with the numerous, seemingly unrelated new findings, which he needs to know to cope most effectively with modern life. Many of us have thought about what might be done. Some of us saw in computers a new resource of possible value in this regard.

The problem of organizing information has recently become one of great concern to government and industry. More than 600 projects are listed in the National Science Foundation's annual compendium of summaries, *Current Research in Scientific Documentation, No. 14.* Most of these are government-supported. The data-processing industry looks for its next large market among those who can be aided by computers in improving the management of their increasingly complex organizations and particularly in the use of the written records that are necessary to run these organizations.

Several universities have recently established programs in "information science"; others have included information-retrieval courses in departments called "computer science" or "communication science." This selection of readings originated in a graduate-level seminar on information-retrieval systems theory which I taught in the Communication Sciences Department at the University of Michigan. I compiled a 175-item bibliography of books and papers; about 50 of these items were chosen by the students for a presentation and a critical discussion in class. The selections included in this book are based, in part, on the critical evauation and interests of the students in this seminar.

Some of the papers and excerpts included here proved to be very difficult to obtain, even in the excellent library community at the University of Michigan. This is one reason for compiling them into a book. If the sample of students in my seminar is representative of the next generation of leaders in this field, and if such a book would have greatly facilitated their access to this part of the literature, then it should provide convenient access for a larger community of students and scholars with similar interests and backgrounds.

This book is intended for two audiences. First, it is intended for students at all levels who are interested in the mechanisms behind the growth, organization, and use of knowledge as a natural phenomenon. This includes students interested in the impact of technology on these natural information processes, as well as those students likely to accomplish the technological innovations that may drastically alter these processes. It also includes students with interests outside science or engineering who feel the need to critically appreciate the ideas and accomplishments in this field as part of their general, cultural background.

Familiarity with mathematics, computer lore, engineering, or science, though helpful, is not a prerequisite for the profitable use of this book. Although a few selections can be fully appreciated only by the college graduate or the exceptional high-school graduate, the majority of the selections should be easily intelligible to anyone with a normal high-school education. Whether the central message of these selections is recognized depends more on the imaginativeness with which this subject is approached than on formal education.

This book is also intended for use by professional practitioners and researchers in education, librarianship, documentation, the behavioral sciences, law, medicine, and administration. This audience includes, above all, every curious, intelligent, and responsible person, when not acting in the role of a specialist. The book may also be of some service to physical and biological scientists, to scholars in the humanities and history, and to those interested in technology, either as contributors to the development or as users of improved information-retrieval services. It is not intended to serve information-retrieval specialists, engineers, or programmers who are concerned solely with the computerization of information retrieval, or operations researchers who are concerned with library automation for its own sake.

The aim of this book is to provide such a mixed audience with a coherent compilation of articles that are either of lasting value or that give a snapshot of the quality, excitement, and controversy of current, highly dynamic activity in information retrieval. This book is meant to be conveniently usable in the following ways: (1) as a source of stimulation and guidance for fresh direction, ideas, viewpoints, historical perspective, and judgment; (2) as a means of attracting new creative talent to advance the relevant arts and sciences; (3) and as a ready reference in the preparation of papers, proposals, speeches, and criticisms, or in teaching.

Some leading specialists in this field feel that information retrieval is no longer concept-limited, that there have been significant accomplishments, that attracting high-level, creative talent or searching for fresh and fundamental directions and ideas is no longer the most critical need. There are critics who feel that little of solid practical or scientific merit has been accomplished, that the general quality and intellectual level of research in information retrieval is low, that future efforts are in dire need of redirection and problem definition. The position taken in this book, although aligned neither with that of the extreme enthusiast nor with that of the extreme critic, veers more toward that of the critic. The reader who does not share this view can obtain a better acquaintance with the positive accomplishments in information retrieval from the excellent recent compendium, *Annual Review of Information Science and Technology, Volume 1,* Carlos Cuadra, editor.*

If, after taking an accurate pulse of the current state of creative technical activity in information retrieval by critically studying the specialized literature, the reader agrees that there is need for attracting fresh ideas and new creative talent into this area, he will be better able to appreciate the present selection of readings. Hence this book stresses ideas more than concrete results, although at least two papers describe accomplishments that rank among the best in the field.

The selections offered here support a definite position. The issue is whether or not research and development should continue to proceed solely in the direction of information-dispensing systems. By this we mean the providing of efficient procedures for dispensing pertinent and only pertinent information in immediate response to queries by researchers at the frontiers of their specialty. The stand taken here is to suggest an alternative goal for information-retrieval systems which deserves greater priority than the dispensing of information. This alternative is to assimilate and weld newly generated knowledge into a coherent overall image at sufficient speed, so as to counteract the tendency of knowledge to scatter centrifugally into isolated fragments; to impart understanding rather than dispense information; and to aim to serve primarily the interested nonspecialist and only secondarily the skilled specialist. Whereas the keyword of

* John Wiley and Sons, New York, 1966.

most enterprises and projects in information retrieval is *access*, the keywords proposed here as an alternative are *evaluation* and *synthesis*.

This position is important. It needs to be explicitly stated and elaborated. It may well provide the urgently needed direction for the concentration of our presently scattered resources in this area to obtain a greater effect. It may, indeed, express what is already an undercurrent of implicit agreement and understanding among some key thinkers in this area. It is, nonetheless, neither a popular view, nor one that is well understood or explicitly recognized.

There seems to be no other single document that meets these needs. To achieve its aim, this book is organized into three parts. Part One contains articles that elaborate on the great central idea of an "encyclopedia system," which was first strongly espoused by H. G. Wells. This idea is the main theme running through the remainder of the book. Also included in Part One are, by contrast, some of the numerous ideas that characterize the mainstream of current thought on information retrieval. Part Two brings together articles that are concerned with the more scientific foundations for the realization of an encyclopedic information-retrieval system. They sample our current "know-what" underlying what H. G. Wells called constructive sociology. Also included, because of what they could teach information-retrieval system planners about the way in which nature may embody the same functions, are articles on the physiology and biochemistry of information storage and retrieval. Part Three sketches the current state of "know-how" underlying constructive sociology. These articles describe the technological resources that could be brought to bear on the building of an encyclopedic information-retrieval system.

To many, the connection between such seemingly diverse papers as "Parkinson's Law," the article by Carnap, and that by O. Schmitt may appear remote. The value of any of these three articles to anyone interested in information retrieval may not be immediately apparent. Nor will the controversial issues of Carnap's positivistic philosophy or of some modern biochemical theories of memory be noticeable to those who do not have some training in these fields. The two dozen selections in the book were obviously written by authors who have different goals, who use different methods to attain these goals, and who have different audiences in mind. The more profound connections among all these authors may not be obvious to any but the most perceptive and imaginative minds. The various papers do not speak for themselves about what they have in common. Although I have attempted in the connecting passages to suggest the unifying basis, I do not claim that a common framework has here been firmly established. These are, however, the previously mentioned advantages of conveniently assembling all these interesting and important articles in one volume.

Special acknowledgment is due to H. G. Bohnert, who first introduced me to the book by H. G. Wells and with whom I have had some stimulating discussions about digital encyclopedia systems. The idea of a "digital encyclopedia system" or "tutorial information system" had occurred to me prior to my acquaintance with Wells in my search for a sound, basic direction for research in information retrieval. The advice of colleagues, such as P. Baxendale, H. P. Edmundson, M. M. Flood, R. Lindsay, M. E Maron, J. Miller, J. Platt, G. Salton, R. Simmons, and L. Uhr, has influenced this book, although many of the views expressed here are contrary to theirs. I am particularly grateful to L. Uhr for his interest and help. I also wish to thank R. Tagliacozzo for her valuable help in locating the most appropriate selections and B. Segur for his careful and critical reading of the entire manuscript. Special thanks are due to my wife for her valuable help in preparing it for publication. I also thank the various publishers for granting permission to reprint the articles that appear in this book.

MANFRED KOCHEN

Ann Arbor, Michigan
January 1967

Contents

PART THREE

Introduction

A seven-year-old child asks how an amphibian breathes. A space-suit designer needs to know the maximum and minimum temperature that the space-suit would attain at the surface of the moon at any time and spot. Providing suitable answers to these queries are services expected of information-retrieval (IR) systems. It is mostly the traditional library and the modern information center that provide information-retrieval services today. Neither would always provide the most satisfactory answer to the kind of question posed by either the seven-year-old or the space-suit designer.

An engineer, needing a high-intensity light source, wishes to know how a laser works. His query has more in common with that of the seven-year-old than with that of the space-suit designer. Both the engineer and the seven-year-old wish to satisfy their curiosity and to increase their understanding at a level commensurate with their ability to comprehend. The engineer will be as little satisfied by references to gas lasers, relay lasers, or injection lasers as the child would be by references to gills or lungs.

A historian's quest for the exact year of Homer's birth has more in common with the space designer's query than with that of the seven-year-old. Neither of them seeks to modify significantly his image of an aspect of the world; they both seek a reasonably well-specified isolated datum. Both might be satisfied by pairs of numbers on appropriate scales.

The responses of an information-retrieval system to such queries as the four above may take many forms. An ideal form of the response to the seven-year-old's query might be a television tape that describes, at a level of a seven-year-old, how amphibians breathe. The person to whom the query is posed would be able to display the answer on a readily available television set, which is furnished with a special tape reader, within at most a few minutes after the query is first expressed. The tape for a seven-year-old would differ from the tape for a ten-year-old asking the same question. Even if it were possible to catalog and use an immense library of such tapes in this way, it would still not be possible to anticipate all queries. Furthermore, the child should be allowed to interrupt the showing with his questions. He should be able to elicit from the IR system a response that may be composed of several prerecorded fragments. It may give the child a bird's-eye view, or it may go into as much detail as the child's curiosity demands.

An ideal response to the space-suit designer's query might be a documented statement that gives the required maximum and minimum temperatures, as well as the pertinent references to documents on which the validity of these answers is based. The designer may wish to examine the documents. He may need photocopies or displays of the text on a cathode-ray tube or on the translucent screen of a microfilm or similar projector. He would need these with minimum delay and without the inconvenience of going to a library or to a special station with equipment. He will be irked if he has to wade through many pages of irrelevant or distracting material. He will be even more annoyed if, years later, he discovers the prior existence of a document with a more accurate measurement than any given him by his IR system. He is not interested in undocumented information.

Servicing the child's question is the task of what we shall call an encyclopedic or tutorial information system. To illustrate the distinction between a tutorial information system—the need for which this book advocates—and what is now generally understood by an information-retrieval system, let us consider a practical question asked not by the child but by his mother. She seeks guidance about, "flu shots." She wants more guidance than is usually obtained from the opinions of friends or the frequently not much more thoughtful opinions of doctors. Were she to compile a collection of articles pertinent to the topic—even if she could do this rapidly, conveniently, without obvious irrelevancies, and without important omissions—she might well be faced with several dozen more or less technical articles. Even if she tried to read them all, which is unlikely, some of them would be immediately recognized by her as being beyond her capacity or interest. Of the remainder, she might possibly misunderstand a significant fraction without realizing this. Of the remaining dozen papers, the message of which would be understood, perhaps half might argue *for* preventive influenza inoculations, the other half *against*. The mother does not really want to study all the pros and cons. She would like help in making an intelligent decision, as a voter might like help in making an intelligent decision when casting his vote. She would most of all appreciate a thoughtful author's compilation of all the pros and cons, perhaps recommending a carefully and clearly reasoned position. She may accept this recommendation not because of the author's authority, but because he *taught her just what she needs to know* to make the decision. The final decision and responsibility is hers, not the author's. The author's task has been to sift, compile, evaluate, screen, combine, and tie together into a teachable, coherent whole the previously bewildering mass of detailed facts and diverging opinions. The need of a doctor for a good clinical picture of effects and side effects of a new drug for a certain type of cancer, the need of a lawyer to understand the use of the word "obvious" in patents, and the needs of a legislature in seeking to comprehend the attitude of

Southern whites toward school integration are all best served by this type of information-retrieval system.

Servicing the space-suit designer's question is the task of what we shall call an information-dispensing system. Its function is to store and retrieve references to documents, to retrieve documents themselves, and to extract answers from relevant documents. Nearly all current efforts are directed toward developing this type of information-retrieval system. There is little doubt that such a system serves many important needs. The simplest, yet most frequent use to which it is likely to be put is that of document recall. Most of the requests received by a reference librarian involve determining the presence and precise location of a document which the user knows to exist; either he has incomplete or erroneous bibliographic data or is unacquainted with the library's cataloging or filing procedures. Most requests serviced by an information center entail the use of lengthy topical bibliographies, in some cases annotated. Extraction, by computer, of an answer such as that required by the space-suit designer from the machine-readable text of documents in such a bibliography is still a long-range goal of research in this direction being vigorously pursued by creative investigators.

But is this goal worthy of *all* the resources, or even of the larger part of the resources allotted to information-retrieval? If, after having read this book, the reader has gained better grounds for his stand on this issue, or at least has become more aware of the issue than he was before, the book will have served its main purpose. If an occasional reader who can influence the allocation of resources in this area is swayed by the arguments presented here toward an increased emphasis on encyclopedic systems, a useful impact will have been made.

In planning, designing, building, maintaining, and using an IR system there are so many diverse problems that it is difficult to conceive of information-retrieval as a single topic. There are problems in the physics and chemistry underlying photographic, photochromic, thermoplastic, and holographic technologies for efficient microform image storage and transport. High-capacity, high read/write-rate magnetic or photoscopic stores for digital data present special problems in engineering, chemistry, and physics. High-intensity light sources and display techniques entail difficult problems in optics. Pneumatic or other means of transporting microforms or hard copies present challenging problems in mechanical engineering. The achievement of electronically controlled, high-speed high-quality multifont printers and low-cost yet sophisticated input facilities for a time-shared computer system presents formidable problems of electrical engineering. Low-cost, high-speed, high-capacity buffers and less expensive modulator-demodulator subsets for high-speed data channels all involve solvable engineering problems. Far more difficult are the linguistic and logical problems in assigning elements of an indexing/query-language to stored documents and relating them to anticipated queries.

Most of these problems are common to both encyclopedic and information-dispensing systems. Other formidable problems are unique to each of the two systems. For an information-dispensing system to be really useful to the researcher at the frontier of his specialty, it should not only contain index terms shortly after they have proved to be significant, but should, indeed, anticipate such terms. "Categorical algebra," for example, should now, in 1966, be included in the subject-authority list of a good cataloging system by a "cataloger" who is sufficiently sensitive to significant trends and has sufficient understanding and critical judgment, as well as up-to-the-month current awareness of the literature, to predict the pioneering and bandwagon effects of the paper by McLane and the book by Freyd on this subject. His prediction may, of course, be wrong, as may his judgment. But his making the prediction, wrong or right, may have some influence on the growth of the subject. Moreover, he must relate the index term "categorical algebra" to enough other terms so as to make its existence known to contemporary mathematicians who are working on this or related topics and to others who are groping for knowledge that falls under this topic, but who are all unaware that such a topic is emerging as a new subfield. Although the expert researcher is more likely to be aware of these trends at the frontier of his specialty than any cataloger could be, he feels uneasy about the possibly enormous volume of documented data in his specialty that he might need to know if he knew it existed. He is not concerned with the dozen or so key documents that might account for more than half of his interest; he is concerned about the thousands of documents which, *together*, account for the other part of his more marginal interests. He is also concerned about being able to recall accurately (without miss), precisely (without extraneous findings), and efficiently (quickly, conveniently) documented data with which he does not want to clutter and overburden his own memory but which he wants to file in a memory external to his own for ready recall when needed, so that he must only memorize the fact of their existence when he first learns of these data.

To be useful to the "average" person, an encyclopedic system must be enormously flexible and adaptable to patterns of use and to the growth of our collective understanding and wisdom, much more so than our present educational system. It must play an active rather than an entirely passive part in the man–IR system relation. It must transform knowledge into understanding not only in the way in which an individual scholar builds for himself a coherent organized image from and about what he knows, but also in the way in which a community of scholars evolve a theory. Machines would, of course, play only a part in such an encyclopedic system. It is still the society of scholars who have the responsibility for such a synthesis, as well as for representing it in the variety of forms suitable for effective communication, inspiration, and so on. The key problem is how to organize such a society of scholars. What roles should various types of machine assistance play?

There are other types of IR systems besides what we have called the encyclopedic and the information-dispensing systems, although these two might reflect the opposite poles of a spectrum. The first system aims at the integration of knowledge, at imparting understanding to practitioners of all kinds. The second system aims at collecting the isolated fragments of knowledge and channeling them to where they are needed when they are needed, as messages in a giant switching net would connect authors—past and present—to their audiences. Few papers in the literature contain clear formulations of the key problems in the attempt to understand the functioning of such information-retrieval systems; even fewer provide definite solutions. Even so, most of the literature is addressed toward novel techniques which are useful in building information-dispensing systems. The little literature there is on encyclopedic systems is mostly older and at the idea-level in the form of eloquent verbal discourse rather than precise definitions of problems, solutions, or descriptions of accomplishments. Nevertheless, the most important half of the papers in this book are in the latter category: on the encyclopedia system idea.

The selections presented here are primarily articles that describe plans and speculations rather than definite results and accomplishments. For many readers who are stimulated by far-reaching ideas expressed in non-technical language, philosophical speculation has a more positive connotation than it does for technical specialists.

This collection of readings invites the reader to share an adventure in ideas. As such it may prove more stimulating to many than reports of statistical data, theorems, and algorithms of moderate importance.

PART ONE

Directions for Information-Retrieval Research

We consider it significant to divide the ideas and problems of information retrieval into two major and distinct categories. The first revolves about the "encyclopedic idea." The second deals with "libraries of the future" or "information dispensing."

The idea of encyclopedic systems as a reasonable goal for IR systems development is not new. More effort has been expended in eloquent elaboration of the idea than in solid scientific research to realize this goal. The imperative need for systems of the encyclopedia type has been stressed in the speculative literature with compelling force. On the other hand, the large effort toward realizing practical systems—if it had any direction at all—was aimed toward the other class, "information-dispensing" systems. Actually, in much of the constructive effort on the implementation side there has been manifest the need for a clear, reasonable direction. Paradoxically, the "encyclopedia idea" as a goal was either totally unknown to those in search of direction or deliberately ignored, grossly misunderstood, or perhaps even violently opposed.

The various, scattered ideas for information-dispensing systems, automated information centers, and libraries of the future have led more to clever innovation and construction than to clearly stated, reasonable goals for *what* information-retrieval systems to build. They leave us today with an impressive know-how but with considerable confusion about the applications merited by it.

The first half of Part One deals with papers that elaborate a worthwhile[1] goal for IR systems development. This goal could provide direction for the large number of clever, well-trained people interested in research and development in information-retrieval who are in need of enterprises worthy of their best. In a way, this section traces the historical development of the encyclopedia system idea from H. G. Wells to the Weinberg report.

The second half of Part One samples a few of the major disparate ideas toward libraries and information centers of the future that have exerted considerable influence during the past five years and have led to spectacular advances in technology and systems know-how.

[1] The worthwhileness of this idea—especially considering the fears of centralized, authoritarian control and bureaucracy that it arouses—is subject to debate, and requires discussion and elaboration beyond the scope of this book.

PART ONE

A. The Encyclopedia System Idea

This idea seems to have been first expounded in a serious way by that great integrative thinker, H. G. Wells, who was concerned with the enormous disparity between mankind's growing physical strength (because of power-amplifying technology) and mankind's collective wisdom to put this power to use wisely. This imaginative author-historian conceived of a way to bring the collective wisdom to bear on the everyday management of our lives. He foresaw the potentialities of the relevant technology of his day—1937—which was microfilm. He envisaged a system—not unlike the original conception of the university—in which a board of editors would screen, sift, commission works of synthesis, and organize and disseminate all of the world's knowledge so as to reflect, in coherent, maximally useful form, mankind's total image of itself and its environment.

The few authors who have written on this idea seem to have been unaware of what Wells considered the major idea in his life. Even O. Neurath,[1] who tried to implement a closely related idea on an ambitious scale, in collaboration with some of the world's leading integrative thinkers, did not once cite Wells' *World Brain*. Perhaps it was the choice of the title for Wells' book; perhaps the association in the readers' minds of what he called "World Encyclopedia" with conventional encyclopedias; perhaps it was the untimeliness of Wells' idea. Today, we have, in addition to power-amplifying technology, intelligence-amplifying technology and thus the potential means to realize Wells' dream of narrowing the gap.

The central idea of an encyclopedic system reappears—discovered apparently independently—in the classic, pioneering paper of V. Bush. Here the idea is coupled with boldly imaginative speculations about computer technology, which was then—in 1947—just beginning. He not only foresaw its potential but also postulated a novel idea for storing information items in relation to all other items. He called this brilliant conception the memex, and it is still an elusive target for computer science and technology. Note, for example, the beginning of Section VIII in Bush's article; "Wholly new forms of encyclopedias will appear . . . ." In assessing such predic-

---

[1] Neurath, Otto, "Unified Science as Encyclopedia Integration," in *International Encyclopedia of Unified Science*, Vol. 1, No. 1. Chicago: The University of Chicago Press, 1947.

tions, we would do well to heed Licklider's warning[2] about our universal tendency to overestimate what can be done in one year and to underestimate what can be done in ten.

A variant of the encyclopedia system idea appears again—also arrived at independently—in the famous Weinberg report.[3] This thoughtful report had greater influence in intellectual circles than among the innovators of information technology. Note that the central theme, in PART 2B of the Weinberg report, stresses the information process as being part and parcel of the process of discovery and innovation; it asserts that the essence of the information problem is to maintain knowledge as a viable unity and that the basic information processes are those of sifting, reviewing, and synthesizing information. In the spirit of this report we would think no more seriously of a fully automatic information-retrieval system than we would think of a discovery machine. In the words of the report—the title of Part 32—"Mechanization Can Become Important But Not All-Important."

Among the few authors who were cognizant of Wells' book and were determined to develop the idea further was W. Davis. Even prior to Wells, he translated his own ideas into practice by founding and directing the Science Service (an institution for the popularization of science) in 1921. One of his most recent papers presents the major theme which recurs throughout his writings and which, like Wells' book, should exert a greater impact than it seems to have done to date.

Among those who were groping for the encyclopedia system idea without explicitly building on the prior ideas of Wells is de Grazia. He proposed the "Universal Reference System" and edited the *American Behavioral Scientist*. The September 1962 issue of this journal was devoted entirely to encyclopedism, without a single reference to Wells' *World Brain*. It did, however, contain a pellucid article on the encyclopedia idea, by van Doren, which is reprinted here, because it describes in more detail the objectives of an ideal encyclopedia in contrast to lower-priority objectives.

[2] Licklider, J. C. R., *Libraries of the Future*, M.I.T. Press, Cambridge, Mass., 1965.
[3] A variety of reports from similar government task forces are described in the most recent one, *Recommendations for National Document Handling Systems in Science and Technology*, by the Committee on Scientific and Technical Information (COSATI) of the Federal Council for Science and Technology (AD 624 560, November 1965).

World Encyclopaedia[1]

by H. G. Wells

Most of the lectures that are given in this place to this audience are delivered by men of very special knowledge. They come here to tell you something you did not know before. But tonight I doubt if I shall tell you anything that is not already quite familiar to you. I am here not to impart facts but to make certain suggestions. And there is no other audience in the world to which I would make these suggestions more willingly and more hopefully than I do to you.

My particular line of country has always been generalization and synthesis. I dislike isolated events and disconnected details. I really hate statements, views, prejudices and beliefs that jump at you suddenly out of mid-air. I like my world as coherent and consistent as possible. So far at any rate my temperament is that of a scientific man. And that is why I have spent a few score thousand hours of my particular allotment of vitality in making outlines of history, short histories of the world, general accounts of the science of life, attempts to bring economic, financial and social life into one conspectus and even, still more desperate, struggles to estimate the possible consequences of this or that set of operating causes upon the future of mankind. All these attempts had profound and conspicuous faults and weaknesses; even my friends are apt to mention them with an apologetic smile; presumptuous and preposterous they were, I admit, but I look back upon them, completely unabashed.

Somebody had to break the ice. Somebody had to try out such summaries on the general mind. My reply to the superior critic has always been—forgive me—"Damn you, *do it better.*"

The least satisfactory thing about these experiments of mine, so far as I am concerned, is that they did not at once provoke the learned and competent to produce superior substitutes. And in view of the number of able and distinguished people we have in the world professing and teaching economic, sociological, financial science, and the admittedly unsatisfactory nature of the world's financial, economic and political affairs, it is to me an immensely disconcerting fact that the *Work, Wealth and Happiness of Mankind* which was first published in 1932 remains—practically uncriticized, unstudied and largely unread—the only attempt to bring human ecology into one correlated survey.

Well, I mention this experimental work now in order that you should not think I am throwing casually formed ideas before you tonight. I am bringing you my best. The thoughts I am setting out here have troubled my mind for years, and my ideas have been slowly gathering definition throughout these experiments and experiences. They have interwoven more and more intimately with other solicitudes of a more general nature in which I feel fairly certain of meeting your understanding and sympathy.

I doubt if there is anybody here to-

SOURCE: *World Brain*. Garden City, New York: Doubleday, Doran & Co., Inc., 1938, pp. 3–35.

[1] Read at the Royal Institution of Great Britain Weekly Evening Meeting, Friday, November 20, 1936.

night who has not given a certain amount of anxious thought to the conspicuous ineffectiveness of modern knowledge and—how shall I call it?—trained and studied thought in contemporary affairs. And I think that is mainly in the troubled years since 1914 that the world of cultivated, learned and scientific people of which you are so representative, has become conscious of this ineffectiveness. Before that time, or to be more precise before 1909 or 1910, the world, our world as we older ones recall it, was living in a state of confidence, of established values, of assured security, which is already becoming now almost incredible. We had no suspicion then how much that apparent security had been undermined by science, invention and sceptical inquiry. Most of us carried on into the War, and even right through the War, under the inertia of the accepted beliefs to which we had been born. We felt that the sort of history that we were used to was still going on, and we hardly realized at all that the War was a new sort of thing, not like the old wars, that the old traditions of strategy were disastrously out of date, and that the old pattern of settling up after a war could only lead to such a thickening tangle of evil consequences as we contemplate today. We know better now. Wiser after the events as we all are, few of us now fail to appreciate the stupendous ignorance, the almost total lack of grasp of social and economic realities, the short views, the shallowness of mind, that characterized the treaty-making of 1919 and 1920. I suppose Mr. Maynard Keynes was one of the first to open our eyes to this world-wide intellectual insufficiency. What his book, *The Economic Consequences of the Peace,* practically said to the world was this: *These people, these politicians, these statesmen, these directive people who are in authority over us, know scarcely anything about the business they have in hand. Nobody knows very much, but the important thing to realize is that they do not even know what is to be known. They arrange so and so, and so and so must ensue and they cannot or will not see that so and so must ensue. They are so unaccustomed to competent thought, so ignorant that there is knowledge and of what knowledge is, that they do not understand that it matters.*

The same terrifying sense of insufficient mental equipment was dawning upon some of us who watched the birth of the League of Nations. Reluctantly and with something like horror, we realized that these people who were, they imagined, turning over a new page and beginning a fresh chapter in human history, knew collectively hardly anything about the formative forces of history. Collectively, I say. Altogether they had a very considerable amount of knowledge, uncoordinated bits of quite good knowledge, some about this period and some about that, but they had no common understanding whatever of the processes in which they were obliged to mingle and interfere. Possibly all the knowledge and all the directive ideas needed to establish a wise and stable settlement of the world's affairs in 1919 existed in bits and fragments, here and there, but practically nothing had been assembled, practically nothing had been thought out, practically nothing had been done to draw that knowledge and these ideas together into a comprehensive conception of the world. I put it to you that the Peace Conference at Versailles did not use anything but a very small fraction of the political and economic wisdom that already existed in human brains at that time. And I put it to you as rational creatures that if usage had not chilled our apprehension to this state of affairs, we should regard this as fantastically absurd.

And if I might attempt a sweeping generalization about the general course of human history in the eighteen years that have followed the War, I believe I should have you with me if I described it as a series of flounderings, violent ill-directed mass-movements, slack drifting here and convulsive action there. We talk about the dignity of history. It is a bookish phrase for which I have the extremest disrespect. There is no dignity yet in human history. It would be pure comedy, if it were not so often tragic, so frequently dismal, generally dishonourable and occasionally quite horrible. And it is so largely tragic because the creature really is intelligent, can feel finely and acutely, expresses itself poignantly in art, music and literature, and—this is what I am driving at —impotently knows better.

Consider only the case of America during this recent period. America when all is said and done, is one of the most intelligently *aware* communities in the world. Quite a number of people over there seem almost to know what is happening to them. Remember first the phase of fatuous self-sufficiency, the period of unprecedented prosperity, the bloom, the crisis, the slump and the dismay. And then appeared the new President, Franklin Roosevelt, and from the point of view of the present discussion he is one of the most interesting figures in all history. Because he really did make an appeal for such knowledge and understanding as existed to come to his aid. America in an astounding state of meekness was ready to be told and shown. There were the universities, great schools, galaxies of authorities, learned men, experts, teachers, gowned, adorned and splendid. Out of this knowledge mass there have since come many very trenchant criticisms of the President's mistakes. But at the time this—what shall I call it—this higher brain, this cerebrum, this grey matter of America was so entirely uncoordinated that it had nothing really comprehensive, searching, thought-out and trustworthy for him to go upon. The President had to experiment and attempt this and that, he turned from one promising adviser to another, because there was nothing ready for him. He did not pretend to be a divinity. He was a politician—of exceptional goodwill. He was none of your dictator gods. He showed himself extremely open and receptive for the organized information and guidance . . . *that wasn't there.*

And it isn't there now.

Some years ago there was a considerable fuss in the world about preparedness and unpreparedness. Most of that clamour concerned the possibility of war. But this was a case of a most fantastic unpreparedness on the part of hundreds of eminent men, who were supposed to have studied them, for the normal developments of a community in times of peace. There had been no attempt to assemble that mechanism of knowledge of which America stood in need.

I repeat that if usage had not dulled us into a sort of acquiescence, we should think our species collectively insane to go about its business in this haphazard, planless, negligent fashion.

I think I have said enough to recall to any one here, who may have lapsed from the keen apprehension of his first realization, this wide gap between what I may call the at present unassembled and unexploited best thought and knowledge in the world, and the ideas and acts not simply of the masses of common people, but of those who direct public affairs, the dictators, the leaders, the politicians, the newspaper directors and the spiritual guides and teachers. We live in a world of unused and misapplied knowledge and skill. That is my case. Knowledge and thought are ineffective. The human species regarded as a whole is extraordinarily like a man of the highest order of brain, who through some lesions or defects or insufficiencies of his lower centres, suffers from the wildest uncoordinations; St. Vitus's dance, agraphia, aphonia, and suffers dreadfully (knowing better all the time) from the silly and disastrous gestures he makes and the foolish things he says and does.

I don't think this has ever been so evident as it is now. I doubt if in the past the gap was so wide as it is now between the occasions that confront us, and the knowledge we have assembled to meet them. But because of a certain run of luck in the late nineteenth century, the existence of that widening gap and the menace of that widening gap, was not thrust upon our attention as it has been since the War.

At first that realization of the ineffectiveness of our best thought and knowledge struck only a few people, like Mr. Maynard Keynes, for example, who were in what I may call salient positions, but gradually I have noted the realization spreading and growing. It takes various forms. Prominent men of science speak more and more frequently of the responsibility of science for the disorder of the world. And if you are familiar with that most admirable of all newspapers, *Nature,* and if you care to turn over the files of that very representative weekly for the past quarter of a century or so and sample the articles, you will observe a very remarkable change of note and scope in what it has to say to its readers. Time was when *Nature* was almost pedantically special and scientific. Its detachment from politics and general affairs was complete. But latterly the concussions of the social earthquake and the vibration of the guns have become increasingly perceptible in the laboratories. *Nature* from being specialist has become world-conscious, so that now it is almost haunted week by week by the question: "What are we to do before it is too late, to make what we know and our way of thinking effective in world affairs?"

In that I think it is expressing a change which is happening in the minds of—if I may presume to class myself with you—nearly all people of the sort which fills this theatre tonight.

And consider again the topics that have been dealt with at the latest gathering of the British Association. The very title of the Presidential Address: "The Impact of Science upon Society." Sir Josiah Stamp, as you will remember, stressed the need of extending endowment and multiplying workers in the social sciences. Professor Philip dealt with "The Training of the Chemist for the Service of the Community." Professor Cramp talked of "The Engineer and the Nation," and there was an important discussion of "The Cultural and Social Values of Science" in which Sir Richard Gregory, Professor Hogben and Sir Daniel Hall said some memorable things. There can be no doubt of the reality of this awakening of the scientific worker to the necessity of his becoming a definitely *organized* factor in the social scheme of the years before us.

Well, so far I have been merely opening up my subject and stating the problem for consideration. We want the intellectual worker to become a more definitely organized factor in the human scheme. How is that factor to be organized? Is there any way of implementing knowledge for ready and universal effect? I ask you to examine the question whether this great and growing gap of which we are becoming so acutely aware, between special knowledge and thought and the common ideas and motives of mankind can be bridged, and if so how it can be bridged. *Can* scientific knowledge and specialized thought be brought into more effective relation to general affairs?

Let us consider first what is actually going on. I find among my uneasy scientific and specialist friends a certain disposition—and I think it is a mistaken disposition—for direct political action and special political representation. The scientific and literary workers of the days when I was a young man were either indifferent or conservative in politics, nowadays quite a large proportion of them are inclined to active participation in extremist movements; many are leftish and revolutionary, some accept the strange pseudo-scientific dogmas of the Communist party, though that does no credit to their critical training, and even those who are not out on the left are restless for some way of intervening, definitely as a class, in the general happenings of the community. Their ideas of possible action vary from important-looking signed pronouncements and protests to a sort of strike against war, the withholding of services and the refusal to assist in technical developments that may be misapplied. Some favour the idea of a gradual supersession of the political forms and methods of mass democracy by government through some sort of *élite*, in which the man of science and the technician will play a dominating part. There are very large vague patches upon this idea, but the general projection is in the form of a sort of modern priesthood, an oligarchy of professors and exceptionally competent people. Like Plato they would make the philosopher king. This project involves certain assumptions about the general quality and superiority of the intellectual worker that I am afraid will not stand scrutiny.

I submit that sort of thing—political activities, party intervention and dreams of an authoritative *élite*—is not the way in which specialists, artists and specialized thinkers and workers who constitute the vital feeling and understanding of the body politic can be brought into a conscious, effective, guiding and directive relationship to the control of human affairs. Because—I hope you will acquit me of any disrespect for science and philosophy when I say this—we have to face the fact that from the point of view of general living, men of science, artists, philosophers, specialized intelligences of any sort, do not constitute an *élite* that can be mobilized for collective action. They are an extraordinarily miscellaneous assembly, and their most remarkable common quality is the quality of concentration in comparative retirement—each along his own line. They have none of the solidarity, the

customary *savoir faire*, the habits arising out of practices, activities and interests in common that lawyers, doctors or any of the really socially organized professions for instance display. A professor-ridden world might prove as unsatisfactory under the stress of modern life and fluctuating conditions as a theologian-ridden world.

A distinguished specialist is precious because of his cultivated gift. It does not follow at all that by the standards of all-round necessity he is a superior person. Indeed by the very fact of his specialization he may be less practised and competent than the average man. He probably does not read his newspaper so earnestly, he finds much of the common round a bother and a distraction and he puts it out of his mind. I think we should get the very gist of this problem if we could compare twelve miscellaneous men of science and special skill, with twelve unspecialized men taken—let us say—from the head clerk's morning train to the city. We should probably find that for commonplace team-work and the ordinary demands and sudden urgencies of life, the second dozen was individually quite as good as, if not better than, the first dozen. In a burning hotel or cast away on a desert island they would probably do quite as well. And yet collectively they would be ill-informed and limited men; the whole dozen of them would have nothing much more to tell you than any one of them. On the other hand our dozen specialists would each have something distinctive to tell you. The former group would be almost as uniform in their knowledge and ability as tiles on a roof, the latter would be like pieces from a complicated jig-saw puzzle. The more you got them together the more they would signify. Twelve clerks or a hundred clerks; it wouldn't matter; you would get nothing but dull repetitions and a flat acquiescent suggestible outlook upon life. But every specialized man we added would be adding something to the directive pattern of life. I think that consideration takes us a step further in defining our problem tonight.

It is *science* and not *men of science* that we want to enlighten and animate our politics and rule the world.

And now I will take rather a stride forward in my argument. I will introduce a phrase *New Encyclopaedism* which I shall spend most of the rest of my time defining. I want to suggest that something—a new social organ, a new institution—which for a time I shall call *World Encyclopaedia,* is the means whereby we can solve the problem of that jig-saw puzzle and bring all the scattered and ineffective mental wealth of our world into something like a common understanding, and into effective reaction upon our vulgar everyday political, social and economic life. I warn you that I am flinging moderation to the winds in the suggestions I am about to put before you. They are immense suggestions. I am sketching what is really a scheme for the reorganization and reorientation of education and information throughout the world. No less. We are so accustomed to the existing schools, colleges, universities, research organizations of the world; they have so moulded and made us and trained us from our earliest years to respect and believe in them; that it is with a real feeling of temerity, of alma-matricidal impiety, so to speak, that I have allowed my mind to explore their merits and question whether they are not now altogether an extraordinarily loose, weak and out-of-date miscellany. Yet I do not see how we can admit, and I am disposed to think you have admitted with me, the existence of this terrifying gap between available knowledge and current social and political events, and not go on to something like an indictment of this whole great world of academic erudition, training and instruction from China to Peru—an indictment for, at least, inadequacy and inco-ordination if

not for actual negligence. It may be only a temporary inadequacy, a pause in development before renascence, but inadequate altogether they are. Universities have multiplied greatly, yes, but they have failed to participate in the general advance in power, scope and efficiency that has occurred in the past century.

In transport we have progressed from coaches and horses by way of trains to electric traction, motor-cars and aeroplanes. In mental organization we have simply multiplied our coaches and horses and livery stables.

Let me now try to picture for you this missing element in the modern human social mechanism, this needed connection between the percipient and informative parts and the power organization for which I am using this phrase, World Encyclopaedia. And I will take it first from the point of view of the ordinary educated citizen—for in a completely modernized state every ordinary citizen will be an educated citizen. I will ask you to imagine how this World Encyclopaedia organization would enter into his life and how it would affect him. From his point of view the World Encyclopaedia would be a row of volumes in his own home or in some neighbouring house or in a convenient public library or in any school or college, and in this row of volumes he would, without any great toil or difficulty, find in clear understandable language, and kept up to date, the ruling concepts of our social order, the outlines and main particulars in all fields of knowledge, an exact and reasonably detailed picture of our universe, a general history of the world, and if by any chance he wanted to pursue a question into its ultimate detail, a trustworthy and complete system of reference to primary sources of knowledge. In fields where wide varieties of method and opinion existed, he would find, not casual summaries of opinions, but very carefully chosen and correlated statements and arguments. I do not imagine the major subjects as being dealt with in special articles rather hastily written, in what has been the tradition of Encyclopaedias since the days of Diderot's heroic effort. Our present circumstances are altogether different from his. Nowadays there is an immense literature of statement and explanation scattered through tens of thousands of books, pamphlets and papers, and it is not necessary, it is undesirable, to trust to such hurried summaries as the old tradition was obliged to make for its use. The day when an energetic journalist could gather together a few star contributors and a miscellany of compilers of very uneven quality to scribble him special articles, often tainted with propaganda and advertisement, and call it an Encyclopaedia, is past. The modern World Encyclopaedia should consist of selections, extracts, quotations, very carefully assembled with the approval of outstanding authorities in each subject, carefully collated and edited and critically presented. It would not be a miscellany, but a concentration, a clarification and a synthesis.

This World Encyclopaedia would be the mental background of every intelligent man in the world. It would be alive and growing and changing continually under revision, extension and replacement from the original thinkers in the world everywhere. Every university and research institution should be feeding it. Every fresh mind should be brought into contact with its standing editorial organization. And on the other hand its contents would be the standard source of material for the instructional side of school and college work, for the verification of facts and the testing of statements—everywhere in the world. Even journalists would deign to use it; even newspaper proprietors might be made to respect it.

Such an Encyclopaedia would play the rôle of an undogmatic Bible to a world culture. It would do just what our scattered and disoriented intellectual organizations of today fall short of doing. It would hold the world together mentally.

It may be objected that this is a Utopian dream. This is something too great to achieve, too good to be true. I won't deal with that for a few minutes. Flying was a Utopian dream a third of a century ago. What I am putting before you is a perfectly sane, sound and practicable proposal.

But first I will notice briefly two objections—obstructions rather than objections—that one will certainly encounter at this point.

One of these is not likely to appear in any great force in this gathering. You have all heard and you have all probably been irritated or bored by the assertion that no two people think alike, *"quot homines, tot sententiae,"* that science is always contradicting itself, that theologians and economists can never agree. It is largely mental laziness on the defensive that makes people say this kind of thing. They don't want their intimate convictions turned over and examined and it is unfortunate that the emphasis put upon minor differences by men of science and belief in their strenuous search for the completest truth and the exactest expression sometimes gives colour to this sort of misunderstanding. But I am inclined to think that most people overrate the apparent differences in the world of opinion today. Even in theology a psychological analysis reduces many flat contradictions to differences in terminology. My impression is that human brains are very much of a pattern, that under the same conditions they react in the same way, and that were it not for tradition, upbringing, accidents of circumstance and particularly of accidental individual obsessions, we should find ourselves—since we all face the same universe—much more in agreement than is superficially apparent. We speak different languages and dialects of thought and can even at times catch ourselves flatly contradicting each other in words while we are doing our utmost to express the same idea. And self-love and personal vanity are not excluded from the intellectual life. How often do we see men misrepresenting each other in order to exaggerate a difference and secure the gratification of an argumentative victory! A World Encyclopaedia as I conceive it would bring together into close juxtaposition and under critical scrutiny many apparently conflicting systems of statement. It might act not merely as an assembly of fact and statement, but as an organ of adjustment and adjudication, a clearing house of misunderstandings; it would be deliberately a synthesis, and so act as a flux and a filter for a very great quantity of human misapprehension. It would *compel* men to come to terms with one another. I think it would relegate *"quot homines, tot sententiae"* back to the Latin comedy from which it emerged.

The second type of obstruction that this idea of a World Encyclopaedia will encounter is even less likely to find many representatives in the present gathering and I will give it only the briefest of attention. (You know that kind of neuralgic expression, the high protesting voice, the fluttering gesture of the hands.) "But you want to *stereotype* people. What a dreadful, dreadful world it will be when everybody thinks alike"—and so they go on. Most of these elegant people who want the world picturesquely at sixes and sevens are hopeless cases, but for the milder instances it may be worth while remarking that it really does not enhance the natural variety and beauty of life to have all the clocks in a town keeping individual times of their own, no charts of the sea, no time-tables, but trains starting secretly to unspecified destinations, infectious diseases without notification and postmen calling occasionally when they can get by the picturesque footpads at the corner. I like order in the place of vermin, I prefer a garden to a swamp and the whole various world to a hole-and-corner life in some obscure

community, and tonight I like to imagine I am making my appeal to hearers of a kindred disposition to my own.

And next let us take this World Encyclopaedia from the point of view of the specialist and the super-intellectual. To him even more than to the common intelligent man World Encyclopaedia is going to be of value because it is going to afford him an intelligible statement of what is being done by workers parallel with himself. And further it will be giving him the general statement of his own subject that is being made to the world at large. He can watch that closely. On the assumption that the World Encyclopaedia is based on a world-wide organization he will be—if he is a worker of any standing—a corresponding associate of the Encyclopaedia organization. He will be able to criticize the presentation of his subject, to suggest amendments and re-statements. For a World Encyclopaedia that was kept alive and up to date by the frequent re-issue of its volumes, could be made the basis of much fundamental discussion and controversy. It might breed swarms of pamphlets, and very wholesome swarms. It would give the specialist just that contact with the world at large which at present is merely caricatured by more or less elementary class-teaching, amateurish examination work and college administrations. In my dream of a World Encyclopaedia I have a feeling that part of the scheme would be the replacement of the latter group of professional activities, the college business, tutoring, normal lecturing work and so on, by a new set of activities, the encyclopaedic work, the watching brief to prevent the corruption of the popular mind. In enlightening the general mind the specialist will broaden himself. He will be redeemed from oddity, from shy preciousness and practical futility.

Well, you begin to see the shape of this project. And you will realize that it is far away from anything like the valiant enterprise of Denis Diderot and his associates a century and a half ago, except in so far as the nature of its re-action upon the world's affairs is con-cerned. That extraordinary adventure in intellectual synthesis makes this dream credible. That is our chief connection with it.

And here I have to make an inciden-tal disavowal. I want to make it clear how little I have to do with what I am now discussing. In order to get some talk going upon this idea of an Encyclo-paedia, I have been circulating a short memorandum upon the subject among a number of friends. I did not think to mark it *Private,* and unhappily one copy seems to have fallen into the hands of one of those minor pests of our time, a personal journalist, who at once rushed into print with the announcement that I was proposing to *write* a brand new Encyclopaedia, all with my own little hand out of my own little head. At the age of seventy! Once a thing of this sort is started there is no stopping it— and I admit that announcement put me in my place in a pleasantly ridicu-lous light. But I think after what I have put before you now that you will acquit me of any such colossal ambition. I implore you not to let that touch of personal absurdity belittle the greatness and urgency of the cause I am pleading. This Encyclopaedia I am thinking of is something in which manifestly I have neither the equipment nor the quality to play any but an infinitesimal part. I am asking for it in the rôle of a common intelligent man who needs it and under-stands the need for it, both for himself and his world. After that you can leave me out of it. It is just because in the past I have had some experience in the assembling of outlines of knowledge for popular use that I realize, perhaps bet-ter than most people, the ineffectiveness of this sort of effort on the part of indi-viduals or small groups. It is something that must be taken up—and taken up very seriously—by the universities, the learned societies, the responsible edu-cational organizations if it is to be brought into effective being. It is a super university I am thinking of, a world brain; no less. It is nothing in the nature of a supplementary enterprise. It is a completion necessary to modern-ize the university idea.

And that brings me to the last part of this speculation. Can such an Encyclo-paedia as I have been suggesting to you be a possible thing? How can it be set going? How can it be organized and paid for?

I agree I have now to show it is a possible thing. For I am going to make the large assumption that you think that *if it is a possible thing* it is a desirable thing. How are we to set about it?

I think something in this way: To begin with we want a Promotion Organ-ization. We want, shall I call it, an Encyclopaedia Society to ask for an Encyclopaedia and get as many people as possible asking for an Encyclopaedia. Directly that Society asks for an Ency-clopaedia it will probably have to resort to precautionary measures against any enterprising publisher who may see in that demand a chance for selling some sort of vamped-up miscellany as the thing required, and who may even trust to the unworldliness of learned men for some sort of countenance for his raid.

And next this society of promoters will have to survey the available mate-rial. For most of the material for a modern Encyclopaedia exists already— though in a state of impotent diffusion. In all the various departments with which an Encyclopaedia should deal, groups of authoritative men might be induced to prepare a comprehensive list of primary and leading books, articles, statements which taken together would give the best, clearest and most quint-essential renderings of what is known and thought within their departments. This would make a sort of key bibliog-raphy to the thoughts and knowledge of the world. My friend Sir Richard

Gregory has suggested that such a key bibliography for a World Encyclopaedia would in itself be a worthwhile thing to evoke. I agree with him. I haven't an idea what we should get. I imagine something on the scale of ten or twenty thousand items. I don't know.

Possibly our Encyclopaedia Society would find that such a key bibliography was in itself a not unprofitable publication, but that is a comment by the way.

The next step from this key bibliography would be the organization of a general editorial board and of departmental boards. These would be permanent bodies—for a World Encyclopaedia must have a perennial life. We should have to secure premises, engage a literary staff and, with the constant co-operation of the departmental groups, set about the task of making our great synthesis and abstract. I must repeat that for the purposes of a World Encyclopaedia probably we would not want much original writing. If a thing has been stated clearly and compactly once for all, why paraphrase it or ask some inferior hand to restate it? Our job may be rather to secure the use of copyrights, and induce leading exponents of this or that field of science or criticism to co-operate in the selection, condensation, expansion or simplification of what they have already said so well.

And now I will ask you to take another step forward and imagine our World Encyclopaedia has been assembled and digested and that the first edition is through the press. So far we shall have been spending money on this great enterprise and receiving nothing; we shall have been spending capital, for which I have at present not accounted. I will merely say that I see no reason why the capital needed for these promotion activities should not be forthcoming. This is no gainful enterprise, but you have to remember that the values we should create would be far more stable than the ephemeral encyclopaedias representing sums round about a million pounds or so which have hitherto been the high-water of Encyclopaedic enterprise. These were essentially book-selling enterprises made to exploit a demand. But this World Encyclopaedia as I conceive it, if only because it will have roped in the large part of the original sources of exposition, discussion and information, will be in effect a world monopoly, and it will be able to levy and distribute direct and indirect revenue, on a scale quite beyond the resources of any private publishing enterprise. I do not see that the financial aspects of this huge enterprise, big though the sums involved may be, present any insurmountable difficulties in the way of its realization. The major difficulty will be to persuade the extremely various preoccupied, impatient and individualistic scholars, thinkers, scientific workers and merely distinguished but unavoidable men on whose participation its success depends, of its practicability, convenience and desirability.

And so far as the promotion of it goes I am reasonably hopeful. Quite a few convinced, energetic and resourceful people could set this ball rolling towards realization. To begin with it is not necessary to convert the whole world of learning, research and teaching. I see no reason why at any stage it should encounter such positive opposition. Negative opposition—the refusal to have anything to do with it and so forth—can be worn down by persistence and the gathering promise of success. It has not to fight adversaries or win majorities before it gets going. And once this ball is fairly set rolling it will be very hard to stop. A greater danger, as I have already suggested, will come from attempts at the private mercenary exploitation of this world-wide need—the raids of popular publishers and heavily financed salesmen, and in particular attempts to create copyright difficulties and so to corner the services and prestige of this or that unwary eminent person by anticipatory agreements. *Vis-à-vis* with salesmanship the man of science, the man of the intellectual *élite*, is apt to show himself a very Simple Simon indeed. And of course from the very start, various opinionated cults and propagandists will be doing their best to capture or buy the movement. Well, we mustn't be captured or bought, and in particular our silence must not be bought or captured. That danger may in the end prove to be a stimulus. It may be possible in some cases to digest and assimilate special cults to their own and the general advantage.

And there will be a constant danger that some of the early promoters may feel and attempt to realize a sort of proprietorship in the organization, to make a group or a gang of it. But to recognize that danger is half-way to averting it.

I have said nothing so far about the language in which the Encyclopaedia should appear. It is a question I have not worked out. But I think that the main text should be in one single language, from which translations in whole or part could be made. Catholic Christianity during the years of its greatest influence was held together by Latin, and I do not think I am giving way to any patriotic bias when I suggest that unless we contemplate a polyglot publication—and never yet have I heard of a successful polyglot publication—*English* because it has a wider range than German, a greater abundance and greater subtlety of expression than French and more precision than Russian, is the language in which the original text of a World Encyclopaedia ought to stand. And moreover it is in the English-speaking communities that such an enterprise as this is likely to find the broadest basis for operations, the frankest criticism and the greatest freedom

from official interference and government propaganda. But that must not hinder us from drawing help and contributions from, and contemplating a use in every community in the world.

And so far I have laid no stress upon the immense advantage this enterprise would have in its detachment from immediate politics. Ultimately if our dream is realized it must exert a very great influence upon everyone who controls administrations, makes wars, directs mass behaviour, feeds, moves, starves and kills populations. But it does not immediately challenge these active people. It is not the sort of thing to which they would be directly antagonistic. It is not ostensibly anti-*them*. It would have a terrible and ultimately destructive aloofness. They would not easily realize its significance for all that they do and are. The prowling beast will fight savagely if it is pursued and challenged upon the jungle path in the darkness, but it goes home automatically as the day breaks.

You see how such an Encyclopaedic organization could spread like a nervous network, a system of mental control about the globe, knitting all the intellectual workers of the world through a common interest and a common medium of expression into a more and more conscious co-operating unity and a growing sense of their own dignity, informing without pressure or propaganda, directing without tyranny. It could be developed wherever conditions were favourable; it could make inessential concessions and bide its time in regions of exceptional violence, grow vigorously again with every return to liberalism and reason.

So I sketch my suggestion for a rehabilitation of thought and learning that ultimately may release a new form of power in the world, recalling indeed the power and influence of the churches and religions of the past but with a progressive, adaptable and recuperative quality that none of these possessed. I believe that in some such way as I have sketched tonight the mental forces now largely and regrettably scattered and immobilized in the universities, the learned societies, research institutions and technical workers of the world could be drawn together in a real directive world intelligence, and by that mere linking and implementing of what is known, human life as a whole could be made much surer, stronger, bolder and happier than it has ever been up to the present time. And until something of this sort is done, I do not see how the common life can ever be raised except occasionally, locally and by a conspiracy of happy chances, above its present level of impulsiveness, insincerity, insecurity, general under-vitality, under-nourishment and aimlessness. For that reason I think the promotion of an organization for a World Encyclopaedia may prove in the long run to be a better investment for the time and energy of intelligent men and women than any definite revolutionary movement, Socialism, Communism, Fascism, Imperialism, Pacifism or any other of the current *isms* into which we pour ourselves and our resources so freely. None of these movements have anything like the intellectual comprehensiveness needed to construct the world anew.

Let me be *very* clear upon one point.

I am not saying that a World Encyclopaedia will in itself solve any single one of the vast problems that must be solved if man is to escape from his present dangers and distresses and enter upon a more hopeful phase of history; what I am saying—and saying with the utmost conviction—is this, that without a World Encyclopaedia to hold men's minds together in something like a common interpretation of reality, there is no hope whatever of anything but an accidental and transitory alleviation of any of our world troubles. As mankind is, so it will remain, until it pulls its mind together. And if it does not pull its mind together then I do not see how it can help but decline. Never was a living species more perilously poised than ours at the present time. If it does not take thought to end its present mental indecisiveness catastrophe lies ahead. Our species may yet end its strange eventful history as just the last, the cleverest of the great apes. The great ape that was clever—but not clever enough. It could escape from most things but not from its own mental confusion.

As We May Think

by Vannevar Bush

As Director of the Office of Scientific Research and Development, Dr. Vannevar Bush has coördinated the activities of some six thousand leading American scientists in the application of science to warfare. In this significant article he holds up an incentive for scientists when the fighting has ceased. He urges that men of science should then turn to the massive task of making more accessible our bewildering store of knowledge. For years inventions have extended man's physical powers rather than the powers of his mind. Trip hammers that multiply the fists, microscopes that sharpen the eye, and engines of destruction and detection are new results, but not the end results, of modern science. Now, says Dr. Bush, instruments are at hand which, if properly developed, will give man access to and command over the inherited knowledge of the ages. The perfection of these pacific instruments should be the first objective of our scientists as they emerge from their war work. Like Emerson's famous address of 1837 on "The American Scholar," this paper by Dr. Bush calls for a new relationship between thinking man and the sum of our knowledge.

This has not been a scientist's war; it has been a war in which all have had a part. The scientists, burying their old professional competition in the demand of a common cause, have shared greatly and learned much. It has been exhilarating to work in effective partnership. Now, for many, this appears to be approaching an end. What are the scientists to do next?

For the biologists, and particularly for the medical scientists, there can be little indecision, for their war work has hardly required them to leave the old paths. Many indeed have been able to carry on their war research in their familiar peacetime laboratories. Their objectives remain much the same.

It is the physicists who have been thrown most violently off stride, who have left academic pursuits for the making of strange destructive gadgets, who have had to devise new methods for their unanticipated assignments. They have done their part on the devices that made it possible to turn back the enemy. They have worked in combined effort with the physicists of our allies. They have felt within themselves the stir of achievement. They have been part of a great team. Now, as peace approaches, one asks where they will find objectives worthy of their best.

I

Of what lasting benefit has been man's use of science and of the new instruments which his research brought into existence? First, they have increased his control of his material environment. They have improved his food, his clothing, his shelter; they have increased his security and released him partly from the bondage of bare existence. They have given him increased knowledge of his own biological processes so that he has had a progressive freedom from disease and an increased span of life. They

SOURCE *Atlantic Monthly*, **176**, No. 1, July 1945, pp. 101–108.

are illuminating the interactions of his physiological and psychological functions, giving the promise of an improved mental health.

Science has provided the swiftest communication between individuals; it has provided a record of ideas and has enabled man to manipulate and to make extracts from that record so that knowledge evolves and endures throughout the life of a race rather than that of an individual.

There is a growing mountain of research. But there is increased evidence that we are being bogged down today as specialization extends. The investigator is staggered by the findings and conclusions of thousands of other workers—conclusions which he cannot find time to grasp, much less to remember as they appear. Yet specialization becomes increasingly necessary for progress, and the effort to bridge between disciplines is correspondingly superficial.

Professionally our methods of transmitting and reviewing the results of research are generations old and by now are totally inadequate for their purpose. If the aggregate time spent in writing scholarly works and in reading them could be evaluated, the ratio between these amounts of time might well be startling. Those who conscientiously attempt to keep abreast of current thought, even in restricted fields, by close and continuous reading might well shy away from an examination calculated to show how much of the previous month's efforts could be produced on call. Mendel's concept of the laws of genetics was lost to the world for a generation because his publication did not reach the few who were capable of grasping and extending it; and this sort of catastrophe is undoubtedly being repeated all about us, as truly significant attainments become lost in the mass of the inconsequential.

The difficulty seems to be, not so much that we publish unduly in view of the extent and variety of present-day interests, but rather that publication has been extended far beyond our present ability to make real use of the record. The summation of human experience is being expanded at a prodigious rate, and the means we use for threading through the consequent maze to the momentarily important item is the same as was used in the days of square-rigged ships.

But there are signs of a change as new and powerful instrumentalities come into use. Photocells capable of seeing things in a physical sense, advanced photography which can record what is seen or even what is not, thermionic tubes capable of controlling potent forces under the guidance of less power than a mosquito uses to vibrate his wings, cathode ray tubes rendering visible an occurrence so brief that by comparison a microsecond is a long time, relay combinations which will carry out involved sequences of movements more reliably than any human operator and thousands of times as fast—there are plenty of mechanical aids with which to effect a transformation in scientific records.

Two centuries ago Leibnitz invented a calculating machine which embodied most of the essential features of recent keyboard devices, but it could not then come into use. The economics of the situation were against it: the labor involved in constructing it, before the days of mass production, exceeded the labor to be saved by its use, since all it could accomplish could be duplicated by sufficient use of pencil and paper. Moreover, it would have been subject to frequent breakdown, so that it could not have been depended upon; for at that time and long after, complexity and unreliability were synonymous.

Babbage, even with remarkably generous support for his time, could not produce his great arithmetical machine. His idea was sound enough, but construction and maintenance costs were then too heavy. Had a Pharaoh been given detailed and explicit designs of an automobile, and had he understood them completely, it would have taxed the resources of his kingdom to have fashioned the thousands of parts for a single car, and that car would have broken down on the first trip to Giza.

Machines with interchangeable parts can now be constructed with great economy of effort. In spite of much complexity, they perform reliably. Witness the humble typewriter, or the movie camera, or the automobile. Electrical contacts have ceased to stick when thoroughly understood. Note the automatic telephone exchange, which has hundreds of thousands of such contacts, and yet is reliable. A spider web of metal, sealed in a thin glass container, a wire heated to brilliant glow, in short, the thermionic tube of radio sets, is made by the hundred million, tossed about in packages, plugged into sockets—and it works! Its gossamer parts, the precise location and alignment involved in its construction, would have occupied a master craftsman of the guild for months; now it is built for thirty cents. The world has arrived at an age of cheap complex devices of great reliability; and something is bound to come of it.

II

A record, if it is to be useful to science, must be continuously extended, it must be stored, and above all it must be consulted. Today we make the record conventionally by writing and photography, followed by printing; but we also record on film, on wax disks, and on magnetic wires. Even if utterly new recording procedures do not appear, these present ones are certainly in the process of modification and extension.

Certainly progress in photography is not going to stop. Faster material and lenses, more automatic cameras, finer-grained sensitive compounds to allow an extension of the minicamera idea, are all imminent. Let us project this trend ahead to a logical, if not inevitable, out-

come. The camera hound of the future wears on his forehead a lump a little larger than a walnut. It takes pictures 3 millimeters square, later to be projected or enlarged, which after all involves only a factor of 10 beyond present practice. The lens is of universal focus, down to any distance accommodated by the unaided eye, simply because it is of short focal length. There is a built-in photocell on the walnut such as we now have on at least one camera, which automatically adjusts exposure for a wide range of illumination. There is film in the walnut for a hundred exposures, and the spring for operating its shutter and shifting its film is wound once for all when the film clip is inserted. It produces its result in full color. It may well be stereoscopic, and record with two spaced glass eyes, for striking improvements in stereoscopic technique are just around the corner.

The cord which trips its shutter may reach down a man's sleeve within easy reach of his fingers. A quick squeeze, and the picture is taken. On a pair of ordinary glasses is a square of fine lines near the top of one lens, where it is out of the way of ordinary vision. When an object appears in that square, it is lined up for its picture. As the scientist of the future moves about the laboratory or the field, every time he looks at something worthy of the record, he trips the shutter and in it goes, without even an audible click. Is this all fantastic? The only fantastic thing about it is the idea of making as many pictures as would result from its use.

Will there be dry photography? It is already here in two forms. When Brady made his Civil War pictures, the plate had to be wet at the time of exposure. Now it has to be wet during development instead. In the future perhaps it need not be wetted at all. There have long been films impregnated with diazo dyes which form a picture without development, so that it is already there as soon as the camera has been operated.

An exposure to ammonia gas destroys the unexposed dye, and the picture can then be taken out into the light and examined. The process is now slow, but someone may speed it up, and it has no grain difficulties such as now keep photographic researchers busy. Often it would be advantageous to be able to snap the camera and to look at the picture immediately.

Another process now in use is also slow, and more or less clumsy. For fifty years impregnated papers have been used which turn dark at every point where an electrical contact touches them, by reason of the chemical change thus produced in an iodine compound included in the paper. They have been used to make records, for a pointer moving across them can leave a trail behind. If the electrical potential on the pointer is varied as it moves, the line becomes light or dark in accordance with the potential.

This scheme is now used in facsimile transmission. The pointer draws a set of closely spaced lines across the paper one after another. As it moves, its potential is varied in accordance with a varying current received over wires from a distant station, where these variations are produced by a photocell which is similarly scanning a picture. At every instant the darkness of the line being drawn is made equal to the darkness of the point on the picture being observed by the photocell. Thus, when the whole picture has been covered, a replica appears at the receiving end.

A scene itself can be just as well looked over line by line by the photocell in this way as can a photograph of the scene. This whole apparatus constitutes a camera, with the added feature, which can be dispensed with if desired, of making its picture at a distance. It is slow, and the picture is poor in detail. Still, it does give another process of dry photography, in which the picture is finished as soon at it is taken.

It would be a brave man who would predict that such a proces will always remain clumsy, slow, and faulty in detail. Television equipment today transmits sixteen reasonably good pictures a second, and it involves only two essential differences from the process described above. For one, the record is made by a moving beam of electrons rather than a moving pointer, for the reason that an electron beam can sweep across the picture very rapidly indeed. The other difference involves merely the use of a screen which glows momentarily when the electrons hit, rather than a chemically treated paper or film which is permanently altered. This speed is necessary in television, for motion pictures rather than stills are the object.

Use chemically treated film in place of the glowing screen, allow the apparatus to transmit one picture only rather than a succession, and a rapid camera for dry photography results. The treated film needs to be far faster in action than present examples, but it probably could be. More serious is the objection that this scheme would involve putting the film inside a vacuum chamber, for electron beams behave normally only in such a rarefied environment. This difficulty could be avoided by allowing the electron beam to play on one side of a partition, and by pressing the film against the other side, if this partition were such as to allow the electrons to go through perpendicular to its surface, and to prevent them from spreading out sideways. Such partitions, in crude form, could certainly be constructed, and they will hardly hold up the general development.

Like dry photography, microphotography still has a long way to go. The basic scheme of reducing the size of the record, and examining it by projection rather than directly, has possibilities too great to be ignored. The combination of optical projection and photographic reduction is already producing some results in microfilm for scholarly purposes, and the potentialities are highly suggestive. Today, with microfilm, reductions by a linear factor of 20 can be employed and still produce full clarity when the material is re-enlarged for examination. The limits are set by the graininess of the film, the excellence of the optical system, and the efficiency of the light sources employed. All of these are rapidly improving.

Assume a linear ratio of 100 for future use. Consider film of the same thickness as paper, although thinner film will certainly be usable. Even under these conditions there would be a total factor of 10,000 between the bulk of the ordinary record on books, and its microfilm replica. The *Encyclopaedia Britannica* could be reduced to the volume of a matchbox. A library of a million volumes could be compressed into one end of a desk. If the human race has produced since the invention of movable type a total record, in the form of magazines, newspapers, books, tracts, advertising blurbs, correspondence, having a volume corresponding to a billion books, the whole affair, assembled and compressed, could be lugged off in a moving van. Mere compression, of course, is not enough; one needs not only to make and store a record but also be able to consult it, and this aspect of the matter comes later. Even the modern great library is not generally consulted; it is nibbled at by a few.

Compression is important, however, when it comes to costs. The material for the microfilm *Britannica* would cost a nickel, and it could be mailed anywhere for a cent. What would it cost to print a million copies? To print a sheet of newspaper, in a large edition, costs a small fraction of a cent. The entire material of the *Britannica* in reduced microfilm form would go on a sheet eight and one-half by eleven inches. Once it is available, with the photographic reproduction methods of the future, duplicates in large quantities could probably be turned out for a cent apiece beyond the cost of materials. The preparation of the original copy? That introduces the next aspect of the subject.

III

To make the record, we now push a pencil or tap a typewriter. Then comes the process of digestion and correction, followed by an intricate process of typesetting, printing, and distribution. To consider the first stage of the procedure, will the author of the future cease writing by hand or typewriter and talk directly to the record? He does so indirectly, by talking to a stenographer or a wax cylinder; but the elements are all present if he wishes to have his talk directly produce a typed record. All he needs to do is to take advantage of existing mechanisms and to alter his language.

At a recent World Fair a machine called a Voder was shown. A girl stroked its keys and it emitted recognizable speech. No human vocal chords entered into the procedure at any point; the keys simply combined some electrically produced vibrations and passed these on to a loud-speaker. In the Bell Laboratories there is the converse of this machine, called a Vocoder. The loudspeaker is replaced by a microphone, which picks up sound. Speak to it, and the corresponding keys move. This may be one element of the postulated system.

The other element is found in the stenotype, that somewhat disconcerting device encountered usually at public meetings. A girl strokes its keys languidly and looks about the room and sometimes at the speaker with a disquieting gaze. From it emerges a typed strip which records in a phonetically simplified language a record of what the speaker is supposed to have said. Later this strip is retyped into ordinary language, for in its nascent form it is intelligible only to the initiated. Combine these two elements, let the Vocoder run the stenotype, and the result is a machine which types when talked to.

Our present languages are not especially adapted to this sort of mechanization, it is true. It is strange that the inventors of universal languages have not seized upon the idea of producing one which better fitted the technique for transmitting and recording speech. Mechanization may yet force the issue, especially in the scientific field; whereupon scientific jargon would become still less intelligible to the layman.

One can now picture a future investigator in his laboratory. His hands are free, and he is not anchored. As he moves about and observes, he photographs and comments. Time is automatically recorded to tie the two records together. If he goes into the field, he may be connected by radio to his recorder. As he ponders over his notes in the evening, he again talks his comments into the record. His typed record, as well as his photographs, may both be in miniature, so that he projects them for examination.

Much needs to occur, however, between the collection of data and observations, the extraction of parallel material from the existing record, and the final insertion of new material into the general body of the common record. For mature thought there is no mechanical substitute. But creative thought and essentially repetitive thought are very different things. For the latter there are, and may be, powerful mechanical aids.

Adding a column of figures is a repetitive thought process, and it was long ago properly relegated to the machine. True, the machine is sometimes controlled by a keyboard, and thought of a sort enters in reading the figures and poking the corresponding keys, but even this is avoidable. Machines have been made which will read typed figures by photocells and then depress the corresponding keys; these are combinations of photocells for scanning the type, electric circuits for sorting the consequent variations, and relay circuits for interpreting the result into the action of solenoids to pull the keys down.

All this complication is needed because of the clumsy way in which we have learned to write figures. If we recorded them positionally, simply by the configuration of a set of dots on a card, the automatic reading mechanism would become comparatively simple. In fact, if the dots are holes, we have the punched-card machine long ago produced by Hollorith for the purposes of the census, and now used throughout business. Some types of complex businesses could hardly operate without these machines.

Adding is only one operation: To perform arithmetical computation involves also subtraction, multiplication, and division, and in addition some method for temporary storage of results, removal from storage for further manipulation, and recording of final results by printing. Machines for these purposes are now of two types: keyboard machines for accounting and the like, manually controlled for the insertion of data, and usually automatically controlled as far as the sequence of operations is concerned; and punched-card machines in which separate operations are usually delegated to a series of machines, and the cards then transferred bodily from one to another. Both forms are very useful; but as far as complex computations are concerned both are still in embryo.

Rapid electrical counting appeared soon after the physicists found it desirable to count cosmic rays. For their own purposes the physicists promptly constructed thermionic-tube equipment capable of counting electrical impulses at the rate of 100,000 a second. The advanced arithmetical machines of the future will be electrical in nature, and they will perform at 100 times present speeds, or more.

Moreover, they will be far more versatile than present commercial machines, so that they may readily be adapted for a wide variety of operations. They will be controlled by a control card or film, they will select their own data and manipulate it in accordance with the instructions thus inserted, they will perform complex arithmetical computations at exceedingly high speeds, and they will record results in such form as to be readily available for distribution or for later further manipulation. Such machines will have enormous appetites. One of them will take instructions and data from a whole roomful of girls armed with simple keyboard punches, and will deliver sheets of computed results every few minutes. There will always be plenty of things to compute in the detailed affairs of millions of people doing complicated things.

IV

The repetitive processes of thought are not confined, however, to matters of arithmetic and statistics. In fact, every time one combines and records facts in accordance with established logical processes, the creative aspect of thinking is concerned only with the selection of the data and the process to be employed and the manipulation thereafter is repetitive in nature and hence a fit matter to be relegated to the machines. Not so much has been done along these lines, beyond the bounds of arithmetic, as might be done, primarily because of the economics of the situation. The needs of business, and the extensive market obviously waiting, assured the advent of mass-produced arithmetical machines just as soon as production methods were sufficiently advanced.

With machines for advanced analysis no such situation existed; for there was and is no extensive market; the users of advanced methods of manipulating data are a very small part of the population. There are, however, machines for solving differential equations—and functional and integral equations, for that matter. There are many special machines, such as the harmonic synthesizer which predicts the tides. There will be many more, appearing certainly first in the hands of the scientist and in small numbers.

If scientific reasoning were limited to the logical processes of arithmetic, we should not get far in our understanding of the physical world. One might as well attempt to grasp the game of poker entirely by the use of the mathematics of probability. The abacus, with its beads strung on parallel wires, led the Arabs to positional numeration and the concept of zero many centuries before the rest of the world; and it was a useful tool—so useful that it still exists.

It is a far cry from the abacus to the modern keyboard accounting machine. It will be an equal step to the arithmetical machine of the future. But even this new machine will not take the scientist where he needs to go. Relief must be secured from laborious detailed manipulation of higher mathematics as well, if the users of it are to free their brains for something more than repetitive detailed transformations in accordance with established rules. A mathematician is not a man who can readily manipulate figures; often he cannot. He is not even a man who can readily perform the transformations of equations by the use of calculus. He is primarily an individual who is skilled in the use of symbolic logic on a high plane, and especially he is a man of intuitive judgment in the choice of the manipulative processes he employs.

All else he should be able to turn over to his mechanism, just as confidently as he turns over the propelling of his car to the intricate mechanism under the hood. Only then will mathematics be practically effective in bringing the growing knowledge of atomistics to the useful solution of the advanced problems of chemistry, metallurgy, and biology. For this reason there will come more machines to handle advanced mathematics for the scientist. Some of them will be sufficiently bizarre to suit the most fastidious connoisseur of the present artifacts of civilization.

V

The scientist, however, is not the only person who manipulates data and examines the world about him by the use of logical processes, although he sometimes preserves this appearance by adopting into the fold anyone who becomes logical, much in the manner in which a British labor leader is elevated to knighthood. Whenever logical processes of thought are employed—that is, whenever thought for a time runs along an accepted groove—there is an opportunity for the machine. Formal logic used to be a keen instrument in the hands of the teacher in his trying of students' souls. It is readily possible to construct a machine which will manipulate premises in accordance with formal logic, simply by the clever use of relay circuits. Put a set of premises into such a device and turn the crank, and it will readily pass out conclusion after conclusion, all in accordance with logical law, and with no more slips than would be expected of a keyboard adding machine.

Logic can become enormously difficult, and it would undoubtedly be well to produce more assurance in its use. The machines for higher analysis have usually been equation solvers. Ideas are beginning to appear for equation transformers, which will rearrange the relationship expressed by an equation in accordance with strict and rather advanced logic. Progress is inhibited by the exceedingly crude way in which mathematicians express their relationships. They employ a symbolism which grew like Topsy and has little consistency; a strange fact in that most logical field.

A new symbolism, probably positional, must apparently precede the reduction of mathematical transformations to machine processes. Then, on beyond the strict logic of the mathematician, lies the application of logic in everyday affairs. We may some day click off arguments on a machine with the same assurance that we now enter sales on a cash register. But the machine of logic will not look like a cash register, even of the streamlined model.

So much for the manipulation of ideas and their insertion into the record. Thus far we seem to be worse off than before —for we can enormously extend the record; yet even in its present bulk we can hardly consult it. This is a much larger matter than merely the extraction of data for the purposes of scientific research; it involves the entire process by which man profits by his inheritance of acquired knowledge. The prime action of use is selection, and here we are halting indeed. There may be millions of fine thoughts, and the account of the experience on which they are based, all encased within stone walls of acceptable architectural form; but if the scholar can get at only one a week by diligent search, his syntheses are not likely to keep up with the current scene.

Selection, in this broad sense, is a stone adze in the hands of a cabinetmaker. Yet, in a narrow sense and in other areas, something has already been done mechanically on selection. The personnel officer of a factory drops a stack of a few thousand employee cards into a selecting machine, sets a code in accordance with an established convention, and produces in a short time a list of all employees who live in Trenton and know Spanish. Even such devices are much too slow when it comes, for example, to matching a set of fingerprints with one of five million on file. Selection devices of this sort will soon be speeded up from their present rate of reviewing data at a few hundred a minute. By the use of photocells and microfilm they will survey items at the rate of a thousand a second, and will print out duplicates of those selected.

This process, however, is simple selection: it proceeds by examining in turn every one of a large set of items, and by picking out those which have certain specified characteristics. There is another form of selection best illustrated by the automatic telephone exchange. You dial a number and the machine selects and connects just one of a million possible stations. It does not run over them all. It pays attention only to a class given by a first digit, then only to a subclass of this given by the second digit, and so on; and thus proceeds rapidly and almost unerringly to the selected station. It requires a few seconds to make the selection, although the process could be speeded up if increased speed were economically warranted. If necessary, it could be made extremely fast by substituting thermionic-tube switching for mechanical switching, so that the full selection could be made in one one-hundredth of a second. No one would wish to spend the money necessary to make this change in the telephone system, but the general idea is applicable elsewhere.

Take the prosaic problem of the great department store. Every time a charge sale is made, there are a number of things to be done. The inventory needs to be revised, the salesman needs to be given credit for the sale, the general accounts need an entry, and, most important, the customer needs to be charged. A central records device has been developed in which much of this work is done conveniently. The salesman places on a stand the customer's identification card, his own card, and the card taken from the article sold—all punched cards. When he pulls a lever, contacts are made through the holes, machinery at a central point makes the necessary computations and entries, and the proper receipt is printed for the salesman to pass to the customer.

But there may be ten thousand charge customers doing business with the store, and before the full operation can be completed someone has to select the right card and insert it at the central office. Now rapid selection can slide just the proper card into position in an instant or two, and return it afterward. Another difficulty occurs, however. Someone must read a total on the card, so that the machine can add its computed item to it. Conceivably the cards might be of the dry photography type I have described. Existing totals could then be read by photocell, and the new total entered by an electron beam.

The cards may be in miniature, so that they occupy little space. They must move quickly. They need not be transferred far, but merely into position so that the photocell and recorder can operate on them. Positional dots can enter the data. At the end of the month a machine can readily be made to read these and to print an ordinary bill. With tube selection, in which no mechanical parts are involved in the switches, little time need be occupied in bringing the correct card into use—a second should suffice for the entire operation. The whole record on the card may be made by magnetic dots on a steel sheet if desired, instead of dots to be observed optically, following the scheme by which Poulsen long ago put speech on a magnetic wire. This method has the advantage of simplicity and ease of erasure. By using photography, however, one can arrange to project the record in enlarged form, and at a distance by using the process common in television equipment.

One can consider rapid selection of this form, and distant projection for other purposes. To be able to key one sheet of a million before an operator in a second or two, with the possibility of then adding notes thereto, is suggestive in many ways. It might even be of use in libraries, but that is another story. At any rate, there are now some interesting combinations possible. One might, for example, speak to a microphone, in the manner described in connection with the speech-controlled typewriter, and thus make his selections. It would certainly beat the usual file clerk.

VI

The real heart of the matter of selection, however, goes deeper than a lag in the adoption of mechanisms by libraries, or a lack of development of devices for their use. Our ineptitude in getting at the record is largely caused by the artificiality of systems of indexing. When data of any sort are placed in storage, they are filed alphabetically or numerically, and information is found (when it is) by tracing it down from subclass to subclass. It can be in only one place, unless duplicates are used; one has to have rules as to which path will locate it, and the rules are cumbersome. Having found one item, moreover, one has to emerge from the system and re-enter on a new path.

The human mind does not work that way. It operates by association. With one item in its grasp, it snaps instantly to the next that is suggested by the association of thoughts, in accordance with some intricate web of trails carried by the cells of the brain. It has other characteristics, of course; trails that are not frequently followed are prone to fade, items are not fully permanent, memory is transitory. Yet the speed of action, the intricacy of trails, the detail of mental pictures, is awe-inspiring beyond all else in nature.

Man cannot hope fully to duplicate this mental process artificially, but he certainly ought to be able to learn from it. In minor ways he may even improve for his records have relative permanency. The first idea, however, to be drawn from the analogy concerns selection. Selection by association, rather than by indexing, may yet be mechanized. One cannot hope thus to equal the speed and flexibility with which the mind follows an associative trail, but it should be possible to beat the mind decisively in regard to the permanence and clarity of the items resurrected from storage.

Consider a future device for individual use, which is a sort of mechanized private file and library. It needs a name, and, to coin one at random, "memex" will do. A memex is a device in which an individual stores his books, records, and communications, and which is mechanized so that it may be consulted with exceeding speed and flexibility. It is an enlarged intimate supplement to his memory.

It consists of a desk, and while it can presumably be operated from a distance, it is primarily the piece of furniture at which he works. On the top are slanting translucent screens, on which material can be projected for convenient reading. There is a keyboard, and sets of buttons and levers. Otherwise it looks like an ordinary desk.

In one end is the stored material. The matter of bulk is well taken care of by improved microfilm. Only a small part of the interior of the memex is devoted to storage, the rest to mechanism. Yet if the user inserted 5000 pages of material a day it would take him hundreds of years to fill the repository, so he can be profligate and enter material freely.

Most of the memex contents are purchased on microfilm ready for insertion. Books of all sorts, pictures, current periodicals, newspapers, are thus obtained and dropped into place. Business correspondence takes the same path. And there is provision for direct entry. On the top of the memex is a transparent platen. On this are placed longhand notes, photographs, memoranda, all sorts of things. When one is in place, the depression of a lever causes it to be photographed onto the next blank space in a section of the memex film, dry photography being employed.

There is, of course, provision for consultation of the record by the usual scheme of indexing. If the user wishes to consult a certain book, he taps its code on the keyboard, and the title page of the book promptly appears before him, projected onto one of his viewing positions. Frequently-used codes are mnemonic, so that he seldom consults his code book; but when he does, a single tap of a key projects it for his use. Moreover, he has supplemental levers. On deflecting one of these levers to the right he runs through the book before him, each page in turn being projected at a speed which just allows a recognizing glance at each. If he deflects it further to the right, he steps through the book 10 pages at a time; still further at 100 pages at a time. Deflection to the left gives him the same control backwards.

A special button transfers him immediately to the first page of the index. Any given book of his library can thus be called up and consulted with far greater facility than if it were taken from a shelf. As he has several projection positions, he can leave one item in position while he calls up another. He can add marginal notes and comments, taking advantage of one possible type of dry photography, and it could even be arranged so that he can do this by a stylus scheme, such as is now employed in the telautograph seen in railroad waiting rooms, just as though he had the physical page before him.

VII

All this is conventional, except for the projection forward of present-day mechanisms and gadgetry. It affords an immediate step, however, to associative indexing, the basic idea of which is a provision whereby any item may be caused at will to select immediately and automatically another. This is the essential feature of the memex. The process of tying two items together is the important thing.

When the user is building a trail, he names it, inserts the name in his code book, and taps it out on his keyboard. Before him are the two items to be joined, projected onto adjacent viewing positions. At the bottom of each there are a number of blank code spaces, and a pointer is set to indicate one of these on each item. The user taps a single key, and the items are permanently joined. In each code space appears the code word. Out of view, but also in the code space, is inserted a set of dots for photocell viewing; and on each item these dots by their positions designate the index number of the other item.

Thereafter, at any time, when one of these items is in view, the other can be instantly recalled merely by tapping a button below the corresponding code space. Moreover, when numerous items have been thus joined together to form a trail, they can be reviewed in turn, rapidly or slowly, by deflecting a lever like that used for turning the pages of a book. It is exactly as though the physical items had been gathered together from widely separated sources and bound together to form a new book. It is more than this, for any item can be joined into numerous trails.

The owner of the memex, let us say, is interested in the origin and properties of the bow and arrow. Specifically he is studying why the short Turkish bow was apparently superior to the English long bow in the skirmishes of the Crusades. He has dozens of possibly pertinent books and articles in his memex. First he runs through an encyclopedia, finds an interesting but sketchy article, leaves it projected. Next, in a history, he finds another pertinent item, and ties the two together. Thus he goes, building a trail of many items. Occasionally he inserts a comment of his own, either linking it into the main trail or joining it by a side trail to a particular item. When it becomes evident that the elastic properties of available materials had a great deal to do with the bow, he branches off on a side trail which takes him through textbooks on elasticity and tables of physical constants. He inserts a page of longhand analysis of his own. Thus he builds a trail of his interest through the maze of materials available to him.

And his trails do not fade. Several years later, his talk with a friend turns to the queer ways in which a people resist innovations, even of vital interest. He has an example, in the fact that the outranged Europeans still failed to adopt the Turkish bow. In fact he has a trail on it. A touch brings up the code book. Tapping a few keys projects the head of the trail. A lever runs through it at will, stopping at interesting items, going off on side excursions. It is an interesting trail, pertinent to the discussion. So he sets a reproducer in action, photographs the whole trail out, and passes it to his friend for insertion in his own memex, there to be linked into the more general trail.

VIII

Wholly new forms of encyclopedias will appear, ready-made with a mesh of associative trails running through them, ready to be dropped into the memex and there amplified. The lawyer has at his touch the associated opinions and decisions of his whole experience, and of the experience of friends and authorities. The patent attorney has on call the millions of issued patents, with familiar trails to every point of his client's interest. The physician, puzzled by a patient's reactions, strikes the trail established in studying an earlier similar case, and runs rapidly through analogous case histories, with side references to the classics for the pertinent anatomy and histology. The chemist, struggling with the synthesis of an organic compound, has all the chemical literature before him in his laboratory, with trails following the analogies of compounds, and side trails to their physical and chemical behavior.

The historian, with a vast chronological account of a people, parallels it with a skip trail which stops only on the salient items, and can follow at any time contemporary trails which lead

him all over civilization at a particular epoch. There is a new profession of trail blazers, those who find delight in the task of establishing useful trails through the enormous mass of the common record. The inheritance from the master becomes, not only his additions to the world's record, but for his disciples the entire scaffolding by which they were erected.

Thus science may implement the ways in which man produces, stores, and consults the record of the race. It might be striking to outline the instrumentalities of the future more spectacularly, rather than to stick closely to methods and elements now known and undergoing rapid development, as has been done here. Technical difficulties of all sorts have been ignored, certainly, but also ignored are means as yet unknown which may come any day to accelerate technical progress as violently as did the advent of the thermionic tube. In order that the picture may not be too commonplace, by reason of sticking to present-day patterns, it may be well to mention one such possibility, not to prophesy but merely to suggest, for prophecy based on extension of the known has substance, while prophecy founded on the unknown is only a doubly involved guess.

All our steps in creating or absorbing material of the record proceed through one of the senses—the tactile when we touch keys, the oral when we speak or listen, the visual when we read. Is it not possible that some day the path may be established more directly?

We know that when the eye sees, all the consequent information is transmitted to the brain by means of electrical vibrations in the channel of the optic nerve. This is an exact analogy with the electrical vibrations which occur in the cable of a television set: they convey the picture from the photocells which send it to the radio transmitter from which it is broadcast. We know further that if we can approach that cable with the proper instruments, we do not need to touch it; we can pick up those vibrations by electrical induction and thus discover and reproduce the scene which is being transmitted, just as a telephone wire may be tapped for its message.

The impulses which flow in the arm nerves of a typist convey to her fingers the translated information which reaches her eye or ear, in order that the fingers may be caused to strike the proper keys. Might not these currents be intercepted, either in the original form in which information is conveyed to the brain, or in the marvelously metamorphosed form in which they then proceed to the hand?

By bone conduction we already introduce sounds into the nerve channels of the deaf in order that they may hear. Is it not possible that we may learn to introduce them without the present cumbersomeness of first transforming electrical vibrations to mechanical ones, which the human mechanism promptly transforms back to the electrical form? With a couple of electrodes on the skull the encephalograph now produces pen-and-ink traces which bear some relation to the electrical phenomena going on in the brain itself. True, the record is unintelligible, except as it points out certain gross misfunctioning of the cerebral mechanism; but who would now place bounds on where such a thing may lead?

In the outside world, all forms of intelligence, whether of sound or sight, have been reduced to the form of varying currents in an electric circuit in order that they may be transmitted. Inside the human frame exactly the same sort of process occurs. Must we always transform to mechanical movements in order to proceed from one electrical phenomenon to another? It is a suggestive thought, but it hardly warrants prediction without losing touch with reality and immediateness.

Presumably man's spirit should be elevated if he can better review his shady past and analyze more completely and objectively his present problems. He has built a civilization so complex that he needs to mechanize his records more fully if he is to push his experiment to its logical conclusion and not merely become bogged down part way there by overtaxing his limited memory. His excursions may be more enjoyable if he can reacquire the privilege of forgetting the manifold things he does not need to have immediately at hand, with some assurance that he can find them again if they prove important.

The applications of science have built man a well-supplied house, and are teaching him to live healthily therein. They have enabled him to throw masses of people against one another with cruel weapons. They may yet allow him truly to encompass the great record and to grow in the wisdom of race experience. He may perish in conflict before he learns to wield that record for his true good. Yet, in the application of science to the needs and desires of man, it would seem to be a singularly unfortunate stage at which to terminate the process, or to lose hope as to the outcome.

Science, Government, and Information

by Alvin Weinberg

The Nature of the Information Problem

Science and technology can flourish only if each scientist interacts with his colleagues and his predecessors, and only if every branch of science interacts with other branches of science; in this sense science must remain unified if it is to remain effective. The ideas and data that are the substance of science and technology are embodied in the literature; only if the literature remains a unity can science itself be unified and viable. Yet, because of the tremendous growth of the literature, there is danger of science fragmenting into a mass of repetitious findings, or worse, into conflicting specialties that are not recognized as being mutually inconsistent. This is the essence of the "crisis" in scientific and technical information.

Inasmuch as the Federal Government now supports three-fourths of all science and technology of the United States, it has a responsibility to prevent our scientific-technical structure from becoming a pile of redundancies or contradictions simply because communication between the specialized communities or between members of a single community has become too laborious. Moreover, since good communication is a necessary tool of good management, the Federal Government, as the largest manager of research and development, has a strong stake in maintaining effective communication.

The problem of course is not the Federal Government's alone. Science and technology are the business of many who are outside Government: the professional technical societies, the universities, private industry. Each of these communities has developed methods to cope with the difficulties in communication, some (notably the physical scientists) more successfully than others; yet because these communication systems have grown up in isolation, they too often tend to further fragment our already disjointed scientific structure. The Federal Government alone interacts with all of the elements of our information systems; it is uniquely able to examine the overall problem from a properly general viewpoint and to guide and otherwise support measures for unifying our communication and so preserving that unity of science and technology that is indispensable to their effective pursuit.

Another reason for the Federal Government's interest in maintaining the health of our scientific communication systems has to do with the validity of our science. Modern science and technology cost our society dearly, and our society is justified in demanding its money's worth. Much of the return from science and technology is tangible and obvious: better defense, better food, more abundant energy. But the many

SOURCE: *Science, Government, and Information: The Responsibilities of the Technical Community and the Government in the Transfer of Information,* President's Science Advisory Council, U.S. Government Printing Office. Washington, D.C.: 1963, pp. 7–37.

technical activities that do not directly lead to tangible gains must also justify their existence to the society that supports them. Here the process of scientific communication, with its long tradition of ruthless self-criticism, plays an indispensable role. The existence of a healthy, unified, impartial, and sophisticated system of scientific communication—indeed, of scientific criticism—helps to assure society that the science it supports is a responsible and worthwhile undertaking and not merely an avenue of self-expression for an elite group.

The Government's attitude toward dissemination of scientific information is necessarily affected by the influence of science upon our national posture. The idealistic motivation for science and the most compelling one for the creative individual is intellectual curiosity; a society that ignored this motivation would still achieve some material progress for a brief interval, but would have stifled the spark of the deepest human aspirations. But science is not pursued solely for human edification or even for improvement of our social and material well-being; parts of research and of development are aimed at maintaining our military strength to keep the peace. Results from these technical efforts cannot be transmitted as freely as can non-military science and technology; on the other hand, within the circle of military research establishments, quick, discriminating communication of discoveries is essential. The conflicting demands of secrecy and of free exchange, reflecting as they do the diversity of our technical and scientific goals, complicate the problem of effective communication.

Both the legislative and the executive branches of the Federal Government have already devoted considerable attention to the mounting problem of handling information. On the legislative side, the Senate Committee on Government Operations and its Subcommittee on Government Reorganization and International Organizations have studied the problem and have issued several reports dealing with it. On the executive side a previous Panel of the President's Science Advisory Committee (PSAC) under the chairmanship of W. O. Baker has examined the question of whether the Federal Government should establish a single all-encompassing centralized science information service, similar in scope to the U.S.S.R.'s All-Union Institute of Scientific and Technical Information, as a means of coping with the threatened breakdown in scientific communication. The Baker Panel concluded that no such drastic action was called for at the time, but that the National Science Foundation's role as a coordinator of science information services ought to be strengthened. Central to the recommendation of the Baker Panel was the establishment of the Office of Science Information Service (OSIS). The OSIS has been in existence since 1959 and has performed many of the functions envisioned for it by the Baker Panel. This Panel also urged the independent professional societies to participate aggressively in an expanded science and engineering communication system.

The scope of the present Panel study is somewhat broader than that of the earlier PSAC Panel since, among other things, the present Panel can assess how the earlier recommendations have turned out. In addition to considering the role of the Federal Government and the relation between the Federal Government's information systems and the non-Government systems, we have tried to examine the scientific communication process itself: how information is generated, stored, retrieved, summarized. Our report and recommendations are addressed therefore not only to the Federal agencies but also to private agencies, and to individual working scientists and engineers. We hope to apprise scientists and technologists of the current information problem and to arouse them to personal as well as group action in dealing with it.

How Much Communication Is Needed?

Everyone engaged in science—the working scientist, the scientific administrator, the head of a scientific agency —recognizes that scientific communication is necessary; the question is: how much is necessary? To expand an information system or to establish one where none now exists takes money and manpower. Since there are no unequivocal criteria for deciding what is a sufficient information system, why should one decide the appropriate size of his infor-especially if it means spending less on something else or if one's efforts are useful mainly to someone else? How does the head of a Federal agency decide the appropriate size of his information service? How does a professional society through its publication committee decide on a new journal? For that matter, how does a working scientist decide whether to spend more time in the library? Because of the elusive quality of scientific communication, because there are few criteria available to decide how much communication is enough, such decisions are generally made intuitively if not haphazardly. To the working scientist or engineer, time spent gathering information or writing reports is often regarded as a wasteful encroachment on time that would otherwise be spent producing results that he believes to be new. To the scientific administrator, the need for scientific communication is one of many competing needs— to be weighed against the need for additional computing equipment, or for more scientists, or for more stenographers.

It is no wonder that the scientific administrator, especially at the highest level in Government, so often fails to be impressed with the urgency of the communication problem or with the necessity of spending more to improve the situation. He is importuned on every hand by professional specialists to each of whom the situation in his specialty appears to be in a state of crisis that can be eased only by more spending. Communication is only one such professional specialty; it suffers by comparison with other services, such as, say, computing, in that the output of a computer as a rule demonstrably affects the course of a technical enterprise, whereas the output of an information system usually affects the course of a technical enterprise less directly and over a longer period.

We have been unable to make much progress in deciding how much communication is about right. Evidently, some knowledge is better recreated than retrieved. For example, most scientists recompute the square of a number rather than looking it up in Barlow's Tables. On the other hand, even in a well-equipped laboratory one would ordinarily look up the melting point of LiF rather than measure it. Thus the question of when to re-create a scientific result and when to use the information system is a matter of relative cost and familiarity with the system. A scientist resorts to the information system if he believes it is easier, or more illuminating, to consult the written record rather than to do the experiment himself. Yet the scientist's own estimate of what he wants by way of information may be inconsistent with what he should have to pursue his work most effectively. The anomalies of our information system have conditioned some scientists to active resistance to being informed.

An operational analysis of the process of technical discovery made by the Panel suggests that the individual theoretical scientist will, on the average, maximize his overall productivity if he spends half of his time trying to create new scientific information and half of his time digesting other work and communicating his own. This result seems to be rather insensitive to the values of the parameters that were used to characterize the processes of information retrieval and creation. We would therefore suspect that mathematical models of similar flavor might throw some light on the question of how much effort ought to be put into an information system, whether an individual's, a professional society's, or a Government agency's. But this is a speculation that further work can verify or deny. In the meantime, we have only commonsense to tell us that considerable effort—in most cases more than is now expended —must go into scientific communication, and that the effort required will grow.

Good Scientific Communication Is No Substitute for Good Management

Because information about what is going on is necessary for making management decisions, improvement in scientific information systems is sometimes represented as a panacea for bad management of research and development. Though it is true that poor management can and does occur with the best of communication systems, poor communication almost always leads to bad management.

We belabor this point because some articulate and concerned spokesmen have, at least by implication, confused the problem of communication with the problem of management of research and development. In some discussions of the advisability of establishing a single Department of Science, deficiencies in the scientific communication system have been invoked to help justify the merging of all Government science into a single department. But this is surely an oversimplification of a perplexing problem. Whether bringing the Government's total information system under a single organizational roof would improve communication is in the first place conjectural; in any case, even if the desired improvement were thereby achieved, better management of research and development would not automatically fol-

low. Information is one of many tools that the manager of research and development must have; the *use* to which he puts the information—indeed, the diligence and responsibility he shows in unearthing needed information—is determined only by his own skill as a manager. To expect miracles of management to follow from centralization of the information system is unjustifiably optimistic, especially since many important aspects of research and development management are, and must remain, decentralized.

PART II

Attributes and Problems of the Information Transfer Chain of Information Systems

The information problem is many separate problems because the information process is many separate processes. Moreover, information is handled in many different systems, and each information system serves many different communities, each with its own interests and outlook. In this part of our report we shall describe some attributes, and the corresponding problems, of information processing and of the systems, governmental and nongovernmental, that have evolved to handle scientific and technical information. Suggestions for solving the problems, both by individual and Government action, will be considered later.

The basic scientist, the technologist, and the administrator see the dimensions and nature of the scientific communication problem differently. Most basic scientists confine their interests to one or a few rather narrow specialties; the extent of each specialty is largely determined by the effectiveness of the scientist's communication system. If communication with a neighboring field becomes too difficult, the basic scientist imperceptibly narrows his interest to those matters on which he believes he can keep himself informed. Thus the information dilemma appears relatively remote to the basic scientist. But even in basic science, narrowing of the scientist's interests is a dangerous course. As we have already said, science is really indivisible; if it fragments into a host of wholly unconnected specialties, each specialty narrowing and the number of specialties increasing with time, science as an instrument for probing nature will be greatly weakened. Moreover, in spite of the obstacles to proper communication, modern science tends to become more and more interconnected. Though a scientist chooses to narrow his specialty, science itself creates an ever-increasing number of potential points of contact between the scientist's narrow specialty and the surrounding fields. As time goes on, successful pursuit of a narrow specialty requires effective contact with more and more diverse parts of the literature.

The technologist is at the other extreme from the basic scientist. He cannot afford the luxury of accommodating the size of his field of interest to what his information system can handle. His job is to design a rocket or a communication system or a reactor, and his customer will not be satisfied with inadequate design because some knowledge was out of his field. He must be receptive to cues from all fields of science and technology. He ignores related art at great peril, especially when the hardware that he creates is expensive. The problem of information access falls upon him more heavily than it does upon the basic scientist.

The information needs of the technical administrator overlap those of the scientist and the technologist, but the emphasis is different. He too must encompass large segments of technical information; yet the manager needs not only the technical results of a given investigation but also knowledge of what is being done by whom, and who is available for doing what. This kind of information we shall call "scientific intelligence." At every level of management, either in Government or in a research organization, scientific intelligence is used by the administrator when he draws up a research program, proposes a new project, or decides to cut back on an old one.

In a sense, every individual scientist or technologist is a research manager. At the beginning of a new research he must decide on his strategy (including allocation of his personal resources); he must even decide whether or not to do the research. In making such judgments, he too uses scientific intelligence; since these judgments are divided among so many more people than those made by the full-time research manager, his needs for scientific intelligence, though equally important in the aggregate, are not so clearly felt.

The Information Transfer Chain

The information process comprises separate steps or "unit operations": generation, recording and exposition, cataloging, storage and dissemination, retrieval and exploitation by the user. Since the steps are linked in the sense that the later steps depend on the earlier, the entire information process is chainlike; we shall call it the Information Transfer Chain. The first two steps in the chain—generation, and recording and exposition—are performed by the technical man and the organizations that support him, the later steps by the professional documentalists and the organizations that handle information, as well as by the users.

The information chain operates like a switching system. The ultimate aim is to connect the user, quickly and efficiently, to the proper information and to only the proper information. But perfectly precise switching is neither possible nor desirable. One cannot define in advance exactly what information is proper; the switching system must always allow for some browsing in neighboring areas. Moreover *the capacity of the user to absorb information limits the system.* Evidence is accumulating that the amount of scientific literature the user will pay attention to is limited; one survey conducted by *Biological Abstracts* suggests that on the average a biologist can scan journals or titles or abstracts involving 5,000 papers per year. Thus the information switching system, to be effective, must be more than a passive switch: it must select, compact, and review material for the individual user so that he *actually assimilates* what he is exposed to, and he is not exposed to too much that is unimportant or irrelevant. Its fundamental task is switching *information*, not documents.

Most of what is written about the information problem is concerned with the later steps in the information transfer chain; that is, analyzing information for the purpose of identification, placing information in its proper place in a classification system, storing information, alerting, and matching stored information with requests for information. The elaborate automated systems described in the popular press and the art and science of librarianship are concerned exclusively with these later steps in the handling of information already generated and not at all with the initial generation of information. It is our belief that the information problem is aggravated by this separation between what is done by the documentalist and what is done by the author: that the earlier and later steps in the chain are not as separate as tradition holds them to be, and that improvement in the former, especially with a view toward subsequent retrieval, would undoubtedly ease the latter.

The Information Process as Part of the Research Process

Carrying further the thread of argument of the previous paragraph, we come to perhaps the most essential attribute of the information process: *the information process is an integral part of research and development.* Research and development cannot be envisaged without communication of the results of research and development; moreover, such communication involves in an intimate way all segments of the technical community, not only the documentalists. The attitudes and practices toward information of all those connected with research and development must become indistinguishable from their attitudes and practices toward research and development itself. This is the central theme of our report.

We place special stress upon what seems an obvious point because, in the early days of science, the problem of communication could be managed casually. Each individual scientist could work out his own private communication system, suitable to his own needs, and, since the requirements were relatively small, the whole matter could be treated rather incidentally. But with the growth of science a casual attitude toward communication can lead only to insufficient communication. Scientists individually, technical societies, agencies supporting research and development, will have to recognize that adequate communication no longer comes free. Communication cannot be viewed merely as librarians' work; that is, as not really part of science. An appreciable and increasing fraction of science's resources, including deeply motivated technical men as well as money, will inevitably have to go into handling the information that science creates.

Science can ultimately cope with the information expansion only if enough of its most gifted practitioners will compact, review, and interpret the literature both for their own use and for the benefit of more specialized scientists. The Panel believes that such activities may eventually achieve a position in the science of the future comparable to that of theoretical physics in modern-day physics. Recognition of the importance of such scientific middlemen is discernible in the proliferation of the so-called specialized information center where information is digested and interpreted. The Panel views the specialized information center as one key to ultimate resolution of the scientific information crisis.

The Discipline-Mission Duality

Information generated for one purpose is often useful for quite different purposes. The documentalist is therefore faced with a difficult problem of classification: according to what fundamental scheme ought he to label a segment of knowledge so as to make it available to all who need it, yet avoid redundant announcing, abstracting, and identifying?

Scientific knowledge, by the middle of the 19th century, was divided into classical disciplines such as chemistry, physics, physiology, etc., each with its own communication system. As long as there were few points of contact between the disciplines, each disciplinary system operated in fairly strict isolation from the systems of other disciplines. As science has become interdisciplinary and as the literature has grown, the weaknesses in the strict disciplinary classification of knowledge have become apparent. Chemists as well as physicists used information on the infrared spectra of hydrocarbons; abstracts of the same articles on infrared spectra began to appear therefore in both *Chemical Abstracts* and *Physics Abstracts*. The secondary literature expanded, and thus added to the information problem.

The growing importance of interdisciplinary fields has caused some duplication in information systems. However, much more overlapping has resulted from the extraordinary growth of mission-oriented science, especially science supported by Government agencies with fairly well-defined missions. Thus research and development supported by the National Aeronautics and Space Administration furthers the applied mis-

sion of the agency; namely, the exploration of space. The work itself falls into almost all the traditional disciplinary fields—chemistry, physics, astronomy, biology, etc. The workers in the field are *space* scientists or engineers, dedicated to achieving the mission of NASA; they are also rocket chemists, guidance physicists, weightlessness physiologists, and the like. The information collected by these diverse specialists very properly should be collected, disseminated, and controlled in a mission-oriented (in this case, space) information system, since what the physiologist learns about weightlessness affects the engineer's design of a space capsule. But the knowledge discovered by the physiologist about weightlessness is also useful to the basic physiologist interested in the kinesthetic sensory system. The basic physiologist is not likely to read, nor should he be expected to read, the space literature; hence the information contained in the mission-oriented NASA system must also appear in the discipline-oriented American Physiological Society system. Obviously the situation is reciprocal: in many cases the information originating in the discipline-oriented system must also find its way into the mission-oriented system. Thus we recognize a fundamental mission-discipline duality in information systems that is familiar to all who have worked in a large laboratory where a related duality often goes under the name of systems-components. The technical community itself has responded to the mission-discipline duality by organizing itself into horizontal discipline-oriented societies such as the American Physical Society and into vertical mission-oriented societies as the American Rocket Society. A physicist working on rockets will ordinarily belong to both the American Physical Society and the American Rocket Society. He will communicate the same results to his colleagues in both societies, in the one case flavoring his communication with more physics than rocketry, in the other case with more rocketry than physics.

The mission-discipline duality, even though it has evolved gradually and is inherent in modern scientific communication, imposes many complications upon the information switching system. In the first place, it implies a duplication of effort, albeit a necessary duplication. The same individual must often present his paper twice, once to his discipline-oriented colleagues and once to his mission-oriented colleagues. This places a burden not only on the communicator but also, after publication, on his ultimate audience. For the literature has now grown by two papers instead of one, and retrieval has become more complicated. Secondly, the compacted literature—that is, abstracts, keyword indexes, titles—of the one system must eventually appear in the other. This inevitably introduces delays. Finally, even though a mission system overlaps with several discipline-oriented systems, the overlap is incomplete. Would the physicist interested in nuclear structure find better coverage in the nuclear section of *Physics Abstracts* or the physics section of *Nuclear Science Abstracts?* Not knowing the answer a priori, many physicists consult both.

The mission-discipline duality also raises fundamental questions concerning the Government agency information systems. Government agencies usually have fairly well-defined applied missions. Presumably all the technologists or research and development administrators who work for the agency are united by a single interest—achievement of the agency's mission. For this technical audience, held together by a common purpose, a mission-oriented internal information system run by the Government agency makes good sense. But what about Government agencies whose mission is so broad (as for example the Department of Defense) as to comprise almost all science as well as many, many sub-missions? What of

the Government agency such as the National Science Foundation whose primary mission is support of basic research in all fields? In the case of the National Science Foundation, just who would be served by an information system, complete with abstracting service and bibliographic controls that covered only those parts of basic research that are paid for by NSF and almost every useful item of which would ultimately appear in the standard disciplinary systems? Source of support is no valid criterion for bibliographic classification. Aside from the practical fact that agency systems are usually quicker than disciplinary systems, information systems based on the criterion of source of support can have relatively little use to the basic scientist unless the source of support is so broad that the information system brings the great bulk of a scientific field under its control. Thus the NSF supports only a small part of all the American work in nuclear physics, and an information system that covered only what NSF supported would be of little use to a nuclear physicist; on the other hand, AEC supports most of the country's work in nuclear physics, and an AEC information system, especially when not wholly confined to AEC-supported research, can be quite useful to the nuclear physicist, both inside and outside AEC.

But there are other than purely scientific uses to which Government information systems are put. To the administrator, research and development manager, company trying to get a contract, or congressional investigator who wishes to know what is going on—not because he can make detailed scientific use of the material but because he needs the information to form management judgments—such collections of information are invaluable. The collection, however, is then being used as a source of scientific intelligence, not of scientific information, and ought to be so recognized. Many research institutions as a matter of custom and etiquette periodically present their work as a whole, even though the work lies in many different fields; such "reports to the trustees" are traditional in the scientific world. To some extent the agencywide information system, especially in the basic sciences, is a continuing report to the agency's management, giving the management an idea of what is being done by whom. As an effective bibliographic tool in the basic sciences, such reports, because of their limited coverage, are at a serious conceptual disadvantage.

The agencywide system generally has much more validity in technology than in basic science, since technology is itself strongly mission oriented and depends upon many disciplines. An information system oriented around the same mission as the technology is therefore natural and proper. Moreover, the technological literature generally is less well organized than is the purely scientific; technological literature, being often in the form of informal reports, may find no bibliographic home outside an agency information system. Were they not collected in agency systems, many specialized technical reports would never be recorded and would be lost forever.

The Relation Between the Various Information-Handling Communities; Financial Problems

The diversity of information systems raises many jurisdictional, and financial, questions. As we have seen, information is generated and handled by many different communities: the technical societies, Government agencies, private publishers, technically oriented companies. The functions of many of these organizations overlap, partly because some of the groups are organized around a mission and some are organized around a discipline, partly because in a free society, overlap and blurring of sharp lines is inevitable. Thus some Government agencies act in many respects like a full-fledged technical publishing house. For example, AEC arranges for the publication of books, monographs, and journals that it deems to be relevant to atomic energy. Again in the field of atomic energy, parallel publication efforts have been launched by numerous private publishers: in English, there are now three series of monographs on atomic energy of which one is originated and partially subsidized by AEC, two are issued by private publishers. Similarly, where a mission-oriented technical society has sprung up to meet the requirements of people working for a given Government agency, the communication programs of the technical society and of the Government often overlap. For example, when all of atomic energy was classified, all communication in the field—reports, meetings, even journals—was published by AEC. Now that large parts of atomic energy are unclassified, much of the communication process has been taken over by the mission-oriented societies that cluster around atomic energy—the American Nuclear Society, the Health Physics Society, the Radiation Research Society, the Society of Nuclear Medicine. But the takeover is not complete; AEC continues to keep the whole literature of nuclear science under bibliographic control, and to provide other information services that are not available from non-Government sources.

Overlapping of private and public services, in this case information systems, is traditional in our society. Can we identify criteria according to which we decide which segment of the information system ought to be the Government's direct responsibility, which parts ought to be subsidized by the Government but remain under private control, which parts ought to be completely private? The Government agency information systems have evolved without any Government-wide policy concerning the relative roles of the private and public enterprises, and some guidance on this tricky issue is needed.

Many Government information systems are better financed than non-Government ones—at least the Government is often better able to absorb the expense of an information system that does not visibly pay its own way than is a private institution, either profit or nonprofit. In the hands of a vigorous information system director and a sympathetic agency administrator, Government information systems therefore could well be more expansionist than are the non-Government ones, and this expansion by Government could aggravate the financial distress of the non-Government systems. We must ask whether such encroachment exists, and if it does, is it, on the whole, desirable— is the overall result a more effective or a less effective information system?

Not that the financial distress of our non-Government information organs is in any real degree caused by Government competition; the main cause is that the volume of information has grown too fast. *Chemical Abstracts* in 1930 contained 54,000 abstracts; a private subscription cost $7.50 per year, an institutional subscription cost $12 per year. In 1962 *Chemical Abstracts* published 165,000 abstracts and the 1963 price was $500 per year to American Chemical Society members and to colleges and universities, and $1,000 per year to all others. Though these prices fully pay for publication of *Chemical Abstracts,* they leave nothing to pay for badly needed experimentation in new ways of abstracting and indexing chemical literature. Insofar as the Federal Government is the main sponsor of both basic and applied research, it has responsibility for the financial viability of the communication network whether it is within or without Government: if *Chemical* or *Biological Abstracts* were about to cease publication because they had no money to continue, the Federal Government could not idly stand by.

Finally we come to a most delicate,

and perhaps crucial, issue in the discussion of the relative role of Government in the technical communication system. The traditional communication channels, organized generally by discipline, are strongly under the control of the practicing technical people. A communication system controlled by the people it serves may in some respects be less efficient than a monolithic government system; it has, however, the overriding merit of being sensitive to the needs of its customers. It was as much as anything to preserve this essential quality of the present rather haphazard information system that the Baker Panel recommended against establishing an all-encompassing, Government-operated information system in which control, however well meaning and beneficent its intent, is removed from the practitioners. Much thoughtful attention must be given to the point raised by the Baker Panel before one embarks on a great expansion of the Government's own information system. Nevertheless, we must recognize that our primary concern is to maintain the strength of our science and technology. We must search for the means by which we can improve the efficiency of our communication system without sacrificing the values inherent in our traditional methods and organizations.

The Emergence of the Report and Preprint Literature

To many professional librarians, especially those who became librarians before informal research and development reports assumed their present dominant position, the technical report is the crux of the current information crisis insofar as the Government is concerned. And the professional librarian has real cause for alarm. About 100,000 informal Government reports, of which 75,000 are unclassified, are written each year in the United States as compared to 450,000 papers in standard American technical journals. Material that appears in standard journals is kept under bibliographic control; it is generally abstracted and made part of the permanent record. This is too infrequently the case with research and development reports, most of which record work done for the Government either in its own laboratories or under contract. The documentation community has taken an equivocal attitude toward informal reports; in some cases the existence of these reports is acknowledged and their content abstracted in the abstracting journals. In other cases informal reports are given no status; they are alleged to be not worth retaining as part of the permanent record unless their contents finally appear in a standard hard-copy journal. Whether this position is tenable even in the basic sciences is open to question; it certainly is no longer tenable in technological development. Here the informal report, rather than the formal paper, has always been the main vehicle of publication. Most companies doing development had fairly elaborate internal report systems long before the war-born deluge of Government reports. Because so much development is now done by Government, a large fraction of all technical, especially development, information is now contained in the Government report literature: what was a minor problem when Government development was minor has become a major headache now that Government-sponsored development dominates all development.

Some basic scientists see in a variant of the formal report—the preprint—the beginning of the breakdown of the basic-science communication system. In many highly competitive, fast-moving fields of basic science, such as molecular biology, the machinery of publication in standard journals moves too slowly to serve fully the needs of the scientific community. It has therefore become customary for scientists to circulate preprints of articles among their colleagues. Such informal circulation, which harks back to the earliest days of science when new results were communicated by personal letter, has the advantage of speed. But it also has within it the seeds of serious disorders for science; for such distribution of scientific knowledge is controlled neither with respect to content nor bibliographically (to the point where many librarians are unaware of its existence). The distribution list for preprints usually consists of a few hundred of the author's colleagues, and this militates against the publicness of science. A preprint does not have to pass a critical referee; the preprint "literature" is therefore irresponsible, and cannot serve, as does the refereed literature, to assure society that the science it supports is a responsible enterprise. Altogether the preprint system has created an information problem in some parts of basic science which, in its way, is as serious as the problem created by the informal report system: in both cases the product is unedited; it is privately distributed; it is not abstracted; and it is difficult to retrieve. The scientific community must devise ways of retaining the timeliness of the preprint and yet reducing its privateness and irresponsibility. Rapid publication of preprints in standard journals and discarding of preprints that have been already printed are practices that would obviously help.

Development of Information-Handling Technology

The growth of published information has fostered the invention of many new handling and searching techniques and concepts. Best known are the retrieval systems based on automatic machinery. In addition, there are imaginative new ways of listing titles; for example, permuted titles,[1] of gaining access to the literature (citation indexes), of preparing abstracts or translations (by ma-

---

[1] The earliest reference found to this principle appears in A. Crestadoro's *Art of Making Catalogs of Libraries,* London, 1856.

chine), of compacting the physical size of the record (microfilm and micro-fiches), of duplicating printed material.

The invention of the new retrieval methods is beginning to affect our traditional modes of communication. The traditional forms of the book, journal, and reprint may eventually give way to the machine storage of graphical and digital information and machine-generated copy. The technical publishing business may gradually be transformed into the *information handling* business in which the printing press as a means of mass production of identical documents no longer plays a dominant role.

The mechanical devices are divided into two types, graphical and digital. The former handle photographs of documents directly, and they require human interpretation (i.e., reading) to retrieve the information contained. The devices which handle information in digital form cover a wide spectrum.

At one extreme, the automated index compacts the intellectual content of a document into a few index terms or key-words that are stored in the machine. These systems can retrieve mechanically the desired information if the query can be represented adequately in such primitive terms. However, the human effort required to index in depth any significant body of information (e.g., 10,000 man-years of work by B.S. chemists would be needed to index all U.S. chemical patents) is a serious shortcoming of such systems.

At the other extreme, the whole text could be put into digital form, say from the monotape used to prepare a book. Practically nothing has been accomplished in developing adequate search strategies for purely mechanical retrieval from such a store, although there is likelihood that such methods will be developed in the next decade.

A characteristic of any nontrivial information retrieval system is the large volume of information in terms of bits of storage required and the small amount of processing (relative to numerical data processing). Equipment directed to these characteristics is not yet available, although it is technically feasible.

Because most of the schemes and devices for handling information are so new, their limitations are still not fully understood; in particular, it is not usually appreciated that the new systems generally retrieve *documents* rather than *information*. The proponents of new systems often urge them on the information community with zeal and enthusiasm, and the documentalist or administrator must decide how much to accept and how much to reject. Elaborate automation systems have been bought both within and without Government before the real usefulness of the systems has been assessed. It will therefore be important to understand the promise and limitation of automatic information retrieval systems. Administrators and documentalists will have to improve their grasp of modern information-handling technology so that they do not look upon elaborate and expensive computers as magical panaceas for their information-handling woes.

The Student

The size of the information problem as well as the developments in information-handling techniques place new burdens upon the student. He must learn much more about his subject and he must learn more about how to keep in touch with his subject than did students of earlier generations. Would we not ameliorate the information problem if we required each new scientist or technologist to understand the techniques of communication just as we are beginning to require him to understand computer-technology? Courses in the use of literature and in technical communication have been sporadically offered in many schools of science and engineering. Would more such courses and further modernization of course content help to keep up with new technologies? These questions are pursued in Part 3 of this report.

International Aspects of Scientific Information

Finally we touch briefly on problems created because science and technology are international enterprises. Historical accident has fragmented the world politically, and this political fragmentation is fundamentally inconsistent with the unity of science. Nevertheless scientists have through the years developed rather effective methods for overcoming their political and geographic isolations— they have formed international unions, they exchange reprints, they hold many international meetings. But the burgeoning of science has complicated the workings of the international instruments that have grown up to help scientists in one country exchange views with those in another. All the problems that beset domestic communication beset international communication, but with certain additional complication; most obvious is the diversity of languages. Considerable progress is being made in machine translation of scientific material, and the Panel believes that machine translation may reduce the need for learning languages.

Geographic fragmentation further complicates the mission-discipline duality: superposed on the information systems organized by mission and discipline are information systems organized by geographic division, and switching between the systems is cumbersome. Thus each of the atomic energy commissions —the French, the British, the Russian, for example, as well as the American— has its own information system. Unclassified reports generated within the French and British, and to some extent within the Russian, systems are eventually collected and abstracted in the American system, and vice versa; but the foreign reports sift into the domestic system relatively slowly and there is much duplication. What is true of the atomic energy information system is even more true of information systems in fields that have a long tradition of independent national publication: there is overlapping duplication, and general inefficiency. A step toward improvement worthy of study would be to establish a number of technical depositories abroad, comparable to the 12 regional depositories being established in the United States with the cooperation of the Department of Defense, National Aeronautics and Space Administration, Atomic Energy Commission, and National Science Foundation. These centers furnish convenient facilities for reference to Government reports, and would help unify our existing information facilities in many countries.

One aspect of the international communication system gives it a unique importance. Science as one of mankind's common undertakings has great potential as a generator of international good will. The international scientific organizations, like the international unions, were originally created to cope with the problem of scientific communication; and, in general, international cooperation in the sciences has meant primarily cooperation in communication of scientific results. Any further rationalization of the international system of scientific communication will go right to the center of the whole matter of international cooperation in science and will have a corresponding effect in fashioning science into a stronger instrument of international understanding.

PART III

Suggestions: The Technical Community

In the previous section we identified several unsolved problems of our information system. In this and in the next section we offer suggestions to the technical community and to the Government agencies for correcting some of the deficiencies we have identified. Our suggestions to the technical community will be concerned mostly with rationalizing the information transfer process itself insofar as this process depends on the written, rather than the spoken, word; our suggestions to the Government will be aimed at strengthening the Government organizations that handle information.

Authors Must Accept More Responsibility for Information Retrieval

We have seen that the information transfer chain can be split into those parts carried out by the author (initial generation) and those parts carried out by the documentalist and the user (dissemination, cataloging, storage, and retrieval). Traditionally, authors have assumed little responsibility for the later links in the information transfer chain. This sharp separation of tasks aggravates the difficulties of information retrieval: authors ought to prepare their papers with much more sensitive regard for subsequent dissemination and retrieval than has been their custom. The managers of primary publication (editors, publishers, technical societies) must likewise do their part to ease retrieval of the information they publish.

The individual author can help in many ways. Thus the title of a technical paper should be one of the simplest and most effective devices for announcement and retrieval; yet titles, particularly of patents, are often meaningless. The value of a title as a bibliographic device depends on how well, and how succinctly, it conveys the sense of the papers. Authors should use specific and meaty words that would be positively helpful to a person trying to judge the content of a paper from its title. Referees, journal editors, and patent examiners often demand that poorly written papers or patents be rewritten; they must demand that poorly titled papers or patents be retitled.

Closely related to titles are keywords and thesaurus classifications. Many journals now require their authors to label their articles with keywords taken from an assigned thesaurus. In some fields, notably nuclear spectroscopy, the data fall into such well-defined and unvarying categories that authors, by assigning keywords, can provide a very complete index to the content of their papers. Even in such broad fields as engineering, keyword indexing is being undertaken with considerable success. The American Institute of Chemical Engineers now requires keywords on each article, and the Engineers' Joint Council is preparing an engineering thesaurus. Some fields, especially those that have strong interdisciplinary implication, do not lend themselves as well to keyword classifications; nevertheless, the utility of keywords, particularly for retrieval by computer, encourages their widest possible use.

What is true of titles and keywords is also true of abstracts; no one can abstract an article as economically as can the author; yet many journals do not require an author abstract. We would suggest that every paper be accompanied by an author abstract that is acceptable to the editor of the journal, and that each editor insist (perhaps by detached reviewing) on abstracts the form and characteristics of which best serve the users in the particular field served by the journal.

Unnecessary Publication Should Be Eliminated

A simple but urgent suggestion to authors is to refrain from unnecessary publication. The literature has been and always will be cluttered with poor and redundant articles. In final analysis the quality of what is published reflects the taste and judgment of the individual author. Admonition to authors to restrain themselves from premature, unnecessary publication can have little effect unless the climate of the entire technical and scholarly community encourages restraint and good taste. But there are many pressures to publish quantity, fewer pressures to publish quality. Those supporting research can much more easily judge how many papers have been published than they can judge how good the papers are. When the volume of publication in a field becomes so great that many of the papers remain unread, the prestige that can be properly assigned to the writing of a paper diminishes; the technical paper as a unit of currency for measuring the merit of a scientist becomes devalued, and administrators must consider this when they insist on frequent publication.

Inadequate means of switching between information systems also encourages redundant publication. If those who will be interested in specific results of a scientist do not belong to the readership of some one journal, there is pressure for the scientist to publish similar material not once but twice or even more. As the information transfer network now exists, with main emphasis on journals to switch the information, such duplication is essential if the information is to be transferred to those who need it. The need for duplicate publication can be reduced by improving alerting systems of all kinds so that they will be more dependable and more widely used.

Some duplicate publication will always be necessary; in particular, because of the mission-discipline duality, the same material must, one way or another, be readily available to users of both the mission-oriented and discipline-oriented systems. But the needs of the users of both kinds of systems could more frequently be served by publication in only one system if the switching devices—title announcements, abstracts, referral services—between the two systems were fast and efficient. Improvements in switching mechanisms, for example, in fast exchange of permuted title lists, are even now technically feasible and they should be widely used.

Many Government agencies have tried to avoid publication of the same primary material in both their report system and in overlapping technical society systems

by encouraging primary publication i the open (usually, discipline-based) li erature. Reprints of material so pul lished are acquired by the agency syste and the reprints are recorded and a nounced in the agency system's regul title or abstract journal. The schem works well where the paces of th agency system and of the discipline oriented systems are comparable. Unfo tunately, especially in technology, a fas moving agency cannot gear the pace its information system to that of a archival, discipline-oriented, technic society. Nevertheless, agencies shoul rely upon *open* literature for primar publication to the greatest extent feas ble, and they should be ready to ado better switching mechanisms betwee their system and the open literature a those become available.

American Technical Books Must Be Improved

The previous suggestions relate t those parts of the information transfe chain in which the overlap betwee author and documentalist is clearl recognized. In other parts of the chai the author's job does not overlap s clearly with the job of the documen talist; these parts have to do with th content and manner of expression o what the author seeks to communicate whether it be information already avail able or new information. Briefly, we be lieve that clearer and more succinc writing will in itself smooth the avenue of communication and the mechanism of retrieval.

We are convinced that too man scientific books are written hastily an with much less care than the subject deserve. Writing a good book takes a immense amount of time and work. I implies the clarification of many idea that one has been willing to leave alon for awhile; the review of a large, repe titious, and often unclear literature; an the careful arrangement and rephrasin of the whole subject. A major task fac ıg our American technical community to write not only more books but ьetter books.

One way to get better books would be ɔ commission their writing by recognized authorities, and to pay the authors ∋ally well for their efforts. We would rge agencies, both governmental and on-governmental, to sponsor the writ-ıg of surveying and summarizing books ɪ the same way as they now sponsor ∍search. We believe agencies ought to dopt policies regarding the reimburse-ıent of authors that encourage, rather ıan hinder, the writing of books by ompetent people who are supported by ıe agencies. In particular, we believe ;overnment-sponsored fellowships for ∍search and training grants should be vailable for the writing of books.

ʰe Technical Community Should ;ive Higher Status to the Reviewer

Scholarly reviews, articles, and critical ∍ibliographies also play an important ›art in easing the information crisis. ʰey serve the special needs of both ʰe established workers in a field and ʰe graduate student entering the field, s well as the general needs of the non-ɔecialist. Review writing is a task vorthy of the deepest minds, able to ∍ecast, critically analyze, synthesize, and Iluminate large bodies of results. The ∍lation of the reviewer to the existing ɔut widely scattered bits of knowledge ∍sembles the relation of the theorist to vailable pieces of experimental infor-ıation. In order to emphasize the grow-ıg importance of the reviewer and also ʰe growing difficulties that he faces, cientific and technical societies should ∍ward his work with good pay and with ʰe regard that has been reserved here-ɔfore for the discoverer of experimental ıformation. Those asked to write re-iews or to give invited papers review-ıg a subject should be selected by the cientific societies with the same care s are recipients of honors or of appoint-ıents to the staff of a university.

Hand in hand with the increasing recognition of the review author should go an increasing realization by him of his growing responsibilities. He should view his subject dispassionately, paying equal attention to his own contribution and to the contributions of others. He should search for remaining problems and the most fruitful areas of further work as diligently as he emphasizes existing accomplishments. He should also point to areas where further work is necessary.

Modern Psychological Insights Into Communication Should Be Exploited

New information could be made easier to assimilate, and in this sense easier to retrieve, if authors wrotr better. We do not understand the communication process well enough to know how our natural language can be made into an instrument for the most effective presentation of scientific and technical information, but progress is being made. Advances in our understanding of the communication process should become known to authors and to the information-handling community, and should be put to work in the improvement of our technical writing. Nor should devices other than improvements in the natural language be ignored. Recognizing the danger of creating too many highly specialized languages, we point out nevertheless that symbols or conventions to replace wordly clichés or to describe commonly used methods of instrumentation could reduce the volume of the literature and help ease its retrieval. Or judiciously used journalistic techniques, such as different type fonts, display boxes, different colors, might help to make the technical literature easier to assimilate. Many of these techniques might be repugnant to those brought up in the conservative scholarly tradition, yet if further study and experiment shows them to be effective, the technical community ought to consider their adoption.

Our Scientists and Engineers Must Express Themselves Clearly

Much more obvious than any deficiency in our understanding of the communication process itself, or in the possible application of journalistic techniques, is our inability to use natural English properly. This Panel is gravely concerned, as are many others who have written on the information problem, that so many American scientists and technologists can neither speak nor write effective English, that the new language of science and technology is turgid, heavy, and unclear. This is a problem that goes beyond what the Panel has set out to do. The seeds of articulateness are sown in the home and at the elementary and high school level. Nevertheless we strongly suggest that science and engineering departments demand much more expository writing as part of regular courses, and that ability to communicate well be made a firm requirement for graduation from our technical schools.

The Technique of Handling Information Must Be Widely Taught

But our schools and colleges will have to do more than insist on proficiency in handling the language. They will also have to insist on some proficiency in the techniques of information retrieval. The technical man, as an author, contributes to the information explosion; as a user of information, he is overwhelmed by the explosion. He must therefore be able not only to express himself clearly and succinctly and with proper regard for subsequent retrieval of what he writes; he must also be acquainted with the new tools and techniques of information handling. Imparting such skills to our new generation of technical people is the job of our colleges, universities, and technical schools. They will have to teach, much more aggressively than they have in the past, the techniques of technical communication.

Schools of science and technology have offered some training in use of the literature and in the techniques of communication, but their efforts have been sporadic. Only in those fields, notably chemistry, where the information crisis has been clearly discerned, has much formal training in literature retrieval been given. Some chemistry departments have for years required their students to take short courses in the use of the literature, and many have adopted the more effective procedure of making active use of the literature a necessary part of the work in such courses as Qualitative Organic Analysis. It is probably no accident that the practicing chemist subsequently demonstrates greater proficiency in using the literature than do most of his colleagues in other disciplines. Engineers, on the other hand, receive virtually no training in literature techniques, and they pursue their daily work unmindful of the powerful resources awaiting their call. We are glad that the Engineers' Joint Council has recognized this serious lack and is formulating plans to fill the need. We would go a step further and suggest that all professional societies in the sciences and in engineering adopt an official policy calling for training in the preparation and use of literature as part of the curriculum. Accreditation teams should subsequently inquire not only into the adequacy of the library, as in the past, but also into the ways in which its use is promoted and facilitated. This has been done for many years by the American Chemical Society's Committee on Professional Training. Government agencies supporting research at a university should recognize support of the library as a legitimate expense.

Attempts to provide more adequate training in scientific communication and information retrieval encounter several problems. The support of the college administration and department heads must be gained. There are too few professors who are themselves sufficiently knowledgeable in the use of the literature to be able to teach the modern techniques effectively. Students themselves must acquire enthusiasm for learning how to cope with the information problems they will surely encounter in their careers. It should not be overlooked that neophytes in the scientific and engineering professions usually pattern their professional behavior after the behavior of the professional tutor. Only if the technical community itself becomes information minded will its students become information minded.

We recognize and support NSF's programs aimed at training teachers in the field of scientific documentation. We also urge that more teaching material, especially books, be prepared as texts for courses in technical communication. It is true that books on this subject are already available. However, most of them were written at a time when the scientific information problem was less critical than it now is; they generally aim at helping the author put across his ideas and his personality. What are needed in addition are books that cover the author's entire role in the information transfer chain, and that describe recent developments both in information-handling technology, and in those parts of psychology and information theory that bear on the communication problem.

The Technical Documentalist Must Be Recognized and Supported

Even though the individual scientist and engineer becomes more proficient in handling the literature, there is obviously more published literature than the average individual can master in all its detail. The technical man therefore needs the continuing and growing support of professionals who really know how to exploit the literature fully, and who are able to invent imaginative new approaches to the techniques of information transfer.

We therefore strongly support NSF's efforts to develop college and university programs aimed at attracting more science and engineering students to careers in technical information. A science or engineering degree with an option in technical documentation may be an appropriate pattern. We also recommend that secondary school guidance officers learn more about career opportunities in modern technical librarianship. The library profession has so far given only a token nod to the challenge presented by the radically new systems for organizing, storing, and retrieving technical information. We believe this shortcoming would be overcome if more able scientists and engineers went into technical librarianship.

New Switching Methods Must Be Explored and Exploited

In the previous paragraphs we have proposed some measures that authors could take to smooth the transfer of information from author to user. We consider now what can be done to improve those steps in the information transfer chain that are more directly under the control of the documentalist and the user; these include dissemination, storage and retrieval.

As we have already said, the basic problem of literature access can be considered a switching problem—switching information, not documents. The basic need is to connect each customer, as nearly as possible, to the information he needs, plus a little more. The information-handling community has come up with many inventions, both in hardware and in technique, that hold promise in this connection. Some of these schemes, such as citation indexing, or issuing a daily scientific newspaper, have either not been tried, or are being tried on a small scale. Permuted title indexes are beginning to spread with *Chemical Titles* and the indexes in each issue of *Biological Abstracts* leading the way. Data and information centers have caught on widely. In the following paragraphs we shall discuss some of these new-switching methods. Our main purpose is not so much to recommend one specific scheme over another as it is to emphasize the need for innovation, imagination, and courage. New techniques must be tried and new attempts supported. Mistakes, some of them costly, will occur. Yet to do nothing new is perhaps the worst mistake; the flood of undigested information will surely engulf our science and shatter it into isolated fragments unless we change the traditional methods that we use to handle the flood. Some societies, notably the American Physical Society and the American Chemical Society, have shown admirable initiative in trying new schemes; others have been much less venturesome. We urge all organizations concerned with technical information to investigate the new techniques and ideas and to take a sympathetic attitude toward innovation in handling of information. We wish especially to commend the NSF for its support of research in this field, and in particular for its support of practical tests of new modes of technical communication.

Centralized Depositories Are an Attractive Possibility

An attractive *technical* solution to the problem of the dissemination and retrieval of documents is the centralized depository. This would acquire documents in a field of its responsibility; it would broadcast abstracts in a regular announcement bulletin; copies of the full texts would be available on order from the depository. Papers sent to the depository would be freely available for journal publication, thus encouraging journals to continue and to expand their vital function of selection and quality leadership. This system is now in partial effect for Government reports put out by AEC, DOD, and NASA. Individual grantees and contractors of these agencies also participate in it, especially for the dissemination of technical reports not published elsewhere.

The central depository has some ad-

vantages as a substitute for, or better, as a supplement to, conventional publication. It is extremely fast; it rationalizes the preprint; it compacts the circulating literature; it funnels the accumulation from a given field in one place for efficient retrieval. By relieving the conventional journals of their implicit obligation to process every contribution that might be conceivably useful to science, it can leave them with the more creative and manageable responsibility of selecting and encouraging the best contributions for wide distribution. Centralized facilities can also be the focal points for the development of automatic processing techniques that are uneconomical for widely scattered services. The Atomic Energy Commission and the Armed Services Technical Information Agency (ASTIA) repository systems have already proved their effectiveness for technical reports. ASTIA fulfills requests for documents in 3 to 6 days and soon plans to give faster service. The quality of print retrieved from microfilm with new copying equipment used by the large depositories is close to that of the original document.

Despite the technical and possibly even the economic advantages of a switching center based on a central depository, a number of problems must be solved before this method can be considered seriously as the primary method of dissemination. Perhaps the main obstacles to its more general adoption may come from the attitudes of some elements of the technical community itself. It is not certain how scientists would react to the establishment of such a system, since all previous experiments (for example, the American Documentation Institute) have lacked some features essential to a successful central depository: adequate coverage; broadcast announcement; auxiliary select journals and retrieval services; adequate financial support; approbation by scientific and governmental leadership. Some members of the Panel are more optimistic than others about the facility with which the hard-copy journal, with the prestige that purportedly goes with publication in the conservative traditions, can be led to share its functions with the depository, even on the grounds of broader concern for the unity and effectiveness of science. In any event, coordinated systems developed on the initiative of scientific societies are preferable, for many reasons, to those based on centralized judgment of a Government bureaucracy. In fact, in fields such as basic physics and chemistry, in which strong scientific societies have evolved, the outlook for effective communication systems involving the gradual evolution of a depository approach is relatively optimistic. These efforts should be given every possible encouragement as answers to the communication problem in which scientists play the most effective part.

We are much impressed with the ingenious "halfway solution" to the central depository problem that the American Physical Society has devised. The society divides its contributions into those that are very timely and particularly important and those that are less timely and more archival. The former are published in abbreviated form with less than a month's delay in *Physical Review Letters*. The latter are published in extenso in *The Physical Review* with a 4 to 6 months' delay; abstracts of articles appearing in *The Physical Review* are distributed as an abstract bulletin with *Physical Review Letters*. *The Physical Review* is becoming a sort of central depository; more and more physicists read only the abstract bulletin, and consult the full articles in their library, or obtain reprints from the author. In another experiment the American Chemical Society has reported the outstanding popularity of an advance reprint service for *Industrial and Engineering Chemistry;* contributions to the journal are promptly announced and reprints are made available even before articles are published. From these arrangements to the full-fledged depository appears

to us to be a relatively small step. Once individual scientists become accustomed to consulting abstract or title bulletins for the purpose of current awareness, the magic of the unique hard copy, with its very long delay, ought to disappear.

The outlook in other fields, for example, in biology and medical research, is dimmed by the complex interrelationship of the subjects with which biologists deal and the lack of comprehensive technical organizations comparable to the American Chemical Society or the American Physical Society. The problem of communication in this field may not be solved until the workers in the field evolve, possibly with Government support, comparably strong central organizations.

More and Better Specialized Information Centers Are Needed

The centralized document depository is primarily a clearinghouse for documents; in general, it does not try to glean information from the documents it handles, but merely provides appropriate documents to users. But retrieval of documents is not the same as retrieval of information; a technical specialist really needs the information contained in the published literature, not the published literature itself. To retrieve information, as contrasted to documents, the technical community has devised the specialized data and information center.

A specialized information center makes it its business to know everything that is being published in a special field —such as nuclear spectroscopy or the thermophysical properties of chemical compounds; it collates and reviews the data, and provides its subscribers with regularly issued compilations, critical reviews, specialized bibliographies, and other such tools. Its input is the output of the central depository. There are now in the United States about 400 such centers; the net number is growing, though some specialized information centers can and should die because the fields of science they serve cease to be active. As originally conceived, the centers compiled data as opposed to ideas or knowhow; one of the earliest *data* centers compiled the *International Critical Tables.* Many of the data centers have evolved into *information* centers that not only compile data but also keep abreast of all developments in a field.

We believe that the specialized information center, backed by large central depositories, might well become a dominant means for transfer of technical information. It therefore behooves the technical community, at this early stage in the proliferation of specialized centers, to learn what makes a good specialized center, and to plan new centers accordingly.

Specialized information centers, to be fully effective, must be operated in closest possible contact with working scientists and engineers in the field. The activities of the most successful centers are an intrinsic part of science and technology. The centers not only disseminate and retrieve information; they create new information. Making a discriminating selection of data, as was done in preparing the *International Critical Tables,* requires scientific insight of high order, and is itself an essential scientific activity. The process of sifting through large masses of data often leads to new generalizations. The Nuclear Data Center that collects and distributes information on the static properties of nuclei contributed notably, for example, to the development of the shell model of the nucleus, one of the major theoretical underpinnings of modern nuclear physics. What is true of the Nuclear Data Center is undoubtedly true of other centers. In short, knowledgeable scientific interpreters who can collect relevant data, review a field, and distill information in a manner that goes to the heart of a technical situation are more help to the overburdened specialist than is a mere pile of relevant documents. Such knowledgeable scientific middlemen *who themselves contribute to*

science are the backbone of the information center; they make an information center a technical institute rather than a technical library. The essence of a good technical information center is that it be operated by highly competent working scientists and engineers—people who see in the operation of the center an opportunity to advance and deepen their own personal contact with their science and technology. Proliferation of the specialized information centers will therefore require many such "information scientists": dedicated and knowledgeable technical men who help interpret and assimilate the literature for others working in the field.

Since the technical information center in this sense must be part of science and technology, it is natural that it be located where relevant science is flourishing. The Panel therefore urges that new information centers be established at public and private technical institutions, not as adjuncts of general libraries, or of publishing ventures, or of central depositories. Where research and development is done for the Government —at Government laboratories, national laboratories, universities, or industrial laboratories—information centers in related fields ought to find a congenial atmosphere. We note with approval that AEC has already established about a dozen such centers at its national laboratories, and we believe this practice should be encouraged by other Government agencies.

Mechanization Can Become Important But Not All-Important

Emergence of the information center with its emphasis on retrieval of information as contrasted with retrieval of documents does not mean that document retrieval is unnecessary. On the contrary, the growing volume of publications places more and more pressure on the technical community to come up with ingenious schemes for switching documents efficiently—if not to individual users, then to information centers.

In fact, the proliferation of the information centers will undoubtedly increase the pressure on the general document wholesalers—libraries and Government agencies—to strengthen and rationalize their document-retrieval systems.

Retrieval of documents requires both "hardware" and "software." Hardware connotes those mechanical devices (ranging from edge-punched cards to elaborate digital computers) that identify labels for, and may even deliver originals or copies of, documents once the documents have been properly indexed or otherwise identified. Software connotes the increasing variety of ways by which retrieval systems may selectively reach the document: conventional catalog entries, keywords, abstracts, permuted title indexes, citation indexes, etc.; and the programing systems that would let us take full advantage of such modes of access. Without adequate software, hardware cannot help and sometimes can hurt.

Where the software exists or can be made available in time, the possibilities of hardware improvements are indeed impressive, but the demands are also impressive. The Library of Congress, for example, contains over 10 million identified accessions, corresponding to 10^{13} bits of recorded information. Each accession requires some 2,000 bits of information to catalog it. A memory of several tens of billions of bits' capacity is required to store the catalog alone. Current use requires 200 accesses a minute, from 200 simultaneous users. An easily attainable improvement in service would require a tenfold increase in capacity (e.g., more cross-referencing) and could accommodate a tenfold increase in use. These characteristics are not met by existing commercially available equipment, but are now technically feasible.

Although a system for the Library of Congress could cost as much as $50 million, we believe that, since the advance in the technology of retrieval achieved by automating the Nation's largest library or at least its Division of Science and Technology will be available to all libraries, such an expenditure could be well worth while. We therefore recommend that the recent report recommending automation of the Library of Congress, prepared under the auspices of the Council of Library Resources, be reviewed carefully with a view to possible implementation of its findings.

The NSF, recognizing that a central advisory service where documentalists and others concerned with information problems can go for impartial advice as to what computers can and cannot do would be very helpful, supported the setting up of such a service at the National Bureau of Standards in 1959. We urge documentalists, especially within the Government, to consult this service before committing themselves to very expensive and complicated automatic document-retrieval systems. Insofar as Government information services are concerned, there is a need to provide information about other, less exciting but very important aspects of retrieval hardware such as reproducing and microphotographing equipment; we are pleased to note that the Bureau offers information on such devices as well as on computers. The Panel urges that the Bureau's services be widely used and perhaps better publicized.

Citation Indexing Should Be Useful

Along with development of hardware, much ingenious thought must obviously go into software; i.e., indexing and other preparation of the documents for subsequent retrieval. Of the new approaches to software, the Panel is particularly impressed with the citation index; we wish to call the technical community's attention to this apparently powerful, though relatively little used, new searching tool.

All of us are familiar with lists of references at the end of an article. Such lists enable the reader to trace backward in time the antecedents of the article being perused. Every scientist has used such lists to delve more deeply into the subject he is studying. But reference lists only go backward in time; they give no hints as to the influence a given article has had on the development of the subject after the article appeared in print. The citation index is a list of the articles that, subsequent to the appearance of an original article, refer to or cite that article. It enables one to trace forward in time the same sort of interconnections with the literature that, by means of lists of references, one now traces backward in time. Because the indexing is based on the author's, rather than on an indexer's, estimate of what articles are related to what other articles, citation indexes are particularly responsive to the user's, rather than to the indexer's, viewpoint.

Lawyers have used a citation index, Shepard's Citations, for more than 100 years. Each year Shepard's lists all appellate decisions that have cited any previous cases. Since the law is unified in somewhat the same way as is science in that the rule of precedent connects what happens later with what happened earlier, it is not surprising that a bibliographic tool so useful to the lawyer could also be useful to the scientist.

The National Science Foundation is sponsoring trials of citation indexing in genetics and in statistics and probability. The genetics index, for example, will cover all the genetics literature from 1959 through 1963 and will be published in a single volume; it will be kept up to date by yearly supplements. The Panel believes that citation indexing, particularly in combination with permuted title indexing, will come to be used widely, and that its use will further alter both the way in which we think of the technical literature and the way we manage it.

The Importance of Compatibility

Growth in amount and diversity of literature will inevitably bring us more major switching elements, divided between specialized information centers, abstract journals, central depositories, and technical libraries; and an increased flow of documents, abstracts, title and keyword lists, divided between conventional journals, letter journals, reports, and deposited manuscripts. As the system grows, obstructions to easy flow will become more and more disabling. The greatest of these obstructions is incompatibility.

Overlapping information systems can surely gain by replacing exactly synonymous keywords by identical ones. And the identical abstract may be usable in two or more abstract journals. As larger and larger parts of the information system are considered, the problems become more difficult. How widely can the same principles for the selection of keywords or the writing of abstracts be used? When must two systems analyze the same paper from different points of view?

The National Science Foundation, recognizing the importance of uniform abstracting and indexing, has sponsored the National Federation of Science Abstracting and Indexing Services (NFSAIS). This forum of some 20 different nonprofit and Government services works to achieve more uniformity among the many overlapping services. Because most services developed their own habits and traditions in isolation, NFSAIS has encountered understandable difficulties in achieving uniformity. Nevertheless the Panel believes that much can be done, and it commends both NSF and NFSAIS for undertaking to create more order in a chaotic sea of nonuniformity.

Gains from either mechanization or compatibility are greater when the other is present. To the extent to which editors, of both primary and abstract journals, can agree on compatible formats and can assign page numbers to articles before they are printed, photographic reproduction in abstract journals could be used to bring many abstracts out as soon as, or even before, the papers are published. Exchange of lists of titles and keywords between mechanized systems is easy when title formats and keywords are compatible—i.e., easily inter-translated—and very difficult otherwise. Exact agreement offers still further gains, though not as much as for hand systems. Transfer and merging of compatible title and keyword lists can be greatly speeded by mechanization; if mail exchange of tapes proves inadequate, direct communication between rapid access memories is possible. Actual trials, such as the Medlars (Medical Literature Analysis and Retrieval System) scheme for switching between the National Library of Medicine and satellite centers in specialized fields of medicine, will soon help to guide us as to how far and fast we should move toward such complete mechanization. The Panel believes that adequate means for rapid switching, the first among which is compatibility, can greatly ease the burden caused by overlapping systems—agency with discipline, agency with agency, or discipline with discipline.

Non-Government Technical Publication Will Require Government Support

How shall we pay for our non-Government information systems? Obviously, since the Government now supports three-fourths of all scientific and technical work, publication even in non-Government media will eventually be largely paid for by Government. One question is how to choose the fairest means for transferring Government money to the technical publications. In particular, which is sounder public policy—to allot Government funds directly to a nonprofit publication, or to allot the money indirectly via the page charge?

The Federal Government, through the Federal Council for Science and Technology, has already taken a stand in favor of page charges. As yet, not all technical societies have accepted the principle of page-charge financing. To many scientists the page charge is repellent because it represents a change in a comfortable and longstanding custom. To many in industry it appears to be in conflict with the fundamental assumption of the patent system that the discoverer of technical information should be rewarded for making the information public. This view is contrary to the one we have emphasized in this report. We believe information is part of research: that the links in the information transfer chain are welded together, and that in this age of information crisis, the creator of information must assume as much responsibility as possible for subsequent dissemination and retrieval of the information he creates. The page charge imposes on the technical author a financial responsibility that is consistent with this view of the information transfer chain. We therefore urge technical societies, regardless of their tradition, to turn to page-charge financing.

The page charge does not serve the needs of secondary publication—abstracting and indexing. Article charges (perhaps a flat fee per article) that would go to support abstracting and indexing by related secondary media have been suggested as a way of supporting media of secondary dissemination. At first glance, since foreign abstracts account for almost half of the content of many American abstract journals, it might seem that article charges would be an unfair way to provide such support. But when we consider that each article, if carefully prepared, has already drawn upon the efforts of secondary publications, article charges appear much more reasonable. In any case, except in the few cases where subscriptions pay the actual cost of abstracting, we see no other alternative to direct Government subsidy of secondary media. Such subsidy might cost as much as $30 million per year by 1970.

The Universal Brain: Is Centralized Storage and Retrieval of All Knowledge Possible, Feasible, or Desirable?

by Watson Davis

One of the great dreams of mankind has been an intellectual world in which everyone can have the opportunity of knowing everything past and present in order to plan and predict for the future. A universal brain, tappable and intelligible to everyone who aspires, is a concept which is perhaps too Utopian and grandiose.

Knowing what has been and what is is more achievable in certain fields of human knowledge than others. Without minimizing the difficulties of the organization of scientific and technical knowledge, it is fair to assume that science and technology information can be marshalled with greater success and usefulness than the content of other cultures such as politics, poetry, and religion.

The conception of bringing together all the knowledge of the world is very old. In the 19th century and the early 20th century, there were those individuals and organizations who thought big and aspired to the bringing of knowledge into one set of coordinates. It goes back to the famous library in Alexandria, Bacon's *Novum Organum,* and the Encyclopedias. More recently there were such ambitious and unrealized projects as the Royal Society's *Index of Scientific Literature* and *Concilium Bibliographicum.* The *Concilium Bibliographicum* took the form of a gigantic card index

and was drowned in a sea of card bits of information, largely because of the immensity of attempting to handle such compilations long before the invention of automation and computers. The Royal Society of London produced over a period of years its index in bound volume form. It, too, found the task too great and too costly.

Today we have the specialized and limited, but extremely useful, modern abstracting efforts. The great libraries of the nations including in America the Library of Congress, the National Medical Library, the National Agricultural Library, and the great depositories at Harvard, Yale, and other such centers, in a very real sense are partial attempts to collect, order, and make available the world's knowledge.

Under the prodding of human advance and the expansive growth of research results, the day of individual or limited attempts to marshal the knowledge of the world has long since passed. Fortunately, it will be possible to utilize the intellectual memory and science of most of the efforts past and present in building what can be called a universal or world brain.

We have, in our technology of information, the kinds of mechanisms that allow us again to aspire to bringing all knowledge together usefully.

SOURCE: Paper delivered before the National Microfilm Association, Sheraton-Cleveland Hotel, Cleveland, Ohio, Thursday Afternoon, May 13, 1965.

Microfilm is one of the greatest of these mechanisms. The electronic computer, in all of its many ramifications, is another prime mechanism. Link these devices or methods together and feed them into print-out devices and it is quite possible to visualize the kind of service to the intellectual, scientific, and scholarly world that past generations have envisioned.

Conventional books on shelves and card indexes (essentially a great American invention) are and will continue to be prime data tools. There are now available microfilm, facsimile copying, and the complex and evolving mechanisms for filing and retrieval based upon the electronic computer and similar mechanisms.

We have the hardware and the mechanisms to bring together the information of the world for scientific, technologic, and administrative use. The problem is to make what we have available and to fill in the uncovered areas, and concurrently to make this material available promptly to scientists and technologists, engineers, students, administrators. The general public wishes to know. For the distribution of scientific information through newspapers, magazines, radio-TV, and even gossip is amazingly effective.

It may not be a realistic and the best procedure to attempt to do the whole task of world information, even in the field of science, in any one place. So many of the parts of the operation already exist somewhere with considerable completeness.

Speed and versatility of computers and their ramifications, various systems of classification, the many forms of recording information and making the output available, can be blended into what will amount to one large system from the standpoint of utilization. Care must be exercised to discover what already exists in the way of information gathering and processing, how it can be fitted into an overall plan. There should be

used the dreams, encouragement, and enthusiasm of many thousands of dedicated individuals and institutions all over the world for the accomplishment of the common goal, for the creation of what H. G. Wells in 1937 called engagingly a "world brain." This must be the concern of all peoples, governments, and organizations throughout the world.

We need to enlist the efforts of our friends and foes alike. The information activities of Moscow and Peking must eventually be made a part of the world plan, and the sooner the better. If there can be utilized non-American brains, resources, and manpower to do part of the great operation, this will be overall gain. If we can persuade the Russians not to poison the atmosphere, it should be even simpler to convince them that cooperation in enriching the human information sources on a world basis would be possible.

The first approach to the objective of the proposals upon which this hearing is being held would seem to be a hard look at what is and is not being done, unencumbered by preconceived ideas as to how the overall and essential objective is to be achieved.

To aid this objective, I suggest possibilities, as I have on numerous occasions since the 1930's when *Science Service* took the conceptual and operational initiative in what is now called documentation. It would seem that some of the possibilities would be obvious and easily accomplished without a large financial expenditure.

My impatience causes me to wonder why it takes so long to materialize four ideas which had their promising beginnings three decades ago. These are:

1. What I have called "one big library." This does not contemplate moving a single book or consolidation as the term might imply.

2. An unpatentable invention (of which I am very proud) that is called auxiliary or demand publication, which

can solve the publication jam and save millions.

3. The idea of "one big journal," a conception that I wish to develop further a little later.

4. The "world brain" of the universal storage and retrieval of information.

Because the public is the ultimate user of all the scientific information and knowledge of the world, it is essential that there be reporting, interpretation, and popularization of the old and the new scientific discoveries and applications.

Another field in which immediate and low cost accomplishments can be made is that of language. There has been created, out of a regularizing and simplifying of existing languages, a world language, called Interlingua, which has been demonstrated as practical as a bridge or auxiliary language. It could save millions of dollars in translation costs and immediate accessibility of foreign science information, if we can persuade scientists writing in other languages to append, as we are doing, summaries in Interlingua to their original articles. Summaries in Interlingua allow the specialist direct access to the literature without intervention of translators. This has been demonstrated in over a score of medical journals and many international congresses.

"One Big Library"

The concept of "one big library" has not been fulfilled widely and adequately. It is still not possible for the scientist or scholar to order in facsimile or microfilm from the nearest library the literature he desires with assurance of receiving it promptly and at reasonable price. It was perhaps actually easier than now to do this just before World War II when the American Documentation Institute was operating copying cameras in four major Washington libraries and exchanging orders with other libraries. The "one big library" concept does not involve any physical consolidation or change in libraries or the creation of new libraries.

Is cooperation between librarians and organizations so difficult that "one big library" can not be accomplished? A little organization, cheerful argument, and gentle pressure from users and financial supporters such as government and foundations would make it possible. The know-how exists and we only need the let's-do.

From the standpoint of distribution of knowledge for scholarly, scientific, engineering, and industrial utilization, a good case can be made for the operation of extract copying use of libraries—the one big library concept—without charge to all of those who have need to know. Government contractors with the Department of Defense already can obtain without money payment documents that originate in the extensive research program of the Department of Defense.

The Carnegie Free Libraries are one of the earliest and outstanding examples of spreading knowledge among those who wish to know, and an equivalent of the free loan of books, the extraordinary conception of Andrew Carnegie, needs to have a rebirth. If a potential user desires to have a copy of something that exists in a library, no matter where, in the interest of the advance of knowledge it should be furnished to him without charge.

An argument could be made that it would cost less to institute a properly supervised free service than to operate a complex sales system. Be that as it may, it would be useful and beneficial to scientific research and scholarship to provide this service freely. Large subsidies are being paid by the Government, the National Science Foundation, for example, to promote translations of foreign literature, to subsidize the publication of scientific research results, and to index and provide bibliographies of research results. All of these functions are in a sense secondary in comparison to the providing of copies of actual materials in journals, books, and manuscript collections.

Copies of research reports provided in this way, would be just as useful as new laboratory buildings and equipment which are being subsidized wisely, by governmental and foundation funds.

There should be enacted into the Copyright Law a version of the "Gentleman's Agreement" of the 1930's that will allow single copy reproduction for scholarly and scientific purposes. It was recognized in the formative period of microfilm that use of photography, in lieu of copying by hand or typewriting, was a legitimate exercise of reader's right.

Copying of extracts of journal articles and books by photographic means, whether by direct facsimile or enlargement from microfilm, should become a major aid to research and scholarship.

Auxiliary publication as operated since the late 1930's is a successful documentation invention that has not been utilized as widely as it should be. It has been extensively utilized to deposit thousands of documents so that copies of them can be had on demand. It needs continuous explanation and promotion, particularly to editors of scientific scholarly and learned journals. So long as money for slick and obese journals is obtainable from government, foundations, libraries, and even the producers of research, auxiliary publication will not be used as it should be. Money is being wasted on unnecessary conventional publication and it is time that those setting policy by money control realize that auxiliary publication can be used to reduce publication costs.

The technique of auxiliary publication has happily been used to make other large masses of documents available, notably the World War II enemy documentation and current government research reports through the Department of Commerce and theses through University Microfilms, Inc.

Could the facilities and techniques developed for auxiliary publication be urged upon professional societies, journal editors, and research organizations? Participation of the professional journal is necessary in auxiliary publication. The announcement by notice through published summary or condensed article of the availability of the deposited document is essential. The specialist can learn of the existence of the document he may need by reading about it in the journal of his specialty.

The perpetual availability of the document at the announced price should be guaranteed.

"One Big Journal"

The concept of "one big journal" perhaps can not be realized but the idea should be expounded and explored. There are admittedly too many journals. For economy of publication the largest press runs and the least costly printing methods are needed. This would seem to require low price and use of newspaper printing with linotype setting and rotary presswork on newsprint. Before microfilm, printing nonephemeral material on newsprint was unwise. The permanency of microfilm makes it practical to use newspaper printing, which is a great complex of inventions.

For instance, the National Science Foundation has financed a gigantic program of translating Russian literature. The possibility of saving millions by using newspaper techniques was pointed out, but ignored. A fresh look should be taken at this and other publication efforts to determine the part that better distribution and printing methods might play.

Too many new journals are being brought into the world and not enough consolidation of existing journals takes place in order to speed and facilitate scientific publication. Birth control of journals is needed.

Too frequently organizations come into being for the purpose of starting new journals and often the motive of a new journal is to give prestige to a scientist who wishes to become an editor. There is money in prestige and the reputation of being an editor, for at least the editor may by that fact win a higher salary within his university.

So long as subsidies are available, it can not be hoped that financial difficulties will slow down the multiplication of new journals.

It is not likely that it will be possible to put the research record of even relatively limited areas of research into one journal unless there are developments which will bring about financial limitations.

A large weekly publication, of the magnitude perhaps of the *New York Times,* could carry the original publication of a considerable volume of the scientific and technical research reports of the nation. Published in large editions on newspaper rotary presses, probably it would be possible to replace many individual journals, and the cost of this publication to the consumer would undoubtedly represent a considerable saving. One should not be optimistic, however, as to the practicality of such a development even though it would be economically advantageous. It would undoubtedly speed communication among scientists and would, in the long run, result in economy to the Government, industry, and the professional societies.

"World Brain"

Organizing the knowledge of the world into a "world brain" is still the prime need that could be filled. The great computer and information systems, added to advanced microfilm, developed in recent years makes this more technically possible. But has the vision perished and the desire dulled? Is preoccupation with minutiae preventing the big view and broad effort? If the mechanisms are so wonderful, can we encourage the kind of human brains and

aspirations that gave birth to them to assume the greater task of ordering and arranging for use the magnificent creation of the intellect? Shall we read the plans of past decades and then proceed to build them with the tools that were not then fashioned?

While knowledge is immortal and human beings have a fondness for imagining that ultimate truth can be achieved, there is a life expectancy that can be estimated for most scientific papers and reports. Most of the scientific publication of more than a decade or two ago, if it is important, has become infused in later reports and found its way into citations in later scientific papers. Important scientific advances move into general knowledge even faster, although the period of development of many devices based upon scientific research requires many years, far more than the period of the gestation of an elephant. This makes it probable that magnitude of the "world brain" creation can be kept within comprehensible limits by handling the current output of publication and working backward so far as found necessary.

In our fascination with electronic gadgetry, marvelous as it is, we should not overlook the wonders of the human brain which still is the most wonderful "computing" mechanism that has ever been created. The electronic variety of computer may work faster, but for the purpose of bringing to bear upon a problem an immense multitude of details and relating them when they seemingly are unrelated, the human brain is unparalleled and probably will remain supreme in the foreseeable future. An expert with years of training in a particular field, equipped with the rare insight which is a gift not given to many, is a supreme scientific tool essential to creative work. The gathering and arranging of facts, which is the purpose of the project about which we are talking, will only be useful as it fits into these great creative human mechanisms.

Scientists are such modest and undemanding individuals that they overlook the possibility of utilizing the marvelous communication devices that science and technology have created. When a researcher is "hot" after an idea, he should search for the facts and information that he needs wherever they might be found. He should pick up the telephone and, if necessary, talk across the continent or across the oceans to the three or four colleagues who know what he is trying to do and who could possibly help him in his research. The total cost would be small compared with the possible results. The military quite properly has extensive communication lines of telephone and teletype connecting its installations. Great research laboratories, on the battle front of man's fight for more knowledge, should be given equivalent facilities. "Hot" lines between research laboratories may well be as important as that between the White House and the Kremlin.

We must not overlook the mass media which are the great communicators of ideas and facts to the intellectual world as well as to the public at large. It was not out of character for *Science Service* to be interested in documentation for it is the institution for the dissemination and popularization of science. The fundamental task of informing the public through newspapers, magazines, radio, and TV is as important as primary scientific publication and the filing and finding that keeps the technical record in order and useful. To both the creative worker and the applier of new knowledge, the everyday information that everyone reads in newspapers is more effective than a thousand general indexes. This kind of browsing is the way many ideas are synthesized. The human brain can store and retrieve billions of bits of information, combine them in often almost unbelievable ways, and create concepts and knowledge that never before existed. To do this, the most diverse and detailed input is needed. If any justification is needed for general communication, it is that it is perhaps the most powerful ingredient of the information formula.

The Idea of an Encyclopedia

by Charles Van Doren

An analysis of a great modern encyclopedia permits Mr. Van Doren to establish several themes and ideals of the encyclopedist: teaching over informing, art over reference, human over scientific-literary, the "curious average man" target, reformism over the intellectual and social status quo.

What is the idea of an encyclopedia?

It is not surprising that the editors of encyclopedias are asking themselves this question. In some sense the old idea of an encyclopedia, whatever that was, is now outmoded, and both the old aims and the old ability to serve them, whatever those aims and abilities were, are declining. It should not be surprising, either, that the French have been among the first to see these truths. The French have often been ahead of the rest of the world in ideas, and their experience as encyclopedists is second to none. *L'Encyclopédie française*, a work which was begun in the early 1930's and is not yet complete because of the war, is a response to those questions in France. Its sponsor was Anatole de Monzie, first Minister of National Education; its editor was Lucien Febvre, professor in the College de France.

L'Encyclopédie française has an idea. The work is based on an overall conception of what an encyclopedia is and should be. This situation is rarer than one would suspect. Most encyclopedias, particularly the American ones, have little or no idea of themselves. They just grow; they are not created. The idea of the French work is also radical. It appears to be statable in five propositions, each of which may sound strange to the reader of an ordinary encyclopedia. The five propositions are these:

1. The primary aim of an encyclopedia should be to teach. It should seek only secondarily to inform.

2. An encyclopedia should be primarily a work of art. It should be only secondarily a work of reference.

3. The point of view of an encyclopedia should be primarily human. It should be only secondarily historical and/or scientific and/or literary.

4. The ideal reader of an encyclopedia should be primarily the curious average man. He should only secondarily be the specialist and/or the high school student.

5. An encyclopedia should be primarily a document that hopes to change the world for the better. It should be only secondarily a document that accurately reflects the knowledge, opinions and prejudices of its time.

It appears to be the opinion of the editors of *L'Encyclopédie française* that each of these points is essential to the idea of an encyclopedia, and that if any one of them is ignored, the idea itself is vitiated. It is our opinion, also, that this is the case.

We shall discuss each of these points

SOURCE: *The American Behavioral Scientist,* **6,** No. 1, September 1962, pp. 23–26.

in turn, making reference as we go to the two prefaces, one by Febvre, the other by de Monzie, that introduce the French work.

The Idea of an Encyclopedia as an Educational Institution

L'Encyclopédie française intends to teach. M. Febvre emphasizes this point. *Enseigner, pas renseigner,* he insists, and he takes for his motto: *Faire comprendre* (make comprehensible), not *Faire connaître* (make known). The end is unabashedly educational, and M. Febvre apparently does not fear that this fact will drive away any class of readers.

His view of education is revolutionary. He does not believe in teaching "subjects." Probably he believes that "subjects" cannot be taught. He suggests that *savants* will be included among his reader-students, as well as average men and schoolchildren. He evidently feels that *savants* need education as much as anyone else.

But how can this be, since it is *savants* who will create the encyclopedia? M. Febvre means that what is required is not more "knowledge"—specialized information, of which *savants* already have a great deal—but a synthesis, an underlying theory: *the universe,* as he puts it, *seen from very far away.* "In preparing the elements of a total synthesis," he writes, "we may render visible to all, and, most important, to the *savants* themselves, the analogous nature of methods and problems, and the obvious convergence of results." He hopes by this means to restore confidence in the power of the mind.

The aim of the typical American encyclopedia is to inform, *renseigner;* it intends to make known, not to make comprehensible. Even if it is true that this kind of book is a great educational tool, it is so only secondarily. Education is too important to be a mere secondary end. More than that, education involves the understanding that some things are more important than others. One who reads an alphabetical encyclopedia through, from A to Zygote, would indeed learn many important things. But he would know a great deal that he did not need to know to be educated, and he would undeniably not know much that an educated man must know.

The key to the problem lies in M. Febvre's "total synthesis." Education in the West, particularly higher education in America, has almost lost the ability *to see the universe from very far away.* The universe and, consequently, almost any part of it, is now considered too vast for the feeble human intellect. But, as M. Febvre says, the world is only "unthinkable because unthought"; the failure is human, it is not in the nature of things. It takes a brave man to master more than one discipline nowadays; bravery is not totally absent from our society, and so heroes can be found. But the man who attempts to find the principles which underlie two or more disciplines is considered not brave, but mad or subversive. Those whom graduate schools have put asunder, let no man join together!

The fragmentation which is so marked a characteristic of American encyclopedias is a function of the fragmentation of the American university. Interdepartmental squabbling would be amusing if it did not imply the breakdown in conversation between scholars of what were, only a few years ago, closely allied "fields." Perhaps the game should not yet be given up. And since contemporary scholars seem inclined away from rather than toward such a synthesis, it may be that the world cries out for an encyclopedia to do the job. The editors of *L'Encyclopédie française* certainly feel that this is so.

The editors of American encyclopedias can find good reasons, some of them even selfish, for undertaking such a synthesis. In the opinion of many younger academicians American encyclopedias are on the decline. This is because they appear, though they actually do not, to undertake a synthesis merely by the fact that they include "all knowledge" in one set of books. In the present state of opinion even physical propinquity is suspect. Thus an overarching encyclopedia is said to be impossible because it is thought that any synthesis is impossible.

But even those who say they believe this, might value the attempt if it were made with the authority that at least some American encyclopedias have behind them—an authority derived from a tradition of dedication to truth and completeness. Many academicians who fear the unknown most actively at the same time desire to conquer their fear and make knowledge once more one. Such a great and, at the beginning, perhaps Quixotic program might strike fire in the imaginations of many of those on whom an encyclopedia would depend for its reputation. Respectability seems safe. But what will be respectable in thirty years seems *avant-garde* now. If an encyclopedia hopes to be respectable in the year 2000 it must appear daring in the year 1963.

The Idea of an Encyclopedia as a Work of Art

M. Febvre emphasizes that *L'Encyclopédie française* will be *une oeuvre*—and he adds that the word connotes *esprit* (intellect or understanding).

Most encyclopedias are "great dictionaries of Letters, Sciences and Arts," he says, and as such *not* works of art.

M. Febvre does not refer to the quality of writing in such "great dictionaries." He does refer to their attitude toward themselves, an attitude which he expects his encyclopedia *not* to have. That is, they do not believe that an encyclopedia can be a work of art. They do not admit that an intellectual principle of unity exists which is vast enough, or overarching enough, to encompass articles on such diverse subjects as, for example, backgammon and crystallog-

raphy. But this is because the present encyclopedias do not propose as an end a synthesis of thought in our time. If they did, the first order of business would obviously be to find just such a unity. The assumption of its existence would constitute the first big step toward finding it. Everything contained in the volumes would then be there for a reason deriving from the inherent idea of the work. At present many articles are included in encyclopedias merely because their subjects are in some sense *there;* they must be covered. If a synthesis were sought and achieved, there would be valid reasons for including and excluding. The encyclopedia would insofar become a work of art.

The encyclopedist can have two basic approaches to his subject, taking as that subject "all knowledge." A passive approach assumes that knowledge, the body of what is known by men, has inherent in it the principle of its own ordering. Science, it is true, is said to be "ordered" knowledge. But the world of scholarship has not yet attained that heaven wherein there is only one Science, of which the various disciplines are merely parts fitting neatly together to make a whole. In fact, despite the progress made in the ordering of knowledge in the last two centuries, experts seem to disagree as much as ever about the limits of the various sciences, about their true and proper spheres, and about their relative importance. The passive solution to the problem is, practically, to consider each of the disciplines as a distinct Science, to treat them as organic wholes, and to ignore any duplications and overlappings among them. The task of deciding whether chemistry is a part of biology or biology a part of chemistry, and so forth, is so difficult that the old terms are used, terms which in many cases have little relation to present reality but which are sanctified by ages of confusion and laziness. Is linguistics a part of language, philosophy, or psychology? Books have recently been published that argued for each of these possibilities. Admitting that it would mean a different thing to say that it was a part of any of them, we must point out that the typical encyclopedia's practice of writing a separate article on linguistics and placing it in alphabetical order seems hardly daring as a solution to the problem.

We are not sure where linguistics ought to go in an ideal encyclopedia, but it ought to go somewhere, and to discover its proper place by thought and discussion would be to use what we term the active, or creative, approach to the making of an encyclopedia. Having this approach it becomes necessary to evolve a method, to construct a synthetic formulation of "all knowledge." The creation of this structure is the most important task that faces the editors of an encyclopedia. When it is done, the main job is done.

There remains the question whether an encyclopedia can be both a work of art and a useful work of reference. On one level the answer is certainly yes. All that is needed is a good index. On a higher level, it must be recognized that the answer is no. If "to make known" becomes a secondary rather than a primary aim, then value as a reference tool will have to be sacrificed. But it must be said that American alphabetical encyclopedias at present leave much to be desired as reference works. For subjects of no great importance, which can be covered in short articles, they are admirable. In general, however, the more extensive the treatment (and thus the more important the subject), the more difficult it is to use modern encyclopedia articles for reference purposes. So an encyclopedia might not be losing as much as it sometimes seems to fear if its aim were converted from *faire connaître* to *faire comprendre*.

The Point of View of an Ideal Encyclopedia

MM. Febvre and de Monzie agree that the point of view of their encyclopedia should be "humanist" and not literary. The distinction may mean more to a Frenchman than to an American. "Humanist" has become a questionable word in the western hemisphere, partly because we are subjected to so much nonsense about "human values" in popular art and philosophy.

Nevertheless, the tone of American encyclopedias is often fiercely inhuman. It appears to be the wish of some contributors to write about living institutions as if they were pickled frogs, outstretched upon a dissecting board. Most encyclopedias are seldom amusing or easy reading. Their tone is "academic" and "scientific"—no compromises are made with ignorance, and one has the feeling that contributors expect readers to be almost as learned, dull and unenthusiastic as themselves.

L'Encyclopédie française is sometimes dreadfully dull. But it contains many amusing and interesting articles such as the ones, in Vol. XVII, on "The Profession of the Artist" and "The Profession of the Composer." These articles include descriptions of the difficulty artists have in finding suitable places to display their work, the high commissions agents demand for handling the canvases of young painters, and the costs of hiring a music hall. With this goes highly imaginative use of illustrations. Accompanying the article on the artist's profession are full-page photographs of the working palettes of several eminent modern painters. One can feel sure that a reader who wanted to know what it was like to be a painter in our age would be fascinated by such a display.

The most striking difference between the points of view of most American encyclopedias and of the French work is that the latter's is intentionally unhistorical. There is a good deal of history in *L'Encyclopédie française*. Two volumes of its nineteen are devoted to a history of man and his institutions. But the emphasis is usually on the present day. Volume XVIII, *Religions et Philosophies*, hardly discusses these matters as before about 1875. The same is true of the volumes devoted to art and literature, in which only modern painting, writing, composing and performing are covered. When an historical allusion is necessary it is inserted, and the contributors by no means give the impression that they are ignorant of the past. But the great interest of the articles, as well as their sometimes racy style, is at least partly due to the extremely controversial quality of their subjects. Hardly anyone becomes very angry now about the character writers of the 17th Century in England, but it is easy to grow warm over the relative merits of modern playwrights, and the French work joins battle as often as it does not. This is less irresponsible than it sounds, for most of the contributors are unquestioned authorities in their fields. Indeed, the encyclopedia has a higher proportion of world-famous names among its contributors than we have ever seen. This is additional evidence that many *savants* might not be opposed to the idea of an encyclopedia attempting a synthesis, for the French work attempted it, and the *savants* wrote for it.

It is this intention of bringing philosophy down to the market place and, indeed, into coffeehouses and drawing rooms that is meant by M. de Monzie when he says that the point of view of his encyclopedia is man "as common center." We know of no more appropriate center of an encyclopedia, which is, as its name tells us, a circular view of the world.

The Ideal Reader of an Ideal Encyclopedia

Publishers of encyclopedias, as producers of consumer goods, are worried about their market. Who reads encyclopedias? Who uses them? Who needs them?

Insofar as encyclopedia-making is a business these questions are as valid as they are for any business. But an encyclopedia is more than a business enterprise. Any encyclopedia is, more or less, an instrument of enlightenment, and an ideal encyclopedia would be an educational institution of the highest importance, with a far-reaching effect. In short, an encyclopedia is a worthwhile intellectual undertaking. This is usually not true of a business enterprise. There the only justification is sales. But an encyclopedia means something in and for itself.

Thus we may, and should, adjust the questions that are to be asked about the market for which an encyclopedia is intended. For whom should an encyclopedia be intended? Who should use it? Who should need it?

The usual answers—that the prime users of these reference works are high school students and specialists seeking additional information—seem inadequate. Given the choice between these two "ideal" readers, we might have to admit that we were not intensely interested in educating either of them.

M. de Monzie has another idea. The French encyclopedia, he says, is intended for "the curious average man."

Who is the average man? Of course, we all know. M. Febvre says that he is "a judge, lawyer, doctor, businessman, technician, or administrator"—in fact, he is ourselves. The *curious* average man is, he says, such a one who carries about with him the weight of an unsatisfied desire to understand the civilization in the eddies of which he flounders, without being able to raise himself high enough to see its total form.

Our ideal reader is not a specialist. Specialists are often bored by knowledge and have lost the ability and desire to understand freshly. Our ideal reader is not a high school student, either, who does not yet know enough to be intelligently curious. The ideal reader is knowledgeable, enthusiastic and demanding. He cannot be given too much, but he must be met halfway. Most important, he is not familiar with the terms of discourse of the subjects about which he is reading. He only knows that he wants to understand them, and their relation, to the other things that he knows.

The Idea of an Encyclopedia as a Revolutionary Document

There remains to be considered perhaps the most important statement of all in the two prefaces to *L'Encyclopédie française*, that in which M. de Monzie defines the work as "an instrument of understanding and of action."

It is, he says, an invitation to the present generation to examine its intellectual conscience.

Present day American encyclopedias do not have a mission. They are, taken as a whole, essentially conservative documents. They seek to "sift the vast store of available knowledge and render its essential part accessible to all who read." They are thus mnemotechnic, to use M. de Monzie's term. They are, essentially, machines that remember for us. They do not create anything. They satisfy the desire of a generation and of a culture which would rather look backward than forward.

Because the world is radically new, the ideal encyclopedia should be radical, too. It should stop being safe—in politics, in philosophy, in science. It should create a synthesis where none is thought to be possible. It should carve a new order out of the chaos that has swept away the old. It should think of itself as an important—perhaps even the most important—tool for the reconstruction of a world that has meaning.

Perhaps the only practical way to create such a work would be to form an entirely new organization of scholars, who might or might not—but it would probably be better if they did—consider themselves a kind of university. The new organization ought to be able to compete for talent with any university or college in the country. The writing of encyclopedia articles at two, three, four or even five cents a word is not an attractive proposition to young and imaginative minds.

Finally, it is important that the work, if attempted, be thought of as a kind of message for the future. "This is the way it was," it would say. "We give you this world; now make it your own." It would speak to the next century rather than to this. It would attempt to interpret the twentieth century for the twenty-first. Such a document would provide an educative synthesis from which the "curious average man" could successfully encounter the novel complexities of the present, and build a future that is good for man.

B. Ideas Toward Libraries of the Future

The preceding five articles have expounded and traced a single great idea, or variants of this idea. The ideas described next are several, and no single one of them compares in beauty or stature to the magnificent conception of an encyclopedia system. Discussion of these ideas can be found in two recent significant books—Overhage and Harman's *Intrex* and Licklider's *Libraries of the Future*. They reflect several important current trends. One is the feeling that remote, on-line access to computers—and time-sharing in particular—could help solve some information problems. Another trend seems to be a feeling of growing impatience with hundreds of separate, unconnected research projects and a sense of urgency to consolidate and to launch significant new enterprises that either test many research findings available to date in a critical-size operational service or start afresh. Information retrieval is still a "field" in which the newcomer of high prestige from another field can have the greatest impact.

These trends toward consolidation, evaluation in an operational environment, and use of time-sharing technology are evidenced in at least three significant new projects and enterprises: INTREX, EDUCOM[1] and the government's plans for information nets. Similar, less well-publicized schemes that are now being hatched are too numerous to mention. One of the most influential forces shaping these trends was the elaboration and support by J. C. R. Licklider of the idea of a man-machine partnership resembling symbiosis. These ideas are related to information-retrieval

[1] EDUCOM is a corporation of more than forty United States universities. Its purpose is to keep its members cognizant of developments in information technology, to represent the interests of the academic community vis-à-vis government and industry, and to put into action, by means of task forces, plans for resource sharing beyond that available to member universities by themselves. Like IN-TREX, an EDUCOM task force on networks has prepared a proposal for large-scale immediate implementation of some kind of computer-based network. These first steps are expected eventually to have a significant impact on all aspects of university activities, such as aids to experimental research (e.g., on-line data recording, control of stimulus presentation), aids to theoretical research (e.g., on-line simulation, correction of computer programs, computations), aids to library management, retrospective searching and current awareness, and aids to publication. EDUCOM might yet come to realize that its top priority objective may well be to aid in the evaluation and synthesis of knowledge and to help to reestablish the university community in the sense of the original word "university," rather than the fragmented assemblage of specialized departments that characterizes a university today. EDUCOM would seem to have a unique opportunity for furthering the great idea that is the theme of this book.

problems in *Libraries of the Future*. They are also central to project INTREX, as described in the first selection in this part of the book. Although many of the ideas in this book have been elaborated before,[2] bringing them all together presents a very exciting and challenging picture.

The excerpt from *Intrex,* like all the other selections in Part One, is included in the hope that it will stimulate criticism of and spirited public debate about the underlying technical ideas. This excerpt is especially interesting in contrast to the ideas in the first half of Part One. It is followed by a description, by W. T. Knox, of COSATI's current and organizational ideas and plans for national information nets. Information-retrieval specialists all too easily lose sight of the fact that in creating a viable information-retrieval system the entrepreneurial problems are at least as important as the technical ones. Appropriate managerial judgments can determine the technical problems that must be solved, even though significant innovations and research findings could influence managerial judgment. Time-sharing is such an innovation, but it is as yet far from the complete practical reality that many enthusiasts seem to believe it to be.

The third selection, *Automation and the Library of Congress,*[3] is considerably less speculative and deals with the more immediate problem of bibliographic control. Again, it is included to elicit constructively critical public discussion at a time when this can contribute significantly to important decisions. It recommends the introduction of information technology in realistic yet bold steps toward a major increase in the utilization of United States Information Resources.[4]

The last selection in this part is an article by H. P. Luhn, which many consider to be his best. This creative inventor and pioneer in information retrieval developed systems like SDI (Selective Dissemination of Information) and KWIC (a permuted title index), both of which are exerting significant commercial impact. The NASA five-million dollar investment in an SDI system is probably one of the most significant current accomplishments.

Each of the nine articles in Part One has a partly transient and a partly lasting aspect. They all are plans, ideas, and suggestions, rather than re-

[2] For example, Kochen, M., "Some Ideas and Pertinent Research Activities Toward an Automated Encyclopedic Information Service," IBM Report RC-921, March 31, 1963, Th. J. Watson Research Center, Yorktown Heights, N.Y.

[3] In the deliberations about the functional goals of the Library of Congress that would be most enhanced by automation, the encyclopedia idea was suggested by the Survey team, (in particular by the editor of the present book) which produced the final report and the book. The idea appears almost parenthetically on pages 22–23 of the book.

[4] A major systems specification effort for automation is now underway at the Library of Congress, as well as a modest experimental effort to produce a magnetic tape record of some catalog cards as a by-product of the process of generating them.

ports or descriptions of work done. It is the fate of such plans to undergo numerous revisions and elaborations before a few of them are selected to be implemented on a scale that would constitute a significant test. It is, of course, relatively easy to speculate and difficult to evaluate proposals in the absence of an underlying discipline or much experience.

Nor is the needed discipline likely to come *solely* from discussions at the level of the ideas presented so far. A certain boldness in undertaking the implementation of such significant-scale (and very costly) enterprises, even when there is hardly any rationale for making the important design decisions, is therefore in order. This will at least provide the necessary experience, and, at best, lead to the eventual emergence of an underlying scientific discipline. Yet, there is a danger that the ideas are lost to sight in the excitement of executing a large enterprise, and it is of great value to debate, appreciate, and criticize the ideas for their own sake before seizing one of them and putting it to work.

The On-Line Intellectual Community
and the Information Transfer System
at M.I.T. in 1975

by Carl F. J. Overhage and R. Joyce Harman

Introduction

Five years ago, "The On-Line Intellectual Community" was a fragmentary dream in a very few minds. Today it borders on actuality, though only in a primitive way and in a very few places. Five years from now, we think, it will be a significant force in, and some years after that the very basis of, scholarship, science and technology. In any event, the concept of the on-line intellectual community has been one of the three main influences in the planning of Project Intrex.

The essential bases of the on-line intellectual community are man-computer interaction and computer-facilitated cooperation among men. To state it just that way, and not to say that the essential basis is the digital computer itself, implies two things that we consider significant in the conceptual foundations for Project Intrex that we have developed during the Planning Conference.

The first is that the digital computer, together with computer programs, is now recognized not only as an essential tool but as a facility of absolutely first-rank importance for almost any individual or organization whose product depends heavily upon execution of complex but definite procedures.

The second is that the capabilities of computers themselves (as now designed and programmed) are great only within the domain of the execution of pre-defined algorithms; that new plans and new formulations must stem from men (or from the domain of heuristics in which men are still unchallenged masters), and that the solving of difficult problems can be greatly facilitated by coupling closely together the heuristic contributions of intelligent men and the algorithmic contributions of well-programmed computers.

Even in the mid-1950's, there was, in the minds of most of those who had worked closely with computers, no longer any question about the first of the foregoing propositions—about the great value of the then-still-new devices. By the end of the decade, many people had seen what computers could do, and the problem was not to convince skeptics but to calm enthusiasts. Now, five years later, enough responsible people have had the opportunity to enter into, and to sense the power of, (limited) intellectual partnerships with computing machines that the validity of the second proposition—the three-part proposition of which the last part asserted the importance of man-computer interaction is firm enough to support that proposition as a basis for significant decisions. In short, it is now evident that much of the creative intellectual process involves moment-by-moment interplay between

SOURCE: *Intrex*. Cambridge, Mass.: M.I.T. Press, 1965, pp. 25–51.

heuristic guidance and execution of procedures, between what men do best and what computers do best. On the basis of that realization, it seems reasonable to project to a time when men who work mainly with their brains and whose products are mainly of information will think and study and investigate in direct and intimate interaction with extensively programmed computers and voluminous information bases.

With computer facilitation of cooperation among men—the second of the two concepts underlying the on-line intellectual community—we have had less experience than we have had with partnerships between an individual man and a computer. Nevertheless, some essential features of community-computer interaction have emerged and are seen clearly enough to convince some of us that this second part of the conceptual foundation will be even stronger than the first.

Evidently many major achievements, although they may be crystallized by the work of one or two great men, result from the accumulation and the melding of the contributions of many. Because communication among men is fallible, and because heretofore men did not have effective ways of expressing complex ideas unambiguously—and recalling them, testing them, transferring them, and converting them from a static record into observable, dynamic behavior—the accumulation of correlatable contributions was opposed by continual erosion; and the melding of contributions was hampered by divergences of convention and format that kept one man's ideas from meshing with another's. The prospect is that, when several or many people work together within the context of an on-line, interactive, community computer network, the superior facilities of that network for expressing ideas, preserving facts, modeling processes, and bringing two or more people together in close interaction with the same information and the same behavior—those su-

perior facilities will so foster the growth and integration of knowledge that the incidence of major achievements will be markedly increased. Perhaps as stated (or overstated), that is still a dream. But we have been seeing the beginnings of its realization in the cooperative communities that have been developing around pioneering time-sharing computer systems; and we think we see in those communities (most clearly, of course, in the one at MIT, for it is the oldest and we have had the closest view of it) an important part of the solution to the ever-more-pressing problem of timely and effective transfer of information.

The Project MAC Experience

The concept of the on-line intellectual community is in large part a projection of recent experience with time-sharing computer systems, mainly at MIT, but also at the Carnegie Institute of Technology, the System Development Corporation, the RAND Corporation, and (especially during the last year) at several other institutions. Work in time sharing began in the Computation Center at MIT in 1960 and has continued there and in an Institute-wide program known as Project MAC. At the present time, two large computer systems, each comprising a conventional digital computer with several modifications and additions, disc and drum-storage units, and a communication subsystem, together with a considerable number of consoles, most of them located remotely from the computers themselves and in or near the offices of users. There are now more than 150 typewriter and teletypewriter consoles which may be connected to either of the large computers through the Institute telephone system, the external telephone system, or (in the case of the teletypewriters) through the Western Union Telex System. Indeed, if it has authorization, any teletypewriter in the international Telex system can communicate with the computers at

MIT, and—after slight modification of its modulator—any teletypewriter in the country-wide TWX network can do likewise. There are several smaller computers and one quite-elaborate console featuring advanced graphic display devices that constitute, with one large computer, a fairly complex computer network. The foregoing is the hardware base of the program, now five years old, from which have arisen some of the ideas that we now see as fundamental for information transfer networks of the future.

The experience gained by many members of the MIT community through interaction with the time-sharing computers has been so convincing that both of the new, advanced computers (one to be delivered late this year and the other early in 1967) will be machines designed especially for time-sharing and —as turns out to be even more fundamental, memory-sharing—applications. The new machines, a General Electric Model 645 and an IBM System/360 Model 67, will increase the capacity for providing simultaneous on-line service from the present total of 60 consoles (30 for each system) to a total of several hundred.

Although the hardware basis is easier to describe and tends to be described first, even in this late stage in the ascendancy of software, the software basis —the collection of computer programs, documentation and doctrine—is equally important and more directly responsible for the shape and structure of the services rendered by the systems to the users. Because the basic software is the same for both systems, we need describe only one. We shall describe it, not from the structural point of view of a "system programmer," but from the behavioral point of view of a substantively oriented user of the system.

The user sits at his typewriter or teletypewriter and types messages to the system, which sends messages back to him, sometimes cryptic, sometimes full,

long or short, in natural language or in mathematical notation, all depending upon the nature of the program that is running in the computer for the user at the time. While the user upon whom our attention is here focused is interacting with the computer, other users are interacting with it too—up to 29 others, and usually precisely 29 others—under the rules that are presently in force. Actually, of course, since there is only a single processor in each of the present main computers, the programs of the 30 users do not run precisely simultaneously. The computer operates one, and then another, and then another, each for a brief interval, in a sequence determined by a set of rules incorporated in a program called the "scheduling algorithm." However, the intervals are short enough that no user ever need wait very long for his program to have a turn; moreover, each user can type to the system, and the system can type back to each user, even when the processor is working on another user's work, which is possible because the system's communications with users are handled by a separate communication subsystem, and that subsystem can time-share its facilities among the users.

The computer program with which the user communicates when he first "logs in" to work on-line, and whenever he wishes to switch from one course of action to another, is the supervisory program. That program is quickly available to him at all times because it always resides in the primary, directly processible memory of the computer and because all communications between the user and other programs (and other people) are monitored by the supervisory program. The supervisory program not only does what its name suggests it should do, but also does what one would expect an arrangements secretary and a recording secretary to do. It responds to a "command language" that includes about a hundred basic commands. Examples are:

List the names of the files in my private sector of the store, and show me the records of their recent use.

Accept the following, under the name "_____," as input to my file.

Fetch me the editing program and tell it that I wish to edit "_____."

Tell me how many consoles are currently active.

Save this information that I am going to use, now, so I may recover it if my test goes awry and destroys the test copy.

Start up program "_____" from just the state in which I left it when last I used it.

Explain command "_____" to me in greater detail.

Compile (i.e., prepare for execution) the program called "_____" with the "_____" compiler.

Operate the program called "_____," using the data called "_____."

The user does not have to type such long statements, of course. To have a castle-planning program named "Ludwig" compiled by the Michigan Algorithmic Decoder, for example, the user need type only "MAD LUDWIG."

The services arranged for by the supervisor are actually fulfilled, of course, by other computer programs. The set of these other programs, and hence the set of services, is open-ended and continually increasing. Most of the programs are devised by users of the system to meet needs encountered in their work. Such programs begin their existences in the private files of their originators and then are copied into the private files of other users who discover their convenience and modify them to meet broader ranges of requirements. Then, when the programs have proved themselves in use and have been "documented" well enough to meet the standards set for "public programs," they are recognized by the Editorial Committee and admitted into the public files. The same course is being followed, now, with data that are likely to be useful to many people, with data including, many users are pleased to note, instructions on how to use the timesharing system. Thus the community of users is creating something that no single individual (indeed, no affordable centralized group of system specialists) could possibly create: a broad, comprehensive, and continually expanding system of information and information-processing services that is at the hunt and peck of any member of the community of users, either for employment "as is" or for modification or specialization to his own particular requirements. Note that the services include facilities for retrieval of information and for retrieval of processors and for applying the processors to the information (which is the immediate source of the strength of the system) and for improvement and augmentation of the services themselves (which is the generic source of the strength).

The "services" of which we have been speaking are the clerical and quasiclerical functions and operations involved in creative intellectual work. (Some of them are too sophisticated to be called merely "clerical." The "on-line mathematical assistant" can carry out symbolic integrations about as well as most graduating seniors can.) Examples of areas in which services are available to aid the on-line user are:

Preparing and editing text and running off clean copy.

Graphic design of structures and devices.

Modeling or simulation of dynamic and stochastic processes.

Planning of highways, buildings, water-resource systems, and the like.

Understanding of systems of mathematical and logical interrelations and constraints.

Examining and tracing bibliographic information in the field of physics.

Preparing, testing, revising, and documenting computer programs.

Each of these services performs for the user, quickly and responsively, functions that are essential to the development of his line of thought or investigation but that would be prohibitively time-consuming if he had to carry out all the operations himself or wait for a conventional computer center to return the result pertinent to each elementary step before he could move on to the next.

The time-sharing systems of Project MAC and the Computation Center are computing systems primarily, of course, and not library systems. The experience with them has therefore not been an experience with precisely the spectrum of classes of information and information processes with which Project Intrex will be concerned. Nevertheless, the experience has been much more directly relevant to library and information-network topics than most foresaw at the outset. Indeed, the time-sharing systems include small "libraries"—millions of "computer words," not millions of documents—and information-retrieval and information-dissemination subsystems. The main features that are seen, as a result of the time-sharing experience, to be essential for future libraries and information networks, are the on-line mode of operation, the open-endedness, the capability of examining and acting upon information through programs, and the facilitation of coherent interaction and cooperation among the members of the community of users.

The Concept

We try to distinguish clearly in our thinking between the actual experience thus far gained in on-line computing and the concept of the full-fledged, online intellectual community of unspecified future date. The experience has provided a concrete foundation for the concept and attested to the feasibilities and values of some of its parts; but the over-all concept is as much an idealization, based on perception of our wants and needs, as it is a projection of experience in community-computer interaction.

In the concept, all the members of the university community—undergraduate students, graduate students, faculty members, full-time researchers, scientists and engineers in associated industry, and, indeed, librarians and administrators—work in close and frequent interaction with the information system. The system is at once a store, a processor, and a transmitter of information: the central nervous system of the community. Unlike the central nervous systems known in biology, however, the information system of the local university community is a node in a larger network that serves the complex of communities and organizations that support the intellectual life of the society. Each member of the local university community therefore works, in a real and effective sense, "on-line to the public informational resources of the world."

As members of intellectual communities have done for many years, the members of the on-line intellectual community think, study, teach, learn, experiment, publish, develop, invent, organize and analyze, solve problems, make decisions, and carry out all the other ill-defined processes of cognition, overt and covert. They carry out those processes mainly at their desks (which is to say, their consoles) in close interaction with the information processors and the information bases of the network, and sometimes through the network with other members of the community or the community of communities.

The contributions made by the network are largely clerical and quasi-clerical, in the sense already mentioned; but one of the main features of the concept is that the system delivers much of its help "inside the thought cycle" and ready for integration within the structure of the user's thinking. That is the essential advantage of being on-line.

That is what so greatly facilitates the melding of the heuristic guidance and evaluation provided by the man and the precise memory and rapid processing provided by the computer.

The list of services that the system (network) affords begins with access to stored information. Whenever a user needs to employ a fact or refer to a document that is "in the network," he has only to specify the fact or the document uniquely; and, if it is not buried down in a little-used sector of the memory or separated from the request by imposing obstacles, it is delivered. If the cost of delivery would be great, the cost is presented, rather than the fact or document itself, and a negotiation between the user and the system is thus opened. If the user does not specify the fact or document uniquely, then a negotiation is opened to refine the retrieval prescription or to give the user a notion of how many facts or documents he may receive if the system follows through to meet his request. The fact-retrieval capability postulated here is based upon the assumption that the system contains a store of information organized in a more readily processible form than that of natural-language text or, alternatively, that great strides have been made beyond the present level of understanding the syntactic organization (and, more especially, the semantics) of natural language. The document-retrieval capability, on the other hand, is based approximately upon the present state of the art. Whether one contents himself with document retrieval, or assumes retrieval of facts from fact stores organized by men, or goes on to postulate inference from natural-language text, the conclusion must remain the same: that retrieval of stored information is the basic service upon which all the facilities of the on-line system must depend.

The second fundamental service is processing of retrieved information with the aid of computer programs. It is essential to the concept of the on-line intellectual community that there exist, within the on-line system, an extensive library of computer programs that can be called upon by any user, specialized (through commands given in a convenient language) to meet his immediate purposes, and directed upon any body or bodies of information he cares to name. If he knows how to write computer programs, the user can add to the publicly available armamentarium and process information in ways of his own particular choosing. If he commands the services of a programmer, the user can have programs custom-made. By and large, however, users of the system here envisioned are able to retrieve, from the library of programs, all the processes and procedures that they need—and, from the library of documents and data, all the information that they need to process. For example, in filling out an automobile registration form, one might ask the system to divide the nominal curb weight of his 1959 Mercedes 190 Sedan by 100, round to the nearest integer, and then multiply the result by $1.00. The system would "know" the weight of the automobile and therefore be able quickly to give him the registration fee. However, the system would know, also, the formula for computing the fee, and, indeed, it might very well know everything, both fact and procedure, required to fill out the form. But then, of course, there should be no form, for all the information would be "in the system," and there would be no need to disturb the automobile owner at all. This line of discussion can go on to embrace bank accounts, credit, and other nonintellectual aspects of life. For the present purpose, however, it suffices to illustrate the projected capability of the system to apply pre-defined procedures to information contained within its stores.

A third fundamental service deals with display of information to the user. This service, also, is controlled by a language, designed to be natural enough for the user and formal enough for the computer, that deals with entities to be displayed, with the selection of display devices, and with the specification of formats. Through this language—or sublanguage as it should be called, since it can be embedded in other languages— he can have alpha-numeric text presented to him as soft (ephemeral) copy on a special alpha-numeric display or typed out for him on a printer, and he can call for graphs, diagrams, sketches, and the like, mixed with alpha-numeric text, on various display screens, and have the information captured photographically or xerographically for later reference.

The fourth and final basic service is control. The user controls the system, or addresses requests to it, through a few familiar devices: a keyboard, a pen-like stylus, a microphone, and a small assortment of buttons and switches. Through those devices, he can communicate in strings of alpha-numeric characters, by pointing, by writing clearly, by sketching or drawing, and by speaking distinctly in a limited vocabulary. His communication with the system is carried out, as suggested earlier, in languages that are somewhat more constrained and formal than the open, natural language of everyday speech among men.

Built upon the basis of the four services just described are many derivative services. It will have to suffice to mention only a few of them, and briefly. There are arrangements, patterned after the Sketchpad programs developed at the MIT Lincoln Laboratory, that facilitate the design of structures and devices. There are programs to facilitate the preparation and editing of text. There are programs to facilitate the preparation, editing, testing, modification, and documentation of computer programs. There are special-purpose languages, together with facilities for carrying out instructions given in the languages, for modeling or simulating complex processes. (The modeled processes may then be set into action and viewed in operation on the display screens.) There are arrangements to facilitate communication among members of the on-line community—arragements for viewing the same dynamic model on screens at different consoles, for authorizing access to otherwise private files, for merging texts and pooling data, and the like. There are many courses and many techniques of computer-assisted instruction, including some that instruct the user in the operation of the on-line system and in the preparation of computer programs in various procedure-oriented and problem-oriented languages. Indeed, there are even programs that will play chess, checkers, and Kalah, for example, with anyone who challenges them; and some of the game-playing programs will play at any specified level of mastery and with any specified style.

The foregoing description of the system's possibilities is not complete. There are many other services, such as programs for statistical analysis of data, programs to facilitate conducting experiments through the system, and programs that conduct tests of all kinds. The description is based upon something more than free invention of desiderata, for each of the services mentioned (except possibly the game-playing service, as elaborated) is an achievable extension of programs that already exist in demonstrable form in one computer system or another. It would be much better, if it were possible, to substitute demonstration (even of primitive precursors that are in operation now) for this description, because many of the demonstrations are quite striking and quite clearly extrapolable to services of the kind described here, whereas the description in mere words may sound as much like science fiction as like a reasonable projection.

Be that as it may, the members of the on-line intellectual community work in close partnership with the system—with the computer(s) and the information base(s)—in almost all their work, whether it be formulative thinking, or experimentation involving the control of apparatus, or teaching, or learning, or any of the other things in the list of their activities. Many of the members of the community are skilled in the art of computer programming and fluent in a number of programming languages. These people contribute in an important way to the improvement or extension of the system whenever, in the course of their work, they come to points at which the existing facilities are less than satisfactory—and prepare new procedures to fulfill the required functions or to meet the new circumstances. In that way, they add to the processing capabilities of the system. Other members of the community, not given to programming, may nevertheless add materially to the capability of the system; they do so by introducing new facts, new data, and new documents into the store.

The system is augmented not only through the contributions of its users, of course, but also through the contributions of full-time organizers, programmers, and maintainers of the system. The contributions of the system professionals were greatest during the early years of the development of the system. During the later years, the fact that the substantively oriented users predominate so greatly in sheer number offsets the greater concentration and, on the whole, greater skill of the professionals. In many instances, however, it is difficult to distinguish clearly between the contributions of the substantively oriented users and the contributions of the system professionals, for the professionals monitor the contributions of the users and often modify substantially, and usually polish, the techniques and programs and the sets of data that are offered to the public files.

The functions of the network that are of greatest relevance to Project Intrex are, of course, those that involve contribution to and consultation of the stored record. Let us examine briefly a few such functions.

Phillips, an experimenter in the psychology laboratory, is conducting an experiment on manual control. A subject, seated before a display screen, is trying to keep a stylus in contact with a point of light that moves about the screen. The trajectory of the point of light is calculated and controlled by a computer. The subject's response is recorded and analyzed by the computer, and the results are displayed graphically to the experimenter. The experimenter guides the execution of the experiment and controls the analysis of the data.

In the memory of the computer are three dynamic models of the manual-control process, three competitive theories of what goes on when a man tries to keep a stylus on a moving target. Two of the models were retrieved through the network, the other formulated by the experimenter at his console. The same target motion that is being displayed to the human subject is being fed to the three models. The responses of the models are recorded and analyzed in parallel with the response of the human subject. The computer adjusts the parameters of each model to maximize the correspondence between the model's behavior and the subject's. The computer keeps records of the degrees of correspondence achieved and displays the situation to the experimenter. Seeing the shortcomings of the models under test, the experimenter devises another model and tests it with the same target courses.

At the end of the session, the experimenter remains at his console to examine, organize, document, and file the records. After several such sessions, he assembles the entire accumulation of records, devoting particular attention to ensuring their retrievability and their convertibility from static to dynamic form. As a precaution, he exercises each of the models with test inputs and puts the parameter of the models under the parameter tables. Then he calls a type-and-edit program and prepares first draft of a report.

The report is a document, of course, complete with references and figures. The writer does not have to type out the references, for they are "in the system" —he merely points to the ones he wants and to the places in the text to which they are relevant, and the computer captures them and numbers (and, when a new reference is added, re-numbers) them. Some of the figures are dynamic. When the models, for example, are displayed on the screen, their input signals flow and the models "behave." Most figures have several forms. The reader can select detailed, real-time behavior or summary statistics. In some instances, the information contained in the figure is displayed from store. In other instances, a generating function is stored, and the figure is displayed from concurrent calculation.

The report is typed just once—when the author writes the initial draft. Indeed, in writing the initial draft, he employs some material that he prepared earlier for use in the experiment itself. He does not re-type it; he has the computer copy it, and perhaps he edits it a bit. In any event, a thing is typed just once and thereafter only modified. Because editing with the aid of the editing program is quick and easy, and because the current approach to computer "understanding" of natural language is more demanding than human readers are for excellence of style and rigorous adherence to stated conventions, important articles are revised and re-revised.

In the on-line community, publication is a multi-stage process. Even while a manuscript is in preparation, it can be as accessible to on-line colleagues as the author cares to make it so.

As soon as the manuscript is completed, it is available for retrieval with the aid of tags the author has tentatively attached to it. (Usually the author consults through the system with a docu-mentation expert during the final phase of preparing the manuscript.) If the manuscript is read (and "operated") by several members of the community, it is likely to pick up attachments: comments affixed to it by readers. The author may take them into account when he revises his manuscript, inserting "credit pointers" at the appropriate places in the text. (Credit pointers, attachments, and various other interactive paraphernalia become visible only in certain modes of display. The reader can call for them or inhibit them, whichever he likes.)

When it is ready for more formal publication, the author may submit his manuscript to any journal that operates within the network. (The author could submit it simultaneously to several journals, but, even if he were to try to hide his skullduggery by putting a separate copy into the store for each submission, a monitor program would probably find him out and attach all the submission records to each copy.) Editors use the network in their communications with reviewers, and that speeds up the review process.

In addition to its human reviewers, each journal uses a reviewing program that checks that all matters of format are in order. The program is most insistent that the author include suggested retrieval tags. Usually, the author interacts with the review program on-line. He may use it in a programmed-instruction mode to find out why it complains about a particular "period-quotes-closed" punctuation. He may find that the review program has looked up the quotation and discovered that the original version does not end in a period. Most journals that operate within the network have long since adopted stylistic conventions designed to preserve information—rather than, for example, to facilitate typesetting—and, in the case of the period and the quotation mark, that meant adopting the British practice.

Publication in a good journal within the network carries some guarantees of accessibility. Recent issues of *Physical Review,* for example, are never more remote than the third echelon of the local store. Publication in a good journal also ensures that the information contained in the document will be processed by one of the groups engaged in reorganizing the body of knowledge—that the information will be introduced into one of the new computer-processable information structures that promise in a few years to displace natural-language text as the main extra-neural carrier. Finally, publication in a good on-line journal guarantees publication and distribution in print. That is still important because the on-line network is not yet worldwide and because print-and-paper books still have advantages over consoles for a few non-negligible purposes.

The report is not stored all in one place. The title, abstract, references, etc., are held in a more readily accessible file than the body. Keyed to the body (and to some of the figures) are sets of data. The sets of data are stored in a data bank. Whereas data used to be relegated to vaults—preserved on the off-chance that some scholarly skeptic might re-examine the experiment in detail—now that there are means for working with data effectively, for analyzing or summarizing them in new ways without going through hours of drudgery, stored data are as often retrieved and examined as are stored documents.

The information contributed by the author to whose manuscript we have been directing our attention can be retrieved in several forms: document, set of data, dynamic model, answers to questions. Associated with each article is a description telling what things are available and in what forms. Part of the description is for potential users; it gives them the over-all picture. Part is for computers; it provides detailed instructions for operation of models, retrieval of associated data, and the like.

Phillips's article on manual control has now been published in (on-line)

"Human Factors." In Los Angeles, Dennis and Fry are writing a general on-line review of manual control and, in St. Louis, Rodehafer is conducting an experiment on manual control. Dennis and Fry have long since found and examined Phillips's article, of course; it was retrieved by their very first prescription. The way they incorporate Phillips's material into their review is worth examining briefly. They do not "rehash" it. They do not copy figures. Their introduction to Phillips's work sets it into perspective, defining its relation to other work in the field. Almost every sentence of the introduction contains pointers which, when activated, lead through the retrieval system to the relevant work. Their discussion of the work itself is organized around several basic theoretical questions. The discussion is full of pointers, too. Some of them lead to theoretical articles. Others lead to the figures and tables of Phillips's article. There is no need to copy those items and store them as part of the review article, for they are already in the memory of the network and readily recoverable from it. The review article is therefore in large part an associative structure of the kind Vannevar Bush envisaged in his 1945 description of "Memex."

In their review, Dennis and Fry mention Rodehafer's on-going experiment. They found out about it by following retrieval trails recorded within the system. (Each user has the option of leaving his trails open to inspection or covering them up. A tradition of "open trails" is developing within the academic community, whereas many business and industrial firms follow a policy intended to protect proprietary interests.) The review mentions the unfinished experiment but does not, of course, draw any conclusions from it. However, Dennis and Fry file a "suspense" message that will call to their attention the completion of Rodehafer's report. They do that because an on-line review article is not a one-shot effort. The reviewers have accepted a commitment to keep their review up-to-date for a period of five years.

Rodehafer, meanwhile, is using parts of the in-process review. He has become acquainted with Fry through the system. He disagrees with Fry's method of analyzing a basic theoretical problem. He is expanding his experiment to include a comparison of Fry's version of a pursuit model and his own.

The discussion between Fry and Rodehafer leads Fry to relearn some Laplace transform theory. He studies it partly with the aid of programmed instruction, partly by reading retrieved texts, and partly by asking questions. At one point, for example, Fry asks:

What is the rule or law: stability, servomechanism, locus, origin, Nyquist diagram or plot?

The question-answering system has a bit of trouble with that. It has to ask a question in reply:

Does the rule or law deal with: complex plane, Nyquist criterion?

Fry says that it does, that "Nyquist criterion" is the phrase he was trying to think of. The question-answering system then tells him that the Nyquist criterion is 10 years out of date, that the modern criteria are given by the root-locus method. The system then presents instructional material on the root-locus method. Fry is brought up-to-date and, incidentally, into better agreement with Rodehafer's analysis, which had been based on current concepts. Fry learns to use the system's on-line root-locus programs. He introduces Dennis to them. The review is saved from prenatal obsolescence.

The foregoing example mixes content appropriate to 1965 with question-answering capability not available in 1965. However, the postulated question-answering capability is far from sophisti-

cated. It assumes only a very simple syntax and nothing more advanced then lexicographic semantics. The service available to the on-line intellectual community of the 1980's will be considerably more complex and sophisticated than the services we have suggested here.

Complexity and sophistication, however, are not crucial to the main theme of the concept. The essentials are:

The "on-lineness"—the quick responsiveness that permits integration into the on-going line of thought.

The breadth of the spectrum of the services.

The fact that the services supplement the capabilities of men.

The fact that the network promotes coherent interaction among the members of the intellectual community.

The Influence of the Concept

The idealized concept of the on-line intellectual community is by no means a goal of Project Intrex. If it were a goal, it would certainly not be achievable on the time scale that has been laid down for the Project. The idealized concept is, like the Project MAC experience, an influence that has played a role in shaping the program of research that is recommended for Project Intrex to carry out. Whereas the MAC experience served as a base from which to project, the idealized concept of the on-line intellectual community serves as a check-list of attractive features, many of them not achievable on the Intrex time scale, but all of them worth examining for relevance and feasibility.

The single consideration that has most severely inhibited the tendency to reach as far as possible toward the idealized concept in the planning for Project Intrex was the difficulty of converting a truly large body of information from the presently modal form of print-on-paper into the digital code required for computer processing. There is some spread of opinion within the Planning Conference as to the extent to which that difficulty will be overcome during the next few years, but there was general agreement that it would not be feasible to convert all the contents of all the documents in the MIT libraries, or even all the contents of all the documents that would be required for a model library capable of supporting significant experiments. The conclusion was that every effort should be made to capture newly generated information directly in computer-processible form. Much of it exists in that form at one point or another during the process of preparation, editing, typesetting, and printing, and almost all of it—all that is typewritten—could be gotten into computer-processible form with only a little additional expenditure of time and facilities. Therefore, new information should go directly into the digital store. All the information in the apparatus of bibliographic control must be converted into computer-processible form, even though the conversion may require considerable labor. As for the contents of the documents that are already in the library, however, large-scale conversion at the present time does not seem practicable. It seems better to wait for the development of effective and economical character-reading machines—and perhaps even for devices and programs capable of encoding line drawings, if not pictures—before pressing forward to complete the task of conversion. That set of conclusions severely limits the distance Project Intrex can go toward realizing a computer system of the kind required to support a full-fledged, on-line intellectual community.

The other major restraining factor is the primitive state of understanding of natural language. Men appear to communicate with one another in natural language rather well, but even the most sophisticated linguists do not fully understand the syntax; and there is almost no semantic theory at all that is capable of supporting engineering applications. It is evident that, although linguistics is recognized as an important and challenging field, and although it is the focus of much activity, the basic problems will not be solved to the point of engineering applications on the time scale that has been set for Project Intrex and the operational information network to which it is to lead. This consideration adds its weight to that of the text-conversion difficulty in limiting the use of the on-line intellectual community as a model.

Despite these constraining effects, the concept of the on-line intellectual community remains a strong influence on Project Intrex. The concept has registered itself upon many creative minds in the Cambridge area, and too forcefully upon those minds not to shape the Intrex program in many ways. Enough members of the Cambridge intellectual community want to be members of an on-line intellectual community to keep the idea from lying dormant. Therefore, even though the on-line intellectual community will not come into existence as a result of Project Intrex, it will become a nearer prospect, and advances made during the 1970's might well remove the constraints and permit, during the 1980's, an essential realization of the concept.

The Information Transfer System at M.I.T. in 1975

Three main streams of progress in the information transfer field were intensively discussed at the Project Intrex Planning Conference:

The modernization of current library procedures through the application of technical advances in data processing, textual storage, and reproduction.

The growth, largely under Federal sponsorship, of a national network of libraries and other information centers.

The extension of the rapidly developing technology of on-line, interactive computer communities into the domains of the library and other information centers.

The information transfer system that we visualize at MIT in 1975 is a forward projection of these developments based on the assumption that Project Intrex will aim to merge them into a balanced combination.

In attempting a description of the principal features of the system of 1975, we have been mindful of the universal tendency to overestimate what can be done in a single year, and to underestimate what can be done in ten. Thus our ten-year leap into the future of information transfer may have the appearance of an overly bold flight of fancy. We present it with diffidence and we caution the reader against confusing it with MIT policy. But we also point out to the reader that a factual description of today's computer operations at MIT would have seemed fantastic to him in 1955.

A Central Computer

The flow of information in the system of 1975 will be controlled by means of a time-shared digital computer. Sharp distinctions must be drawn among at least four different ways in which computers are now being used and certainly will be used by the university of 1975. This is necessary for two reasons. In the first place, we wish to set limits to the fields of interest to which Project Intrex will address itself. Secondly, an early discussion is required to avoid confusion on the extent to which these different applications can or should share common computational facilities, either during the development phase or operationally.

Four applications which are already clearly distinguishable are related to (1) the needs of the universities for computational and data-handling facilities in the conduct of their organizational businesses, such as payrolls, scheduling classes, and so forth; (2) the computational needs of the members of the university community in the pursuit of their intellectual endeavors; (3) the use of computers for what has now come to be called computer-aided instruction (CAI); and, finally, (4) the use of the computer for information retrieval. It is, of course, this last category that is the proper concern of Project Intrex, although the storage and retrieval of the text used for CAI can probably be also considered a part of the Intrex responsibility. We further note that all four of these applications can and will make use of computers operating in a time-sharing mode and that, in principle, they all could share a single common facility. While this might seem to be a desirable state of affairs in the interest of economy, it seems highly unlikely that all four different groups of users could work together satisfactorily, particularly in the early, developmental stages.

The Information Store

A university has access to a great many sources of information. Much of the information is recorded in books, pamphlets, and so forth, and resides in the present-day library. Some of the information is retained in the minds of the community itself, and is communicated to the student body in the normal teaching processes, and to colleagues via seminars and informal discussion. The information transfer system of 1975 might have provisions for tapping this latter source of knowledge just as it obviously must have facilities for tapping the information stored in the library.

In predicting the form in which the "recorded" portion of the information will be stored, we have assumed that by 1975 we shall be roughly half-way in the transition from the library of the present time to a completely on-line intellectual community as already described, at least so far as the science and engineering holdings are concerned; that is, approximately half the scientific information actually transmitted to the user would be stored in books or on microfilm, and half in some computer-accessible form. A word of caution: We are talking here not about the total information available but that portion of the information that the user actually makes use of. Obviously, the heritage of the existing library will not be easily duplicated or replaced, and most of the archival type of information will still exist in printed form.

A large portion of library information will be available in image microform. This main image store will be accessed by address only. Microform copies of equal size or of larger format (for inexpensive viewers) and hard copy will be available locally within seconds on demand. Although local viewing of the microform may possibly be done by mechanical transport of the microform, remote viewing will be possible by high-resolution facsimile or CRT display.

Certainly, we are not going to take the present library holdings and transfer them *en masse* into a machine-readable form by 1975, if, in fact, this is ever done. Much of the material that is created between now and 1975 will be produced in hard-copy form. However, it is not at all unreasonable to assume that the most often-used portion of this information will either be initially produced in machine-readable form or be converted into machine-readable form and will be available to an on-line intellectual community through terminals of some sort. And since a large part of the scientific community is concerned with recent information rather than archival information, we will assume that up to 50% of the *active* information will be stored, transmitted or reproduced in coded form.

This coded material will consist of source documents in the present-day sense and of derived material in the form of card catalog information, abstracts, indices, bibliographies, concordances, critical reviews, summary information and condensations. There is, of course, a present-day tendency to consider such information as being distinct from the documents themselves, but we will assume that by 1975 the amount of such material will have grown disproportionately and that it will no longer be considered separately. We can anticipate that it will be necessary to index, abstract, and condense the normal indexing and abstracting documents themselves.

Access Techniques

Physical Aspects

In the information transfer system of 1975, the user will have a choice of means by which he can obtain access to the information stored in the system. It is highly unlikely that he will borrow books from the library as he does at present. If he needs the actual document itself, he will obtain a copy of it. This copy may be prepared by the publisher in the usual fashion, and we can think of the bookstore and the library as having coalesced, at least in the university community. If the desired document is out-of-print at the time of the request, the library will duplicate it by one of the many duplicating facilities that it will then possess. We are, of course, assuming that progress will have been made toward resolving the legal aspects of the situation, and toward developing methods of fairly reimbursing the authors and publishers.

Because of the difficulties of handling books of different sizes, one might think that the leading libraries will have standardized on a fixed book size both for storage and for distribution. But this could have been done with profit at any time within the last 300 years, and it seems that a general law may be at work, the consequence of which is that it is easier to introduce a distinctly new system than to modify slightly an old one. We have little confidence that the actual format of ordinary books will be very much modified by 1975. Books for storage purposes could be produced with high-quality materials which would no longer be subject to the high deterioration rates which affect our present materials.

As a second type of service, we will assume that many users will want to read specific pages of a given document but will not have any need for the possession of the actual document. These users will be served through a variety of consoles with cathode-ray tube or other method of presentation of page material. It seems reasonable to assume that the costs of such consoles will be still quite high and that they will not have wide distribution. However, in a community the size of MIT, it would not be unreasonable to assume that there may be as many as 50 to 200 such terminals scattered around the campus at strategically located positions, in branch libraries or student reading rooms and places of that sort.

A third class of service to be provided will be that of producing hard copy by typewriters or printers (mechanical and nonmechanical) at remote locations, quite analogous to the typewriter output now obtainable through the MAC computer, but at a higher output speed. Again, making an estimate as to the magnitude of this service, it would seem not unreasonable to assume that substantially every faculty member would have such a terminal available to him and that there might be between 100 and 1000 available to the student body.

A fourth form of service will be through the medium of terminals designed primarily for CAI use. This service will resemble that provided by the third class of terminals with however serious restrictions on the speed of output printer, dictated by cost considerations as noted earlier. There may be 1000 of these terminals in use at MIT by 1975.

And as a final form of output, we will certainly have available a Touch-Tone push-button input and voice-answer-back system. By 1975 we can expect that each student will have a telephone available either on his own study desk or, at worst, shared with another student in his dormitory room.

In effect, access by telephone and by any of the other terminals would be independent of geographical location and there would be as many terminals on the information transfer system as there are telephones.

Intellectual Aspects

We have talked about access in terms of physical devices. Now let us turn our attention to the intellectual aspects of providing access to stored information.

In the information transfer system of 1975, an augmented catalog (author, subject, title; table of contents, abstract, citations, etc.) will be available via the computer in machine-readable form.

In addition, the Touch-Tone telephone with voice-answer-back could, of course, be used for obtaining certain types of catalog information. It is not unreasonable to assume that by 1975 a fairly elaborate voice-answer-back technique will have been developed, based on the "twenty-question" idea so that the input required of the user will be minimized and limited to occasional pushing of one of the ten buttons that will then exist on many telephones.

This same system would, of course, be employed extensively in instructional use. We can envision the situation by 1975 in which all lectures are stored, at least temporarily, and that the student who has missed a lecture in person can have it repeated to him over the telephone. Implied in all this, although not stated so far, is the assumption that this telephone answer-back service—and, indeed, all the mechanized aspects of the library—will be available on a 24-hour basis, so that the student at any time during the preparation of his next assignment could refresh his memory as to the exact happenings in the class the day before.

The typewriter output service which

now bulks so large in on-line systems such as Project MAC will, probably by 1975, have ceased to have so large a significance, although here again it may well be that very rapid printers, facsimile printers, and the like will have been developed as of this time, in which case this service will still be important. This service will be used to obtain extracts of documents abstracts, condensations, and material which requires detailed study on the part of the student. The absence of effective graphics will, however, be a serious drawback as of 1975 unless major developments are made which cannot at the present be fully anticipated.

Turning now to the most elaborate form of terminal which, as indicated earlier, will probably contain both typewriter input and rapid output, and a cathode-ray tube display with a light pen or some other graphic input device, we note there are essentially no limits to the intellectual scope of the activity that can be carried on by means of these terminals. The user will be able to have displayed, on his scope, catalog information, extract information, or complete portions of complete documents, depending on his needs at the moment.

We might pause here to note that the same terminal facilities that provide access to these various classes of services should also provide access to computational facilities as now provided by Project MAC or by the Computation Center at MIT, and that this dual function should continue and be undoubtedly much enlarged by 1975. We might well require the user to dial a separate number for extensive computational services since it may be unreasonable to require the information-retrieval computer to handle the transcription of the input and output between the user and the computational facilities.

From what has been said, it is evident that we anticipate a situation in 1975 in which the on-line intellectual community will, in effect, have come into existence, still with terminals inadequate because of economic considerations. It is also highly unlikely that the system will be able to serve all the potential users or that it will contain a completely adequate corpus of information in machine-readable form, but it will be a start. This would provide the evolutionary aspect of the system, enabling it to expand to provide all the desired services at some future time.

The conventional library as a storehouse for books would, of course, continue to exist and will continue to be extremely useful to the user of 1975, although it seems possible that, by this time period, character-reading equipment may have been developed such that most archival information could be translated on demand into machine-readable form. However, we will assume that this would not be done on a routine basis but only on a request basis.

The routine operational procedure in the book aspect or document-storage aspect of the complete information transfer system would consist largely of making and distributing reproductions, either page reproductions or entire volume reproductions, to requesting users. These reproductions would, however, not necessarily be in full-size copies. It is uncertain at the present time what these forms will ultimately be and what the mechanism of their enlargement for ultimate use will be but, again, it seems reasonable to assume that we will be in a transition stage with most forms of services presently available, or conceptually available today, in rather widespread use. Many users will desire that the documents be delivered to them in their full size. For storage reasons, the library will, however, probably not save all source documents in their full size but will be well along in an orderly process of converting a large share of source material into microforms. The user who then requests full-size copies will have the enlargements made for him at the library and they will be delivered to him in this form.

Other users, of course, will want to retain a larger volume of material. These users will ask for the material to be delivered to them in a microform package and will then have locally available enlarging equipment for viewing.

The viewing equipment of 1975 will undoubtedly provide for rapid page-turning of microdocuments in such a fashion that the user will be able to thumb through a book, in much the fashion that he now thumbs through a physical book, and to make use of all the quick-scanning procedures that users employ today.

Selective Dissemination

Many of the difficulties which currently plague selective dissemination systems will have been obviated by 1975. We can therefore expect with confidence that there will be at least two forms of selective dissemination for which the system must make provision. The simplest form of such a system will consist of notifications sent to the user whenever there are new acquisitions that fit his profile. However, we can predict that, for a limited class of users, the actual documents will be sent on arrival as soon as the profile match has been observed. The systems, at least the more advanced systems, will undoubtedly provide for machine determination of reader profile based on his initial assessment of his interest, as modified by his actual use of the library system. From one really extreme point of view, a request by a user for a specific document to the library indicates either that the user's profile has changed with time or that the system is not functioning properly.

New Publishing Patterns

The editing programs and typesetting programs that have been implemented at various places on a time-sharing computer will have very great impact on the entire publishing and library field. Using the report-editing facilities which will be available, many of the MIT staff will undoubtedly use the on-line facilities as a means for first recording their potentially publishable information; and, in fact, potential books may go through several editions before ever appearing between hard covers, being available only to the users of the system via the terminals.

A development of automatic library systems will undoubtedly lead to rather profound changes in the methods by which documents are prepared for library use. In all probability by 1975, the major publishers will be able to supply copies of most of their publications in a microform, and it is highly likely that this form will replace book acquisition, as such, to a very large measure. Many publications, handbooks and the like, might even be distributed in magnetic form for use in data-retrieval systems rather than in document-retrieval systems, and be, therefore, available to the library of the future in this form.

Changes in periodicals may also be rather profound. It is possible that periodicals will publish reprints rather than completely bound journals, and libraries may prefer to subscribe to a reprint service of this sort rather than to have the bound volumes of the journal in their possession. On the other hand, the incremented cost of an additional copy in microform will be so much less than that of actual volumes that every library in the field may well acquire a microform version for reference and copying. Depending upon the publishing economics as of that time, the library may acquire a large enough supply of printed reprints to supply them to potential users, or they may acquire only one or two such documents (preferably in microform) and produce the desired copies on demand in microform or hard copy.

Integration with Other Information Sources

The information transfer system of 1975 will easily extend the reach of its users beyond the resources of the local system. There will be communications networks tying university systems together and providing connections with national resources. Facsimile transmission schemes will provide for the rapid interchange of document images in situations where coded information is not available.

The Role of the Librarian

Naturally, collections of art books, posters, original manuscripts and letters, phonograph records, etc., will have to be maintained, acquired and loaned— much as they are at present. It will be wrong to imagine, however, that the librarian's only function in the 1975 environment will be to care for the more recalcitrant members of the collection. Certainly, the librarian of 1975 will be less involved than now with the individual transaction between user and book, but our whole purpose is to increase very greatly the utility of the information-transfer system. The librarian will be of primary importance in the acquisition of new material, in cooperative cataloging, in organizing the collection, instructing users of the library, and in modifying the rules and programs to maximize the services provided to the user over the long run. The librarian will be able to operate with greater freedom by having control over advanced machinery. The librarian will be much involved with the arrangement of channels with other libraries and facilities and with the presumption and provision to users of proper and economical terminals or other means of access to the system. Vastly more material than now will be available to the user of the library, and there will be a need for professional librarians at all levels in the system. It seems likely that to be a librarian in 1975 will be very fruitful and exciting.

The Information Transfer Budget of 1975

The information transfer system that has been described as a conceptual pattern for 1975 is vastly different from the library of today in the scope of the services it seeks to provide. While no cost estimates for such a system can be made until there has been extensive experimental investigation, it is clear that substantially larger budgets will be required for such an information transfer complex than would be available under a normal extrapolation of today's library budgets. The Planning Conference has indulged in some speculation on the proper magnitude of an MIT information transfer budget for 1975, and has arrived at a figure of $15 million by two different routes.

It is a well-known phenomenon that the amount of published information doubles approximately every 13 years. Since scientific information increases at a somewhat higher rate, and since libaries should, if anything, increase their relative holdings, it seems not unreasonable to assume that the amount of material available to the typical library, assuming no changes were made in its function, would in 1975 be at least double the amount now contained.

Project Intrex will, of course, result in an increased emphasis on libraries at MIT; and we can reasonably expect to see an increase in the relative size of the MIT library compared to other universities (it has been decreasing steadily since 1930). With due allowance for all these factors, we might expect the total amount of stored information in the MIT information-transfer system of 1975 to be more than ten times as large as it is in the library of today. We conclude that the magnitude of the information available in 1975 could demand a 15-fold increase in the budget of the library.

While the advances sparked by Project Intrex could result in a decrease in the actual budget, a more probable outcome, if past experience is any guide, will be a very great increase in the services rendered. Thus we might expect that the total budget for information transfer services at MIT will be of the order of $15 million in 1975.

Alternatively, we can base an estimated budget on an assumed size of the MIT community in 1975, and on the needs of the individual in the community. For this purpose, we shall take the community to contain 15,000 people: students, faculty, research staff, and some of the surrounding community. With increased mechanization that makes other services available and with the increase in total available information, it is not unreasonable to expect that the total expenditure for information services per user will increase. There is, of course, a very wide difference in annual expenditure per user at different universities. An estimate of $1000 per user of the future MIT information transfer system would bring us to the same $15 million figure previously cited for 1975.

The Government Makes Plans

by William T. Knox

In discussing information-system development, I feel, in a way, like a missionary. I don't mean in the sense of propagating the faith some of us have that progress in science and technology can result from better information handling. I mean, rather, in advocating a partnership of the government and the private sector in fashioning the tools—the information systems—that will meet our present and future needs. I stress the word *partnership* because I sincerely believe that although *federal*-information-system improvement is a vital ingredient, the larger need is *national*-information-system improvement. In this positive sense, then, I describe myself as a missionary seeking to convert your curiosity into interest and your interest into action. Without your participation in the planning and execution of national systems, progress will continue to be slower than it need be.

In a nutshell, we who are studying the problem for the federal government are convinced that in your professional and in the public interest every physicist has a role to play in the development of national systems for scientific and technical information.

I am chairman of one of the committees of the Federal Council for Science and Technology, the Committee on Scientific and Technical Information, commonly called "COSATI." Let me give you a word picture of what COSATI does and how the COSATI Task Group on National Systems for Scientific and Technical Information is

proceeding. I will tell you about some problems we face and trends we must consider. I will outline some of the actions undertaken and some being planned by the government. I will highlight to you my interest that organizations such as the American Institute of Physics and its member societies must participate in the program of developing a national system and that the stakes are high for us as a nation as well as for physicists as individuals. You are invited to join in a dialogue—to make your thoughts known.

What Is an Information System?

Now, I have been referring to information systems and perhaps we need a definition. Information systems, as I use the term, refers to that large, somewhat amorphous complex under the general heading of scientific and technical information activities. I think "systems" is a better concept, because it is through a series of related systematic functions that information is transferred to promote the progress of science and technology.

Too often there has appeared to be an emphasis on scientific and technical information systems without relating them to the cause the systems serve, the reason for their existence—the progress of science and technology.

President Kennedy focused on the real issue when he said, "One of the major opportunities for enhancing the effectiveness of our national scientific and technical effort, and the efficiency

SOURCE: *Physics Today*, **19**, No. 1, January 1966, pp. 39–44.

of government management of research and development lies in the improvement of our ability to communicate information about current research efforts and the results of past efforts. Strong science and technology is a national necessity and adequate communication is a prerequisite for strong science and technology."

Arising out of that basic declaration of opportunity and purpose, those federal government organizations concerned with overall plans and policies for research and development have for some years been working on specific programs to improve scientific-information systems. That effort is now greater than ever before.

The Government Effort

The Federal Council for Science and Technology is the overall advisory and coördinating mechanism for activities within the executive branch of the federal government for science and technology. I also assist Dr. Donald F. Hornig, the President's Special Assistant for Science and Technology and Director of the Office of Science and Technology. OST advises and assists the President in overall coördination, planning, and evaluation of federal programs in science and technology. COSATI is the principal mechanism for obtaining individual agency views and reaching agency consensus on desirable activities and programs of the federal government with respect to information systems for science and technology. The Office of Science and Technology provides an executive device for implementing the recommendations of COSATI.

Let me first outline the scope of COSATI'S concerns. They are very broad because they are related to all scientific and engineering disciplines and to all of technology. The breadth of problems being studied by COSATI can be understood better by considering the work areas of its panels:

Operational techniques and systems.

This panel is concerned with acquisition, accession, abstracting, indexing, announcement, distribution, terminology control, equipment compatibility and convertibility, wholesale and retail resources, specialized information centers, libraries, and depositories. This is our "workhorse" panel, charged with improving the quality of performance and coördination of current and near future federal agency programs.

Information sciences technology. The missions assigned to this panel are to make recommendations for orderly development of information-sciences technology and orderly transition from current to improved systems. "Orderly development" means avoiding unnecessary duplication of agency research and development efforts and identifying gaps in those efforts.

Education and training. This panel helps us look for improved education and training of information specialists and means for increasing their supply. It will also recommend programs to help educate scientists and engineers and managers in the use of information resources and systems.

International information activities. This country needs information produced by scientists and engineers in other countries. In these days of plans for computerized information systems serving an international community, it is important to have a panel to help coördinate federal-agency activities to set standards for systems, to recommend international exchange policy and procedure and to improve the many translation programs carried on in and out of government.

Also under consideration are other panels dealing with the problems associated with production and use of information and with relations between federal and nonfederal information activities.

COSATI'S concerns thus embrace not only systems that actually transfer documents and information from one user to another. They also embrace (*a*) initial publication processes and producers of information, (*b*) user groups with their varying information needs, (*c*) education and training of information-system operators, and (*d*) producer-user groups of modern information systems. Information systems also have their own large research and development programs.

The size of the federal-government program is not easy to determine. The reason is that it is difficult to make a distinction between some information activities and the research or engineering activities of which they are an integral and essential part. To all scientists and engineers information transfer is an inseparable part of their science and engineering. Recognizing, however, the difficulties in separating information services from other aspects of research and development, COSATI has developed some very rough budget estimates for information programs of executive-branch agencies for fiscal year 1966 (Table 1).

TABLE 1

Activity	Cost ($ millions)
Publication and distribution	130
Bibliographic and reference service	80
R&D information sciences and systems	60
Symposia and technical meetings	40
Information centers	20
Management and training	20
Audio and visual media	10
Budget issues	10
Translations	5
Support publications	5
Total	380

The numbers are rounded. They are estimated obligations, not expenditures.

Actions by Federal Agencies

A number of actions have been taken by federal agencies to improve information systems as a result of COSATI studies and recommendations. Some of these are:

1. A uniform policy to guide federal agencies on financial help to nonprofit, nongovernment scientific publications. This is the so-called "page-charge" policy, whereby federal agencies pay certain costs of publication if requested by the publishers

2. A standard for microforms of technical reports. We call these "microfiche," and we look for this new standard to create a new, large market and thus lower unit costs

3. A uniform method for identifying federal reports. This is called "descriptive cataloging," and the technique is of particular help to those people who have to store and retrieve reports

4. Finally, a subject-category list to be used throughout the federal government for the announcement of reports. This will make it easier for users of federal reports to locate information.

These COSATI actions do not have the glamor of a space walk, but they are very significant actions in bringing about better coördination of federal and nonfederal information activities. We will have to follow their implementation and modify and correct them when necessary. We are also working hard on other standards and policies.

In addition to the above-mentioned actions whereby individual agencies and nongovernment organizations have been enabled to make their own information systems more effective and more efficient as components of the total national network, COSATI has been the mechanism by which, or with whose endorsement, several new organizations have been created to carry out special functions of the national network. These new central organizations are

1. the Clearinghouse for Federal Scientific and Technical Information,

2. the Science Information Exchange,

3. the National Referral Center for Science and Technology, and

4. the National Standard Reference Data System.

An Overall National Complex

About a year ago, following several suggestions from committees of the Congress that the executive branch exercise stronger, more aggressive leadership in this area, an interdepartmental COSATI task group began to develop the conceptual framework for a plan to improve the overall complex of scientific and technical information activities in the United States.

To develop a realistic conceptual framework, one had to consider activities inside and outside the federal establishment because nonfederal and federal activities are mutually dependent on one another, and much federal money goes directly or indirectly in support of these activities (and vice versa, of course). Very early in the deliberations of the COSATI task group, we recognized the importance of continuing dialogues with representatives of various nongovernment components of the information-system complex.

Accordingly we have already participated in a number of special meetings held to present the task group's preliminary thinking regarding a *concept* toward which United States information systems could develop. These meetings have been held with top-level representatives of scientific and engineering professional societies, industrial and trade associations, the technical and business press, and library groups.

Although there are many other areas of interest, the task group has focused its efforts so far on formalized communications mechanisms, primarily document-handling mechanisms. In part this emphasis is due to the relatively organized subsystem of document-handling activities, compared to the less structured nondocument systems for information transfer. The task group has been assisted by a study team from the System Development Corporation, and the first report became publicly available recently.

What have we developed so far? First, we have concluded that the far-flung, widespread nature of the information system can be roughly conceived as in part analogous to the telephone network, which is a mechanism for connecting people who want to know or to talk with other people who either have the desired information or are willing to listen. The telephone network is a mechanism completely at the service of its users, and one needs only an elementary knowledge to be able to use it. The telephone operates on a real-time basis, however, and this is a big difference from information systems, which in part transfer knowledge acquired some years ago to today's users.

Partly to recognize this difference in user need and partly because of the different functions and types of people involved, we have, in our preliminary thinking, divided the body of the national network of information systems into two parts: first, a complex of library systems (document-oriented, as are traditional libraries) and second, a complex of information evaluation and retrieval systems (information-oriented).

A Copy of Each Significant Document

A basic proposition has been put forth by the task group for further consideration within the government: namely, that the federal government has responsibility for ensuring accessibility within the United States of a copy of all significant worldwide literature in science and technology. This does not mean federal *operation* of the document-handling system but only federal *responsibility* for ensuring an effective system.

Apparently we need several libraries at the national level, handling *documents* in such fields as medicine, agriculture, engineering, earth sciences, physical sciences, behavioral sciences, etc. Each of these libraries would be concerned with acquiring all the pertinent literature in its field, cataloging or indexing it, announcing the availability of the literature, and providing copies if requested. These would be structured, operated, and administered to meet some standard system requirements or specifications, but they would not necessarily be operated by the government. Each national library would be the responsibility of a federal agency with primary mission responsibilities in its field of interest, such as the National Library of Medicine, which responds to the mission of the Department of Health, Education and Welfare. Coördination and compatibility among the libraries would be a primary goal from the beginning, and a question for early decision is the mechanism for bringing about this coördination.

Because of the size of our population and the diversity of demands made on libraries for documents, ranging from help to the teenage student to the needs of the lay adult to the needs of small and large business and the professions, the rest of the library network will be essentially retailers of documents. Other library systems (federal, college and university, public, specialized, industry, institutes, schools, etc.) would, as now, look to the national libraries for loan of documents, catalogs, etc., as may be appropriate, and would, in turn, provide some of the input to those libraries. But their main role would be to serve those users who will be satisfied with documents.

Evaluation and Retrieval

The other part of the system—the complex of evaluation and retrieval systems—would consist of those activities of government agencies, universities, industries, and societies (professional, scientific, and trade) that are concerned with providing information, as opposed to documents, to specific audiences directly concerned with science and technology. Elements of this system would be expected to

1. provide secondary current awareness, such as abstracts bulletins;
2. analyze and evaluate information, not only the information contained in documents but that information just developed and still unpublished;
3. facilitate searching of the literature through deep indexing and other means;
4. retrieve specific information on request, that is, answer on-the-spot questions.

These activities are normally much more closely identified with the research and development programs and the scientific disciplines than are the document-oriented activities centered on libraries. They require scientific and technical orientation and competence of the participating personnel. Here, too, we need an improved mechanism for bringing about the desired coördination of effort, and here especially the government needs the advice, assistance, and active involvement of nongovernmental groups. The task group will begin active study of this part of the national network very soon.

We look forward to continued progress in interagency coördination and to increasingly productive coöperation with the nongovernmental community.

Problems: Money, Men, Management

There are, however, some difficult problems to be solved. For example, the advent of national computer-based information systems will raise new issues. Because of the federal government's deep involvement in the national effort in science and technology and its close relation to and financial support of the extensive nongovernmental activities in so much of the information network, the Congress will ultimately have to decide what parts of the evolving modern information network are appropriately federal-government responsibilities and to what degree. As the report[1] of the President's Science Advisory Committee said, "Government involvement in scientific communication is going to grow, just as governmental involvement in science and technology is growing. We must always seek to ensure on behalf of both the federal government and the technical community, that the federal information system remains adequate but does not overwhelm the existing nongovernment systems and that our government and nongovernment systems continue to develop into an effectively interwoven instrument that is always responsive to the changing needs of our science and technology."

Other difficult problems are the sources and mechanisms for financial support for the information network.

Federal-agency information services are usually subsidized by the general tax-paying public for the benefit of the service users. This is sometimes justified on the grounds of eliminating billing costs and collection of charges for many small items—sometimes on the grounds that more use is encouraged if the services are provided free, sometimes because it is judged to be for the general welfare. It is common experience that people associate value with cost to them, and in most cases people are willing to pay for something they really need. In the absence of a cost-controlling mechanism, an information service, like other services, is likely to become unwieldy and cumbersome and unresponsive to

user needs. Such a situation could lead to overemphasis on the production or processing side and underemphasis on the true needs of the user, which is the marketing side. A mechanism by which users of an information service are made to pay some part of the costs for the service is a valuable control device. It also acts as a spur to the information-service managers.

There are other serious problems, too, such as the lack of adequate skilled manpower for the modernized information network and the lack of adequate information facilities on our college and university campuses, where the future users of the system are being trained.

But the problem demanding greatest attention at present is creating a permanent mechanism for ensuring the effective, efficient management of the vast, far-flung, almost incredibly complicated series of functions that together make up the national information network.

Let me mention a few possibilities for a central management mechanism. These are (*a*) a COMSAT-like corporation deeply involved in the actual operation of the information network with both governmental and private interests, (*b*) a new federal agency managing all agency science and technology information services much as the General Services Administration handles other services, (*c*) a new federal agency restricted to top-level planning and evaluation with existing agencies continuing to manage their internal information systems, (*d*) assignment of top-level planning and evaluation functions to an existing federal agency, and (*e*) a continuation of the present multifaceted management. These possibilities, and others, are now being examined closely by the COSATI task group and the System Development Corporation.

[1] Weinberg, A. M., et al., *Science, Government, and Information: The Responsibilities of the Technical Community and the Government in the Transfer of Information*, January 10, 1963; available from Superintendent of Documents, Washington, D.C. 20402.

Automation and the Library of Congress

by Gilbert W. King

Assessment of Need

The Research Library Today

One of the notable changes in our culture over the past two decades has been the growth in academic and technical activity. The number of people drawn into this activity has increased at least tenfold. The effect has been to make information a critically important national product. By its nature, information is heavily dependent upon itself, that is, upon prior information; thus, improving its use can have tremendous implications in our future academic and technical growth. If automation can bring about such improvement, it will surely be justified by its contribution to the quality of a large and important part of our national effort.

Research librarians face a range of serious problems which stem from the rate at which information is accumulating and from the changes in its production and use in our society. For example, almost every research library now has some arrearages in the processing of newly acquired materials. In some research libraries these arrearages constitute a very serious backlog of partially processed or unprocessed material. The acquisitions procedures of research libraries have become ponderous and slower than is desirable because of the mass of detail that must be managed.

Serial publications present increasingly complex problems in ordering, the prompt claiming of missing issues, and the fiscal management and bibliographical identification of titles; yet serial publications are rapidly increasing in number and in importance for research. There is a need for more intensive subject analysis of periodicals and other kinds of research material than is now possible for economic and other reasons. Concomitant with the growth and size of library collections is the growth in size and complexity of the card catalog which is getting more and more difficult to use merely because of its size and dispersion. Reorganization of the card catalog and the book collection are almost impossible under present conditions.

Most libraries have severe problems of space; buildings are relatively inflexible structures and accommodation to the growing collection is difficult. Any attempt to make a useful distinction between widely used material and little used or useless material is very difficult within the framework of present techniques and practices. Present library systems cannot accommodate easily to providing a range of response times geared to the requirements of their users. Requests which should receive responses in a matter of minutes are generally handled by the same methods

SOURCE: *Automation and the Library of Congress.* Washington, D.C.: 1963, pp. 1–24.

[1] G. W. King was chairman of a survey team that studied automation at the Library of Congress from 1960 to 1963 and produced the book excerpted here. The other coauthors were H. P. Edmundson, M. M. Flood, M. Kochen, R. L. Libby, D. R. Swanson, and A. Wylly

and techniques as those for which a delay of a day or two is acceptable. Manual techniques make it altogether impractical to provide the very rapid response required in many instances of manipulating and examining catalogs or bibliographies. Moreover, the size of card catalogs has so strongly dictated two or three, rarely four or more, access points to a given work, that rigid cataloging systems (both subject and descriptive) have persisted. Subject headings and subject heading lists cannot be maintained at the level of currency required for effective retrieval. Finally, there is too much duplication of effort among the various research libraries that make up our national capability for communicating recorded knowledge. This multiplication of effort pervades the cataloging process, the production of bibliographies, the function of acquisition, and even the contents of the collections.

In science and technology the technical report literature has not found its way, other than by exception, into the general corpus of research library materials and services. Almost all of the subject analysis of the scientific and technical periodical literature is provided by services operated outside research libraries. Certain classes of literature, including reprints, preprints, specialized reports, abstracts, etc., are increasingly collected and circulated by decentralized and subject-specialized information centers. It is appropriate to raise the issue as to what extent specialized and tailor-made information services should be provided by the general research library if it is to avoid the role of a mere repository or a passive adjunct to the academic process.

The resources of research libraries should be used more extensively than they now are in a great many of the present research activities in the arts and sciences, but in order for this to happen new technological aids for the library must be introduced.

There is no simple measure of the usefulness of libraries, but their effect is observable in the quality of our intellectual endeavors. Large research libraries, mainly centered in the academic community, have always played a vital role in the training of succeeding generations of leaders in every field of knowledge and enterprise. Libraries support academic research. They are the adjunct of our expanding culture and provide the connection with other cultures now and in the past. Despite their importance, however, they generally have had extremely limited resources made available to them. The burden of effective exploitation has thus always been, and will always be, on the user himself, but substantive techniques for lightening this burden have fallen far short of what could be done with increased resources. The "information explosion" has resulted in disproportionate increases in the complexity of subject interrelatedness, so that the user is faced with penetrating an almost impossibly complex reference maze that is growing more complex. The need for greater depth of subject control has made it increasingly difficult for librarians to organize their materials for the user's benefit, and the specialized indexing and abstracting services have filled only a part of this need. To some significant degree, a lack of rapport between large research libraries and the new class of information users has developed. For example, numerous specialized documentation centers have been established in industrial organizations. The cost of this, in duplicated acquisitions alone, is very high, and the effect on intellectual activities may be profound.

It is possible to identify many different kinds of library users and user needs. They range from the individual who enters the library for intellectual recreation or self-improvement to the investigator who requires answers to a specific question stemming from his research. More often than not the investigator knows that he is unlikely to find a specific answer, but he goes to the library to obtain clues and suggestions. It is generally assumed by librarians that, within wide bounds, all purposes and interests have equal value, so that the serious research worker often competes for library service on virtually equal terms with all other users. In the future there should be greater focus upon the user who requires library facilities for support of his research work, whatever the field of endeavor. As libraries become more responsive to research needs, they are certain to be used much more extensively, and with greater efficiency, for research purposes. Thus, the total cost of automation must be judged against the anticipated, rather than the present, experience of library use.

For the most part, the library today has completed its task when its materials are stored in an orderly fashion and when an item with probable relevance to the subject of inquiry can be identified and delivered to the user. The library of the future should be one that actively participates by predicting the areas for which information will be needed and in minimizing the time the user must spend in ascertaining pertinence of library materials to his special interests. Several years ago optimism prevailed about what could be done in the area of automatic indexing, abstracting, etc., and much of the research in information retrieval currently in progress was started then. This optimism has been somewhat dissipated because solutions have been slow in coming or have not come at all. It has also been recognized that work to solve the more immediate problems of libraries has been underemphasized. In this report the point is made that both the immediate and future problems have a common source —the explosion in research activity— and have to be considered as a whole. The present systems for the bibliographic organization and display of the resources

of large research libraries are not sufficiently adaptable to rapidly changing requirements, and they no longer lead the serious investigator easily and directly to pertinent information. Changes are clearly needed if the incalculably valuable information housed in large research libraries is to be put to use by society.

Publication patterns have been changing, particularly since World War II, with the advent of the research report to the Government. Libraries have been criticized for their inability to assimilate new kinds of material within their traditional processing techniques. Also they have faltered, or depended upon other information services, in the indexing of serial literature. Essentially they have retained the book as the focus of their indexing and classification techniques, but books cannot have the currency that the modern tempo in research requires. Even journals are becoming too sluggish. The latest development is the growth in importance of preprints and mimeographed memoranda. Libraries will have to develop capabilities for processing these new materials. Their nature does not differ in any substantial way from other library materials, but they can be looked upon as added burdens to the functions of acquisition, cataloging, and reference for which library resources are already minimal. Since the unpublished report literature is not subjected to the same editorial sanctions or critical review processes as are published journal articles, it might be argued that these materials are of lower quality and do not deserve the same attention as other library materials. However, since there is much valuable information in the unpublished report literature that is not available elsewhere, this does suggest that more effort must be invested in identifying that portion which is of suitable quality for preservation. Automation can potentially contribute to the problem area of quality identification, descriptive cataloging, and subject indexing, and to storage and distribution through microform techniques.

Because of the nature of modern technology, the benefits of automation would be realized first, and the cost supported, by the very large libraries. The libraries of the United States, and indeed of other countries as well, hope that leadership for the evaluation and the implementation of automation will come from the Library of Congress.

This brings us to the central question of our inquiry: Can automation be of help in an important way? Mechanization of current functions is not primarily what is meant, since, if this were to be the limit of the effort, many users would obviously be neglected because the intellectual environment has changed, and they find themselves with needs not currently satisfied. Moreover, the real potential of automation would be sacrificed. Automation, even in areas where it is well established, can still be expected to yield much more than it has already. In the library, which is as yet virtually untouched, it is particularly important to avoid merely perpetuating past practices. Future possibilities and alternative ways to realize them must be kept in mind at every step of the way. In assessing the usefulness of automation, what we hope to achieve in the future is as important as what we know can be done now.

Automation's Promise

There is a spectrum of functions which automation can improve, ranging from purely routine processing chores, such as circulation control and the maintenance of serial records, to advanced information retrieval techniques. The routine processing operations of large research libraries are complex and are basic to all effective service to readers, but it is believed by the members of the team that the efficiency of many of these functions can be substantially improved

with the assistance of automated procedures and equipment, and therefore these matters are not stressed in this report, although some details are given in the Appendix. Rather, emphasis is placed upon those catalog-searching and bibliographic functions which could greatly assist the user and expand the usefulness of large libraries in present-day research activity. A simple example is the assistance automation could give the user in establishing search trails through the various catalogs, indexes, and files. It is most important to observe that the immediate interests and demands of both the recordkeeping and bibliographic functions should be studied within the framework of a single system. There are many potentially serious pitfalls in the independent automation of the many separate functions, since this might result in creating grave difficulties in the ultimate realization of a totally integrated system. In the design study phase, it is recommended that both the routine processing and the assistance-to-search functions be considered simultaneously. Whether or not these are finally implemented with the same equipment is yet to be determined.

What then can be looked for? What are reasonable future goals toward which it is possible now to take at least some first steps? A general goal that influences all others is to make the library a more active organism. The catalogs of libraries must be transformed into dynamic files of records that assist in their own use. Catalogs, however, only direct the user to documents. We should also envision services that go at least one step further, that is, directly to information or at least to fragments or portions of documents. Depth of subject control is at the basis for this hope and it should be recognized that such depth, although facilitated by automation, is not an inevitable consequence thereof. Through improving the flexibility of bibliographic control and through increasing subject coverage in depth, particularly in many areas of science and technology, the possibility emerges that we can add a new dimension to the library's usefulness and to its value as a national resource. Automation will contribute to this new dimension by making practical and economic certain functions that would be extravagant within the framework of existing methods.

Assessment of Feasibility

General Requirements

In terms of information processing technology, the requirements of the Library of Congress may be categorized as follows:

1. Storage of very large quantities of material in digital form (i.e., in a form machines can "read").

2. High-speed processing to manipulate the stored digital information.

3. Storage of vast quantities of graphic material in a form which can be easily and quickly manipulated (principally photographs of pages of documents).

4. File conversion, e.g., the conversion of information now in card catalogs to machine-readable form.

5. Retrieval of the documents themselves, i.e., printed books, periodicals, etc.

6. Communication and display to the user of the various types of information within the system, both digital and graphic, e.g., catalog entries.

7. Output printing, ranging from publication of the National Union Catalog to "throw-away hard copy" of individual bibliographies, etc.

8. Communications with other libraries.

Storage and Processing Requirements

The distinctive feature of the Library of Congress, from the viewpoint of its impact on automation, is the enormous size of its holdings, totaling almost 42

million pieces (as of June 1962), and requiring approximately 270 miles of shelving and containing the equivalent of perhaps 10^{14} bits of information.[1] The present catalog files for this collection, if converted, would require 10^{11} bits of memory capacity;[2] a memory capacity of 10^{12} bits would probably be required to describe the Library's holdings at the anticipated rate of growth through the next generation. Vastly improved image storage in microphotographic form will also be necessary, for a long while, to complement the descriptive digital store. Here the objective should be to make microform more convenient for the user than a book. These demands for storage are a challenge to the information-processing industry.

On the other hand, the rate at which the stored material is changed is relatively low. Currently, on the order of 10^7

[1] A "bit" is the unit in which information is measured in communications and data-processing activities. It is an element in the simplest (two-element) code and is easily represented in a machine by the on-off of a switch, the presence or absence of magnetization, etc. To encode digitally an average English word requires about 30 bits. A few extra bits, as prefixes, are required to accommodate other alphabets, font styles, etc.

The Library collection consists of 42 million pieces of which 13 million are books, bound newspapers, and serials; 18 million are manuscripts, leaving a remainder of material as diverse as maps, microprints, music, and photographs. To determine the total contents of the collection an arbitrary estimate of 100 pages per item and 1,000 words per page was made. This gives a total of 4×10^{12} words in the Library. At a minimum of 5 characters per word, this would amount to about 10^{14} for full conversion of the *text* of the contents of the Library of Congress.

[2] Exhibit 35 in the Appendix to this report to convert the 50 words of the average main entry card for each of the estimated 6,600,000 titles in the Library of Congress catalog would require conversion of 2×10^9 characters. At a minimum of 6 bits per character the digital conversion would require 10^{10} bits; additional index files required by the system would yield a figure of at least 10^{11}.

(at most 10^8) bits are changed or added per day in the course of Library operations[3] as compared to 10^{10} bits which are merely looked through without alteration.[4] Thus the processing requirement, though certainly not trivial, will be much less difficult to meet than the requirement for storage and access.

Multiple-Access Requirement

The diversity of users of libraries has already been noted. As the files and contents of traditional libraries are divided into a large number of separate physical units (cards, books, etc.), each user has somewhat independent access and the opportunity for an independent adjustment in his mode of use. The preservation of such flexibility in an automated library, where an enormous amount of information must be concentrated in one or only a few machines, is necessary, but will pose an extremely difficult problem of access.

One approach to the problem is to design the central machines, stores, and

processors to meet concurrent demands from a multiplicity of terminals, with appropriate equipment at such terminal points. The terminal sets will have to be simple to use, yet provide a variety of possible interactions with the system. Many of these interactions will be very simple, for example, the request for a specific identifiable book, and for these a simple keyboard will suffice as a console. Other types of interactions will be of a more complex nature and will require an extensive dialogue between the user and the machine system. The console for this purpose will include a display device of some kind (possibly a cathode-ray tube) connected to the digital display or the microform viewer. It is possible that a third type of console intermediate in complexity between the two just described will be required.

A detailed study must be carried out to determine the relative importance, in terms of the workload, of the various console functions to be performed by the user. The system should then be designed to minimize the idle time of all consoles and to avoid the use of expensive or complex consoles for carrying out relatively simple operations. The use of consoles should be avoided altogether, when it can be done without loss of response time and flexibility.

A large fraction of the bibliographic product of the Library of Congress can be produced on an assembly-line basis with printed catalogs and bibliographies as the output. For many requests placed on the system by users, a printed catalog may serve the purpose as well as a console, and the choice as to which facility is provided should then be based largely on economic factors.

Most consoles should have a simple intercommunication system or telephone to provide communication with reference librarians. Reference librarians should, in turn, have access to other librarians in the country by means of a communication network, for example, a teletype.

---

[3] According to the analysis presented in Section IV of the Appendix about 4 million operations involving record alteration are now performed each year in the Library. (These operations include posting serial receipts, maintaining circulation records, etc.). With 3,000 hours of operation per year, 1.3×10^3 such operations are performed hourly. If we assume that for each operation an average of 10^3 bits of information is changed, then 1.3×10^6 bits of information are changed each hour; in an 8-hour workday this would amount to at least 10^7 bits of information altered or added.

[4] According to figures used for the cost study, the present catalog use is about 50 per minute for look-up operations. If we assume that one card is selected for each use and assume that 1,500 bits of information is average per card, then about 8×10^4 bits of information are selected each minute, or about 4×10^7 operations per day. With the reasonable assumption that to select the desired card at least 100 bits of information are scanned on 10 cards, then 10^{10} is a reasonable approximation of the present daily look-up operation.

Printing Requirements

The Library of Congress provides a valuable service to other libraries through the distribution of its printed catalog cards, lists of holdings, and book catalogs. The availability of an automated catalog will permit the computer to be used to compile special bibliographies and to produce, as required, specialized catalogs of various kinds.

Where depth of subject control is desirable, these catalogs or bibliographies should exploit to the extent practical the products of subject-specialized indexing and abstracting services. Printed and bound supplements to *The National Union Catalog* should be issued bimonthly and cumulated at least quarterly, yearly, and on a 5-year basis. Production quantity should be between 1,000 and 5,000 in order to provide multiple-copy distribution to 60 or so major research libraries and single-copy distribution to other research libraries and public libraries.

Under the present system, subject headings are continually being added or revised, but the subject heading list incorporating these changes is printed only every few years, with supplements issued between editions. This list should be revised and reprinted yearly; distribution in the hundreds is required.

The printing and production of specialized bibliographies will be another major requirement of the system. Many of these bibliographies will be produced in editions of less than 100 copies and may vary in length from 1 to 50 pages. It is roughly estimated that possibly up to 1,000 per day would have to be produced. Further detailed study is necessary in order to determine this volume.

Part of this demand for special bibliographies will be met directly at the user console, where a brief bibliography may be produced in hard copy as an immediate response to a request. The bulk of the bibliographies produced, however, will be on a time scale of a half day or so, rather than on an immediate demand basis. In the Appendix to this report data are given, on the basis of which volume estimates of the required printing load may be made.

Legibility to permit the rapid scanning of the printed product is an important requirement that implies a capability for printing in a variety of type fonts and sizes. Output printers for computer systems have adequate speed but poor readability; for the most part, they print in a single style and only in uppercase letters. A variety of type styles, weights, and sizes are needed to meet the standards of Library publication.

A remote printing capability may also be needed to provide rapid access to holdings for libraries using the Library of Congress as a repository; however, a careful study must be made of response times actually required, since quite possibly they can be met with centralized printing and mail distribution.

The requirement for high-speed, high-quality, multifont printers has been recognized by several designers of other systems both in Government and commerce. It is believed that equipment meeting the needs of the proposed system for the Library will be available in the near future.

Feasibility of Storage, Processing, and Input

Within recent years technology has addressed itself to the foregoing problems; the technical feasibility of meeting all the requirements outlined can be demonstrated in development laboratories.

Specifically, it is now feasible to meet storage and access requirements for catalogs and indexes suitable for an automated Library of Congress system (from 10^{11} to 10^{12} bits). Equipment with rapid access to over a billion bits is already commercially available, and it is a reasonable assumption that the demands of a library system could be met in the near future at a reasonable cost.

The data-processing requirements (on the order of 10^9 bits daily) are already being met in somewhat similar systems that must provide "on demand" services. The terminal sets, for both input and output functions, are technically feasible, but they need more development work to be adapted to the functions of the Library of Congress system.

Communications media for the transmission of digital and graphic material have been developed recently at the technical level to be practical for the system visualized, and a variety of transducers for conveying information between terminal sets or data processors and communications networks are now available.

Feasibility of File Conversion

The process of converting information from textual form to machine-readable form, which is necessary for both the transition to an automated system and its continual updating, is itself a subject of considerable importance. This conversion could be accomplished with traditional methods of keypunching or typing with simultaneous punching on paper tape.

The conversion of catalog cards[5] is an enormous task; the National Union Catalog, for example, contains about 15 million cards with an average of approximately 50 words per card. Running text can be keypunched and verified at roughly one cent per word. At this rate the complete conversion of the National Union Catalog would cost about $7.5 million. However, the heavy mixture of numerals and the necessity for a certain amount of formatting, error correction, and quality control suggest that the one-cent-per-word figure may be somewhat low.

The automatic conversion of stenotyping is being actively pursued with the aim of reducing the cost of file conversion. Automatic print-reading devices are under development and may at some future date provide a partial solution to the problem.

The technique of file conversion requires further research and development. This activity will undoubtedly result in a method of converting the Library's catalogs into machine-readable form in the near future at an acceptable cost.

Microform Storage

The microform storage of page images and graphic records has been addressed traditionally to preservation of materials, saving of space, and facilitating the duplication and distribution of library materials. The miniaturized record is intended for human consumption and of itself has nothing to do with the machine processing of information.

The problems of cataloging, indexing, and classifying, as well as the coding and recording of such information, can be considered independently of the question of microstorage. To be sure, there are systems of microform storage which combine both a digital code and a graphic image in a single record, but these systems represent particular approaches which must be evaluated on a speed and cost basis when a detailed systems design study is undertaken. It should be noted that text words in stored micro-images are not accessible to machine processing any more so than are words on a printed page.

The issue of microform storage and its applicability within large research libraries depends strongly on the question of economics. The expense of storing a bound full-size book must be compared with the expense of recording it in microform plus producing enlarged hard copy as necessary. The speed of access in the two cases must be compared with the requirement for access.

Requirements for access time cannot be explicitly formulated at this stage, but certain observations can be made. Immediately following a catalog search, or the production of a brief special bibliog-

---

[5] Current (1967) estimates of the size of the LC official catalog are: 11,450,000 cards for 4 million titles, 440 characters/ card (Ed.).

raphy, the requester may wish to examine certain portions of books before requesting the books themselves. Portions might include title page, table of contents, index, or perhaps a few selected pages of text which would permit judging the level of technical detail or other characteristics of the work.

Ideally, this graphic material should be delivered for perusal within seconds. If a batch of contiguous material is requested, such as successive pages of a report, then a more stringent requirement exists for sequencing back and forth from a page in about $\frac{1}{5}$ of a second.[6] To make a few essential pages from each work available, and with only partial selection of books, journals, newspapers, and reports within the Library of Congress, it will still be necessary to record upwards of 5 million images, and perhaps eventually several times this amount; any given page-image must be accessible within several seconds.

Microstorage for certain types of archival material or complete books will have access-time requirements that may vary from minutes up to a day or so. The volume requirement here is difficult to estimate, but will depend primarily on the economic balance between the cost of hard-copy storage and the cost of miniaturization and subsequent enlargement. This basic form of storage has long been used in libraries, but with primitive mechanization and very slow access.

In the past decade great strides have been made so that the technology is certain to be of greater importance to libraries than it has been. Automatic stores holding millions of images are available. Their drawbacks are low speed and high cost. Images can be located and reproduced from these stores in seconds, but even this may be too slow for compatibility with other aspects of auto-

mation and the mode of use envisioned. The feasibility of devices in the required speed range has already been proved in research and development laboratories and with technology that does not appear to be inherently expensive.

Feasibility of Automated Stack Storage and Retrieval

A significant feature that poses difficulty in most large research libraries is the inflexibility of the "marriage" between the bibliographic catalogs and the physical arrangement of library holdings. There should be a complete independence of the physical location of items from their descriptive mapping in the catalogs and files. Such independence will encourage the physical storage of material on the basis of probability of use, where this is practical, or in special compact storage, browsing, or reference collections. Automation can facilitate such independence.

There is the possibility that the form in which knowledge is recorded, stored, and distributed will change appreciably within the next decade. Progress in reproduction techniques, particularly from microfilm, has been so rapid that the circulation of most documents in their printed form may become unnecessary. There is also likely to be a trend toward publication "on demand" from text prepared in machine-readable form. With the possibility of such radical changes to take into account, there is some question as to whether or not it would be worth automating the physical retrieval of books from the collection in its present form.

Present methods of physically retrieving library holdings certainly leave much to be desired and will seem worse as automation increases the speed of bibliographic access. The problem can be simply stated. The time required to extract a book from the stacks and deliver it to a central point should be substan-

[6] To the reader a delay of more than $\frac{1}{5}$ of a second is sufficiently annoying to reduce the appeal, and hence the use, of the system.

tially reduced. The advanced state of technology in the area of mechanical manipulation is an inducement for change. Nevertheless, the investment that would be required, in terms of both money for equipment and effort for the transitional description, appears too great to expend except in new or renovated libraries.

A hidden danger is that such an investment might tend to deter the adoption of the far more significant changes in storage and publication technology mentioned above. Thus, while the desirability for improved physical handling cannot be denied, the exact requirement will depend on the consequences of changes in information handling, which must be given priority. The door, however, should be left open to clever invention. No approach yet proposed appears to have sufficient merit to justify implementation, but new ideas could still change the picture.

State of Information Science

Intimately connected with technical feasibility is the understanding of how information should be organized in the files and processed to answer the demands on the system. The nature of the data is quite different from that which the computing industry encountered in business and scientific work and learned to handle so well. Libraries consist essentially of collections of words in text. These words are combined and have significance to humans that, in our present state of knowledge, cannot be expressed in terms of machine rules. Thus they cannot be normalized or put in uniform format without their character being changed and information lost.

Present automation techniques do not deal adequately with raw text. At the outset only catalogs, inventory files, and indexes should be considered for automation. Even here, to use these in a sophisticated manner, it may be necessary (and there should be no reluctance) to insert manual processing and human

decisions when they are essential or too expensive to replace.

The economic and technical feasibility of automatically retrieving information directly from the text of documents has not yet been established and is an extremely complex subject. For this reason, there is likely to be greater emphasis for some years on the retrieval of bibliographic information. The initial objective in the proposed Library system is to use automation to discover which documents are related to the user's information needs. Even during the initial stages, however, automation should allow much richer cross-referencing and descriptive labeling.

A most desirable goal, and a feasible one, is a system that could accept the user's experience as feedback and thus evolve toward greater capability. This could be achieved in several ways. Users' annotations on subject classification or assignment of subject headings could be accepted as input at the console, subjected to further review and editing by a librarian and then incorporated, as desirable, in the system. Users could also comment on the similarity or relatedness of specific papers, reports, or books which they utilize. The idea of accepting user experience as a feedback to the system can be looked upon as amplifying or supplementing citations made by the author. Author citations have traditionally served as valuable reference tools.

A fairly wide range of novel techniques of this kind deserves further study and exploration in order to insure that future automated libraries will be highly flexible in adapting themselves to user requirements.

Conclusion

The automation of the bibliographical control of the Library of Congress is not only technically feasible but could provide a system more responsive to users and more adaptive to changes in user needs, Library operating conditions, publication practices, the national research library system, and information technology.

For some time, however, costs will remain a problem for all the data-processing and microstorage equipment, but they can be predicted to follow a postdevelopmental curve downward. A further pull downward could be exerted if demands from libraries and similar systems were consolidated to allow a uniform manufacturing attack. A cost study based on actual and estimated prices shows that by 1972 the cumulative costs for automation of the central bibliographic control functions of the Library of Congress system would be comparable to costs for continuing the current manual system.[7]

Projection of a System

In order to assess feasibility and to estimate costs, a partially automated library is described, completely implementable by 1972 and capable of working in parallel with the existing system on a transitional basis by 1969. Many systems may be hypothesized; no claim is made that the one presented is ideal, since designing an appropriate system will be part of the task of implementing the recommendations of the survey team. It is, however, a reasonable system in terms of short- and long-range goals, and is used solely to illustrate the possibilities of automation concretely in terms of present Library of Congress operations.

The survey team identified the following as functions that could be im-

proved by automation, and the proposed system was designed to facilitate these as a minimum.

1. Accounting and management control.
2. Record management for procurement and processing activities, including serials.
3. Development of cataloging aids (authority files, etc.).
4. Cataloging and catalog maintenance.
5. Searching of catalogs and files.
6. Circulation control.
7. Presentation of information to librarians and users.
8. Publication of cards, catalogs, bibliographies, and indexes.
9. Communications with other libraries and agencies.

Operational Description

The projected system consists of a variety of files, heterogeneous in nature, but susceptible to examination with the same equipment and mode of search. A set of input-output consoles allows both user and librarian to have essentially instantaneous access to any file.

The computer program, a part of which may be thought of as linking the consoles and stored files, provides a method of search for each question, adapting the search sequence to the user's needs. Thus, the system can be regarded as both a learning machine and a teaching machine.

Notwithstanding the emphasis given here to the console mode of operation, it should be understood that there are many processing requirements in the system which will not depend upon use of a console. Many, if not most, of the bibliographies produced in multiple copy will be associated with relatively long response times, such as a day or so, or else will be prepared in accordance with standing requirements for which there may well be a weekly cycle. Even longer cycles pertain to the prep-

---

[7] Reported in Appendix I. Sections VI, VII, and IX of the study are most pertinent to cost problems. Note that this study shows a break-even point by 1972 for those operations included in the $30 million cost estimate. The team recommends that $50 to $70 million be spent to provide, in addition, automation of operations not now performed by the Library. For these operations no comparable manual system exists, nor was one projected for the purpose of cost comparisons.

aration of large catalogs and possibly to large bibliographies. Accordingly, many computer programs for searching the automated catalog, preparing an initial bibliography, editing such bibliography, and finally formatting to produce a printed product must be written.

Systems such as those in operation at the National Library of Medicine and at the Office of Scientific and Technical Information of the National Aeronautics and Space Administration should be studied thoroughly during the systems design phase and the lessons learned therefrom appropriately taken into account. None of the services or products of these centers should be duplicated within the Library of Congress, but operations with similar purposes should be established in areas not covered by such specialized services.

A major task of the systems design effort is to insure that the technology recommended is suitable for both the console mode of operation and the required assembly-line method of production.

CATALOGING. The function of matching an item of information in hand against the information in files and catalogs is one that is present in virtually every library operation. This search and match process is used to determine whether a recommended item is in the Library's collections, whether a received item is the one that was ordered, whether an author entry has been previously established, whether the work is present in another edition, etc. Undoubtedly cataloging is of prime importance in generating the tool to support this search function. The detailed manner in which the proposed system converges on the cataloging process is shown in Exhibit 1 of the Appendix. The system permits the cataloger to have rapid access to any portion of the authority file, the central library catalog, and other files that he might not otherwise have approached. Searching can thus be reduced to a minimum, freeing the cataloger for the more intellectual aspects of descriptive and subject analysis.

The expansion of subject analysis in greater depth will become possible. This is impractical in existing libraries because of the bulkiness of card catalogs and the inconvenience to humans working with very large files. With an expanded file the necessity for the user to learn the librarian's language may be reduced. Another advantage will be that special catalogs and bibliographies can be produced on a more sophisticated basis, without the need for special procedures. All the responses which the card catalog can now give will be retained, but these do not approach the complexity or variety of questions a research investigator is capable of posing. An automated card catalog can meet more demands, even guiding users in their line of inquiry (as explained in the following paragraphs on the use of consoles).

It should not be supposed, however, that depth in subject analysis is a necessary and inevitable consequence of automation, nor should it be assumed that such depth will be uniform throughout the holdings of the Library of Congress. It should be noted that considerable depth of subject control already exists in many of the specialized indexing and abstracting services.

Even in a future system, however, it will not be economically sensible to attempt to control every page in every book, document, and journal article in the Library of Congress to the same depth as is currently done by these services. Automation will make less costly the expansion of subject control to areas not presently so covered, but, in the last analysis, the decision as to which areas, and how extensively, will have to be made on an economic basis. Furthermore, depth in control should in no case duplicate any of the functions performed outside of the Library of Congress by the more specialized services.

Rather, the system should be designed to accommodate the output of these specialized services and to provide similar services in areas not now covered.

USE OF CONSOLES BY LIBRARY CLIENTS. In the fully operational system, the query console is intended for the individual user. Because some experience will be required for effective manipulation of the console, it would be desirable at the outset to have a reference librarian perform the console manipulation. Careful consideration during the design study should be given to the workload corresponding to the various console operations. With such data, design criteria for several types of consoles, from simple numerical keyboards to intricate display and input devices, can be developed. The following functional description applies primarily to the more sophisticated consoles. User access to the console will provide a catalog-browsing capability which will be enhanced by the ability of the system to provide hard copy of any item displayed on the console screen. Thus, in viewing a given sequence of bibliographic entries, the user will be able to retain copies of those entries which interest him for further consideration or for record purposes.

A capability for relatively elaborate dialogues between the user and the catalog is an important requirement for the more complex consoles. The query-input keys should essentially be of two types, "process-keys" that initiate entire computer subroutines, and "data keys" that permit the entry of alphabetical and numerical data. The alphanumeric keyboard should include a local display to permit the immediate checking of keyed information before it is finally entered into the computer system. The displays themselves must be alphanumeric, but a line drawing capability is not required. Particular care must go into the design of the process keys and into the computer programs that they implement, because in this area lie the

means to the simplicity and flexibility which are so necessary to the user-console approach. Information displayed in response to commands initiated at the console should provide statistical and bibliographical data of maximum use to the requester in formulating the next stage of his request.

If the query is too broad or vague, the system should not deluge the questioner with all the references available but should indicate to him first the fact that he has asked too broad a question. For example, the reader might ask for an edition of Shakespeare's *Hamlet*. The first response from the system might be that the Library has 374 editions of this work and that a printed bibliography is available. A display on the console screen indicates to the user ways in which he could narrow his query, e.g., by specifying language, date, type of edition: translation, illustrated, abridged, student edition, etc. The user can then "fill in the blanks" and indicate that he is, for example, interested only in recent English-language student editions. The system would then indicate the number of editions which filled this criteria and, depending on the number and the user's needs, he could further refine his query, scan the catalog entries for the relevant editions on the console screen, or request a printed listing of the entries.

If the reader decides to scan the catalog entries, the equivalent of a catalog card or a set of several cards would be displayed on the console screen. The operator could then press the "Sequence" key and immediately the following "cards" would be presented. This could be repeated until the end of the sequence for the given author's name.

If the operator at any point wishes to refer to a previous card, he may do so by pressing the "Back Sequence" key. Each console will have available to it a buffer file (for example a magnetic disk) that records the information received from the central catalog store. A standard type of buffer might hold the contents of 100 cards (roughly 200,000 bits). Thus, the operator, by a query or succession of queries, will be able to build up a private "card" file, then readily refer to the material he has collected by pressing the "Sequence" and "Back Sequence" keys.

This mode of operation is intended as an example only and other possibilities can be envisioned. A user may choose to specify that only a portion of the information on each catalog card, such as author and title, be listed in order to permit viewing many more at the same time and minimize the back and forth sequencing operation. In effect then, he is presented with a trial bibliographic listing; he may then call for additional information, such as may be present on a complete catalog card, or he may require a display (probably from a microform image) of selected pages of the work itself. The buffer is also suggested as an example only, since alternative ways of providing the required capability may be conceived. The buffer may possibly be an allocated portion of the main memory, which may or may not be time-shared among several consoles, depending upon workload factors.

After the perusal of this visual material, the user may decide to record the information, i.e., copy the "catalog cards." The "Hard-Copy" key may be pressed, with the result that a printout of the information is automatically produced at the console on a piece of paper for the user.

The user may decide to obtain the item indicated on the display from the collection. Several alternatives are possible. In the transition period, he could obtain the hard-copy printout, take it to the call desk, and obtain the item by the present manual method. In a more automated system he could press the "Call" key. The item number or numbers that he designated on the display would automatically go through the system and result in the items being physically delivered to him at or near the console.

So far we have assumed that the requester's requirement was for a specific identifiable book or report and that he knew the author's name. The system must also accept various other kinds of descriptive tags, such as date, language, publisher, etc., in order to present to the user a bibliography of all items which meet a stated request, even though such request may contain only a part of the information normally required in a conventional system.

Another kind of request is one in which the user needs subject access to the library holdings. In this situation he would key in a subject name and press the "Subject File" key. Here we have a more complicated matter, for the user may specify terms which differ from those used by the cataloger. Thus, the first thing the system must do is transform the user's terms, by a process similar to that now used for language translation, into terms meaningful to the system. For example, if "insurgence" were keyed in as a subject term, it might be translated to one or several headings, for example, "insurrection." This term would be displayed to the user for his information and would also augment his original word as the subject of search. In many instances there will be ambiguities. A research worker may be expert in the terminology of his own field without being aware that some of these terms have quite different meanings in other subject fields. If, for example, the user keys in "bonds," the display might show:

"adhesives"
"bonding agencies"
"chemical valence"
"securities"

The user would then select one or more by pressing appropriate keys, which then cause the subject file to be searched automatically. Again, the first display would probably be the number of items under this heading and a suggestion for further restriction of the question.

At first the display will be equivalent to catalog cards or to a bibliographic listing, as noted earlier. As additional files are assembled and integrated into the system, the catalog will be made a far more flexible tool. In time the system will be capable of suggesting that a given subject is analyzed in a different or deeper way in the catalog of another library. It will also be able to indicate that the subject is well treated in certain encyclopedias, and, as a convenience, it should allow the user to call for the pertinent article from either a digital or microform file and display it for him. It is essential that this system be compatible with the trend to convert documents to film by microphotography. The first use of microform images to extend the library catalog will be in displaying title pages and tables of contents.

USE OF CONSOLES BY LIBRARY STAFF. The console for use by the library staff, in the acquisitions and cataloging operations, may or may not be identical to one of the several types of user consoles, but in any event the requirements for its use are somewhat different. For reference assistance to the user, it is assumed here that the librarians will have access to a user console. To illustrate the use of the staff console, consider the process of descriptive cataloging.

The basic input to the system is the title page data typed in by the cataloger. Edit programs for the processor would be written to execute most of the normalization of the data on the title page to the form of a Library of Congress card. These operations consist of properly arranging information, selecting font styles, referring to the authority file, the National Union Catalog, etc. An accession or item number would be automatically generated and displayed. A preliminary "card" would very rapidly be written by the program and displayed at the console, together with unresolved questions. The cataloger would then edit this material at the console until a per-

fect Library of Congress "card" would be displayed, at which point, by a control, he would send it to temporary (quick writing) storage. Here it would be used in another program, and material would be developed from its contents for assignment to all appropriate files—author, subject, etc. No typing or preparation of paper documents or cards would be necessary.

Librarians in other libraries would have consoles similar to those at the Library of Congress and would be able to use them for monitoring the status of processing. This would be necessary because, with high-speed capability, the Library of Congress would be able to do the cataloging for almost all new items. For items not in the Library of Congress but held by other libraries, cataloging information could be transmitted for inclusion in the Library of Congress catalog. If this information were fragmentary, it could be fully elaborated by the automated cataloging system at the Library of Congress for retransmission to the initiating library. Furthermore, other libraries in the system could then obtain the complete data, possibly via display consoles if rapid response were needed, in order to prepare catalog cards for their own files. Librarians at the outlying libraries, however, would not have the capability of changing any of the basic Library of Congress files. Further study of remote console use should be carried out during the design of the system since it can be foreseen that a good part of the requirement of communication with outlying libraries can be met by a communications system (e.g., teletype, dataphone, etc.) and with response times much longer than are implied by display consoles.

METHODS OF SEARCH. So far the system has been described as consisting of two basic elements: means of storing catalog and index information, and means of display, with rapid access, to the user. There is a third element, the implementation of a search procedure. These search procedures may be very simple, but the capability for very complex searches should exist. The system must therefore be designed to accommodate, without radical changes in equipment or undue additional expense, the advent of new search techniques developed either by experience with the system itself or as a result of research in the field of library and information science.

In order to be usable, material within a library must be indexed, classified, and cataloged, by all methods, both subject and descriptive, that are commonly used to gain access to bibliographic materials. This analysis is done either extrinsically by assigning labels, e.g., subject headings, or intrinsically by the direct use of words occurring within the material itself. Under present cataloging practices, titles and authors' names represent the limit of intrinsic indexing. It has to be recognized that to improve retrieval of information more extensive intrinsic indexing is mandatory. In fact, it is desirable for certain types of material that portions of the text itself be made accessible. A minimal requirement for all material in the library is for intrinsic indexing to include at least the present descriptive information, such as title, authors, publisher, imprint date, etc.

With regard to extrinsic indexing, such indexes as shelf number and accession number can be generated automatically. Subject analysis at present requires human effort, and is a processing bottleneck. Nevertheless it clearly must be expanded and improved. It is obvious that present subject analysis by the Library of Congress makes no pretense at coverage in depth. The average number of subject headings assigned to a book is between one and two, even though a dozen subjects may be dealt with. It has been mentioned that any decision to achieve subject control in depth will be limited by economic fac-

tors, and that maximal advantage should be taken of output already provided in specialized subject areas by indexing and abstracting services. Certain initial and limited steps should be further studied, for example, recording the tables of contents of books and journals in machine-readable form. An automatic indexing procedure then could permit a reasonably accurate assignment of subject descriptors. Some experimental evidence exists to indicate that this technique, applied to highly technical material, is as successful as human subject analysis in depth of similar material.

A fundamental principle of library systems analysis is that the indexes to the intellectual content of a document be divorced conceptually from the physical storage of that document. As the future automated library is conceived here, index material should be recorded in a memory specifically designed for digital storage. Independence of digital index data from graphic records generally provides a flexibility not otherwise possible, and certainly not practicable at present in the Library of Congress. For example, under the existing system, if a change of classification is desirable, not only the book labels must be changed and all changes reflected in the card catalogs, but the books themselves must be moved. By giving the physical documents merely a permanent accession number and arranging the library by manipulating records within the machine, changes can be made at low cost and high speed. In this context, "changes" means desirable regroupings of index material with growth of the library, with changes in human knowledge and in the analysis of it, and with the advances in information retrieval.

Another important feature of the system, as currently conceived, is that, by proper construction of the files, different schemes of subject analysis, including those of specialized libraries, can be used in the system simultaneously. Then the user of the system will have the choice and be advised of different analyses of the material in which he is interested. A large variety of indexes must be made available; the cost and space requirements of storage in a machine must be studied and compared with what would be required to house and manipulate equivalent card files or book catalogs.

The design objective in automation should center on responsiveness to the user and not on automation as an end in itself. The basic user requirements involve searching for desired material in response to a specific need, and this implies that the files must not be dead lists but must provide their own references while still accommodating decision and choice of path by the user. The files will be dynamic in the sense that the search is automatically transferred from one reference to another until a satisfactory compilation of selective material is achieved. Further study must be conducted on efficient methods for storing and searching for information. This must be done as part of the design study in close coordination with the planning of equipment, since the particular methods of search to be implemented may depend strongly on the equipment itself. The following description of a series of tables in which a search process is referred from one to the next in a serial fashion is intended as an example only.

SEARCH TABLES. It is simpler to begin with the final stage of the search, which is the location of the required item. This will be accomplished by a table relating two indexes, the item number (permanently assigned to an item and physically attached thereto), and its current location number. The latter may reflect that the item is checked out or at the bindery. Thus upon looking up an item by its number, the first step will be a reference (e.g., in the not-on-shelf file). The result of this look-up is an automatic reference to the next subsidiary table

to be searched—various process files, circulation files, etc.

The identification of an item leading to its location and use can also be accomplished through table look-up. In support of a central file of numbered items described in essentially the form consonant with accepted library practice (but not constrained thereby), there will be tables which relate authors, titles, subjects, and other attributes to item numbers. These tables will be approached (automatically) sequentially to effect identification of single items or groups of items by author, subject, or other discriminating criteria (year of publication, language, etc.). When the author's exact name or the exact form of the subject term is lacking, the system would provide automatic reference to other tables or files which will make the needed names or terms available. In addition there will be tutorial tables describing to the user facts about the system and suggestions for directing his search.

A feature which must be emphasized in characterizing all of these files is their formal nature as tables giving logical steps to be taken next. Specifically, each entry has an index by which it is searched, an outcome which may or may not be presented on a console, and a reference to the next table which should be referred to, either automatically or at the choice of the user of the console.

USE OF MICROFORM STORAGE. It has been pointed out earlier that the traditional purpose of microform storage has been to save space and permit easier duplication and distribution of library materials. The graphic record produced is for human consumption, not for machine processing; thus provision must be made for rapid mechanical handling and access to these graphic records for presentation to humans.

Depending upon the particular equipment used to implement such access, there may be considerable flexibility in the organization of the microform file in order to accommodate new accessions without a burdensome interfiling process. Items may be entered into the store merely in some convenient order (e.g., chronologically by accession) and assigned a location number, which will be placed in the automated catalog. Thus, after the system finds a desired item in the catalog, the user will have it displayed immediately on the console by specifying its location number. The capability to retrieve microform images of title pages, tables of contents, and indexes, as well as sample pages taken from the work itself, will be exceedingly useful in supplementing catalog searching as part of the browsing process. It is essential therefore that, to meet this requirement, the system respond within a few seconds in sending the images called for. Successive pages of a single work should be presented with a still faster response time.

The nature of the material to be stored in microform covers a wide spectrum, and the limit is one of economics. It may be practical to put catalog cards in this form for some purposes. However, even at the start, it will be necessary to have this information in digital form as well, for manipulation by computer programs. Other reference materials, such as encyclopedias, bibliographies, newspapers, journals, book title pages, chapter headings, abstracts, and indexes, will be stored in microform as the system develops. Ultimately the complete text of many books will be stored in microform, although the balance between this and conventional hard-copy techniques will be governed by cost factors. A great potential of microform storage is that it may permit methods of publication whereby an individual could assemble a tailormade book on any desired topic from a variety of references. The assembly feature will be part of the retrieval program, and

editing could be carried out at the console.

The automated library system as projected will provide for only minimal use of microform at the outset but will be designed to accommodate substantial growth in this phase of its operation, as needs, funds, and technology permit.

System Characteristics

The paragraphs above contain some hints of radical changes in library functions. It is therefore worth reemphasizing that the proposed system has as its primary aim the improvement of certain present library functions, specifically those functions listed on page 112. The only gain to be realized initially will be in processing rates and the degree to which holdings are made accessible. As a byproduct, however, the system should generate a complete record of its transactions, thus allowing an evaluation of its performance to an extent that is presently impossible.

The system as proposed will be much more functionally flexible than the present manual system. Basic alterations in the present system are too cumbersome to consider, and even experimentation requires too much effort. With the streamlining of clerical operations and the high speed of response, it will become practical to experiment with parallel analyses and descriptions of the same material. In time the user should be able to search for needed information in catalogs organized from several different points of view, that is, he should have many information systems at his disposal rather than a single system.

There must be compatibility between the Library of Congress and other research libraries, particularly with respect to the kinds of equipment developed. There is some urgency with respect to this compatibility since some efforts at automating individual libraries are already underway. The effort of establishing compatibility, or at least appropriate interfaces, is probably small compared to expected benefits. In regard to the "software," that is, indexing, classification, etc., there is no need to constrain individual libraries. A specialized medical library cannot be expected to organize its holdings in the same way as the medical collection of a large general library. In an automated system, it should be possible to provide necessary transformations from one system to another. There should be no reason for destroying the user's sense of the history or peculiar qualities of any collection. Unique indexes should not be lost in an overall national indexing system but should be made available to any user of the automatic system.

The projected automated system is designed to permit an orderly transition to more advanced modes of response to the user's needs. As the quality of indexing increases so will the user's resourcefulness in searching. At the outset, then, machines can hardly be expected to give much more than clerical assistance. In time their power will come to be applied more widely to assist the cataloging, indexing, and assembling of information. As machine processes are improved for these functions they will also become increasingly adaptive to the user's needs.

Implementation of a System

Management of the Transition

The first step to be taken in the automation program is the establishment within the Library of Congress of a management group to insure effective control, coordination, monitoring, and evaluation of activities leading to the successful procurement of a working system. This group will procure a detailed system design that will entail flow charting of essential processes and the determination of machine programming requirements, manpower requirements, machine and machine-hour require-

ments, throughput volumes, and throughput rates. These design activities should result in a set of performance specifications for the system as a whole and for system components as necessary. The development, installation, and testing of the working system will be based on these specifications.

The transition to the new system admits a variety of alternatives, whose choice will be conditioned by consideration of costs of converting all or part of the present catalogs and related files into machine-readable form, by factors of availability of requisite funds and space, and also by certain development requirements that may make parts of the system available at different times. It is envisioned that the new system, or parts of it, will be operated in parallel with the old, since it would be impossible to make the transition in a short period of time.

Auxiliary Research and Development Needs

The implementation of a system at a cost that is not prohibitive will require that emphasis be placed on the following areas of research and development as early as possible. These areas essentially require engineering development rather than basic technological advances insofar as equipment is concerned.

TRILLION-BIT MEMORY. Storage in, and access to, an automated catalog containing on the order of 10^{11} to 10^{12} bits is a formidable engineering problem, although equipment can be demonstrated in the laboratory which apparently indicates a promising direction for such a development. There is a requirement for further engineering development, but probably no major basic research or new development programs are needed.

CONSOLES. Display consoles suitable for functions similar to those envisioned here are available now, but they are by no means entirely satisfactory. Their cost is high for library applications, particularly since perhaps thousands of consoles will be needed for the national library system. New ideas, not just engineering or production changes, are required to overcome both cost and performance obstacles in the same development.

Visual display consoles appear to be desirable, but whether they are to be of the cathode-ray-tube type is not as important as whether, at least, the equivalent of a library card (roughly 1,000 characters) can be displayed, and changed, on the order of one second. Similarly, the display method must allow some form of selection by a "marker" from a multiple-choice array to keep user keying to a minimum.

Temporary storage, either at the console or the central computer, of at least 100 library card equivalents should be provided, with the user able to call for a sequential display of the stored contents. A keyboard supplemented with marker and process keys would be required.

The "process" keys would be used to institute queries to specific portions of the automated catalog and to respond to the next steps suggested by the automated system. At least a 120-character or symbol set would be desirable, in contrast with the 64 characters typically available now. This means that effort will have to be placed on new or improved and certainly more economical means of character generation.

There should also be some means, whether at the console or central processor, of automatic format control and a means of automatic transliteration of words in digital storage to the Roman alphabet, regardless of the source language alphabet. Lastly, economical methods of providing "scratch pad" copies of displayed information to the console user must be sought.

The foregoing requirements refer to the most complex type of consoles. Again it should be emphasized that several forms of consoles should be developed, depending upon the workload associated with various functions required.

GRAPHIC OUTPUT EDITING AND COMPOSING. Automation of the Library of Congress and the National Union Catalog bibliographic information system holds promise for providing catalog production service on a national basis. Machine methods of editing, spelling correction, type selection, page formatting, and line justification have all been demonstrated. Stress must be placed on software techniques for editing and page composition. Computer graphic composer equipments must be made capable of providing high quality, reproducible copy at rates of several hundred characters per second with a large repertory of symbols, characters, and type sizes.

USER-SYSTEM TUTORIAL INTERACTION. Both console and system logic design should stress an "open-endedness" about the possibilities of providing tutorial interaction between the machine system and the user. The near future will bring considerable progress in this area. Although there are no revolutionary ideas on the horizon, the increased labeling and cross referencing made possible by mechanical stores should allow for fruitful experimentation. In addition to labeling schemes, optimum search strategies must be sought. It is not enough that machines and men interact so as to converge upon a mutual understanding of what the system contains and what the searcher seeks. They must converge rapidly and economically, without tedious exploration. If these ends can be attained, increased indexing will be done by the user in the course of use, and not by increasing the indexing staff.

Further study on the possible dialogues between the user and the automated catalog is needed. These dialogues must be developed in considerable detail, flow charted, and then used as the basis for computer programming. Several novel techniques proposed within the last few years certainly hold sufficient promise to justify inclusion in some form in the proposed system. The use of citation indexing and the maintenance of user records represent particularly valuable sources for different approaches to information. A thorough study should be made of present descriptive cataloging rules to determine whether they should be modified in order to build maximum flexibility of use into the system and permit effective exploitation of the capability provided by automation and if so, how?

COMMUNICATION TECHNOLOGY. It is unlikely that the needs of research libraries could appreciably affect developments in the area of communication technology. However, the reverse is not true. Centralized research libraries which provide service over telephone or telegraph lines are feasible now and are certain to become more attractive economically as communication technology advances. It is thus likely that, even at the outset, data communication facilities will be used, but quite sparingly, say, for priority information to the more important cooperating libraries. The research and development needs are minor, with the possible exception of terminal sets. The following questions need to be answered prior to large-scale use: To what extent is there a need for an extensive communication net? Will there be user acceptance? At what rate will the cost-performance ratio improve? Can orderly growth in facilities be achieved?

TEXTUAL DATA CONVERSION METHODS. Large-scale conversion of textual information into machine-readable form currently appears to cost on the order of one cent per word and proceeds at human typing rates. The development of flexible, multifont print readers, promising character-by-character conversion at several hundred characters per second, is being fostered by several Government agencies. However, the automatic conversion of files, such as the National Union Catalog, which contain considerable heterogeneous symbolism, is not likely in the near future. New methods

for accomplishing catalog conversion should be given emphasis.

Consequences of Automation

Impact on the National Library System

INFORMATION FLOW. It is evident that automation of the Library of Congress alone would not be a complete solution of all national research library problems. On the one hand, the Library of Congress does not hold everything published. Other libraries (the National Agricultural Library, the National Library of Medicine, etc.) have more complete collections in certain topical areas, and indexes to their holdings are better organized or are in more descriptive depth for the specialist's use. On the other hand, other libraries have come to depend upon the Library of Congress for assistance in carrying out their functions. The Library of Congress provides catalogs, lends books, distributes cards, and offers varied reference, bibliographic, and consultant services.

Thus it is desirable to conceive of a library network, a national research library system, incorporating the telecommunications necessary to accommodate the flow of information to all its branches. Technical developments in the last year or so have greatly improved this situation, and there is no doubt that intercommunication of the information considered here is technically feasible and economically reasonable.

At the present time, all information that is useful for the purposes intended to be served by the large research libraries of the United States is not stored in those libraries. For example, in the field of scientific research, technical reports and memoranda often are never brought into the library system or are brought in too late to be of maximum value. In this respect the importance of information centers (such as exist for handling technical literature dealing, for example, with nuclear science, aerospace, or military research) should be recognized and the relation of those centers to a national research library system examined. In many fields, especially those in which knowledge is accumulating most rapidly, the centers are serving a user need that libraries have neglected. It is not apparent, however, that information centers are able to do much more than provide an alerting function. If this is correct, then the research library system can assume the very important tasks of stimulating a fresh and useful flow from these newer information sources, and it can also provide orderly bibliographic control over their products so that they have long-term use.

INTERLIBRARY COOPERATION. Cooperation among libraries exists in acquisition, cataloging, particular bibliographic projects, library lending, and in many other areas. This cooperation is an attempt to make maximum use of limited resources. Libraries cooperate to improve service and in the interest of the common good, but the test to justify cooperation is usually an economic one. Automation will permit a change in outlook.

The centralized cataloging possibilities implicit in an automated library system could be realized only through a major reorganization of effort in individual libraries. Even acquisition attitudes will have to change as information on holdings is more and more rapidly exchanged and reproduction simplified. The benefits of integrating resources will, in general, be more difficult to ignore. The argument that libraries cannot effectively use the fruits of cataloging efforts performed elsewhere because the results do not meet their own local requirements is far less persuasive in an automatic system. This is so because of the possibility of the central cataloging function accommodating itself to a variety of user needs and perhaps performing special editing processes by machine in order to deliver a tailormade product to certain libraries having such a requirement.

Numerous advantages will accrue to individual libraries because of their having direct access to the National Union Catalog. If their own systems are automated, and they have provided for maintaining a use-frequency history within their collection, they can rely more heavily on the Library of Congress for the less frequently used books in order to keep valuable space in local libraries allocated to the active part of the collection.

Impact on the Library User

The library-user relationship will be significantly affected, although all possible consequences cannot be foreseen. Clearly, services will become much more closely geared to the user's needs. Emphasis will be placed on saving the user time in finding and examining items of interest to him. The user will be assured a more comprehensive search and more selective service. As the users acquire experience with consoles, and as the system and its programs are designed to take into account the users' annotations, comments, and the use history of a variety of users and a variety of works, the system itself will become more responsive. In short, what will be accomplished is a much closer intellectual interaction between the user and the library. Only with this kind of improved interaction can the task of communicating recorded knowledge be performed with a high degree of effectiveness, so that major portions of it are not lost to posterity.

In a certain sense, the automatic library described here can be viewed as both a learning and a teaching machine, and in this way would have a great influence in enhancing the level of our culture.

Effect on Availability of Scientific and Technical Information

The nation's problem of scientific and technical information has been of growing concern to the defense establishment and to the Congress.[8] Most recently the President's Science Advisory Committee published a report entitled *Science, Government, and Information,* in which the fragmentation of scientific literature by speciality is pointed out as demanding some counteracting consolidating force in communications:

Though a scientist chooses to narrow his specialty, science itself creates an ever-increasing number of potential points of contact between the scientist's narrow specialty and the surrounding fields. As time goes on, successful pursuit of a narrow specialty requires effective contact with more and more diverse parts of the literature.

To see what the effect of automation might be, let us examine the three levels through which information passes in the publication process.

First, at the generation or first-publication level, individual workers or small groups record information that they have assembled by creative thought, experiment, or literature research in a publishable article, paper, or communication. Examples of this first-publication level are individual journal articles, doctoral dissertations, contract-reporting documents, industrial research reports, and so forth.

Without question, the input of knowledge to the generation level must exist as a diverse and spontaneous activity, and it is reasonable to expect that the publishing effort for this level will similarly remain diverse and essentially uncoordinated, even though the basic mechanisms of such publication may change appreciably over the years.

The second level is the book. Here, some major topic is comprehensively brought into a cohesively organized form summarizing and referring to prior published knowledge. At the book level, information, usually 2 to 10 years old, is assembled into a packaged form generally having some unifying theme. Periodicals are increasingly devoting entire issues to the treatment of all aspects of some topic. Such special issues, being equivalent to books but unlike them in their multiple authorship, suggest a decline of books as research sources. A comprehensive, mechanized reference and indexing system should allow such special-issue documents to be rapidly compiled and narrowly focused. One can also foresee the pruning of the now too prevalent weaker articles in such collections and, eventually, even the pruning of weaker portions of articles. The efforts of the Atomic Energy Commission, National Institutes of Health, Defense Documentation Center (formerly Armed Services Technical Information Agency), National Science Foundation, National Aeronautics and Space Administration, and others will assist and encourage this aspect of the organization and consolidation of knowledge.

The third level, the preparation of encyclopedias and treatises is declining, relative to growth of publication. Private enterprise has certainly provided an adequate encyclopedic effort when "encyclopedia" is considered in its popular sense. However, with a few exceptions, the job of summarizing knowledge in particular subject areas in a systematic way has not been successfully attacked. It is this aspect of the organization of knowledge that could be undertaken under the aegis of an automated research library system. The consoles and machine-aided search strategies would greatly facilitate this work.

---

[8] See, for example, the following reports: U.S. *Congress. Senate. Committee on Government Operation.* Documentation, indexing, and retrieval of scientific information; a report. Washington, U.S. Govt. Print. Off., 1960. 283 p. (86th Cong., 2d sess. Senate. Document no. 113.) Addendum to this report issued as 87th Cong., 1st sess. Senate. Document no. 15.

U.S. *Congress. House. Committee on Science and Astronautics.* Dissemination of scientific information. Washington, U.S. Govt. Print. Off., 1959. 12 p. (86th Cong., 1st sess. House. Report no. 1179.)

Organization of the Collections

The Library of Congress and most research libraries shelve books in a classified array. The purpose is to place books on the same subjects together for stack control, delivery, special collections, browsing, etc. This mode of shelving has been questioned for a number of reasons: It is wasteful of space. Books are not usually written on a single subject, yet must be placed in only a single location. The number of books on a given subject in a large research library defeats browsing. It has even been said that browsing is an admission of defeat in indexing. Against this background of readiness for change, automation might be at least as welcome as it is disturbing.

Certainly, mechanization will impose a change, because a large research library, automatically controlled to insure the effective location and delivery of its holdings, cannot permit open-shelf operation. Browsing can now be freed of its dependence on classification, from which most of its ills stem, and given a functional orientation. Special browsing collections can be assembled of most frequently used materials or materials of established value for research in given subject fields. These collections can be seeded with analogous or related materials which the librarians believe to be of value and can be weeded, updated, and organized to make the browsing yield more effective and valuable.

A capability for browsing by use of the console should be of even greater significance. The opportunity to examine statistical data on the number of entries in a bibliography, the bibliography itself, and then selected pages of particular items which may include title pages, tables of contents, and indexes, all on a successive rapid response basis and coupled with subject access to whatever depth economics permits, will provide a far more flexible intellectual interaction between the user and the collection than occurs in wandering through the stacks as though one were shopping in a supermarket.

Measurement and Feedback of Library Effectiveness

It is a curious and unfortunate fact that libraries of today have virtually no way of knowing how well they are performing from the point of view of what the user ought to be getting from the system. In general, there is no way of knowing how much information responsive to a subject-oriented request is not found. Possibly one of the most important consequences of automation will be to provide a capability for maintaining use history and for implementing measurements on a sampling basis in order to install a good system of quality control in the library's operations. With such quality control measurements, the possibility for improvement-feedback then exists. It is unlikely that industry could operate today without an adequate system of quality control over its products. Why then should not libraries, with perhaps far more important products, stand to benefit by such a philosophy?

Concluding Comment

Certain trends toward decentralization and specialization of collections in both the arts and sciences are partial evidence of the difficulties which research libraries are encountering in rendering adequate service. The most serious problem is that of characterizing documents to facilitate their retrieval and the retrieval of their contents within the bounds of a manual system. Many of the mechanical limitations could be overcome by the application of current or imminent technical advances. One can also be optimistic about increasing the sophistication of library use and, more importantly, the knowledge of how to use them by the advent of machines.

This survey has been very conservative in its appreciation of technology and science applicable to document and information retrieval, but some of the team have more optimism about future developments than can be documented by today's equipment and methodology. The need for automation in libraries will create advances in these areas.

It is a general conclusion of this survey that research libraries are lagging behind in the application of existing technology to their information handling problems, principally because of insufficient funds. Based on its investigation, the survey team asserts that existing and imminent technology can bring about major improvements in the service of the Library of Congress, and that an automated system accomplishing this can be made operable within the next few years. The survey team has therefore recommended that immediate efforts be made to automate research library functions. It is also strongly recommended that the Library of Congress, because of its central role in the Nation's library system, take the lead in the automation venture.

A Business Intelligence System

by Hans P. Luhn

Abstract: An automatic system is being developed to disseminate information to the various sections of any industrial, scientific or government organization. This intelligence system will utilize data-processing machines for auto-abstracting and auto-encoding of documents and for creating interest profiles for each of the "action points" in an organization. Both incoming and internally generated documents are automatically abstracted, characterized by a word pattern, and sent automatically to appropriate action points. This paper shows the flexibility of such a system in identifying known information, in finding who needs to know it and in disseminating it efficiently either in abstract form or as a complete document.

Introduction

Efficient communication is a key to progress in all fields of human endeavor. It has become evident in recent years that present communication methods are totally inadequate for future requirements. Information is now being generated and utilized at an ever-increasing rate because of the accelerated pace and scope of human activities and the steady rise in the average level of education. At the same time the growth of organizations and increased specialization and divisionalization have created new barriers to the flow of information. There is also a growing need for more prompt decisions at levels of responsibility far below those customary in the past. Undoubtedly the most formidable communications problem is the sheer bulk of information that has to be dealt with. In view of the present growth trends, automation appears to offer the most efficient methods for retrieval and dissemination of this information.

During the past decade significant progress has been made in applying machines to the processes of informa-tion retrieval. Automatic dissemination has so far been given little considera-tion; however, unless substantial por-tions of human effort in this area can be replaced by automatic operations, no significant over-all improvement will be achieved. Even the information retrieval processes mechanized so far still require appreciable human effort to organize the information before it is entered into machines.

It is believed that techniques now being developed will greatly contribute to the solution of the problem by ex-tending automatic processes to the pre-paratory phases of mechanical informa-tion-retrieval systems, to the area of dis-semination and to associated functions. Ideally, an automatic system is needed which can accept information in its original form, disseminate the data promptly to the proper places and fur-nish information on demand.

The techniques proposed here to make these things possible are:

1. Auto-abstracting of documents.
2. Auto-encoding of documents.

SOURCE: *IBM Journal of Research and Development,* **2,** No. 4, October 1958, pp. 314–319.

127

3. Automatic creation and updating of *action-point* profiles.

All of these techniques are based on statistical procedures which can be performed on present-day data processing machines. Together with proper communication facilities and input-output equipment a comprehensive system may be assembled to accommodate all information problems of an organization. We call this a *Business Intelligence System*.

Objectives and Principles

Before the system operation is described, the term *Business Intelligence System* should be defined and the objectives and principles stated.

In this paper, *business* is a collection of activities carried on for whatever purpose, be it science, technology, commerce, industry, law, government, defense, et cetera. The communication facility serving the conduct of a business (in the broad sense) may be referred to as an *intelligence system*. The notion of *intelligence* is also defined here, in a more general sense, as "the ability to apprehend the interrelationships of presented facts in such a way as to guide action towards a desired goal" (1).

The term *document* is used to designate a block of information confined physically in a medium such as a letter, report, paper or book. The term may also include the medium itself.

The objective of the system is to supply suitable information to support specific activities carried out by individuals, groups, departments, divisions, or even larger units. These are the *action points* previously referred to. To this end the system concerns itself with the admission or acquisition of new information, its dissemination, storage, retrieval and transmittal to the action points it serves.

More particularly the object of the system is to perform these functions speedily and efficiently, taking advantage of novel procedures which utilize the inherent capabilities of electronic devices.

One of the most crucial problems in communication is that of channeling a given item of information to those who need to know it. Present methods of accomplishing this are inadequate and the general practice is to disseminate information rather broadly to be on the safe side. Since this method tends to swamp the recipients with paper, the probability of not communicating at all becomes great. The Business Intelligence System provides means for selective dissemination to each of its action points in accordance with their current requirements or desires. This is accomplished by the mechanical creation of *profiles* reflecting the sphere of interest of each point and by updating these profiles as dictated by changes in the attitude of the respective action points and as recorded by the system on the basis of certain transactions.

Another problem in communication is to discover the person or section within an organization whose interests or activities coincide most closely with a given situation. Presently, the difficulty of finding such relationships often results in improper decisions, wrong actions, inaction, or duplication. An objective of the Business Intelligence System is to identify related interests by use of profiles of action points.

The problem of discovering information which has a bearing on a given situation has probably received the most attention in recent years, and various mechanical systems have been developed and put into operation. This phase of communication is commonly referred to as *information retrieval* or, more broadly, as the *library problem*. Information retrieval is necessarily a major function of the Business Intelligence System. Means are provided not only to integrate this function with the rest of the system but also to produce additional useful functions, as will be described later.

The achievement of these objectives is governed by principles essential to effective service and convenience of the user. Some of these are listed below:

1. Information admitted to the system includes communications, addressed to action points individually, which contain information of potential interest to other action points.

2. New information which is pertinent or useful to certain action points is selectively disseminated to such points without delay. A function of the system is to present this information to the action point in such a manner that its existence will be readily recognized.

3. Transmittal of information either as a result of dissemination or of retrieval is to be guided by progressive stages of acceptance by an action point. This procedure saves the recipient's time by reducing the amount of material to be transmitted and eliminating the non-pertinent material.

4. The system is to provide means for quickly discovering similarity of interests and activities that might exist amongst action points so that subjects and problems of common concern may be discussed and advanced through direct interchange of ideas between such points, if so desired.

5. The system is not to impose conditions on its user which require special training to obtain its services. Instead the system is to be operated by experienced library workers. Thus, in the case of an inquiry, the user will be required only to call the librarian, who will accept the query and will ask for any amplification which, in accordance with his experience, will be most helpful in securing the desired information.

6. Similarly, information lingering at an action point but of potential value to other action points is *mobilized* for efficient communication through inquiries of skilled reporters.

Description of the Business Intelligence System

The following description is given in rather general terms, and references to any specific type of *business* have been substantially avoided. Furthermore, the fact that certain devices are being referred to as implementation of the system should not be interpreted as implying a specific size of the operation.

The description is given in accordance with main functional sections of the system, each illustrated by the diagram. Our assembly of these functional sections into a complete system is shown in Fig. 1.

Document Input

Each document entering the system shown in Fig. 1 is assigned a serial number and is photographically reproduced on some medium such as microfilm. In those cases where the document has been addressed specifically to an action point, the original is promptly transmitted to the addressee. In all other cases the original is stored in a file for a reasonably short time and thereafter destroyed, unless there are reasons for preserving it for longer periods.

The microfilm copy of the document is transcribed onto magnetic tape by a human transcriber or a print-reading device. In those cases where the original document is available in machine-readable form, the transcription is done mechanically. The document is now available both as a microfilm copy and a magnetic tape record.

The microfilm copy is then recopied onto the storage medium of a *document microcopy* storage device. The microfilm record is stored elsewhere to constitute a microfilm master file which may serve to regenerate records in cases of emergency.

The magnetic tape record is now introduced into the auto-abstracting and encoding device. This device submits

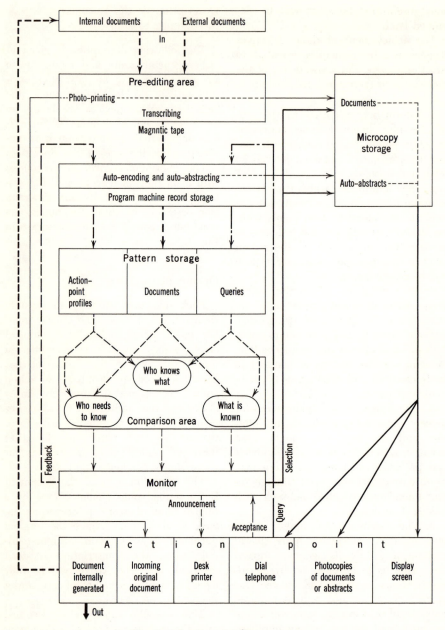

Fig. 1. A business intelligence system.

the document to a statistical analysis based on the physical properties of the text, and data are derived on word frequency and distribution. From these data the device then selects certain sentences of the document to produce an auto-abstract (2). This is printed out, together with the title, author, and document serial number. This printout is photographically transferred onto the storage medium of the *auto-abstract microcopy storage* device.

The process of creating auto-abstracts consists of ascertaining the frequency of word occurrences in a document. A predetermined portion of the words of highest frequency is then given the status of *significant words* and an analysis is made of all the sentences in the text containing such words. A relative value of sentence significance is then established by a formula which reflects the number of significant words contained in a sentence and the proximity of these words to each other within this sentence. Several sentences which rank highest in value of significance are then extracted from the text to constitute the auto-abstract.

As soon as the auto-abstract has been created, the statistical data are further processed to derive an information pattern which characterizes the document. This process of *encoding* constitutes a further abstraction and involves procedures such as the categorization of words by means of a thesaurus (3).

Useful patterns may be derived by listing a given portion of the words of highest frequency together with a selection of specific words. The interrelationship of words may also be indicated and certain frequently occurring combinations of words may be noted. Because of variation of word usage amongst authors the normalization of such words becomes an important function of encoding. Index lookup in a thesaurus-like dictionary will replace words, including those of foreign languages, by a notional family designation. The selection of specific words may also be accomplished by index lookup.

The document pattern derived by the above process is then transferred into a special pattern-storage device together with the title, author, and document serial number. This information is stored in coded form on a medium that may be subjected to serial scanning. As an alternative the resulting pattern may be rearranged and be distributed over a storage array to permit random access according to characteristics.

The tape or film transcript of the document may be stored in a library for reference if it later becomes necessary to change the method or scope of encoding.

Action-Point Profiles

As indicated earlier, one of the basic requirements of the system is the ability to recognize by mechanical means the sphere of interest and the type of activities that characterize each of the action points the system is to serve. This is accomplished by means of an information pattern similar to that of the documents.

Initially, the creation of these action-point profiles is best accomplished by having each action point create a document describing the various aspects of its activities and enumerating the types of information needed. Such documents are then introduced at the input of the system and are identified by action-point designation. The machine-readable transcripts of these documents are then described in connection with the document input. The resulting patterns are then stored in the Pattern Storage area in a special profile-storage device. Also stored, with each of these profile patterns, is the date of entry.

Selective Dissemination of New Information

Based on the document-input operation and the creation of profiles, the system is ready to perform the service function of selective dissemination of new information.

As soon as a new document has been entered into the system and its pattern developed, this pattern is set up in a comparison device which has access to all of the action-point profiles. The comparisons are carried out on the basis of degree of similarity, expressed in terms of a fraction, for each of the profile patterns. This fraction is subject to change as time goes on, depending upon conditions to be explained later.

Whenever a profile agrees to a given extent with a given document pattern, the serial number, title, and author of the affected document, together with the action-point profile designation, are transferred and stored in a monitoring device. This procedure is repeated for any subsequent similar occasion. The monitor is substantially a random-access storage device and has the functional capabilities of performing inventory operations. In this capacity it will transmit the serial number, title and author of the document in question to the desk printer at the selected action point and keep a record of this transaction.

Of the various ways in which such an announcement may be transmitted to the affected action points, the most effective one is by means of a printing device at each action-point location. An objective of the system is to command attention of the recipient. The use of individual printing devices is more effective than are centrally located devices serving several action points.

Selective Acceptance of Disseminated Information

The dissemination of information so far has consisted in furnishing the action point with the serial number, title, and author of documents selected for it. This selection, however, is considered to be a provisional one, and the system withholds any further information if the action point can determine, on the basis of information given so far, that certain of the selected subjects are not of sufficient interest. If an announcement is of interest, and more detailed information on the subject is desired, the system will produce such information on demand. This step is initiated when the action point connects itself by telephone to the monitor and dials the serial numbers of the documents affected. Upon receipt of this message the monitor will relay an instruction to the microcopy storage device to produce photoprints of the auto-abstracts of these documents and to mark them with the action-point designation. The auto-abstracts are then transmitted to the action point either in the form of a paper copy or by speedier means, such as Telefax or TV display.

The action point may now peruse the abstracts to determine which of the documents are desired in their entirety. These decisions are then entered into the system in the form of *acceptances*. An acceptance is made at an action point by dialing the document number, prefixed by a code symbol, whereupon the monitor will instruct the microcopy storage device to produce a photocopy of the complete document, properly marked with the action-point designation. These photocopies are then delivered to the action point.

The monitor will record the incidence of acceptance by modifying the affected records contained in its storage. At the same time the monitor will also instruct the auto-encoding device to transfer copies of the code patterns of the affected documents to the profile section of pattern storage, together with the identification of the action point involved and the date of transferral.

As a result of these operations the profile of a given action point has been updated to reflect interest in a currently communicated subject. As time goes on there is the probability that an increasing number of new documents will be announced to an action point because of possible shift of interests. In order to avoid such cumulative effects, the system is so arranged that the response to past interests is gradually relaxed. This relaxation is related to the date affixed to each new pattern that is superimposed on an action point's profile. Depending on the age of each of these patterns, an adjustment is made on the fraction of similarity that must be met in the comparison process of new documents. The older the profile pattern, the closer an agreement is needed for selection for dissemination, and consequently the fewer documents are selected. On the other hand those documents selected are more closely related to the original subject.

Information Retrieval

This phase of the system concerns itself with the retrieval of those stored documents which might be relevant to a topic under consideration by an action point. The information to be discovered may vary widely and may consist of anything ranging from factual data to an extensive bibliography on a broad subject. Under the supervision of an experienced librarian the process of information retrieval is performed in the following way.

An action point telephones the librarian and states the information wanted. The librarian will then interpret the inquiry and will solicit sufficient background information from the action point in order to provide a document similar in format to that of documents normally entering the system. This query document is transmitted to the auto-encoding device in machine-readable form. An information pattern is then derived from the query document in a manner similar to that used for normal documents.

The resulting query pattern, together with a serial number and designation of the originating action point, is then sent to the queries section of the pattern-storage device. Subsequently a copy of this query pattern is set up in the comparison device and is compared with all of the document patterns stored in the document-pattern storage device. This operation is similar to the one described in connection with selective dissemination. In the present case, the query pattern replaces the profile pattern.

Whenever similar patterns are detected by this means, the document designation is transmitted to the monitor, where it is registered and then announced to the action point.

Although the service of a librarian is considered a convenience to the action point, in certain cases, means may be provided at the action-point location to permit direct access to the system. This would be justified where many of the inquiries concern lookup-type retrieval of data.

When an action point desires information relative to a given document, the number of the document at hand would be dialed and instructions for search given to the monitor. Thereupon the monitor would select the corresponding pattern from document-pattern storage and provide instruction for use as a query pattern in the ensuing comparison operation.

Selective Acceptance of Retrieved Information

The considerations which prompted the step-by-step acceptance of documents in the dissemination process are also applied to information retrieval. The processes employed, therefore, are identical.

The function of information retrieval, however, differs from that of dissemination in that the choice is not that of accepting or rejecting one document, but rather a selection of one or several from a special group of potentially relevant documents. Although in some cases a first search may have produced satisfactory references, in other cases the material produced may not be satisfactory. The action point must then relay this fact to the librarian and discuss with him how the searching procedure or the query should be modified so as to improve the probability of getting relevant material.

In those cases where pertinent information has been discovered, the acceptance of the complete documents of such information will cause the updating of the action-point profile, as was the case in dissemination. The query pattern will be impressed on the profile as a matter of course, whether or not the inquiry has been satisfied, so that new documents relevant to the subject of the inquiry will be made known subsequently.

Detection of an Action Point Having Given Characteristics

In the process of transacting business it is often desired to determine who concerns himself with a given subject. The usual type of question asked is: "Who does or knows a certain thing?" A function of the Business Intelligence System is to answer questions of this type.

The manner in which this function is performed by the system is similar to the information retrieval procedure. However, instead of simulating a document pattern, a profile pattern is developed which represents most closely the characteristics of an action point sought. This synthetic profile is then compared with those in the profile storage and when a given degree of similarity is discovered, the identification of the affected action point is transferred to the monitor, together with the identification of the inquirer point. Thereafter the identities are announced by the tape-printing device at the inquiring action point so that personal contacts may be made.

Document Output

The functions described so far have concerned themselves with documents admitted or acquired by the system from the outside. The document-output phase deals with internally generated documents. This type of document is essentially the product of action points and may be addressed to other action points within the organization or to external points. An objective of the system is to facilitate selective dissemination and retrieval of such documents in substantially the same way as for outside documents.

When a document has been created at an action point, a copy is produced, preferably in machinable form. This copy is then dispatched for processing to the input point of the system and the original is sent to the addressee.

Since this type of document is an indication of the interest of the originating action point, the information pattern derived by the auto-encoding process is not only stored in document-pattern storage but also is impressed on the profile of its originator, thereby updating it.

In the dissemination process this internally created document is announced to other action points in the same fashion as were outside documents.

Miscellaneous Functions of the System

The comprehensive system for the various functions so far described is illustrated by Fig. 1. A number of additional useful functions which may be derived from the system are briefly described here.

It might be desirable to check each new document for duplication by comparing it with all of the documents in storage. Similarly a list of related documents may be prepared to serve as references applying to a new document.

When retrieving information it might be found advantageous to compare a query first with all the queries stored, in order to discover whether similar queries have been submitted in the past. If a list of the documents retrieved is available, the process of retrieval may be greatly simplified. This method may also be used to bring together the respective inquirers to furnish an opportunity to discuss the problems which apparently brought about similar inquiries. Periodic analysis of the profiles may also furnish valuable information on trends and possible overlapping of activities or interests.

Since a history of the usage of the system is stored in the monitor, an analysis of its records will disclose the efficiency of system operation. The findings may serve to adjust the system for optimum efficiency.

There are many details which might have to be provided to adjust the general form of the system to specific applications. One such requirement might be classification, by an editor, of documents with regard to security, proprietary interests and proper utilization of information.

A plurality of systems may be organized in hierarchical fashion, in which a first system would serve a number of more specialized systems. In this case the specialized system would each assume the role of an action point in the mother system.

It also appears quite feasible to share the system equipment among a number of organizations.

Prospects for Establishing a Business Intelligence System

The system described here employs rather advanced design techniques and the question arises as to how far away such systems may be from realization. It may therefore be of interest to review the state of system and machine development.

The availability of documents in machine-readable form is a basic requirement of the system. Typewriters with paper-tape punching attachments are already used extensively in information processing and communication operations. Their use as standard equipment in the future would provide machine-readable records of new information. The transcription of old records would pose a problem, since in most cases it would be uneconomical to perform this job by hand. The mechanization of this operation will therefore have to wait until print-reading devices have been perfected.

The type of equipment required for processing information in accordance with the system is presently available as far as the functions are concerned. It is safe to assume that special equipment will eventually be required to optimize the operation.

The auto-abstracting and auto-encoding systems are in their early stage of development and a great deal of research has yet to be done to perfect them. Perhaps the techniques which ultimately find greatest use will bear little resemblance to those new visualized, but some form of automation will ultimately provide an effective answer to business intelligence problems.

REFERENCES

1. *Webster's New Collegiate Dictionary,* G. & C. Merriam Co., Springfield, Mass.
2. Luhn, H. P., "The Automatic Creation of Literature Abstracts," *IBM J. Res. Develop.,* **2,** No. 2, 159 (April 1958).
3. Luhn, H. P., "A Statistical Approach to Mechanized Encoding and Searching of Literary Information," *IBM J. Res. Develop.,* **1,** No. 4, 309 (October 1957).

PART TWO

Disciplines Underlying Constructive Sociology of Information-Retrieval Systems

What, precisely, is the "encyclopedia system" idea? Do we understand the concepts that are involved in this idea with the degree of logical precision necessary for a thorough analysis of such a system and for its realization. Could we specify conditions under which one form or another of the system would function as intended, or under which it would provide socially useful services? When would it malfunction? What is a good way in which to implement the idea?

Are there any answers to these and related questions? Are there any scientific findings or techniques that can be brought to bear on obtaining such answers?

D. Swanson once stated that information retrieval has produced answers, but not yet the questions to which they pertain. From ideas such as those contained in Part One significant questions can be expected to arise. It appears that, at best, only very indirect and partial answers are available in the literature. These develop for the most part from more or less remote analogies between the organization, storage, and retrieval of knowledge in society and the organization, storage, and retrieval as studied by the biologist, the biochemist, the neurophysiologist, and the psychologist. It is in this area that exciting scientific progress, in the traditional sense of science, seems to hold considerable promise. A sample of four articles of this nature is presented in the second half of Part Two.

The little science underlying the rational construction of encyclopedic information systems that are to grow into viable social systems is sampled by the five articles in the first half of Part Two. The numerous "answers to which there are no questions"—mostly impressive accomplishments in technology and inventions in techniques for file organization and indexing —are not sampled here. They are adequately covered by the books of Becker and Hayes, Cuadra, Sharp, Borko, and Bourne and by journals such as *American Documentation* and *Communications of the ACM*.

PART TWO

A. Relevant Background

Many valuable data about the information needs,[1] reading patterns and literature-search habits of scientists have been compiled since the time of Bernal—by Ackoff,[2] Menzel, Garvey, Wolfe, Rosenbloom, Wuest, Price, Marquis, and many others.[1] Machlup's estimates of the size of the United States "knowledge industry" surprised many of us by showing the unexpectedly rapid growth of this industry and the large share in the economy that this most recently detected sector has assumed. Much of the data is in need of reduction and integration into a coherent and teachable form. Although many of the papers are technically excellent and some embody clever new techniques for data collection (for example, Ackoff[2]), the article by Price seemed the most suitable for inclusion here because of its breadth and depth. This paper also covers the very important work on citation indexing by Garfield, Tukey, Kessler, and Osgood-Xhingesse. The structure of a citation network reveals much about the processes of organizing knowledge, the ways in which new literature is synthesized from the old.

Creating and using a citation index is an example of what H. G. Wells called "constructive sociology." The paper by Price is a good example of work in the scientific discipline underlying information-retrieval system design.[3] The next selection, by C. N. Parkinson, although on the surface it may seem unrelated, is another good example of a finding in the necessary underlying discipline. There has been much talk about the "information explosion or crisis," little careful thought about a precise problem formulation, much less about what might be the real causes of all the current concern with information. Could it be that beneath the anxiety directed at the growth of literature is a deeper fear about our ability to manage the increasingly complex and dangerously powerful organizations due to

---

[1] Auerbach Corp., Final Tech. Report 1151–TR3 to ARPA, DOD User Needs Study, Philadelphia, Pa., May 1965.

[2] Ackoff, Russell L., and Michael H. Halbert, *An Operations Research Study of the Scientific Activity of Chemists.* Cleveland: Case Institute of Technology, Operations Research Group, 1958.

[3] Another important author who regards libraries, information centers, information exchanges, information distribution and dissemination systems, and invisible colleges as social institutions is Meier, R. L.; for example, see "Efficiency Criteria for the Operation of Large Libraries," *The Library Quarterly,* 31, No. 3, July 1961, pp. 215–234.

growth of population and technology? Although most of the literature stresses the information problems of scientists and science (for example, the article by Price), it is perhaps the vast remainder of society that has information problems of at least equal magnitude and import to those of scientists. In a world of several billion people, where much routine and some skilled labor can be done more efficiently and economically by machines, the average man of the future must discover suitable new roles for himself and must be able to avail himself of the collective wisdom of mankind to best fill these roles. The continued tendency of men to aggregate into organizations in which they primarily create work for one another not only complicates the search for roles with human dignity, but also the information problem. For most of the work that officials make for one another is paper work (Parkinson's second axiom). It is estimated that in one year, the United States Government alone generates 3.8×10^{11} records,[4] and this number increases faster than the population.

The article by Parkinson could well be taken seriously as an example of a scientific law central to the scientific discipline underlying information-retrieval systems design. It provides considerable insight into one of the mechanisms of document growth.

There is little question that logic and linguistics are basic to constructive sociology of information systems. Much of the corpus on which an information-retrieval service is based is in the form of natural language text. The language in which those seeking education or information interact with the system (via a catalog, a reference librarian, a special searcher, or a terminal device connected to an automated search system) is often far more constrained than that used in everyday conversation. Certain types of data to be stored for retrieval, or for compilation into a coherent unity, could be represented more advantageously in an English-like but formal language suitable for automatic processing. A language modeled after mathematical logic might facilitate, with the help of computers, the deduction of inferences from stored information, allowing retrieval of answers to a far greater class of questions than would retrieval without such inferential capability.

Modern linguistics has made great strides toward an understanding of syntactic structure,[5] an area in which it overlaps with the theory of programming languages and certain aspects of logic. But it has not made equally significant advances in that area of linguistics which is the most pertinent to information retrieval. To be sure, significant progress in computational linguistics has recently been reported by Kuno.[6] He demon-

[4] Barcan, A., "The Battle of the Bulk," *New York Times*, March 28, 1964, Section 12, p. 8.

[5] Chomsky, Noam, *Aspects of the Theory of Syntax*. Cambridge: The M.I.T. Press, 1965. *Syntactic Structures*. The Hague: Morton and Company, 1957.

[6] Kuno, S., "The Predictive Analyzer and a Path Elimination Technique," *Communications of the ACM*, 8, No. 7, July 1965, pp. 453–462.

strated that a large computer can provide all the parsings of a sample of 20 typical English sentences in approximately 2.6 minutes, about two thirds of which is input-output time. Another sample of 13 rather complex sentences from 40 to 56 words long was analyzed in 3.8 minutes. Although this is an impressive advance over previous results of this nature, it is but a modest step toward information retrieval. Suppose for a moment that automatic indexing based on the full text of a document digitally coded and stored in a computer were a reasonable goal. Let us also make the highly questionable assumption that the information on which to base the sound selection of indexing terms were contained among the words of the text. Because a text might contain 200 sentences, about half an hour of computer time per article would be required for parsing alone. There is still a long road from the phrase markers of the sentences to a good set of index terms. At current rates, one half hour of computer time can cost about $50 to 100. It is true that the result might be more consistent and perhaps "better" than that produced by most human indexers, but that is not an adequate basis for comparison. Possibly, with further research such as Kuno's and with faster, cheaper machines the $50 figure can be much reduced, but there will be a theoretical lower bound that may still be intolerably high because we are using basically arithmetical machines to perform a nonarithmetic processing task.

The third selection in the first half of Part Two is one of Carnap's famous works on the logical analysis of language. It is deeper and more technical than many of the other articles in this book. Much of the work on modern syntactic analysis seems to be modeled after the methods used by Carnap and long used in logic, for example, the use of rules of formation and transformation. There has been much research on some of the important technical details since this work. Later even Carnap was much less positivistic. Although this approach to languages of science is now understood to be limited in how much of actual science it can account for, it may apply to the design of languages for storage and retrieval of facts in a limited domain of discourse.

The fourth article, by Swets, draws on yet another established discipline that contributes toward a scientific foundation for the design of information retrieval systems: mathematical statistics. It is an application of elementary decision theory to evaluate the performance of certain retrieval systems, similar to the one that had been previously made by the author to develop signal detection theory. This article, together with Salton's, comes closest to the mainstream of the literature being produced by information-retrieval specialists. Since the article was written, the evaluation methodology has been applied to Salton's experimental data.[7] This method-

[7] Salton, G., "The Evaluation of Automatic Retrieval Procedures—Selected Test Results Using the SMART System," *American Documentation,* **16**, No. 3, July 1965.

ology does not seem to discriminate ineffectiveness among half a dozen rather different retrieval procedures that were tried by Salton. This resembles an earlier finding by Cleverdon,[8] who did not use so sophisticated a methodology, to the effect that retrieval effectiveness did not depend much on which of several classification systems was used.

Beneath this sophisticated methodology are basic questions that are quite obscure, such as the operational definition of relevance and the question of what performance variables such as hit-rate (recall ratio), acceptance-rate (relevance-ratio), miss-rate, and false-drop rate really measure. These measures do not help to evaluate a system for a biochemist who wishes to "keep up." The papers he may want—syntheses of several related papers—probably do not exist, and he seeks aid not with hopeless searches for such works of evaluation and synthesis but in their creation. Nonetheless, this paper exemplifies the best of the contributions toward the needed scientific disciplines, even if it is more relevant to the answers in search of questions than to the solution of real problems.

A good language, to be constructed for use in expressing queries and indexing documents, should not be as heavily constrained as are the languages of programming or mathematical logic; nor can it be as unconstrained as conversational English. It should have a sufficiently rich vocabularly and intricate structure to express most of the queries that can be anticipated during design. It should be able to take advantage of the logical processing speeds and storage capacity made possible by modern information technology. It should resemble the language spoken by its users so that it is convenient to use and easy to learn. Above all, it should be flexible so that its vocabulary and syntax can adapt to changes in use or to patterns of use as these become better known.

Such a language[9] was developed in the AMNIP[10] System. The idea of this system, later rediscovered independently by many others,[11-13] is described in the next paper. This system is now being implemented at

[8] Cleverdon, Cyril W., "Report on the Testing and Analysis of an Investigation into the Comparative Efficiency of Indexing Systems," Cranfield (Eng.): ASLIB Cranfield Research Project, 1962.

[9] An earlier paper with a similar language appeared in a Soviet publication which was hard to obtain: Uspenskii, V. A., "The Problem of Constructing a Machine Language for an Information Machine," in *Problems of Cybernetics*, Vol. II, A. A. Lyapunov (Ed.). New York: Pergamon Press, 1961, pp. 356–371.

[10] An acronym for "Adaptive Man-Machine Nonarithmetic Information Processing." This was the central theme around which the information-retrieval project at the IBM Research Center was organized under the direction of the editor from 1961–1963. It was also the dominant theme of the book *Some Problems in Information Science*, by M. Kochen, Scarecrow Press, New York, 1965.

[11] Levien, R., and M. E. Maron, "Relational Data File: A Tool for Mechanized Inference Execution and Data Retrieval," RAND Memorandum RM-4793 PR, December 1965.

[12] Bodnarchuk, V. G., T. A. Grinchenko, and V. I. Kolinko, "On a Reference Type Information System," *JPRS*, 33, 991, Translation from Russian of paperbound *Problems of Theoretical Cybernetics*, 1965, pp. 110–119.

RAND Corporation, and much more sophisticated systems should soon be possible as clever new data structures[13] and techniques for analyzing them[14] are being invented and implemented at M.I.T. and in other time-sharing systems throughout the country.

This paper relates previous work on algorithms for concept and hypothesis formation with information storage and retrieval. It deals primarily with data retrieval, including bibliographic data about documents, biographic data about authors, and thesaurus-type data coupling subject headings with one another. Fundamentally, it stresses the changing nature of all files and the interrelations among items in files. The main reason that implementation of this system at IBM did not materialize was the requirement to demonstrate the power of a photoscopic read-only technology.

The kind of system now being implemented differs little from AMNIPS, and it is currently quite popular. The AMNIPS paper presents a plan, an idea, which is related to the idea of an encyclopedia system, so that it might have been placed in the first half of Part One. But it is also the design of a novel and unique experimental tool with the purpose of enabling information-retrieval investigators, who are at the same time users of the system, to "grow" a system. If information-retrieval systems can be arranged along a spectrum where the right-most system is centralized, with the central doing all the indexing, dissemination, abstracting, synthesizing (preferably automated with a central computer) and with more or less passive users at the periphery, and where the left-most system is one in which each user is active, cooperating with a select group of others, both as contributor and recipient of services, then AMNIPS is to the left of center. The dissemination systems DICO and SASIDS,[15] which grew out of the AMNIPS project, are examples of systems further to the left, whereas SDI is to the right of center.

[13] Feldman, J. A., "Aspects of Associative Processing," Lincoln Lab. Tech. Note, April 1965.

[14] Holt, Anatol W., "Notes for Computer and Program Organization," University of Michigan Summer Conference, No. 6613 Ann Arbor, 1966.

[15] Kochen, M. *Some Problems in Information Science*, Scarecrow Press, New York, 1965, pp. 271–288.

Networks of Scientific Papers

by Derek J. de Solla Price

This article is an attempt to describe in the broadest outline the nature of the total world network of scientific papers. We shall try to picture the network which is obtained by linking each published paper to the other papers directly associated with it. To do this, let us consider that special relationship which is given by the citation of one paper by another in its footnotes or bibliography. I should make it clear, however, that this broad picture tells us something about the papers themselves as well as something about the practice of citation. It seems likely that many of the conclusions we shall reach about the network of papers would still be essentially true even if citation became much more or much less frequent, and even if we considered links obtained by subject indexing rather than by citation. It happens, however, that we now have available machine-handled citation studies, of large and representative portions of literature, which are much more tractable for such analysis than any topical indexing known to me. It is from such studies, by Garfield (1, 2), Kessler (3), Tukey (4), Osgood (5), and others, that I have taken the source data of this study.

Incidence of References

First, let me say something of the incidence of references in papers in serial publications. On the average, there are about 15 references per paper and, of these, about 12 are to other serial publications rather than to books,

theses, reports, and unpublished work. The average, of course, gives us only part of the picture. The distribution (see Fig. 1) is such that about 10 percent of the papers contain no references at all; this notwithstanding, 50 percent of the references come from the 85 percent of the papers that are of the "normal" research type and contain 25 or fewer references apiece. The distribution here is fairly flat; indeed about 5 percent of the papers fall in each of the categories of 3, 4, 5, 6, 7, 8, 9, and 10 references each. At the other end of the scale, there are review-type papers with many references each. About 25 percent of all references come from the 5 percent (of all papers) that contain 45 or more references each and average 75 to a paper, while 12 percent of the references come from the "fattest" category—the 1 percent (of all papers) that have 84 or more references each and average about 170 to a paper. It is interesting to note that the number of papers with n references falls off in this "fattest" category as $1/n^2$, up to many hundreds per paper.

These references, of course, cover the entire previous body of literature. We can calculate roughly that, since the body of world literature has been growing exponentially for a few centuries (6), and probably will continue at its present rate of growth of about 7 percent per annum, there will be about 7 new papers each year for every 100 previously published papers in a given field. An average of about 15 references

SOURCE: *Science*, **149**, July 30, 1965, pp. 510–515.

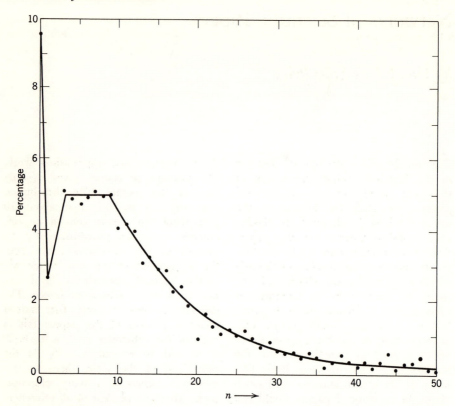

Fig. 1. Percentages (relative to total number of papers published in 1961) of papers published in 1961 which contain various numbers (n) of bibliographic references. The data, which represent a large sample, are from Garfield's 1961 *Index* (2).

in each of these 7 new papers will therefore supply about 105 references back to the previous 100 papers, which will therefore be cited an average of a little more than once each during the year. Over the long run, and over the entire world literature, we should find that, on the average, *every scientific paper ever published is cited about once a year.*

Incidence of Citations

Now, although the total number of citations must exactly balance the total number of references, the distributions are very different. It seems that, in any given year, about 35 percent of all the existing papers are not cited at all, and another 49 percent are cited only once ($n = 1$) (see Fig. 2). This leaves about

16 percent of the papers to be cited an average of about 3.2 times each. About 9 percent are cited twice; 3 percent, three times; 2 percent, four times; 1 percent, five times; and a remaining 1 percent, six times or more. For large n, the number of papers cited appears to decrease as $n^{2.5}$ or $n^{3.0}$. This is rather more rapid than the decrease found for numbers of references in papers, and indeed the number of papers receiving many citations is smaller than the number carrying large bibliographies. Thus, only 1 percent of the cited papers are cited as many as six or more times each in a year (the average for this top 1 percent is 12 citations), and the maximum likely number of citations to a paper in a year is smaller by about an

order of magnitude than the maximum likely number of references in the citing papers. There is, however, some parallelism in the findings that some 5 percent of all papers appear to be review papers, with many (25 or more) references, and some 4 percent of all papers appear to be "classics," cited four or more times in a year.

What has been said of references is true from year to year; the findings for individual cited papers, however, appear to vary from year to year. A paper not cited in one year may well be cited in the next, and one cited often in one year may or may not be heavily cited subsequently. Heavy citation appears to occur in rather capricious bursts, but in spite of that I suspect a strong statistical regularity. I would conjecture that results to date could be explained by the hypotheses that every year about 10 percent of all papers "die," not to be cited again, and that for the "live" papers the chance of being cited at least once in any year is about 60 percent. This would mean that the major work of a paper would be finished after 10 years. The process thus reaches a steady state, in which about 10 percent

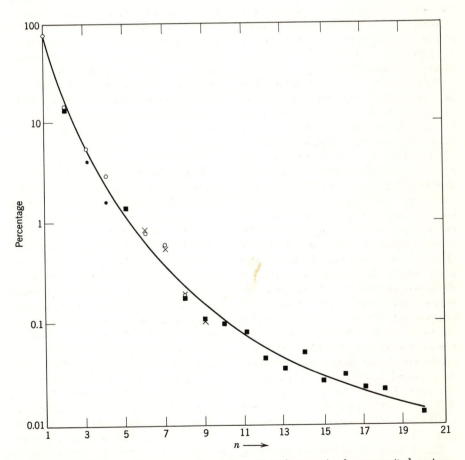

Fig. 2. Percentages (relative to total number of cited papers) of papers cited various numbers (n) of times, for a single year (1961). The data are from Garfield's 1961 *Index* (2), and the points represent four different samples conflated to show the consistency of the data. Because of the rapid decline in frequency of citation which increase in n, the percentages are plotted on a logarithmic scale.

of all published papers have never been cited, about 10 percent have been cited once, about 9 percent twice, and so on, the percentages slowly decreasing, so that half of all papers will be cited eventually five times or more, and a quarter of all papers, ten times or more. More work is urgently needed on the problem of determining whether there is a probability that the more a paper is cited the more likely it is to be cited thereafter. It seems to me that further work in this area might well lead to the discovery that classic papers could be rapidly identified, and that perhaps even the "superclassics" would prove so distinctive that they could be picked automatically by means of citation-index-production procedures and published as a single U.S. (or World) Journal of Really Important Papers.

Unfortunately, we know little about any relationship between the number of times a paper is cited and the number of bibliographic references it contains. Since rough preliminary tests indicate that, for much-cited papers, there is a fairly standard pattern of distribution of numbers of bibliographic references, I conjecture that the correlation, if one exists, is very small. Certainly, there is no strong tendency for review papers to be cited unusually often. If my conjecture is valid, it is worth noting that, since 10 percent of all papers contain no bibliographic references and another, presumably almost independent, 10 percent of all papers are never cited, it follows that there is a lower bound of 1 percent of all papers on the number of papers that are totally disconnected in a pure citation network and could be found only by topical indexing or similar methods; this is a very small class, and probably a most unimportant one.

The balance of references and citations in a single year indicates one very important attribute of the network (see Fig. 3). Although most papers produced in the year contain a near-average number of bibliographic references, half of these are references to about half of all the papers that have been published in previous years. The other half of the references tie these new papers to a quite small group of earlier ones, and generate a rather tight pattern of multiple relationships. Thus each group of new papers is "knitted" to a small, select part of the existing scientific literature but connected rather weakly and randomly to a much greater part. Since only a small part of the earlier literature is knitted together by the new year's crop of papers, we may look upon this small part as a sort of growing tip or epidermal layer, an active research front. I believe it is the existence of a research front, in this sense, that distinguishes the sciences from the rest of scholarship, and, because of it, I propose that one of the major tasks of statistical analysis is to determine the mechanism that enables science to cumulate so much faster than nonscience that it produces a literature crisis.

An analysis of the distribution of publication dates of all papers cited in a single year (Fig. 4) sheds further light on the existence of such a research front. Taking [from Garfield (2)] data for 1961, the most numerous count available, I find that papers published in 1961 cite earlier papers at a rate that falls off by a factor of 2 for every 13.5-year interval measured backward from 1961; this rate of decrease must be approximately equal to the exponential growth of numbers of papers published in that interval. Thus, the chance of being cited by a 1961 paper was almost the same for all papers published more than about 15 years before 1961, the rate of citation presumably being the previously computed average rate of one citation per paper per year. It should be noted that, as time goes on, there are more and more papers available to cite each one previously published. Therefore, the chance that any one paper will be cited by

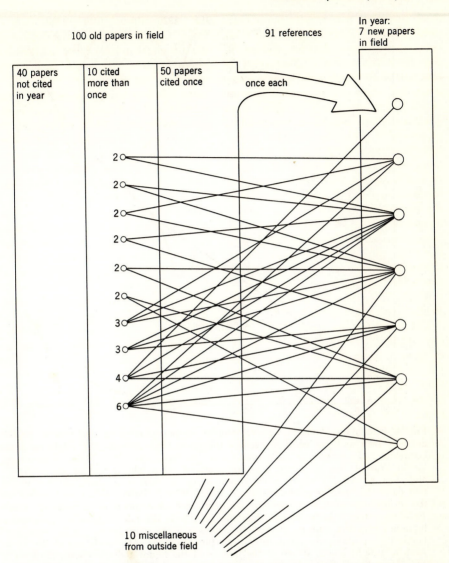

Fig. 3. Idealized representation of the balance of papers and citations for a given "almost closed" field in a single year. It is assumed that the field consists of 100 papers whose numbers have been growing exponentially at the normal rate. If we assume that each of the seven papers contains about 13 references to journal papers and that about 11 percent of these 91 cited papers (or ten papers) are outside the field, we find that 50 of the old papers are connected by one citation each to the new papers (these links are not shown) and that 40 of the old papers are not cited at all during the year. The seven new papers, then, are linked to ten of the old ones by the complex network shown here.

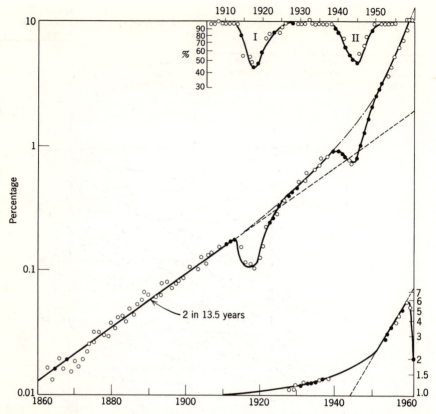

Fig. 4. Percentages (relative to total number of papers cited in 1961) of all papers cited in 1961 and published in each of the years 1862 through 1961 [data are from Garfield's 1961 *Index* (2)]. The curve for the data (solid line) shows dips during World Wars I and II. These dips are analyzed separately at the top of the figure and show remarkably similar reductions to about 50 percent of normal citation in the two cases. For papers published before World War I, the curve is a straight line on this logarithmic plot, corresponding to a doubling of numbers of citations for every 13.5-year interval. If we assume that this represents the rate of growth of the entire literature over the century covered, it follows that the more recent papers have been cited disproportionately often relative to their number. The deviation of the curve from a straight line is shown at the bottom of the figure and gives some measure of the "immediacy effect." If, for old papers, we assume a unit rate of citation, then we find that the recent papers are cited at first about six times as much, this factor of 6 declining to 3 in about 7 years, and to 2 after about 10 years. Since it is probable that some of the rise of the original curve above the straight line may be due to an increase in the pace of growth of the literature since World War I, it may be that the curve of the actual "immediacy effect" would be somewhat smaller and sharper than the curve shown here. It is probable, however, that the straight dashed line on the main plot gives approximately the slopes of the initial falloff, which must therefore be a halving in the number of citation for every 6 years one goes backward from the date of the citing paper.

any other, later paper decreases exponentially by about a factor of 2 every 13.5 years.

For papers less than 15 years old, the rate of citation is considerably greater than this standard value of one citation per paper per year. The rate increases steadily, from less than twice this value for papers 15 years old to 4 times for those 5 years old; it reaches a maximum of about 6 times the standard value for papers 2½ years old, and of course declines again for papers so recent that they have not had time to be noticed.

Incidentally, this curve enables one to see and dissect out the effect of the wartime declines in production of papers. It provides an excellent indication, in agreement with manpower indexes and other literature indexes, that production of papers began to drop from expected levels at the beginning of World Wars I and II, declining to a trough of about half the normal production in 1918 and mid-1944, respectively, and then recovering in a manner strikingly symmetrical with the decline, attaining the normal rate again by 1926 and 1950, respectively. Because of this decline, we must not take dates in the intervals 1914–25 and 1939–50 for comparison with normal years in determining growth indexes.

The "Immediacy Factor"

The "immediacy factor"—the "bunching," or more frequent citation, of recent papers relative to earlier ones—is, of course, responsible for the well-known phenomenon of papers being considered obsolescent after a decade. A numerical measure of this factor can be derived and is particularly useful. Calculation shows that about 70 percent of all cited papers would account for the normal growth curve, which shows a doubling every 13.5 years, and that about 30 percent would account for the hump of the immediacy curve. Hence, we may say that the 70 percent represents a random distribution of citations of all the scientific papers that have ever been published, regardless of date, and that the 30 percent are highly selective references to recent literature; the distribution of citations of the recent papers is defined by the shape of the curve, half of the 30 percent being papers between 1 and 6 years old.

I am surprised at the extent of this immediacy phenomenon and want to indicate its significance. If all papers followed a standard pattern with respect to the proportions of early and recent papers they cite, then it would follow that 30 percent of all references in all papers would be to the recent research front. If, instead, the papers cited by, say, half of all papers were evenly distributed through the literature with respect to publication date, then it must follow that 60 percent of the papers cited by the other half would be recent papers. I suggest, as a rough guess, that the truth lies somewhere between—that we have here an indication that about half the bibliographic references in papers represent tight links with rather recent papers, the other half representing a uniform and less tight linkage to all that has been published before.

That this is so is demonstrated by the time distribution: much-cited papers are much more recent than less-cited ones. Thus, only 7 percent of the papers listed in Garfield's 1961 *Index* (2) as having been cited four or more times in 1961 were published before 1953, as compared with 21 percent of all papers cited in 1961. This tendency for the most-cited papers to be also the most recent may also be seen in Fig. 5 (based on Garfield's data), where the number of citations per paper is shown as a function of the age of the cited paper.

It has come to my attention that R. E. Burton and R. W. Kebler (7) have already conjectured, though on somewhat tenuous evidence, that the periodical literature may be composed of two dis-

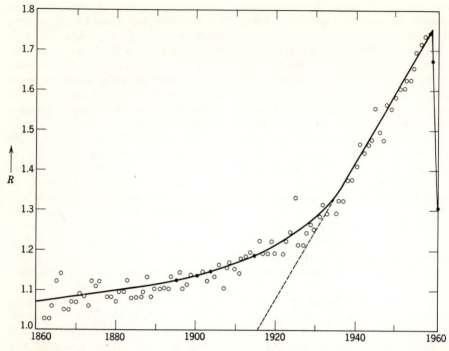

Fig. 5. Ratios of numbers' of 1961 citations to numbers of individual cited papers published in each of the years 1860 through 1960 [data are from Garfield's 1961 *Index* (2)]. This ratio gives a measure of the multiplicity of citation and shows that there is a sharp falloff in this multiplicity with time. One would expect the measure of multiplicity to be also a measure of the proportion of available papers actually cited. Thus, recent papers cited must constitute a much larger fraction of the total available population than old papers cited.

tinct types of literature with very different half-lives, the classic and the ephemeral parts. This conjecture is now confirmed by the present evidence. It is obviously desirable to explore further the other tentative finding of Burton and Kebler that the half-lives, and therefore the relative proportions of classic and ephemeral literature, vary considerably from field to field: mathematics, geology, and botany being strongly classic; chemical, mechanical, and metallurgical engineering and physics strongly ephemeral; and chemistry and physiology a much more even mixture.

Historical Examples

A striking confirmation of the proposed existence of this research front has been obtained from a series of his-

torical examples, for which we have been able to set up a matrix (Fig. 6). The dots represent references within a set of chronologically arranged papers which constitute the entire literature in a particular field (the field happens to be very tight and closed over the interval under discussion). In such a matrix there is high probability of citation in a strip near the diagonal and extending over the 30 or 40 papers immediately preceding each paper in turn. Over the rest of the triangular matrix there is much less chance of citation; this remaining part provides, therefore, a sort of background noise. Thus, in the special circumstance of being able to isolate a "tight" subject field, we find that half the references are to a research front of recent papers and that the other half are to papers scattered uniformly through the literature. It also appears that after every 30 or 40 papers there is need of a review paper to replace those earlier papers that have been lost from sight behind the research front. Curiously enough, it appears that classical papers, distinguished by full rows rather than columns, are all cited with about the same frequency, making a rather symmetrical pattern that may have some theoretical significance.

Two Bibliographic Needs

From these two different types of connections it appears that the citation network shows the existence of two different literature practices and of two different needs on the part of the scientist.

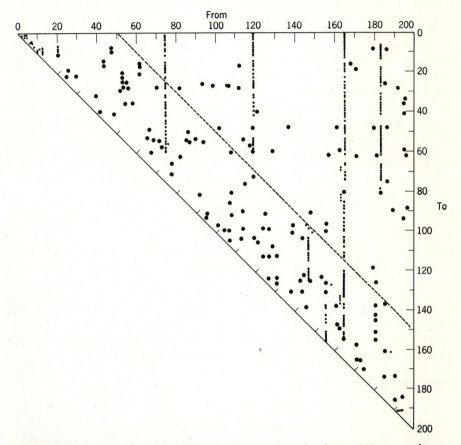

Fig. 6. Matrix showing the bibliographical references to each other in 200 papers that constitute the entire field from beginning to end of a peculiarly isolated subject group. The subject investigated was the spurious phenomenon of N-rays, about 1904. The papers are arranged chronologically, and each column of dots represents the references given in the paper of the indicated number rank in the series, these references being necessarily to previous papers in the series. The strong vertical lines therefore correspond to review papers. The dashed line indicates the boundary of a "research front" extending backward in the series about 50 papers behind the citing paper. With the exception of this research front and the review papers, little background noise is indicated in the figure. The tight linkage indicated by the high density of dots for the first dozen papers is typical of the beginning of a new field.

(1) The research front builds on recent work, and the network becomes very tight. To cope with this, the scientist (particularly, I presume, in physics and molecular biology) needs an alerting service that will keep him posted, probably by citation indexing, on the work of his peers and colleagues. (2) The random scattering of Fig. 6 corresponds to a drawing upon the totality of previous work. In a sense, this is the portion of the network that treats each published item as if it were truly part of the eternal record of human knowledge. In subject fields that have been dominated by this second attitude, the traditional procedure has been to systematize the added knowledge from time to time in book form, topic by topic, or to make use of a system of classification optimistically considered more or less eternal, as in taxonomy and chemistry. If such classification holds over reasonably long periods, one may have an objective means of reducing the world total of knowledge to fairly small parcels in which the items are found to be in one-to-one correspondence with some natural order.

It seems clear that in any classification into research-front subjects and taxonomic subjects there will remain a large body of literature which is not completely the one or the other. The present discussion suggests that most papers, through citations, are knit together rather tightly. The total research front of science has never, however, been a single row of knitting. It is, instead, divided by dropped stitches into quite small segments and strips. From a study of the citations of journals by journals I come to the conclusion that most of these strips correspond to the work of, at most, a few hundred men at any one time. Such strips represent objectively defined subjects whose description may vary materially from year to year but which remain otherwise an intellectual whole. If one would work out the nature of such strips, it might lead to a method for delineating the topography of current scientific literature. With such a topography established, one could perhaps indicate the overlap and relative importance of journals and, indeed, of countries, authors, or individual papers by the place they occupied within the map, and by their degree of strategic centralness within a given strip.

Journal citations provide the most readily available data for a test of such methods. From a preliminary and very rough analysis of these data I am tempted to conclude that a very large fraction of the alleged 35,000 journals now current must be reckoned as merely a distant background noise, and as very far from central or strategic in any of the knitted strips from which the cloth of science is woven.

REFERENCES AND NOTES

1. E. Garfield and I. H. Sher, "New factors in the evaluation of scientific literature through citation indexing," *Am. Doc.* 14, 191 (1963); ———, *Genetics Citation Index* (Institute for Scientific Information, Philadelphia, 1963). For many of the results discussed in this article I have used statistical information drawn from E. Garfield and I. H. Sher, *Science Citation Index* (Institute for Scientific Information, Philadelphia, 1963), pp. ix, xvii–xviii.

2. I wish to thank Dr. Eugene Garfield for making available to me several machine printouts of original data used in the preparation of the 1961 *Index* but not published in their entirety in the preamble to the index.

3. I am grateful to Dr. M. M. Kessler, Massachusetts Institute of Technology, for data for seven research reports of the following titles and dates: "An Experimental Study of Bibliographic Coupling between Technical Papers" (November

1961); "Bibliographic Coupling Between Scientific Papers" (July 1962); "Analysis of Bibliographic Sources in the *Physical Review* (vol. 77, 1950, to vol. 112, 1958) (July 1962); "Analysis of Bibliographic Sources in a Group of Physics-Related Journals" (August 1962); "Bibliographic Coupling Extended in Time: Ten Case Histories" (August 1962); "Concerning the Probability that a Given Paper will be Cited" (November 1962); "Comparison of the Results of Bibliographic Coupling and Analytic Subject Indexing" (January 1963).

4. J. W. Tukey, "Keeping research in contact with the literature: Citation indices and beyond," *J. Chem. Doc.* **2**, 34 (1962).

5. C. E. Osgood and L. V. Xhignesse, *Characteristics of Bibliographical Coverage in Psychological Journals Published in 1950 and 1960* (Institute of Communications Research, Univ. of Illinois, Urbana, 1963).

6. D. J. de Solla Price, *Little Science, Big Science* (Columbia Univ. Press, New York, 1963).

7. R. E. Burton and R. W. Kebler, "The 'half-life' of some scientific and technical literatures," *Am. Doc.* **11**, 18 (1960).

Parkinson's Law or the Rising Pyramid

by Cyril N. Parkinson

Work expands so as to fill the time available for its completion. General recognition of this fact is shown in the proverbial phrase "It is the busiest man who has time to spare." Thus, an elderly lady of leisure can spend the entire day in writing and dispatching a postcard to her niece at Bognor Regis. An hour will be spent in finding the postcard, another in hunting for spectacles, half an hour in a search for the address, an hour and a quarter in composition, and twenty minutes in deciding whether or not to take an umbrella when going to the mailbox in the next street. The total effort that would occupy a busy man for three minutes all told may in this fashion leave another person prostrate after a day of doubt, anxiety, and toil.

Granted that work (and especially paperwork) is thus elastic in its demands on time, it is manifest that there need be little or no relationship between the work to be done and the size of the staff to which it may be assigned. A lack of real activity does not, of necessity, result in leisure. A lack of occupation is not necessarily revealed by a manifest idleness. The thing to be done swells in importance and complexity in a direct ratio with the time to be spent. This fact is widely recognized, but less attention has been paid to its wider implications, more especially in the field of public administration. Politicians and taxpayers have assumed (with occasional phases of doubt) that a rising total in the number of civil servants must reflect a growing volume of work to be done.

Cynics, in questioning this belief, have imagined that the multiplication of officials must have left some of them idle or all of them able to work for shorter hours. But this is a matter in which faith and doubt seem equally misplaced. The fact is that the number of the officials and the quantity of the work are not related to each other at all. The rise in the total of those employed is governed by Parkinson's Law and would be much the same whether the volume of the work were to increase, diminish, or even disappear. The importance of Parkinson's Law lies in the fact that it is a law of growth based upon an analysis of the factors by which that growth is controlled.

The validity of this recently discovered law must rest mainly on statistical proofs, which will follow. Of more interest to the general reader is the explanation of the factors underlying the general tendency to which this law gives definition. Omitting technicalities (which are numerous) we may distinguish at the outset two motive forces. They can be represented for the present purpose by two almost axiomatic statements, thus: (1) "An official wants to multiply subordinates, not rivals" and (2) "Officials make work for each other."

To comprehend Factor 1, we must picture a civil servant, called A, who finds himself overworked. Whether this overwork is real or imaginary is immaterial, but we should observe, in passing, that A's sensation (or illusion) might easily result from his own decreasing

SOURCE: *Parkinson's Law*. Boston, Mass.: Houghton Mifflin Company, 1957, pp. 2–13.

energy: a normal symptom of middle age. For this real or imagined overwork there are, broadly speaking, three possible remedies. He may resign; he may ask to halve the work with a colleague called B; he may demand the assistance of two subordinates, to be called C and D. There is probably no instance in history, however, of A choosing any but the third alternative. By resignation he would lose his pension rights. By having B appointed, on his own level in the hierarchy, he would merely bring in a rival for promotion to W's vacancy when W (at long last) retires. So A would rather have C and D, junior men, below him. They will add to his consequence and, by dividing the work into two categories, as between C and D, he will have the merit of being the only man who comprehends them both. It is essential to realize at this point that C and D are, as it were, inseparable. To appoint C alone would have been impossible. Why? Because C, if by himself, would divide the work with A and so assume almost the equal status that has been refused in the first instance to B; a status the more emphasized if C is A's only possible successor. Subordinates must thus number two or more, each being thus kept in order by fear of the other's promotion. When C complains in turn of being overworked (as he certainly will) A will, with the concurrence of C, advise the appointment of two assistants to help C. But he can then avert internal friction only by advising the appointment of two more assistants to help D, whose position is much the same. With this recruitment of E, F, G, and H the promotion of A is now practically certain.

Seven officials are now doing what one did before. This is where Factor 2 comes into operation. For these seven make so much work for each other that all are fully occupied and A is actually working harder than ever. An incoming document may well come before each of them in turn. Official E decides that it falls within the province of F, who places a draft reply before C, who amends it drastically before consulting D, who asks G to deal with it. But G goes on leave at this point, handing the file over to H, who drafts a minute that is signed by D and returned to C, who revises his draft accordingly and lays the new version before A.

What does A do? He would have every excuse for signing the thing unread, for he has many other matters on his mind. Knowing now that he is to succeed W next year, he has to decide whether C or D should succeed to his own office. He had to agree to G's going on leave even if not yet strictly entitled to it. He is worried whether H should not have gone instead, for reasons of health. He has looked pale recently—partly but not solely because of his domestic troubles. Then there is the business of F's special increment of salary for the period of the conference and E's application for transfer to the Ministry of Pensions. A has heard that D is in love with a married typist and that G and F are no longer on speaking terms —no one seems to know why. So A might be tempted to sign C's draft and have done with it. But A is a conscientious man. Beset as he is with problems created by his colleagues for themselves and for him—created by the mere fact of these officials' existence—he is not the man to shirk his duty. He reads through the draft with care, deletes the fussy paragraphs added by C and H, and restores the thing back to the form preferred in the first instance by the able (if quarrelsome) F. He corrects the English—none of these young men can write grammatically—and finally produces the same reply he would have written if officials C to H had never been born. Far more people have taken far longer to produce the same result. No one has been idle. All have done their best. And it is late in the evening before A finally quits his office and begins the return journey to Ealing. The last of the office lights are being turned off in the gathering dusk that marks the end of another day's administrative toil. Among the last to leave, A reflects with bowed shoulders and a wry smile that late hours, like gray hairs, are among the penalties of success.

From this description of the factors at work the student of political science will recognize that administrators are more or less bound to multiply. Nothing has yet been said, however, about the period of time likely to elapse between the date of A's appointment and the date from which we can calculate the pensionable service of H. Vast masses of statistical evidence have been collected and it is from a study of this data that Parkinson's Law has been deduced. Space will not allow of detailed analysis but the reader will be interested to know that research began in the British Navy Estimates. These were chosen because the Admiralty's responsibilities are more easily measurable than those of, say, the Board of Trade. The question is merely one of numbers and tonnage. Here are some typical figures. The strength of the Navy in 1914 could be shown as 146,000 officers and men, 3249 dockyard officials and clerks, and 57,000 dockyard workmen. By 1928 there were only 100,000 officers and men and only 62,439 workmen, but the dockyard officials and clerks by then numbered 4558. As for warships, the strength in 1928 was a mere fraction of what it had been in 1914—fewer than 20 capital ships in commission as compared with 62. Over the same period

the Admiralty officials had increased in number from 2000 to 3569, providing (as was remarked) "a magnificent navy on land." These figures are more clearly set forth in tabular form (Table 1).

The criticism voiced at the time centered on the ratio between the numbers of those available for fighting and those available only for administration. But that comparison is not to the present purpose. What we have to note is that the 2000 officials of 1914 had become the 3569 of 1928; and that this growth was unrelated to any possible increase in their work. The Navy during that period had diminished, in point of fact, by a third in men and two-thirds in ships. Nor, from 1922 onward, was its strength even expected to increase; for its total of ships (unlike its total of officials) was limited by the Washington Naval Agreement of that year. Here we have then a 78 percent increase over a period of fourteen years; an average of 5.6 percent increase a year on the earlier total. In fact, as we shall see, the rate of increase was not as regular as that. All we have to consider, at this stage, is the percentage rise over a given period.

Can this rise in the total number of civil servants be accounted for except on the assumption that such a total must always rise by a law governing its growth? It might be urged at this point that the period under discussion was one of rapid development in naval technique. The use of the flying machine was no longer confined to the eccentric. Elec-

TABLE 1. Admiralty statistics

Year	Capital Ships in Commission	Officers and Men in R.N.	Dockyard Workers	Dockyard Officials and Clerks	Admiralty Officials
1914	62	146,000	57,000	3249	2000
1928	20	100,000	62,439	4558	3569
Increase or decrease	−67.74%	−31.5%	+9.54%	+40.28%	+78.45%

trical devices were being multiplied and elaborated. Submarines were tolerated if not approved. Engineer officers were beginning to be regarded as almost human. In so revolutionary an age we might expect that storekeepers would have more elaborate inventories to compile. We might not wonder to see more draughtsmen on the payroll, more designers, more technicians and scientists. But these, the dockyard officials, increased only by 40 per cent in number when the men of Whitehall increased their total by nearly 80 percent. For every new foreman or electrical engineer at Portsmouth there had to be two more clerks at Charing Cross. From this we might be tempted to conclude, provisionally, that the rate of increase in administrative staff is likely to be double that of the technical staff at a time when the actually useful strength (in this case, of seamen) is being reduced by 31.5 percent. It has been proved statistically, however, that this last percentage is irrelevant. The officials would have multiplied at the same rate had there been no actual seamen at all.

It would be interesting to follow the further progress by which the 8118 Admiralty staff of 1935 came to number 33,788 by 1954. But the staff of the Colonial Office affords a better field of study during a period of imperial decline. Admiralty statistics are complicated by factors (like the Fleet Air Arm) that make comparison difficult as between one year and the next. The Colonial Office growth is more significant in that it is more purely administrative. Here the relevant statistics are as follows:

1935	1939	1943	1947	1954
372	450	817	1139	1661

Before showing what the rate of increase is, we must observe that the ex-

tent of this department's responsibilities was far from constant during these twenty years. The colonial territories were not much altered in area or population between 1935 and 1939. They were considerably diminished by 1943, certain areas being in enemy hands. They were increased again in 1947, but have since then shrunk steadily from year to year as successive colonies achieve self-government. It would be rational to suppose that these changes in the scope of Empire would be reflected in the size of its central administration. But a glance at the figures is enough to convince us that the staff totals represent nothing but so many stages in an inevitable increase. And this increase, although related to that observed in other departments, has nothing to do with the size—or even the existence—of the Empire. What are the percentages of increase? We must ignore, for this purpose, the rapid increase in staff which accompanied the diminution of responsibility during World War II. We should note rather, the peacetime rates of increase; over 5.24 percent between 1935 and 1939, and 6.55 percent between 1947 and 1954. This gives an average increase of 5.89 percent each year, a percentage markedly similar to that already found in the Admiralty staff increase between 1914 and 1928.

Further and detailed statistical analysis of departmental staffs would be inappropriate in such a work as this. It is hoped, however, to reach a tentative conclusion regarding the time likely to elapse between a given official's first appointment and the later appointment of his two or more assistants.

Dealing with the problem of pure staff accumulation, all our researches so far completed point to an average increase of 5.75 percent per year. This fact established, it now becomes possible to state Parkinson's Law in mathematical form: In any public administrative department not actually at war, the staff increase may be expected to follow this formula:

$$x = \frac{2k^m + l}{n}$$

k is the number of staff seeking promotion through the appointment of subordinates; l represents the difference between the ages of appointment and retirement; m is the number of man-hours devoted to answering minutes within the department; and n is the number of effective units being administered. x will be the number of new staff required each year. Mathematicians will realize, of course, that to find the percentage increase they must multiply x by 100 and divide by the total of the previous year, thus:

$$\frac{100 (2k^m + l)}{yn} \%$$

where y represents the total original staff. This figure will invariably prove to be between 5.17 percent and 6.56 percent, irrespective of any variation in the amount of work (if any) to be done.

The discovery of this formula, and of the general principles upon which it is based has, of course, no political value. No attempt has been made to inquire whether departments *ought* to grow in size. Those who hold that this growth is essential to gain full employment are fully entitled to their opinion. Those who doubt the stability of an economy based upon reading each other's minutes are equally entitled to theirs. It would probably be premature to attempt at this stage any inquiry into the quantitative ratio that should exist between the administrators and the administered. Granted, however, that a maximum ratio exists, it should soon be possible to ascertain by formula how many years will elapse before that ratio, in any given community, will be reached. The forecasting of such a result will again have no political value. Nor can it be sufficiently emphasized that Parkinson's Law is a purely scientific discovery, inapplicable except in theory to the politics of the day. It is not the business of the botanist to eradicate the weeds. Enough for him if he can tell us just how fast they grow.

Logical Foundations of the Unity of Science

by Rudolf Carnap

What Is Logical Analysis of Science?

The task of analyzing science may be approached from various angles. The analysis of the subject matter of the sciences is carried out by science itself. Biology, for example, analyzes organisms and processes in organisms, and in a similar way every branch of science analyzes its subject matter. Mostly, however, by "analysis of science" or "theory of science" is meant an investigation which differs from the branch of science to which it is applied. We may, for instance, think of an investigation of scientific *activity*. We may study the historical development of this activity. Or we may try to find out in which way scientific work depends upon the individual conditions of the men working in science, and upon the status of the society surrounding them. Or we may describe procedures and appliances used in scientific work. These investigations of scientific activity may be called history, psychology, sociology, and methodology of science. The subject matter of such studies is science as a body of actions carried out by certain persons under certain circumstances. Theory of science in this sense will be dealt with at various other places in this *Encyclopedia;* it is certainly an essential part of the foundation of science.

We come to a theory of science in another sense if we study not the actions of scientists but their results, namely, science as a body of ordered knowledge. Here, by "results" we do not mean beliefs, images, etc., and the behavior influenced by them. That would lead us again to psychology of science. We mean by "results" certain linguistic expressions, viz., the statements asserted by scientists. The task of the theory of science in this sense will be to analyze such statements, study their kinds and relations, and analyze terms as components of those statements and theories as ordered systems of those statements. A statement is a kind of sequence of spoken sounds, written marks, or the like, produced by human beings for specific purposes. But it is possible to abstract in an analysis of the statements of science from the persons asserting the statements and from the psychological and sociological conditions of such assertions. The analysis of the linguistic expressions of science under such an abstraction is *logic of science.*

Within the logic of science we may distinguish between two chief parts. The investigation may be restricted to the forms of the linguistic expressions involved i.e., to the way in which they are constructed out of elementary parts (e.g., words) without referring to anything outside of language. Or the investigation goes beyond this boundary and studies linguistic expressions in their relation to objects outside of language. A study restricted in the first-mentioned way is called *formal;* the field of such formal studies is called formal logic or *logical syntax.* Such a formal or syntactical analysis of the language of science as a whole or in its various branches

SOURCE: *International Encyclopedia of Unified Science*, 1, No. 1, July 1938, pp 42–62.

will lead to results of the following kinds. A certain term (e.g., a word) is defined within a certain theory on the basis of certain other terms, or it is definable in such a way. A certain term, although not definable by certain other terms, is reducible to them (in a sense to be explained later). A certain statement is a logical consequence of (or logically deducible from) certain other statements; and a deduction of it, given within a certain theory, is, or is not, logically correct. A certain statement is incompatible with certain other statements, i.e., its negation is a logical consequence of them. A certain statement is independent of certain other statements, i.e., neither a logical consequence of them nor incompatible with them. A certain theory is inconsistent, i.e., some of its statements are incompatible with the other ones. The last sections of this essay will deal with the question of the unity of science from the logical point of view, studying the logical relations between the terms of the chief branches of science and between the laws stated in these branches; thus it will give an example of a syntactical analysis of the language of science.

In the second part of the logic of science, a given language and the expressions in it are analyzed in another way. Here also, as in logical syntax, abstraction is made from the psychological and sociological side of the language. This investigation, however, is not restricted to formal analysis but takes into consideration one important relation between linguistic expressions and other objects—that of designation. An investigation of this kind is called *semantics*. Results of a semantical analysis of the language of science may, for instance, have the following forms. A certain term designates a certain particular object (e.g., the sun), or a certain property of things (e.g., iron), or a certain relation between things (e.g., fathership), or a certain physical function (e.g., temperature); two terms in

different branches of science (e.g., "homo sapiens" in biology and "person" in economics, or, in another way, "man" in both cases) designate (or do not designate) the same. What is designated by a certain expression may be called its *designatum*. Two expressions designating the same are called *synonymous*. The term "true," as it is used in science and in everyday life, can also be defined within semantics. We see that the chief subject matter of a semantical analysis of the language of science are such properties and relations of expressions, and especially of statements, as are based on the relation of designation. (Where we say "the designatum of an expression," the customary phrase is "the meaning of an expression." It seems, however, preferable to avoid the word "meaning" wherever possible because of its ambiguity, i.e., the multiplicity of its designata. Above all, it is important to distinguish between the semantical and the psychological use of the word "meaning.")

It is a question of terminological convention whether to use the term "logic" in the wider sense, including the semantical analysis of the designata of expressions, or in the narrower sense of logical syntax, restricted to formal analysis, abstracting from designation. And accordingly we may distinguish between logic of science in the narrower sense, as the syntax of the language of science, and logic of science in the wider sense, comprehending both syntax and semantics.

The Main Branches of Science

We use the word "science" here in its widest sense, including all theoretical knowledge, no matter whether in the field of natural sciences or in the field of the social sciences and the so-called humanities, and no matter whether it is knowledge found by the application of special scientific procedures, or knowledge based on common sense in everyday life. In the same way the term "language of science" is meant here to refer to the language which contains all statements (i.e., theoretical sentences as distinguished from emotional expressions, commands, lyrics, etc.) used for scientific purposes or in everyday life. What usually is called science is merely a more systematic continuation of those activities which we carry out in everyday life in order to know something.

The first distinction which we have to make is that between *formal science* and *empirical science*. Formal science consists of the analytic statements established by logic and mathematics; empirical science consists of the synthetic statements established in the different fields of factual knowledge. The relation of formal to empirical science will be dealt with at another place; here we have to do with empirical science, its language, and the problem of its unity.

Let us take "physics" as a common name for the nonbiological field of science, comprehending both systematic and historical investigations within this field, thus including chemistry, mineralogy, astronomy, geology (which is historical), meteorology, etc. How, then, are we to draw the boundary line between physics and biology? It is obvious that the distinction between these two branches has to be based on the distinction between two kinds of things which we find in nature: organisms and nonorganisms. Let us take this latter distinction as granted; it is the task of biologists to lay down a suitable definition for the term "organism," in other words, to tell us the features of a thing which we take as characteristic for its being an organism. How, then, are we to define "biology" on the basis of "organism"? We could perhaps think of trying to do it in this way: biology is the branch of science which investigates organisms and the processes occurring in organisms, and physics is the study of nonorganisms. But these definitions would not draw the distinction as it is

usually intended. A law stated in physics is intended to be valid universally, without any restriction. For example, the law stating the electrostatic force as a function of electric charges and their distance, or the law determining the pressure of a gas as a function of temperature, or the law determining the angle of refraction as a function of the coefficients of refraction of the two media involved, are intended to apply to the processes in organisms no less than to those in inorganic nature. The biologist has to know these laws of physics in studying the processes in organisms. He needs them for the explanation of these processes. But since they do not suffice, he adds some other laws, not known by the physicist, viz., the specifically biological laws. Biology presupposes physics, but not vice versa.

These reflections lead us to the following definitions. Let us call those terms which we need—in addition to logico-mathematical terms—for the description of processes in inorganic nature *physical terms*, no matter whether, in a given instance, they are applied to such processes or to processes in organisms. That sublanguage of the language of science, which contains—besides logico-mathematical terms—all and only physical terms, may be called *physical language*. The system of those statements which are formulated in the physical language and are acknowledged by a certain group at a certain time is called the physics of that group at that time. Such of these statements as have a specific universal form are called *physical laws*. The physical laws are needed for the explanation of processes in inorganic nature; but, as mentioned before, they apply to processes in organisms also.

The whole of the rest of science may be called *biology (in the wider sense)*. It seems desirable, at least for practical purposes, e.g., for the division of labor in research work, to subdivide this wide field. But it seems questionable whether any distinctions can be found here which, although not of a fundamental nature, are at least clear to about the same degree as the distinction between physics and biology. At present, it is scarcely possible to predict which subdivisions will be made in the future. The traditional distinction between bodily (or material) and mental (or psychical) processes had its origin in the old magical and later metaphysical mind-body dualism. The distinction as a practical device for the classification of branches of science still plays an important role, even for those scientists who reject that metaphysical dualism; and it will probably continue to do so for some time in the future. But when the after-effect of such prescientific issues upon science becomes weaker and weaker, it may be that new boundary lines for subdivisions will turn out to be more satisfactory.

One possibility of dividing biology in the wider sense into two fields is such that the first corresponds roughly to what is usually called biology, and the second comprehends among other parts those which usually are called psychology and social science. The second field deals with the behavior of individual organisms and groups of organisms within their environment, with the dispositions to such behavior, with such features of processes in organisms as are relevant to the behavior, and with certain features of the environment which are characteristic of and relevant to the behavior, e.g., objects observed and work done by organisms.

The first of the two fields of biology in the wider sense may be called biology in the narrower sense, or, for the following discussions, simply *biology*. This use of the term "biology" seems justified by the fact that, in terms of the customary classification, this part contains most of what is usually called biology, namely, general biology, botany, and the greater part of zoölogy. The terms which are used in this field in addition to logico-mathematical and

physical terms may be called biological terms in the narrower sense, or simply *biological terms.* Since many statements of biology contain physical terms besides biological ones, the *biological language* cannot be restricted to biological terms; it contains the physical language as a sublanguage and, in addition, the biological terms. Statements and laws belonging to this language but not to physical language will be called *biological statements* and *biological laws.*

The distinction between the two fields of biology in the wider sense has been indicated only in a very vague way. At the present time it is not yet clear as to how the boundary line may best be drawn. Which processes in an organism are to be assigned to the second field? Perhaps the connection of a process with the processes in the nervous system might be taken as characteristic, or, to restrict it more, the connection with speaking activities or, more generally, with activities involving signs. Another way of characterization might come from the other direction, from outside, namely, selecting the processes in an organism from the point of view of their relevance to achievements in the environment (see Brunswik and Ness). There is no name in common use for this second field. (The term "mental sciences" suggests too narrow a field and is connected too closely with the metaphysical dualism mentioned before.) The term "behavioristics" has been proposed. If it is used, it must be made clear that the word "behavior" has here a greater extension than it had with the earlier behaviorists. Here it is intended to designate not only the overt behavior which can be observed from outside but also internal behavior (i.e., processes within the organism); further, dispositions to behavior which may not be manifest in a special case; and, finally, certain effects upon the environment. Within this second field we may distinguish roughly between two parts dealing with individual organisms and with groups of organisms. But it seems doubtful whether any sharp line can be drawn between these two parts. Compared with the customary classification of science, the first part would include chiefly psychology, but also some parts of physiology and the humanities. The second part would chiefly include social science and, further, the greater part of the humanities and history, but it has not only to deal with groups of human beings but also to deal with groups of other organisms. For the following discussion, the terms "psychology" and "social science" will be used as names of the two parts because of lack of better terms. It is clear that both the question of boundary lines and the question of suitable terms for the sections is still in need of much more discussion.

Reducibility

The question of the unity of science is meant here as a problem of the logic of science, not of ontology. We do not ask: "Is the world one?" "Are all events fundamentally of one kind?" "Are the so-called mental processes really physical processes or not?" "Are the so-called physical processes really spiritual or not?" It seems doubtful whether we can find any theoretical content in such philosophical questions as discussed by monism, dualism, and pluralism. In any case, when we ask whether there is a unity in science, we mean this as a question of logic, concerning the logical relationships between the terms and the laws of the various branches of science. Since it belongs to the logic of science, the question concerns scientists and logicians alike.

Let us first deal with the question of terms. (Instead of the word "term" the word "concept" could be taken, which is more frequently used by logicians. But the word "term" is more clear, since it shows that we mean signs, e.g., words, expressions consisting of words, artificial symbols, etc., of course with the meaning they have in the language in question. We do not mean "concept" in its psychological sense, i.e., images or thoughts somehow connected with a word; that would not belong to logic.) We know the meaning (designatum) of a term if we know under what conditions we are permitted to apply it in a concrete case and under what conditions not. Such a knowledge of the conditions of application can be of two different kinds. In some cases we may have a merely practical knowledge, i.e., we are able to use the term in question correctly without giving a theoretical account of the rules for its use. In other cases we may be able to give an explicit formulation of the conditions for the application of the term. If now a certain term x is such that the conditions for its application (as used in the language of science) can be formulated with the help of the terms y, z, etc., we call such a formulation a *reduction statement* for x in terms of y, z, etc., and we call x *reducible* to y, z, etc. There may be several sets of conditions for the application of x; hence x may be reducible to y, z, etc., and also to u, v, etc., and perhaps to other sets. There may even be cases of mutual reducibility, e.g., each term of the set x_1, x_2, etc., is reducible to y_1, y_2, etc.; and, on the other hand, each term of the set y_1, y_2, etc., is reducible to x_1, x_2, etc.

A *definition* is the simplest form of a reduction statement. For the formulation of examples, let us use "$\equiv$" (called the symbol of equivalence) as abbreviation for "if and only if." Example of a definition for "ox": "x is an ox $\equiv$ x is a quadruped and horned and cloven-footed and ruminant, etc." This is also a reduction statement because it states the conditions for the application of the term "ox," saying that this term can be applied to a thing if and only if that thing is a quadruped and horned, etc. By that definition the term "ox" is shown to be reducible to—moreover definable by— the set of terms "quadruped," "horned," etc.

A reduction statement sometimes cannot be formulated in the simple form of a definition, i.e., of an equivalence statement, ". . . ≡ . . . ," but only in the somewhat more complex form "If . . . , then: . . . ≡ . . ." Thus a reduction statement is either a simple (i.e., explicit) definition or, so to speak, a conditional definition. (The term "reduction statement" is generally used in the narrower sense, referring to the second, conditional form.) For instance, the following statement is a reduction statement for the term "electric charge" (taken here for the sake of simplicity as a nonquantitative term), i.e., for the statement form "the body x has an electric charge at the time t": "If a light body y is placed near x at t, then x has an electric charge at $t \equiv y$ is attracted by x at t." A general way of procedure which enables us to find out whether or not a certain term can be applied in concrete cases may be called a *method of determination* for the term in question. The method of determination for a quantitative term (e.g., "temperature") is the method of measurement for that term. Whenever we know an experimental method of determination for a term, we are in a position to formulate a reduction statement for it. To know an experimental method of determination for a term, say "Q_3," means to know two things. First, we must know an experimental situation which we have to create, say the state Q_1, e.g., the arrangement of measuring apparatuses and of suitable conditions for their use. Second, we must know the possible experimental result, say Q_2, which, if it occurs, will confirm the presence of the property Q_3. In the simplest case—let us leave aside the more complex cases—Q_2 is also such that its nonoccurrence shows that the thing in question does not have the property Q_3. Then a reduction statement for "Q_3," i.e., for the statement form "the thing (or space-time-point) x is Q_3 (i.e., has the property Q_3) at the time t," can be formu-

lated in this way: "If x is Q_1 (i.e., x and the surroundings of x are in the state Q_1) at time t, then x is Q_3 at $t \equiv x$ is Q_2 at t." On the basis of this reduction statement, the term "Q_3" is reducible to "Q_1," "Q_2," and spatio-temporal terms. Whenever a term "Q_3" expresses the disposition of a thing to behave in a certain way (Q_2) to certain conditions (Q_1), we have a reduction statement of the form given above. If there is a connection of such a kind between Q_1, Q_2, and Q_3, then in biology and psychology in certain cases the following terminology is applied: "To the stimulus Q_1 we find the reaction Q_2 as a symptom for Q_3." But the situation is not essentially different from the analogous one in physics, where we usually do not apply that terminology.

Sometimes we know several methods of determination for a certain term. For example, we can determine the presence of an electric current by observing either the heat produced in the conductor, or the deviation of a magnetic needle, or the quantity of a substance separated from an electrolyte, etc. Thus the term "electric current" is reducible to each of many sets of other terms. Since not only can an electric current be measured by measuring a temperature but also, conversely, a temperature can be measured by measuring the electric current produced by a thermo-electric element, there is mutual reducibility between the terms of the theory of electricity, on the one hand, and those of the theory of heat, on the other. The same holds for the terms of the theory of electricity and those of the theory of magnetism.

Let us suppose that the persons of a certain group have a certain set of terms in common, either on account of a merely practical agreement about the conditions of their application or with an explicit stipulation of such conditions for a part of the terms. Then a reduction statement reducing a new term to the terms of that original set may be used as a way of introducing the new term into the language of the group. This way of introduction assures conformity as to the use of the new term. If a certain language (e.g., a sublanguage of the language of science, covering a certain branch of science) is such that every term of it is reducible to a certain set of terms, then this language can be constructed on the basis of that set by introducing one new term after the other by reduction statements. In this case we call the basic set of terms a *sufficient reduction basis* for that language.

The Unity of the Language of Science

Now we will analyze the logical relations among the terms of different parts of the language of science with respect to reducibility. We have indicated a division of the whole language of science into some parts. Now we may make another division cutting across the first, by distinguishing in a rough way, without any claims to exactness, between those terms which we use on a prescientific level in our everyday language, and for whose application no scientific procedure is necessary, and scientific terms in the narrower sense. That sublanguage which is the common part of this prescientific language and the physical language may be called physical thing-language or briefly *thing-language*. It is this language that we use in speaking about the properties of the observable (inorganic) things surrounding us. Terms like "hot" and "cold" may be regarded as belonging to the thing-language, but not "temperature" because its determination requires the application of a technical instrument; further, "heavy" and "light" (but not "weight"); "red," "blue," etc.; "large," "small," "thick," "thin," etc.

The terms so far mentioned designate what we may call observable properties, i.e., such as can be determined by a direct observation. We will call them *observable thing-predicates*. Besides such

terms the thing-language contains other ones, e.g., those expressing the disposition of a thing to a certain behavior under certain conditions, e.g., "elastic," "soluble," "flexible," "transparent," "fragile," "plastic," etc. These terms—they might be called *disposition-predicates*—are reducible to observable thing-predicates because we can describe the experimental conditions and the reactions characteristic of such disposition-predicates in terms of observable thing-predicates. Example of a reduction statement for "elastic": "If the body x is stretched and then released at the time t, then x is elastic at the time $t = x$ contracts at t," where the terms "stretched," "released," and "contracting" can be defined by observable thing-predicates. If these predicates are taken as a basis, we can moreover introduce, by iterated application of definition and (conditional) reduction, every other term of the *thing-language*, e.g., designations of substances, e.g., "stone," "water," "sugar," or of processes, e.g., "rain," "fire," etc. For every term of that language is such that we can apply it either on the basis of direct observation or with the help of an experiment for which we know the conditions and the possible result determining the application of the term in question.

Now we can easily see that every term of the *physical language* is reducible to those of the thing-language and hence finally to observable thing-predicates. On the scientific level, we have the quantitative coefficient of elasticity instead of the qualitative term "elastic" of the thing-language; we have the quantitative term "temperature" instead of the qualitative ones "hot" and "cold"; and we have all the terms by means of which physicists describe the temporary or permanent states of things or processes. For any such term the physicist knows at least one method of determination. Physicists would not admit into their language any term for which no method of determination by observations were given. The formulation of such a method, i.e., the description of the experimental arrangement to be carried out and of the possible result determining the application of the term in question, is a reduction statement for that term. Sometimes the term will not be directly reduced by the reduction statement to thing-predicates, but first to other scientific terms, and these by their reduction statements again to other scientific terms, etc.; but such a reduction chain must in any case finally lead to predicates of the thing-language and, moreover, to observable thing-predicates because otherwise there would be no way of determining whether or not the physical term in question can be applied in special cases, on the basis of given observation statements.

If we come to *biology* (this term now always understood in the narrower sense), we find again the same situation. For any biological term the biologist who introduces or uses it must know empirical criteria for its application. This applies, of course, only to biological terms in the sense explained before, including all terms used in scientific biology proper, but not to certain terms used sometimes in the philosophy of biology—"a whole," "entelechy," etc. It may happen that for the description of the criterion, i.e., the method of determination of a term, other biological terms are needed. In this case the term in question is first reducible to them. But at least indirectly it must be reducible to terms of the thing-language and finally to observable thing-predicates, because the determination of the term in question in a concrete case must finally be based upon observations of concrete things, i.e., upon observation statements formulated in the thing-language.

Let us take as an example the term "muscle." Certainly biologists know the conditions for a part of an organism to be a muscle; otherwise the term could not be used in concrete cases. The prob-

lem is: Which other terms are needed for the formulation of those conditions? It will be necessary to describe the functions within the organism which are characteristic of muscles, in other words, to formulate certain laws connecting the processes in muscles with those in their environment, or, again in still other words, to describe the reactions to certain stimuli characteristic of muscles. Both the processes in the environment and those in the muscle (in the customary terminology: stimuli and reactions) must be described in such a way that we can determine them by observations. Hence the term "muscle," although not definable in terms of the thing-language, is reducible to them. Similar considerations easily show the reducibility of any other biological term—whether it be a designation of a kind of organism, or of a kind of part of organisms, or of a kind of process in organisms.

The result found so far may be formulated in this way: The terms of the thing-language, and even the narrower class of the observable thing-predicates, supply a sufficient basis for the languages both of physics and of biology. (There are, by the way, many reduction bases for these languages, each of which is much more restricted than the classes mentioned.) Now the question may be raised whether a basis of the kind mentioned is sufficient even for the whole language of science. The affirmative answer to this question is sometimes called *physicalism* (because it was first formulated not with respect to the thing-language but to the wider physical language as a sufficient basis). If the thesis of physicalism is applied to biology only, it scarcely meets any serious objections. The situation is somewhat changed, however, when it is applied to psychology and social science (individual and social behavioristics). Since many of the objections raised against it are based on misinterpretations, it is necessary to make clear what the thesis is intended to assert and what not.

The question of the reducibility of the terms of psychology to those of the biological language and thereby to those of the thing-language is closely connected with the problem of the various methods used in psychology. As chief examples of methods used in this field in its present state, the physiological, the behavioristic, and the introspective methods may be considered. The *physiological approach* consists in an investigation of the functions of certain organs in the organism, above all, of the nervous system. Here, the terms used are either those of biology or those so closely related to them that there will scarcely be any doubt with respect to their reducibility to the terms of the biological language and the thing-language. For the *behavioristic approach* different ways are possible. The investigation may be restricted to the external behavior of an organism, i.e., to such movements, sounds, etc., as can be observed by other organisms in the neighborhood of the first. Or processes within the organism may also be taken into account so that this approach overlaps with the physiological one. Or, finally, objects in the environment of the organism, either observed or worked on or produced by it, may also be studied. Now it is easy to see that a term for whose determination a behavioristic method—of one of the kinds mentioned or of a related kind—is known, is reducible to the terms of the biological language, including the thing-language. As we have seen before, the formulation of the method of determination for a term is a reduction statement for that term, either in the form of a simple definition or in the conditional form. By that statement the term is shown to be reducible to the terms applied in describing the method, namely, the experimental arrangement and the characteristic result. Now, conditions and results consist in the behavioristic method either of physiological processes in the organism or of observable processes in the organism and in its environment. Hence they can be described in terms of the biological language. If we have to do with a behavioristic approach in its pure form, i.e., leaving aside physiological investigations, then the description of the conditions and results characteristic for a term can in most cases be given directly in terms of the thing-language. Hence the behavioristic reduction of psychological terms is often simpler than the physiological reduction of the same term.

Let us take as an example the term "angry." If for anger we knew a sufficient and necessary criterion to be found by a physiological analysis of the nervous system or other organs, then we could define "angry" in terms of the biological language. The same holds if we knew such a criterion to be determined by the observation of the overt, external behavior. But a physiological criterion is not yet known. And the peripheral symptoms known are presumably not necessary criteria because it might be that a person of strong self-control is able to suppress these symptoms. If this is the case, the term "angry" is, at least at the present time, not definable in terms of the biological language. But, nevertheless, it is reducible to such terms. It is sufficient for the formulation of a reduction sentence to know a behavioristic procedure which enables us —if not always, at least under suitable circumstances—to determine whether the organism in question is angry or not. And we know indeed such procedures; otherwise we should never be able to apply the term "angry" to another person on the basis of our observations of his behavior, as we constantly do in everyday life and in scientific investigation. A reduction of the term "angry" or similar terms by the formulation of such procedures is indeed less useful than a definition would be, because a definition supplies a complete (i.e., unconditional) criterion for the term in question, while a reduction statement of the conditional form gives only an incomplete one. But a criterion, conditional or not, is all we need for ascertaining reducibility. Thus the result is the following: If for any psychological term we know either a physiological or a behavioristic method of determination, then that term is reducible to those terms of the thing-language.

In psychology, as we find it today, there is, besides the physiological and the behavioristic approach, the so-called *introspective method*. The questions as to its validity, limits, and necessity are still more unclear and in need of further discussion than the analogous questions with respect to the two other methods. Much of what has been said about it, especially by philosophers, may be looked at with some suspicion. But the facts themselves to which the term "introspection" is meant to refer will scarcely be denied by anybody, e.g., the fact that a person sometimes knows that he is angry without applying any of those procedures which another person would have to apply, i.e., without looking with the help of a physiological instrument at his nervous system or looking at the play of his facial muscles. The problems of the practical reliability and theoretical validity of the introspective method may here be left aside. For the discussion of reducibility an answer to these problems is not needed. It will suffice to show that in every case, no matter whether the introspective method is applicable or not, the behavioristic method can be applied at any rate. But we must be careful in the interpretation of this assertion. It is not meant as saying: 'Every psychological process can be ascertained by the behavioristic method.' Here we have to do not with the single processes themselves (e.g., Peter's anger yesterday morning) but with kinds of processes (e.g., anger). If Robinson Crusoe is angry and then dies before anybody comes to his island, nobody except himself ever knows of this single occurrence of anger. But

anger of the same kind, occurring with other persons, may be studied and ascertained by a behavioristic method, if circumstances are favorable. (Analogy: if an electrically charged raindrop falls into the ocean without an observer or suitable recording instrument in the neighborhood, nobody will ever know of that charge. But a charge of the same kind can be found out under suitable circumstances by certain observations.) Further, in order to come to a correct formulation of the thesis, we have to apply it not to the kinds of processes (e.g., anger) but rather to the terms designating such kinds of processes (e.g., "anger"). The difference might seem trivial but is, in fact, essential. We do not at all enter a discussion about the question whether or not there are kinds of events which can never have any behavioristic symptoms, and hence are knowable only by introspection. We have to do with psychological terms not with kinds of events. For any such term, say, "Q," the psychological language contains a statement form applying that term, e.g., "The person . . . is at the time . . . in the state Q." Then the utterance by speaking or writing of the statement "I am now (or I was yesterday) in the state Q," is (under suitable circumstances, e.g., as to reliability, etc.) an observable symptom for the state Q. Hence there cannot be a term in the psychological language, taken as an intersubjective language for mutual communication, which designates a kind of state or event without any behavioristic symptom. Therefore, there is a behavioristic method of determination for any term of the psychological language. Hence every such term is reducible to those of the thing-language.

The logical nature of the psychological terms becomes clear by an analogy with those physical terms which are introduced by reduction statements of the conditional form. Terms of both kinds designate a state characterized by the disposition to certain reactions. In both cases the state is not the same as those reactions. Anger is not the same as the movements by which an angry organism reacts to the conditions in his environment, just as the state of being electrically charged is not the same as the process of attracting other bodies. In both cases that state sometimes occurs without these events which are observable from outside; they are consequences of the state according to certain laws and may therefore under suitable circumstances be taken as symptoms for it; but they are not identical with it.

The last field to be dealt with is *social science* (in the wide sense indicated before; also called social behavioristics). Here we need no detailed analysis because it is easy to see that every term of this field is reducible to terms of the other fields. The result of any investigation of a group of men or other organisms can be described in terms of the members, their relations to one another and to their environment. Therefore, the conditions for the application of any term can be formulated in terms of psychology, biology, and physics, including the thing-language. Many terms can even be defined on that basis, and the rest is certainly reducible to it.

It is true that some terms which are used in psychology are such that they designate a certain behavior (or disposition to behavior) within a group of a certain kind or a certain attitude toward a group, e.g., "desirous of ruling," "shy," and others. It may be that for the definition or reduction of a term of this kind some terms of social science describing the group involved are needed. This shows that there is not a clear-cut line between psychology and social science and that in some cases it is not clear whether a term is better assigned to one or to the other field. But such terms are also certainly reducible to those of the thing-language because every term referring to a group of organisms is reducible to terms referring to individual organisms.

The result of our analysis is that the class of observable thing-predicates is a sufficient reduction basis for the whole of the language of science, including the cognitive part of the everyday language.

The Problem of the Unity of Laws

The relations between the terms of the various branches of science have been considered. There remains the task of analyzing the relations between the laws. According to our previous consideration, a biological law contains only terms which are reducible to physical terms. Hence there is a common language to which both the biological and the physical laws belong so that they can be logically compared and connected. We can ask whether or not a certain biological law is compatible with the system of physical laws, and whether or not it is derivable from them. But the answer to these questions cannot be inferred from the reducibility of the terms. At the present state of the development of science, it is certainly not possible to derive the biological laws from the physical ones. Some philosophers believe that such a derivation is forever impossible because of the very nature of the two fields. But the proofs attempted so far for this thesis are certainly insufficient. This question is, it seems, the scientific kernel of the problem of vitalism; some recent discussions of this problem are, however, entangled with rather questionable metaphysical issues. The question of derivability itself is, of course, a very serious scientific problem. But it will scarcely be possible to find a solution for it before many more results of experimental investigation are available than we have today. In the meantime the efforts toward derivation of more and more biological laws from physical laws—in the customary formulation: explanation of more and more processes in organisms with the help of physics and chemistry—will be, as it has been, a very fruitful tendency in biological research.

As we have seen before, the fields of

psychology and social science are very closely connected with each other. A clear division of the laws of these fields is perhaps still less possible than a division of the terms. If the laws are classified in some way or other, it will be seen that sometimes a psychological law is derivable from those of social science, and sometimes a law of social science from those of psychology. (An example of the first kind is the explanation of the behavior of adults—e.g., in the theories of A. Adler and Freud—by their position within the family or a larger group during childhood; an example of the second kind is the obvious explanation of an increase of the price of a commodity by the reactions of buyers and sellers in the case of a diminished supply.) It is obvious that, at the present time, laws of psychology and social science cannot be derived from those of biology and physics. On the other hand, no scientific reason is known for the assumption that such a derivation should be in principle and forever impossible.

Thus there is at present *no unity of laws*. The construction of one homogeneous system of laws for the whole of science is an aim for the future development of science. This aim cannot be shown to be unattainable. But we do not, of course, know whether it will ever be reached.

On the other hand, there is a *unity of language* in science, viz., a common reduction basis for the terms of all branches of science, this basis consisting of a very narrow and homogeneous class of terms of the physical thing-language. This unity of terms is indeed less far-reaching and effective than the unity of laws would be, but it is a necessary preliminary condition for the unity of laws. We can endeavor to develop science

more and more in the direction of a unified system of laws only because we have already at present a unified language. And, in addition, the fact that we have this unity of language is of the greatest practical importance. The practical use of laws consists in making predictions with their help. The important fact is that very often a prediction cannot be based on our knowledge of only one branch of science. For instance, the construction of automobiles will be influenced by a prediction of the presumable number of sales. This number depends upon the satisfaction of the buyers and the economic situation. Hence we have to combine knowledge about the function of the motor, the effect of gases and vibration on the human organism, the ability of persons to learn a certain technique, their willingness to spend so much money for so much service, the development of the general economic situation, etc. This knowledge concerns particular facts and general laws belonging to all the four branches, partly scientific and partly common-sense knowledge. For very many decisions, both in individual and in social life, we need such a prediction based upon a combined knowledge of concrete facts and general laws belonging to different branches of science. If now the terms of different branches had no logical connection between one another, such as is supplied by the homogeneous reduction basis, but were of fundamentally different character, as some philosophers believe, then it would not be possible to connect singular statements and laws of different fields in such a way as to derive predictions from them. Therefore, the unity of the language of science is the basis for the practical application of theoretical knowledge.

SELECTED BIBLIOGRAPHY

Logical Analysis

Carnap, R. *Philosophy and Logical Syntax*. London, 1935. (Elementary.)
———. *Logical Syntax of Language*. London, 1937. (Technical.)

Reducibility

Carnap, R. "Testability and Meaning," *Philosophy of Science,* Vols. III (1936) and IV (1937).

The Unity of the Language of Science; Physicalism

Papers by Neurath and Carnap, *Erkenntnis,* Vol. II (1932); *ibid.,* Vol. III (1933). Translation of one of these papers: Carnap, *The Unity of Science.* London, 1934. Concerning psychology: papers by Schlick, Hempel, and Carnap, *Revue de synthèse,* Vol. X (1935).

Information-Retrieval Systems

by John A. Swets

In the past five years, the period of intensive study of information-retrieval systems, ten different measures for evaluating the performance of such systems have been suggested. In this article I review these measures and propose another.

The various measures have much in common. Eight of them evaluate only the effectiveness (accuracy, sensitivity, discrimination) of a retrieval system and are derived completely, in one way or another, from the 2-by-2 contingency table of pertinence and retrieval represented in Fig. 1. The other three measures assess efficiency as well as effectiveness, by including such performance factors as time, convenience, operating cost, and product form.

In some of the measures, in each of the categories just mentioned, the variables considered are combined into a single number. In other measures, of each kind, the separation of two or more variables is maintained, and the numerical value of each is listed. Still other measures consist of a graph showing the relationship between two variables related to effectiveness.

The measure proposed here is one supplied by statistical-decision theory. It compresses the four frequencies of the contingency table into a single number, and it has the advantage that this single number is sufficient to generate a curve showing all of the different balances among the four frequencies that characterize a given level of accuracy. That is to say, this measure, given the

	P	$\bar{P}$	
R	a V_1	b K_1	$a + b$
$\bar{R}$	c K_2	d V_2	$c + d$
	$a + c$	$b + d$	$a + b + c + d$

Fig. 1. The 2-by-2 contingency table of pertinence and retrieval. P and $\bar{P}$ denote, respectively, pertinent and nonpertinent items; R and $\bar{R}$ denote, respectively, retrieved and unretrieved items; a, b, c, and d represent the simple or weighted frequencies of occurrence of the four conjunctions; V_1 is the value of retrieving a pertinent item; V_2 is the value of not retrieving a nonpertinent item; K_1 is the cost of retrieving a nonpertinent item; and K_2 is the cost of failing to retrieve a pertinent item.

validity of the model underlying it, provides an index of effectiveness that is invariant over changes in the breadth of the search query or in the total number of items retrieved. If desired, a second number can be extracted from the fourfold table to characterize the specific balance among the frequencies that results from any specific form of query. This measurement technique has the drawback, at present, that the model on which it is based has not been validated in the information-retrieval setting. The ground for optimism on

SOURCE: *Science*, 141, July 19, 1963, pp 245–250.

this score is the fact that the model has been validated in analogous problems of signal detection studied in electrical engineering and psychology.

Before proceeding to the review and proposal, it should be stated that this article deals only with measures of merit—that is, with the dependent variables of an experiment conducted to evaluate one or more retrieval systems. It is not concerned with methodological issues (such as the number of items in the information store, the means of determining relevance, the number and qualifications of judges, and the form and number of queries) in the design of such experiments.

Review

In this review I present the measures to some extent in the terms of their originators and to some extent in common terms which will make it easier to compare and contrast them with the measure proposed here. A common vocabulary is achieved by coordinating the variables expressed in the various terms of different writers with the quantities of the contingency table as they are represented in Fig. 1. These translated quantities always appear in brackets. Thus, [a] represents the number of pertinent items retrieved. A quantity such as [a/a + c] represents the proportion of pertinent items retrieved and may be taken as an approximation to the conditional probability that a pertinent item will be retrieved—a probability denoted $[Pr_P(R)]$. It is convenient at times to refer to these quantities in words, so I define them as follows:

$$a/a + c = Pr_P(R) = \text{conditional probability of a ``hit.''}$$

$$b/b + d = Pr_{\bar{P}}(R) = \text{conditional probability of a ``false drop.''}$$

$$c/a + c = Pr_P(\bar{R}) = \text{conditional probability of a ``miss.''}$$

$$d/b + d = Pr_{\bar{P}}(\bar{R}) = \text{conditional probability of a ``correct rejection.''}$$

The first measure to be considered is one proposed by Bourne, Peterson, Lefkowitz, and Ford (1), a measure best described as "omnibus." These writers recommend determining a measure of agreement between an aspect of system performance and a related user requirement for each of approximately 10 to 12 requirements. The measures of agreement are then multiplied by weighting coefficients which represent the relative importance of the requirements, and the products are summed to achieve a single figure of merit.

Bourne and his associates report the results of what they regard as a preliminary investigation, and it is true that the measure has not yet been described in sufficient detail for application. The requirements to be included in the measure have deliberately not been fixed; it is suggested that they will represent such factors as amount of pertinent material missed [c], amount of nonpertinent material provided [b], delay, ease of communication, complexity of search logic accommodated, form in which items are delivered, and degree of assurance that items on a given subject do not exist. Bourne and his associates point out that there are not enough quantitative data available to apply the measure now, but they do present data which demonstrate that users tend to disagree on the relative importance of different user requirements. They do not justify the combining of many different kinds of variables on a single metric.

Bornstein (2), in discussing details of experimental design, proposes consideration of the following four variables: (1) the number of pertinent [a], partially pertinent, peripherally pertinent, and nonpertinent [b] responses to each question; (2) the time spent by the user in examining materials in each of the four categories of pertinence; (3) the proportion of acceptable substitutes for "hard copy" which are supplied in each of the four categories; and (4) the actual coincidence and uniqueness of responses on the four-point scale of pertinence.

Bornstein suggests that analyses of variance be carried out for variables 1 to 3 for each point on the pertinence scale, the main effects attributed to the different retrieval systems being compared. He suggests that within-cell variance terms and certain interaction effects will also convey valuable information. This procedure yields only relative measures of effectiveness and efficiency, but Bornstein argues that using a known store of information, which is necessary if absolute measures are to be obtained, requires excessive effort and biases the comparison of different retrieval systems.

Wyllys (3) derives a single figure of merit for the efficiency of a search tool as employed at a given stage in a sequential search process. He proposes to obtain the product of four variables: (1) the "restriction ratio" (which is the number of items retrieved at stage k divided by the number of items retrieved at stage $k - 1$, or the reduction in the number of potentially pertinent items that is effected by the search tool); (2) the cost of using the tool; (3) the number of pertinent documents eliminated from further consideration [c]; and (4) a loss function [K_2].

Wyllys states that the cost variable should be defined in accordance with the local situation to weight correctly such factors as time, money, inconvenience, and indexing costs, and that the loss function should incorporate the degree of pertinence of the pertinent documents eliminated.

Verhoeff, Goffman, and Belzer (4) propose a measure which may be translated as

$$M = [a(V_1) - b(K_1) - c(K_2) + d(V_2)],$$

in which [K_1] and [K_2] are non-negative constants, and for which pertinence is defined by each system user.

These writers would maximize the measure for a given retrieval system, over users with different opinions about pertinence, by defining a critical probability

$$\left[Pr = \frac{K_1 + V_2}{V_1 + K_1 + K_2 + V_2} \right]$$

for each item relative to each query, and by retrieving those items having a probability of pertinence greater than the critical probability. This procedure is germane to system design and use rather than to system evaluation, but I mention it because it bears some resemblance to concepts discussed later in this article.

Swanson (5) has proposed a measure $M = R - pI$, where R is the sum of relevance weights of retrieved items divided by the sum of relevance weights (for a given query) of all items in the store; I is the effective amount of irrelevant material, and is defined as $N - LR$ where N is the total number of items retrieved [$a + b$] and L is the total number of pertinent items in the store [$a + c$]; and p is a penalty [K_1] which takes on arbitrary values.

Borko (6) presented a modification of Swanson's measure in which the irrelevancy score I is redefined. In Borko's measure, I is the number of nonpertinent items retrieved [b] divided by the number of items retrieved [$a + b$], or [$Pr_R(\bar{P})$]. Borko also prefers to do without the arbitrary penalty on nonpertinent retrievals so that the measure is bounded by $+1$ and -1.

Mooers (7) proposes three ratios: (1) the ratio of the number of crucially pertinent items retrieved to the number of crucially pertinent items in the store; (2) the ratio of the number of pertinent or crucially pertinent items retrieved to the number of pertinent or crucially pertinent items in the store;

and (3) the ratio of the number of nonpertinent items retrieved to the number of nonpertinent items in the store.

In more general terms, Mooers proposes consideration of three conditional probabilities—of an important hit, of a hit, and of a false drop. He states that, for an excellent system, the first probability should be high and the last should be simultaneously low. He further states that a system is good if the first is near 1.0, and very good if the last is less than .01. The second variable is said to be of less importance than the other two; it should always closely approach 1.0.

Perry and Kent (8) consider several quantities found in the contingency table but focus on two: (1) the conditional hit probability, $[a/(a+c)]$ or $[Pr_P(R)]$, and (2) the inverse hit probability $[a(a+b)]$ or $[Pr_R(P)]$.

Cleverdon (9) considers the same two variables, which in his terms are the "recall ratio" and the "relevance ratio," respectively. He emphasizes the trading relationship (that is: as the inverse hit probability or relevance ratio increases, the hit probability or recall ratio can be expected to decrease) and suggests that it will be illuminating to plot the recall ratio against the relevance ratio. He expects that a curve will be generated, with an as yet unknown shape, as the restrictiveness of the search query is varied. He has speculated that the curve will look something like the one in Fig. 2. Thus, highly restrictive queries would lead to a relatively high relevance ratio and to a relatively low recall ratio; a less restrictive query would enhance the recall ratio at the expense of the relevance ratio.

Swanson's second proposal (10) is much like the last few discussed. From an experiment on automatic text searching he has plotted the percentage of pertinent items retrieved [or the conditional hit probability, $Pr_P(R)$] against the number of nonpertinent items retrieved [b]. His data follow the curve of Fig. 3. The data points forming this

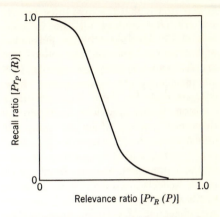

Fig. 2. The plot suggested by Cleverdon (9) to show the trading relationship between the proportion of pertinent items which are retrieved and the proportion of retrieved items which are pertinent.

curve were generated by a procedure analogous to varying the requirements for proximity, in text, of key words, and by specifying either an "and" or an "or" relationship among a variable number of key words.

The proposal made in the next section, discussed later in detail, is that $Pr_P(R)$ be plotted against $b/(b+d)$—that is, against $Pr_{\bar{P}}(R)$—rather than against b, as Swanson has done, or against $Pr_R(P)$, as Cleverdon has done.

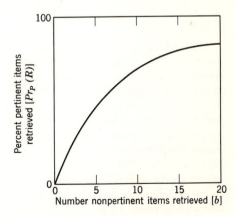

Fig. 3. Curve representing an idealization of data reported by Swanson (10).

One reason is that the quantities $Pr_P(R)$ and $Pr_{\bar{P}}(R)$ contain all the information in the fourfold table of pertinence and retrieval, because the other two, $Pr_P(\bar{R})$ and $Pr_{\bar{P}}(\bar{R})$, are simply their complements. The major point, however, is that, for these axes, statistical-decision theory provides a family of theoretical curves, which are similar in appearance to Swanson's empirical curve, along with two parameters. One of the parameters, the one of major interest, reflects accuracy; it is an index of the distance of a curve from the positive diagonal, the latter corresponding to chance performance. The other parameter reflects the breadth of the query; it indexes a point on a curve by the slope of the curve at that point.

Thus, if it can be generally established that varying the breadth of the query in retrieval systems will generate a curve of the type provided by the theory (and this seems likely), then it is possible to combine the hit and false-drop probabilities, $Pr_P(R)$ and $Pr_{\bar{P}}(R)$, into a single number which is an absolute measure of retrieval-system accuracy, independent of the particular balance between the two probabilities that is struck by any particular form of query, and also to combine the two probabilities in another way into another single number to represent any particular balance between them.

Proposal

The relevance of statistical-decision theory to the problem of information retrieval has been observed before. Maron and Kuhns (11) have suggested "an interpretation of the whole library problem as one where the request is considered as a clue on the basis of which the library system makes a concatenated statistical inference in order to provide an ordered list of those documents which most probably satisfy the information needs of the user." Wordsworth and Booth (12) have applied game theory to the problem of deciding when to stop a search. Here I simply call attention to the possibility that statistical-decision theory will provide a measure of retrieval effectiveness that is preferable to the measures proposed to date.

Decision theory is addressed to the problem of assigning a sample, bearing evidence, to one or the other of two probability distributions—one of two (mutually exclusive and exhaustive) statistical hypotheses is to be accepted. An analogous problem is posed in classical problems of signal detection. The measure taken of the input to a detector, in a particular time interval, must be assigned to one of two events—the detection system reports either that noise (random interference) alone existed or that a specified signal existed in addition to the noise. Similarly, a retrieval system takes a measure of a given item in the store, relative to a particular query, in order to assign the item to one of two categories—the retrieval system rejects the item as not being pertinent or retrieves it.

Decision theory describes the optimal process for making the type of decision with which it deals (13). This process description has been translated directly into a functional specification of the ideal signal-detection device (14) and it has been found to represent quite accurately the behavior of human observers in a variety of detection and recognition tasks (15, 16).

The primary concern here is not with a process, or with system design, but rather with the measurement techniques that accompany the process description. The process model is presented here, though very briefly, because it provides a rationale for the measurement techniques. The model is described in the language of the retrieval problem to display one possible coordination between the elements of the model and the physical realities of retrieval. It is suggested, however, that the measurement techniques may be used to advantage whether or not this particular coordination seems entirely apt.

The model. Let us assume that when a search query is submitted to a retrieval system the system assigns an index value (call it z) to each item in the store (an item can be a document, a sentence, or a fact) to reflect the degree of pertinence of the item to the query. (Maron and Kuhns have described a particular procedure to accomplish this assignment, but let us regard such a procedure, in general, as a feature of all retrieval systems.) Now it may be that for a given need, or for the need as translated into a search query, the items in a given store do in fact vary considerably in pertinence, from a very low value (or no pertinence) to a very high value (or full satisfaction of the need). On the other hand, all of the items may in fact (according to expert opinion or the user's opinion) be either clearly nonpertinent or clearly pertinent to the need. In either case the retrieval system, being imperfect, will view the items as varying over a range of pertinence; indeed, because of the error which will exist in any retrieval system, the value of z assigned to a nonpertinent item will frequently be higher than the value of z assigned to a pertinent item.

Thus, we assume that the retrieval system assigns a fallible index of pertinence, z, and that there exists, apart from the retrieval system, a knowledge of which items are "in truth" pertinent and nonpertinent. We may speculate that the situation is similar to that depicted in Fig. 4. The abscissa represents the degree of pertinence as indexed by z. The ordinate shows the probability of assignment of each value of z. The lefthand function, $f_{\bar{P}}(z)$, represents the distribution of values of z assigned to nonpertinent items, and the righthand function, $f_P(z)$, represents the distribution of values of z assigned to pertinent items. It should be noted that an umpire can determine the condition P or $\bar{P}$ (that is, he can classify all items

as being pertinent or nonpertinent) either because, in his opinion, they all fall clearly into one of these two categories or by virtue of selecting arbitrarily a cutoff along a continuum of pertinence.

Figure 4, as described so far, is intended only to portray the assumptions that the values of z assigned to $\bar{P}$ items vary about a mean, that the values of z assigned to P items vary about a higher mean, and that the two distributions as normal and of equal variance. These assumptions, if justified empirically, facilitate the calculation of a measure of effectiveness, but they are not necessary.

It is clear from the representation of the problem in Fig. 4 that if the retrieval system is to accept (retrieve) or reject each item on the basis of the index value z associated with it, a criterion of acceptance must be established by, or for, the system. A cutoff value of z, denoted z_c, must be established such that all items with $z > z_c$ are retrieved and all items with $z < z_c$ are rejected. It may also be seen in Fig. 4 that a trading relationship exists between the conditional probability of a hit, $Pr_P(R)$ [represented by the area under $f_P(z)$, to the right of z_c], and the conditional probability of a false drop, $Pr_{\bar{P}}(R)$ [the area under $f_{\bar{P}}(z)$ to the right of z_c]. If, for example, the acceptance criterion is made more lenient—that is, if z_c is

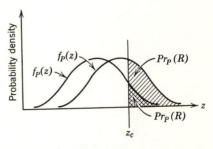

Fig. 4. A representation of the probability distributions, on the index of pertinence z, related to nonpertinent and pertinent items, and of the retrieval criterion z_c.

moved to the left—$Pr_{\bar{P}}(R)$ is increased at the expense of increasing $Pr_{\bar{P}}(R)$.

Just where, along the z axis, the cutoff is best set is determined by the values and costs appropriate to a particular retrieval need. If the user is willing to examine a good deal of nonpertinent material in order to reduce the chance of missing a pertinent item, the cutoff should be low. Alternatively, if time or money is an important factor and a miss is not very serious, the cutoff should be high. Similarly, certain a priori probabilities may affect the level of the desired cutoff. If the user has good reason to believe the store contains the item he wants, he may choose to make a relatively thorough search; if he is doubtful that the store contains the item he requires, he may prefer a token search, of only the items most likely to be responsive to his query. In practice, the level of the cutoff may be set, though imprecisely to be sure, by the choice of a form of query. The choice of an "and" or "or" relationship among a number of key terms, and the selection of the number of key terms, are ways of determining the breadth of the query and thus the level of the z-axis cutoff.

In the next section I derive a measure of the basic effectiveness of a retrieval system that is independent of the level of the acceptance criterion. If the general representation of the problem in Fig. 4 is valid, then the measure presented is the only one that serves the purpose. Measures of the proportion of hits, or the proportion of hits and correct rejections, or the proportion of hits minus the proportion of false drops, or other measures of this kind, are not adequate, and simply observing various values of two variables, such as the proportion of hits and the proportion of false drops, is an unnecesarily weak procedure.

Of course, the assumption that a real retrieval system has a constant effectiveness, independent of the various forms

of queries it will handle, is open to question. It seems plausible, however, that the sharpness of the retrieval system's query language, and its depth of indexing, and also the heterogeneity of items in the store, will determine a level of effectiveness that is relatively invariant over changes in the form of the query. In any event, the assumption is subject to empirical test, and its importance is sufficient to justify the effort of testing. Again, it may be that retrieval systems vary considerably in their ability to handle different forms of query—that is, to adopt different acceptance criteria— some present systems being relatively inflexible. Differences in this respect come under the heading of efficiency, as opposed to effectiveness, and can be taken into account separately. This kind of flexibility will probably be a standard feature of future retrieval systems.

Derivation of the Measure

The proposal made here amounts to a recommendation that retrieval-system performance be analyzed by means of the *operating characteristic* as used in statistics. One form of the operating characteristic is the curve traced on a plot of $Pr_P(R)$ versus $Pr_{\bar{P}}(R)$ as the z-axis cutoff varies. One such operating-characteristic curve, calculated on the basis of the assumptions that the underlying probability distributions (of Fig. 4) are normal and of equal variance, is shown in Fig. 5. The complementary probabilities, of a correct rejection and of a miss, $Pr_{\bar{P}}(\bar{R})$ and $Pr_P(\bar{R})$, are also included in Fig. 5 to emphasize the fact that a complete description of the retrieval system's performance can be obtained from an operating-characteristic curve.

It is evident that a family of theoretical operating-characteristic curves can be drawn on the coordinates of Fig. 5, bounded by the positive diagonal and the upper left-hand corner, that correspond to different distances between the means of the two proba-

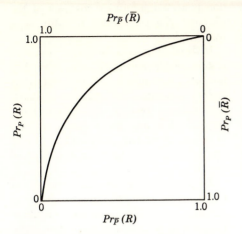

Fig. 5. A typical operating-characteristic curve.

bility distributions, $f_{\bar{p}}(z)$ and $f_{p}(z)$. Since the distance between the means of these two distributions reflects the ability of the retrieval system to segregate nonpertinent and pertinent items, the parameter of this family of curves will serve as a measure of effectiveness.

If the curves are normal, they can be characterized by a single parameter—namely, the distance between the means of the two probability distributions divided by the standard deviation of the distribution of nonpertinent items,

$$\frac{{}^{M}f_{P}(z) - {}^{M}f_{\bar{P}}(z)}{{}^{\sigma}f_{\bar{P}}(z)}$$

It does no harm to adopt the convention that this standard deviation is unity, and then the parameter is just the difference between the means. This measure, which in this context I shall call E, is simply the normal deviate. It is easily obtained from a table of areas under the normal curve. Figure 6 shows a family of operating-characteristic curves and the associated values of E.

It is possible to relax the assumption of equal variance of the two distributions which was made in drawing the curves of Fig. 6. By way of illustration, Fig. 7 shows a family of theoretical

curves calculated on the basis of the assumption that the variance of $f_{p}(z)$ increases with its mean—in particular, that the ratio of the increment in the mean to the increment in standard deviation is equal to 4.0.

I next describe a convenient way of calculating E in practice, and show how an additional parameter may be obtained, if necessary, to represent the ratio of variances. For the present, it is important to note that the assumption of normality will probably be ade-

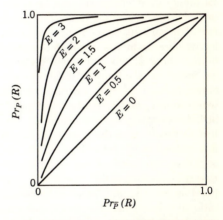

Fig. 6. A family of operating-characteristic curves, based on normal distributions of equal variance, with values of the parameter E.

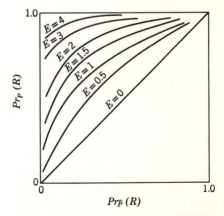

Fig. 7. A family of operating-characteristic curves based on an assumption of increasing variance.

quate, and that curves based on quite extreme variance ratios differ very little. It will, in fact, be difficult to obtain enough data to reject the normality assumption or to distinguish among similar assumptions about variance. With the variance ratio as a free parameter, a normal operating-characteristic curve can be drawn to fit closely any steadily rising function. That a steadily rising curve will be obtained in practice is a reasonable expectation; Swanson's data (Fig. 3) certainly fit such a curve.

Having seen how a given level of sensitivity or effectiveness can be measured by a single number E, independent of a particular acceptance criterion, let us observe in passing that the slope of the curve at any point will serve as an index of the particular acceptance criterion, and of the breadth of the search query, which yielded that point. Strictly speaking, it is assumed in statistical theory that the z axis of Fig. 4 is a scale-of-likelihood ratio, $f_P(z)/f_{\bar{P}}(z)$, and then the value of the slope of the operating-characteristic curve at any point is exactly the value of likelihood ratio at which the acceptance criterion must be set to produce that point. Moreover, if the a priori probabilities $[Pr(P)$ and $Pr(\bar{P})]$ and the values and costs are known, then the optimal setting of the acceptance criterion is at the value of likelihood ratio equal to

$$\frac{Pr(\bar{P})}{Pr(P)} \cdot \frac{(V_2 + K_1)}{(V_1 + K_2)}$$

However that may be, the formal assumptions and the full quantitative power of statistical theory have not been emphasized here; although they may ultimately be found to be of value in the retrieval application, the use of the suggested measures does not depend on this finding. The slope may simply be taken as the measure of the acceptance criterion, empirically, without concern for its precise theoretical basis. It is clear that the difference in the slopes at two points of a steadily rising func-

tion is a straightforward measure of the effective change in the breadth of a search query.

In brief, the operation of a retrieval system yields entries in the cells of a fourfold contingency table and thus yields estimates of four conditional probabilities, two of which are independent. For any given query or form of query, these two probabilities can be plotted as a point in the unit square of Fig. 6.

The parameter of the theoretical curve on which the point falls is a measure of retrieval system effectiveness; the slope of the curve at that point is a measure of query breadth. It is expected that the various fourfold tables which result from systematically varying the breadth of the queries addressed to a given retrieval system will generate a steadily rising function similar to the ones shown in Fig. 6.

Specifics of Measurement Techniques

The most convenient way of converting the conditional probabilities of a hit and of a false drop into a value of E is to plot them on normal coordinates —that is, on probability scales transformed so that the normal deviates are linearly spaced (for example, Codex Graph Sheet No. 41,453). On these scales, as illustrated in Fig. 8, the normal operating-characteristic curve becomes a straight line. The points indicated as A and B illustrate that the difference between the normal-deviate values, one taken from the abscissa and one from the ordinate, is equal to E.

The lines shown in Fig. 8, having unit slope, are based on probability distributions, $f_{\bar{P}}(z)$ and $f_P(z)$, of equal variance. In general, the reciprocal of the slope (with respect to the normal-deviate scales) is equal to the ratio of the standard deviation of $f_P(z)$ to the standard deviation of $f_{\bar{P}}(z)$. Thus, the curves of Fig. 7, if plotted on these scales, would show slopes of less than unity and a decrease in slope with increases in E.

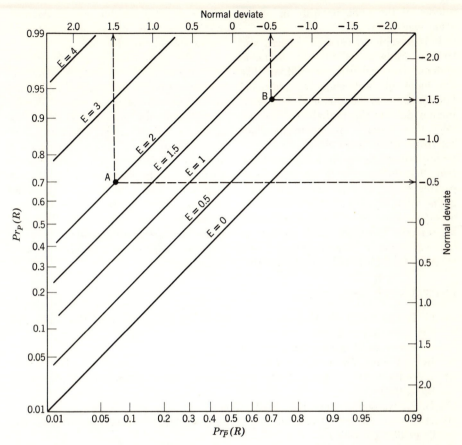

Fig. 8. Normal operating-characteristic curves plotted on double-probability graph paper.

It should be noted that the procedure just given for calculating the value of E—that is, taking the difference between the two normal-deviate values—is not adequate when the operating-characteristic curve has a slope other than unity, for then a single curve will produce different values of E, depending on which point along the curve is chosen. A satisfactory convention often followed in this case is to determine the value of E from the point where the curve crosses the negative diagonal.

Validating Requirements

The validity of the decision-theory model and measurement techniques for a given retrieval system can be tested by determining the operating-characteristic curve experimentally. Four or five data points, spread over a range of $Pr_{P}(R)$ from approximately 0.10 to 0.90, will establish whether or not the curve rises steadily, and, if it does, these four or five points will establish its slope. Each data point must, of course, be based on a large enough sample to provide a fairly reliable point estimate of a probability. This is admittedly a large number of data, more than many investigators would at present consider economically feasible to obtain. There is, unfortunately, no substitute for adequate numbers of data if retrieval systems are to be evaluated on an empirical basis. Perhaps a small offsetting consideration is the fact that results can be pooled for queries of the same breadth, or of the same logical form.

It is possible to conduct further, and stronger, tests of validity. For retrieval systems that calculate something like the index of pertinence, z, additional information can be obtained by determining directly the probability distributions that underlie the operating characteristic. Other tests exist which may be applied appropriately to retrieval systems that do not provide an index comparable to z. An extensive testing program, originally designed for the study of signal detection in psychology, could be directly translated and applied to retrieval systems. A description of this program may be found elsewhere (16).

For most purposes, however, a determination of the operating-characteristic curve should be adequate.

If the empirical operating-characteristic curve obtained from a given retrieval system is reasonably well fitted by a linear function on normal-deviate coordinates, the measure E is appropriate to represent the effectiveness of that system. It is to be expected, on rational grounds, that the model will be found to apply generally to a variety of retrieval systems. If this proves to be the case, there will be many current applications of the measure E. This outcome would greatly facilitate performance-cost analysis of available retrieval systems (17).

REFERENCES AND NOTES

1. C. P. Bourne, G. D. Peterson, B. Lefkowitz, D. Ford, *Stanford Res. Inst. Proj. Rept. No. 3741* (1961).
2. H. Bornstein, *Am. Doc.* **12**, 254 (1961).
3. R. E. Wyllys, *Trans. Congr. Inform. System Sci., Hot Springs, Va., 1st* (1962).
4. J. Verhoeff, W. Goffman, J. Belzer, *Commun. Assoc. Computing Machinery* **4**, 557 (1961).
5. D. R. Swanson, *Science* **132**, 1099 (1960).
6. H. Borko, *System Development Corp., Santa Monica, Calif., Field Note No. 5649/000/01* (1961).
7. C. N. Mooers, *Zator Company, Cambridge, Mass., Tech. Note No. RADC-TN-59-160* (1959).
8. J. W. Perry and A. Kent, Eds., *Tools for Machine Literature Searching* (Interscience, New York, 1958), pp. 3–18.
9. C. W. Cleverdon, *Association of Special Libraries and Information Bureaux, Cranfield, England, Interim Rept.* (1962).
10. D. R. Swanson, paper presented at the Congress of the International Federation of Information Processing Societies, Munich (1962).
11. M. E. Maron and J. L. Kuhns, *J. Assoc. Computing Machinery* **7**, 216 (1960).
12. H. M. Wordsworth and R. E. Booth, *Western Reserve Univ. Tech. Note No. 8, AFOSR-TN-59-418* (1959).
13. A. Wald, *Statistical Decision Functions* (Wiley, New York, 1950).
14. W. W. Peterson, T. G. Birdsall, W. C. Fox, *IRE (Inst. Radio Engrs.) Trans. Information Theory* **4**, 171 (1954); D. Van Meter and D. Middleton, *ibid.*, p. 119.
15. W. P. Tanner, Jr., and J. A. Swets, *Psychol. Rev.* **61**, 401 (1954); J. A. Swets, *Psychometrika* **26**, 49 (1961).
16. J. A. Swets, *Science* **134**, 168 (1961).
17. The preparation of this article was supported by a grant from the Council on Library Resources, Inc. Lewis and Judith Clapp gave helpful advice and greatly facilitated the review of relevant literature.

Adaptive Mechanisms in Digital "Concept" Processing[1]

by Manfred Kochen

1. Introduction

The ability to adapt, like the ability to think, is characteristic of living organisms. But are such abilities unique to life? Part of this puzzle stems from the notions of adaptation and cognition themselves. Attempts to specify machines with such capabilities may at least sharpen our conception of certain adaptive and cognitive mechanisms.

The general question to be discussed here concerns the possibility of a machine which can:

(a) assimilate new information,

(b) channel recorded information to where it should be at the appropriate time and in a suitable representation, and

(c) form hypotheses and modify them with experience.

This paper sketches a theoretical construction within which some key problems can be formulated.[2] Such relevant accomplishments as have been attained are compiled and classified in terms of this model. The relatively new techniques of computer programming in the sense of experimental mathematics, applied to the ideas of concept-processing in a way to be described here, appear sufficiently powerful to demonstrate certain properties of the proposed machine.

The study of such a machine is of interest in its own right. The rate at which recorded knowledge is generated and the need for absorbing it are such that men concerned with intelligence data, patent searches, literature searches in technology, law and medicine, have begun to look to machines for aid. The real problems encountered in such applications may help to formulate and select significant research problems which have, so far, been extremely elusive and ill-defined. Conventional approaches to such information processing needs (36) are based on classifying newly arriving information into preassigned categories. They may have to yield to new methods based on adaptive concept-processing.

The main feature of this paper is the description of a novel information retrieval system. Part of this system has been simulated on the IBM 7090, another part on more advanced equipment.

2. General Problems and Background

An important type of concept is that of a class of objects. Various forms of expression, such as spoken language, provide signs to represent concepts. That human communication is possible at all

SOURCE: *Proc. Joint Automatic Control Conference*, American Institute of Electrical Engineers, 1962, pp. 49–59.

[1] This work was supported by the Air Force Cambridge Research Laboratories under contract AF-19(604)-8446.

[2] The great difficulty of formulating significant and tractable scientific problems in this area accounts, in part, for the scarcity of major theoretical insights, conclusive experiments, or proven practical systems with the above properties.

suggests that there is probably some consistency and lawfulness in the practice of representing concepts by linguistic signs. To effect communication between men and machines, some of these laws must be made explicit. They could then be used to construct a formal intermediate language, in which a person could readily learn to express his ideas, and in terms of which a machine could, perhaps, process its representations of concepts. The first main class of problems in the study of concept-processing concerns the *representation* of concepts: the assignment of signs and lawful combinations of signs in a well-defined language to our ideas.

But how can a store of concepts be built up and organized through experience so that new experiences can be readily related to familiar and analogous concepts? Concept-formation is an inductive process. It is similar to classification. This can be viewed in two ways: first, as the immediate perception of a quality or recognition of a class, such as "twoness" apart from all pairs of objects; second, as successively improving selections of attributes common to a number of objects, mediated by accumulated experiences. The second view led experimental psychologists to find certain strategies used by people in concept-attainment. But knowing that people can obtain concepts from experience is of interest here only insofar as it suggests that, perhaps, there might be machines that could do it too. And the mechanisms for constructing concepts need in no way resemble those of humans. It must be possible for man and machine to communicate about the results of such constructions. The second major class of problems, then, concerns the various strategies for constructing an organized cumulative record of suitably represented experience within which concepts are constructed.

The remaining general class of problems deals with processing concepts in order to answer certain questions. A machine can, of course, process only the signals which represent concepts. It must process these in such a way that relations between concepts correspond to relations between their representations. Questions are interpreted as command statements which specify a sequence of machine operations to be executed. What basic operations should such a machine be enabled to perform? What facilities for constructing compound instructions from such basic ones should be built into the machine? The answer to the latter depends on the kinds of questions which arrive. The addition of new instructions for executing indicated processes should adapt to both the continuing input of information and questions.

In the next three sections, something about what is and what is not known about the answers to the three broad questions posed above will be described.

The general notion of "concept" which is generally accepted by experimental psychologists and which also seems suitable for an exact definition as needed to specify a machine stems back at least as far as J. Locke (ca. 1700): that all ideas are composed of simple phenomena which are presented in sensation and reflection as attributes of substances. To W. James (ca. 1890), concept-formation meant the "dissociation of varying concomitants." In the earliest experiments (ca. 1908), subjects were instructed to look for common attributes. Hull (15), for example, presented his subjects with Chinese characters. A number of these with essentially the same radical were consistently associated with the same nonsense syllable. The subjects then had to spontaneously recognize new characters by assigning the appropriate nonsense syllables. Though the percentage of correct responses increased (up to 56%) with increasing exposure to labeled patterns, neither the subjects nor the investigator could describe a reasonable basis for the choice patterns.

The influence of information theory and the desire to obtain more significant results led later investigators (6) to provide their subjects with precise information about:

(*a*) what attributes of a sample object, such as color, size, shape, etc., they should pay attention to;

(*b*) the possible values of each attribute, e.g. color could be either blue or red, size large or small, etc.; and

(*c*) what kinds of "concepts" they are required to express, such as "all red and large or all blue and square figures."

While such control over experimental variables evaded the difficulties of earlier work by establishing methodologically satisfactory results,[3] it also evaded the key problem of concept-formation: how to abstract relevant attributes from complex experiences and how to express hypotheses about them spontaneously.

3. Representation of Concepts

Representation of Input Sentences

How can immediate sensory experiences involving individual people, objects, places, time periods, organizations be reported and coded in form suitable for machine input? English-like words and phrases probably allow for the expression of human experiences better than any other single form of expression.[4] To report observations or simple facts like "America was discovered in 1492," "Scott is the author of Ivanhoe," sentences of the form name-predicate-name appear satisfactory. Few sentences in any naturally encountered linguistic text—even in the discourse by and to a

two-year-old—are in this form. But it is not unlikely that much of our sensory experience is so organized that it could, without too much difficulty, be expressed in this way.

To construct a formal language $\mathcal{L}$ in which such sentences are defined, consider the following primitive constants:

> All natural numbers 1, 2, 3, . . .
> The letters R and L.

Let r denote a variable, particularly some sequence of the above signs.

Definition 1. r is an $\mathcal{L}$-name if it is R followed by a natural number; R2, for example, is a name.

Definition 2. r is an $\mathcal{L}$-predicate if it is L followed by a natural number; L7, for example is a predicate.

Definition 3. r is an $\mathcal{L}$-sentence if it consists of an $\mathcal{L}$-name, followed by an $\mathcal{L}$-predicate, followed by an $\mathcal{L}$-name, as R2 L7 R5.

Henceforth, unless otherwise indicated, the $\mathcal{L}$ will be understood but omitted as a prefix to these terms.

Informally, the "names" correspond primarily to individual objects, but also to documents, authors, and subject headings.

Predicates of $\mathcal{L}$ correspond to a few selected English phrases, built around an adjective, verb, or preposition, as in "was born on," "authored," "is synonymous with," "is greater than." All the predicates used here are two-place predicates.[5] That is, they serve to assert relations between two names.

---

[3] Most subjects adopted the strategy: form the initial hypothesis by guessing some of the attribute values on the basis of the first instance; do not change the hypothesis in force for confirming instances, but for refuting instances revise it so as to make it consistent with all past data.

[4] Undoubtedly people apprehend experiences not through any *single* form of expression, but through many, such as pictorial imagery, tactile sensations. S. Langer (21) has introduced the notion of a "presentational symbol" to express experiences which cannot be adequately expressed by linguistic means alone.

[5] Some justification for the use of dyadic predicates is provided by a result of Quine (30) showing that, under certain general set-theoretic conditions, arbitrary predicates can be reduced to dyadic ones. It may prove desirable to use only a single "basic predicate," like ϵ, "is a member of," from which, in combination with names, compound predicates can be constructed. Some foundation for this possibility is provided by a result of Kemeny (16), who showed that truth-definition for logical propositions formulated within the framework of simple type theory can also be given within Zermelo set theory.

The information received by subjects in many experiments on concept-formation and models for these can be represented by $\mathcal{L}$-sentences. In one such experiment (18) the subject (or concept-forming mechanism) is shown a finite time-sequence of bits, one bit at a time, such as 01010101, and he is required to guess the next bit. Let Ri symbolize the $(i-2)$th bit for $i = 3, 4, 5, \ldots, L1$ the predicate "has the value of," and let $R1$ and $R2$ symbolize 0 and 1 respectively. Thus on the 5th trial, the subject receives the sentence $R7\,L1\,R1$ and on the 6th trial, $R8\,L1\,R2$, etc.

In other experiments and models (6, 14,19) the subject is shown a time sequence of objects and told to pay attention to n attributes, and to certain possible values for each attribute. For example, consider 3 two-valued attributes describing 8 different objects. Let $R1$, $\ldots, R8$ symbolize these objects. Let $L1$, $L2$ and $L3$ stand for the three attribute predicates "has the color," "has the shape of a" and "has greater area than" respectively. Interpreting the "$=$" sign as "symbolizes," let $R9 = $ "red," $R10 = $ "blue"; $R11 = $ "circle," $R12 = $ "square"; $R13 = $ "one inch square," $R14 = $ "four inch square." The subject, or concept-forming mechanism, then receives a sequence of sentences like ($R1$ $L1\,R9$, $R1\,L2\,R11$, $R1\,L3\,R13$; $R1\,L4$ $R15$) ($R2\,L1\,R9$, $R2\,L2\,R12$, $R2\,L3$ $R13$; $R2\,L5\,R15$) ($R3\,L1\,R10$, $R3\,L2$ $R11$, $R3\,L3\,R14$; $R3\,L5\,R15$). . . . A quadruple of sentences is presented at a time. The fourth sentence indicates, by means of predicates $L4$ ($=$ is a member of) and $L5$ ($=$ is not a member of) and $R15$, the name of a "concept," whether or not the object that the first three sentences describe is a member of some class of objects. To represent such highly formatted input data as this, each object could be characterized as an n-bit word, with an additional bit for the value of the characteristic function of the unknown class for that object. This was done in the computer simulation reported in (19,20). Most other related simulations, such as EPAM (10), "Baseball" (12), accepts data or stimuli in binary coded special format.

An information-retrieval system storing sentences about biographic and bibliographic data in a branch of the computer field was constructed. These sentences were manually prepared with the help of a codebook in which the Ri and Lj are defined. The Ri were primarily names of authors, publishers, places and institutions, titles of articles, journals, dates and topics. No more than about 30 L's were used. Some of them were: "authored," "is affiliated with," "pertains to," etc. There is, of course, no theoretical limit to the number of predicates (or names) that can be used when required to express new facts. This is the most powerful feature of this language compared with formatted modes of expressing data for input.

It would be preferable to enter data as they might "naturally" be expressed, in complex declarative sentences. Techniques such as those developed by Z. Harris (25) could be used to produce complete specification lists, somewhat like the incomplete specification lists used to transform queries in "Baseball" (12). But considerably further and deeper analysis into the syntax of language will be needed before this can be adequately done. Studies on the logic of grammar (3) or machine methods for the "discovery" of a grammar on the basis of a sample of acceptable sentences (33), which is somewhat related to the inductive concept-formation model discussed here, suggest that important contributions in this direction are possible. No attempt to relate $\mathcal{L}$-sentences to English-like sentences is made here. It is assumed that all recorded sentences are meaningful to an English speaking person, as well as true.

Representation of Machine-Constructed Sentences

What in a machine might correspond to the results of human reflection? While $\mathcal{L}$-sentences might represent sensory experience, it will take sentences in a richer language, $\mathcal{L}'$, to represent conceptual experience. Within $\mathcal{L}'$ it must at least be possible to express generalizations based on $\mathcal{L}$-sentences. To this end, consider first an operator, A, for constructing predicate expressions about a class of objects. The expression (Ak) $(Rk\ L1\ R2)$ denotes the set of all named objects, Rk, for which the sentence $Rk\ Lj\ R2$ is on record. Thus, if $L1\ R2$ denotes "has greater area than a 2-inch square," the above expression denotes the class of all objects known to possess this property. This class can be given a name, and sentences involving this name can now be constructed.

It is desirable, however, to consider classes which are more general than the above. To denote the set of all objects such that for at least one among them the sentence $Rk\ L1\ R2$ is on record, a complementation operator N is useful. It can be applied to any class of objects such as the above to form a complementary class. Thus, $N((Ak)\ (Rk\ L1\ R2))$ denotes the class of objects named Rk for which the sentence $Rk\ L1\ R2$ is not on record. It is also useful to have a conjunction and a disjunction operator. It can be applied to any pair of object classes such as the above to produce another class of objects. Thus, $[(Ak)(Rk\ L1\ R2)]$ & $[(Al)(Rl\ L2\ R3)]$ denotes the set of all objects, Rk, for each of which both the sentence $Rk\ L1\ R2$ and the sentence $Rk\ L2\ R3$ is on record. The operator & is commutative and associative. It will not be explicitly written, but understood whenever two expressions are written adjacently.

Nearly everything that has been called a "concept" in the experimental literature and more can be expressed in terms of these three operators applied to classes of objects about which $\mathcal{L}$-sentences are recorded. A "conjunctive concept," like "all red and square objects," could be represented by

$$[(Ak_1)(Rk_1\ L1\ R9)][(Ak_2)(Rk_2\ L2\ R12)].$$

A "disjunctive concept" like "all red or square objects" can be represented by:

$$N\{N[(Ak_1)(Rk_1\ L1\ R9)]\ \&$$
$$N[(Ak_2)(Rk_2\ L2\ R12)]\}$$

which reads: "all objects which are not such that none are both red and square."

A variety of class concepts such as the above can be represented in this notation. While this appears cumbersome, it has the advantage of using only three simple machine operations. Nor do the above examples illustrate the full generality and power of this language for representing concepts.

To express assertions about concepts, the above-mentioned classes are treated as names occurring in $\mathcal{L}$-sentences. To express logically richer assertions and queries, however, operators analogous to the above three are helpful. These are A, the universal quantifier, $\sim$, the denial operator and $\wedge$, the logical "and" which connects two assertions. Sentences using these operators and the primitives of $\mathcal{L}$ are formed according to the rules of predicate calculus. They constitute the language $\mathcal{L}'$.

Definition of Concept

In our view, even the broader notion of "concept" as described in the previous section—which regards a concept as one of a set of well-formed sentences in a formal language like $\mathcal{L}'$, whose specified primitives need have no "meaning"— should be augmented by taking content into account in terms of accumulating experiences. This view can, of course, be traced back as far as Kant (1781) and Cassirer (1923). Thus, to people, the concept of "redness," as evoked by mention of a "trigger" word like "red," is the essence of the sum total of their sensory and reflective experience that is somehow associated.

To begin to capture this notion[6] for

[6] This will not be completed until the manner of storing and processing $\mathcal{L}$-sentences which report observations is explained in the next two sections. "Concepts" are inherently the result of a process, and, though they can be represented by sentences of a language, cannot be defined as such.

the purpose of representation within a machine, let $a(Ri)$ denote the set of all actual $\mathcal{L}'$-sentences involving the $\mathcal{L}$-name Ri. An $\mathcal{L}'$-sentence is said to involve Ri if it explicitly contains Ri or if it contains defined names or predicates, the definitions of which involve Ri. A sentence $r(Ri)$ from set $a(Ri)$ is regarded equivalent to a sentence $r(Rj)$ from set $a(Rj)$ if both have the same number of operators A and N in the same order, and both contain the same $\mathcal{L}$-sentences except for Ri and Rj. Thus, $r(R1)$ is equivalent to $r(R2)$, where $r(R1) = (Ak_1) N(Ak_2) (R1 L1 Rk_1) (N Rk_2 L2 R1)$ and $r(R2) = (Au) N(Av) (R2 L1 Ru) (N Rv L2 R1)$.

The set inclusion relation $\subseteq$ is defined for all pairs of sets, $a(Ri) \subseteq a(Rj)$, as asserting that for every sentence in $a(Ri)$, there is an equivalent sentence in $a(Rj)$. A relation $\leq$, which partially orders the set of all $\mathcal{L}$-names, is defined as: $Ri \leq Rj$ if and only if $a(Ri) \subseteq a(Rj)$. Two names Ri and Rj are identical if and only if $Ri \leq Rj$ and $Rj \leq Ri$. To illustrate this relation, let $R1$ symbolize "Mark Twain" and $R2 =$ "Sam Clemens," with $L1 =$ "is author of," $R3 =$ "Tom Sawyer," $R4 =$ "Huckleberry Finn." Let $a(R1) = \{(R1 L1 R3), (R1 L1 R4)\}$ and $a(R2) = \{(R2 L1 R3), (R2 L1 R4)\}$. These two sets are in $1 - 1$ correspondence, so that $R1$ and $R2$ would be equivalent.

On intuitive grounds, an equivalence class seems too restrictive a notion to represent a "concept." To broaden the notion, let $n(A)$ denote the number of distinct sentences in set A, which is like $a(Ri)$. Consider the following recursive definition.

Step 0. Choose a "trigger"-name, Ri_0, which might, for example, mean "red."

Step 1. Find another name, Ri_1 such that $f_1 = n(a(Ri_1) \cap a(Ri_0))$ is maximum. It is notationally convenient to omit reference to i, and to abbreviate $a(Ri_1) \cap a(Ri_0)$ by $A_{1,0}$.

Step 2. Find another name, Ri_2, such that $c_2 n(a(Ri_2) \cap a(Ri_1)) + c_2 n(aRi_2) \cap a(Ri_0)) + c_3 n(a(Ri_2) \cap a(Ri_1)$

$\cap a(Ri_0))$ is maximum. Here c_2 and c_3 are numerical constants, with $c_3 > c_2$, giving greater weight to names that occur in sentences common to both the previous names Ri_0 and Ri_1. With the further abbreviation, $A_{2,1,0} = a(Ri_2) \cap A_{1,0}$, the expression that Ri_2 should maximize is $f_2 = c_2 n(A_{2,1}) + c_2 n(A_{2,0}) + c_3 n(A_{2,1,0})$. Should there be several Ri_1 for which $n(A_{1,0})$ has the same, maximum value, say Ri_{11} and Ri_{12}, compute both the quantity f_2 with $Ri_1 = Ri_{11}$ and $Ri_2 = Ri_{12}$ and f_2 with $Ri_1 = Ri_{12}$ and $Ri_2 = Ri_{11}$, and select that value for Ri_2, which gives the larger f_2. If there is still a tie, repeat the procedure up to step 3.

Step 3. Find a name Ri_3 such that $c_2 n(A_{3,2}) + c_2 n(A_{3,1}) + c_2 n(A_{3,0}) + c_3 n(A_{3,2,1}) + c_3 n(A_{3,2,0}) + c_3 n(A_{3,1,0}) + c_4 n(A_{3,2,1,0})$ is maximized. Here $A_{3,2} = a(Ri_3) \cap a(Ri_2)$, $A_{3,2,1} = a(Ri_3) \cap A_{2,1}$, $A_{3,2,1,0} = a(Ri_3) \cap A_{2,1,0}$, etc. Deal with ties as above.

Step k. Find Ri_k such that

$$\sum_{m=1}^{k-1} c_{m+1} \sum_{j_1 < k, j_2 < k, \ldots, j_m < k} n(A_{k, j_1, j_2, \ldots, j_m})$$

is maximized and form all the k sets $A_{k,j}$, $j = 0, 1, \ldots, k - 1$; all the $\binom{k}{2}$ sets A_{k,j_1,j_2}, with j_1, $j_2 = 0, \ldots, k - 1$, defined recursively by $A_{k,j_1, j_2} = a(Ri_k) \cap A_{j_1, j_2}$, all $\binom{k}{3}$ sets $A_{k, j_1, j_2, j_3}, \ldots$ etc.

The iteration ceases as soon as

$$a(Ri_k) \subseteq \bigcup_{m=0}^{k-1} a(Ri_m).$$

Call this limit set $C(Ri_0)$ and interpret it as the concept associated with "trigger" name Ri_0. It must be proved that for every name Ri there exists a uniquely defined corresponding concept $C(Ri)$. To abstract the notion of "concept" from the associated trigger names, call two names Ri and Rj "conceptually equivalent" if $C(Ri) = C(Rj)$. This defines an equivalence class of names C' for every concept C.

It remains to be shown that the concept-classes, C' and C, which are formed in this way, group together names and sentences that people would be willing to regard as conceptually related, and discriminate between names and sentences that people would judge conceptually unrelated. Of course the limitations of the predicate calculus are well-known, and other logics are likely to be better suited to specific universes of discourse.

4. Memory

The heart of our hypothetical machine is its memory. It is a cumulative record of names which are richly cross-referenced through the $\mathcal{L}$-sentences in which they occur. It consists of essentially three parts: a store M in which $\mathcal{L}$-sentences are recorded on arrival; a "scratch-pad" store M' in which machine-generated $\mathcal{L}'$-sentences are stored; a dictionary or table lookup store D in which metalinguistic, definitional statements relating $\mathcal{L}$-names and $\mathcal{L}$-predicates to English phrases are recorded.

Input-Sentence File M

Let $t = 0, 1, 2, \ldots$ denote discrete time periods, during each of which a single input $\mathcal{L}$-sentence arrives to be recorded. In the version of the machine currently being simulated, there are two mechanisms for automatically producing new $\mathcal{L}$-sentences from input-sentences wherever possible.

1. For every input sentence $Ri\ Lj\ Rk$, another $\mathcal{L}$-sentence $Rk\ Lj'\ Ri$, which represents a statement in the opposite voice is automatically produced and recorded. Thus, for every predicate Lj, such as "is author of," there is an opposite voice predicate Lj', such as "is authored by."

2. For certain predicates Lj, which are said to be transitive, whenever a pair of $\mathcal{L}$-sentences like either $Ri\ Lj\ Rk$ and $Rk\ Lj\ Rn$ or $Ri\ Lj\ Rk$ and $Rn\ Lj\ Ri$ are on record (including the latest input sentence or its opposite voice), a new $\mathcal{L}$-sentence, either $Ri\ Lj\ Rn$ or $Rn\ Lj\ Rk$, corresponding to the two situations above, is automatically constructed and recorded. An example of a transitive predicate is "is located in" when used in connection with place name pairs, e.g., "Oxford is in Ohio" and "Ohio is in the Midwest," results in "Oxford is in the Midwest" being automatically constructed and recorded.

These two mechanisms enrich M. The first one also ensures that *all* $\mathcal{L}$-sentences beginning with a specified name could be readily found. Although it nearly doubles[7] the memory load with redundant information, there is a compensating gain in search time. The construction and recording of sentences produced by mechanism 2 could be effected at the time a request to search for the presence of such a statement occurs rather than at the time it first becomes possible. There again storage space is "wasted" to save search time (or waiting time on the part of the inquirer).

Dictionary File D

Nearly every new input sentence will contain names that have not been previously encountered. In the present simulation, D consists of a manually maintained codebook. Whenever a sentence involving new names or predicates is entered, a new entry in D is made. Previously used names must be looked up to ensure that the appropriate Ri and Lj are consistently used.

There are two dictionary files, D_R and D_L. Entries in the name file D_R

---

[7] Except for "symmetric" predicates like "co-authored with," which is the same in both active and passive voice.

appear like ("Scott, W." = $R1$), where "=" should be read as "is symbolized by." This file is alphabetically ordered by name. Certain names could be identified by the coder as synonymous and assigned the same $\mathcal{L}$-name, or they could be entered separately with an $\mathcal{L}$-sentence asserting that the $\mathcal{L}$-names are synonymous.

The predicate table D_L is treated similarly, though there are much fewer predicates than names. As explained earlier, some predicates can be compounded from more basic predicates and names. Any statement involving the sign "=" with an $\mathcal{L}$-name to its right and a meaningful English phrase or a mixture of English words and $\mathcal{L}$-words is a legitimate entry to D_L. An analogous remark applies to D_R, with the emphasis that the left side of an entry must be directly meaningful to people through ordinary sensory channels.

$\mathcal{L}'$-Sentence File M'

This is the store which temporarily records tentative hypotheses, partial concepts, logical inferences and intermediate statements needed in logical processing. It contains only machine-generated $\mathcal{L}'$-sentences. It also stores *formal* definitions, in distinction to the notational "definitions" stored by D, which should be properly interpreted as an expanding list of primitive constants for the applied language $\mathcal{L}$. While every sentence in M is to be understood as materially true, the sentences in M' may also be logically true or false. Any conjunctive combination of $\mathcal{L}$-sentences recorded in M up to time t is to be regarded as true. If r is recorded in M, then $\sim r$ cannot be recorded there. But the $\mathcal{L}'$-sentence "not-r or r," could be stored in M'.

In a mixed universe of discourse such as we are dealing with, many meaningless sentences could be formed, such as "Ivanhoe is author of Scott." It is assumed that the input $\mathcal{L}$-sentences are all meaningful and true. This need not

be so for the machine-produced $\mathcal{L}'$-sentences. Certain critical sentences formed by inductive and deductive methods within the machine are displayed from time to time, to be verified or corrected by an editor.

In any implementation of this memory, M and D would be physically combined with the = sign treated as if it were another predicate; both the English phrases and the $\mathcal{L}$-names would correspond to physical states of a finite-state device.

Storage Requirements and Difficulties

To store the wealth of details based on a limitless stream of sensory input information,[8] obviously requires enormous capacities. Existing stores have capacities of up to about 10^9 bits, but this will hardly suffice for any non-trivial application.[9] The kind of store needed here would probably differ greatly from conventionally addressable memories. Current developments in content-selectable memories are more pertinent. Unfortunately none with capacities greater than 10,000 words have been proven technically feasible. It is not obvious that bits are the appropriate units for measuring storage capacity for the kinds of memories we need. The discovery of a more suitable unit for measuring storage capacity of "meaningful" information is an important challenge for theoretical research.

A step toward the kind of memory organization that may be useful stems from the idea of a list-structure (27). A list is a set of symbols, each of which refers to two items:

[8] People, for example, "process" about 2×10^9 natural impulses generated by their visual system alone during every waking second.

[9] A typical book or the average amount of reading done by a scientist in a week would require about 10^6 bits if it were to be stored in conventional codes, with 6 bits/character.

(*a*) either recorded data symbols, or the symbolic name of another list, and

(*b*) the symbolic address of the next item in the list, or a symbol to denote that the list is terminated.

This notion of a list has been claimed to capture the idea of "concept." It is more likely, however, to provide a useful technique for processing representations of concepts, as discussed here. There are a number of programming languages—in the form of interpreters—which are based on this idea: IPLV (28), FLPL (11), LISP (23), COMIT (40) to mention a few. These languages are useful for simulating various proposals for concept-processing mechanisms, among other things. Indeed the memory and processing mechanism described here is being simulated in IPLV. A number of similar models are also being simulated in IPLV, notably "Baseball" (12) and EPAM (10). The "General Inquirer," (35) written in COMIT, aims to facilitate content analysis of verbal material. Prior work by Stevens, using SEAC (34) as well as various studies (9) and early proposals (37) should be mentioned as sources of ideas and techniques used in this paper.

The storage requirements of the dictionary D are not a major limiting factor. The number of entries probably need not exceed a million (upper limit of a person's vocabulary), and very efficient table lookup machines and procedures that can provide millisecond access to dictionaries with over 100,000 entries are in use (17) (8). Similarly, the storage requirements of M' may not be as severe as those of M. Inasmuch as M is a growing, cumulative record, no bounds on its capacity can be specified except arbitrarily. Generally, limits on storage are determined by the machine's users whom it should help with their conceptual processes for obtaining answers to questions posed in natural language. Considerably more experimental evidence about people's capacities in

these tasks than now available is needed for better estimates of storage and access time requirements.[10]

Given a finite storage capacity for M, it is clear that new information can be recorded only if M is purged of valueless sentences and some efficient coding mechanism can be found. As mentioned earlier, eliminating redundant sentences may increase processing time, but this is unimportant when such sentences are not often used in the first place. The theoretical problems of defining value for recorded sentences, and finding efficient purging strategies is very important for large files. In current practice, purging a large file is extremely difficult and costly and it is seldom done. The technique used by Samuel (31) in his checker learning program to purge the store of little used board configurations should prove useful here.

The theoretical problem of how to aggregate the highly interrelated $\mathcal{L}$-names in M into a hierarchy of concept-classes, along the lines discussed in the last section, is fundamental. Such classification can serve as a basis for the maximally efficient packing of coded information in a limited-capacity file.

While it is not yet possible to specify meaningful storage requirements, it may be of interest to summarize our preliminary considerations in terms of some very speculative but suggestive figures. A machine system based on our model, used to help people deal with information in a non-trivial, realistic situation,

---

[10] People can read at a rate of about 10 characters/second and enter information into a keyboard at about 3-5 characters/second. They can "keep in mind" about 7 distinct objects at a time in a counting task. Little, however, is known about the number of different textual statements, among which a person has to make one selection, that could be presented to him simultaneously. Little is known about the way (vocabulary and syntax) people formulate and revise questions in natural situations such as libraries, and in what forms they should receive answers.

might have to: accept information at a rate of perhaps 10^6–10^9 facts per year; answer questions at a throughput of perhaps 10^5–10^8 questions per year. Both might have an exponential growth rate of 7%/year. It should continually "assimilate" new information and continually re-classify stored information into concept-classes at a sufficiently high rate and quality so as to permit purging and processing. The total required storage capacity may be constant at, perhaps, 10^9–10^{12} $\mathcal{L}'$-sentences or their equivalent.

Memory Structure

To analyze the organization of various files, the relation among data segments was represented as a graph. Each node is labeled by Ri for some i and each edge by Lj for some j. The Ri have quite vaguely been called "names" and could designate individual objects, classes of objects, sentences, and any other "namable" entity, while the Lj loosely stood for predicates relating two names Ri and Rk in that order. Thus each edge is directed and colored according to its label, making the resulting graph a "chromatic, oriented linear graph." The Ri could also *represent* other nodes, as addresses represent (name) what they contain. The name of a variable could simply be the address in which it is stored at any one time.

This graph models the structure of M. Techniques used in graph theory and in the study of probabilistic nets are being used to analyze such graphs. Some of the problems amenable to analysis pertain to the degree to which the graph has a non-homogeneous or "cluster" structure; others pertain to changes in the graph as it grows, as machine-produced statements are added. Others deal with the trade-off between computer storage as related to classes of questions, classes of input statements, hardware constraints and different programming designs.

5. Processing

The processing unit of our hypothetical machine has as its main function the execution of operations specified by a request or query. It must also classify and relate previously unencountered names with recorded names on the basis of inductively formed $\mathcal{L}'$-sentences; and, it must continually revise such sentences in the light of new facts.

The purpose of this machine is to amplify people's conceptual abilities in somewhat the way a live "information please" service might. The primary reason for wanting the machine to form representations of concepts is to enable people to usefully communicate with the machine when they need information. People often cannot specify what information they ought to have. A questioner attempts to specify his request in a formal (or perhaps even in "natural") English. If either the machine cannot process this or he has not quite expressed his real need, the machine supplies him with aids, in the form of a display of related vocabulary or suggestions to qualify his request, for revising the query. This "conversation" continues until questioner and machine arrive at a mutually satisfactory query statement. The machine also records the final request, which may be used to up-date D and even M and M'. That is, if the machine is "better informed" about the question than the user—in the sense of having a more fully developed concept-representation rather than having on record the specific answer—it acts as a teaching machine; if it is less well informed, it acts as a learning machine.

Factual Queries

A factual query is an expression for a class of objects followed by the symbol !, which specifies a search for a set of $\mathcal{L}$-sentences in M.

(*a*) If a query contains no free or bound variables, such as $R1\ L2\ R3$! or $(R1\ L1\ R2)$ & $N(R2\ L2\ R3)$!, it specifies that a search be made to determine whether the sentence is (or in the second example, whether the first one is but the second one is not) on record in M.

(b) If a query contains bound variables only, such as (Ak_1) (Ak_2) $Rk_1 Lk_2$ R5!, it specifies the execution of operations to search for and list the indicated sets of sentences. Thus, the above query specifies search for all $\mathcal{L}$-sentences terminating in $R5$.

(c) If a query contains free variables, it is regarded as incompletely specified. The questioner would then be informed of this and, perhaps, given aid to further qualify his request. This may be done by treating the free variable (k) in a query like $R1 Lk R5!$ as bound by (Ak), and displaying to the questioner all possible L's involved with both $R1$ and $R5$ from which he should select. For names this is impractical. With a hierarchic classification of names and predicates, appropriate class names would be displayed, one class level at a time.

The following three types of queries have been simulated so far by means of IPLV subroutines. The query is presently represented to the machine by selecting a number of prepunched cards, one for the name of the subroutine, the others for the specified names and predicates.[11] These are fed into a card reader. The answer is printed in English within seconds.

(a) If an inquiry of the form $R1 L2$ $R3$! is entered, one of the following answers is reported: "Yes," "No," "no sentence starting with $R1 L2$ is recorded" or "no sentence starting with $R1$ is recorded."

[11] The query can also be entered through a console keyboard, but requires an operator who knows the code. Ideally, it should be possible to service the requests of perhaps 100 simultaneous users, without letting anyone wait much more than a few minutes. But difficult practical multiprogramming (as well as theoretical congestion problems) must be solved first.

(b) If an inquiry is of the form (Ak) $R1 L2 Rk!$, all statements beginning with $R1 L2$ are printed out.

(c) If an inquiry is of the form (Ak) (Aj_1) (Aj_2) . . . (Aj_n) $(R1 Lj_1 Rk)$ $(R2 Lj_2 Rk)$ . . . $(Rn Lj_n Rk)$! then all sentences for which the given names $R1$, . . , Rn are linked to a common name through some predicates are printed out. With $n = 1$ all sentences beginning with $R1$ would be printed out.

It is, of course, desirable, to be able to enter the query in reasonably unconstrained English directly through a keyboard. How well this can be done was demonstrated by the "Baseball" program (12). This program transforms one-clause, single-verb queries, with no logical connectives, comparatives or ordinals, into a specification list. The syntactic portion of the program finds the verb, subject, object, etc. It uses some of the algorithms developed at the University of Pennsylvania. (25) Their novel method of using subroutines to deal with the meaning of certain words —words specifying operating instructions —is very important. Thus, a transformed query, such as, "How many games did the Yankees win in July?" specifies a search through a fixed, formatted record of baseball games listing teams, data, place and score.

Logical Queries

Providing answers to very specific factual queries only when those answers are explicitly recorded, though valuable, is not as much as might be accomplished and wanted with machine aid. If a certain fact is sought but not explicitly recorded as such, the machine might, instead, print out other recorded facts from which the user (or the machine) could *deduce* the desired answer. For example, if the value of $\log_2 5{,}000$ or a table of $\log_2 x$ for all integers from 1,000 to 10,-000 were requested, and if it were not recorded as such, the machine would indicate what tables are on record (either by reference or by producing the table, say $\log_{10} x$). It would also display a conversion formula like $\log_2 x = (\log_{10} x)/\log_{10} 2$; or the machine could compute the desired result directly, depending on how long the user wishes to wait before receiving even a partial answer. The difficult task required of the machine is the search for relevant recorded facts from which the desired data can be derived. Obviously not all alternatives can be explored, and efficient search strategies are required. All the necessary "scratch-pad" data would be temporarily recorded in store M', until a program for deducing the desired data from recorded data is constructed by the machine. This program, together with the inquiry, may be (permanently) recorded in M'. (It would be purged if too infrequently used.)

A query requiring logical deduction such as the above is basically different from a query like $r\,!$, where r is an $\mathcal{L}'$-sentence. It will be called a logical query, and denoted by r'', where $''$ is a new primitive added to $\mathcal{L}'$. Such queries are intimately related to requests for a proof[12] of some partially specified "theorem." Thus, "there exists a number y such that $\log_2 5{,}000 = y$" is a theorem, and the two statements $s_1 =$ "$\log_{10} 5{,}000 + 3{,}69897$" and $s_2 = $ "for all x, $\log_2 x = 3.3222 \log_{10} x$" constitute the main steps of a proof. More formally, the logical query r'' specifies search for a deductive proof that the $\mathcal{L}'$-sentence r is either logically true or false. If r is an $\mathcal{L}$-sentence, the main difference between $r\,!$ and r'' is that a negative answer to $r\,!$ means that r has not been recorded in M *up to the time of query;*

[12] These are rules, like modus ponens (If "A implies B" and "A" are both true, so is "B") according to which certain well-formed formulas (e.g., $\mathcal{L}'$-sentences) are immediately derivable, from others. Any finite sequence of well-formed formulas is called a "proof" if each one is either an axiom or immediately derivable from preceding ones. A theorem—the last formula in such a sequence—is called provable if a proof can be specified.

a negative answer (false) to r'' means that r can *never* be recorded as a true statement.

Some important results, both from analysis and from computer simulation studies, toward the possibility of theorem-proving machines have been obtained. Some of these involve new and efficient search techniques, which is the central problem. These results will not be discussed here because of our primary interest in inductive rather than deductive processing, though the latter is very important for our purpose. The fundamental theorems of mathematical logic limit the class of logical queries that can be answered. Gödel's famous theorem asserts that even in so simple a system of logic as needed for number theory, there is at least one well-formed formula which is not provable *and* its negation is not provable either. In a sense, there is no single formalization of number theory which does not miss some fact of number theory. Another very important and interesting result of the same type is Church's theorem. To state it, call a proposition constructive if it will occur somewhere among the list of all possible propositions that could be constructed, given no time limit; call a proposition effective if it can be immediately recognized as belonging to the list. The theorem asserts that there are propositions, with as few as two variables, which are constructive but not effective. For example, whatever method is proposed to test the logical truth of a proposition like "If all children are human, then children's clothes are human clothes," there will be propositions to which this method does not apply.

Factual queries, $r\,!$, are special cases of logical queries because if r is recorded in M, the answer to r'' will be "yes, r is (materially) true." Reconsider the example "There is a y such that $\log_2 5{,}000 = y$" + s_3. Let p be the probability that the $\mathcal{L}$-sentence "$\log_2 5{,}000 = 12.28879$" is recorded in M at any time.

Assume p constant and that all successive $\mathcal{L}$-sentences recorded in M, one at a time, are statistically independent. The probability that the sentence will be recorded by query time t is about $1 - e^{-pt}$. The probability that statements, like s_1 and s_2, from which the truth or falsity of s_3 could be deduced, are on record by time t should be much larger than $1 - e^{-pt}$ in most cases.

General Queries

Consider the question "Was the Declaration of Independence signed in Washington?" Suppose that the sentence s = "The Declaration of Independence was signed in Philadelphia" is recorded in M. Suppose further that there are no recorded statements from which the answer to the above question, interpreted as a logical query, could be rigorously deduced. There is still an important sense in which the question is meaningful. From the many recorded sentences involving "Washington," it may be *inductively inferred*—conjectured with a high plausibility—that Washington is a president, a city, a state, a place; also, that signing the Declaration of Independence is an historic event; also that if an historic event occurs in one place, it cannot occur in another place. This and similar inferences are unlikely to be already explicitly recorded. From these inferences, which are especially constructed to answer this question, the answer can be deductively inferred. But the primary difficulty lies in finding usable premises for such deduction. What makes it a difficulty is the unlimited number of $\mathcal{L}'$-sentences that *could* be constructed, and which obviously cannot be tested for their value as premises—even an infinitesimal fraction of them.

A general query will be represented by r ?, where r is an $\mathcal{L}'$-sentence, and ? is a new primitive added to $\mathcal{L}'$. In the above example, r = "The Declaration of Independence was signed in Washington." A general question r ? specifies

search for the inductive inference leading to "r is probably true (or r is probably false)." Thus, both logical and factual queries are special cases of general queries. If r is an $\mathcal{L}$-sentence, while "No" to r ! means that r is not now on record, "No" to r " that r can never be on record (probability 1), a negative answer to r ? means that it is very improbable that r will ever be recorded.

Concept-Formation

Insofar as all the well-formed formulas of a language like $\mathcal{L}'$ can be enumerated, the principles of how appropriate plausible conjectures can be inductively attained can be studied with a highly simplified but analogous model. At any given time t, the dictionary store D has entries involving a finite number of names (R's or L's), say $n(t)$ of them. Thus, M could contain at most $[n(t)]^3$ different sentences. (This is, of course, a theoretical upper bound since most combinations of R's and L's do not occur.) Since class concepts are represented by a finite sequence of, say $m(t)$, symbols, each either an $\mathcal{L}$-sentence, N, (A), or the unwritten "and," at most $(n(t) + 3)^{m(t)}$ phrases could, theoretically be on record in M'. That is, only concepts (hypotheses, conjectures) that could be represented as one of these phrases can be formed at time t. Assuming, for the sake of argument, that $n(t)$ and $m(t)$ do not change with time, conclusions reached with the simple model described in sections 2 and 3 will also apply. More important, however, is the "experimental mathematics" technique used to obtain these results, which might also apply to the more sophisticated model for concept-formation considered here.

Recall that in the conventional concept-formation paradigm, input statements could be represented by an n-bit word (representing the description of a sample object in terms of n two-valued attributes) together with a Yes/No signal (indicating whether or not the object is an instance of the concept; see p. 188). Purely conjunctive concepts could also be conveniently expressed as a sequence of 0's, 1's or X's, where X in a particular position of the formatted sequence that denotes some fixed attribute (e.g., color) means that this attribute is irrelevant. Thus, the example of "all red and square objects" described in section 3 (p. 188) could also be represented by $0\ 1\ X$. Here 0 in the first position means color red; 1 in the second means shape of a square; X in the third means size could be either that of a one inch square or a four inch square. Thus, $0\ 1\ X$ denotes the set of the two 3-bit words $0\ 1\ 0$ and $0\ 1\ 1$. With n attributes, 3^n different conjunctive concepts would be constructed. As many as 2^{3^n} disjunctions of conjunctions could be constructed, but not all of them are different. This number corresponds to the $(n(t) + 3)^{m(t)}$ possible phrases mentioned earlier.

If all 3^n conjunctive concepts were equiprobable, there is a search or selection strategy—a procedure for sequentially selecting n-bit words for examination and deciding which n-bit word to examine next depending on the Yes/No response—such that the average total number of n-bit words that need be examined does not exceed $\log_2 3^n$ or $1.76n$. Suppose, however, that the sequence of n-bit words cannot be freely chosen but that each word is, for example, chosen by independent random selections (with replacement) from all 2^n equiprobable words. The average number $\bar{N}$ of drawings which need not be exceeded for the sample to contain sufficient information for selecting an adequate conjunctive hypothesis—assuming that the data is consistent with a *conjunctive* concept—could, in principle, be computed. The corresponding optimal strategy for selecting and revising the hypotheses could also be analytically derived.

Because such analyses (39) are very difficult in the general case, computer simulations have been used by the author and others (19, 20, 14). There are a number of simulations which are more or less closely related. The work of Hovland and Hunt (14) is most closely related, but is, like that of Feigenbaum (10), oriented to simulating human concept-formation. Bonner's program (4) examines a time sequence of unclassified n-bit words (representing printed characters), one at a time, and classifies each into one of a predetermined number (e.g., 26) of similarity classes by "exclusive or" comparisons with previous words.

There are many other similar "classification" programs and models with adaptive features, too numerous to be reviewed here. For example, in an important recent study (38) related to the pioneering ideas of Selfridge (32) a pattern-recognition program that generates, evaluates and adjusts its own operators for finding and combining attributes is reported. An interesting approach modeled after mathematical genetics and bearing a striking resemblance to conventional servo-mechanism models is discussed in (5). The technique used in (19) was to write computer programs that reads the labeled n-bit words, one at a time. With each input word, it produces one of the 3^n hypotheses—words of the type $0\ 1\ X$—according to a particular strategy. One such type of strategy was: retain the hypothesis in force if the current input confirms it; if it does not, change the hypothesis as little as possible to make it consistent with all previously recorded inputs. Different strategies are embodied in separate programs. Several random input sequences are generated. There is a count of the number N of input words that had to be examined before the correct conjunctive concept was first found. These counts are averaged over a random sample of such input sequences (random permutations of the same input-words), to obtain $\bar{N}$, the mean minimum number of probe words needed to find the concept. In this way, hypothesis-selection or concept-formation strategies with the following properties were found:

(a) $\bar{N}$ is much less than the mean number of probe words needed to logically determine each of the n positions in the conjunctive concept as being either 0, 1 or X.

(b) There is a function assigning a credibility to each hypothesis on the basis of the accumulated probe words. The mean number of probe words at which this function first shows an unusual increase is closely correlated with $\bar{N}$.

(c) If there is storage capacity for recording only the last T probe words, then $\bar{N}$ plotted against T looks like a sharply dropping curve with a horizontal asymptote; the value of T at which N reaches its limiting values is independent of n.

The measure of credibility which was used satisfies conditions for such a measure analogous to those stated by Polya (29).

1. If an hypothesis, say $01X$, implies an input-word, say (010, Yes), and that input word actually occurs, then the hypothesis is more credible.

2. A positively confirming instance, like 010 for $01X$, which is less probable adds more to the credibility of an hypothesis than another more probable and positively confirming instance.

3. A positively confirming instance which differs greatly from previous inputs adds more to the credibility of an hypothesis than an equiprobable positively confirming instance that differs less from previous inputs.

As already emphasized, the names or concepts—neither their number $n(t)$ nor what they are—should be considered a priori prescribed, as assumed in the foregoing. The machine should be able to "construct" concepts it was not explicitly designed to construct. For this,

the algorithm suggested by the recursive definition of concept in section 3 is to be used. The coefficients c_2 c_3, . . . needed to compute the f's would be determined by successive approximations, based on user responses for evaluation somewhat as in (45). The machine has, of course, the facility for assigning new names to such concepts, namely the $\mathcal{L}$-name $R(n + 1)$, where n is the largest integer used for $\mathcal{L}$-names so far. The definitions of such names are stored in M'.

The general key problem in inductive concept-formation concerns the efficiency of such algorithms. Indeed, efficiency cannot be defined except in terms of the extent to which the concepts (beliefs) so formed can serve to correctly classify (assimilate) future experiences and adequately respond to queries. Efficiency also refers to the extent to which concept-representations can be formed within reasonable constraints on time and storage capacity. Since unavailability of relevant analytic techniques are likely to severely and rapidly limit the extent to which this problem can be attacked, the simulation technique of "experimental mathematics" described above is being used and holds considerable promise.

Manner of Use

The purpose of an adaptive concept-processing machine is to help people with their information needs. People could use it to extend and amplify their memory in the manner of V. Bush's ingenious Memex (7). As such, it could be a personalized information or document storage and retrieval system. This would be inordinately expensive unless shared by a number of people whose personal information needs coincide.

The three most important ways in which a machine, by virtue of its great storage capacity, speed and reliability could help people were mentioned in the very beginning of this paper. The first is to help people cope with the enormous amount of information that they normally encounter, and most of which is not immediately pertinent. If they encounter facts they would like recorded for possible future use, they would enter these into our hypothetical machine in the form of $\mathcal{L}$-sentences within minutes. Many of these facts would be assimilated into the machine's memory more usefully than if the person had tried to remember it himself; this applies particularly to topics in which the person does not have much experience with the basic concepts. To assimilate a new fact means to detect non-superficial logical and other relations to previously recorded facts. Thus, a hitherto unencountered name could be related to previously recorded names not only through the $\mathcal{L}$-sentence in which it was introduced, but through various devices like transitive predicates, and $\mathcal{L}'$-sentences, inductively arrived at, from which inferences can be made.

Secondly, to perform their jobs more effectively, certain people can benefit from pertinent timely information that is either disseminated to them or delivered to them upon request. Both a standing request or a query—the first having no response time specified and resulting in automatic dissemination of newly arrived facts submitted by others or a central source—are entered as either factual, logical or general queries. The most important thing to stress is that the machine does not necessarily supply answers; it supplies the person with enough information in the form of clues and aids for revising a request so that the person can, by "conversing" with the machine, obtain the information he ought to have, not necessarily what at first he states he wants. It is primarily to communicate with a person whose thinking involves concepts, and whose language represents concepts, that a machine, too, must deal with representations of concepts. Similarly, the machine may not be able to provide answers until it, in turn, asks some questions and receives more information from the questioner.

Finally, the machine's representations of concepts change continually, adapting to the continual stream of factual and request inputs from the individuals it is to serve. The machine might inductively form "beliefs"—that is, $\mathcal{L}'$-sentences that serve as plausible conjectures or hypotheses—which could prove useful to people both for what they suggest, and for what these conjectures imply that might be interesting to people. In this way, such a machine, if it proves feasible, could serve to amplify man's non-numerical information processing abilities in somewhat the way that computers have amplified man's arithmetical abilities to the point of permitting computations that could never be attempted before.

REFERENCES

1. Amarel, S., "An Approach to Automatic Theory Formation," *Illinois Symposium on the Principles of Self-Organizing Systems*, May 1960.
2. Bar-Hillel, Y., and R. Carnap, "Semantic Information," *Brit. J. Philos, Science*, 4, August 1953, p. 127.
3. Bohnert, H. "An English-Like Extension of An Applied Predicate Calculus," Technical Note AFOSR-TN-62-3, AF-49(638)-1062, February 1962.
4. Bonner, R., "A 'Logical-Pattern' Recognition Program," *IBM J. Res. Develop.*, in publication.
5. Bremermann, H. J., "The evolution of Intelligence. The Nervous System as a Model of its Environment," TR No. 1, USNRO 43200, July 1958.
6. Bruner, J. S., J. J. Goodnow, and A. A. Austen, *A Study of Thinking*, John Wiley and Sons, Inc., New York, N. Y., 1956.
7. Bush, V., "As We May Think," *Atlantic Monthly*, July 1945, *176*, pp. 101-108.

8. Craft, J. L., E. H. Goldman, and W. B. Strohm, "A Table Look-up Machine for Processing of Natural Languages," *IBM J. Res. Develop.*, **5**, No. 3, July 1961, pp. 192–203.
9. Estrin, G., "Maze Structure and Information Retrieval," Proc. Int. Conf. Science Information, National Acad. Science, 1958.
10. Feigenbaum, E. A., "The Simulation of Verbal Learning Behavior," *Proc. WJCC*, May 1960, pp. 133–144.
11. Gelernter, H., J. R. Hansen, and C. L. Gerberich, "A Fortran-Compiled List-Processing Language," *J. ACM*, **7**, pp. 87–101, April 1960.
12. Green, B. F., Jr., A. K. Wolf, and C. Chomsky, "Baseball: An Automatic Question-Answerer," *Proc. WJCC*, May 1960, pp. 219–224.
13. Hovland, C. I., "A 'communication-analysis' of Concept Learning," *Psychol. Rev.*, **59**, pp. 461–472, 1952.
14. Hovland, C. I., and C. B. Hunt, "Programming a Model of Human Concept-Formation," *Proc. WJCC*, May 1960, pp. 145–156.
15. Hull, C. L., "Quantitative Aspects of the Evolution of Concepts," *Psychol. Monographs*, **28**, No. 1 (Whole No. 123), 1920.
16. Kemeny, J., "Type Theory vs. Set Theory," PhD. Thesis, Princeton, Abstract in *J. Symbol. Logic*, March 1950.
17. King, G. W., "Table Look-up Procedures in Language Processing, Part I, The Raw Text," *IBM J. Res. Develop.*, **5**, 1961, p. 86.
18. Kochen, M., and E. H. Galanter, "The Acquisition and Utilization of Information in Problem Solving and Thinking," *Info. and Control*, **1**, No. 3 (1958), pp. 267–288.
19. Kochen, M., "Experimental Study of 'Hypothesis-Formation' by Computer," *Information Theory*, Butterworth & Co., Ltd., London, 1960, pp. 377–403.
20. Kochen, M., "An Experimental Program for the Selection of Disjunctive 'Hypotheses'," *Proc. WJCC*, May 1961, pp. 571–578.
21. Langer, S., *Philosophy in a New Key*, 3rd ed., Harvard University Press, 1957.
22. Librarian of Congress, Annual Report 1961. U. S. Government Printing Office, Washington, 1961, p. xi.
23. McCarthy, J., "Recursive Functions of Symbolic Expressions," (LISP), *Commun. ACM*, **3**, April 1960, pp. 184–195.
24. McCarthy, J., "Programs with Common Sense," *Mech. of Thought Processes*, Vol. 1, HMS, London, 1959, pp. 75–84.
25. National Science Foundation, "Current Research and Development," in *Scientific Documentation*, No. 9, NSF-61-76, November 1961, pp. 205–207.
26. Neisser, U., "Time-Analysis of Logical Processes in Man," *Proc. WJCC*, May 1961, pp. 579–586.
27. Newell, A., and H. Simon, "Programming the Logic Theory Machine," *Proc. WJCC*, 1957, pp. 230–240.
28. Newell, A., J. C. Shaw, H. Simon, and F. M. Tonge, "An Introduction to Information Processing Language—IPLV," *Commun. ACM*, **3**, April 1960, pp. 205–282.
29. Polya, G., *Mathematics and Plausible Reasoning*, Princeton University Press, Princeton, 1954.
30. Quine, W. V. O., "Reduction to a Dyadic Predicate," *J. Symbol. Logic*, **19**, 1954, pp. 180–182.
31. Samuel, A. L., "Some Studies in Machine Learning Using the Game of Checkers," *IBM J. Res. Develop.*, **3**, No. 3, July 1959, pp. 211–229.

32. Selfridge, O. G., "Pandemonium: A Paradigm for Learning," *Mechanization of Thought Processes,* London, HMSO, 1959, pp. 511–535.
33. Solomonoff, R. J., "An Inductive Inference Machine," *IRE National Convention Record,* Part 2, 1957, pp. 56–62.
34. Stevens, M. E., "A Machine Model of Recall," *Proc. Intern. Conf. on Information Processing UNESCO House,* Paris, 1959, pp. 309–315.
35. Stone, P. J., R. F. Bales, J. Z. Namenwirth, and D. M. Ogilvie, *The General Inquirer: A Computer System for Content Analysis and Retrieval Based on the Sentence as a Unit of Information,* Harvard University, November 1961.
36. Swanson, D., "Information Retrieval: State of the Art," *Proc. WJCC,* May 1961, p. 239.
37. Taube, M., "Storage and Retrieval of Information by Means of the Association of Ideas," *American Documentation,* **6,** pp. 1–18, 1955.
38. Uhr, L., and C. Vossler, "A Pattern Recognition Program that Generates, Evaluates and Adjusts its own Operators," *Proc. WJCC,* May 1961, pp. 555–570.
39. Watanabe, S., "Information-Theoretic Aspects of Inductive and Deductive Inference," *IBM J. Res. Develop.,* **2,** No. 4, April 1960, pp. 208–231.
40. Yngve, V. H., "COMIT as an IR-Language," *Commun. ACM,* **5,** No. 1, January 1961, pp. 19–27.

Appendix: Discussion

by Merrill M. Flood

Dr. Kochen has described the adaptive man-machine non-arithmetical information processing system (AMNIPS) that he and his associates are developing at IBM. This is to be an intelligent machine capable of learning from its users, but intended to serve users primarily as an aid in such tasks as bibliographical and biographical search.

AMNIPS is both a library and a teaching machine. As an adaptive library, the system has the property that its response to a particular user's query at a later time will depend directly upon the kind of use made of it meanwhile by other users. As a teaching machine, the system molds its responses to match the personal characteristics of each user, and even formulates explicit working hypotheses regarding the likely interests

and purposes of each particular user at the time of use.

Dr. Kochen has been very conservative in his remarks. He has described only the equipment and procedures already well along in their development. For example, the IBM photostore is the central memory component for the experimental prototype of AMNIPS. Photostore is a "read only" photoscopic disk memory with a capacity of about 5×10^7 bits and maximum access time of perhaps 20 msec. But IBM has an advanced version of photostore under development with a capacity of 10^{12} bits, and maximum access time of a few milliseconds, or the equivalent of better than 20,000 photostores in a single piece of equipment. Now 10^{12} bits is the equivalent of about one million magnetic core memories, each of 32,000 36-bit words, so memory capacity will surely not limit such systems in the future.

The real difficulties in developing intelligent machines of this type are with software rather than hardware. Unlike the computer, where there was a fully developed scientific discipline to be served, the non-arithmetical machine must perform tasks that only human beings now perform and for which there are as yet no algorithms. There is no general algorithm as yet for language translation, or for literature searching, as there was for matrix inversion, and other arithmetical tasks, when the early computers were under development.

Dr. Kochen has shown us that these difficult software problems can be studied effectively. It is central to his research strategy that he assumes that human users will interact with the intelligent machine, and that machine and user will help each other to improve their permanent stores of information during each such interaction. That this interaction must be communicated by console keyboard for machine input, and by line printing and scope display for machine output, and that such a limited dyadic predicate formal language must be used for input, very seriously restricts the capability of this first experimental version of AMNIPS. However,

I am convinced that Dr. Kochen is wise to start with this relatively modest goal at the outset, and let the course of future developments force him into appropriate extensions and modifications of his experimental system.

Personally, I would urge that AMNIPS be treated about the same as one would treat a curious, intelligent, year-old child who lacked his five main senses but who had a vast and reliable memory. Programming is akin to early training in the structure of a simple formal language, and query subroutines are akin to early training in the acceptance and performance of simple tasks. It takes a great deal of this early training before the child is ready and able to form concepts, make generalizations, and otherwise use his deductive and inductive powers. Furthermore, the child must receive a large basic store of information before he can do much internal processing. With the child, unlike AMNIPS, we already know what language we wish to use eventually; in AMNIPS the creation of a suitable language must be done in parallel with development and training of the system. I fondly hope and trust that some mature AMNIPS of the future will serve me well as a "reference librarian," and help me to keep abreast of the rapidly growing literature on AMNIPS!

B. *Analogies*

What could we learn about improving information systems by observing the way in which nature regulates its information systems? Could mechanisms similar to those found in individual organisms operate in social information systems? The clichés that the airplane was not invented by watching birds in flight, and that the wheel is not found in nature, are not appropriate here. A more apt analogy would be to point out that an artificial limb or hearing aid is to the human body as a retrieval system is to the ongoing social information system. We may not design an artificial limb to be *structurally like* the way nature grew the limb, but we want it to share the *essential functions*. Therefore, an understanding of natural functions is not merely helpful; it is essential.

In a way, when we seek information from an information-retrieval system, we wish to relieve our minds from the strain of trying to remember, recall, organize, and assimilate all the valuable little bits of information that we do not want to lose. If our file drawers are mechanical extensions of our own memories, then both need to be better organized so as to match. It is essential that we know something about how our minds organize, file, and recall that which we keep in the internal memory rather than in the external memory aids.

Two examples of a social information system are an invisible college and a closely knit, library-centered university community. Would a better understanding of how a person organizes his own memory for recall help in the design of filing systems that are to extend, relieve, and amplify his limited memory? Could the organization of a person's private files suggest better ways of designing a public file, such as a library catalog or index?

The eminent biologist Paul Weiss explores a beautiful analogy between knowledge as a growth process and the corresponding growth processes in organisms. The literature contains a number of related papers,[1] but the one chosen is the most eloquent and suggestive article for the purpose of this book. It captures the thesis of this entire book.

Another eminent biologist, O. H. Schmitt, masterfully summarizes much of what is and is not known about physiological bases for memory, storage,

[1] Orr, R. H., "The Metabolism of New Scientific Information: A Preliminary Report," *American Document*, **12**, No. 1, January 1961.

and retrieval. He proposes important directions that may bring information theory and computer lore to bear on the key problems in a significant way.

The greatest strides in our understanding of biological mechanisms for the storage and transfer of information, in particular for genetic information and racial memory, have come from biochemistry. Somewhat in this direction of molecular biology, but more directly concerned with memory and learning behavior during the life of an animal are the very recent and remarkable findings of Albert and others, which are masterfully summarized in a recent article in *Scientific Research*.

On the more molar, psychological level there are numerous papers about memory and retrieval (recall, remembering). Of these, one stands out as a classic. It is pertinent both for the information systems designer concerned with the human engineering aspects and for the information scientist concerned with possible analogies. This is George Miller's famous paper about the number seven as the number of distinct items that can be recalled in a counting task, for example, a seven-digit telephone number.

A very recent paper, by R. Brown and D. McNeill[2], like the Miller[3] paper, should have been included here had it not been for its length and detail peripheral to information-retrieval systems theory. The highly interesting findings of this study are as follows. People, asked to try to recall rarely used English words on being given only the definition of that word, showed that they knew, prior to recall of the wanted word, the following data about it: (*a*) the numbers of letters; (*b*) the number of syllables; and (*c*) the location of primary stress. Sometimes parts of the missing word were recalled first. The features of words to which people seem to pay most attention are those which occur at the beginning or the ending of the missing word.

It would seem that this kind of knowledge is highly pertinent to the designer of a filing system who is concerned with the human engineering aspects.

In the field of "artificial intelligence," there has been growing interest and speculation about automata with the ability to comprehend a natural language. Some of this literature is described in Simmons' survey and is criticized by Kasher in Part Three of this book. The problem of specifying an automaton with functions that are analogous in an essential way to human capabilities for thinking, learning, imagining, reasoning, and linguistic performance is of obvious intellectual interest for information retrieval. It is, like the work on the physiology, biochemistry, and psychology

[2] Brown, R., and D. McNeill, "The 'Tip of the Tongue' Phenomenon," *Journal of Verbal Learning and Verbal Behavior*, 5, No. 4, August 1966, pp. 325–337.

[3] Miller, G. A., The Magical Number Seven, Plus or Minus Two: Some Limits on Our Capacity for Processing Information, *Psychol. Rev.*, 63, No. 2, 1956, pp. 81–97.

of memory, of even greater interest in its own right. There have been no scientific advances in this area comparable to the ones reported by the other papers in this part of the book. But there have been advances in our understanding, in great measure due to the insights of D. M. MacKay. The next selection is the result of a series of intensive discussions to assess the claims and ideas in this area.

Knowledge: A Growth Process[1]

by Paul Weiss

It seems appropriate for a member of the American Philosophical Society for Promoting Useful Knowledge to review for himself on occasion the philosophy by which useful knowledge is promoted. I have indulged in such a private exercise, not as a philosopher, which I am not, but as a practitioner of science. In our day, promotion of knowledge has become a public trust. Its managers and practitioners must see and keep the object—knowledge—in sharpest focus, lest it get blurred in the excitement of a mass-production boom, or get disjointed by progressive parceling among producers, sponsors, distributors, interpreters, administrators, and consumers.

Promoting knowledge can only mean fostering its intrinsic growth. To do this rationally requires insight into the nature of the growth process. I wish to show that, fundamentally, *our knowledge grows the way a living body does.* The kind of knowledge I shall deal with is scientific knowledge, implying no inference to other forms. And even this limited perspective is slanted from the angle of my specialty, the life sciences. Yet, it takes the vantage point of a biologist to recognize the growth of knowledge as truly a mirror image of the growth of organisms. Not long ago, I summed it up as follows: "*Scientific knowledge grows like an organic tree, not as a compilation of collector's items.* Facts, observations, discoveries, as items, are but the nutrients on which the tree of knowledge feeds, and not until they

have been thoroughly absorbed and assimilated, have they truly enlarged the body of knowledge" (1). This thesis I shall now try to expound.

My model is a higher animal. The main steps of its growth process are diagrammed in the upper half of Fig. 1, with boxes indicating material entities, and arrows, the flow of processes, connecting them. Growth converts food from the environment into body substance in a sequence of four major steps: intake, digestion, assimilation, and final utilization. The raw materials are gathered from the environment and either stored or passed on directly for alimentary processing. Digestible items are *broken down* chemically to more manageable compounds, which are then *screened* and *sorted* into useful and useless varieties. The wastes, together with undigestible residues, are eliminated, sharing the fate of spoilage from protracted storage. The useful items, the true nutrients, are circulated to the tissues, whose cells pick what they need, then recombine and modify it to form intermediary products, already bearing specific earmarks of that organism, some to be recirculated for use by other cells, some still to be discharged as waste; and finally, culminating the synthesis, each cell constructs from this supply pool selectively the substances and structures uniquely characteristic of its own kind. In this last step, cells branch in two directions: They either reproduce, that is, add more cells to the body; or

SOURCE: *Science,* **131,** June 10, 1960, pp. 1716–1719.
[1] This article is based on a paper read at the meeting of the American Philosophical Society, Philadelphia, November 13, 1959, and was printed simultaneously in *Science* and in the *Proceedings of the American Philosophical Society,* **104,** No. 2 (1960).

they turn to the manufacture of special products, like fibers, hair, secretions, bone, and such.

This model is abridged and over-simplified. However, it illustrates the essence of the growth process, which is that in its growth an organism never adopts foreign matter outright, but re-organizes and assimilates it to fit its own peculiar pattern. Even a leech must first dissolve the hemoglobin of its meal of blood and then compose its own brand from the fragments. Organic growth is by *assimilation,* not accretion. Food items are not simply stuck on to the body, but, on the contrary, lose their identity and become anonymous and indistinguishably blended into the body's very own type of constituents by the processing chain of extraction, screening, sorting, fitting, and recasting.

How closely this course is mirrored in the growth of knowledge is symbol-ized in the lower half of Fig. 1, be-ginning from its source—experience, still unprocessed. Probing of the environ-ment furnishes the raw data of informa-tion, which are either stored as records for future use or analyzed forthwith. The products of analysis are then screened and sorted according to relevance. Ir-relevant ones go into discard, sharing the fate of records become obsolete. And from this sorting, the pile of data emerges as an ordered system, cata-logued and classified, yet each item still revealing its erstwhile identity. The grandest examples of such ordered sets of data are perhaps the Linnean system of species prior to the theory of evolu-tion, or the Mendelyeev Atomic tables prior to modern physics. In various stages of evaluation, such packaged in-formation is then widely circulated, lead-ing to confluence and critical correlation with countless contributions from other sources. From this synthetic process, hy-potheses emerge, which, upon further verification, turn into integral parts of the body of knowledge—theorems, prin-ciples, rules, and laws—general formulas which not only supersede the itemized accounts of the very data from which they were derived, but can dispense with the further search for items of in-formation, which they predictively sub-sume.

At this stage, data have become as-similated, have lost their individual iden-tities in merging with that higher en-tity—the body of organized knowledge. Sheer listing has given way to under-standing. A patchwork of unrelated facts has been transformed into a rationally connected thought structure of inner con-sistency, viable and durable, subject to the tests of survival and the adaptive improvements of evolution—a veritable model of an organism. As in the organ-ism, the culminating phase is branched: as basic knowledge grows, part of the increment accrues to its own body, yield-ing more basic knowledge, while another part is converted into differentiated prod-ucts—all that is commonly lumped under the attribute "applied."

Note that no separate express tracks connect either foodstuffs directly with functional products in the organism, or informational data with practical results in human affairs but that both must be routed through the common machinery for growth. In knowledge, as in nature, fruit grows on trees and cannot be raised directly on the soil by short cuts by-passing the tree.

Our growth analogy could be ex-panded—tradition standing for heredity; novel ideas, for mutations; the "team" approach, for symbiosis—but the general parallelism will have become clear enough for us now to examine its im-plications.

In the first place, it shows that in-formation is not tantamount to knowl-edge. Information is but the raw ma-terial, the precursor, of knowledge. To hoard a store of unrelated items of in-formation in a mental gullet by rote memory and without sense of relevance —including the ability to regurgitate the data on a quiz master's prompting— should pass for knowledge no more than the stuffing of a hamster's pouch can

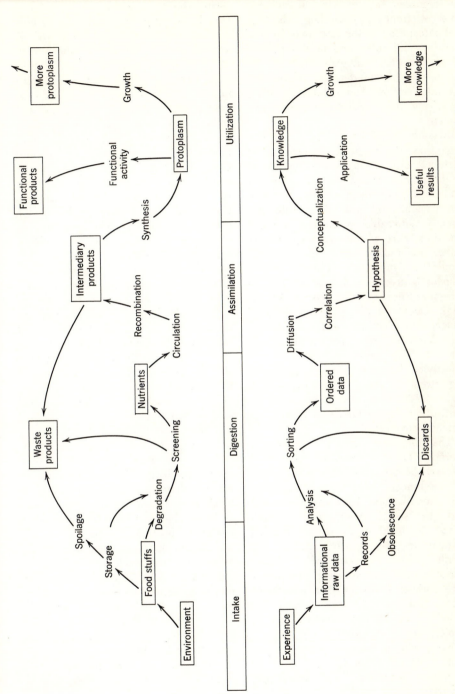

Fig. 1. (*Top*) The growth process of higher animals. (*Bottom*) The growth of knowledge.

be regarded as growth. Knowledge emerges from the distilling, shaping, and integrating of the raw material into concepts and rules, and in this process of condensation and generalization, the number of bits of detailed information dwindles, rather than mounts: a piling up of raw data signals glut rather than growth.

Accordingly, if knowledge grows like organisms, we ought to observe sound dietetics and avoid unhealthy over-stuffing; the symptoms of glut—redundancy, superdetermination, oversophistication, and just plain bulk—are already noticeable in current research practices. Part of the syndrome carries rather undignified names, such as "soft money" or "projectitis." But the crucial ailment is myopic vision, which fails to recognize the true character of knowledge. Once out of sight, the body of concepts to which data collection should be related no longer guides the search for data. The sense of relevance and selectivity becomes atrophic, composing stops at sheer compiling, search becomes pointless, and freedom of investigation degenerates into license for random movements.

The diagnosis calls for preventive therapy. One nostrum proposes that research be governed with social utility as the beacon. Unfortunately, the diet this prescribes for knowledge is of the sort that social insects feed to their larvae to mold them to preordained stations in life, mostly soldiers and sterile workers, instead of nurturing versatile and reproductive specimens. By contrast, I submit that knowledge grows best on a liberal balanced diet based on variety and wide freedom of choice, free of excessive roughage.

Now, who is there to write the formula? We all abhor the notion of an all-wise potentate of knowledge, whether person, institution, or society, to rule on what will, and what will not, promote the growth of knowledge. But there is one wizard, who has the formula and gladly hands it over for the asking—history, which has watched knowledge grow from infancy. It tells us that the key agent in the growth of knowledge has always been the human mind, imaginative, critical, and integrative; devising robots, tools, and techniques merely as aids to extend the limited reach of man's perception and control, but never abdicating the functions of evaluation and invention. Promoting knowledge, therefore, implies giving full scope to the exercise of the faculty for assimilation and synthesis by which the mind converts facts to knowledge. The history of knowledge contains the rules to give those bent on promoting knowledge by either doing or supporting research the necessary cues for intelligent and responsible self-direction. The stress here lies on "self"; there is no need for forcible external steering: bearings for self-steering are needed. But how could the uninitiated self orient itself purposefully if we hide or blur the goal? Or do we expect each self to rediscover the goal for himself by trial-and-error, fumbling and floundering in semidarkness, when we could readily draw on the lessons of the past to illuminate both goal and path?

You realize what I am driving at. As educators we mold tomorrow's promoters of knowledge. We must be far more explicit than we have been lately in teaching them not just the present state of knowledge, but the way in which it has grown up to here, which is the only way in which it can grow further. Inspired teachers teach and practice it, but they are too few. Some students find it by themselves, but not enough of them. So, let us restore to education some fundamentalism—making explicit to the student the fundamental bearings needed for him to chart his own course in clear view of what furthers knowledge and what does not, instead of letting him drift in the cross currents of traditional momenta and alluring fashions. Ideas—yes, even well-founded speculation—should find a respectful place again among the shining gadgets.

And his critical mind, rather than the board room of a fellowship or grants committee, should become again the primary testing and screening ground for relevance. If he finds data, let him explain their meaning. And if he can't he should have a sense of incompleteness, and not of glee over having prevented mental contamination of nature. Let editors encourage, rather than blue pencil, an author's interpretive excursions. And let the whole process of fostering knowledge become refocused on penetration and concentration, instead of sheer expansion and bulk. Or else, knowledge—an organism—might come to share the fate of the dinosaurs.

Yet, notwithstanding this plea for more thorough digestion and mental processing of data, there is another side of nature which is refractory to this treatment and does not fit our analog at all. I am referring to those phenomena whose constellation in space or seriation in time is so unique that generalization would obliterate their most relevant features. We can establish general principles of parasitism, but each species of parasite has its own peculiar life history, which must be known as such. Chemical chain reactions must conform to thermodynamics law. But just what sequence of steps constitutes a given metabolic cycle must still be determined separately in each instance. Despite their common name, each hormone has its own special way of operating, and each disease has its specific course. In other words, the information which in the search for basic knowledge would merely be a way station, becomes a terminal; to remain useful, its itemized character must be preserved.

This seems the proper province of automation, relegating increasingly to technological devices the jobs of recording; scanning, sorting, reducing, storing, and retrieving data. But even here human intelligence will have to judge what to explore and to record. As every single walnut is unique, can we afford to go on indefinitely shelling walnuts and loading down our libraries with records of their physiognomies? Certainly not, unless there is a point to it. To make the point is up to the investigator. But it is up to educators to imbue investigators with a sufficient sense of relevance and responsibility as to abstain from pointless tasks. Self-direction must not be let lapse into self-indulgence. But how draw the line? Whether to stop at pragmatism or to go on to generalize varies, of course, with subject matter, need, and interest but, above all, perspective.

To gain perspective, let us again turn to history. What is—so we may ask— the real fate of plain recorded data? What is their life expectancy, and does it differ substantially for data that can be generalized and those that cannot? Since mere occupancy of library space is no criterion of life, as against mummification, I made a little actuarial study, using as a gauge of relative vitality of data the frequency with which they are referred to in the literature.

For comparison, I chose two biological journals: *Experimental Cell Research*, with a strongly analytical emphasis, and the *Biological Bulletin*, with a larger descriptive bias. I tallied all references, except self-citations, by all authors year by year over a 10-year period and plotted the percentage frequency with which publications were cited lying back 5, 10, 15, 20, and so forth, years. Figure 2 shows the results, which are quite striking (2).

For each of the two journals, the annual percentage frequencies define with remarkable consistency a single curve, whose course expresses the rate of obsolescence of publications. The steepness of its slope should give us pause. No more than 50 percent of the annual references in *Experimental Cell Research* date further back than five years, and still older literature is rapidly lost sight of. By contrast, the flatter curve for *Biological Bulletin* re-

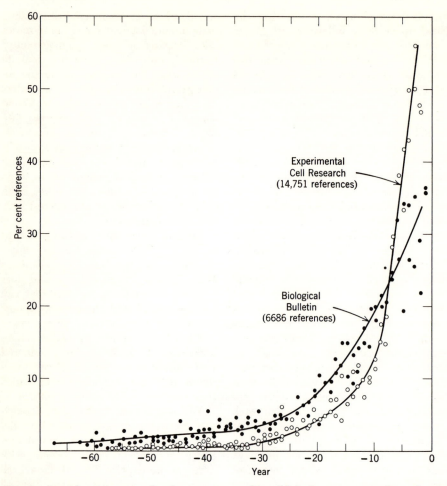

Fig. 2. Annual percentage of references to works published a given number of years previously.

veals a much greater dependence on older records. The difference is highly significant. To validate it further, I plotted the chronological frequencies of back citations during 1952–1954 in the major journals in physiology and in zoology and entomology (Fig. 3) from a report on "Scientific Serials" (3), and obtained an essentially similar pair of curves, both dropping off sharply, but the drop being much steeper in analytical physiology than in its more descriptive biological sister sciences.

The lessons of this actuarial census of literature thus are twofold: in the first place, the active life span of pure

data is at any rate amazingly short: they die of either assimilation or oblivion. And second, the less they lend themselves to assimilation, the longer they remain useful individually.

This leads me to conclude as follows: Each field of knowledge must be accorded its own merit ratio between generalization and particularization, it being taken for granted that assimilation will be driven to the utmost limits compatible with the nature of the field. Yet, in view of the rapid attrition of *all* unassimilated information, a radical reorientation of our publication policies would seem warranted, based on introducing the principle of actuarial tables, about as follows:

In each discipline separate media of publication would be established for classes of communications of different life expectancies. Each author of a manuscript would assess its prospective useful life span—presumably with the benevolent advice of editors—on a rating scale extending from the ephemeral technical note at the low end to the great synthetic opus at the other; the paper would then be allocated to the corresponding fast-aging or slow-aging class of serial. Each serial volume would be kept on library shelves only for the time span allotted to its class, and then discarded, except in a few libraries specifically designated as permanent historical repositories. Some such deliberate scheme would go far in restoring and preserving a reasonable ratio of payload to ballast in our record of knowledge.

Graded in terms of relevance, not every observation is worth reporting; not every report is worth recording; not every record is worth publishing; and not every publication is worth preserving for eternity, except in sample specimens as in Noah's Ark. I submit that this grading can still be left to the investigators and their peers, as long as they are cognizant of the true nature of knowledge as a growth process, of which assembling facts—of food for thought—is but the first preliminary step; a growth process, moreover, which often thrives better on a spare than on an overly rich diet, and in which self-restraint can readily ward off obesity.

So in conclusion, and dropping parabolic language, the effective pursuit of

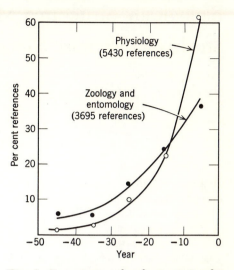

Fig. 3. Percentages of references, in the major journals in physiology and in zoology and entomology, referring to work published a given number of years previously.

knowledge is intimately linked to the old virtue of disciplined research morale which will not countenance the substitution of bigness for greatness, gadget for intellect, projects for ideas, and man-hours for thought; although it must rely to the fullest on technical relief by gadgets and man-hours in those auxiliary services which do not require the intervention of a constructive mind.

As I said at the outset, my comments are confined to *scientific* knowledge. Its steady long-range growth has still immense potential scope. We should not let it get diverted, inflated, and unbalanced by pressures for short-range crash spectaculars. More than ever, our key words should be *balance* and *perspective*.

REFERENCES

1. Weiss, P., "The Message of Science," *Occasional Papers from the Rockefeller Institute No. 1* (1959).
2. The assistance of Mrs. Sybil Bush in compiling the data is gratefully acknowledged.
3. Brown, C. H., "Scientific Serials," *Association of College and Reference Libraries Monograph No. 16* (1956).

Biologically Structured Microfields and Stochastic Memory Models

by Otto H. Schmitt

Despite excellent research directed toward understanding memory processes, we are still spectacularly ignorant of the micro-anatomical, the physiological, and the spatial-temporal systems-organization aspects of memory acquisitions, storage, and retrieval in living organisms.

No very plausible explanation has been advanced to account for the conscious memory system where short-term environmental information transduced into the organism via its sensory receptors is stored and processed.

We are even worse off when we try to understand the operation of racial memory in the context of: Sauer's and Kramer's experiments with bird navigation (1a, b, c); Lorenz's imprinting experiments (2); the experiments of Hasler, Lissmann, and others with fish and insect navigation (3a, b, c). These experiments show an inbuilt, accurate time-and-directional sense as well as an ability to detect and operate decisively on diffuse, weak, and obscure environmental clues (4).

We are only a little better off when we consider genetic memory in its simpler forms where chemical genetics and other macromolecular studies are yielding some pertinent hard information.

We are especially obtuse in discovering the physiological (functional) basis of memory.

There is available, I believe, adequate information about the molecular, cellular, and organismic basis of memory to send us plunging into hundreds of fruitful experiments if we were only freed of the strait jacket of conventional interpretation of function in the structures where memory is known to reside.

As a small nudge toward breaking this log-jam, I propose to explore here two approaches. First, I should like to rephrase some of our common knowledge about biological memory in a form such that the heavy artillery of theoretical and analogical model-making, of information-theory and computing-machine lore can be brought to bear. Second, I should like to present selected biophysical facts and methods of analysis, which, when brought together, could establish a new focal insight into the memory problem.

I. Some Characteristic Properties of Every Biological Information Handling System

1. *Data processing system* (see Fig. 1). Some equivalent of this system must reside in any biomemory system (in the case of subjective experience, output is internal).

These properties imply:

2. The storage system must be compatible with a time-sequence pulse-code modulated information input, because this is the nearly universal common neural (axonal) code. Signals may have digital significance but very often blend

SOURCE: *Macromolecular Specificity and Biological Memory*, F. O. Schmitt, Ed. Cambridge, Mass.: M.I.T. Press, 1962, pp. 7–16.

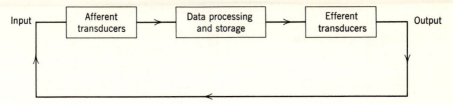

Fig. 1. Data-processing system.

this digital significance into a continuum code and almost invariably carry a positive and a negative quadrature constituent, i.e., integration and differentiation. This means that the code itself has built into it "anticipation" and "nothing new" interpretation.

Some resulting conclusions are:

(*a*) Time-interval measuring must have a biophysical implementation in memory mechanisms.

(*b*) The strong distinction now made between digital and "analog" codes is largely in the analysis rather than in the process.

(*c*) From the ease with which memory makes the conversion of a temporal sequence to a spatial sequence we must look for codes and macromolecular machinery that implement this property. This interchangeability of pattern between space and time co-ordinates is a prime feature of a *wave* function, e.g., the one dimensional form

$$p = f(x - ut)$$

where p is a state of the phenomenon, x is a spatial position, u is a velocity of propagation, and t is time. Notice that wave behavior does *not* necessarily imply periodicity.

3. The innate time sense. The time arrow and the smooth-flowing property of time are not properties that inhere prominently in the world of physical science, but are properties forced upon physics by "common sense," i.e., the physicist's time arrow is primarily a concession to our biological experience.

Among the properties that characterize biological time are:

(*a*) The high temperature coefficient of subjectively estimated time (5).

(*b*) The remarkable temperature independence of bioperiodicity in widely divergent lower and higher animal forms and even in micro-organisms and plants (6*a, b*).

(*c*) No readily acceptable biochemical basis has been found for the circadian biological process which free-runs (7*a, b*) so reliably at nearly a one-day period yet synchronizes readily with environmental clues. No experimental evidence has been found to support the attractive hypotheses that frequency division by counting, or time constant multiplication by feedback, might account for long-term bioperiodicity in terms of short-period biophysical phenomena (8). This last hypothesis contains within it a mechanism for wide-range temperature compensation without requirement for temperature independent reference processes.

4. A less oversimplified representation of a biological input-output system in the scheme of transfer-function analysis is the *Adaptive bioservo system* (9) (see Fig. 2). Some new features emphasized by this representation are:

(*a*) The neglected properties of adaptive feed-ahead loops which permit an approximately exact rather than an asymptotic approach to ideal performance.

(*b*) The feasibility of *ad hoc* reverberatory chains.

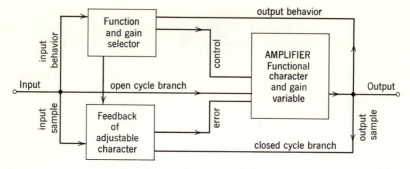

Fig. 2. Adaptive bioservo system.

(*c*) The self-purifying properties of pulsatile codes in closed-loop systems whereby signals are periodically rejuvenated according to fixed patterns, so that they can go on for long periods with virtually no deterioration of message content.

(*d*) The efficiency of a common cross-modality symbolic language (e.g., neural and hormonal codes) for associating and intercorrelating related input and output signals.

(*e*) A convenient classification of biological and technological transfer-function systems which are detailed in Table 1.

II. Biological Information Space—A Modification of the Popular Information Theory Concept Adapted to Life-Science Studies

Included in this category are the following points:

1. A multi-dimensional "phase" space in which a "pattern" or "idea" can have a multiplicity of temporal-spatial representations.

2. In this phase space, distance between points has an interpretation in terms of significance (10).

3. Language and code translations have a direct interpretation in such associated spaces. A very attractive representation of "imagination" and experimentation can be made.

4. "Protection" of an item in this space by redundancy can be illustrated,

and a decision forcing mechanism can be postulated (the trigger-circuit decision analog) (11).

5. This type of informational space invites investigation of matrix-scanning cycles temporal and spatial.

6. It is clearly necessary that biophysical mechanisms for short- and long-term memory be provided which are compatible with the layering of memory, as demonstrated by sequential return of recall under shock therapy.

7. The resolution of ambiguities and the filling in of faulty memory with plausible data by interpolation and extrapolation have a simple representation in this informational space.

8. The informational importance of *coherence*, both temporal and spatial, in biological input systems must not be neglected, as this coherence property is undoubtedly heavily used in biological data analysis.

III. Computer Science Suggests Certain Classes of Memory Processes That May Have Biological Counterparts

1. Simple ephemoral memory, e.g., the fading oscilloscope trace.

2. The ephemoral memory that becomes stable by virtue of feedback, e.g., the bistable trigger circuit.

3. Stable memory vs. energy-maintained stable memory, i.e., passive vs. active memory. The bistable transistor

flip-flop is an energy-maintained stable memory, whereas the magnetic trace is a passively stable memory.

4. Computer memory may be extinguished by the act of interrogation and may disappear or be preserved by immediate reconstitution; alternatively it may survive interrogation unmodified.

5. Circulating memory exists only by virtue of continued circulation of information around a closed path and never exists at one specifiable location.

6. Response-averaging designs with instruction time-dependent loops form attractive models for biological memory.

The prospect of technological computers built in the image of biological memory and information processing and of computers especially designed to make them compatible with the demands of biological application is most attractive (12).

IV. Biologically Structured Microfields

The term "entero transducer" has been applied to miniaturized sensing elements introduced mechanically or surgically into the organism; they usually contain a small radio transmitter to relay environmental information. The responsive transducer or transponder for such applications is currently being developed and permits a classification of information converting systems which is equally applicable in biology and in technology (see Table 1). All classes in this system have practical representation.

TABLE 1. Classes of information converting systems

Transducer	Active
Transponder	Passive
Efferent	Biological
Afferent	Technological

The idea of transponders in contrast to transducers is one of importance to biological scientists in planning their experiments as well as in interpreting them.

A transducer is a device or system which converts information from one code, format, or modality into another, while a transponder is a related informational energy converting system which responds only in response to interrogation.

This classification of information converting systems leads to a novel and productive way of thinking about the communicative interaction between normal biological components of the organism at (1) very short, (2) short, and (3) long ranges.

Evidence has been available since the late 1930s (13) to demonstrate that even the axonal extensions of nerve cells interact with each other through the external electric field, and it is generally agreed that similar electrical interaction plays at least a fairly important role in non-axonal interaction. It is important that theory and experimental techniques be developed to deal with additional electric, electromagnetic, and solid-state interactions between biological information-processing elements.

Steady electric fields cause force to be exerted on charged particles and hence can account for electrophoretic transport, but will not transport dipoles (14). Dipoles can, however, be actively transported in convergent or divergent inhomogeneous fields. Oscillating fields will similarly transport charged particles and dipoles selectively when these charges oscillate at a matched frequency. Macromolecular interfaces are a natural site for action of electric fields, and structuring of such fields temporally and spatially can make them highly selective. In the light of current laser work this strongly suggests the feasibility of active biological communication mechanisms basically powered by common biochemical oxidation-reduction sources but highly selective perhaps in specific system combinations by virtue of detailed macromolecular structure of cellular current activity for long-range effects. The field surrouding a dipole falls off as the inverse *cube* of distance, not as the inverse square. For most practical purposes, the dipole can be thought of as losing its influence at ranges in excess of three times the polar separation. Note that the field around a dipole is *not* zero in the equatorial plane. In the equatorial plane it is opposite in direction to the field along the axis and is just half the strength for any given radial distance beyond the immediate proximity of the dipole. Such dipolar field patterns can be used to build up directional patterns almost like the patterns of directional radio antennas, hence one can selectively extend or shield certain patterns and loci from effects of cellular fields and this shielding can be sharply modulated by slight phase shifts in the pattern of excitation.

A line of dipoles produces a pattern somewhat similar to the single dipole pattern but extending farther from the source for a given total aligned dipole moment.

A sheet of dipoles can produce a field nearly independent of distance near the middle of the sheet.

A structured pattern of excited dipoles can be thought of as sampling a field region and thus representing a selective interrogation of an information reservoir.

Field interaction should not be thought of as confined to the static interaction of charged particles and dipoles but should certainly include the interesting solid-state interactions now being evidenced in physical science studies of laser action, of carrier-and-hole conductions, and of microwave interaction, as well as more familiar band excitation of conduction.

V. Reciprocity and Superposition Theorems

It is desirable wherever possible to formulate field interaction or transfer properties in such a fashion that the superposition property applies and that the systems will be linear in the mathematical sense. Superposition rules for predicting effects produced by dipolar sources apply for either the potential or current formulations if the mathematical procedures are carried out properly, but it is very much more difficult to formalize cellular, intracellular, electric reactions in the potential form. It is therefore recommended that the current dipole be the accepted unit of source (15).

The reciprocity theorems from electricity and magnetism (16) form very powerful tools for study of structured fields as they permit calculation of transfer characteristics with exchange of a source and a measurement position. Otherwise inaccessible measurements can often be performed through such reciprocity inversions.

In such studies as these the Maxwell displacement current often assumes a prominent role. This displacement current is often wholly disregarded in physical chemical and biochemical theorization regarding bio-electric processes. This current which is not accompanied by the physical transport of charged particles may be larger than the total ordinary ionic current. The study of macromolecular and biosystemic relaxation processes from the audio to the microwave or even optical spectral regions offers a powerful tool in discovering microstructural interactions. Particularly important is the exploration of spatial and temporal gradients in these processes.

The conceptual differentiation between electrical potential difference and the circuital concept of electromotive forces is important and often confused (17). The simple electrical transformer with closed ring resistive single turn secondary provides an excellent illustration of this distinction.

VI. The Generalization to Biological Systems of the Transfer Function Concept

The engineer's concept of input-output relationships and indeed of more general transfer functions is ordinarily associated with relationships between a localizable input and a localizable output and is usually restricted to linear or quasilinear relationships (18). Sacrificing the convenience of Laplace transform techniques, a more generalized version of this transfer relationship for biological science application can be made by removing the requirement of linearity and by allowing the transfer to be spatially distributed. An illustration of this approach restricted to the linear case can be found in the transfer impedance function developed for electrocardiographic and electroencephalographic applications (19). Here the transfer impedance is defined by relation

$$E_o = \mathbf{Z}_t \cdot \mathbf{I}$$

Where E_o is the potential difference measured at any pair of potential points determined by any linear combination of output points, $\mathbf{Z}_t$ is the transfer impedance, and $\mathbf{I}$ is the current dipole moment. It will be noted that $\mathbf{Z}_t$ is a vector point function in real space, and $\mathbf{I}$, the source current moment, is correctly treated as a vector quantity. Reciprocity immediately allows this relationship to be inverted without modification of $\mathbf{Z}_t$ without change of scale or dimensions into the form

$$\mathbf{E} = \mathbf{Z}_t \, I_i$$

where I_i is now the current input at the points formerly used for voltage measurement. Current is now considered in the conventional scalar sense, and $\mathbf{E}$ represents the electric field strength in the domain.

This generalized transfer-function approach extended to a phase space leads to a very interesting stochastic memory model, a flexible yet useful algorithm.

REFERENCES

1a. Sauer, E. G. F., and E. M. Sauer, Star navigation of nocturnal migrating birds. The 1958 planetarium experiment. *Cold Spring Harbor Symposia on Quantitative Biology*, **25**, 263–473, 1960.

1b. Matthews, G. V. T., *Bird Navigation. Cambridge Monographs in Experimental Biology*, No. 3. Cambridge University Press, 1955.

1c. Kramer, G., *Experiments on bird orientation. Ibid.*, **94**, 265–285, 1952.

2. Lorenz, K., The comparative method in studying innate behavior patterns. *Symposia of the Society for Experimental Biology. IV, Physiological Mechanisms in Animal Behavior*, Academic Press, Inc., New York, 1950, pp. 220–268.

3a. Hasler, A. D., Perception of pathways of fishes. *Quart. Rev. Biol.*, **31**, 200–209, 1956.

3b. Lissmann, H. W., and K. E. Machin, The mechanism of object location in *Gymnarchus niloticus* and similar fish. *J. Exp. Biol.*, **35**, 451–486, 1958.

3c. Lissmann, H. W., and K. E. Machin, On the function and evolution of electric organs in fish. *J. Exp. Biol.*, **35**, 156–191, 1958.

4. *Cold Spring Harbor Symposia on Quantitative Biology*, **25**, *Biological Clocks*. The Biological Laboratory, Cold Spring Harbor, L. I., N.Y., 1960, 524 pages.

5. Hoagland, H., The physiological control of judgments of duration: evidence for a chemical clock. *J. Gen. Psych.*, **9**, 267–287, 1933.

6a. Hastings, J. W., and B. M. Sweeney, A persistent diurnal rhythm of luminescence in *Gonyavlax polyedra. Biol. Bull.*, **115**, 440–458, 1958.

6b. Bünning, E., *Biological clocks. Cold Spring Harbor Symposia on Quantitative Biology*, **25**, 1–9; Circadian rhythms and the time measurement in photoperiodism, pp. 249–256, 1960.

7a. Halberg, F., The 24-hour scale; a time dimension of adaptive functional organization. *Perspectives in Biol. and Med.*, **3**, 491–527, 1960.

7b. Halberg, F., Temporal coordination of physiologic function. *Cold Spring Harbor Symposia on Quantitative Biology*, **25**, 289–310, 1960.

8. Schmitt, O. H., Biophysical and mathematical models of circadian rhythms. *Cold Spring Harbor Symposia on Quantitative Biology*, **25**, 207–210, 1960.

9. Schmitt, O. H., Biological engineering. *Honeywell Flight Lines*, **5**, No. 1, 1–5. January 1954.

10. Shannon, C. E., Communication in the presence of noise. *Proc. Inst. Radio Eng.*, **37**, 10–21, 1949.

11. Schmitt, O. H., A thermionic trigger. *J. Sci. Instr.*, **15**, 24, 1938.

12. *Bionics Symposium* (*Living Prototypes—The Key to New Technology*). Wright Air Development Division Technical Report 60-600. U.S. Air Force, Wright-Patterson Air Force Base, Ohio, December 1960, 499 pages.

13. Schmidt, O. H., and B. Katz, Electric Interaction between two adjacent nerve fibres. *J. Physiology*, **97**, No. 4, 471, 1940.

14. Pohl, H. A., Nonuniform electric fields. *Scientific American*, **203**, No. 6, 106–112, 1960.

15. Schmitt, O. H., Lead vectors and transfer impedance. In *The Electrophysiology of the Heart*. Annals of N. Y. Acad. Sci., Vol. 65, Art 6, 1092–1109, Aug. 9, 1957.

16. Selgin, P. J., *Electrical Transmission in Steady State*. McGraw-Hill Book Co., Inc., New York, 1946, p. 31.

17. Page, L., and N. I. Adams, *Principles of Electricity*. Van Nostrand Co., New York, 1931, p. 160.

18. Murphy, G. J., *Basic Automatic Control Theory*. Van Nostrand Co., New York, 1957, pp. 129–159.

19. Schmitt, O. H., The biophysical basis of electrocardiography. In *Proceedings of the First National Biophysics Conference*, Yale University Press, New Haven, Conn., 1959, pp. 510–562.

Controversy Grows Over Molecular Basis of Memory

by the Editorial Staff of Scientific Research

The idea that memory is encoded directly in RNA molecules within the neuron (and hence can be transferred from one organism to another) is questioned by those who see memory as a special use of the genetic code.

Beyond making headlines in the popular press the recent "learning transfer" experiments have served to give a new impetus to thinking about one of the major unsolved riddles in biology—the molecular basis of memory. These experiments, in which organisms, such as planaria say, seem to acquire conditioned responses simply by eating the RNA extracted from planaria whose responses had been previously conditioned, suggest a model for the molecular basis of memory that may well lend itself to further experimental tests. To explain the phenomenon of learning transfer reported by a number of investigators (but still disputed by others) McConnell (1) postulates that memory consists of changes in the base sequence of neural RNA (see Fig. 2), these changes being induced directly by electrical impulses impinging on the neuron. The altered RNA molecules then in some unspecified way modify the functioning of the neuron giving rise to the phenomenon of memory at its most fundamental level. Also unspecified are the mechanisms by which the electrical impulses alter the RNA and altered RNA is able to replicate itself. The need for replication stems from the observation that the lifetime of an RNA molecule is much shorter than the rate of decay of memory, and this requirement stands as perhaps the biggest stumbling block for the RNA model of memory. In all known instances, RNA synthesis within the cell is gene-directed; hence proponents of the RNA model are saddled with the burden of demonstrating that in some circumstances RNA is capable of synthesis and self replication independently of genetic control.

Some biologists are so impressed with the unlikelihood of this possibility that a rival model for a molecular basis of memory has been offered that now stands in direct competition with the RNA model. This second theory maintains that memory acquisition must be linked to the genetic apparatus, particularly the mechanism of expression of the genetic information in the DNA molecule. Unlike the RNA model in which there is a single locus of memory transcription (*the* memory molecule), the genetic model regards memory as a special adaptation in nerve cells of a general biological regulatory *process* involving the repression and de-repression of genes in the DNA molecule, like the operation of an "on-off" switch (See Fig. 1).

The way in which genetic messages are played back from DNA storage is highly analogous to the way in which information is stored and information flow is regulated in the electronic digital computer. This mechanism makes for a prefabricated information switching system existing in every neuron. Operating within the framework of this

SOURCE: *Scientific Research*, **1**, No. 6, June 1966, pp. 19–22.

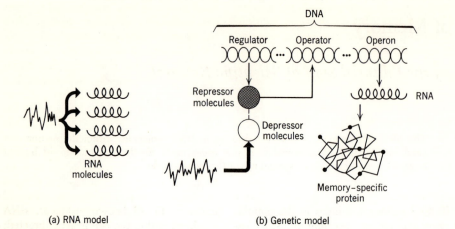

(a) RNA model   (b) Genetic model

Fig. 1. Molecular basis of memory. Memory models differ in role of genes. RNA model (*a*) proposes a direct influence on the base sequence in neuronal RNA by electrical impulses impinging on the neuron. This RNA is proposed to be a unique memory agent, making possible learning transfer from one animal to another. But in all known instances of RNA synthesis in the normal cell, the base sequence in the RNA molecule is specified only by the genetic information in the DNA molecule. Rival hypothesis (*b*) envisions memory acquisition as a special adaptation in the neuron of the general regulatory mechanism of the genetic "switching" system. In the genetic model the instructions for the synthesis of a memory-specific protein are contained in a passage of the genetic codebook, like a digital computer program. This passage can be read out by the de-repression of a repressor molecule. The repressor molecule, which keeps the program from expression, acts by combining reversibly with an operator gene. The de-repressing molecule is seen as somehow being activated by the impinging electrical impulse. The operon is a set of genes switched "on" by the operator to synthesize RNA which, in turn, directs the synthesis of cellular protein.

In both models the mechanism directly connecting the impinging electrical impulses with the molecular alterations remains unknown. Equally mysterious in both models is the connection between the RNA or "specific" protein and the electrical impulse response of the neuron to stimulation.

information system the memory mechanism could be seen as contained in a "passage" of the DNA codebook, a passage which instructs the neuron how to process and "remember" signals impinging on it. Access to these passages in the codebook would require the activation of DNA by the incoming electrical impulses.

Although this model does not as easily explain the learning transfer results as the RNA model, it has the advantage that by including DNA in the memory process the permanency of memory is made feasible. And there is something more plausible to many people about a scheme that is part of the logic

of the general regulation of cell activity than a scheme in which RNA is produced without the direction of DNA.

Still a third memory model has been advanced by a small community of investigators (2), which implicates the glial cells in the memory mechanism —the cells that virtually surround every neuron in the central nervous system of every species, from cockroach to man.

Although the neuro-glial model adheres to the central doctrine that RNA is the essential component in memory acquisition, it sees this RNA as originating in the glial cells with subsequent involvement of the neuron's genetic apparatus through an RNA initiated mechanism of de-repression of a gene. Consequently this model can be considered as a special case of the category of genetic models.

All of the models presented so far fail to be explicit about how the information stored in molecules within the neuron is able to modify the threshold for incoming signals at the synapses of the neuron. The idea that neurons can contribute to the total, macroscopic activity of the brain only through changes at the synapses affecting the rate of neuron firing dates back to Freud (circa 1896) and remains today as the fundamental postulate underlying our concepts of how a brain composed of billions of neurons must function as a system. Presumably the memory model that first explains how the biosynthesis (or alteration) of macromolecules in memory can also affect the synaptic transmission of information between neurons will take a giant step ahead of competing models.

Clearly, this whole field is susceptible of very rapid development.

RNA Model

The development of the view that the RNA molecule is the organic substrate of memory—or that at least it plays a unique role in the encoding process—is chiefly connected with Hydén's early reports (3). In these first publications he showed that the adenine/uracil ratio of the RNA in the cell nucleus of rat neural tissue increased significantly following a learning experiment. It was also stated that an increased amount of RNA per neuron could be observed in rats which had established a learned pattern of sensory and motor abilities. In early theories Hydén proposed the thesis that at the foundation of the memory process there is a change in the bases in the RNA molecule (see Fig. 2). This alteration of base sequence and composition is brought about somehow through the action of the frequency modulated electrical signals received by the neuron at its dendrites. The new pattern in the

RNA molecule then remains and specifies the production of a new protein. Now subsequent electrical stimulation produces rapid dissociation of the newly specified protein. Following this action the dissociated protein combines with a complementary molecule forming a complex, or hybrid structure, influencing the release of transmitter substance in the synapse so that the post-synaptic neuron is excited. In summary the permanent change in the RNA molecule is a response to a characteristic electrical input (frequency modulated waves) describing a sensory experience; when a neuron in an already established memory trace is activated the impulses stimulate the protein (specified by the memory RNA) and release transmitter substance causing the next neuron in the chain to be excited. The connection between the pattern of impulses which make up the basic electrical activity in brain tissue and the nature of the macromolecular changes proposed remains unspecified. This is true of all theories of memory which have been founded on molecular considerations.

Evidence implicating RNA as the memory substrate continues to be brought forth. We can sketch out its history roughly. Corning and John (4) reported that planaria (trained to a classical conditioning task) after being cut in half were allowed to regenerate in ribonuclease (an enzyme catalyzing the breakdown of the RNA molecule) and in pond water. The heads which had been regenerated in ribonuclease retained their conditioning at the same level as that of the head and tail sections regenerated in pond water. But the tail sections which had been regenerated in ribonuclease performed randomly, as if they had lost their conditioning—although these regenerated tail sections could be retrained. In their summary they remarked that the assumption that RNA is the memory molecule remains tenable.

Similar evidence, along with the claim

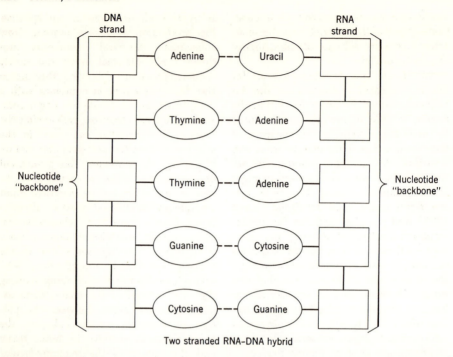

Fig. 2. Ribonucleic acid and the genetic message. Ribonucleic acid (RNA) consists of nucleotide subunits, a nucleotide consisting of a five-carbon sugar molecule (ribose), an attached phosphate group, and a nitrogen-containing base (e.g., ademine, uracil, thymine, etc.). The genetic information in DNA is transmitted to messenger RNA (mRNA) in the nucleus. The two-stranded DNA molecule divides and one of the strands then "hybrids" with mRNA (as shown). The hybrids form in such a way that the base sequence in the RNA is complementary to the base sequence (the genetic code) in DNA. Thus, e.g., if the linear base sequence in RNA is ATTGC. . ., mRNA must have the base sequence UAAGC . . . Bonner (12) suggests that if learning and memory are gene-directed, then the labeled RNA of sensorily affluent mice, distinguished by hybridization, should be different from the RNA of sensorily deprived mice.

of "chemical transfer of learning," i.e., by injecting brain tissue extracts from one animal to another, have appeared subsequently (5, 6). These kinds of investigations were motivated by the early report (1) that planaria trained in a conditioning task and then fed to untrained planaria transferred a measure of their abilities to the naive animals. Albert (7) most recently reports: by producing a spreading depression of neuronal activity in one hemisphere of rat brain the learning of an avoidance response was isolated to the other brain hemisphere; removing some cortical tissue from the trained hemisphere an ex-

tract of brain cells was injected intraperitoneally back into the donor animal and there was observed consequently a savings in learning trials in learning the avoidance response with the untrained hemisphere. The active agent in the injected brain extract was shown to be nuclear RNA and the results suggest therefore that the effect of the injected material was to permit RNA molecules containing the memory code for the learned response to infiltrate the untrained hemisphere and behave there as stored memory.

These reports of transfer of learning by the extraction of nucleic acid from the brains of trained animals and subsequent injection of the extract into naive animals would indeed seem to furnish the first proof of a direct connection between the nucleic acids and memory. There is an indication however that an argument is developing over this whole aspect of the memory question.

To begin with, Hartrey et al. (8) have attacked the planaria work, claiming that in their work with planaria they were unable to demonstrate specific memory transfer from trained to untrained organisms. Bennet and Calvin (9) found it impossible in the first instance to demonstrate any kind of learning at all in planarians. Albert (7), who was able to make an *intra*-animal transfer of learning indicated on the other hand that efforts at *inter*-animal transfer were unsuccessful. Most recently, Luttges et al. (10) extracted nucleic acid from the brains of trained animals and found no transfer phenomenon after intraperitoneal injection into the naive group.

The RNA hypothesis of memory is objectionable however on more general grounds. In the first place, in every case where the biosynthetic origin of RNA in the normal cell has been traced the basic sequence of RNA is dictated by the base sequence (the genetic message) in the DNA molecule. Secondly, it is well known that there are complicated patterns of animal behavior that are of instinctual origin, that is, inherited and not acquired through experience. By definition such behavioral patterns derive from the DNA-directed biosynthesis of RNA, the initial step in the translation of the genetic message. If there is already the framework for a molecular mechanism mediating behavior in the cell, is it appropriate now to introduce a wholly new system seemingly autonomous from the genetic system?

Genetic Model

Schmitt (11), Bonner (12) and Barondes (13), among others, wanting to preserve the concept of a unity of biochemical devices of cellular control from highest to lowest cells, proposed that the memory mechanism fits into the functional scheme of the genetic apparatus.

Bonner's (12) hypothesis of the encoding process involves the principle features of the "switching" mechanisms which have been found to be at the heart of the operation of the reading out of the genetic code (see Fig. 1). In this theory the chemical alteration of the neuron resulting in a memory enscription depends upon the de-repression of a previously repressed gene (or genes). These genes, now free to function, manufacture substances providing for the passage of electrical impulses through specific synapses. In this point of view, as well as that adopted by Barondes (13), there is no memory molecule as such but instead memories are stored as facilitated synaptic connections. These new synaptic connections come about somehow either by virtue of the production of a special protein or the structural modification of already existing proteins.

Bonner's model, which suggests that any RNA synthesized following learning should be a gene product, predicts that the learning-induced RNA can be hybrided (see Fig. 1) with DNA. By contrast, RNA which has not been altered by the genetic DNA could not be hybrided with DNA. The reason for this is that the RNA forms as a hybrid complex molecule with one strand of the divided, formerly two stranded DNA molecule. The formation of this hybrid complex requires adherence to a complementarity principle which restricts the allowed base pairings active in forming the hybrid complex. RNA formed independently of the genomal DNA would not have a sequence of bases complementary to the base sequence in DNA. Bonner (11) suggests a crucial experimental test of the DNA model of memory, at the same time offering a means of refuting the RNA model; if learning and memory are connected with gene de-repression the labeled RNA of sensorily affluent mice, distinguished by hybridization, should be different from the RNA of sensorily deprived mice. If these hybrids can be found then the gene de-repression model could be made very attractive.

Neuro-glial Hypothesis

In later work Hydén (2) became concerned with the relation between the glial cells—surrounding neurons and believed to be responsible for the synthesis of the substance sheathing nerve fibers (axons)—and neurons. Every known nervous system, in cockroach or man, contains two types of cells, glia and neurons, and it has been suggested often that a better terminology would be "glia-nervous system" for the structure in which memory transcriptions are made. While the earlier model (3) did not involve the genetic apparatus in the encoding process Hydén's later theory proposed that RNA from the glia enter the neuron and act as de-repression agents to free a gene or genes for the production of a specific protein which then influences synaptic condition. Gaito (14) has proposed a simple test of this suggestion: inject tritiated uridine, which would be incorporated by RNA, sacrifice the animal at varying times during learning events, extract glial and neural RNA, and determine the amount of label in each. If the neuro-glial model has merit there should be a gradual drift of labeled RNA from glia to neuron.

Inter-Neuron Communication

Current models of memory acquisition make only vague allusions to the relation between the molecular changes in the neuron cell body and the synapses regulating inter-neuron communication. This is not surprising since little is known of these vital structures and there has never been any successful effort to find a permanent alteration of a synaptic molecule or structure which could account for memory and the regulation of information flow between neurons.

Modern theories in cybernetics contend that memory of sensory stimuli can be accounted for by changes in a "synaptic" variable called the "weight" —rather like the amplification factor in an electronic tube. The distribution of such "weights" over an assembly of neurons would be more-or-less unique for each stored sensory pattern. But the "synapses" of cybernetic theories bear little resemblance in their functioning to the supposed functioning of the real synapses between neurons. The cybernetic synapse is merely a storage bin and does not regulate or "gate" the flow of information in the assembly of neurons. It merely reflects the stimulus history of a single neuron. In this sense it is really nothing more than the mathematical model of the biochemical entities now being sought in the individual neuron as the *unit* of memory in a vastly complex network of coupled neurons.

Perhaps the only dynamical model relating memory storage to molecules and the interactions between neurons is the chemical kinetic brain model, proposed by Bernhard (15). This model makes a homolog between an assembly of neurons and a network of catalyzed chemical reactions. The molecular basis of memory in this model is the production of enzymes (proteins) which catalyze the chemical reactions underlying the couplings between neurons. The study of signal ebb and flow in this formulation then becomes a matter of investigating the characteristics of complex chemical networks in which the reaction rate constants are time-varying. It is well known of course that enzymes exert their influence on chemical systems by affecting the rate constant of chemical reaction. Open, catalyzed chemical reaction systems exhibit features of long and short term memory of chemical stimuli.

REFERENCES

1. McConnell, J. V., A. L. Jacobson, and D. P. Kimble, *J. Comp. and Physiol. Psychol.*, **52**, 1 (1959).
2. Hydén, H., in *Macromolecular Specificity and Memory*, F. O. Schmitt, Ed. (MIT Press, Cambridge, Massachusetts, 1962).
3. Hydén, H., in *Neurochemistry*, K. A. Elliott et al., Eds. (C. Thomas, Springfield, 1955).
4. Corning, W. C., and E. R. John, *Sci. Amer.*, **134**, 1363 (1961).
5. Zelman, A., et al., *Worm Runner's Digest*, **5**, 14 (1963).
6. Babich, F. B., et al., *Science*, **149**, 656 (1965).
7. Albert, D. J., *Neuropsychologia*, **4**, 79 (1966).
8. Hartrey, A. L., P. Keith-Lee, and W. Morton, *Science*, **146**, 274 (1964).
9. Bennet, E., and M. Calvin, *Neurosciences Research Program Bull.*, **2**, 3 (1964).
10. Luttges, M., et al., *Science*, **151**, 834 (1966).
11. Schmitt, F. O., *Science*, **149**, 931 (1965).
12. Bonner, J., in *Macromolecules and Behavior*, J. Gaito, Ed. (Appleton-Century-Crofts, New York, 1966).
13. Barondes, S., *Nature*, **205**, 18 (1965).
14. Gaito, J., in *Macromolecules and Behavior*, J. Gaito, Ed. (Appleton-Century-Crofts, New York, 1966).
15. Bernhard, R., *J. Theoretical Biology*, **6**, 244 (1964).

Computers and Comprehension

*by M. Kochen, D. M. MacKay, M. E. Maron,
M. Scriven, and L. Uhr*

Summary

Understanding has both non-linguistic and linguistic aspects. An organism (natural or artificial) may be said to "understand" adequately some feature of its environment if its internal organizing system is set up to take adequate account of it (without, necessarily, having any capacity to express that understanding linguistically). In the linguistic context, a new set of capacities is needed, chiefly related to: (1) the development and use of internal models as such; (2) the distinction between linguistic and direct experiential input; and (3) the capacity to learn. For (2) it is important to distinguish between:

(*a*) The ability to react to indicative utterances as *symptoms* of the state of affairs giving rise to them (i.e., as equivalent to the output of a sensory transducer).

(*b*) The ability to perceive utterances as *descriptions* of that state of affairs (i.e., as semantic tools intended by their originator to set up a state of readiness for the state of affairs in question).

For understanding, whether linguistic or not, the information system must embody something equivalent to an internal model of what is understood. A model, in this sense, is distinguished from a mere mnemonic by virtue of a connection between the structure of the model and the logical relationships between the elements of what is represented. To understand the difference between a description and a mere symptom of a state of affairs, the information system must embody something equivalent to an internal model of the *communication process*.

Four levels of demands for language-handling ability may be distinguished:

(*a*) Routine ability to look up answers to specified questions, without any sign of comprehension of the tokens manipulated, even though the process may be organized and condensed by algorithms or mnemonics.

(*b*) Ability to show an understanding of what the particular discourse is about (referring discourse to an internal model, plastic or otherwise), not of what discourse itself is (e.g., no operational distinction need here be embodied between *being told* something and observing it).

(*c*) Ability to understand the intentional character of linguistic utterances as designed to be used by a motivated interlocutor. This (which requires some internal representation of the interlocutor as goal directed) makes possible evaluation of, and discourse about, the communicative process itself, when this is relevant.

SOURCE: This research was sponsored by the United States Air Force under Project RAND—contract No. AF 49(638)-700 monitored by the Directorate of Development Planning, Deputy Chief of Staff, Research and Development, Hq USAF. Views or conclusions contained in this Memorandum should not be interpreted as representing the official opinion or policy of the United States Air Force. It was published in April 1964 as the RAND Memorandum, RM–4065–PR.

(*d*) Ability to learn, to model itself, and to engage in dialogue of a fully reciprocal character. The last demands the embodiment of a *normative* system accessible to linguistic address, as well as the internal "map" of the domain of discourse, including the interlocutor.

The more sophisticated features discussed in this article are required only of the highest of these levels.

Foreword

The specific topic of the symposium on which this article is based—computers and the comprehension of ordinary language—was chosen by M. E. Maron because of his feeling that the problem of the comprehension of natural language is vital in future computer research. First, an artifact capable of receiving and comprehending messages formulated in ordinary language could fill a growing need in a world where the written word (viz., books, journals, messages, reports, etc.) is inundating workers in science, business, and management. Secondly, it would seem that the ability to comprehend natural language would have to be a necessary characteristic of any artificial entity deserving to be called intelligent. In fact, it might be argued that only by interrogation over a wide range of subjects could one decide whether or not (or to what degree) an artifact was intelligent —and this intercommunication could be carried out effectively with a human interrogator only through the medium of ordinary language.

This article does not consider the logical design of the appropriate programs, dealing only with certain prior considerations on which the programming should be based. The manuscript was originally written by Michael Scriven as an attempt to synthesize the views expressed during the project, and has been subsequently modified in the light of further reflections by all participants. Footnotes contributed as an elaboration, dissent, or qualification are identified by the author's initials. The original RAND report contained several appendixes; in one of these M. Scriven elaborated on the specifications for an entity that can properly be said to understand by examining the dimensions along which a contrast is drawn between understanding and certain other conditions.

The authors wish to express their appreciation to T. E. Harris who conceived the idea for the Working Session in Mathematical Biology, of which the present symposium was a part. The encouragement and support of this symposium given by him and by E. S. Quade, Paul Armer, and W. H. Ware are gratefully acknowledged.

We would like to also thank H. A. Simon and Allen Newell for the time they spent with us in discussing questions relating to computers and comprehension.

Introduction

In recent years, attention in computer research has been shifting from high-speed scientific and business data processing to more sophisticated uses for computing machines. Computers have been programmed to play games, to derive theorems in logic, and to answer questions on the basis of information previously stored in memory. Some of the latter types of computer programs have been described in the literature as "understanding" or "comprehending."[1] There are obviously many differences between computers so programmed and a human being who would be described in the same terms. The purpose of this article is to clarify and examine these differences, and to decide which, if any, are fundamental to the concept of comprehending a natural language.

The paper is concerned with the following: first, it considers criteria for

[1] These terms are here taken to be synonymous.

comprehension, with discussion on comprehension in general and on linguistic comprehension in particular; secondly, it is concerned with some key concepts that enter into these criteria, viz., language, models, and learning. It concludes with a brief discussion of general and practical implications.

Criteria of Comprehension

Types of Criteria

In a well-known application of behaviorism to computers,[2] Turing suggested that cross-examination of an entity through a communication channel is the only legitimate test procedure for evaluating its mental capacity. On this view, if there are no questions the answers to which distinguish a man from a machine, there is no basis for withholding personal language in talking about it.

Other views make physical composition and structure the determining factor. The present authors feel that, although output behavior is crucial, it is entirely legitimate to examine the way in which it is produced, including the structure and its information flow-map, as a way of checking that it is "genuine" and not "rigged" or accidental (1, 2).

On the other hand, it seems unreasonable to make protein composition a prerequisite. If it were possible to produce a human child (in protein) by artificial means, it would be thought implausible to argue that such a being was not really thinking for himself as he solved novel environmental problems of the school room just like his classmates. If then the behavior of such a constructed human could be matched by that of a machine with the same information-processing system, but using inorganic components, it would seem hard to deny that the artificial agent could

[2] See the Appendix for a brief discussion of terminology.

think, etc.[3] So, requiring protein composition seems unreasonable.

Dimensions of Understanding

The following is a list of the contrasts to locate the concept of understanding more precisely and indicate the necessity for careful specification of the kind of understanding that a comprehending artifact is intended to embody.

1. Understanding vs. ignorance.
2. Understanding vs. knowing.
3. Understanding a thing vs. understanding language.
4. Understanding lanugage vs. understanding what language is.
5. Understanding a message vs. understanding a topic.
6. Adequacy, depth, and range of understanding.
7. Understanding vs. memorizing.

Linguistic Understanding

The basic requirement for fully linguistic comprehension of a typical natural language is the ability to perceive language as instrumental,[4] and not merely symptomatic. This is essential, first, because without it the denotative relation cannot be fully understood, and also because many of the concepts expressed in natural language which relate to ways in which language itself is used (e.g., truthfulness, lying, exaggeration, etc.), would otherwise be incomprehensible.

Thus, we could understand the sounds "the sky is blue," if emitted by a photoelectrically-triggered tape recorder, purely as a *symptom* of the physical condition that released the tape. They could for this purpose be replaced by a buzz

[3] Note that "thinking," etc., is something we attribute not to "brains" but to "people" or "agents." It would therefore be nonsense to claim that "machines" think, if by "machine" we meant only the artificial analog of "brain." (D.M.M.)

[4] This point is argued in more detail by MacKay (3).

or any other distinctive noise. Even if the photocell in question were directed to the sky through a blue filter, so that from hearing "the sky is blue" we could correctly infer that the sky was then blue, this inference would not require or demonstrate any linguistic understanding of the sounds. For that, we must know what it would be for an English speaker to *use* the expression "the sky is blue" to serve a *semantic* purpose.

Note, however, that this does *not* mean that an expression cannot be understood linguistically unless its *current* user's purpose is known. An expression can be understood linguistically even when it is not being used, but only mentioned. What is essential for linguistic rather than symptomatic understanding is the perception of the expression as conventionally *having* a purpose; i.e., as a tool, designed to serve a social function whether at the moment used as such or not.

Specific types of utterances, such as statements, commands, requests, questions, warnings, instructions, advice, promises, and the like, can all be distinguished by the processes of evaluation appropriate to them in the computing network of the recipient.

THE UNDERSTANDING OF STATEMENTS. The example of statements may here suffice to indicate the operational approach we favor. We take the *meaning* of a statement to be its selective function on the range of internal states of organization (or conditional preparedness for adaptive action) of the recipients. This is to be distinguished from the magnitude of its *effect*, which will depend on the divergence between the receiver's initial state and the state selected. Its *standard* meaning is the selection function it would conventionally have; its *intended* meaning and *interpreted* meaning are analogously defined (4–7). Sometimes, it is useful to think of a statement as a tool whose purpose is to adjust the recipient's internal representation or model of the world (8–10). The difference between hearing someone *say* the volcano has blown up and hearing (or seeing) it blow is reflected by characteristic differences in the evaluatory filtering operations in the hearer. As soon as input is recognized as being linguistic, its originator and the environment are scanned for cues to authority, reliability, etc., and only when these are established is the message allowed to exercise its adjusting functions. (Of course, further feedback occurs if incompatibility arises.) Short-circuiting can, however, occur through learning, so that single cues (e.g., trusted friend speaking) may automatically open the gate to the recipient's model-adjusting system.

PROPOSITIONS INVOLVING REFERENCE TO SENSATIONS. It is not easy to dismiss the logical intuition that an entity incapable of a certain kind of experience cannot really understand terms referring to it. But it is clear that it can possess and know to be relevant every stateable proposition about such experiences: the blind man knows very very well that "Grass is green" and "The sea is blue" are normally true.[5]

PROPOSITIONS ABOUT AGENCY. Similarly, it can be argued that *with tagging* it must be possible for a computer system to act as the brain of an (artificial) agent who knows that he so acts and hence knows, in principle, how to use agency language even when it refers to personal human experience. It must be emphasized that merely tying the output of a computer to a plotter, for example, and providing an independent feedback which informs the machine of the success of its "intended" actions is only to *implement* agency. For an entity to understand what agency *is*, it requires at least the capacity to analyze its actions in terms of such concepts as intention and achievement, and relate this

---

[5] It would be less plausible to claim that either a blind man or a computer knows what is meant by saying that grass looks green. (D.M.M., M.K., L.U., M.E.M.)

vocabulary to the processes of analyzing the authority of commands and the meaning of descriptions (embodied in the commands or elsewhere) which it may receive or emit. There is no great harm in saying that a plotter, like a dog, understands certain simple commands, even if it lacks these meta-skills; but understanding a natural language certainly requires them. Someone would have to build a good deal into a dog's brain before it could handle this, and it is no more illuminating to say that the plotter "essentially embodies" what is necessary than to say that a dog or a thermostat does.

PROPOSITIONS ABOUT OTHERS. Much of a natural language contains explicit or implicit references to other people. An artificial agent which understood this aspect of language would have to have some internal representation of other agents and know of the similarities and differences between its own status and abilities and theirs. This is to some degree necessary for it to understand the use or concept of language at all; but to understand that, it would need to have little conception of the motivations of others, knowing only that they may sometimes lie or err or be wrong for other reasons. (A good program would recognize the possibility of solipsistic doubt.) One special interest of propositions about others is that they can be handled by using the self as a model.[6] Seeing others as analogous to oneself provides an immediate structure for storage of information about them.[7]

PROPOSITIONS REQUIRING TOPIC UNDERSTANDING. This last subsection illustrates a general class of propositions which are fully understood only by someone with some degree of topic understanding. Topic understanding multiplies the in-

formational impact of a proposition and a special case of this effect occurs when partial message understanding combines with topic understanding to produce complete message understanding via an hypothesis about the speaker's intentions. This procedure is embodied in some programs that are currently referred to as "semantic." They incorporate part of what, in a comprehending entity, would be called checking alternative interpretations of ambiguous input against what is known to be true, and operating on the assumption that the consistent alternative is the correct interpretation. This relatively crude algorithm, nonetheless, considerably improves their efficiency, and a more sophisticated program, which allowed for the occasions when truth is not intended (then selecting the negation as the correct interpretation) and the occasions when truth is irrelevant, etc., would obviously improve efficiency further for certain types of input (e.g., intelligence reports).[8]

So-called "semantic machines" (better called "truth-testing machines") are unable to distinguish experience from statements *about* it and, hence, cannot be said to understand anything like a natural language. Of course, they respond to coded stimuli, but so does a telegraph clacker and a supermarket cash register; calling it a *code* is based on purely anthropomorphic convention. Language is an agreed device, understood and often manufactured by both sides; the number of stones we throw at apples in trees or the keys we hit on a typewriter may signify something and are correlated with the output in a nonrandom way, but the trees and the typewriter could not be said to "understand a language" in this interaction. For that to occur, a quite different order of operation by the recipient is required which makes the distinction between

[6] See MacKay (9), p. 83.
[7] It is perhaps for this reason that primitive man used this model in his attempts to store and relate data about the external world with his anthropomorphic theories and deities. (M.S.)

[8] But note that they *do* handle their intended universes—those where the truth is spoken. (L.U.)

language and significant sensory input (which naturally must itself be coded), and employs the right vocabulary about it.

To the suggestion that this just means more complexity, perhaps the best reply is that complexity and organization are all that distinguish molecules from atoms, monkeys from molecules, and men from monkeys: the *right* kind of complexity is what we are looking for in any program design or analysis task.

Related Concepts

Language and Natural Language

It would require extensive further discussion to uncover and make plausible the case for a *minimum* set of sufficient conditions for a language. But it seems clear that two important necessary conditions can be given.

REFERENTIAL FUNCTION. Language is related to reality (including the numerical, etc., realities of mathematics, subjective realities such as pain, and the hypothesized realities of fiction) in a conventionally recognized way which enables it to function as a medium for communication. It may, of course, be abused or used to mislead, as well as to inform, etc. The perception of clouds to windward evokes expectation of shade via a very simple stored associative connection. The expression "clouds to windward" requires an extra decoder to get its meaning and an extra set of filters and feedbacks to handle the assessment of reliability.

The loose coupling between language and the world which distinguishes statements from symptoms is notably absent in something that has often been called a language—the representation of information in afferent nerve fibers. This is systematic but purely symptomatic, and the relations between "sender," "user," and "referent" are considerably different. The retina cannot exercise an opinion whether to tell the brain what energy has reached it and where; the brain does not consider the possibility of deliberate deception by the retina: neither of these are agents with goals and possible goal-conflicts and, hence, independence of action. Neither knows what the other is doing with the information it receives or even that it receives it as information. There is no common learning of the language, etc. These facts are not incidental to the concept of comprehending or using a language, but central (3, 7); a microwave relay station is neither using nor comprehending the coded information it handles.

COMBINATORIAL POSSIBILITIES. The use of language is often a symptom of some state of the user, but language is not just a set of symptoms (what does "and" symptomatize?; "part of," "number," etc.?). It is crucial that language is a combinatory repertoire with unlimited possible combinations whose meanings can be inferred from a finite set of "rules" governing the components' meaning. (The so-called "rules" are learned as response sets and are only partly formalizable.) Thus, "Ouch!" is either a natural sign of pain and non-linguistic, or else, to the extent that it is a conventionalized sign of the same condition, a wholly atypical linguistic utterance, a limit case, an atom which cannot be combined into molecules.[9]

ANIMAL LANGUAGES. Parrots utter sentences, and some even utter them only on appropriate occasions. But the parrots neither use nor understand language as such, because they do not understand the *words* they use. A dog obeying simple commands can more easily be said to understand them since he does respond to them in several different combinations. But the key test is whether

---

[9] Some linguists (e.g., Hockett, in a private communication) and logicians (e.g., Quine, in *Word and Object*) would argue that "Ouch!" is linguistic. It is an expression of pain, quite unlike a groan or reflexive response. It could, perhaps, be combined into compounds such as, "Ouch and Ouch again," or, "Ugh, Ouch, and Goodbye." (M.K.)

he responds appropriately[10] to a *new* combination of old words. If he does so, he is beginning to understand grammar —i.e., the *structure* of language; and language without structure is hardly language at all.

The "language of the bees" is an interesting intermediate case which apparently does involve recombination, but it is still not clear that the watching workers could handle novel combinations, although their present repertoire appears to be much larger than that of any dog. At least, it must be said that their language (and that of the dolphins as so far disclosed) is extremely limited in its uses (and has no apparent capacity for misuse), although it does clearly demonstrate the crucial social advantages of language.

Natural Language versus Technical Languages

As the natural language springs from the needs of a society of semi-cooperating, semi-competing, semi-romantic, semi-realistic beings, so technical languages spring from certain special needs. Typically, an increase in the number of discriminations needed and the labels for them is involved; frequently, the addition of new organizations and names for them is desirable. Hence, the greater precision[11] and novel concepts of the mathematical sciences and the language of games come about. Such languages may in general be handled more easily

than natural languages by computers, since the resolution of ambiguity typically requires only syntactical, contextual, and semantic cues and not circumstantial ones.[12]

Natural Language

Esperanto and Basic English are synthetic languages designed for basic communication. But they contain enough concepts to require a machine with all the sophistications discussed above. They are *embryonic* natural languages, serving quite a different function from technical languages. If we try to get a technical or artificial language to do the job of natural language, the environment and normal use will soon "contaminate" it.

So natural language may be thought of as being natural in two ways: it deals with natural needs, conflicts, objects, etc., rather than the entities of artificially constructed fields; and, it evolves naturally rather than being invented.

For two reasons, the comprehension of a natural language appears to be a good requirement to set for a computer which is supposed to be capable of understanding.[13] First, we have a good idea how to test the understanding of such material, whereas in an artificial

---

[10] In any general treatment, this would include not responding to meaningless combinations, and responding in the same way at one level, and differently at another, to expressions with the same meaning but made up of different words.

[11] While normative prescriptions for how language users ought to respond to utterances dominate in the case of technical languages (e.g., "Integrate $x^2\,dx$ from 0 to 1!"), descriptive rules for how users do respond to utterances dominate in natural languages (e.g., responses to "Integrate the schools in Atlanta!"). (M.K.)

[12] This may be seen as largely due to the fact that such languages were designed to be written, not spoken, and only partly due to any intrinsic precision, since that is always inexhaustible, or, conversely, is *for certain purposes* as great in the phrase "longer than" as in "one micron longer than." (M.S.)

[13] A third reason making ordinary language of special interest as a vehicle to study comprehension in relation to automata is that it refers to internal models of reality rather than to reality itself. Thus, the term "integrated schools" evokes in listeners internal images—no two listeners having exactly the same ones. Yet, there is enough in common to all these individual internal images to make communication possible. (M.K., L.U.)

language which both we and the computer have to learn, it is highly debatable what constitutes comprehension. That is, success is readily recognizable. Second, the practical applications of a computer which understands a natural language are, sometimes at least, significantly greater than those of the alternatives. That is, success is really valuable.

Natural languages in this sense have been the subject of increasing attention in recent years, in both the philosophical and the computer fields, partly because they have two striking and valuable features, which may be termed flexibility and fertility.

FLEXIBILITY. The function words of English—the conjunctions, participles, copulas, prepositions—have almost no associations for any of us. They are the smooth stones on the river bed, worn free of any growths by the torrent of language which they support. The same is almost true of many high-frequency terms, such as "same," "almost," "many," "high." But words such as "river," "bed," "worn," "free," "growths," are highly associative and are instantly suggested by cues which occur in a new physical or conceptual environment. We naturally and immediately understand the use of river metaphors when talking of time; for example, time "rolls on," "rushes by," "flows smoothly." And, in the same way, we understand the bed metaphor when it is applied to the river. This capacity of a natural language to describe new situations immediately and illuminatingly is its flexibility. It should be appreciated in its mundane aspects as well as its poetic. A child is understood when he calls the referee a policeman, as is Keats when he speaks of "silver snarling trumpets."

FERTILITY. The other side of the flexibility coin is the tendency of connotations in natural language to suggest inferences or associated ideas, some appropriate and some inappropriate; from these, new theories and new philosophical puzzles spring. The "river of time" simile suggests that we ask how fast time flows, and the problem of whether an answer is an introspective datum, is metaphysical nonsense, or is an axiom of physical metatheory, is still unclear. We rely on flexibility and hope for fertility whenever we introduce a new concept in science using old terms—force, energy, information, genetic code, diameter of universe.

So, natural language, apart from its fuzziness (for some purposes) has also a degree of flexibility and fertility which is essential for handling the everyday events and exchanges of normal life.[14]

Models

This section summarizes and expands slightly what is implicit in the earlier discussion. Models can be *embodied* in a computer (from a slide rule up) or a computer program. For a computer system to *have* a model in the sense we do, it must embody a second-order ca-

[14] The contrast between natural and artificial or technical languages has another aspect of some practical interest. Natural language is an excrescent symbolic approximation to a world of experience essentially richer. We try to put experience, advice, etc., into words. Generally, the result enables us to recognize the essential features of the experience, advice, etc., we meant to convey; but equally generally, it leaves us dissatisfied in some detail. In short, in natural language it is the *concepts* that are in command—the words have to shuffle around until they match as best they can. In artificial language, on the other hand, terms are stripped as clean as possible of associations, and stick to their defined meaning. Here, the *words* are in command. The concepts (ideally) are restricted to a set in one-to-one correspondence with formulations. (D.M.M.)

All natural languages seem to have certain basic syntactic features in common which may reflect some basic principles of how internal models are made or of the constituents used to make them. Prepositions seem particularly worthy of study for what they might reveal about representations of the most basic concepts. (M.K., L.U.)

pacity[15] to represent the model itself, to distinguish it from and relate it to reality, to update it on the basis of linguistic and experiential input, to read off required data from it. The merits of modeling are economy and fertility/flexibility: it is suggestive of hypotheses (predictive and otherwise), and is able to accommodate new input without extensive rearrangement.[16]

A mnemonic is a device for improving recall by attaching data in an arbitrary way to a structure that is distinguished only by being easily recalled. A model, on the other hand (in any sense stronger than "descriptive rules"), attaches data via a systematic transformation to a structure which is chosen, not for its ease of recall, but for (a) the fact that *it* is understood, and (b) the fact that a systematic transformation is available which we think will work for present *and* future data. Today's computers which embody a model cannot be said to "have" the model they use as a model in the above sense: they incorporate no more understanding than we have of a subject for which we have only an algorithm.

Computers may have (certainly will have in future) much larger immediate or total storage capacity than a human. This would reduce one need for models, that of economy, but it would not eliminate their desirability nor affect the fact that understanding is often enhanced if coupled with ability to predict.[17] Ability to calculate probabilities for future events is part of understanding of the nature of similar events in the past, and mere rote storage—however large—will not help with that. To understand is to have hypotheses about what is understood, and hypotheses organize expectations as well as memory (17–19). The urge for simplicity in hypothesis-making is an urge for predictive as well as storage efficiency. To have grasped an idea or to understand a phenomenon (to have a theory of it) is partly to have found a model of it which has enough inductive support to make one feel that the extrapolation of its model-relationship is justified so that surprises are unlikely.[18]

Models can be formed to represent conditions at a space-time location different from that of the agent, very different from those now surrounding him, and manipulated verbally and conceptually for purposes of long-range preparedness.[19] (This feature is not necessary in models of family relationships or chess which are aspatial and partly atemporal, although more-localized hypotheses can be built on them.[20]

In a computer program to handle language with this degree of intelligence, mechanisms will be required for forming the triple association between linguistic description, direct experience, and model. They should themselves be subject to description by the user, if our own language, in which we discuss such

---

[15] It might be fruitful to distinguish between two types of programs (or algorithms) and to inquire if the distinction is fundamental. The first is one designed to pass as sophisticated a comprehension test on as large a class of materials as anyone specifies. The second type of program generates programs of the first kind, with capability of receiving or calling for external information. This type of program would run indefinitely. Perhaps, for the second type of program, given *any* comprehension test, there exists a time at which the computer will adequately pass it. For the first type of program, this may not be the case. (M.K.)

[16] See: Craik (11); MacKay (8–10, 12–13); Peirce (14); Uhr (15–16).

[17] Because we count being surprised by X's behavior as a sign of not having fully understood X. (M.S.)

[18] Pasteur's dictum that chance favors the prepared mind implies that it takes a certain understanding to recognize the possibility of surprises in the first place. (M.K.)

[19] Note that here again the agent's own organizing system can serve in large measure to supply the components of the "model" [see MacKay (8–9].

[20] But relations equivalent to spatial and temporal ones are already found in the programs that handle family relations and chess. (L.U.)

matters, is to be understood in all its aspects. The same can be said about the procedure for amalgamating, collapsing, and relating models from different sensory modalities, informants, and fields.

Learning and Motivation

It will already be clear that the capacity to learn is closely connected with the capacity to understand. One may feel that a computer which had all our knowledge and models of things as they are, and our language built into it, but no learning capacity, would be just as superficial and uncomprehending as one with a gigantic but wholly unorganized memory from which it produced the answers to any question it was asked about things as they are. One might suppose that a difference lies in the greater predictive commitment of the former, but the latter is *ex hypothesi* in possession of every fact and consequence of the former. Is it just the greater economy of the former that appeals to us?

Is it rather the fact that the former's information-flow system is better adapted to the world, that it incorporates better understanding in a way that must eventually show up in either faster retrieval, faster updating, or larger reserve storage? At first, this seems to be the cash value of models. But, if we look closely, we see that active learning capacity is already built into the first machine. To the extent that updating capacity exists at all, and we have constantly stressed its importance, learning of one kind is already present. To the extent that it is programmed for analysis of input information and consequent re-indexing of its own storage, it shows active learning. A computer could not possibly be said to understand input if it did not alter what it subsequently output when asked for related information. So understanding entails one kind of learning.

The superstorage computer either reduces to an inefficient form of the comprehending computer, or fails to give correct answers, when we look into its updating routines. If it doesn't update, it will output contradictions. If it does, then it has the lower (storage) level of the other, less neatly arranged, and nothing else.

Such a computer could be programmed to make an active search of literature or to perform experiments in order to "improve its mind" (and its grammar), and this might be described as a search for truth. There would even be some point in describing it as "motivated to seek truth" if its self-perception was appropriately integrated with this claim. In general, the motivation structure of a supercomputer, like its memory, may well be significantly different from that of a man; but, given the usual language of motives, it should naturally extract from any new task-statement the goal involved and relate this to any superordinate goals it may have.[21]

So, the comprehending computer is automatically a learning computer, to some degree (20, 21). To be as intelligent as it could be—to learn as much as it could from the mistakes and successes of itself and others—would require further design improvements. But the question of whether to try to match a baby's capacities or an adult's as a starting point for a comprehending computer is a hard one. The longer the learning process, the more likely that the final performance will continue to match ours, but, in terms of originality, this may be disadvantageous.[22]

Conclusions

General

An examination of the difference between human comprehension and current computer performance has been

---

[21] At this point, we may begin to consider the possibility of its having unconscious motivation; i.e., goal-seeking patterns in its actions which it has not yet perceived itself. (L.U.)

[22] See also Kochen (22); MacKay (12–13).

undertaken. The major conclusion is that there appears to be no barrier in principle to the construction of an entity (an "artificial agent") which could meet all behavioral tests for comprehension,[23] but that this will require the integration of a wholly distinct set of capacities with those embodied in current programs.

These capacities chiefly relate to: (a) the development and use of internal models as such; (b) the distinction between linguistic and direct experiential input; and (c) learning (these capacities are not wholly distinct). The second necessitates the existence of a processing system for linguistic input which can deal not only with the mere possibility of aberrant symptoms (which a sensory channel must be able to handle), but also with the special kinds of unreliability peculiar to language; e.g., lying, misstating, exceeding authority, misunderstanding, exaggerating, acting. In short, the would-be comprehender of a rich language cannot handle those substantial areas where these sources of error are important, nor be said to understand, *in toto*, what a language is, without the implicit recognition that it originates in an entity who *uses* it for certain ends. The language-comprehender must have a model of the language-producer as such.[24]

Practical

It must be said immediately that something as sophisticated as a full comprehender is unnecessary and even possibly inconvenient for many practical information-processing purposes. We can distinguish several types of artifact in

[23] It seems likely that such an entity will have to grow through its experiences. It is too complex to be designed.

[24] These are merely particular instances of the general principle that when a new domain becomes relevant, the entity must distinguish and sufficiently understand that domain. (L.U.)

terms of different demands made on them:

1. The Electronic Dictionary/Grammar/Encyclopedia (EDGE). Efficient design can provide fast lookup in large volumes of natural language text and printout of answers to questions of stereotyped form. The dictionary aspect could be used for translation and abstracting programs. This would suffice for minor early-warning services and relatively unsophisticated fact and document retrieval services.

2. "Semantic Machine." The "Semantic Machine" incorporates a process for resolving input ambiguity by reference to stored data, on the assumption that the true alternative is more probable. It probably represents significant improvement over EDGE for, for example, technical translation purposes, and would have value as an accessory on, for example, the input end of EDGE in increasing its tolerance of non-standard question forms.

3. Dialogue Analyzer. This would be given all the cues available to a human in dialogue via its own detectors or from an informant, including semantic and pragmatic items, and would have a practical model of language-users. It could thus evaluate the probability of lying and other sources of error, etc., where they are relevant, and might be the minimum necessary equipment for efficient military intelligence source-evaluation work, lie-detecting in a courtroom, or analysis of psychiatric protocols.

4. Artificial Agent. Here, the artifact incorporates a self-consistent long-term goal system, full-scale learning routines, self-modeling and self-evaluation procedures and language, etc. The full-scale comprehension involved here might only rarely be essential for practical tasks, but the development of a number of artifacts capable of this would immediately raise the possibility that they could do independent, original work, which might be further improved by real dialogue be-

tween them, for which the above development would be necessary.[25],[26]

Postscript

At the end of his classic paper, "Computing Machinery and Intelligence," Turing says:

We may hope that machines will eventually compete with men in all purely intellectual fields. But which are the best ones to start with? Even this is a difficult decision. Many people think that a very abstract activity, like the playing of chess, would be best. It can also be maintained that it is best to provide the machine with the best sense organs that money can buy, and then teach it to understand and speak English. This process could follow the normal teaching of a child. Things would be pointed out and named, etc. Again I do not know what the right answer is, but I think both approaches should be tried.

In this article, we have tried to indicate part of what is involved in providing a computer with the capacity "to understand and speak [a natural language, such as] English."

Appendix: A Note on Terminology
by D. M. MacKay

In the case of human beings, we do not say that *brains* think, feel, under-

[25] See also Scriven (23).

[26] We might equally well examine a number of additional combinations of basic functions, such as the following, that can be given a machine: (1) sense patterns; (2) store patterns internally; (3) "model" rather than store a rote representation of an external world; (4) output behavior; (5) move toward desired states (thus satisfying a need-value system); (6) output as a function of inputs; (7) output as a function of internal states; (8) output as a function of needs; (9) identify certain inputs as "talking *about*," hence, signs; (10) build up a grammatically structured language system of such signs; (11) identify the emitter of language utterances as an act or like it in one or more of the above respects; (12) identify certain inputs as coming from itself. (L.U.)

stand, etc., but that *people* do. When we come to consider artificial "brains" we meet the difficulty that no word exists for the artificial analog of "people." This can lead to confused debate unless terms are carefully defined and used.

We do have certain terms which embrace both the personal and the mechanical aspect of human beings. A "man," for example, may be said to think, etc., and also to weigh 150 lb and be made up of so many billion cells (though we would more often say the latter of his "body"). A "baby" is a borderline case where we are more inclined to use personal and physical categories indiscriminately.

In earlier papers, I have used the term "artifact" in this all-embracing sense (the artificial analog of "man" or "baby"), as distinct from "machine" or "computer," which I take to be more analogous to "brain" or "body." In doing so, I was not presuming to legislate on usage, but only indicating a distinction which needs to be made in some way if the comparison of natural and artificial information-processors is to be pursued intelligently (1, 8).

Because the term "artifact" can denote artificial constructs other than information-processors, I do not feel it to be ideal. "Automaton" would be better if it did not have the negative flavour of "mindlessness" or the absence of personality. "Robot" is objectionable for the same reason. We need a term that neither implies nor precludes implicitly the fullest human-like characteristics.

The Gordian solution would be to invent yet another neologism, in (historically unjustified) hopes of keeping it free of misleading associations. Rather than make this cut, however, it seems worth considering whether the term "*artificial agent*" would not serve quite well and impartially for our purpose.

The term "android," which is shorter, has been used to denote an artificial *human* agent, and for this restricted purpose it would seem to be ideal (if its various associations could be lived down!). For the more general class of information-processors, however, a less question-begging term is still needed.

An "artificial agent" can be discussed (like a man) in terms of weight, bodily composition, mechanical principles, and the like, and also in terms of purposes, thoughts, understanding, and so forth, without *presupposing* any particular degree of competence at the personal level. With regard to the issues discussed here, the term "artificial agent" would seem to have the virtue of more genuine neutrality than any existing alternative.

In the present paper, we have tended to follow common usage in making "computer" serve as the omnibus analog of "man"; but, wherever questions would thus be intolerably begged, we have used terms like "computer system," "entity," "artifact," or "artificial agent" to preserve the logical distinctions analogous to that between a man and his brain.

REFERENCES

1. MacKay, D. M., "The Use of Behavioural Language to Refer to Mechanical Processes," *Brit. J. Phil. Sci.*, **13** (1962) 89–103.
2. Uhr, L., "Pattern Recognition Computers as Models for Form Perception," *Psychol. Bull.*, **60** (1963) 40–73.
3. MacKay, D. M., *Linguistic and Non-Linguistic "Understanding" of Linguistic Tokens,* The RAND Corporation, RM-3892-PR, March 1964.
4. MacKay, D. M., "Operational Aspects of Some Fundamental Concepts of Human Communication," *Synthese,* **9** (1954) 182–198.
5. MacKay, D. M., "The Place of 'Meaning' in the Theory of Information," *Information Theory,* E. C. Cherry (ed.), Butterworths, London, 1956, pp. 215–225.
6. MacKay, D. M., "The Informational Analysis of Questions and Commands," *Information Theory,* E. C. Cherry (ed.), Butterworths, London, 1961, pp. 469–476.
7. MacKay, D. M., "Communication and Meaning—A Functional Approach," *Cross-Cultural Understanding: Epistemology in Anthropology,* Helen Livingston (ed.), Harper and Row, 1964.
8. MacKay, D. M., "Mindlike Behaviour in Artefacts," *Brit. J. Phil. Sci.,* **2** (1951) 105–121; **3** (1953) 352–353.
9. MacKay, D. M., "Mentality in Machines," *Proc. Aristot. Soc. Suppt.,* **26** (1952) 61–86.
10. MacKay, D. M., "The Epistemological Problem for Automata," *Automata Studies,* Shannon and McCarthy (eds.), Princeton University Press, Princeton, 1955, pp. 235–251.
11. Craik, K. J. W., *The Nature of Explanation,* Cambridge University Press, Cambridge, 1952.
12. MacKay, D. M., "Operational Aspects of Intellect," *Mechanization of Thought Processes,* Her Majesty's Stationery Office, London, 1959, pp. 37–52.
13. MacKay, D. M., "Information and Learning," *Lernende Automaten,* H. Billings (ed.), Oldenbourg, Munich, 1961, pp. 40–49.
14. Peirce, C. S., *Collected Papers,* Harvard University Press, Cambridge, pp. 1934–1958.
15. Uhr, L., "Machine Perception of Printed and Handwritten Forms by Means of Procedures for Assessing and Recognizing Gestalts," *Preprints of 14th National Meeting of Association for Computing Machinery,* Cambridge, Massachusetts, September 1959, pp. 20.1–20.6.

16. Uhr, L., and C. Vossler, "Suggestions for a General Purpose Adaptive Computer Model for Brain Functions," *Behavioral Science*, **5** (1961) 91–97.
17. Kochen, M., "Experimental Study of 'Hypothesis-Formation' by Computer," *Information Theory*, E. C. Cherry (ed.), Butterworths, London, 1960, pp. 377–403.
18. Kochen, M., "An Experimental Program for the Selection of Disjunctive 'Hypotheses'," *Proceedings of the Western Joint Computer Conference (1961)*, Institute of Radio Engineers, New York, 1961, pp. 571–578.
19. Kochen, M., "Some Mechanisms in Hypothesis-Selection," *Mathematical Theory of Automata*, Polytechnic Press, Polytechnic Institute of Brooklyn, 1963.
20. Uhr, L., "The Development of Perception and Language," *Simulation of Personality Processes*, S. Tomkins and S. Messick (eds.), John Wiley and Sons, New York, 1963, pp. 231–266.
21. Vossler, C., and L. Uhr, "Computer Simulation of a Perceptual Learning Model for Sensory Pattern Recognition, Concept Formation, and Symbol Transformation," *Information Processing 1962*, C. M. Popplewell (ed.), North-Holland Publishing Company, Amsterdam, 1963, pp. 413–418.
22. Kochen, M., "Cognitive Mechanisms," *IBM Report*, 1960.
23. Scriven, M. J., "The Compleat Robot: A Prolegomena to Andriodology," *Dimensions of Mind*, S. Hook (ed.), New York University Press, New York, 1951.
24. Kochen, M., "Organized Systems with Discrete Information Transfer," *General Systems*, **2** (1958) 30–47.
25. Kochen, M., "An Information-Theoretic Model of Organizations," *Trans. IRE*, *PG17* (1954) 67–75.
26. Kochen, M., "Logical Nature of an Action Scheme," *Behavioral Science*, **1** (1956) 265–289.

PART THREE

Technological Resources for Information-Retrieval Systems Construction

Real progress in the computer industry has been due more to the clever inventions of engineers and programmers and to the good judgment of entrepreneurial businessmen than to planned pursuit of a particular idea or goal. Having created large digital memories, fast computers, high-speed data communication lines, advanced programming languages, and programs, information technologists are searching for significant uses of their products. These technologists are joined by crusaders in education, library management, and other fields, who seek ways to make optimal use of the latest methods that technology has to offer. As Swanson put it,[1] we have answers in search of a problem. The computer industry wanted imaginative people who could think of sensible uses for the clever creations of their engineers and scientists. Almost by coincidence, we are left with an extremely impressive technology that could now for the first time realize the great encyclopedia idea.

To realize a major goal such as the encyclopedia-system idea discussed in Part One, a large-scale enterprise must be organized. Its success is measured by its own viability as a service. Three types of resources are necessary for its success. The first is a pool of enough people with enthusiasm for the main goal, with the necessary understanding to properly conceive it, and with the skills—technical and organizational—to implement it. The second of these resources is an information technology that consists of large-scale digital and analog stores, high-speed data and film-transport channels, and low-cost yet adequate input-output equipment; also appropriate computer programming packages and standard operating procedures, all of which have met the test of the market place. The third of these resources consists of capital and goodwill together with the skill to manage their investment for maximum value per resource invested.

It may be argued that there are still far too many basic problems—not yet even recognized and little understood—that must be solved by decades of patient research before a *rational* plan for such an enterprise can be taken seriously. Successful enterprises are not, however, always accom-

---

[1] Swanson, D. R., "The Formulation of the Retrieval Problem," in *Natural Language and the Computer*, P. L. Garvin, Ed., New York, McGraw-Hill Book Co., 1963, p. 255.

panied by a rational plan. Sufficient understanding to solve the deeper problems is probably not now available; yet this may be neither necessary nor sufficient for the practical success of the enterprise. The existence of viable, significant information systems may well provide stimulus toward a more rapid development of the underlying knowledge.

The third factor is perhaps the most critical. The majority of the Research and Development projects in information retrieval are subsidized by government funds and seldom turn into viable self-supporting services. They do not aim for this. Nor is there any effective mechanism to transfer what these projects add to our knowledge about information-retrieval systems design to service-oriented organizations. On the other hand, projects aiming at service, if subsidized, seldom aspire to either attain self-supporting status or to utilize the most advanced thinking of information-retrieval research.

The kind of enterprise envisaged by H. G. Wells would require the spark of an entrepreneurial genius in the spirit of Ford or Rockefeller, not a government planning board, nor benevolent philanthropists, nor an academic project (whether it ties together several fragments of one university or many universities). It might well be a novel industrial enterprise, but the public interest is too vitally concerned to risk possible bias and domination by a single private interest. What is called for is a novel type of enterprise, quite unlike any known to date. There seems to be nothing appropriate in the literature to enlighten anyone seeking further discussion of these problems.

The first factor or resource—skilled manpower—is probably ripe and ready. What the existing literature in the encyclopedia-system field proves is that, by now, the first resource is probably available. That is, the increasing number and quality of papers are partial evidence that now there is probably a critical-size pool of qualified people who could be mobilized on a worthwhile project to which they would give their best. Timing is critical. Premature attempts to mobilize resources can set back the date of a successful start. Belated attempts may no longer have the critical force. With either, there is a risk of missing altogether. Choosing when to act is the essence of good strategy.

More convincing evidence that the needed skills are now ready for effective mobilization toward a worthwhile goal is in the following. There is now a large number of highly competent *service-oriented* system engineers.[2] Who they are and what they do is little known. They are less in the public eye than their more research-oriented colleagues working on glamorous new programming languages, heuristic programs, schemes for automatic content analysis, indexing, inference, and language translation. But these system engineers have the know-how that has been the trademark of suc-

---

[2] For an example, see United Aircraft Corporate Systems Center, "A Study of Terminal Devices for Information Storage and Retrieval Systems," SCR **269**, Farmington, Connecticut, April 19, 1966.

cessful American enterprise: they know what equipment exists, they have a realistic appraisal of how it will be used and its cost, and they can implement an operating system providing a visibly useful service. There is a surprising number of such people, and a surprising number of systems created by them have quietly begun to make a real impact during the past year. Time-sharing technology may well greatly increase the productivity of each of these workers.

Furthermore, many highly skilled workers in the "software" field are likely to shift from business and scientific data processing toward non-arithmetic areas, such as automation in libraries and information centers. There is, of course, the argument that "mobilizing" many of the good workers in IR toward a centrally organized, "monolithic" enterprise with a single goal might stifle the free creativity of the best of these workers, who are motivated primarily by the spirit of their own individual intellectual enterprise. But the new enterprise must be such as to enable these highly individualistic workers to *concentrate their coordinated efforts as a team* without sacrificing their personal aspirations. That is, without disrupting the present productivity of the workers, it must be possible to have the combined *results* of their work *together* exceed the combined results of their work *separately*. The achievement of this would, of course, also require managerial genius.

The second factor—technological resources—is just about now reaching its critical size. Indeed, it may be the rapid growth of this factor that could just help bring out from our midst the needed entrepreneurial and managerial geniuses. That is the reason for believing that perhaps now is the time to call for action toward the encyclopedia-system enterprise.

This is the intended message of this book.

The following articles sample our current technological know-how. They are selected to give partial answers to the questions: What can we use to implement the encyclopedia systems idea? What have we done that can qualify as pertinent experience? What is the evidence for the likelihood of success in such an enterprise? The papers in this section will not speak for themselves to give clear answers to these questions. Kasher's answers are undoubtedly negative: there is far too much research to be done before any kind of such implementation should even be considered, especially if it involves automation. A well-conceived enterprise could, however, succeed by circumventing the need to solve all the basic research problems and still provide a significant service and valuable experience.

The first article shows in a realistic way and in historical perspective the recently popularized and major commercial growth of time-sharing systems. The author of this important paper, A. L. Samuel, has contributed as much to the design of the existing computers (IBM 704) as he has to little-known but significant operational IR systems and to computer simulation of learning by using the game of checkers.

The second article by R. Simmons is a survey of a popular topic. It is included because of the frequency with which students who are interested in information retrieval have requested it. It covers a glamorous aspect of information retrieval, one which has attracted some of the most brilliant younger minds. Question-answering by machine is the vehicle by which the most rapid progress in "artificial intelligence" is often expected. In spite of impressive and clever programs and ideas, the hopes in this area still outreach the advances.

The basis for selecting Simmons' article is its representativeness of the recent literature, which is criticized in the next article by Kasher[3] in the same spirit that earlier literature on "document retrieval" has been criticized by Bar-Hillel.[4] Both of these critical surveys stress the fallacies and misconceptions about theoretical specialties which are assumed to underly fundamental problems in data retrieval. These critics, in their selection of what problems are fundamental—sentence ambiguity, decidability, syntactic simplification—are less sensitive to the excitement of creating new services with social impact than they are to the esthetics and traditions of pure theoreticians and their specialties. The reader interested in "data retrieval" would be well-advised to study both the Simmons and the Kasher survey as well as the papers that they review. The actual state of affairs probably warrants neither the optimism of the Simmons paper nor Kasher's conclusion that numerous very basic investigations must precede even an attempt to predict success or failure of an enterprise in this area.

The fourth article, by L. Karel et al., describes one of several major enterprises of national scope that are now in successful operation. The goals of this system were modest—to increase the efficiency of printing *Index Medicus*. Yet over $17 million were expended to develop this system. Its function as an IR system is almost a byproduct.

The MEDLARS system was selected as a sample from a variety of such systems. It is almost a random sample. A somewhat similar but much less publicized system was developed by NASA.[5,6] Whereas today over 470,000 indexed references are on fifteen reels of magnetic tape of MEDLARS, with a new tape reel containing about 30,000 references being produced every two months, NASA's 200,000 publicly available references are listed

[3] Kasher, Asa, *Data-Retrieval by Computer. A Critical Survey*. Jerusalem, Israel: The Hebrew University, January 1966, AD 631 748.

[4] Bar-Hillel, Y., "Theoretical Aspects of the Mechanization of Literature Searching," *Digitale Informationswandler* (W. Hoffman, Ed.). Braunschweig: Vieweg 1962, pp. 406–443; also published as Chapter 19 of Bar Hillel, Y., *Language and Information*. Reading, Mass., and Jerusalem, Israel: Addison-Wesley Publ. Co. 1964, pp. 336–364.

[5] U.S. National Aeronautics and Space Administration, *How to Use NASA's Scientific and Technical Information System*. Washington, D.C.: U.S. Government Printing Office, 1966.

[6] U.S. National Aeronautics and Space Administration, *NASA's Technology Utilization Program* (N65-36350), Washington, D.C.: U.S. Government Printing Office, 1965.

on fourteen reels; the growth rate is some 6,250 documents per month. Similarly, Euratom[7] has been compiling a significant collection of indexed references from *Nuclear Science Abstracts* on magnetic tapes. The much older efforts of the Defense Documentation Center (formerly ASTIA) have joined forces with more recent work—especially on the formation of subject-authority lists and thesauri—by the Engineers Joint Council and the Atomic Energy Commission under the newly formed project LEX.[8] Also, noteworthy are the enterprises by many scientific societies. The significant and specialized systems of the American Chemical Society[9] could have been described in addition to or instead of MEDLARS had it been possible to find a paper of similar quality. The American Psychological Association[10] is taking a large-scale experimental approach. The American Institute of Physics[11] has an ambitious program that could also have been described here, and so has the American Society of Metals[12] (which was one of the earliest), and nearly every other society. Noteworthy for the uniqueness of the materials as well as for the breadth and depth of its coverage is the Index of Christian Art[13] which does not really fit with the other systems mentioned here because it is untouched by automation.

In an attempt to structure these efforts according to subject matter, the following classification seems useful. The fields are ranked so that those with the highest potential demand for aid as well as the greatest possibilities for providing such aid are at the top of the list.

1. Medicine (for example, MEDLARS, hospital records automation[14]).

2. Law (for example, the work of Horty-Kehl[15] and the American Bar Foundation[16]).

---

[7] Rolling, L., *Euratom—Thesaurus*, Euratom CID report, Eur. 500, Brussels, Belgium 1964.

[8] Heald, H., *Project LEX, Manual for Building a Technical Thesaurus*, ONR-25, Washington, D.C., April 1966.

[9] Mellon, M. G., *Chemical Publications; Their Nature and Use*, New York: McGraw-Hill Book Co., 1965, pp. 224–229.

[10] Garvey, W. D., and B. C. Griffith, "Scientific Communication: The Dissemination System in Psychology and A Theoretical Framework for Planning Innovations," *Am. Psychologist*, 20(2), 1965, pp. 57–164.

[11] Williams, V. F., E. Hutchisson, and H. C. Wolfe, "Consideration of a Physics Information System," *Phys. Today*, 19, No. 1, January 1966, pp. 45–52.

[12] Melton, Jessica S., *et al.*, *Automatic Processing of Metallurgical Abstracts for the Purpose of Information Retrieval*, Interim Report NSF-2, Center for Documentation and Communication Research, School of Library Science. Cleveland, Ohio: Western Reserve University, February 1964.

[13] Esmeijer, A. C., and W. S. Heckscher, "The Index of Christian Art," *The Indexer*, 3, No. 3, Spring 1963, pp. 97–119.

[14] Baruch, J. J., and G. Octo Barnett, "Joint Venture at Massachusetts General," *Datamation*, 11, No. 12, December 1965, p. 29.

[15] Kehl, W. B., J. F. Horty, C. R. T. Bacon, and D. S. Mitchell, "An Information Retrieval Language for Legal Studies," *Comm. ACM*, 4, No. 8, 1961, 380–389.

[16] Eldridge, W. B., and Sally F. Dennis, *Report of Status of the Joint American Bar Foundation—IBM Study of Electronic Methods Applied to Legal Information Retrieval*, American Bar Foundation, August 1, 1962.

3. Military (a sample of somewhat related work is published in the proceedings of the MITRE-sponsored Congress in the Information Systems Sciences[17]; also the work of the Defense Documentation Center (DDC) and the Intelligence Data Handling System (IDHS) of the U.S. Air Force.

4. Politics (content analysis, notably the work of Pool[18,19] and political intelligence analysis).

5. Economics (for example, business intelligence).

6. Sociology (for example, aids to crime detection[20,21]).

7. Technology (for example, NASA, LEX, etc.).

8. Education (for example, the various ERIC[22] projects).

9. Science (for example, the work of the above-mentioned societies).

10. Management of large enterprises (for example, SABRE, the American Airlines Reservation System; management information systems[23] internal to large companies or government agencies: IBM has at least three internal systems, U.S. Steel is developing a very large-scale system, etc.).

Management information systems, if really successful, might well go to the top of the list in terms of the demand generated. Such systems are, however, hard to create for really successful use in an on-going enterprise. Most of the literature in IR has stressed the "information crisis" in science, which should have placed science near the top. The really first-rate scientists, however, do not clamor for "better" *access* to the literature.

There is a large literature on research and development in information retrieval. Because it is so heterogenous—in subject-matter, level, and quality—it did not seem desirable to include more than one sample. Not even the references to the variety of clever ideas or experimental systems can be sampled adequately. The best course for the interested reader is to con-

---

[17] Spiegel, J. P., and D. Walker (Eds.), *Proceedings of the Second Congress of the Information System Science.* Spartan Books, Washington, D.C.: 1965.

[18] Pool, Ithiel de Sola (Ed.), *Work Conference on Content Analysis, Monticello, Ill., 1955.* Urbana: University of Illinois Press, 1959.

[19] Pool, Ithiel de Sola, and A. R. Kessler, "Crisiscom—Computer Simulation of Human Information Processing During Crisis," *IEEE—Trans. on Systems Science & Cybernetics,* SSC-1, No. 1, November 1965, pp. 52–58.

[20] Martin, R., "Computers for Cops: Police in Many Cities Try Electronic Brains to Curb Soaring Crime," *Wall Street Journal,* 166, No. 1. August 25, 1965.

[21] *Western City* for January 1965 features articles on the use of electronic data processing by police departments of various California cities.

[22] Burchinal, L. G., and Harold A. Haswell, "How to Put Two and a Half Tons of Research into One Handy Little Box," *Am. Education,* 2, No. 2, February 1966, pp. 23–25.

[23] *Management Information Systems. Index,* Amer. Data Processing, Inc., Detroit, 1962.

[24] National Science Foundation, *Current Research and Development in Scientific Documentation,* No. 14, NSF Office of Science Information Service, Washington, D.C., 1966.

sult the series of publications by the NSF,[24] and the first annual review of information science and technology.[25]

The fifth article, by Salton et al., illustrates one of the most extensive uses of computers to derive a variety of experimental results about the performance of different automatic indexing schemes.

The last article is an attempt to summarize some of these diverse activities by indicating how systems that are now commercially feasible might be used. It places particular emphasis on the use of "systems arithmetic" to assess conditions under which a proposed system is technically and economically advantageous. In doing so, it samples some of the latest advances in information-processing equipment, the programming arts, and standard operating procedures. It also outlines some of the key technical and scientific problems and hurdles to be attacked.

As a whole, the articles in Part Three are more representative of actual work in information retrieval than those in Parts One and Two. Even so, each article is written for a different audience, attacks different problems, and uses different methods and ideas. This diversity applies to content as well as to level and quality of work done. They constitute a representative sample of the information-retrieval literature.

By contrast, the five articles in the first half of Part One, which discuss the theme and the most important idea of this book, are not representative of the information-retrieval literature. Nor are they representative of modern scientific literature in fields other than information retrieval, for example of the literature sampled by the articles in Part Two. They are, however, nearly all that has been written on the "encyclopedia systems" idea; the importance and quality of the idea as such exceeds the quality of research and actual work based on it, which warrants the inclusion and emphasis of these five articles. The four articles in the second half of Part One resemble those of in the first half in that they also do not report actual work or high-quality research, but are representative of the speculative literature in information retrieval, which has once more become quite influential.

---

[25] Cuadra, C., Ed., *Annual Review of Information Science and Technology,* Vol. 1, John Wiley and Sons, New York, 1966 (Amer. Documentation Institute).

Time-Sharing on a Computer[1]

by Arthur L. Samuel

Making modern computing facilities instantly available to large numbers of users, each with a console in his own office, depends upon the development of general-purpose systems for performing many tasks apparently simultaneously on a single machine. Current experimental approaches are here described.

Why all of this sudden interest in time-sharing? Computers are usually shared by many users. In fact, one of the significant trends of the last several years has been the development of elaborate supervisory programmes, the so-called operating systems, which manage the computer installation and schedule the work for various users with a minimum of human intervention. This scheduling takes various forms, but the more common form involves stacking of jobs according to their expected operating times. Small jobs are given priority during the normal working day and each job in turn is run to completion if this is at all possible.

Recently, an earlier form of operating system known as "time-sharing" has come back into favour and is receiving a great deal of attention, particularly in the United States. It may be of some interest to survey the current state of the art in this old, but now very new way of using computers, and perhaps make a few predictions as to the future trends.

First, a word or two by way of definition. The term "time-sharing" is used to identify a computing system with a number of independent, concurrently-usable consoles, or operating panels. These consoles are serviced by a supervisory programme, which provides each user with the illusion that he has a direct line to the computer and that he can make use of this computer more or less as if he were the sole user. This illusion is achieved either by limiting the size or type of job that the system will accept, or by commutating the services of the computer between the various users. Actual systems differ with respect to the frequency with which each user is serviced but, in general, an attempt is made to limit the maximum delay experienced by the user to a time commensurate with his reaction time. Given the proper balance between computing speed and the total number of users allowed on the system, it may still be possible to do enough computing for each individual user to meet his needs or to match the input and output speed capabilities of his console. He may, therefore, be quite unaware of the quasi-simultaneous use of the computer by the other users. Restricting the term "time-sharing" to describe this particular form of computer operation is, of course, somewhat inexact (multiple-console, on-line computing would be preferable), but this is what "time-sharing" has come to mean.

SOURCE: *New Scientist* 26, No. 445, May 27, 1965, pp. 583–587.

[1] Work reported herein was supported (in part) by Project MAC, an M.I.T. research program sponsored by the Advanced Research Projects Agency, Department of Defense, under Office of Naval Research Contract Number Nonr-4102(01).

Two, or perhaps three, distinct types of time-sharing installations are already discernible. We can avoid misunderstandings if we draw a sharp distinction between these different kinds of systems.

The first type, and the one meant more often than not when the term "time-sharing" is used, is the "General-Purpose System." A general-purpose, time-sharing system attempts to provide each user with the full range of capabilities (except perhaps for speed) which he would have if he were the sole user of a general-purpose computer. The user should be able (1) to use all

Uses a Q-32 computer with a PDP-1 as a terminal interface. The scheduler handles two queues, one having a one-second response time, the other longer. Languages: LISP, IPL, JOVIAL, SLIP, MACHINE. See "Introduction to the System Development Corporation Time-Sharing System," by Jules I. Schwartz, SDC document SP-1722, September 14, 1964. (Published also in *Datamation*, November-December 1964.)

Fig. 1. Systems Development Corporation time-sharing system.

One-language system with up to 40 terminals on an IBM 7040/7044. Designed for engineering and scientific problems in the desk calculator to small computer range. Available for customer installations and also as leased service through terminals installed on customer premises.

All man-machine communication in the source language (compatible FORTRAN subset) and in a conversational mode. Incremental translator with powerful debugging features but with substantial degradation in execution efficiency.

See "Remote Computing—An Experimental System," Part 1, T. M. Dunn and J. H. Morrissey; Part 2, J. M. Keller, E. C. Strum and G. H. Yang; *Proceedings Spring Joint Computer Conference*, 1964, pp. 413–443.

Fig. 2. QUIKTRAN.

components of the computer system, (2) to work in any desired programming language, (3) to use programmes and subroutines which were written, originally, for other (presumably non-time-sharing) systems, with little or no change, (4) to wait for the results or to have the computation continue either in his absence or while he turns his attention to a quite different task using the same console, (5) to communicate freely with the computer both via a conventional typewriter and through some graphical device (a cathode ray tube with a light pen attachment, or the equivalent), (6) to store large amounts of data and programme material within the system to which he can gain access as desired on a moment's notice, and finally, (7) to have the use of a large library of service routines and "debugging" aids. Like it or not, the term "debugging" is now generally used to describe the process of locating programming errors. There is in existence no system which actually provides all of these services (the SDC time-sharing system comes very close, Fig. 1), but this is the goal.

A second type of system sometimes goes by the name of a "Dedicated System," but a better name would be a "One-Language System." Here, no attempt is made to allow the user a variety of languages, and indeed he is constrained to use but a single language which may, for example, be simplified FORTRAN (as in IBM's QUIKTRAN, Fig. 2), or an even simpler language (JOSS, as used by the RAND Corporation, Fig. 3). In effect, the user is presented with a special computer which is literate in but a single language.

Finally, we might distinguish a third class of systems in which the language of the computer is still further restricted and specialized to deal with a restricted set of problems, a common library facility, or a common data base. The SAGE air defence system was an early system of this type. The SABRE airline reservation system is a more recent example, as are the many information retrieval systems that are being talked about. Computer-based instruction systems also properly fall into this third category, although there is a tendency to think of them as being quite unique. In the "Common-Data-Base System" the user can pose only a restricted class of questions about the data base, solve only certain types of problems, for which the solution methods are already available within the system, or provide data in the form of answers to questions which the system itself may ask.

We will devote most of our attention to the general-purpose, time-sharing system. Here, by far the best-known example is the MIT compatible time-sharing system (CTSS), particularly as now used in Project MAC. MAC is an acronym standing for Multiple-Access Computer or, as some prefer, Machine-Aided Cognition. This project is supported by the Advanced Research Projects Agency of the US Department of Defense through the Office of Naval Research. We will, accordingly, refer to it when we wish to be specific (Fig. 4).

A bit of history may be in order. The Bell Telephone Laboratories operated some of their early relay computers with remote consoles, and so deserve the credit for the first "time-sharing" sys-

tems. I have yet to find a reference to time-sharing in Charles Babbage's published work but I am still looking. This early operating procedure was then largely replaced by the elaborate operating systems to which reference has already been made. An Englishman, Mr. Christopher Strachey, in 1959 was one of the first to advocate the time-sharing idea as applied to the large general-purpose computer. Others in the United States, and in particular Dr. J. McCarthy, Dr. J. C. R. Licklider, and Dr. F. J. Corbato, were prominent about the same time in promoting time-sharing. In retrospect, it is perhaps sur-

Serves up to eight users simultaneously at the RAND Corporation on the 1951–53 built Johnniac, responding typically in a fraction of a second to all but extended computing requests. The user may give direct commands or indirect instructions in a stored programme. The system features rapid interaction, exact input, decimal arithmetic, exact output, results appearing in report-quality format, and happy users. See J. C. Shaw, "JOSS: a Designer's View"; *Proceedings Fall Joint Computer Conference, 1964.*

Fig. 3a. JOSS (Johnniac Open-Shop System).

Users' request; typed in green on system

1. 1 Type x, sqrt(x), log(x), exp(x), (x+.25)/x in form 1.
Form 1:

| — | _._____ | _._____ | —._____ | —._____ |

Do step   1. 1 for x = 1(1)4

Machine reply; types in black on system

1	1.00000000	.00000	2.7183	1.25000
2	1.41421356	.69315	7.3891	1.12500
3	1.73205081	1.09861	20.0855	1.08333
4	2.00000000	1.38629	54.5982	1.06250

Fig. 3b. An example of JOSS in operation.

```
login †104 samuel
W1407.9
PASSWORD
    T0104   2484 LOGGED IN  01/28/65   1408.1

    CTSS BEING USED IS          MAC112
SHIFT           MINUTES
        ALLOTTED        USED SINCE 01/28/65  1335.2
    1     100       0.5
    2     100       0.0
    3     100       0.0
    4     100       0.0
LAST LOGOUT WAS 01/28/65   1354.3
TRACK QUOTA =        P,      1500 0.    0023 TRACKS USED.
R 8.483 + .666

resume mon04 5
W 1410.4

    CTSS UP AT 1332.9 01/28/65.

    NUSERS = 35  TIME = 1410.5
    1.8      1.8   BACKGROUND,
    70.5     70.5  FOREGROUND,
    16.9     16.9  SWAP TIME,
    10.8     10.8  LOAD TIME,
    30.7     30.7  USER WAIT,
    13.3     13.3  SWAP WAIT,
    7.5      7.5   LOAD WAIT.

    NUSERS = 35  TIME = 1415.6
    0.       1.5   BACKGROUND,
    68.6     70.3  FOREGROUND,
    17.8     17.0  SWAP TIME,
    13.6     11.1  LOAD TIME,
    30.4     30.7  USER WAIT,
    13.9     13.4  SWAP WAIT,
    8.3      7.6   LOAD WAIT.
    QUIT,
R .350 + 1.016

logout
W 1416.1
    T0104   2484 LOGGED OUT  01/28 /65   1416.1
    TOTAL TIME USED =    00.4 MIN.
```

Fig. 4. An example of MIT's CTSS in operation in Project MAC. Here the computer is monitoring the state of affairs in the system.

prising that this idea should have remained virtually unused for twenty years until its reintroduction by these workers. Undoubtedly many factors were involved, but economic considerations certainly played a part and the development of successful time-sharing systems had to wait for advances in back-up stores, and in large, fast stores.

The argument goes something like this: in the early days, computers were really very expensive, both absolutely and in terms of the cost per operation. The art of programming (preparing instruction lists) was not very advanced and users could, and usually did, require substantial amounts of time between runs to analyse their results and to locate programme errors. Furthermore, there was a tendency to apply computers to problems which were repetitive in nature, and problems once programmed were usually run a great many times. Through the years, the computers have become very much faster and the cost per operation has decreased precipitously. Programming has become a recognized profession with the insatiable demands for programmers currently outstripping the supply. A job which would take several hours on an early computer now may take only five minutes, programming costs have risen, and computers are now being used for many one-shot problems. This has led to the development of problem-oriented programming languages and the development of larger and better operating systems.

More recently, we have seen an increase in emphasis on "turn-around" time as compared with "through-put" rate. We are discovering that it is no longer wise to let the user wait for service on a computer, and now we can, with equanimity, make some sacrifices in computer efficiencies if we can offer the user immediate access to the computer. Since the conventional operating system does not permit this immediate access, a change in operating procedures seems indicated.

Such a change would not be practical were it not for the recent development of large random-access storage devices, particularly in the form of disc files. Magnetic tapes require substantial amounts of operator time to mount and unmount and they must be read serially. When these were used exclusively for programme and data storage and as back-up stores it was impracticable to try to interleave several programmes at one time. The disc file, storing data measured in millions of words and allowing random access, altered the balance, and one can now store an entire programme library for many users within the machine. One can also maintain

several programmes in a running condition by giving each user a small quantum of time in a round-robin fashion. The only constraint is set by the ratio of "swap time" (defined as the time required to transfer one user's programme from the high-speed store to a back-up store and to load the high-speed store with a second user's programme) to running time, which must be kept within tolerable limits.

While we have normally assumed that each user's programme will require the entire fast store of the machine, even this assumption is no longer necessary with the availability of larger and larger fast stores. It is now becoming possible to "space-share" the fast store and so greatly reduce the need for "swapping." In fact, it is possible to overlap the execution of one programme with the swapping of two other programmes so that little or no time is lost. Whether or not there are several users' programmes in the high-speed store at the same time, a certain amount of space-sharing is, of course, essential to permit the supervisor programme to remain in control of the system while a user programme is being run. The CTSS system, as currently operated in Project MAC, makes but limited use of space-sharing; but at least one current system, the IBM TSM system (Fig. 5), makes rather extensive use of this principle. Still another system, the IBM 44X (Fig. 6), was specifically designed to permit the study of various possible space-sharing tech-

Experimental, general-purpose system. 20 users on a 7090 via 1050 consoles. Multi-queue scheduling with space sharing. Few seconds response time. Languages: FAP, FORTRAN, GPSS, PAT. See "The Time-Sharing Monitor System" by H. A. Kinslow: *Proceedings Fall Joint Computer Conference, 1964, pp. 443–454.*

Fig. 5. IBM TSS system.

> Experimental system on a modified IBM
> 7044 with extended addressing capability
> and multiple-register relocation facilities
> for pagination. Variable number of IBM
> 1050 terminals via IBM 7750. Large-
> capacity core store.
>
> Designed specifically for experimental
> study of various time-sharing, space-
> sharing and multi-programming opera-
> tions.

Fig. 6. IBM 44X.

niques. Substantially, all of the new systems now under development will space-
share. This, then, is a third factor responsible for the current interest in the
time-sharing idea.

Professor Corbato, of MIT, emphasizes yet a fourth factor, having to do
with the unusually high degree of equipment reliability required for satisfactory
on-line service, a degree of reliability
that was not always obtainable on some
of the earlier computers and that is only
now being routinely achieved. Not only
is the on-line user more dependent upon
continued operation of the system than
is the stacked-job user, but maintenance
problems are also much more difficult on
a time-shared system, since the concate-
nation of circumstances leading to performance errors and failures can usually
be neither determined nor reproduced.

There is one additional hardware requirement which must be met before
one can build a truly successful time-
sharing system. This is the requirement
for a satisfactory storage-protection
scheme. Each user, and each user's programme, must be restricted so that he
and it can never "access" (read, write,
or execute) unauthorized portions of the
high-speed store, or of the auxiliary store.
This is necessary (1) for privacy reasons,
(2) to prevent a defective programme
from damaging the supervisor or another
user's programme, and (3) to make the
operation of a defective programme independent of the state of the rest of the
store. This last reason is often over-

looked by the uninitiated, but debugging
a programme on a time-sharing system
without storage protection can be a
most frustrating experience. Storage protection can, of course, be obtained
through programing means, but not,
however, without some loss in operating
efficiency. It is now generally conceded
that storage protection can best be
handled by special hardware in the computer.

Storage-protection hardware already
comes in a variety of forms, and new
forms are still appearing. The IBM
7094, as used in the MIT system, contains a relocation register and upper and
lower bound registers whose contents
are alterable only by the supervisory
programme. This is, perhaps, an essential minimum. Access to the disc store
and to all peripheral equipment is usually controlled by the supervisor through
the medium of a directory, and each
user refers to his storage regions by file
name rather than by location. Many
time-sharing systems do not assign fixed
storage locations to each user, but make
contiguous blocks of storage available on
demand up to previously assigned quotas
by means of a list-structuring procedure.
More elaborate systems make the auxiliary store appear to the user as a simple
extension of the fast store (the one-level
store idea) with the mechanics of transferring programme and data from the
auxiliary store to the high-speed store
handled automatically. Many commercial computers offer hardware facilities
which simplify this procedure. A well-
known British example is the ATLAS.

We will be able to discuss but one
more aspect of a typical time-sharing
system—this having to do with the so-
called "scheduling algorithm." The
scheduling algorithm is that set of rules,
or more strictly its embodiment in a
programme, which govern the frequency
with which each user is serviced and
the length of time each programme is
permitted to run before it is interrupted.
We can note two extreme situations, the

one in which each user programme is run to completion, and the second in which the time slot is so short that many periods are required before even the shortest job can be completed. Some time-sharing systems actually operate in accordance with the first scheme. These differ from the conventional stacked-job system only in their use of a number of independent consoles. The illusion of immediate access can still be maintained, by setting stringent limits on the maximum permissible size of programmes, in terms of running time. MIT's CTSS is perhaps more typical in that it maintains a series of queues and runs each programme for only a short period of time. The correct form for a scheduling algorithm is one of the most hotly discussed aspects of a time-sharing system, and a great deal of experimental work will still have to be done before the question can be settled.

It will be apparent to even the casual observer that it requires much more than the bare hardware to make a successful time-sharing system. In the first place there must be a supervisor programme if the user is to be able to control his apparent computer through the medium of a remote console. Besides the supervisor itself, there must be a large library of service routines which can be called by name and which will do for the user many of the things which he might ordinarily handle by his own programming efforts. Associates from whom he might borrow routines are no longer close at hand and he is more or less forced to limit his input and output to an amount consistent with the speed of his console. For example, the library of service routines accessible to each user on the Project MAC computer is in excess of 500,000 words. Establishing a usable general-purpose time-sharing system is a horrendous job and most systems are evolutionary in concept. Here is another reason why time-sharing was slow in catching on. Actually, the task is relatively simple if one is willing to settle for something less than complete generality.

Let us now turn our attention to the user of a time-sharing system. We have been tacitly assuming that this user would be attempting to solve the same class of problems as he previously solved on a stacked-job installation. This certainly is part of what he will want to do, but it is not all. The rapid response time of the time-sharing system leads to changes in programming methods and, more important, it makes possible a redistribution of work between the human problem solver and the computer.

This redistribution is particularly useful in dealing with problems that are not well structured. It often happens that more time is involved in formulating a problem than in solving it. Frequently, as Dr. Richard Hamming, of the Bell Telephone Laboratories, has said, "The purpose of computing is not to get numbers but to gain understanding." When we use a computer to gain understanding, it still gives us numbers and a major part of our task is to formulate the problems so that the numbers do indeed lead to understanding. When confronted with a long turn-around time and a high fixed-overhead charge per run, one must either wrestle with this aspect for a long time before assigning the problem to the computer or risk the expenditure of needlessly large amounts of computer time and the production of large amounts of useless output.

By way of contrast, when one can have access to the computer on an unscheduled basis, when one can observe the course of a computation and alter it at any time, and when it is no longer uneconomic to solve a problem piecemeal or pose very small problems, one can have numbers available in all stages of the problem formulation. For example, if one has doubts about the convergence of some approximate method, one simply tries it out. Instead of spending several hours checking a programme for clerical errors, one lets the "assembly" programme list the errors for him. If a programme does not seem to be giving the right kind of answers or if it simply takes too long, one stops it. Instead of asking for a memory dump, one asks to see the particular items which are thought to be significant. Instead of wasting time printing out all of the output from a run, one leaves the output stored on the disc and simply prints out the numbers needed at the time. One procedure, now only but dimly envisioned, has to do with cooperative procedures enabling several people to work on different parts of a single problem, with the coordination of their efforts and the interchange of information between the workers effected by the computer. Mr. Jules Schwartz, of the Systems Development Corporation, is a strong advocate of this usage. Even more drastic changes in our conventional methods of formulating and solving problems are sure to evolve as time-sharing systems are perfected and become more generally available.

Does this mean the demise of batch processing and its replacement by time-sharing? The world is never this simple. Many of the larger computer users have individual jobs which run for hours. It may not be sensible to split such a job into small portions interspersed with other jobs. Some users must have large amounts of outputs. Some tasks recur on a fixed schedule, or run for a fixed length of time. Still others have such overriding priority that they must have the exclusive use of the computer. Conventional systems work well under these conditions. Some of the newer operating systems of the conventional sort offer many of the advantages of so-called time-sharing systems and many *avant-garde* time-sharing systems, after the first blush of novelty has worn off, are developing a tendency to run short jobs to completion. Just as the competition in the past between "scientific" and "commercial" computers has disappeared with the development of universal computer systems,

such as the IBM SYSTEM/360, the GE compatible series, and the RCA Spectra 70, so we can expect an evolutionary trend toward a new system concept which combines the better features of time-sharing systems.

Let us return for a moment to consider the details of the MIT time-sharing system known as CTSS. While there are actually several different time-sharing installations at MIT, two of these use the CTSS and are substantially identical; one is in use at the MIT Computation Center and the other is at Project MAC. The MAC computer has more users (over 200), serves a few more users simultaneously (30) and provides more hours of time-sharing service a day (approximately 20 hours per day, 7 days a week). Each of these systems uses an IBM 7094 with two 32,000-word core memory banks. Only one of these banks is accessible to the user, the other bank is used by the supervisory programme. "Polling" (commutation between terminals) and some terminal-code conversion functions are performed by an IBM 7750. The user consoles, which can be connected to either system, are about equally divided between teletype machines and IBM typewriters. Some of the latter have both card and paper-tape reading and punching equipment. There are also facilities for connecting to the TWX and TELEX networks and there are a few additional special-purpose consoles in use and under development. While many of these terminals are in the same building with the main computer or in other buildings on the MIT campus, several consoles are in staff members' homes at some distance from the campus and a few people are using the system from quite remote locations ranging from Norway to California.

It will be instructive to follow the course of events as viewed by a user at a typewriter. He must, of course, first get a connection established between his console and the 7750. If he is on the campus, he can dial the computer directly; if outside, he may dial MIT through the ordinary telephone system and ask the local telephone operator to connect him with the computer, or he may dial directly on the TWX or TELEX networks. When the connection is established, he hears a 1000 c/s tone, whereupon he pushes a button to disconnect his telephone and connects the typewriter. He then types LOGIN and gives his problem number and his name. The computer responds by requesting a password and temporarily disconnecting his printing mechanism so that no printed record appears as he responds with his assigned 6-character alphanumeric private identification. If he gives a valid password and if there are fewer than 30 users at the time, the computer acknowledges that he is logged in and supplies him with a brief summary of the state of his files and of the system. He is then free to use the computer in any way he may desire.

For example, he may wish to resume a programme which he had interrupted at an earlier session and saved by typing "SAVE IAN" (IAN being the name he had arbitrarily assigned to the particular programme). If so, he simply types "RE-SUME IAN" and the programme continues from the interruption point. Or he may wish to edit a programme. If so, he calls upon one of the several available editing programmes by typing its name, followed by the name of the programme to be edited. These editing programmes allow him many convenient features— the ability to print out portions of the programme, to correct single characters (identified either by location or by context), to add new material, etc. As still another example, he may now be ready to "compile" a programme, in which case he types the name of the "compiler" he wishes to use, again followed by the name of the programme to be compiled. As a final example, the user may wish to start the operation of an already compiled programme and perhaps have it "stop at" some specified point, or he may wish to invoke some one of the many debugging aids which the system provides.

The user has a "quit" button on his console which enables him to interrupt his programme at any time. This allows him to communicate with the supervisor programme without in any way affecting the interrupted problem programme (except, perhaps, for the loss of some output information which was being typed at the time of the interruption). He can type "SAVE IAN" if this is his wish, invoke the debugging aids, or simply restart the interrupted programme by typing "START." Finally, service is terminated by typing "LOGOUT." The general appearance of the output as typed on a 1050 terminal is shown in Fig. 4, which incidentally shows a five-minute run of a monitoring programme that gives one-minute-averaged and cumulatively averaged percentage statistics for the system at a time when there were 35 users on-line.

Other systems differ in detail but offer much that is similar to the system just described. The interested reader may obtain some insight into these other systems by the brief synopses given in the figures or he may wish to refer to some of the original papers given in the references.

Now for a word or two more about one-language systems. While some people might quarrel with the classification of the IBM QUIKTRAN system as a time-sharing system, since more attention is paid to system through-put and less to time-slicing than is the case with the systems just described, QUIKTRAN is a typical one-language, time-sharing system within the broad definition given earlier. This system has been made publicly available for use on standard IBM equipment and will undoubtedly be widely used. A better known, but not generally available, one-language system is the JOSS system of the Rand Corporation, shown in Fig. 3. Still another system is being offered in the Boston area by Charles Adams Associates (Fig. 7). The Western Union Corporation has also announced a system which is believed to be of the same general type.

The design considerations behind common-data-base systems are perhaps of less immediate interest to the reader than are the previously described types. Common-data-base systems frequently use specially designed terminals, adaptable for handling the special class of service which they provide. In IBM's SABRE system, as installed for American Airlines, there are over 1000 consoles now in use which communicate with the central computer and enable the agents to inquire regarding the availability of

---

On-line packaged commercial data processing, FORTRAN and other engineering languages, on a PDP-6.

Initially 16 leased-line teletype terminals with planned expansion to 256. Dynamic core allocations, interpretative processing. Service on first come, first served basis either to completion or to a needed drum or disc access.

Response time should not exceed ¼ sec more than 10 percent of time.

Fig. 7. Adams Associates—Keydata System.

space on aircraft and to make and cancel reservations at a rate in excess of 1500 inputs per minute. It is characteristic of most common-data-base systems that the system programme remains in control at all times and in effect treats the user's request as input on which the system programme operates. The user may, of course, pose a fairly complicated problem but he does not actually write his own programme as he does for the general-purpose time-sharing system.

Returning to the subject of general-purpose systems, the question uppermost in many people's minds relates to the maximum number of users who can conveniently be serviced in this way on a specific computer and, hence, the cost

---

PDP-1D computer, FASTRAND drum and data channel, independent core stores. User programmes on high-speed drum. 30 simultaneous teletypewriter users. On-line MIDAS assembler plus version of J. C. Shaw's JOSS (q.v.). Multi-level queues; typical maximum response time ½ second. Supervisor includes extensive common sub-routines to enable user programmes to be prepared quickly.

Fig. 8. Bolt, Beranek and Newman Hospital Computer System.

per user. Accurate figures are hard to get, and they are unreliable at best, since most of the existing systems are still experimental. One of the earliest systems in operation, the BBN time-sharing system (Fig. 8), served five typewriters on a PDP-1 computer. Predictions based on this experience as to the number of users who could be served on a larger computer, the 7094 for example, have not been borne out in practice. This is not because the predictions were wrong, but simply because niceties of system design have been sacrificed in order to get the existing systems into operation. The "swapping time" problem and the need to space-share the high-speed store were usually not given due consideration and it is only now that people are facing up to these problems. Two other systems that may be of interest are the ATS (Fig. 9) and the STSS (Fig. 10).

Time-shared text-editing system available to all users of IBM 1440 or 1460 systems. Provides basic editing and desk calculator functions, paging, line-width adjustment, line justification, multi-font features, character, word, line and section deletion, replacement or insertion, etc.

Up to 40 IBM 1050 terminals can be used simultaneously, working on the same or different projects.

Fig. 9. Administrative Terminal System.

Opponents of time-sharing argue that a properly designed, stacked-job operating system can, by its very nature, always outperform a time-shared system in terms of through-put. The proponents of time-sharing counter by objecting to the choice of raw through-put as a valid measure of system utility, by pointing out that time-sharing offers the user a service that simply is not available with the conventional system, and by claiming that this new service is worth all that it costs. They prefer to measure utility in terms of user satisfaction, turn-around time, programming efficiencies and net system through-put, defined not in "meg-ops" (millions of computer operations) but in terms of the useful output from the total man-machine complex as measured against all of the operating costs. The argument continues, and at

Computers: PDP-1, 7090.

Number of stations: 20; 12 cathode-ray tube + 8 teletype.

Swap time: 34 m sec PDP-1, 6 sec. 7090.

User files: IBM 1301 disc.

Languages: MACRO, GOGOL, LISP on PDP-1, BALGOL, FORTRAN, FAP, LISP on 7090.

Uses: Teaching machine laboratory, general computing, on-line data reduction 5 user system—July 1964, 20 users —April 1965.

Fig. 10. Stanford Time-Sharing System.

the moment time-sharing seems to be winning. Time-sharing has been made to work; it is still not strictly economical but it promises to be so in the very near future.

Answering English Questions by Computer: A Survey[1]

by Robert F. Simmons

Fifteen experimental English language question-answering systems which are programmed and operating are described and reviewed. The systems range from a conversation machine to programs which make sentences about pictures and systems which translate from English into logical calculi. Systems are classified as list-structured data-based, graphic data-based, text-based and inferential. Principles and methods of operations are detailed and discussed.

It is concluded that the data-base question-answerer has passed from *initial* research into the *early* developmental phase. The most difficult and important research questions for the advancement of general-purpose language processors are seen to be concerned with measuring meaning, dealing with ambiguities, translating into formal languages and searching large tree structures.

I. Introduction

The last decade has seen many varied approaches toward computer processing of natural languages. The largest number of projects have been concerned with mechanical translation between languages. Document retrieval systems based on computers have become fairly common and more recently programs which support stylistic and content analysis of documents have been built. In the course of this still early development of natural-language-processing techniques, more than a dozen systems which attempt to answer English questions have been reported.

The term *question-answering machine* is used here rather loosely to include general-purpose language processors which deal with natural English statements and/or questions. These vary from conversation machines to machines which generate sentences in response to pictures, and systems which translate from English into logical calculi. All of these may be interpreted in some sense as attempting to use natural English in a manner very closely related to the question and answer pattern.

Research toward natural language question-answering systems has a history dating only from 1959. Currently, 15 or 16 programs exist which answer some type of English question. It must be emphasized that all of these are experimental devices, often significant and exciting in their implications for future developments, but not in themselves practical devices to do the world's work. In a sense, the status of these question-answering systems is like the status of television in the 1930's; a number of breadboard devices exist, each of which shows that some aspects of the panorama of verbal meaning can be success-

SOURCE: *Communications of the ACM*, 8, No. 1, January 1965, pp. 53–70.

[1] This survey was conducted by System Development Corporation's language processing research project, Synthex, under ARPA Contract SD-97.

fully reproduced by machine, but none as yet offers general solutions to the problem of high-quality language processing or attacks the engineering problems which a practical device would encounter.

A harshly critical review could say of each question-answering system so far built that it deals only trivially with a trivial subset of English. Nevertheless, each does answer some subset of English questions, and in the early stages of a research discipline, the effectiveness and generality of the systems developed is of considerably less interest than are the principles which emerge from the experimentation. In reviewing five years' accumulation of question-answering systems, this paper takes a tolerant viewpoint. It is concerned primarily with explaining and extracting principles and techniques of question answering and with communicating to a wider audience the state of the art of language processing.

II. A Logic of Questions and Answers

Most languages have a small set of rules which can be used for transforming any statement into a question. In English the question mark, intonation, and the rearrangement of subject and verb accomplish this function. In addition to transformational rules, a vocabulary of special question words—who, why, where, etc.—exists which provides clues as to the nature of the answer that is desired. Linguistic differences between declarative statements and questions are well catalogued and understood (Lees, 1960).

For logical differences the situation is not so clear-cut. A recent attractive idea is that a question is a special subclass of assertions whose propositional truth or falsity can be determined. Harrah (1961) and Belnap (1963) use this viewpoint as a basis for beginning a logical analysis of questions and answers. For opposing arguments see Hamblin (1963) and MacKay (1961).

This logic offers both a consistent way of looking at questions and a classification scheme for questions and answers.

In the Belnap classification a question has two parts; one part delineates a *set of alternatives,* the other makes a *request.* The request part of the question indicates the acceptable form of a *direct answer* by showing which and how many of the alternatives must be present. A direct answer is that particular set of alternatives which are a complete answer to the question. For example, in the question, "What are two primes between 1 and 10?" the set of numbers between 1 and 10 are presented as an alternative from which an answer is to be selected. The request states that two and *any two* of these will be a direct answer. There exist also partial answers, eliminative answers, corrective answers and relevant answers. Each of these responses offers something less than the questioner hoped for.

Questions may also be classified as complete (disjunctive), e.g., "Is Brown the governor of California?" and as incomplete, "Who is the governor of California?" It is also desirable on occasion to classify questions as safe, risky, foolish, etc. A safe question is one that divides the universe in two as in "Did she wear the red hat or not?" Whatever in fact occurred there is a direct answer to this class of question. A foolish question is one which cannot have a direct answer, e.g., "What is the largest number?" Risky questions include those with built-in assumptions such as "Have you stopped beating your wife?"

Closely related to questions are imperative statements. "Go to the store," "Set course 180, speed 500," and "Set Dodgers equal win over Boston at Detroit" are all imperatives. Most often the imperative calls for a physical action not involving language while a question usually dictates a language response. In terms of question-answering programs however, the difference becomes mainly one of output mode; the analysis phase for each type of statement is similar. Like the question, the imperative contains a request and outlines an environment of alternatives. In such commands as "Name the signers of the Constitution," where the desired behavior is linguistic, the difference disappears entirely. An important implication for language-processing machines is that the logic developed for question-answering systems applies almost directly to machines for doing useful nonlinguistic work in response to English commands.

In summary, a question may be considered as a special subset of imperative statements where the desired response is linguistic. Questions are composed of two parts, one which describes the set of alternatives which include the answer and another which makes a request for a particular subset of these alternatives. A direct answer is a complete answer to the question and all other answers provide less information than the questioner desired. In the analysis of question-answering systems which follows, the main features of the Belnap classification system are either implicitly or explicitly recognized and dealt with. It will be seen that the distinction between commands and questions tends to be of minor importance for these machines.

III. Precursors

Machines and programs which attempt to answer English questions have existed for only about five years. But the desire to translate language statements into symbols which can be used in a calculus has existed as long as formal logic. Attempts to build machines to test logical consistency date back at least to Ramon Lull in the thirteenth century. Several logic machines for testing the validity of propositions were constructed in the nineteenth century. For the interested reader, Gardner's book *Logic Machines and Diagrams* (1958) offers a fascinating technical history of this line of development. However these machines, although they an-

swer questions, do not deal directly with natural languages. Only in recent years have attempts been made to translate mechanically from English into logical formalisms and these will be briefly outlined in Section VII.

In this section two programs reported in 1959 will be described as foreshadowing the principles developed more fully in later question answerers.

THE CONVERSATION MACHINE. This program by L. Green, E. Berkeley and C. Gotlieb (1959) allows a computer to carry on a seemingly intelligent conversation about the weather. The problem was originally posed in the context of Turing's definition that a computer could be said to be thinking if it could carry on a conversation with a person in another room in such a manner that the person could not tell if he was speaking to a real person or not. By choosing a conversational topic as stereotyped as weather, the experimenters hoped to gain some experience with the meaning of Turing's idea.

The conversation machine dealt with three factors: meaning, environment, and experience. Meaning is expressed in terms of dictionary entries for words, combinations of these entries for remarks, and preference ratings (like or dislike) for certain types of weather. The environment of the system is an input of the day's weather, and its experience is a general knowledge of the type of weather experienced at various times of the year.

Words are categorized as *ordinary*, e.g., snow, rain, etc.; *time*, e.g., today, December, etc.; and *operator*, e.g., not, change, stop. The meaning of each word is stored as an attribute-value pair. For time words the attribute is type of time, calendar or relative, and the value is a code for the amount. For operator words the attribute is a code for a function to be accomplished and the value is the degree to which it is to be executed. Thus "change" and "stop" call a subroutine for negation but the degree code for "stop" is greater than that for "change." Such ordinary words as "dew," "drizzle" and "rain" are coded for successively higher values of the attribute "wetness."

The meaning of a remark is calculated by looking up each word and coding it by its attribute-value pair from the dictionary. In the case of words not in the dictionary, defined as meaningless words, the code zero-zero is assigned. The set of codes for words in a remark represents its meaning. The program compares the meaning of a remark with its own store of knowledge and experience which has been similarly coded, then selects a stereotyped reply frame and fills in the blanks with words originating from the remark, from its experiences or from its preference codes.

As an example the authors present, "I do not enjoy rain during July." The "not" operator word acts on "enjoy" to give "dislike" which is a meaningful word to the program. The resultant meaning for the remark is the set, "dislike," "rain" and "July." Looking up the time word "July," the program discovers that "July" is associated with "heat" and "blue skies." Since these two terms do not relate to "rain," the program records an *essential disagreement*. On this basis it selects a reply frame and fills in the blanks as follows:

Well, we don't usually have *rainy* weather
in *July*
so you will probably not be disappointed.

The conversation machine avoids the whole problem of syntactic analysis and is obviously limited to a few simple constructions. However it does manage to analyze a statement into a set of meaningful parameters which are then used to select an answer. Its principle of coding the meaning of words as an attribute-value pair is still basic to far more recent and advanced question systems.

THE ORACLE. As a Master's thesis under John McCarthy, then at M.I.T.,

A. V. Phillips programmed an experimental system to answer questions from simple English sentences (1960). Its mode of operation is to produce a syntactic analysis of both the question and of a corpus of text which may contain an answer. This analysis transforms both the question and the sentence into a canonical form which shows the subject, the verb, the object, and nouns of place and time. The system was written in LISP which simplified the programming task.

Its principle of operation can be appreciated by following the example in Fig. 1. The example sentence is analyzed into subject, verb and (essentially) object. The analysis is limited to simple sentences and breaks down if the sentence has two or more subjects or objects. The first stage of analysis is to look up each word in a small dictionary to discover its word class assignment. At this point such words as school, park, morning, etc., are also coded as time or place nouns. During the analysis the question is transformed into declarative order and auxiliary verbs are combined with their head verbs so that both question and potential answering statement are in the canonical form, subject-verb-object, as shown in Fig. 1.[2]

A comparison is then made to determine if the elements of the sentence match those of the question. In the example all three elements match and the program would print out "to school" followed by the entire sentence. Had the input been a complete question, i.e., "Did the teacher go to school?" the Oracle would have modified its behavior to respond "Yes."

As an early question answerer, the Oracle is a competent example of the principle of answering questions by structural matching of syntactic-semantic

[2] Details of the types of syntactic analysis commonly used will usually not be discussed here. For a survey of the various methods used on computers, see D. Bobrow (1963).

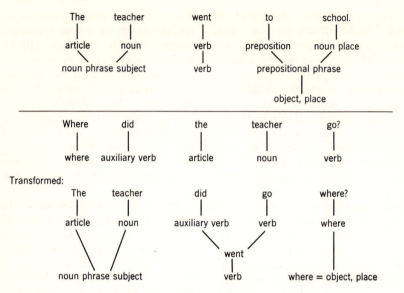

Fig. 1. Oracle-type analysis of question and answer.

codes. Within the range of very simple English structures the method is uncomplicated and easily achievable. The principle of double coding for syntactic and semantic word class—will be seen to generalize to much more complicated structures than Oracle used.

The conversation machine and the Oracle are two prototypes of question-answerers, which even in 1959 demonstrated that *if* statements could be coded semantically and syntactically they could be matched to discover how closely they resembled each other. For the conversation machine the match was against a coded data base and the selection of a reply to a remark was a function of the type of correspondence between the remark after coding and the program's coded knowledge. For the Oracle the comparison was between an English question and an English sentence, both of which were inputs.

IV. List-Structured Data-Base Systems

A *list-structured data-base question-answering system* is one that deals with data that are strongly organized into list

form. SAD SAM reads Basic English[3] sentences and extracts from them data which can be appended to a list-structured data base. The BASEBALL system answers questions from lists which summarize a Major League's season's experience. The recent DEACON system is designed both to build a data structure from English sentences and to answer English questions from it. All of these programs illustrate and explore the principle of well organized but limited information structures as a basis for experimenting with methods of answering English questions.

SAD SAM. This acronym stands for Sentence Appraiser and Diagrammer and Semantic Analyzing Machine. It was programmed in IPL-V by R. Lindsay (1963) as part of a dissertation at Carnegie Institute of Technology. SAD SAM is divided into two parts, a parsing section and a section for handling meanings. The system is designed to accept simple sentences limited to a Basic Eng-

---

[3] Basic English is a subset of English limited to a vocabulary of 300–1600 words and the simplest grammatical constructions. See Ogden (1962).

lish vocabulary concerning family relationships. The data base is in the form of a family tree represented in the program by a hierarchical set of lists. As a sentence is read, it is parsed and the information that a person bears a relationship of brother, mother, father, etc., to someone else is extracted, and the name so represented is appended to the appropriate lists or branches of the family tree.

The parsing system is an independent program which uses a form of the predictive-analysis techniques which have been described in detail by Oettinger and Kuno (1963). Although it was designed for relatively simple structures, Lindsay reports that it can handle relative clauses and at least some appositional strings. As a result of the parsing, the input to the semantic analysis program is (1) a sentence whose parts are labelled noun, verb, noun phrase, etc., and (2) a tree structure showing the relationships among these grammatical features.

The semantic analyzer searches for subject-complement combinations which are connected by the verb "to be" and cross-references these to indicate that each is equivalent to the other. Words which modify such equivalent words are then grouped together. The vocabulary of Basic English provides only eight words to characterize kinship relations so these are then sought in the sentence. Thus, for the sentence,

John's father, Bill, is Mary's father.

the term, "John's father" would be set equivalent to the complement, "Mary's father." The two kinship terms would be recognized and the proper names which modify them would then be discovered. The word "Bill" modifies the subject and since subject and object are equivalent it also modifies the object. Triplets are constructed to show the relationship between each pair of names as follows:

Bill (father) John
Bill (father) Mary

These relationships are added to the family tree which then has the following structure:

Family unit (name)	
(Attribute)	(Value)
Husband	Bill
Wife	Unknown
Offspring	John, Mary
Husband's parents	Unknown
Wife's parents	Unknown

Since this data structure is in the form of IPL lists, instead of actual names of family members, pointers may be used to indicate the location of a different family list which contains the names. The result is an interlocking data structure which allows a fairly significant level of inference. In the example above, since John and Mary are offspring of a common parent, it is known that they are siblings. If a following sentence states that Jane is Bill's wife, it will be immediately known that Jane is the mother of John and Mary (since no multiple marriages are permitted).

Lindsay's primary interest was in machine comprehension of English and he attempted to show that an important component of understanding lay in building large coordinated data structures from the text which was read. He found it necessary to use a syntactic analysis to discover relationships between the words which his program was able to understand and then to transform the portions of the sentence which were understood into a form which could map onto his data structure.

BASEBALL. This is a program originally conceived by Frick, Selfridge and Dineen and constructed by Green, Wolf, Chomsky and Laughery (1963). It answers English questions about the scores, teams, locations and dates of baseball games. The input questions are restricted to single clauses without logical connectives such as "and," "or" or "but" and excluding such relation words as "most" or "highest." Within the limitations of its data and its syntactic capability, Baseball is the most sophisticated and successful of the first generation of experiments with question-answering machines. It is of particular interest for the depth and detail of its analysis of questions.

Baseball is programmed in IPL and uses list structures to organize data. The data are set up with a major heading of months. For each month there is a list of places in which games were played. For each place there is a list of days, for each day a list of games, and for each game a list of teams and score values, exemplified by the following data format:

```
Month = July
  Place₁ = Boston
    Day₁ = 7
      Game Serial # = 96
        Team = Red Sox, Score = 5
        Team = Yankees, Score = 3
```

The program also contains a dictionary which includes the part of speech of a word, its meaning, an indication of whether it belongs to an idiom, and a code to show if it is a question word. The first part of the program's task is to use the dictionary, parsing routines and content routines to translate from the English language question into a specification (or spec) list which is similar in format to the data structure.

The first step is to substitute dictionary codes for the English words. A parsing using a modification of Zellig Harris's approach (1962) results first in bracketing the phrases of the question, then in determination of subject, object and verb. For example, the question "How many games did the Yankees play in July?" gives the following bracketing:

(How many games) did (the Yankees) play (in (July))?

The brackets distinguish noun phrases and prepositional phrases and locate the data which are needed for the spec list. The parsing phase resolves some ambiguities of the noun-verb type while others such as "Boston = place" or "Boston = team" are resolved later. Some, of course, are not resolvable.

A semantic analysis phase actually builds the spec list from the parsed question. In this phase the dictionary meanings of the words are used. The meaning may be an attribute which is part of the data structure, as in "team" means "team = (blank)," or "who" means "team = ?"; or the meaning may be a call to a subroutine, as for example "winning" means "routine A1" which attaches the additional condition "winning" to "team" on the spec list. The output of these routines is a spec list which is used to search the list structures of the data store for an acceptable answer.

After the spec list is completed, the processing phase takes over. In some cases, this requires the simple matching of a blank item on the spec list such as the place in which a given team played on a given day. In other cases, as with the words "every," "either," and "how many," processing is a very complicated searching and counting procedure. The output of the program is in the form of a *found* list which shows all of the acceptable answers to the question.

In the Baseball system three aspects of the question-answering problem stand out clearly. A first phase of syntactic analysis merges into the second phase, semantic analysis. However, for the first time a third logical processing phase becomes explicit. In this phase, even though the relations between words and the meaning of words are already known, a wide range of operations are performed as a function of these meanings.

Having considered the manner in which Lindsay's SAD SAM reads text to append data to a list structure similar to that used by the Baseball system, it is apparent that Baseball could become a completely self-contained (though limited) automatic language processor. To achieve this goal, factual statements would be read and analyzed into their spec lists and a new processor would be required to add the data to the storage lists.

THE DEACON BREADBOARD. At General Electric's TEMPO, F. Thompson (1964) and J. Craig (1963) have reported on DEACON[4]—a data-based question answerer which is part of a man-machine communication system that may eventually allow operators to communicate with each other and with the computer in a subset of natural English. The question answerer is programmed in a special list-processing language, KLS-II, developed at TEMPO for this system. At this writing, many aspects of the natural-language programs have been checked out and the authors expect a complete question answerer to be operable soon.

In general, DEACON depends on a list-structured data base. Thompson makes explicit the importance of a well-understood data structure and introduces a principle of equivalence between the word classes of syntactic analysis and the semantic categories of the data base. As a result his programs do not break neatly into a parsing system, a semantic analyzer, and a data processor, although these phases are still distinguishable. His language analysis parses a sentence into the names of lists and the calls to operations to be performed on the lists. These operations are performed immediately and the resulting sublists are tested for their truth value in the last phase of data processing.

An example presented by Thompson

[4] DEACON stands for Direct English Access and control.

(1964, pp. 17–23) will clarify the operation of these programs.

Question: The cost of what Air Force shipments to Omaha exceeds 100,000 dollars?

The data base from which this question is to be answered is outlined in Table 1. This table can be read as a list structure of shipments with sublists of Air Force, Army and Navy shipments. Each of these sublists has attributes of cost, origin and destination and values as shown in the cells of the table.

The first step in analyzing the question is that of assigning word classes as follows:

the	F	to	F
cost	A	Omaha	V
of	F	exceeds	$R(V, V)$
what	F	100,000	N
Air Force	M	dollars	A
shipments	L	?	

The word "shipment" is classified L as a major list. The term "Air Force" is classified M as a list modifier (or major sublist). "Cost" and "dollars" are assigned A for attribute. "Omaha" is designated V for value and "100,000" is designated N for number. Each of the words coded F represents some function for the system to perform. The parsing is accomplished with a phrase structure grammar in which each rule is accompanied by a transform to operations on the data list structure. For example, the following rule,

$$L_1 = M + L : T_1(M, L)$$

TABLE 1

Shipments	Cost	Origin	Destination
Air Force			
Shipment a	$ 39,000	Detroit	Washington
Shipment b	103,000	Boston	Omaha
Army			
Shipment a	—	—	—
Shipment b	—	—	—
Navy			
Shipment a	—	—	—
Shipment b	—	—	—

means that when the combination of word classes $M + L$ is found, substitute for L_1 the list which is generated by T_1 operating to extract the sublist M from the major list L. The word "what" is a function word interpreted as a quantifier which generates all cases of the structure which it modifies. At the conclusion of the analysis there is the rule,

$$T = V + R(V, V) + V : T_7(V, R, V).$$

This rule translates roughly into "Is it true that the value of the data generated in the first clause exceeds the value of the data generated in the second clause?"[5] By the time this rule is applied, the first and second clauses are each represented by a list. $R(V, V)$ is a function which tests a member of the first list as greater in value than a member of the second. In this case the second list has one entry, value 100,000 dollars, and for each member of the first list the indicator for true or false is assigned as a result of the comparison.

The TEMPO system accepts the occurrence of ambiguous analyses but usually these are resolved in terms of the data context of the sentence. Each remaining analysis is dealt with as a separate statement or question. It generalizes to a broad range of data and to a reasonably complex subset of English. The system is self-contained in that it both reads its own data and answers questions. It makes explicit the principles of structure and question analysis which although previously implicit in such systems as BASEBALL, SAD SAM and the PLM were not then fully conceptualized. It is theoretically important in showing the continuity between syntactic, semantic and symbolic-logical analyses of English in a data base system.

OTHER DATA-BASE APPROACHES. Work by Walker and Bartlett (1962), and by

[5] For example, is clause 1 (cost of AF shipments, etc. = 103,000) greater than clause 2 (100,000 dollars = 100,000); thus, is 103,000 > 100,000?

Sable (1962) and several classified systems under development by the Air Force are further examples of attempted systems which query a data base in some more or less restricted set of English. The outline of a special problem-oriented language for translating from a subset of English into operations on a data base was reported by Cheatham and Warshall (1962) and other computer language developments are also of interest in this area. In general, however, these are not primarily studies of question answering in natural language.

V. Graphic Data-Base Systems

Two interesting systems which depend on graphic data bases are described in this section. One clearly shows the power of translating from English or from graphic data into a subset of the predicate calculus. The other takes a probabilistic learning approach toward the generation of valid English statements from the diagrams it reads. Together they add further support to the idea, suggested earlier by Lindsay (1963) and others, that a well-structured data base offers great potential for making inferences as well as for providing explicitly stored data.

THE PICTURE LANGUAGE MACHINE (PLM). At the National Bureau of Standards, R. Kirsch (1964), D. Cohen (1962), B. Rankin (1961) and W. Sillars (1963) have devised a program system which accepts pictures and sentences as input. It translates both the pictures and the English statement into a common intermediate logical language and determines whether the statement about the picture is true. This set of programs is of particular interest in this review since it seems to be one of the first to explore the principle of translating from a subset of English into a formal language and to point out a reasonable method for doing so.

The PLM is composed of three subsystems—a parser, a formalizer, and a predicate evaluator. Its language is limited to a small subset of English suitable for making statements and asking questions about three geometric figures. The parsing system is based on an immediate-constituent grammar that includes the discontinuous-constituent operator. Parsing is accomplished by a recognition routine which successively substitutes symbols for the dictionary for words in the sentence or for an intermediate symbol string until the top of the parsing tree is reached.

After the sentence has been parsed to produce one or more tree structures representing it, the formalizer translates the parsed sentence into the formal language. The formal language is a first-order functional calculus with a small number of constant predicates. The primitives of the language include brackets, parentheses, the terms "and," "if . . . then," "for all," "there exists," "not," "identity," certain other quantifiers, variables and finally three types of predicates. The singular predicates are typified by the following examples:

Cir(a) a is a circle
Bot(a) a is at the bottom
Bk(a) a is black

Some typical binary and ternary predicates follow:

Bgr(a,b) a is bigger than b
Lf(a,b) a is to the left of b
Smc(a,b) a is the same color as b
Bet(a,b,c) a is between b and c
Mort(a,b,c) a is more to the right of b than c
Mmid(a,b,c) a is more in the middle of b than c

The formalizer is designed to work with each parsing that the grammar produces. For each rule in the grammar there is a corresponding rule of formalization. The translation process is primarily one of substituting formalization symbols for grammar symbols beginning at the top of the parsed tree and working down. More than simple substitution is required to insert quantifiers and impli-

cation symbols, but essentially the process of translating to the formal language bears a great similarity to that of generating a language string from a phrase structure grammar. For each parsing of a sentence the translation into the formal language results in a unique, unambiguous, well-formed formula. An example sentence "All circles are black circles" has only one parsing which finally translates into the following formal statement:

$$[(\forall X_1)\,\mathrm{Cir}(X_1) \supset (\exists X_2)$$
$$\cdot [\mathrm{Cir}(X_2)\ \&\ \mathrm{Bk}(X_2)\ \&\ (X_2 = X_1)]].$$

The structure of this formula is explicit and unambiguous; the relationships between the geometric variables are clearly specified and the truth value may be tested by the predicate evaluator. If true, the answer to the implied question "Are all circles black?" is *yes*.

The predicate evaluator translates from pictures to the formal language. It is designed to accept inputs that have been processed by SADIE, a scanning device which is used as an input to a computer. The inputs are limited to three sizes each of triangle, square or circle, each of which may be in outline or filled in. A technique called *blobbing* is used to distinguish objects resulting from the scan and each such object is then circumscribed with a rectangle. Maximum and minimum x-y coordinates are computed and the ratios of these serve to distinguish triangles from circles or squares. Circles are distinguished from squares on the basis of covering less area. A *black* figure is one whose area is filled in while a *white* figure is an outline. These relatively simple computations suffice to generate the valid predicates from the picture matrix.

Some of the interesting features of the PLM can be appreciated only by close study of its documentation. For example, the grammar used is a modified phrase structure system with a remarkably compacted notation (Kirsch, 1963). The problem of ambiguity of syntactic analysis is accepted and each possible interpretation of the sentence is tested for validity as a well-formed formalization. There is a practical scheme for translating at least a small subset of English into the predicate calculus and an equally feasible system for testing the formalization against that resulting from the picture matrix.

NAMER. Simmons and Londe (1964) at SDC programmed a system to generate natural-language sentences from line drawings displayed on a matrix. The primary intent of this research was to demonstrate that pattern recognition programs could be used to identify displayed figures and to identify the relationships among them. After this had been established, a language generator was used to generate simple sentences such as "The square is above, to the right of, and larger than the circle." The sentences that are generated are answers to the various relational questions which could be explicitly asked.

The pattern recognition aspects of Namer were derived from work by Uhr and Vossler (1963). When a picture is presented on the input matrix, a set of 96 characteristics is computed. The algorithms or operators compute these as functions of the size, shape and location of the pattern in the matrix. Typical characteristics that are derived include one-bit indications of the presence or absence of parts of the figure in sections of the matrix, of protuberances, of holes in the pattern (as in a circle), and of indentations as in a "u." A first-level learning stage of Namer selects a small subset of the 96 characteristics—those which correlate most highly with correct recognition of the name by which the experimenter designates the pattern.

The second level of Namer operates in a comparable fashion to obtain characteristics of the sets of coordinates representing two patterns. At this level the operators generate characteristics of comparative size, separation, density, height,

etc. Subsets of these 96 characteristics are learned in the same fashion as at the earlier level to correlate with such relation terms as above, below, thicker than, to the right of, etc.

The language generator uses a very brief phrase structure grammar to generate simple sentences which are true of the picture. For example,

The dog is beside and to the right of the boy.
The circle is above the boy.
The boy is to the left of and taller than the dog.

There is a great variety of drawings that can be learned and once a relationship is learned between any two figures it usually generalizes successfully to most other pairs of figures.

Both the PLM and Namer show the capability of making geometric inferences based on a set of computational operations on line drawings. Unique sets of characteristics resulting from the computations can be mapped onto English names and words expressing spatial relationships. In this respect these systems anticipate some recently developed inference systems (see Section VII on SQA). The PLM has the additional feature of being able to answer questions about those English language statements which are permissible in its grammar. Since it can translate from English into a formal statement, the formalization for the question can be compared to that for the proposed answer. By the addition of predicates which go beyond simple spatial relations, the PLM may generalize into a much broader inference system than any yet available.

Namer on the other hand is not strictly a question answerer. In order to answer English questions selectively it would be necessary to match the valid statements that can be generated against an analysis of the specific question. However, Namer offers a probabilistic learning approach for learning names and relationships in a data base. This approach may generalize far beyond spatial relationships and their expression in language and may suggest a method for dealing with inference in nongraphic data bases as well.

VI. Text-Based Systems

In the previous two sections, question answerers which query a well-structured but limited data base have been described. The text-based systems, in contrast, attempt to find answers from ordinary English text. As a consequence, neither the language to be used nor the data to be queried lend themselves to fractionation into convenient small packages of vocabulary or simple syntax. Although current experimental text-based systems in fact deal with relatively small amounts of text (from 100–500 thousand words) they are designed with much larger amounts in mind. To some extent they resemble more ordinary information retrieval systems in their use of indexing and term-matching techniques, but they deal at the level of English questions and sentences instead of term sets and documents. In addition, the text-based question answerer adds linguistic and semantic processing phases to evaluate the material discovered in the retrieval phase.

Three such systems will be described here—Protosynthex, the Automatic Language Analyzer and the General Inquirer. Since this area is closely related to that of fact and document retrieval systems, references will be provided to lead the interested reader deeper into that area.

PROTOSYNTHEX. At SDC, Simmons and McConlogue with linguistic support from Klein (Simmons, Klein, McConlogue, 1963) have built a system which attempts to answer questions from an encyclopedia. The problem in this system was to accept natural English questions and search a large text to discover the most acceptable sentence, paragraph or article as an answer. Beginning at the level of ordinary text, Protosynthex

makes an index, then uses a synonym dictionary, a complex intersection logic, and a simple information scoring function to select those sentences and paragraphs which most resemble the question. At this point, both the question and the retrieved text are parsed and compared. Retrieved statements whose structure or whose content words do not match those of the question are rejected. A final phase of analysis checks the semantic correspondence of words in the answer with words in the question.

Beginning with natural text that has been keypunched, an indexing pass is made and an index entry is constructed for each content word in the text. A root-form logic is used to combine entries for words with similar forms; for example, only one index entry exists for govern, governor, government, governing, etc. The contents of the entry are a set of VAPS numbers which indicate the Volume, Article, Paragraph and Sentence address of each occurrence of the indexed word.

The first step in answering the question is to look up all of its content words in the index and so retrieve all of the appropriate VAPS numbers. At this stage a dictionary of words of related meaning is used to expand the meaning of the question's words to any desired level. Thus the question, "What animals live longer than men?" might result in the following lists of content words as a query to the index.

Word	*Words of Related Meaning*
animals	mammals, reptiles, fish
live	age
longer	older, ancient
men	person, people, women

The intersection test finds the smallest unit of text, preferably a sentence, in which the greatest number of words intersect. A simple information score based on the inverse of the frequency of occurrence of the word in the large sample of text is used to weight some words more heavily than others in selecting potential answers. All of this computation is done with the VAPS numbers that were obtained from the index. The highest scoring five or ten potential answers are then retrieved from the tape on which the original text was stored. These comprise an information-rich set of text which roughly corresponds to the set of alternatives proposed by the question (within limits of the available text).

The question and the text are then parsed using a modification of the dependency logic developed by D. Hays (1962). For example, Fig. 2 shows the dependency structures of a question and some potential answers which were retrieved. In passing it should be noted that the parsing system learns its own

word classes as a result of being given correctly analyzed text. The human operator interacts frequently with this parser to help it avoid errors and ambiguities. In the simple examples in Fig. 2, the principle of dependency structure matching can be seen. All of the potential answers included "worms" and "eat," the content words from the question. But only those statements in which the dependency of "eat" on "worms" is maintained need be considered further as possible answers.

The actual matching is accomplished by a fairly complex set of programs which build a matrix containing all the words from the question and from its possible answers. The matrix is examined

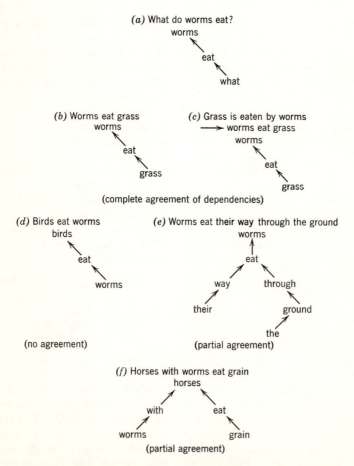

Fig. 2. Dependency structure of a question and some potential answers PROTOSYNTHESIS.

to discover the structure matches and the part of the statement which corresponds to the question word. For the example question, this evaluation program would output as follows:

worms = worms
cat = cat
what = grass
what = their way
what = through the ground

A semantic evaluation system is now required to score each of the words in phrases corresponding to "what." This system is essentially a dictionary lookup whose entries can grow as a function of use. If certain words are found to be answers to "where" questions they will be so coded in the dictionary. If the question had been "Worms eat what food?" the words "ground," "way" and "grass" would have been looked up and compared in semantic coding with "food." Those which corresponded most closely would have been scored as best answers. The semantic evaluation system is still in early stages of experimentation but is expected to resemble the parsing system in that its dictionary will be developed and modified as a function of experience with text under the control of an online operator.

The approach of Protosynthex is to successively filter out more and more irrelevant information, leaving ultimately only statements which have a high probability of being answers to the question. This system is an attempt to deal with a large and syntactically complex sample of natural text. It is a symbiotic system in which a man works with the computer to help resolve both syntactic and semantic ambiguities. Only in this fashion is the program able to overcome the problems associated with multiple, apparently valid interpretations of the same sentence or question.

THE AUTOMATIC LANGUAGE ANALYZER (ALA). From Indiana University a series of quarterly reports by Householder et al. (1960–62) and a final technical report by Thorne (1962) describe the progress toward completion of a rather complicated automatic language analysis system.[6] This system is designed to handle the breadth and complexity of language found in a book on astronomy. As a question-answering system, it introduces a variation of the principle of translating from English into an intermediate language which bears a strong relationship to dependency structure. When translated to the intermediate language, FLEX, the question or text is also augmented by semantic codes obtained from *Roget's Thesaurus*—or from a specially constructed thesaurus. The degree of matching between question and text is then computed to select a best answer.

The primary information store for the ALA is a preanalyzed set of sentences stored on tape. The preanalysis includes assignment of FLEX codes and of thesaurus references. The thesaurus is a list of clusters each of which indexes the portions of the text in which members of the cluster appear. A dictionary of word-stems and phrases provides cross-references to clusters in which the word appears. The sequence of operations is that the question is first analyzed and assigned FLEX and thesaurus codes, then sentences are selected and matched, and finally the paragraphs that contain supposed answering sentences are printed out with their scores.

The transformation of English into the FLEX language is begun by looking up each word in a dictionary to assign ordinary syntactic word classes. At this point a great deal of effort is spent to resolve word class ambiguity by use of special routines which use additional cues available in the sentence. The next phase is to order the words into clauses and phrases and to check the accuracy of this ordering. The breaking into clauses is accomplished by the use of marker words such as verbs and absolute markers such as "because," "how,"

[6] For the sake of convenience, this has been abbreviated to the ALA system and the present summary is based on the final report by Thorne.

"if," "what," "when," etc. When the sentence has been analyzed into subject, verb, and their qualifiers, the translation into FLEX is accomplished as shown below.

The old man ate stale food reluctantly.

S1	S2	P1	P2	P3
man	old	ate	food	stale
			reluctantly	

The notation is to be read, "S1 means subject, S2 is the first qualifier, P1 means the verb, and P2. . . . Pn refer to verb modifiers." The importance to the sentence of each FLEX symbol is rated separately for subject and predicate in order of the numbers assigned. Thus an S1 or a P1 are most heavily weighted in the later comparison process.

Each word also carries a semantic coding. This code is simply a list of the thesaurus clusters in which it is found. For semantic matching of words *a* and *b,* the following formula is used:

$$\text{Semantic correlation} = \frac{n_{ab}}{\sqrt{(n_a \times n_b)}}.$$

where n_a and n_b are respectively the number of clusters in which *a* and *b* are found, and n_{ab} is the number they share in common. When a question and a sentence are matched, *mutual relevance* is scored by considering the following three comparisons in a weighting scheme: (1) relative importance of the category (i.e., S1 or P1 more important than S2 P2), (2) match of FLEX category (S1 = S2 better than S1 = S3, etc.), and (3) cluster matching score (according to the above formula). The paragraphs containing the best scoring sentences and their scores are then recovered and printed out.[7]

Although programming of this system is apparently not yet completed, and it may be claimed that the FLEX transformation leaves much to be desired as

an intermediate language, the ALA is unquestionably one of the more ambitious and sophisticated systems so far described. At this stage of experimentation it is worth wondering how well the semantic correlations will in general correspond to meaning matches between statements. In any case it is a clearly formulated realization of what has hitherto been a rather vague idea that a thesaurus may be helpful in question answering.

THE GENERAL INQUIRER. A paper by P. Stone et al. (1962) at Harvard University describes a COMIT program system useful for analyzing the content of text. As a question-answerer, the General Inquirer recovers all sentences containing a given set of concepts. As in the Householder-Thorne ALA, a thesaurus is used for coding words as to concept membership and, if desired, an intermediate language may be used which makes explicit the syntax of the text and question. However, the General Inquirer differs from most of the systems so far described in that any syntactic manipulations are done as a manual pre-editing phase for the text and the questions.

Probably the most interesting feature about these programs is the dictionary and thesaurus operation. The thesaurus is built especially for the content to be studied. For example, a thesaurus for psychological studies includes headings such as Person, Behavioral Process, Qualities, etc. As subheadings under Behavioral Process, such cluster tags as the following are found: react, see, hear, smell, defend, dream, escape, etc. For an anthropological study the thesaurus would contain many different headings.

The dictionary includes about 3000 common English words and words of special interest to any particular investigation. The dictionary lookup is accomplished by first filtering out function words such as and, or, to, of, etc., then looking up the remaining portion of text (about 50 percent) in the complete dictionary. Each of the words in the main

---

[7] For other associative scoring techniques see Doyle (1963).

dictionary is defined by the thesaurus tags or clusters to which it belongs. Thus the dictionary entry for "abandon" has the following format:

ABANDON = GO+REJECT+END
+DANGER+ALONE

In the processing phase each word in the text to be examined may be tagged by its cluster memberships and matched against the terms of the request.

Content analyses may be as simple as frequency counts of tag-concepts in a discourse or they may be requests for all sentences in the discourse with the tags "reject" and "person." A great deal of useful analysis can be accomplished using just the semantic portion of the General Inquirer. However, to avoid apparent matches which are structurally dissimilar (as in the overworked example, man bites dog vs. dog bites man) a syntactic analysis is often desirable.

The following interesting semantic-syntactic categories are used in the manual pre-editing phase.

1. Subject and incorporated modifiers
2. Nonincorporated subject modifiers
3. Predicate verbs
4. Verb modifiers including time referents
5. Object and incorporated modifiers
6. Nonincorporated object modifiers
7. Indirect object and modifiers
8. Attributive nouns
9. Attributive verbs

The following example (from a suicide note) will illustrate how these codes are actually used.

IN THE LAST/4 WEEK/4 A NUMBER/1 OF OCCUR-RENCES/1 HAVE FORCED/3 ME/5 INTO A POSITION/4 + WHERE I/8 FEEL/9 MY LIFE/1 IS NOT WORTH/3 CONTINUING/3.

The "+" separates two clauses which were coded as separate "thought se-quences." For the case of pronouns or ellipses the referent words are added in parentheses. It is to be noticed that the grammar distinguishes between meta-phrases such as "I feel that" and declara-tive statements about apparent facts.[8] Like the Householder-Thorne ALA, the General Inquirer finds that only a limited syntactic analysis is sufficient for its pur-pose.

Additional applications of the General Inquirer or simulations of it can be found in North et al. (1963), and Ford (1963). It has already proved itself to be a system useful in supporting several types of content analysis.

REMARKS ON TEXT-BASED SYSTEMS. The three systems described in this sec-tion introduce some principles not usu-ally dealt with in data-base machines. The first of these is a semantic principle of indexing large bodies of text at a depth such that words in a question or their semantic tags can serve as queries to the index. The text processors each faced the problem of bringing explicit organization into the relatively loose flow of ordinary English and each at-tempts to solve it by use of some com-bination of indexing, and syntactic and semantic analysis. The dependency struc-ture matching principle of Protosynthex and the translation into the FLEX lan-guage of ALA or the "thought se-quences" of the General Inquirer are each examples of analyses which go be-yond the purely syntactic. In all three systems, additional semantic coding is explicitly undertaken. The data organiza-tion in each of these systems is dis-tributed among indexes, thesauruses and synonym dictionaries, and among the rules for text analysis. Nevertheless a strong data organization is present al-though information categories are over-lapping rather than unique as in the data base questioners.

OTHER TEXT QUESTIONERS. Swanson

[8] With codes 8 and 9, *attributive* mean-ing metaphrase.

(1963) has attempted to measure the effectiveness of natural language queries for retrieving documents. G. Salton (1962) has considered aspects of the structure-matching principle and means for measuring its degree in a given pair of sentences. Guiliano (1962) and J. Spiegel et al. (1962) have given a great deal of consideration to the use of word associations as a basis for question-answering and retrieval systems. There is some indication that associative indexing may prove a valuable adjunct to other techniques of comparing questions and their answers. The association nets described by Doyle (1963) also offer an interesting point of view toward question answering. Finally the whole area of classification systems, autoabstracting and document retrieval can be expected to contribute increasingly toward the development of general-purpose question answerers.[9]

VII. Logical Inference Systems

An approach of demonstrated usefulness, transformation from English to a quasi-logical formulation is represented by one long-term project and by five of the most recently developed question-answering programs. The earliest work in this area is reported in a paper by T. Williams (1956) concerned with translating from natural English to the predicate calculus. More recent work by Williams (1962) and a series of papers by Bohnert (1962, 1963) develop algorithms for translating from important small subsets of English into predicate calculus forms. Bohnert's Project LOGOS at IBM (Yorktown Heights) has developed computer programs which do this translation for such samples of English as a simple language to be used in a marriage bureau and a "war novel" command language. Bohnert's 1963 paper is notable for the clarity with which it presents arguments for the de-

sirability and feasibility of making such transformations as well as for its development of several algorithms for handling difficult aspects of English.

The five most recently developed question-answering systems resemble each other in their use of explicit rules of logical or mathematical inference. Four of these are associated with artificial intelligence or linguistic laboratories at M.I.T. All are programmed in forms of COMIT or LISP, and all suggest a line of descent from McCarthy's Advice Taker model (1959) and bear a relationship to the family of problem-solving and theorem-proving systems.

THE DARLINGTON LOGIC PROGRAMS. A series of COMIT programs by J. Darlington (1964) at the M.I.T. Mechanical Translation Laboratory translate a subset of English into various forms of the propositional and predicate calculi. They then test the validity of arguments using a modification of the Davis-Putnam algorithm. The propositional system is able to discover clause separations and so recognize propositions using only an elementary type of syntactic analysis. A more complete phrase structure analysis is accomplished in programs concerned with translating relational statements into the predicate calculus.

The first phase of the translation is a dictionary lookup which assigns one of two word classes to each word in the text. A word is either a P for punctuation or a W for all other types. The P type are such words as the following: if, then, and, or, but, therefore, either, neither, nor, that, and several others which have significance as logical separators. At later stages additional word class subscripts are assigned. The P words are further subcategorized as to the type of connection or separation that they perform and as to the particular subroutine which is to be called for special processing. For example, "or," "nor" and "and" call a special subroutine which looks for "either . . . or," "neither . . . nor" and "and . . . both," respectively. The W

[9] See also a recent discussion by Jane Robinson (1964).

words are assigned syntactic word classes such as: noun plural, auxiliary verb, adjective, gerund, etc.

At this point the verbs and gerunds are simplified into abbreviated infinitive forms (to be = be), and some sentences are expanded. For example, "The box and the chair are wooden" is processed into the transform, "The box be wooden and the chair be wooden." Every string of W words separated by a P word is then examined to determine if it is a sentence. These strings qualify as sentences only if each contains at least one noun and one verb. Propositional symbols such as A/V, B/V, etc., are then substituted for each string of W words following a P word. These strings are then compared and, where identical, are assigned the same propositional symbol.

Each proposition is then parenthesized according to a fairly complex set of priority rules in accordance with the P words which separate them. The output is then ready to feed into the program which uses the modified Davis-Putnam algorithm to test the validity of the propositions. The modifications to this algorithm simplify and speed up the process of testing consistency by eliminating redundant clauses.

In the functional logic translation program, sentences are parsed into a phrase structure tree whose nodes are labelled in a manner that makes transformation to quasi-logical formulae a simple process. For example the sentence "All circles are figures" transforms into the quasi-logical formula,

All + Variable $\quad$ A + Noun $\quad$ Phrase $\quad$ 1A + is + some + Variable A + Noun Phrase 2A.

This formula is then transformed to the logical format by looking up its elements in a table of equivalents. The logical analysis proceeds through three levels. At the most detailed level all elements of the sentence will have been transformed into relational terms and existence assertions. Darlington is presently working toward the development of an algorithm which the system can use to choose automatically the level of analysis required to prove or disprove the argument.

The Darlington system can be appreciated as a specialized question answerer which tests a verbal argument for internal consistency. The example "All circles are figures. Therefore all who draw circles draw figures." was translated into logical form and proved valid in a total of about .3 minutes. (Note that "Do all who draw circles draw figures?" is the question that is being answered.)

Weaknesses of the Darlington system are the usual ones of limited ability to handle such complexities of English as pronominal reference, ellipsis, metaphor, etc., and its use of a tiny subset of the language. Its approach to syntactic analysis tends to be rather rough-and-ready using assumptions which over-simplify the problem and cast some doubts on the generality of the solutions. However, the system does exemplify a well-rounded attack on the problem of translating a small segment of English into logical notation and then evaluating the arguments. It indicates quite clearly that logical translators are an interesting and profitable line of research toward the aim of high-quality language processing by computers.

THE COOPER SYSTEM. An elegant example of translation from simple English statements into Aristotelian logic has been programmed in COMIT at IBM (San Jose, Calif.) by William Cooper (1964). This system accepts a small subset of statements such as "Magnesium is a metal," "Gasoline burns rapidly," and "Magnesium oxide is a white metallic oxide." Such statements, or questions in the same form, are translated into one of the four basic Aristotelian sentence types, "All x is y, no x is y, some x is y, and not all x is y." The resulting logical form is tested for deducibility from the information already in the system.

Cooper very carefully defines the subset of English and of English grammar with which he is working. This subset includes adjectives, modifying nouns, substantives, "is" predicates and intransitive verb predicates. He also defines a logical language L^*. Within this logical language, a certain amount of syllogistic inference is possible. The translation algorithm includes phases of syntactic analysis and transformation into forms belonging to L^*. In rough outline the process of parsing and transformation is comparable to those already described in the Darlington system and the Kirsch PLM (1964). The system correctly answers "false" to the assertion "sodium chloride is an element" having already been given the statements, "sodium chloride is salt," "salt is a compound," and "elements are not compounds." It also discovers that "magnesium is a metal that burns rapidly" is true, after finding in its information store that "magnesium is a metal" and "magnesium burns rapidly."

Cooper's system is a carefully thought out and well-described example of translating from a subset of English into Aristotelian syllogistic logic. Obvious limitations in the generality of the approach, the usefulness of the subset of English, and the efficiency of the proof algorithm do not detract from the propaedeutic value of a system simply devised and clearly executed.

In this area of translation from natural language to logical formalisms, books by Reichenbach (1947) and Copi (1959) are basic texts. Recent papers by Kochen (1962), Krulee et al. (1962) and Travis (1963) each discuss important aspects of the problem of building question-answering systems which are based on formal languages.

THE SPECIFIC QUESTION ANSWERER (SQA). At Bolt Beranek and Newman, F. Black (1964) programmed the SQA to find brief answers to short English questions. It is called a *Specific Question Answerer* because it can extract only brief specific answers that are either directly stated in or deducible from its corpus of text. The program consists of a basic system written in LISP and a corpus which contains formal and informal rules of inference as well as declarative statements. In most of his examples Black avoids the problems of syntactic analysis by requiring exact matching of structure between questions and possible answers. (In the latest version, the input is in a formal language.)

The corpus is organized as a set of conditional statements of the form, "If —— then ——." A declarative statement such as "Mercury is a planet" is considered to be a conditional with an empty antecedent. A typical corpus is made up of such declarative statements and such complete conditionals as the following:

Mercury is next smaller than Pluto
Pluto is next smaller than Mars
Mars is next smaller than Venus
If X is next smaller than Y, then X is smaller than Y.
If X is next smaller than Y and Y is smaller than Z then X is smaller than Z.

Primitives of the system include variables such as X, Y, etc.; words (which include variables as well as English words such as Mars, Venus, is, next, etc.); and phrases which are strings of words.

The system operates by comparing a question with each of the *consequents* in the corpus. For example, the question "What is next smaller than Pluto?" matches immediately with the first consequent of the corpus, "Mercury is next smaller than Pluto." If the question were "Pluto is smaller than what?," the answering process is more difficult. In this case there are two matches with the consequents, "X is smaller than Y" and "X is smaller than Z." The word "Pluto" may immediately be substituted for X in each consequent. The first antecedents for each of these two consequents are then used as questions, i.e., "If Pluto is next smaller than Y and Y is smaller than *Z*" for the first question and "If Pluto is next samller than *Y* (then Pluto is smaller than *Y*)" for the second. (Parentheses indicate that the enclosure is not an antecedent.) It will be left as a tree-searching exercise for the reader to follow the resulting net to obtain the answers, "Mercury and Venus."

Recent work with minor modifications to this program has shown that it can solve at least some of the Advice Taker problems (McCarthy 1959). Black has also suggested that the parsing of English syntax may be dealt with by conditional substitutions. For example, one question transform is "If *X* is a *Y*, then is *X* a *Y*?" This rule transforms from one form of question to one form of declarative statement. To what extent such a transformational approach will actually account for English syntax remains to be supported by experimental evidence. Although the inference approach is undeniably powerful, two drawbacks remain. The first is that the SQA requires an exhaustive search of the network of matching consequents, and with even a few hundred consequents the time requirement must be very large. The second is the apparent requirement that the corpus of consequents be internally consistent. However, Black has suggested approaches toward easing these difficulties.

THE SEMANTIC INFORMATION RE-TRIEVER (SIR). From the point of view of exploring a model of meaning as communicated in natural language, B. Raphael (1964) has built a program which accepts a class of simple English statements and, in interaction with the questioner, answers some questions about them. The model considers English words as objects and certain relationships as holding between them. The formalization of the model is a limited relational calculus. The model also takes advantage of the property list characteristics of LISP. Although only a few meanings are specifically dealt with, Raphael suggests that by modeling words in their

interrelationships, the meaning is preserved for a human reader.

This program avoids the complexities of syntactic analysis by limiting itself to a small number of fixed formats for sentences. The present system recognizes about 20 simple sentence formats which include both interrogative and declarative types. By comparison with these basic patterns an input sentence such as "Every boy is a person" is translated into the logical form: SETR (Boy Person). This means that "person" is in a superset relation to "boy." If a sentence or question does not correspond to a known format, it is rejected by the program with an appropriate comment to the operator.

Figure 3 shows a set of example inputs to this program and the resulting data structure for them. In answering the question, "How many fingers are on John?" the system is able to match the question form "(finger, John)" successively with "(finger, hand)," "(hand, person, 2)," "(John, boy)" and "(boy, person)." The "How many" requirement was not fully satisfied so it asks for further information. With the additional data "(finger, hand, 5)" in the numerical part-whole relation, it is able to calculate the answer, 10.

The Raphael program is another example of a system which uses a limited set of logical predicates such as subset, part-whole, left-right, etc., to allow study of deducing or inferring answers to questions. Like the Black program this one essentially ignores syntactic problems, and depends on internally consistent data. However, Raphael's model tests a sentence for consistency before accepting it as data and it also makes explicit the interaction with the questioner.

Both the SQA and SIR are examples of deductive systems which understand some aspects of the meaning of words. They put particular emphasis on various relational terms and use rules of logical inference to follow trees of axioms and

Input Statements:	Formalization:
Every boy is a person	SETR (Boy, Person)
John is a boy	SETR (John, Boy)
Any person has two hands	PARTRN (Hand, Person, 2)
A finger is part of a hand	PARTR (Finger, Hand)
Question:	
How many fingers are on John?	PARTRNQ (Finger, John)
Computer Response:	
How many fingers per hand?	
Input Statement:	
Every hand has five fingers	PARTRN (Finger, Hand, 5)
Answer:	
The answer is 10	

Fig. 3. An example from the Raphael program.

theorems. In both cases, if the statement form of the input question can be deduced from information in memory, the answer is "yes;" if its negation is deduced, the answer is "no." If the statement cannot be deduced the answer is "don't know." SIR recognizes when information is missing and requests it, but is limited to those relational terms for which it has corresponding functional routines.

The SQA seems to be a more general approach, in that it can accept a very broad range of relational terms without the necessity of reprogramming. That is, the SQA, following the Advice Taker paradigm, allows the question asker to program the machine by giving it additional information. Both systems provide relatively simple and comparatively efficient algorithms for deducing answers to questions.

STUDENT. D. Bobrow (1964) for an M.I.T. doctoral thesis has programmed an algebra problem solver which accepts problems phrased in a limited subset of English and transforms these into equations which can be solved arithmetically. The limited subset of English is mainly sufficient to account for the phrasing found in a high-school algebra text. The system is programmed in LISP and is currently operable on the timeshared 7094 computer system at M.I.T.'s Project MAC.

STUDENT is based on a theoretical relationship model whose objects are variables such as words, numbers, or phrases which name numbers. The relations are the ordinary arithmetic operations of adding, subtracting, multiplying, dividing, exponentiation, equality, etc. The means for expressing the relations among objects are sets of simultaneous equations. The problem that STUDENT attacks is that of transforming a set of English statements in which a set of equations is implicit into an explicit formulation of those equations.

Background data which help STUDENT to "understand" the meaning of certain words and phrases are provided by a part of the system which accepts simple English statements such as "twice always means two times" or "three feet equals one yard." This subprogram builds what is essentially a dictionary of transformations from one form of English into an equivalent formalism which the program can use, or into a form which is identical with a form used previously in a problem.

Bobrow's first step in transforming an English statement into a set of equations is to make mandatory substitutions such as "two times" for "twice," "square" for "the square of," and several others. His next step is to identify terms such as "plus," "percent," "times," etc., and to tag them as operators. In addition to tagging operators in this phase, the program also identifies certain verbs, question words, and the terminal question mark. The process is accomplished by dictionary lookup. After these operations an example problem appears as follows:

IF THE NUMBER (OF/OP) CUSTOMERS TOM (GETS/VERB) IS 2 (TIMES/OP 1) THE (SQUARE/OP 1) 20 (PERCENT/OP 2) (OF/OP) THE NUMBER (OF/OP) ADVERTISEMENTS (HE/PRO) RUNS, AND THE NUMBER (OF/OP) ADVERTISEMENTS (HE/PRO) RUNS IS 45, (WHAT/QWORD) IS THE NUMBER (OF/OP) CUSTOMERS TOMX (GETS/VERB) (QMARK/DLM)

A most critical phase of the processing is the next step, in which two simple heuristics are used for breaking the problem statement into simple sentences. The first is to look for an "if" followed by anything followed by a comma followed by a question word and transform it to two sentences. For example:

If . . . customers Tom gets . . . is 45,
     What is . . . QMARK
transforms to
     . . . customers Tom gets . . . is 45.
          What is QMARK.

The second heuristic, applied after the first, is to divide strings followed by ", and" into two simple sentences. After these operations the following simple sentences result from the example above:

THE NUMBER OF CUSTOMERS TOM GETS IS 2 TIMES THE SQUARE

20 PERCENT OF THE NUMBER OF ADVERTISEMENTS HE RUNS. THE NUMBER OF ADVERTISEMENTS HE RUNS IS 45. WHAT IS THE NUMBER OF CUSTOMERS TOM GETS

                              QMARK

The operators and function terms are underlined in the above sentences.

All of the simple sentences are now of the form, "P1 is P2." In the first sentence, P1 represents "The number of customers Tom gets" and P2 is the remainder following "is." (In cases of sentences in the form "X does/has Y" the program transforms them to "The *thing* X does/has is Y.")

Each of the operators now calls for a special function to be performed. For example (OF/OP) checks to see if "of" is immediately preceded by a number; in that case it will be treated as the multiplication operator. Otherwise its operator tag will be stripped off and it will be ignored. A (PERCENT/OP2) looks at the preceding number and divides it by 100. Other such operators are not only more complicated but require consideration of precedence levels. The result of applying these operations is to put the equations into the explicit form that LISP can use in solving them.

Many hazards may still exist to block the explicitness of the equations. Because of pronouns, ellipsis, shift in measuring units (as from feet in inches, or from dollars to cents), or because of synonymic reference such as "people for customers," the variables and units in the equations may not match. If these difficulties arise, STUDENT takes recourse to its memory of background data which can be manipulated by the user to provide unit transformations, sentence transforms, and synonyms. Heuristics for guessing the referent of pronouns are also provided.

There are numerous interesting features about STUDENT, not the least of which are its use of a fund of background information and its substitution of a heuristic approach to sentence analysis for the more usual analytic one. The meaning of a problem is first resolved into simple sentence units, then into variables and operators. The meaning of the operators is the function they cause to be performed. For variables, the only pertinent question is "does the string Pi identically correspond to the string Pj." If not, possible transformations are considered to bring about such a result.

Although the system is obviously limited to a well-controlled, specialized subset of English, it has proved sufficiently versatile to solve a large number of high school algebra word problems. It contributes significantly to language-processing technology in its heuristic approach to syntactic analysis, its use of background information, and its direct approach toward translating a small class of English operator words into their mathematical equivalents.

Analysis and Conclusions

PRINCIPLES OF QUESTION-ANSWERING SYSTEMS. Although the question answerers described express a wide variety of approaches, there are in fact striking similarities in processing requirements. A strong organization of data storage is a common requirement. (Even in the case of English text questioners an additional phase of index processing is usual to obtain this degree of organization.) The language must be analyzed syntactically and in the more sophisticated systems semantic analysis is also required. Question and data are transformed into some canonical form and a matching and sometimes a scoring is undertaken to determine whether or not an answer is present. In the list-structured data-base systems, the output is usually a list of the matching terms from the lists which were the referent of the question. In addition, for each of the systems, there may be a level of inference-drawing although only a few make this level explicit.

DATA STRUCTURES. The data-base programs understand text and/or questions by transforming them into the categories and subcategories of a well-structured data storage system. Usually this data system is in terms of lists in which each headlist has sublists which have attributes and values. The chief advantage of

this structure is that a given item may be a member of many lists which address it (and so interrelate it) while the item need be recorded only once. The papers by Lindsay (1963) and by Thompson (1963) make explicit the value and importance of coding information by the structure in which it is embedded. The resulting structural relations permit some degree of inference.

In the text-processing programs, the natural English language text has an additional organization imposed upon it through a preprocessing phase of indexing, usually supported by lists of synonyms and a dictionary of concept codes. The data structure in these systems is less explicit and less centralized but quite as essential as in the list-structured data-base programs.

SYNTACTIC ANALYSIS. Although this paper has not emphasized the description of the special techniques of syntactic analysis, it is an important phase in all question-answering systems. (Even in those where simplifying assumptions are used to avoid it!) Generally an immediate-constituent model is used and generally the problem of ambiguous interpretations is encountered. In the data-base systems, where a small subset of English constitutes the vocabulary, the problems of ambiguity sometimes can be resolved in terms of the referent data structures. In the text processing systems, great effort is taken to resolve syntactic ambiguity before attempting to answer the question. Whether either of these approaches to resolving problems of ambiguity will in fact prove successful remains to be shown.

SEMANTIC ANALYSIS. The phase of a question answering program devoted to semantic analysis is often not clear-cut and usually merges into the syntactic analysis and matching phases. In the data-base systems the meaning of a word is usually the denotation of either a data category or of a subroutine. This meaning is typically a coded entry associated with the word in a dictionary. In the text-processing systems the meaning of a word is generally a list of attribute codes (as the Roget cluster numbers in the Householder-Thorne ALA). By controlling syntactic correspondence the correlation or commonalities of meaning for corresponding words in two statements can be measured in terms of corresponding codes and accumulated across the sentences.

While semantic analysis is much more clearly understandable in terms of the data-base systems, it is apparent that not all subtleties of language can map onto an unambiguously defined data structure. The matter of coding the meanings of words and calculating the meanings of sentences is an area in which only the dimmest of understanding currently exists. However, theoretical work by Katz and Fodor (1963) and by Quillian (1963) suggest avenues of approach, and surely a direct attack on problems of meaning is probably most profitable.

OBTAINING AND EVALUATING ANSWERS. Syntactic and semantic analyses are undertaken to transform the question and the answering text into some canonical form in which they can be easily compared. Generally this form is a syntactically-ordered list of the semantic units with which the system deals. In the data-base systems, the standard form is a set of list names; in the text processors the units may be English words, their synonyms or semantic codes corresponding to words or terms. Several of the more recent systems use something approaching the format of the predicate calculus as a standard form.

However, even when both question and answer exist is canonical form, there are still serious problems in comparing the two. In the data-base systems there is generally the problem of actually processing the data structure and in some cases making inferences (such as, if X and Y are "offspring" of the same parent they are siblings—or, is 300,000 more than 100,000?). In the text-proc-

essing systems really good comparisons of questions and possible answers depend on far better semantic coding than has been presently developed and on a much-increased understanding of how to order the units for comparison. Although these systems are also potentially adept at making language inferences (by generating and answering additional questions and by using dictionaries of rules of linguistic inference) actual experiments in this direction are still largely lacking.

In Kirsch's PLM and Thompson's TEMPO systems, the meaning of a statement is accumulated substructure by substructure and the result is finally tested for truth value. In STUDENT, the Algebra Word Problem Solver, the portions of meaning which are pertinent to solving the algebra problem are accumulated until a well-formed mathematical formulation is available. These systems certainly suggest the way in which meaning (as far as a particular machine function is concerned) can be extracted and accumulated. However to generalize these suggestions to a fairly large set of English words and constructions remains a formidable task for the future.

OUTLOOK. Although research on question-answering systems is only five years old, it is possible to conclude that already enough important principles are understood to offer assurance that the next five or ten years will be even more rewarding. For immediate development the large data-base system, controlled and queried by a small subset of English which can vary freely, looks most promising. Until now data-base systems have worked with a very limited variety of data. The next major step is to experiment with systems which have a wide variety of data in their structure. Such systems would unavoidably be rather large, but the author believes that their problems can be mastered.

The outlook for text-processing systems is also promising but it would be overoptimistic to expect any developmental model with practical utility for some time to come. Questions of semantic coding, of accumulating and representing the meaning of statements, and of performing inference effectively are still very much in the initial research stage. The two general systems which so far exist (Protosynthex and the ALA) are intriguing early demonstrations of ultimately valuable language processors. Those systems which study question-answering methods by using rules of inference are a most recent and potentially attractive feature of the language processor, but a great deal of research into rules of logico-linguistic inference and into methods of translating from English into clarifying forms such as the predicate calculus remains to be done.

In summary, steady, even rapid, progress is being made toward the development of practical question answerers and general language processors. The most difficult questions are now becoming apparent. How does one characterize the meaning of a sentence? How are ambiguous interpretations, both syntactic and semantic, to be dealt with? How are inferences to be made without exhaustive tree searches? How are partial answers, widely separated in the text, to be combined? To what extent can we or should we translate from English into formal languages? Can these studies be attacked from a theoretical point of view or do they yield best to the empirical approach of building large question answerers and language processors as test vehicles? Even partial answers to these questions will contribute to the eventual development of high quality, general purpose language processors.

*

ACKNOWLEDGMENTS. There is today an "invisible college" of language-processing researchers. Those engaged in research on question answering are a relatively new and close-knit group in this college. Thanks to the intensive exchange of information among members of this group, this review of question-answering systems shows fewer of my own biases and gaps of knowledge than would otherwise be true.

I am particularly indebted to Russell Kirsch who called my attention to several approaches to question answering which might not otherwise have been cited. Larry Travis has attempted to allay some of my ignorance in the area of translating from English into formal languages. Dan Bobrow (1963) by his competent survey, *Syntactic Analysis of English by Computer,* has saved me a great deal of detailed exposition of how each question answerer did its parsing. Discussions with several of the researchers cited in this review have helped me understand their various approaches.

REFERENCES

Belnap, N. D., Jr. *An analysis of questions: preliminary report.* Doc. TM-1287, System Development Corp., Santa Monica, Calif., June 1963.

Black, F. S. *A deductive question-answering system.* Ph.D. Thesis, Div. Eng. Appl. Phys., Harvard U., Cambridge, Mass., June 1964.

Bobrow, D. G. *Natural language input for a computer problem-solving system.* Proc., Fall Joint Comput. Conf., **25** (1964). Also available as Ph.D. Thesis, Math. Dept., M.I.T., Cambridge, Mass., 1964.

———. *Syntactic analysis of English by computer—a survey.* Proc. Fall Joint Comput. Conf., **24** (1963), Spartan Books, Baltimore, pp. 365–387.

Bohnert, H. G. *An English-like extension of an applied predicate calculus.* AFOSR-TN-62-3, IBM Corp., Yorktown Hts, N.Y., February 1962. See also: "High-Speed Document Perusal," Final Technical Report, AFOSR-2817, May 1962, M. Kochen, principal investigator pp. 11–19.

————. *Logical-linguistic studies for machine text perusal.* Proj. LOGOS, IBM Corp., Yorktown Hts, N.Y., Tech. Status Rep., May-December 1963.

Cheatham, T. E., Jr., and S. Warshall. Translation of retrieval requests couched in a "semiformal" English-like language. *Comm. ACM,* **5,** 1 (January 1962), pp. 34–39.

Cohen, D. *A recognition algorithm for a grammar model.* Rep. 7885, Nat. Bur. Stand., Washington, D.C., April 1962.

————. *Picture processing in a picture language machine.* Rep. 7885, Nat. Bur. Stand., Washington, D.C., April 1962.

Cohen, F. What is a question? *Monist,* 39 (1929), pp. 350–364.

Cooper, W. S. Fact retrieval and deductive question-answering information retrieval systems. *J. ACM,* **11,** 2 (April 1964), pp. 117–137.

Copi, I. *Symbolic Logic.* Macmillan, New York, 1959.

Craig, J. A. *Grammatical aspects of a system for natural man-machine communication.* RM63TMP-31, TEMPO, General Electric Co., Santa Barbara, Calif., July 1963.

Darlington, J. L. *A COMIT program for the Davis-Putnam algorithm.* Res. Lab. Electron., Mech. Transl. Grp., M.I.T., Cambridge, Mass., May 1962.

————. *Translating ordinary language into symbolic logic.* MAC-M 149, Proj. MAC Memo., M.I.T., Cambridge, Mass., March 1964.

Doyle, L. B. The microstatistics of text. *J. Inform. Storage and Retrieval,* **1,** 4 (1963), pp. 189–214.

Ford, J. D., Jr. *Automatic detection of psychological dimensions in psychotherapy.* Doc. SP 1220, System Development Corp., Santa Monica, Calif., July 1963.

Gardner, M. *Logic machines and diagrams.* McGraw-Hill, New York, 1958.

Giuliano, V. E. *Studies for the design of English command and control language system.* Rep. CACL-1, Arthur D. Little, Inc., Cambridge, Mass., June 1962.

Green, B. F., Jr., A. K. Wolf, C. Chomsky, and K. Laughery. Baseball: an automatic question answerer. In *Computers and Thought,* E. A. Feigenbaum and J. Feldman (Eds.), McGraw-Hill, New York, 1963, pp. 207–216.

Green, L. E. S., E. C. Berkeley, and C. Gotlieb. Conversation with a computer. *Computers and Automation,* **8,** 10 (1959), pp. 9–11.

Hamblin, C. L. Questions. *Australian J. Phil.,* **36,** 3 (1958), pp. 160–168.

————. Questions aren't statements. *Phil. Science,* 30 (1963), pp. 62–63.

Harrah, D. A logic of questions and answers. *Phil. Sci.,* **28,** 1 (1961), pp. 40–46.

Harris, Z. S. *String analysis of sentence structure.* Mouton, The Hague, Netherlands, 1962.

Hays, D. G. Automatic language data processing. In *Computer Applications in the Behavioral Sciences,* H. Borko (Ed.), Prentice-Hall, Englewood Cliffs, N.J., 1962, pp. 394–423.

Householder, F. W., Jr., J. Lyons, and J. P. Thorne. *Quart. rep. on automatic language analysis,* 1–7. ASTIS, Indiana U., Bloomington, Ind., 1960–1962.

Katz, J. J., and J. A. Fodor. The structure of a semantic theory, Part I. *Lang.,* **39,** 2 (1963), pp. 170–210.

Kirsch, R. A. *The application of automata theory to problems in information retrieval (with selected bibliography).* Rep. 7882, Nat. Bur. Stand., Washington, D.C., March 1963.

————. Computer interpretation of English text and picture patterns. *Trans. IEEE-EC* (August 1964). In press.

————, Ray, L. C., L. Cahn, and G. H. Urban. *Experiments in processing pictorial information with a digital computer.* Rep. 5713, Nat. Bur. Stand., Washington, D.C., December 1957.

————, and B. K. Rankin, III. *Modified simple phrase structure grammars for grammatical induction.* Rep. 7890, Nat. Bur. Stand., Washington, D.C., May 1963.

Kochen, M. *Adaptive mechanisms in digital "concept" processing.* Proc. Amer. Inst. Electr. Eng., Joint Autom. Contr. Conf., 1962, pp. 49–59.

Krulee, G. K., D. J. Kuck, D. M. Landi, and D. M. Manelski. Natural language inputs for a problem-solving system. *Behav. Sci.,* **9,** 3 (1964), pp. 281–288.

Kuno, S., and A. G. Oettinger. *Syntactic structure and ambiguity in English.* Proc. Fall Joint Comput. Conf. **24** (1963), Spartan Books, Baltimore, pp. 397–418.

Lees, R. B. The grammar of English nominalizations, Part II. *Intntl. J. Amer. Ling.,* **26,** 3 (1960).

Lindsay, R. K. Inferential memory as the basis of machines which understand natural language. In *Computers and Thought,* E. A. Feigenbaum and J. Feldman (Eds.), McGraw-Hill, New York, 1963, pp. 217–233.

MacKay, D. M. The informational analysis of questions and commands. In *Information Theory, Fourth London Symposium,* Colin Cherry (Ed.), Butterworths, Washington, D.C., 1961, pp. 469–477.

McCarthy, J. *Programs with common sense.* Proc. Symp. Mechanisation of Thought Processes, **1,** London, England, HM Stationary Off., 1959, pp. 75–91.

North, R. C., et al. *A system of automated content analysis of documents.* Rep. of Stanford Studies in International Conflict and Integration, Stanford U., Stanford, Calif., March 1963.

Ogden, C. K. *The General Basic English Dictionary.* W. W. Norton, New York, 1962.

Phillips, A. V. *A question-answering routine.* Memo. 16, Artif. Intell. Proj., M.I.T., Cambridge, Mass., May 1960.

Quillian, R. *A notation for representing conceptual information: an application to semantics and mechanical English paraphrasing.* Doc. SP-1395, System Development Corp., Santa Monica, Calif., October 1963.

Rankin, B. K., III. *A programmable grammar for a fragment of English for use in an information retrieval system.* Rep. 7352, Nat. Bur. Stand., Washington, D.C., June 1961.

Raphael, Bertram. *SIR: a computer program for semantic information retrieval.* Fall Joint Comput. Conf. **25** (1964). Also available as Ph.D. Thesis, M.I.T., Math. Dept., Cambridge, Mass., June 1964.

Reichenbach, H. *Elements of symbolic logic.* MacMillan, New York, 1947.

Robinson, J. J. *Automatic parsing and fact retrieval: a comment on grammar, paraphrase and meaning.* Memo. RM-4005-PR, RAND Corp., Santa Monica, Calif., February 1964.

Sable, J. D. Use of semantic structure in information systems. *Comm. ACM,* **5,** 1 (January 1962), pp. 40–42.

Salton, G. Manipulation of trees in information retrieval. *Comm. ACM,* **5,** 2 (February 1962), pp. 103–114.

Sillars, W. *An algorithm for representing English sentences in a formal language.* Rep. 7884, Nat. Bur. Stand., Washington, D.C., April 1963.

Simmons, R. F. Synthetic language behavior. *Data Process. Management,* **5,** 12 (1963), pp. 11–18.

————, and D. Londe. *Namer: a pattern recognition system for generating sentences about relations between line drawings.* Doc. TM-1798, System Development Corp., Santa Monica, Calif., March 1964; *Proc. ACM Twentieth Nation Conf.,* August 1965, pp. 162–175.

————, S. Klein, and K. L. McConlogue. Indexing and dependency logic for answering English questions. *Amer. Documentation,* **15,** 3 (1964), pp. 196–204.

————, and K. L. McConlogue. Maximum-depth indexing for computer retrieval of English language data. *Amer. Documentation,* **14,** 1 (1963), pp. 68–73. Also available as Doc. SP-775, System Development Corp., Santa Monica, Calif.

Spiegel, J., E. Bennett, E. Haines, R. Vicksell, and J. Baker. Statistical association procedures for message content analysis. In *Information System Language Studies,* No. 1, SR-79, MITRE Corp., Bedford, Mass., October 1962.

Stone, P. J., R. F. Bales, J. Z. Namenwirth, and D. M. Ogilvie. The general inquirer: a computer system for content analysis and retrieval based on the sentence as a unit of information. *Behav. Sci.,* **7,** 4 (1962), pp. 1–15.

Swanson, D. R. *Interrogating a computer in natural language.* In Proc. IFIP Cong., Munich, 1962, C. M. Popplewell (Ed.), North Holland, Amsterdam, 1963, pp. 288–293.

Thompson, F. B. *Semantic counterpart of formal grammars.* TEMPA General Electric Co., Santa Barbara, Calif.

————, et al. *DEACON breadboard summary.* RM64TMP-9, TEMPO General Electric Co., Santa Barbara, Calif., March 1964.

Thorne, J. P. *Automatic language analysis.* ASTIA 297381, Final Tech. Rep., Arlington, Va., 1962.

Travis, L. E. Analytic information retrieval. In *Natural Language and the Computer,* P. Garvin (Ed.), McGraw-Hill, New York, 1963, pp. 310–353.

Uhr, L., and C. Vossler. A pattern recognition program that generates, evaluates, and adjusts its own operators. In *Computers and Thought,* E. A. Feigenbaum and J. Feldman (Eds.), McGraw-Hill, New York, 1963, pp. 251–268.

Walker, D. E., and J. M. Bartlett. The structure of languages for man and computer: problems in formalization. Proc. First Cong., Inform. System Sciences, Sess. 10, MITRE Corp., Bedford, Mass., November 1962.

Williams, T. M. Translating from ordinary discourse into formal logic: a preliminary study. ASTIA 98813, Avion Div., ACF Indust., Alexandria, Va., September 1956.

————, R. F. Barnes, and J. W. Kuipers. *Discussion of major features of a restricted logistic grammar for topic representation.* Lab. Rep. 5206-26, ITEK, Lexington, Mass., February 1962.

Data-Retrieval by Computer:
A Critical Survey

by Asa Kasher

Foreword

During the last five years, a steadily growing group of researchers has come to the fore among those mathematicians and linguists, scientists and engineers in various other fields, librarians and documentalists, systems-analysts and programmers who all deal with different aspects of information storage and retrieval. The members of this group are investigating methods of data-retrieval, methods which seem, to them and to many others, to offer new, exciting and revolutionary possibilities for storage and retrieval of information.

In the field of data-retrieval (to be abbreviated henceforth as DR), as in other fields of artificial intelligence research, initial experiments were soon performed, a number of more advanced methods were developed, and a certain semi-technical terminology emerged. After a few years of research, evaluations of both actual and potential achievements in the field began to appear.

These evaluations were unequivocal. All, without exception, were uncritical and laudatory. Moreover, a comprehensive descriptive survey of work in the field has recently been published (43), of which only a small part is devoted to evaluation—written in the by now typical strain of approval.

Our survey will be, in the main, critical. It will not be comprehensive, but confine itself primarily to certain theoretical issues.

The survey is not descriptive, and therefore a certain familiarity with the field is assumed; the minimum requisite familiarity may be obtained from the descriptive survey of Simmons, (41) or (43).

To some extent, this paper is a continuation of Professor Yehoshua Bar-Hillel's paper "Theoretical Aspects of the Mechanization of Literature Searching" (4). I am indebted to Professor Bar-Hillel for his remarks on the rough draft of this survey. My thanks are also due to Mr. David Louvish for his help in preparing the final draft of the Report.

Introduction: What Is a Mechanized Data-Retrieval System?

Every scientific or technical library and every good news service is faced with the need to respond to various kinds of requests for information. For example, the librarian of an atomic energy commission may be asked to prepare a complete list of all books, papers and technical reports in the library dealing with the subject "Resonance radiation and excited atoms." Or, an employee of an economic news service may be asked to answer a question of the

SOURCE: This report first appeared as paper No. 22, prepared for the U.S. Office of Naval Research, Information Systems Branch, under Contract N62558-4695, NR 049-130/6, at the Hebrew University of Jerusalem, Israel, January 1966.

type: "What is the turnover of the John Doe Investment Company in the industrial field?"

These information requests are not only distinct; they also belong to distinct categories of such requests. The difference is obvious if we consider the different structure of the responses to these requests. The librarian must provide the scientist with a bibliographical list of publications, or an actual collection of publications, whereas the news service employee must give his customer direct information, processed from information at the disposal of the service.

A retrieval system which provides reference-lists or collections of publications dealing with a certain subject is known as a *reference-providing retrieval system*.

A retrieval system which answers questions, and does so by processing information at its disposal, is called a *data-providing retrieval system* (DR-system).

We postulate that a DR-system should, ideally, comprise the following features: A data-processing system is called a *DR-system* if and only if it fulfills the following conditions:

1. *The syntax of the input language is capable of distinguishing between (declarative) statements and questions.*

This condition implies, first and foremost, the existence of some formalization of the terms "(declarative) statement" and "question" within a partial formalization of the input-language. It does not imply that the input-language has some *fixed* means of identifying statements or questions; on the contrary, the syntax may be changed (e.g., by learning programs); but, in any event, formal syntactic distinction between these types of expressions must be possible.

It is certainly not to be assumed on the basis of this condition that any other component of the input-language (such as its vocabulary) is fixed. Neither does

it follow that the input-language is, partially or wholly, either artificial or natural.

By virtue of this condition a DR-system is capable of receiving both statements and questions; i.e., the system can accumulate information and receive certain requests for information.

2. *The syntax of the output-language is such that formal production of (declarative) statements and questions is possible.*

This condition is essentially the twin of the preceding one.

3. *When activated the system produces, in the output-language, a statement or a question. There is a formal syntactic connection between any question and its answer.*

This condition implies formalization of the notion, "answer to a question."

In accordance with these three conditions, a DR-system reacts, producing a statement or a question in its output-language, whenever it receives information or a request for information. Let us elucidate.

When information is transmitted to a DR-system, it may emit some standard response, such as: "I understand," or "The information is unclear." Alternatively, it may ask a question, such as "In the preceding sentence, was the word 'have' used in its connotation of possession or constitution?"—in the event that the system is unable to distinguish on its own between the different connotations of "have" in sentences such as "I have three dollars" and "I have ten fingers."

When a DR-system is asked a question, it may emit a statement, again of standard form, such as: "The answer to the question is . . ." or "The question is ambiguous." Or, again, it may ask a question aimed at clarifying the original question; or voice a request for further information, such as: "How many fingers are there in a hand?"

For certain formal reasons a DR-system is not permitted to remain silent after the reception of information.

4. *The input- and output-languages are identical.*

The purpose of this condition is to insure that whoever provides the system with information and asks it his questions should be able to understand the system's answers and requests for clarification.

The possibility that the output-language be a proper subset of the input-language is, seemingly, not expedient; the reason is that any information supplied the system must be available for inclusion in an answer to some future question. It is improbable that the set of questions to be asked of the system is such that it utilizes the whole input-language as information while utilizing only a proper subset in formulating all the answers. For similar reasons, the possibility that the input-language be a proper subset of the output-language is also excluded.

Since the questions asked by the system (for clarification purposes or in order to make answers possible where not enough information is available) depend on the information currently stored by the system, it is evident that any request for information received by the system is also liable to be emitted—under completely different circumstances—for purposes of clarification etc., and *vice versa*.

5. *The system contains a formal, nontrivial, inference-mechanism.*

This condition implies that a DR-system can also answer questions to which there is no *direct* answer based on the information currently at its disposal. The inferences produced by this mechanism are reached on the basis of existing information in a formal manner, not necessarily uniquely determined (i.e., not necessarily by means of a deductive, as opposed to an inductive, process, or *vice versa*, etc.).

The condition of nontriviality implies that the system is able to draw inferences using at least, for instance, the classical sentential calculus or an appro-

priate section of it. This ends the list of conditions.

We now mention a number of properties of data-processing systems which need not be included among the properties of DR-systems:

(*a*) The input- and output-languages of the system are natural languages, or, at least, sizable portions thereof.

(*b*) There is a semantic connection between any question which the system is asked and the answer given.

(*c*) The system contains a mechanism which checks the compatibility of information in storage with any new information.

(*d*) The system does not forget information, once received.

Property (*a*) is not characteristic of DR-systems since we must consider the possibility that such a system receive information and answer questions posed in some artificial language, such as, for example, an extension of ALGOL by the addition of questions.

As for (*b*), conditions 1 to 5 determine a certain syntactic connection between questions asked a data-retrieval system and the relevant answers. The question of the semantic connection between the question and its answer seems to us to be one of *evaluation* (is the system reliable, is it degenerate, is it "clever") rather than of characterization.

Property (*c*) is left out because DR-systems are faced with the need to use contradictory pieces of information, without having to decide which of them are reliable and which unreliable.

We have omitted property (*d*) so as not to exclude from our discussion DR-systems which receive anew pieces of information, answer appropriate questions, and then erase everything. [Cf., for example, (10).]

In the sequel additional reasons for the omission of properties (*a*) to (*d*) from our characterization will come to light, though we shall not mention this explicitly.

It must be emphasized that when we say that a certain property is not characteristic of DR-systems, we do not mean thereby that the absence of this property is necessary. For example, DR-systems may include a compatibility mechanism, and then again they may not.

As mentioned above, the input/output-language of a DR-system may be an artificial language. The task of such a language is to permit storage of information and answering of questions pertaining to a specific field; thus it may be different from a given natural language; it may be a part of it, or the two may be disjoint. The orginators of all known DR-systems have selected a subset of English as the input/output-language. The main reason for this seems to be that these systems have all been set up with a view to practical use. Accordingly, we shall deal with such systems only, and with the problems arising from the fact that the input/output-language is English or a subset thereof; however, in our opinion this property is not characteristic of DR-systems. In the sequel, then, the words "data-retrieval system" should be construed subject to this qualification.

Is it possible to indicate existing data-retrieval systems which fulfill all five of the above conditions (using English or a subset thereof as their input/output-language)? The reader may easily convince himself that any municipal information bureau constitutes such a system.

By a *mechanized* data-retrieval system we mean a DR-system all of whose activities are performed formally and mechanically. To be precise—it is a DR-system which receives information and questions mechanically; which seeks the answer to the questions asked, on the basis of the information currently at its disposal, mechanically; draws conclusions from this information, mechanically; and phrases the answer to each question mechanically. Do there exist

mechanized DR-systems? In this paper we shall attempt to examine systems that claim to be mechanized DR-systems, and to determine to what degree this claim is justified.

1. Problems Arising from Ambiguity

Sentences may possess various distinct types of ambiguity.

If a given sentence may be assigned, within the framework of a given grammar, more than one syntactic analysis, it is called *syntactically ambiguous* or *polystructural*.

If a given sentence may be assigned, within the framework of a given semantic system, more than one semantic analysis, it is called *semantically ambiguous* or *amphibolous*.

These two types of ambiguity are *formal*—that is to say, the specific ambiguity-type of a given sentence is determined solely by the sentence itself and by the given grammatical or semantic system.

Sentences may also possess ambiguity of a pragmatic nature; such sentences are called *context-dependent*. Context-dependence is a pragmatic form of ambiguity in that it stems from a multiplicity of admissible modes of passage from the sentence to its meaning. The choice of any one such mode depends on the context.

Context-dependence is not a formal type of ambiguity. In other words, not every sentence obtained by substitution of the name of a sentence for "—" in the sentential form "The sentence "—" is context-dependent" is formally verifiable. For, if this were possible for every sentence-name, it would be possible to determine formally whether a given sentence is context-dependent or not. However, this is generally *impossible*, for the following reason. A sentence is context-dependent only *in relation to a set of contexts*. These are the contexts which must be considered (in a specific context) when dealing with the meaning of the sentence. A sentence may be context-dependent relative to one context-set, while not context-dependent relative to another. Now, the appropriate context-set cannot, in general, be expressed formally, and thus, the context-dependence of a sentence cannot be determined formally.[1]

Nevertheless, formal determination of the context-dependence of certain types of sentences is possible. Examples are sentences using demonstrative pronouns or adjectives ("this," "that," "above-mentioned," etc.), or various other word-categories (e.g., "I," "here," "now").

As an alternative to the above classification, ambiguous sentences may be classified according to the means by which their ambiguity can be resolved.

The ambiguity of a sentence may be resolvable on the basis of a specific *verbal context,* any member of a specific set of verbal contexts, or any verbal context whatsoever. A conversation or an article are examples of verbal contexts.

On the other hand, ambiguity may be resolvable on the basis of a *non-verbal context,* relative to some verbal context, if the resolution depends on information which cannot be derived, by standard means, from the given verbal context. In this case, as in the former, one may need either a specific non-verbal context, a set of such contexts or an arbitrary context, relative to a specific verbal context, to a set of contexts or to an arbitrary context.

The two classifications given above are not equivalent. It is quite possible to give an example of a sentence in the framework of a paragraph, whose syntactic ambiguity (within a given grammar) may be resolved on the basis of the grammatical structure of the other

sentences in the paragraph. On the other hand, one may exhibit a sentence in a paragraph, whose semantic ambiguity may not be resolved on the basis of the semantic structure of the other sentences. At the other extreme, there exist context-dependent sentences whose ambiguity, within a certain verbal context, may be resolved on the basis of any non-verbal context. Again, there exist context-dependent sentences whose ambiguity, in certain verbal contexts, cannot be resolved on the basis of certain non-verbal contexts.

When discussing the possibilities of mechanical resolution of sentence-ambiguities, one must determine, first and foremost, the categories to which each sentence belongs according to the above classifications. The ignoring of this requirement has led some investigators to make unjustifiable assumptions. Thus Simmons (42) writes:

Our hypothesis is that computer systems can develop the capability for making unambiguous syntactic analyses by the following methods:
1. By developing their own word classes based on co-occurrence patterns of words in a large sample of preanalyzed text . . . (page 21).

And he goes on to assert:

The ultimate development expected from this phase of research is a context-sensitive grammar that will resolve ambiguities of syntactic analysis on the basis of the context in which a particular category of words appears (page 23).

The basic assumption underlying this approach may be interpreted thus: Let's disregard the possibility that the syntactic ambiguity of a sentence may be resolved, in any verbal context, (solely) on the basis of a non-verbal context. The verbal context contains—within the framework of a given grammar and a given semantic theory—both syntactic and semantic information about the sentence. It is not plausible to suppose that

---

[1] Moreover, many misunderstandings result from the fact that the context-set, relative to which the meaning of a sentence is determined, is not common, for example, to both participants in a dialogue, or is not sufficiently clear to one of them.

these two types of information are completely independent. On the contrary, semantic information may well be of assistance in determining the appropriate grammatical analysis, and it is quite possible that such information is at times *essential* to this object; cf. (40).

[In parentheses, we remark here, following J. Katz and P. Postal (27, page 3), that "the problem of whether an adequate discovery procedure for syntactic components must employ semantic considerations" has nothing to do with the problem of a precise distinction between the different components, syntactic and semantic, of any theory of linguistic descriptions; or with the problem "of intercomponential justification," that is, the question of the legitimacy of the method in which "arguments based upon semantic considerations . . . are . . . offered in order to establish something about the syntactic component," or *vice versa.*]

But even if semantic information is also taken into account for purposes of syntactic analysis, the picture is still incomplete.

Raphael (37), whose express purpose is to investigate "How much semantic or contextual information is needed to resolve ambiguities . . ." (page 142), says:

An expanded version of SIR might be able to resolve ambiguous sentence structure on the basis of the meanings . . . of the words in the sentence. Thus the system could be as effective as people in recognizing the structural difference between sentences like, "Bring me the bottle of milk which is sour," and Bring me the bottle of milk which is cracked" (page 141).

The existence of syntactically or semantically ambiguous sentences whose ambiguity may be resolved, in any verbal context, only on the basis of non-verbal context, is not disputed. But it is known that at present we cannot envisage a mechanical simulation of the process of resolution of ambiguities on the basis of non-verbal context.

The same may be said of the possibilities of mechanical simulation of ambiguity-resolving processes for context-dependent sentences based on non-verbal context. Our grounds for this assertion are as follows.

Firstly, it must be noted that information derived from non-verbal context with a view to resolution of ambiguities is not of a uniform nature. At times the date or locality of an occurrence may be needed; or the information may have to do with the identity of the participants in a conversation; alternatively, general information (knowledge) is needed. The necessity that certain parts of the information be provided by a non-verbal context *may* be inferred from the sentence itself; e.g., when the latter contains words of a demonstrative character. But, in general, the fact that a sentence is context-dependent is not determined by demonstrative words alone, and it is reasonable to say that one cannot decide on the basis of the sentence alone what information is necessary for the resolution of its ambiguity.

Secondly, it is difficult to envisage an adequate formalization of non-verbal context (in general), such that the information necessary for ambiguity-resolution is always derivable from the formalized context. Such context-types as are easily formalizable—date, location, names of participants, etc.—are insufficient, as mentioned above.

To summarize, mechanical resolution of ambiguities on the basis of non-verbal context does not seem to be feasible.

Similarly, in (14), Cooper claims:

Ambiguous sentences require a more complicated logical analysis if the ambiguity is to be fully taken into account. For restricted purposes, however, it suffices simply to select one of the interpretations of an ambiguous sentence—perhaps the commonest interpretation—and treat the sentence as though it had no other interpretation (page 120).

In the first place, this suggestion is obviously unacceptable as far as context-dependent sentences are concerned. No nontrivial DR-system will be fulfilling its function if it attaches the same interpretation to such sentences as "I'm hungry," "This fruit is sweet," etc., in all their occurrences.

Neither is the suggestion acceptable with regard to syntactically ambiguous sentences. There is no need to indicate sentences for which no one "commonest interpreptation" may be selected. We confine ourselves to mentioning the fact that "accepted interpretation" cannot be considered without recourse to some set of non-verbal contexts.

Moreover, it is essential to distinguish between two ways of attaching an accepted interpretation to a sentence. On the one hand, it is possible to select in advance some set of contexts, with regard to which the interpretation of each sentence is determined. On the other hand, one may attempt to attach an accepted interpretation to each sentence on its own, i.e., to correlate with each sentence a characteristic set of contexts relative to which the interpretation of the sentence is the accepted one. Neither of these possibilities is worthy of consideration in connection with mechanical resolution of ambiguities. The first is incapable of insuring the non-occurrence of sentences that have different interpretations in different subsets of the pre-selected context-set; when this happens, how is the accepted interpretations to be determined? On the other hand, the selection of a characteristic context-set for each sentence seems to be extremely difficult from a logical point of view, not to speak of the impossibility of its practical implementation. In addition, both the above possibilities raise the difficult problem, mentioned above, of a general formalization of non-verbal contexts.

At the present time, and indeed in the near future, then, it seems that not much can be done on the basis of non-verbal context. But this is not the only diffi-

culty. Resolution of the ambiguity of sentences with the aid of syntactic and semantic information does not seem feasible either, as far as the present and the near future are concerned.

We mention one point in this connection. In his survey (43) Simmons remarks:

The matter of coding the meanings of words and calculating the meanings of sentences is an area in which only the dimmest of understanding currently exists (page 67).

But he immediately adds:

However, theoretical work by Katz and Fodor (1963) and by Quillian (1963) suggests avenues of approach, and surely a direct attack on problems of meaning is probably most profitable.

However, an examination of the explication given by Katz and Fodor for the notion of "semantic theory" (26) leads to discouraging conclusions as regards its use in mechanical resolution of ambiguity in sentences.

According to Katz-Fodor, every semantic theory contains a dictionary having a special structure. This dictionary contains, for each word, complete syntactic and semantic information, in that it takes into account all contexts in which the word is liable to appear in different syntactic or semantic situations. Two different semantic theories may differ from each other in the semantic categories constituting the last rows of the trees of the lexicographic description [cf. (26), Fig. 2, page 494]. In addition, every Katz-Fodor theory contains projection-rules whose function is to permit passage from the meanings of the words in a sentence to the meaning of the sentence itself. With the aid of these rules, which are in effect rules of inference, it is possible to carry out a semantic analysis of any given sentence, on the basis of its syntactic structure and the above-mentioned dictionary.

Now, the compilation of an appropriate dictionary and semantic projection-rules in such a way that the semantic theory will be a good approximation of the semantic behavior-system is a complicated, perhaps difficult, task. In any event, it is obvious that the compilation of a dictionary and projection-rules suitable for mechanical use is as yet unattainable.

In effect, we may repeat here, *mutatis mutandis*, all the reasons which have been given for the non-feasibility of compiling a *syntactic* grammar and dictionary for mechanical use.

For example, leaving aside the question of the theoretical adequacy of the Katz-Fodor model of the semantic dictionary and projection-rules, we may expect the following fact to come to the fore in the near future: If one wants to increase the degree of approximate practical adequacy of such semantic theories, one has to pay an enormous price for this; namely, a proliferation of projection-rules (partly, but not wholly, caused by a proliferation of semantic categories) of truly astronomic nature. The dialectics of the situation is distressing: the better the understanding of linguistic structure (syntactic and semantic) of a natural language, and the greater our mastery of it—the larger the set of projection-rules we need for an adequate semantic theory, the heavier the work necessary for preparation of the theory, and the costlier the machine operations of storing and working with these rules.

The foregoing paragraph is an almost complete paraphrase of the second paragraph on page 216 of (5), which deals with syntactic theories.

The analysis of Katz and Fodor is, looking far ahead, a step towards an understanding of the structure of a semantic theory, perhaps also towards an investigation of the possibilities inherent in the utilization of semantic theories in mechanical processes. Nevertheless, their analysis undoubtedly exposes, in no uncertain manner, our difficulties in setting up a mechanical system comprising a grammar and semantic rules adequate for

the practical analysis of a modern natural language (not to mention considerations of cost).

We now consider an additional subject mentioned in the above passages from Simmons' survey. Whereas in the first paragraph he deals with the resolution (to some extent) of ambiguities with the aid of syntactic and semantic information about the verbal context, in the second he makes mention of context-sensitive grammars (CSG). Now the latter are not relevant to the problem, as long as resolution of ambiguities in sentences is under consideration. We shall support our thesis in a semi-formal manner.

Parikh has shown in (34) that there exist context-free grammars (CFG) such that the languages represented by them are not derivable from any unambiguous CFG. These languages generate words of the form $\alpha^{n'} \beta^{m'} \alpha^{n} \beta^{m}$ where $n' = n$ or $m' = m$. ($m, m', n, n' > 1$.) In the case $n = m$ there are two possible derivations and thus such words are polystructural. On the basis of this example it transpires that it would be possible to avoid the syntactical ambiguity of certain sentences in these languages, if one could count the number of occurrences of a letter (or word) in a given verbal context and proceed with the development of the syntactical-derivation-tree in accordance with the results of this counting.

Since the number of derivation-rules of a grammar is finite, it is impossible to state within the grammar a counting rule, which would presumably be of a form similar to the following:

$$\alpha^m \times \beta^m \to \alpha^m \gamma \beta^n \qquad m = 1, 2, \ldots$$
$$\alpha^m \times \alpha^n \to \alpha^m \gamma \alpha^n \qquad m \neq n.$$

Thus, it would seem that these languages are not derivable even from an unambiguous CSG. We have no formal proof for this statement, but it is plausible. [A formal proof would be quite difficult, to judge from the algebraic characterization of this set of languages, given by Ginsburg-Ullian (20).]

On the other hand, it is obvious that these languages may be obtained by syntactic inferences from the text, in such a way that to each sentence corresponds a unique derivation—with the aid of a formalism that permits counting (in a certain sense). It is thus clear that CS-grammars do not constitute an adequate explication for dependence on syntactic context.

At any rate, it is evident that the transition, in Simmons' paper, from one type of grammar to the other, must be ruled invalid.

As a first step with a view to overcoming this difficulty we suggest an attempt to investigate grammars of the following type:

Definition. A *context-α sensitive grammar* G is a system of unrestricted rewriting rules fulfilling the following conditions:

(1) If $\varphi \to \Psi$ is a rule of G, then there are non-null symbols $a_1, \ldots, a_m, b_1, \ldots, b_n$, where $m \leqslant n$, such that $\varphi = a_1 \ldots a_m$ and $\Psi = b_1 \ldots b_n$. [This is Chomsky's first condition in (13, page 360).]

(2) If $\varphi \to \Psi$ then there exists a sequence $\omega_1, \omega_2, A, \beta$, where A is a single letter, β is a nonempty word and $\langle \omega_1, \omega_2 \rangle \epsilon \alpha$, such that:

(a) $\varphi = \omega_1 A \omega_2$; $\Psi = \omega_1 \beta \omega_2$.

(b) For every ω', ω'' such that ω', $\omega'' \epsilon \alpha$, we have

$$\omega' A \omega'' \to \omega' \beta \omega''.$$

(3) G contains no rule $X_1 A X_2 \to X_1 \omega X_2$, where ω is a single nonterminal symbol. [Chomsky's third rule (*ibid.*, page 366), due to Parikh.]

α is a binary relation over words; for example, $\alpha = \{\langle \omega_1, \omega_2 \rangle | \omega_1 = \omega_2$, or length $(\omega_1) =$ length (ω_2), or $\omega_1 = a^{m_1}$ and $\omega_2 = a^{m_2}$ and $m_1 = m_2 + 1\}$.

It seems to us that these languages are of theoretical interest; their definition is a natural generalization of the definition of ordinary CS-languages. On the other hand, their practical interest is, we believe, obvious.

It is important to distinguish between explicatum and explicandum. Failure to do this has led to confusion.

It is quite probable that mathematicians, as the providers of explications, "help" to involve others in the results of this error by considering natural languages as complicated formal languages.

For example, Machover (33) writes:

In Leśniewski's grammar, a proper symbol has no pre-assigned syntactic category . . . but the category (as well as the meaning) of each of its occurrences must be determined in (and by) context. This feature is, in a way, a very natural one: at least, it is shared by most (if not all) natural languages . . . (page 2).

We conclude this section with some remarks on a related subject, namely, the problem of *semi-grammatical sentences* (in Chomsky's terminology) or *semi-sentences* (in the more appropriate terminology of J. Katz).

It is well known that in everyday conversation one uses not only sentences, i.e., well-formed utterances, but also semi-sentences, i.e., utterances which are not well-formed utterances of the language in question, from a syntactic and/or semantic point of view. The use of such semi-sentences is standard and does not in general affect comprehension.

For instance, one has no difficulty in understanding semi-sentences such as "He gave me his hand and greeted me" or "Work will continue day and night," despite the fact that the first is semantically defective and the second—syntactically.

A theory of semi-sentences should satisfy the following two conditions, according to the analysis of Katz (26a).

1. The theory determines a partition of the set of ungrammatical strings into two disjoint and jointly exhaustive subsets; the one contains those strings, and

only those, which are semi-sentences, and the other—all "nonsense" strings.

Katz agrees that a theory which determines an ordering of semi-sentences with respect to their degree of deviation from well-formedness "might be considered preferable to one that does not" (*ibid.*). However, this condition is not, in his opinion, necessary, in contrast to condition 1.

In our opinion, condition 1 is certainly sufficient for the first stage of the formation of theories of semi-sentences. However, at a more advanced stage one must require, in addition to condition 1, that the theory determine necessary and sufficient conditions for the truth of assertions of the form "Semi-sentence A is more well-formed than semi-sentence B." Only at an even more advanced stage will a numerical level of well-formedness be necessary. It seems that Katz has not taken the above-mentioned intermediary step into consideration, despite the fact that it is standard in the methodology of concept (and theory) formation.

The second condition is:

2. "A theory of semi-sentences explicates the speaker's knowledge of the patterns of deviation from grammaticality that preserve intelligibility" (*ibid.*, page 403).

These two conditions clarify the connection between the problem of semi-sentences and that of DR-system construction.

In dealing with programs whose aim is the reception of verbal material—given utterances in a natural language—one is faced with two demands which are, in a certain sense, contradictory: on the one hand, the program accepts only part of the sentences and semi-sentences, of the language in question, whose acceptance is desired; on the other hand, it also accepts semi-sentences and nonsense which do not accord, and may even clash, with the aims of the program. Thus, it is necessary on the one hand to

enlarge the set of admissible strings, and on the other—to restrict it. The determination of an "equilibrium-point" between these two conflicting tendencies is, of course, one of the most difficult problems in this field.

It is possible that a theory of semi-sentences, such as developed by Katz in his paper (26a), will be of assistance in the determination of such an equilibrium-point, according to the following working principle: The system should contain, besides the syntactic and semantic components whose function is to determine sentences (well-formed utterances), various types of (meta-)rules of deduction (or identification). The system will determine in a natural way (according to (26a)) the meaning or meanings not only of sentences but also of semi-sentences. An utterance will be adjudged a nonsense-utterance if and only if the system accords it an infinite number of meanings or no meaning at all.

Thus it will be possible to enlarge the set of utterances accepted by the system, and the problem of undesirable semi-sentences and nonsense accepted by the system will become less serious. To a certain extent, this will diminish the practical importance attached to the distinction between sentences and non-sentences. It should, of course, be possible to carry out a precise evaluation of the meaning or meanings associated with semi-sentences by the system, with the aid of the above-mentioned deviation-rules.

The adoption of this method involves, to be sure, problems of both principle and execution such as problems of ambiguity and the complex details of the deviation-rules.

It seems to us that this line of thought should be carefully investigated. Despite the fact that the problem of semi-sentences appears "between the lines" in papers dealing with DR [though never explicitly; cf., for example, Bobrow (10, pages 83–84)], they contain no serious attempt to investigate it.

2. Data-Based Versus Text-Based Systems

In his survey (41), Simmons distinguishes between two types of DR-systems:

A data-based[2] question-answering system is one that deals with data that are strongly organized into tabular or (more usually) list form (page 16).

The text-based systems, in contrast, attempt to find answers from ordinary English text (page 59).

This distinction is worded in terms of the character of the material upon which the systems base their answers to questions. Such terminology appears explicitly in the second definition; it is implicit in the first, since the special structure of the data is aimed at enabling the system to draw inferences thereby.

As a result, it is clear that this distinction sets no *a priori* limits to the range of subjects with which any one system may deal, whatever the type of the system. Thus, any valid comparison of these types must be carried out for systems having similar ranges of subject-matter.

Let us assume, as indeed do all workers in the field (for the present we do not mean to consider to what degree this assumption is justified) that we are dealing with systems having an average or wide range of subjects.

What is the processing procedure in a practical data-based system? The system is presented with material in verbal form. At the time of reception, an attempt is made to "translate" the material into the structure-language of the system. If the attempt is successful, the information is accepted in this structure-language, and if not—it is rejected, or sent for manual processing so as to insure the success of a further attempt. A similar procedure obtains in the case of a question. The system then attempts to arrive, on the basis of the information expressed in the structure-language, at an answer to the question.

In a text-based system the procedure is different. The system absorbs all material with which it is presented, in verbal form, whether this material is "informative" or constitutes a question. When attempting to answer a given question, the program tries to "translate" the sentences stored in its memory into a certain structure-language, with a view to drawing inferences about the given question. Any sentence to which corresponds an appropriate structure under this "translation" process is checked for relevance to the question; a sentence for which the attempt fails is disregarded or rejected for rewriting so that the next attempt to accord it an appropriate structure may be more successful.

Both types of system, then, contain a procedure of translation from the verbal language in which the primary information is given into a special structure-language, in which the information is arranged with a view to drawing inferences therefrom. However, whereas in a data-based system the translation is effected at the time of reception and untranslatable material is rejected simultaneously, the translation in a text-based system occurs when the question is being answered and untranslatable material cannot be utilized at the same time.

In order to permit utilization of all the material given to a system of either of the above two types, manual pre-editing is necessary. The results of such pre-editing come to light, in the case of a data-based system, when the material is accepted; in the case of a text-based system—only after the question is answered.

The above remarks suggest that Simmons' distinction between these two types of systems is of significance much more as regards description of prevalent techniques than from a methodological viewpoint.

---

[2] In (43) the wording was changed here to "list-structured data-base systems"; however, this does not affect the considerations below.

Nevertheless, there is a certain interest in the technical advantages of each type over the other.

The advantage of the data-basing method is obvious—it permits drawing of inferences at greater speed, therefore at smaller cost, since the translation is effected once for all when new material is received.

The advantage inherent in the text-basing method is a little less obvious. It seems that the main advantage is in the superior form of the output, since such systems formulate the answer as a certain combination of previously received sentences, that is to say, sentences in a natural language.

Obviously, the advantage of the one type is the disadvantage of the other. In text-based systems the translation process must be repeated for each answer. On the other hand, the repeated translation process—from the special structure-language into the natural language—needed in data-based systems in order to formulate the answer, can produce only such sentences of the natural language as are derivable from an extremely weak grammar. This point is worthy of emphasis.

The foregoing argument is based on the fact that mechanical simulation of translation from a natural language to a special structure-language is not too advanced; the same is true of the reverse process. The reason for this is obvious— our understanding of the processes of syntactic and semantic analysis and our ability to develop programming-languages are not sufficient for a complete representation of the content of natural language sentences in a *formal* structure-language. What *is* represented in such a language is only a part of that information, and only this part is expressed in the output-language. In other words, the output-language is a good index of the efficiency of the syntactic and semantic analysis mechanism of the input.

The above considerations do not apply, of course, to those systems whose originators are not interested in a process of retranslation and, consequently, are satisfied with a weak output-language, for example, Raphael (37).

The importance attached to Simmons' distinction between two types of DR-systems may possibly be explained as follows.

When dealing with the two types of systems, one is actually not interested in the form of the stored material alone. When data-based systems are under consideration, one is usually interested in systems having an extremely restricted range of subjects. Examples are Lindsay's SAD SAM (32), BASEBALL (22), Thompson's DEACON (47), Bobrow's STUDENT (10), and others. On the other hand, text-based systems usually have a wide range of subject-matter and a correspondingly small inference ability. *Correspondingly*—since, considering the wide range of subject-matter, it is difficult, perhaps even impossible at present, to achieve an efficient internal structure; and in order to overcome this difficulty the inference-methods are weak, probabilistic—typified, e.g., by checking occurrences of similar words, relative frequencies of word-pair occurrences, and so on. Thus, Simmons' definitions are not relevant to what he claims to describe.

From a point of view of appraisal, the foregoing considerations lead to an important conclusion: At present it is not known how to set up a DR-system having both a wide range of subject-matter and good inference-ability.

Good inference-ability is determined by a special structure-language. The efficiency of such a language depends on the particular subject treated. On the other hand, a wide range of subjects is not possible unless this dependence on structure is avoided.

Possibly, structures will be discovered such that the languages based on them will be efficient for an unrestricted range of subjects. List-languages, more advanced than the existing ones, may fulfill such a function. However, before this can be done, it is imperative to carry out thorough investigations of advanced programming-languages, and even more—of the relevant subject-matter itself, since each structure-language must be appropriate to its subject. Such investigations of the structure of languages descriptive of a given subject are a lengthy, though important, matter. As knowledge of these matters deepens, it will be possible to attempt setting up systems having less restricted subject-ranges and nontrivial inference-ability.

At the same time, it must be remembered that there exists a theoretical bound to the possibilities of extension of the field of subject-matter for any given system. We refer to theorems of the following type: The binary predicate calculus of the first order is undecidable (19, page 303 ff.). These theorems indicate a theoretical bound to extension possibilities for DR-systems.

Many investigators fail to adequately recognize that characterizing the meaning of a sentence, in the context of DR-system construction, depends very strongly on the specific field with which one is dealing. 'Characterization of meaning' is an archetypal context-dependent term. It is quite obvious that a lack of acquaintance with this point may well lead one to envisage a considerable extension of subject-matter for DR-systems. In other words, the transition from a DR-system dealing with a specific field, where the information is representable in a specific structure-language, to a DR-system dealing with a number of fields, for which the most efficient structure-languages may be different—is not a quantitative transition. The chances for success do not depend on the quality of the computers at our disposal, but first and foremost on our ability to describe different universes of discourse within one general structure-language. This ability seems at present unattainable, at least with regard to subjects which are

of interest in connection with practical DR-system construction.

Furthermore, it should be emphasized that in this context the term "universe of discourse" has a most restricted connotation. In fact, the term refers here to an extremely restricted type of question, answerable on the basis of an extremely restricted type of information. Even a small branch of physics, for example, cannot be considered in this connection as a universe of discourse. (Consider, for instance, the type of questions that the system BASEBALL is capable of answering.)

In this connection, there is no significant difference between data-based and text-based systems. For reasons to be elucidated elsewhere, systems such as the latter, based on statistical principles, are not capable of attaining an above-average level of efficiency [cf., however, (18)].

3. The Ambivalent Attitude to Theoretical Results

Workers in the field of data-retrieval are either unfamiliar with or unappreciative of theories (often well-known ones) in mathematical, linguistic, logical specialties believed to be relevant by the author.

Some but not all the constructors of DR-systems attempt to carry out—"practically and efficiently"—enterprises which may be proved impossible of execution. Others claim (this is approximately the converse of the foregoing) that whatever they cannot do is valueless from a theoretical point of view. And, as in other parts of "artificial intelligence," we find authors of various pseudo-theories or theories whose main function is decorative.

Below are examples of these vagaries. We believe that a critical reader can immediately recognize this type of theorizing. There are symptoms of this even in good papers which are of interest in connection with DR [see for instance, our review (7) of Lindsay's paper (32)].

The problem of ensuring consistency of a system of stored information concerns some of the researchers in the field. Cooper (14), for instance, writes:

If there is a danger of inconsistency here, a more elaborate algorithm must be devised which will warn the user of any inconsistencies related to his query which might be of concern to him. Accidental inconsistencies originating with blunders on the part of those preparing the bank of information-sentences to be stored could be caught at the time of storage by using the computer in its capacity of inconsistencies-detector (page 122).

This problem cannot be ignored by those who plan DR-systems, especially if these systems are meant for practical use. Nevertheless, it may be avoided, to some extent, by following the method of Raphael (37):

General information about 'all the elements' of a set is considered to apply to particular elements only in the absence of more specific information about those elements (page 85).

Such an *exception-rule* may be of assistance in reducing the seriousness of the consistency-problem for information-systems, in cases where the inconsistency stems from use of the particularization rule

$$(x)P(x) \rightarrow P(t),$$

where t is a term which is, to use Kleene's terminology (31), free for x in P. However, the use of this exception-rule is not devoid of difficulties. In the first place, when the information at hand is of the form

$$(x)P(x); \quad \sim P(t_0)$$

is it prohibited to use the first, universal proposition in connection with any question involving t_0, or is it prohibited only when appearing as the antecedent of a particularization-rule? For example, if the given information is of the form

$$(x)P(x); \quad (x)(P(x) \rightarrow Q(x)); \quad \sim P(t_0)$$

is $Q(t_0)$ an admissible conclusion from this information, is it refuted thereby, or is it perhaps undecidable on the basis of the given information? A decision in favor of the second possibility—and this is the most natural decision where such an exception-rule is admitted—is more problematic than it seems.

To elaborate: inconsistency of the above type may arise as a result of information of the following form:

$$(x_1)(x_2)P(x_1, x_2); \quad \sim P(t_1, t_2)$$

by two successive applications of the particularization-rule. Are all such applications invalid with regard to any question about (t_1, t_2), or only some of them? And if only some, which are they? There is no point in invalidating some of the applications, such as the first, since the order of occurrence of the quantifiers in the universal sentence is immaterial. Therefore the same obtains for the order of applications of the particularization-rule and there is no reason to invalidate any one of the applications occurring in the proof. On the other hand, invalidating *all* applications is no panacea either. For example, suppose the information at hand is of the form

$$p \ \& \ q \rightarrow p; \quad (x)P(x) \ \& \ (x)Q(x); \\ \sim P(t_0) \ \& \ Q(t_0).$$

Then, to invalidate all applications of the particularization-rule would mean that it would be impossible to derive even the particular sentence admitted by Raphael's exception-rule. The difficulty will be more readily seen if we invalidate everything that appears in the proof of the universal sentence $(x)P(x)$.

If use of the universal sentence *is* allowed in cases where it contradicts a particular sentence, similar difficulties are encountered. For example, suppose the information is of the form

$$(x)P(x); \quad (x)P(x) \to (x)Q(x); \quad \sim P(t_0);$$
$$P(t_0) \leftrightarrow Q(t_0).$$

If it is permissible to use the sentence $(x)P(x)$ in answering a question involving t_0, then we obtain contradictory information regarding $Q(t_0)$.

For reasons similar to the above, we must reject the possibility that particular sentences refutable in this way are undecidable on the basis of the information at hand; this would be tantamount to saying that inconsistency implies incompleteness, whereas this is of course incorrect.

It is possible to formulate *ad hoc* exception-rules which would avoid the difficulties arising in the above examples, but it is not difficult to show that similar difficulties are inherent in any such exception-rule.

Another interesting difficulty arising from the use of exception-rules stems from the dependence of the truth-value of a particular sentence on its proof. If the proof contains the sentence only as an axiom (i.e., as information received, intact, from outside the system), the sentence is accepted as true; but if an application of the particularization-rule is made, it may still happen that the system will adjudge it false.

Because of this dependence, information which is obtained, not from outside but by the action of the deductive part of the system, must be stored together with its proofs. The need for such storage may well affect, in an essential way, the efficiency or even the practicality of a DR-system containing an exception-rule of the form proposed by Raphael.

There is no need to dwell on the fact that an exception-rule of the above form does not prevent appearance of other types of inconsistency. In fact, there is reason to believe that the majority of inconsistencies arising from information-sets is indeed not of this type. The full

seriousness of the problem indicated in Cooper's paper is therefore quite clear.

Cooper, it is true, does propose a solution, but this solution is somewhat questionable. If we are dealing with a DR-system having a special structure-language, such as the family trees of SAD SAM (32), it is possible to set up a decision-method for the consistency of a finite set of particular sentences formulated in the structure-language. But if we are dealing with more general systems, having a less specialized structure-language, capable of expressing general propositions and of defining new terms, for example by recursion, then the existence of a decision-method is not *a priori* insured. Moreover, even systems possessing quite a simple structure-language may be capable of defining all primitive-recursive functions; if they are also able to express sentences containing existential quantifiers, then there is *no* decision-method for the consistency of a finite set of sentences of the language.

Cooper's suggestion is thus devoid of practicality in an essential way, as far as general DR-systems are concerned.

To the foregoing observations may be added another, no less serious. There exist quite simple structure-languages for which no decision-method for the consistency of finite sets of sentences exists. Examples are provided by the elementary theories of certain binary relations, since these theories are for the most part undecidable.

The foregoing discussion shows that the efficiency of DR-systems is quite restricted. Various methods have been suggested with a view to avoiding the difficulties.

One of the most popular suggestions of researchers in the field—and one of the most interesting from the point of view of artificial intelligence research—is the following: if there is no decision-method, let's try to find heuristic methods. This direction of research is of interest, and it may be useful even in cases where a decision-method exists but is too complicated or long (and therefore too costly).

However, the situation with regard to research in this subfield of artificial intelligence research is no better than that pertaining to data-retrieval. Any such reduction of the problem would, at this stage of research, miss the mark completely.

Moreover, even if we do eventually achieve understanding of heuristic methods sufficient for application in connection with consistency of finite sets of sentences, such application will not be devoid of difficulties.

The main difficulty seems to me to be in determining the "cost" of such methods. A heuristic method, replacing a non-existent decision-method, may pronounce a given sentence inconsistent with a given set of sentences when it is actually consistent with them. Such an occurrence is not very probable; heuristic methods for determination of consistency will pronounce a sentence inconsistent with a set of sentences only if they discover a contradiction between the sentence and the inferences from the set. But the reverse may well happen. The procedure may determine that a sentence is consistent with the set whereas in actual fact it is not. This would permit incompatible information to "infiltrate" the system. Such information will not of course entail a contradiction discoverable by the heuristic method, but it is not possible to evaluate in advance, in a simple manner, the "accumulating" damage to the system.

To make this clearer, let us consider a related problem. Suppose we have a sentential calculus from which may be derived a sentence and its negation, but that this is not possible by a proof having less than a thousand steps. We are given two sets of sentences; one contains sentences whose proofs in the calculus all contain less than a thousand steps; the other contains sentences whose proofs in the *ordinary* sentential calculus contain less than a thousand steps. The

problem is to find the *measure of divergence* of the first set from the second. In addition, it is required to find the *threshold of divergence* which determines the boundary between *admissible* and *inadmissible* calculi. Obviously, the problem is one of explication, and quite difficult.

Cooper makes a second suggestion toward evading the problem:

If some natural language with its associated rules of logical inference were found to be undecidable . . . then it would in all likelihood contain a decidable sublanguage so extensive as to be coterminous with it for all practical purposes (page 121).

But there is no solution here either. It is true that every recursively enumerable set contains a recursive set, so that every undecidable calculus contains a sub-calculus (with infinitely many different sentences) which is decidable; but the claim that this sub-calculus may be sufficient for all practical purposes is unfounded. Furthermore, the problem of the "cost" involved in substituting a sub-calculus for the original calculus is as serious as that of substituting a heuristic method for a decision-method. In fact, it is possible to reduce the heuristic-method solution to the sub-calculus solution, and *vice versa*, though each has certain (decorative) advantages of its own as regards representation, apart from certain technical differences.

It would seem that the only way out is to accept the following solution: the system admits every sentence with which it is presented. After the syntactic and semantic translation procedure of the sentence, the results are tested for compatibility with the current information, by means of heuristic methods. Anything adjudged invalid by these methods is rejected. Admissible material, on the other hand, is processed *manually*. After manual confirmation the new information is stored in the system. Whenever the system is requested to provide information, it communicates all it knows, without checking the consistency of the answers. The test for consistency of the sentences constituting the answer to the question is again performed *manually*. Exception-rules—such as Raphael's—are used only at the stage of the preliminary heuristic tests.

Even some of the best workers in the field seem to ignore significant theoretical results. Bobrow (10) writes:

A basic postulate of our theory of language is that a listener understands a discourse by transforming it into an equivalent (in meaning) sequence of simpler kernel sentences. A kernel sentence is one which the listener can understand directly (page 27).

He does admit that "The use of kernel sentences in this way is controversial. . . . The theory is proposed . . . not necessarily as a model for human behaviour" (*ibid.*). And he adds:

It has been useful . . . to describe the theory in terms of the properties and actions of a hypothetical speaker and listener. All statements about speakers and listeners should be interpreted as referring to computer programs which respectively, generate and analyze coherent discourse (*ibid.*).

How are such assumptions consistent with the proofs of the existence of sentences which cannot be simplified syntactically (8), or of the severe theoretical restrictions on mechanical simplification of sets of sentences (25)?

In (8) it was shown that there is no sentence which is logically equivalent to the sentence $S_n = (\ldots ((p_1 \rightarrow p_2) \rightarrow p_3) \rightarrow \ldots p_n)$ whose degree of self-embedding (within a given natural derivation-grammar) is smaller than that of S_n. The idea of transforming each sentence into an equivalent, simpler sentence is not feasible for any S_n, $n = 1$, 2, ...

The same result holds for the degree of nesting of sentences, within the same grammar. Since the degree of self-embedding, or at least that of nesting, must

be taken into consideration in any explication of *syntactic simplification*, Bobrow's claim cannot, obviously, be taken seriously *as a whole*. In other words, in order to implement his program he must give up either the generality of the syntactic structure of admissible sentences, or the connection and equivalence between the concepts of syntactic simplicity and the corresponding psycholinguistic and logical concepts.

In (25, page 9) it was shown that if the syntactic-complexity function imposes a general order on a language, then either (semantic) equivalence is a recursive relation or no simplification function is recursive. Although the question of efficiency of his system is in itself of interest, this result makes the practical results of Bobrow's proposal almost trivial. For, if there exists a recursive simplification function, then the equivalence relation must be recursive; in other words, there exists a decision procedure for equivalence, and thus the whole system is decidable. Moreover, if Bobrow intends to generalize his system and deal with an unlimited field of subject-matter using the technique of the present system, he will find himself in conflict with other results of (25), which place unavoidable restrictions on simplification possibilities.

Some of these results relate also to the question of the "cost" of utilizing some recursive function for simplification purposes, in cases where a general simplification function is not available. Part of the price to be paid stems from the danger of "counterfeit" simplification. The simplification-function is general recursive and it associates with each sentence a sentence whose degree of syntactic complexity is smaller (where this is at all possible); but the resulting sentence is not always logically equivalent to the given one. Moreover, other results (25) show that the theoretical possibilities of avoiding or discovering such cases are quite restricted.

The explications used in several data-retrieval systems exhibit serious theoretical difficulties. In the first place, those systems which contain a complex deductive mechanism, such as those of Darlington (17) or Cooper (14), use conventional sentential or functional calculi as explications of logical relations between sentences. It has long been known that material implication cannot provide an adequate explication for the relation of logical inference; thus, one would expect constructors of DR-systems to have recourse to other calculi. Such calculi do exist and most of them have been developed rigorously [cf. (1) and the bibliography given therein]. Some of them —the bulk of the sentential calculi—are even decidable. The situation with regard to functional calculi is more complicated, but then it must be remembered that the conventional functional calculus is undecidable.

Since the form of implication used by these calculi is superior, as far as explication is concerned, to material implication, it is difficult to accept the claims of DR-system constructors about the deductive capabilities of their systems; these utilize, in effect, the conventional calculi, which cannot provide a basis for adequate explication of the required concepts. This criticism is aimed especially at DR-systems which are claimed to be of practical use.

The foregoing is an example of inadequate explication in which the fault stems from the fact that the explicatum is more inclusive than the explicandum. The error in the following example has its source in the reverse state of affairs. Raphael (37) writes:

Quine continues that the elusive meaning of "The door is open" is some complete intuitive set of circumstances surrounding a particular occasion on which the statement . . . was uttered. Clearly this kind of concept does not lend itself to computer usage. In order to construct a computer system which behaves as if it understands the meaning of a statement, one must find specific words and relations which can be represented within the computer's memory, yet which somehow capture the significance of the statement they represent (page 14).

It is quite possible that Quine's explanations are obscure or even faulty, as an attempt to propose an explication of the concept of "meaning"; but the fact that this explication "does not lend itself to computer usage" cannot be regarded as a fault stemming from inadequacy *qua* explication for the given concept. The only possible rejoinder to Raphael's complaint is "So what?"

The source of the error is to be found, it seems, in a confusion between formal and practical, mechanical requirements. An adequate explication must be formal, but we cannot demand that it "lend itself to computer usage"—not even when we are dealing with a concept such as "understanding" which is closely connected with the logic of computer usage.

A similar situation is evident in the work of Katz and Fodor (26, page 502).

In the same paper, Raphael also writes:

SIR, unlike SYNTHEX, does not require grammatical analyses which become more detailed and more complicated as a system expands. Instead, question-answering is based on semantic relationships (page 126).

The paper of Katz and Fodor rejects the possibility of giving an adequate linguistic description of a sentence in a natural language without having recourse to both a grammatical and a semantic system. The task of the semantic system is to provide linguistic information which the grammatical system is incapable of providing; on the other hand, the semantic system itself is largely dependent on the structure of the grammatical system. Thus, Raphael's claim, quoted above, and any other such claim, must be viewed with suspicion. The source of this claim is quite amazing. He writes:

SIR solves the semantic parsing problem by recognizing only a small number of sentence forms, each of which corresponds in specific ways to particular relations . . . (page 55).

The output is defined, in effect, by a finite sequence of *rules,* each of which contains a *sentence-form,* a list of *variables* appearing in the sentence-form, and so on. A sentence is *accepted* by the system if it is of a form appearing in one of the rules of the system. These conditions define a grammar; a very simple one, to be sure, but there is quite a difference between a simple grammar and no grammar at all.

We do not mean here to criticize the decision to set up a certain number of grammatical forms as the only ones to be accepted by the system. On the contrary, in the sequel we hope to show that there is no way, at present, to avoid such restrictions.

4. What Are "Questions" and "Answers"?

In the foregoing we have criticized *extant* explications connected with DR-theory. We now critically examine one of the most serious difficulties in the theory of data-retrieval: the *lack* of adequate explications for the notions "question" and "answer." This deficiency is responsible for the air of finality, so to speak, which is a common trait of most existing DR-system descriptions; we are tempted to ask of these systems: "Where do we go from here?" The technical details of some of these systems are open to improvement, but in order to enhance their abilities to a reasonable degree a change in the theoretical basis is necessary. Of course, it is possible to regard each specific DR-system as furnishing an explication of these concepts, but such explications are of necessity quite faulty.

One way to evade the faults inherent in these explications is to interpret them as if they dealt not with *questions* and *answers,* but rather *with questions of type A about subject B* and *answers of*

type A etc.; however, such explications are not too interesting, as is obvious from consideration of the subject-matter treated by systems such as BASEBALL.

The attempt to set up a general formalization for DR-systems has not been too successful. The work of L. E. Travis (48) contains, it is true, observations and hints of theoretical importance, but most of the formal part of his paper does not transcend the trivial. Very few interesting theoretical observations are possible using a trivial formalism; this is the situation with regard to both mechanical translation (3) and information retrieval (2, 4), and there is no reason to suppose that it will be any different with regard to data-retrieval.

Serious attempts at preliminary explications of the notions in question have been made. The work of Harrah, Belnap and others [cf. Belnap (9) and references in Harrah (24)] constitutes a substantial contribution, though rather restricted in extent, to the achievement of an adequate explication. The restricted character of these explications is a result of the need to classify questions according to types, with each of which a different logical structure is associated. A similar classification obtains for answers. Harrah's explication deals only with two types of question—questions given in the form of exclusive disjunction and "which"-questions. The answer to a question of the first type is of course one (and only one, since the disjunction is exclusive) of the components of the disjunction; the answer to a question of the second type is a complete list of individuals having the property to which the question refers.

Harrah's formalizations fulfill six general conditions which he imposes on any explication of the notions "question" and "answer."

We shall not take up here a detailed critical analysis of the explication proposed by Harrah; nevertheless in order to demonstrate the difficulties involved we shall indicate some doubtful points in the wording of his conditions for adequacy of the explicatum [section 6 in Harrah (24)], and in his claim that the explicatum proposed does indeed fulfill these conditions (*ibid.*, section 10). The first condition is worded thus:

The theory should explicate "question" in such a way that the user of L [the receiver's language] can effectively construct, for each one of his interests, a question which . . . corresponds to this interest in a reasonable way . . . (page 25).

The expression "the user of L" stands for whoever is using L as a *sole* means of verbal expression. Harrah's claim that his explicatum fulfills this condition must be rejected; we shall see that it leads to a contradiction.

Harrah admits that "why"-questions, for instance, "correspond to the receiver's interest in a reasonable way." Such questions may be represented, he says, as "which"-questions, expressed not in the language L but in its metalanguage ML. It thus follows that "why"-questions in the metalanguage ML may be represented as "which"-questions in the meta-metalanguage MML. However, it is impossible to speak of representing "why"-questions as questions in a metalanguage ML if we are dealing with a person whose sole means of verbal expression is L. (It is improbable that Harrah's explication involves the construction of languages which contain their metalanguage; in particular, this is not true of the language L described in detail by Harrah.)

In other words, we have two exclusive possibilities: *Either* the proposed explicatum is inadequate, since it provides no means of describing legitimate "why"-questions; *or* the description of the explicandum is inaccurate, since we are not dealing with a person who uses a certain language exclusively, but with a person who uses the language *and* the metalanguage of any language he uses. It is therefore necessary to alter the explicatum by extending the range of

questions definable thereby, or to alter the explicandum by allowing the use of the metalanguage of any language used.

In favor of the latter suggestion, it may be claimed that only a small number of transitions from a language to its metalanguage is necessary, and that this small number may be feasible for a natural language which can serve as a meta- . . . . -metalanguage of itself, for a restricted number of occurrences of "meta" in place of " . . . . ".

But when dealing with formalized languages, such as Harrah's language L, the formalization of metalanguages and the determination of their metamathematical properties (mainly—their consistency) involve considerable technical difficulties; such a solution should therefore be avoided. These difficulties are surely known to Harrah, and it is therefore surprising that despite his recognition of the problem of "why"-questions he claims his explication is adequate.

The second condition imposed by Harrah is the following:

The theory should explicate "question" in such a way that for every question there is a reply which answers the question in some reasonable sense (page 26).

In the formulation of this requirement, and in the properties of the explicatum aimed at its fulfillment, Harrah ignores the fact that the existence of an answer to a given question depends on the given context. Moreover, whether or not a sentence constitutes an answer "in some reasonable sense" also depends on the context.

The most extreme example of such context-dependence is dependence on the theoretical framework. Theories may differ from each other by virtue of the proper names of the theoretical and observable entities appearing in them. For instance, while one theory may contain proper names of entities having a certain property, another may contain the name of that same property but not the names of entities which may conceivably, within the theory, have the property. Thus the existence of an answer to a question concerning this property and the plausibility of a sentence as an answer to it depend on the given context. These possibilities are taken into consideration neither in the explicandum described by Harrah, nor, *a fortiori*, in his explicatum.

The fifth adequacy condition is:

The theory should explicate various relations of relevance among questions . . . It should yield a containment relation . . . and an equivalence relation . . . (page 27).

In order to fulfill this condition, Harrah presents the following definition:

A question q_1 *answer-contains* a question q_2 *relative to* a wff F if and only if every (answer to q_1) d_1 is such that $(F \& d_1)$ L-implies some (answer to q_2) d_2. Two questions are *answer-equivalent relative to* a wff F if and only if each answer-contains the other relative to F (page 40).

(In contradistinction to his treatment of the two preceding conditions, Harrah here takes into account the possibility that the relation he defines may depend on the given context. This dependence is manifest in the appearance of the wff F in both definitions.)

In his commentary on these definitions, Harrah asserts that they are important in that they reduce the number of necessary questions, since if $(F \& d_1) \rightarrow d_2$ then there is no need to ask both q_1 and q_2—it suffices to ask q_1.[3]

---

[3] These economizing possibilities are not as simple as they seem. If the questioner asks both q_1 and q_2 he receives a direct answer to both, whereas if he asks q_1 alone he will receive an answer to it and will have to infer therefrom an answer to q_2. He must try to obtain any answer to q_2, since he does not know in advance what it is. Now apart from implicit assumptions about the structure of the explicandum, and apart from the strong formal conditions to be fulfilled, necessarily, by the explicatum, this procedure raises grave doubts as to the advantages inherent in the definitions. The

Obviously, the above definitions fulfill the condition that the explication contain definitions of a transitive inclusion relation and an equivalence relation; however, in no way can they be regarded, utilizing the conventional inference-notion of the first-order predicate-calculus, as making a serious contribution to the clarification of any relevance concept. Indeed, the main criticism of material implication as an explication for the concept of logical inference is based on the fact that the conclusions may be irrelevant to the premises.

Harrah is thus leaning upon a rather crude explication of "relevance"; this is unjustifiable, since more refined ones are available. For instance, the explicatum proposed by Anderson and Belnap (1) may be efficacious in setting up an explicatum for the term "relevant question." Harrah's definitions and theorems can be retained in this framework, except, perhaps, the transitivity of the inclusion relation. Indeed, a little reflection will show that this apparent defect may be construed as an advantage: if an explicatum of relevance between questions is being sought, it would seem that there is no need for this transitivity.

The above three examples indicate faults, difficulties and misgivings not only with regard to the explication given by Harrah. They appear in every one of the existing DR-systems; as remarked above, each such system may be regarded as a realization of an explicatum for a restricted type of question and answer. Every existing system is defective, or at best vague, as to the language in which the questions, information and answers are expressed; as to the logical structure of the questions and answers; as to the logical relations between a question and its answer(s); and as to

---

effort expended to infer the answer to q_2 from that to q_1 may well be greater than the effort needed to obtain a direct answer, measuring the effort by any numerical estimating function. However, this difficulty is not of special interest to us at this point.

the determination of relevance and logical inference relations between sentences.

We conclude our discussion of the various explicata of "question" and "answer" with some remarks on the work of Bobrow and Simmons. According to Bobrow (10):

We assume that a speaker has some model of the world in his information store . . . The basic components of the model are a set of objects, a set of functions, a set of relations, a set of propositions . . . One may think of [some of] these propositions as the beliefs of a speaker about what relationships between objects he has noticed are true in the world (page 28).

And his definitions are:

A *closed question* is a relational label . . . $R_i{}^n$ and an ordered set of n objects. The answer to this question is affirmative if the proposition . . . is in the model . . . (page 29).

An *open question* consists of a relational label for an n-argument relation $R_i{}^n$ and a set of objects corresponding to $n - k$ of these arguments, where $n \geqslant k \geqslant 1$. An answer to an open question is an ordered set of k objects, such that if these objects are associated with the k unspecified arguments of $R_i{}^n$, the resulting proposition is in the model . . . (*ibid.*).

The answer to a closed question may be affirmative, negative or undefined. On the other hand,

An open question may have no answers, or may have one or more answers (*ibid*).

At first glance these definitions resemble Harrah's. In a way, a closed question plays the role of Harrah's disjunctive question, and an open question—that of the "which"-question. However, further reflection shows that there are considerable differences between the two sets of definitions, which indicate the superiority of Harrah's.

The main difference is that according to Harrah's definitions distinct types of questions and distinct types of answers have a similar logical structure, while Bobrow's definitions accord them completely different logical functions. For Harrah, all questions and answers are sentences. The difference between different types lies in their syntactic structure; this is true of both questions and answers. On the other hand, according to Bobrow the answer to a closed question is a truth-value—"affirmative," "negative" or undefined, whereas the answer to an open question is an ordered set of objects. These different logical structures complicate the explicatum, and, as is clear from Harrah's explication, this complication is unnecessary.

It must be remarked that these differences are not crucial for the DR-system constructed by Bobrow, since the theoretical distinction does not occupy a central position in the practical system. Simmons (43) writes:

The best answer to an English question from a given text may be obtained by selecting portions of that text such that the following characteristics are maximized (page 29).

And he proceeds to give a list of five characteristics. Now, a maximization requirement implies that some kind of measure is to be associated with the characteristic to be maximized. As far as the five characteristics enumerated by Simmons are concerned, this is quite difficult, if not impossible.

The first characteristic is:

Words of the selected text correspond to words, synonyms, and meanings of content words in the question.

By "correspondence of words to words" Simmons means, seemingly, an external similarity between the words appearing in the questions and those appearing in the given text; but the interpretation to be accorded "correspondence between words and meanings of other words" is not at all self-evident;

even less so is the interpretation of the "maximization" of such a correspondence.

This is a typical case of "reduction" to a more complicated state of affairs; an attempt is made to obtain an explication of a certain notion on the basis of the explication of another, whose representation is no less difficult than that of the original notion.

The second characteristic demanded by Simmons is:

The matching units of the selected text maintain the dependency relations of these units in the question.

Now any demand for maximization of correspondence of grammatical dependency relations implies readiness to accept, as the best answer selected from a given text, a sentence in which not all dependency relations correspond to those of the question. It is not at all clear what the maximal admissible lack of correspondence should be—to what extent a sentence in which the dependency relations differ from those of the question may constitute an answer to that question. Maximization relative to the set of sentences of a given text is out of the question: a sentence obtained in this manner may well prove incapable of answering the given question despite its having dependency-relations corresponding (in part) to those of the question. The development of a measure to determine the limits of admissible non-correspondence seems difficult, though not to the extent of constituting an impassable obstacle to the construction of an explication.

The same is true of the following requirement:

The answering phrases corresponding to the question's query (what name, how many, etc.) correspond in semantic coding to that of the query.

Here again a measure is necessary to determine the minimal correspondence required of the answering sentences.

No hint of such measures is given in Simmons' paper or in other papers. There exist in general implicit practical measures, but nowhere are they discussed or delineated in an adequate fashion.

Any talk of maximization becomes completely meaningless in relation to the next characteristics. For example,

Where matches between question and selected text are incomplete, questions are automatically generated to discover additional pertinent information.

What meaning can we attach to "maximization of automatic generation of questions, etc."? Do there exist measures which determine the level of ability of a given system to generate questions in order to discover additional information, in case of an incomplete match between a question and sentences which may constitute answers to it? Without the construction of such measures any talk of maximization seems pointless. If they can be constructed—and it seems to me that this would involve complex investigations—the maximization will depend on the specific measure used, and again there is no point in demanding maximization in general, without mention of the context (i.e., the measure). In such an event, the accepted answer should not be called "the best," but rather "the best, relative to the measure X."

The same is true of the next condition:

Semantic coding of the text vocabulary is such that it provides a capability for inference.

Again, the maximization requirement is meaningless unless related to a given measure. In the case of systems with nontrivial inference ability, the construction of such a measure seems to be quite difficult. It would have to take into account cases of considerable complexity, theoretically speaking: a system may be, for instance, undecidable while containing a decidable sub-system. It is quite probable that if the measure must take complex cases into account, then the computation of its value for a given system will be ineffective—this will of course render it useless.

5. Turing and Conversation-Programs

There is a clear tendency among those dealing with DR-systems to ignore the difference between systems whose purpose is to answer questions and those that carry on a conversation with a human source.

In his famous paper "Computing Machinery and Intelligence" (49), Turing writes:

I propose to consider the question "Can machines think?" . . . I shall replace the question by another, which is closely related to it and is expressed in relatively unambiguous words. The new form of the problem can be described in terms of a game which we call the "imitation game." It is played with . . . a man (A), a woman (B), and an interrogator (C) who . . . is apart from the other two. [C has] to determine which of the other two is a man and which is the woman. . . . It is A's object in the game to try to cause C to make wrong identification . . . and for B to help the interrogator.
We now ask question, "What will happen when a machine takes the part of A in this game?" Will the interrogator decide wrongly as often when the game is played like this as when the game is played between a man and a woman? These questions replace our original, "Can machines think?" (section 1).

In the sequel, Turing enumerates a number of types of objection to the thesis that the answer to the question "Can machines think?" (in its new version) is "Yes."

One type of objection is worded roughly as follows: "I agree that you can make computers do such and such a thing, as you have said. But you can never make a computer do X," where X is, for instance: to be polite, to have a sense of humor, to be in love, to learn from experience, to think about itself, and so on.

Turing attempts to meet objections of this type by giving an appropriate interpretation to each phrase of the type "make a computer do X." He creates the impression that it is possible to program a computer (which is rapid enough, has enough storage-space, etc.) in such a way that what the computer does may be interpreted as doing X, whatever X may be.

It seems to me that this impression, coupled with a careless disregard for Turing's precise wording, is the root of the aforementioned lack of distinction between conversation systems and question-and-answer systems.

For example, Simmons writes, in discussing conversation programs:

This program by L. Green, E. Berkeley and C. Gotlieb, allows a computer to carry on a seemingly intelligent conversation about the weather.
The problem was originally posed in the context of Turing's definition that a computer could be said to be thinking if it could carry on a conversation with a person in another room in such a manner that the person could not tell if he was speaking to a real person or not (43, page 54).

In this paragraph Simmons does not make the above-mentioned lack of distinction—but claims that Turing phrases his definition in terms of a *conversation*, rather than in terms of asking questions and obtaining answers to them.

An interpretation closely related to the above may be found in Cooper (14), who enumerates the properties required of any interesting DR-system:

A fact retrieval system must normally accept most of its information to be stored, and also its queries, in the form of natural language sentences . . . rather than in some artificial language selected for the purpose (page 118).

I do not mean to deal seriously with the reasons given by Cooper to justify this adequacy requirement; they all have to do with the difficulties arising when artificial languages are used for expression of information or questions expressible in some natural language. Since problems of worthwhileness are involved, such a discussion would have to investigate the results of his method and compare them thoroughly with those of the other methods; considerations of worthwhileness cannot decide in favor of one method if neither method has been investigated. As for the absurdity of Cooper's claim itself, we could as well formulate, as an adequacy requirement, the requirement that information and questions be presented to DR-systems in some artificial language, possessing a special structure, since, as is well known, it is difficult to process verbal material using existing computers and programs.

We believe that the same lack of distinction between "conversation" and "cross-examination" is at the root of Cooper's adequacy requirement. The motivation for the formulation of such requirements is the wish to construct systems which may be said to carry on a conversation.

To the credit of Harrah's work it must be mentioned that, since he defines *communication-events* by means of *momentary question-sets*, he does not go on to define a *conversation*, but rather an *interview*, argument, etc. [Cf. (24), Chapter 12.]

To some extent, the same misunderstanding is evident in the work of Raphael, who makes the following claim with respect to his programs:

Judging from its conversational ability, SIR is more "intelligent" than any other existing question-answering system (37, page 3).

We shall not deal with the claim that SIR is more "intelligent" than other existing programs, but with the claim, implicit in the above, that this program has "conversational ability." We do not think that SIR may be considered to have such ability, for three reasons.

In the first place, the answers are inferred formally from the questions. This is necessary in any automatic system which must answer given questions on the basis of either a given text or information given in a specific form; however, this is not so with respect to ordinary conversations. On the contrary; a conversation fulfilling this condition is of a very special character—an interview, quiz, or the like. Ordinary conversations do not fulfill it unless they are degenerate (in a certain sense, which may be formulated within Harrah's theoretical framework, though he has not done so).

Secondly, the answers to the questions asked of the system are determined in a parametric form. That is to say, the system's reactions to the material with which it is presented and which it receives are produced by putting processed portions of this material and of previously known material in the appropriate places in some member of a finite set of sentential forms. Again, such parametrization does not restrict the system's ability with regard to questions and answers, but it cannot fulfill any principal function in a conversation-system.

We emphasize that in the two foregoing paragraphs the words "questions" and "answers" refer, in effect, to material presented to the system and to its reactions, respectively; Raphael's system, for example, receives both information-sentences and questions, and reacts to both types of sentence if they are expressed in the proper form.

Our third reason is the following. A program may be regarded as having conversational ability only if when it is activated twice in *parallel*, it will produce something that may reasonably be termed a "conversation." That is to say, if two systems of the same structure can carry on a conversation with each other. Raphael's system is incapable of conversing with a twin system in any reasonable manner. For example: After one of the systems has emitted the words "I understand . . ." for the first time (and to judge from the structure of the parametric answers this answer will appear at an early stage), the "conversation" will degenerate (if it continues at all) into an interminable repetition by both systems of sentences each beginning with a sequence, unlimited in length, of assertions "I understand," and whose continuations differ from each other only very slightly. It is difficult to call this a "conversation."

The above criticism is aimed not only at the work of Raphael, but also at other programs which are claimed to have conversational ability. Another example is the weather-conversation program mentioned above by Simmons. (A demonstration of the truth of the assertion contained in our third reason above, in the case of this system, would be quite complicated; nevertheless, it is, to our mind, possible.)

6. Two Graphic Data-Based Systems

This section will be devoted to some remarks about a class of systems which should be discussed in conjunction with DR-systems. We refer to systems whose input is wholly or partially two-dimensional, in contrast with verbal input, which is linear. (The term "two-dimensional" is to be understood in a specific way, quite distinct from the everyday usage by which, for example, the letters on this page are two-dimensional; we shall not go into this in detail.)

The systems in question are not such as receive chemical formulae or handwritten material, etc., and respond by supplying certain information about the input; their function is to relate a graphical input with a certain verbal description thereof. To illustrate: the system of R. Kirsch et al. [(29) to (30)] receives a drawing and a sentence and determines the correspondence between them. The system of Simmons-Londe, on the other hand, is [according to the heading of (45)] "A pattern-recognition system for generating sentences about relations between line drawings."

Simmons himself hints, in (43), at the mutual relevance of discussion of the two types of system, pointing out the similarity of certain components in two-dimensional systems to components customary in DR-systems. In the latter we have translation from a sublanguage of English to an applied first-order predicate calculus with identity, while the former react to the reception of a drawing by emitting an English sentence about it. Simmons also indicates the interest in these systems as systems constituting well-structured data-based systems. However, it would seem that there is another fundamental similarity which enhances the interest in systems of this type and accords the relevant research a primary importance. We allude to the conception of Kirsch et al. [cf. (24) to (27) in the bibliography given in (29)] of syntactic description of pictorial sources. A simple example is given in (24, page 371) of (29) of deduction-rules such a system may contain.

The development of this idea necessitates theoretical investigation of the nature of two-dimensional grammars. Such investigations seem to be interesting, complex, difficult and no less "dangerous" than the manifold research on the subject of grammars in the conventional technical sense. The work of Kirsch, Simmons, Londe et al. has been carried out, of course, with no such theoretical background. Its importance is, therefore, that of preliminary experiments, indicating a set of problems and providing a certain experimental background for the discussion of their solution.

In the systems under discussion there is a dependence, stronger than usual, upon the form of the input. A system that receives, for instance, pictures in two colors only, may be able to distinguish a black disc on a white background, while it cannot distinguish, without adjustment, a white disc on a black background. If more than two colors are desired, the situation becomes correspondingly more difficult. If the identification-logic of the system NAMER, for instance, is adapted to deal with absolute values of color-differences or the like, it will be necessary to re-examine its learning ability. It is reasonable to suppose that this will be reduced. For this reason (among others, of course), it is probable that NAMER will be adept at identification of graphs.

Another problem arising in this connection is that of the relations which describe the components of a picture. It is one thing to derive from the structure of the picture a description of the form: "The girl is standing to the right of the dog with her head turned left"; it is quite another to derive a description such as *"The girl is looking at the dog which is on her left."* It is doubtful whether all such relations may be based on the spatial relations between the components of the picture. Moreover, even if our doubts are unfounded and the answer to the question is in the affirmative, dictionaries of unfeasible length will be involved.

Looking far ahead, and having in mind the practical utilization of these systems for DR, it must be remarked that, among other things, if the system is to learn from verbal descriptions of objects and relations appearing in pictures (which descriptions will be supplied, for practical purposes, "during" a sizable amount of input-material), then it may well transpire that in certain quantitative circumstances there will be no need to expend any effort on the learning section of the system. The reason is that the work of preparation, consisting in verbal description of all material up to a given time, will be so extensive that parallel work will be able to answer the demands of a system with no learning properties and yet capable of fulfilling all retrieval purposes.

These problems, and many others besides, must be investigated continually and thoroughly before any significance can be attached to this interesting field of research. The above-mentioned papers constitute a first step in this direction, which, though modest, is not devoid of significance.

7. The Fallacy of Economic Considerations

In the preceding sections we have not dealt with the economic questions bound up with any evaluation of the nature of the DR-systems we have considered. We shall now attempt to justify this omission.

The problem of storage and retrieval of information may be formulated as follows:

How can we determine—efficiently—whether a given collection of data contains information that may be of assistance in the logical and efficient solution of a given problem? And if the collection contains such information, how can we determine—again, efficiently—which of the documents contain this information, or what it actually is (4)?

One of the crucial points in this formulation of the problem is thus the emphasis on efficiency. The meaning of the word "efficient"—or, for that matter, of the word "worthwhile"—is not unambiguous in this context. The ways in which one determines whether a given system is efficient or worthwhile depend in an essential manner upon the system's field of discourse. It is not difficult to think of fields in which it is not worthwhile to invest above a certain sum, whatever the utility of the information supplied by the system. Conversely, other fields merit quite large investments even if the system in question supplies no more than a reasonable probability that information will be obtained.

Thus, it is necessary to discuss different systems in a comparative manner, in the framework of which essential importance is attached to details of the systems and minute details of their possible modes of practical use, against the background of worthwhileness considerations characteristic of each specific field. It is thus clear that there is no justification for a general discussion of the expediency of some specific device in DR-systems. It is improbable that there are reasons *pro* or *con* some feature which apply equally to all systems in discussions of worthwhileness.

We illustrate briefly. In (16), Donald H. Kraft expresses the opinion that "Because of the consistency and redundancy inherent in computer KWIC indexing the author believes the legal searcher would rate such an index high in findability. . . ."

Now, in evaluating the worthwhileness of this system as against that of others, in the legal context to which our illustration belongs, one must first take into account the legal system used in the location where the DR-system is to be of assistance. For if every remark appearing in a verdict handed down in a certain court is to be regarded as binding for all lower courts, then the use of KWIC indexing may well result in the lack of essential information. Similarly, one must distinguish between an auxiliary system developed by the Bar Association and a parallel system serving an individual lawyer, the former constituting a central device serving the Association and the latter aimed at the advancement of the lawyer's interests—financial, social, political, or otherwise. Again, the preferences of two individual lawyers will differ; for instance, contrast a lawyer whose main business is with cases where the stakes are high with another who deals mostly with civil suits with moderate financial stakes.

There is no doubt that the lack of sufficient attention to such distinctions results in scientific, financial, military, etc., losses; the sins are of both commission and omission. Propagandistic slogans of commercial companies, for instance, which describe various methods as "economically worthwhile" bring about positive decisions of doubtful value; while generalizations stemming from critical descriptions result in negative decisions which are not always justified.

We are therefore of the opinion that the claims appearing from time to time in the literature as to the efficiency or worthwhileness of specific IR- or DR-systems cannot be taken at face value. Such claims, unless accompanied by careful analysis of the economic context of the systems in question, are unfounded.

Another type of statement, also quite common, is to be regarded with even more suspicion. We refer to such claims as "The IR- (or DR-) system to be constructed in the next stage of the project will be efficient." (In general, such declarations are accompanied by a remark to the effect that the planning and coding of the next stage has been completed, while the work of debugging the routines will be completed quite soon.) These claims involve a well known fallacy—they assume for the most part, and without any justification, that the difference between the ability to carry out a certain intelligent action in *some* way and the ability to do so in a *reasonable* way (for practical purposes) is not essentially greater than the difference between complete non-ability to do what is required and the ability to do it somehow. [Cf., e.g., (4), for a critical illustration of this fallacy in connection with IR.]

Despite what has been said; we must emphasize that no negative decision with respect to the construction of IR- or DR-systems can be based exclusively upon this paper or others of its ilk. Such critical surveys may indicate that certain systems do not supply an output appropriate to current needs; they may evaluate the feasibility of systems approximating such an output; they may offer similar criticism in subjects related to these systems. However, they cannot supply the justification for practical decisions, since they attempt no analysis of the relevant economic contexts. This point should be clearly understood.

Conclusion

We preface these concluding remarks with the assertion that *they cannot be based on summaries of papers and reports dealing with the description of DR-systems*. It is only seldom that most scientists are confronted with such a state of affairs; however, those who deal with artificial intelligence or other departments of information processing are quite familiar with it. This state of affairs consists in a divergence between the description of a data-processing system given by its originator, on the one hand, and a *faithful* description, on the other. This divergence is in evidence even in papers worthy of considerable appreciation despite their use of manifestly careless language.

For example, it is not at all clear why a serious report [of work carried out under Project MAC (37)] should commence with statements such as these:

The computer system . . . exhibits some humanlike conversational behavior and appears to have certain cognitive abilities. . . . (It is a) prototype of a general-purpose "understanding" machine. (It) demonstrates how conversational and deductive abilities can be obtained through use of a model which can represent semantic content from a variety of subject areas.

We do not mean to treat the reasons for this state of affairs in detail; we would only point out that what is involved is the uncritical use of technical terms. The researcher, in attempting to simulate the conversational process, uses the word "conversation" in a technical sense whose extension is far narrower than in everyday language; however, in describing his work or summarizing his achievements he does not bother to emphasize that the word is being used in this technical sense. Thus, the untrained reader of the research report assumes that he has to do with the everyday meaning of the word "conversation," whereas the results of the report are appropriate only to the narrower technical meaning. Obviously, this may well lead to a much exaggerated evaluation of the report.

The situation is similar with regard to evaluation of the possibilities for development of DR-systems and their practical utilization. According to *Fortune* (12), Professor M. Minsky

has predicted that in thirty years the computer will in many ways be smarter than man. . . . In ten years . . . we may have something with which we can carry on a reasonable conversation. If we work hard, we may have it in five. If we loaf, we may never have it (page 130).

And behind the Iron Curtain, L. Gutenmacher (23) asserts that

In the future an encyclopaedic machine will *undoubtedly* be developed containing all the known. . . . New results . . . can be introduced into the machine after the machine checks it for novelty . . . (page 158).

We believe that the reader will have no difficulty in discovering the reasons for this situation.

We do not think there is any need to speak in this context of "scientific aberrations," as does Professor Mortimer Taube; the situation is, however, not in the best traditions of science. There are those who consider [cf. (43)] that

a harshly critical review could say of each question-answering system so far built that it deals only trivially with a trivial subset of English.

We hope that the foregoing criticism has made it clear that the fault of existing DR-systems is not that they deal "only trivially with a trivial subset of English." The faults are far more serious, in that they stem from grave difficulties of principle. We also hope that our criticism will not be taken for harshness.

On the basis of the foregoing criticism, we are of the opinion that the only hope for success in the near future is in well-structured data-based systems, having a special internal structure appropriate to a specific field, a reliable technical language, and a competent inference-mechanism, the latter taking account of the special internal structure and based, as far as possible, on nonclassical calculi.

And our positive conclusion implies an analogous negative: We do not believe that there is any real hope for success, in the near future, of DR-systems purporting to deal equally well with any field of discourse, or for that matter with one extensive field. The advance from successful construction of systems of the first type to that of the second involves lengthy and difficult basic research; such research must investigate the syntax and semantics of natural languages, methods of formalization and structuring of the fields of discourse, non-classical logical calculi. Moreover, applied research is necessary in the mechanization of syntactic and semantic analysis of sentences in natural languages, of translation from natural languages to special structure-languages and *vice-versa*, and of theorem-proving; achievements to date in these subjects are insufficient. Since the need is for fundamental investigations so numerous and so basic, we feel there is no point in trying to predict either success or failure. The only statement one can make with any degree of certainty is that, judging from the normal pace of research in these fields, one *cannot* predict far-reaching possibilities for DR-systems (of the second type mentioned above) in the near future (barring some "breakthrough," which may of course occur; though no on account is such a

hypothetical occurrence to be relied upon in advance).

It must be mentioned that an opinion similar to that expressed here has been given by V. E. Giuliano, in his comments (21) on Simmons' survey (43). We derive some encouragement, in addition, from W. Cooper's paper (15) in which he expounds a viewpoint differing from that of his own previous paper (14). We are quite willing to accept his formulation of the problem of applicability of DR-systems:

Are there areas . . . in which it would be natural and useful to apply deductive fact retrieval systems with restricted English input? . . . Important applications . . . will probably not be easy to find . . . It is to be hoped that a wide spectrum of researchers will ask themselves "Could fact retrieval, under its present limitations, be useful to me in my field?" . . . (page 86).

We hope that our critical remarks will be of some help in redirecting this young and interesting field of research, with a view to putting it on a firmer theoretical basis and placing its genuine, and in some respects valuable results more readily at the disposal of the community of information-users.

REFERENCES

1. Anderson, A. R., and N. D. Belnap, Jr., Enthymemes, *J. Philos.*, **58**, 23 (November 1961), pp. 713–723.
2. Bar-Hillel, Y., A logician's reaction to theorizing on information search systems, *Am. Doc.*, 3 (1957), pp. 103–113; appeared also as Ch. 18 of (6), pp. 313–329.
3. Bar-Hillel, Y., The present status of automatic translation of languages, *Advances in Computers*, Vol. I (F. L. Alt, Ed.), New York, 1960, pp. 91–163; Sections 1.2–1.5 appeared also as Ch. 11 of (6), pp. 166–173.
4. Bar-Hillel, Y., Theoretical aspects of the mechanization of literature searching *Digitale Informationswandler* (W. Hoffman, Ed.) Braunschweig: Vieweg 1962, pp. 406–443; appeared also as Ch. 19 of (6), pp. 330–364.
5. Bar-Hillel, Y., *Four Lectures on Algebraic Linguistics and Machine Translation*, Hebrew University, Jerusalem, 1963; appeared also as Ch. 14 of (6), pp. 185–218.
6. Bar-Hillel, Y., *Language and Information, Selected essays on their theory and applications*, Addison-Wesley Publishing Co., Reading, Mass., 1964.

7. Bar-Hillel, Y., and A. Kasher, a review of Lindsay (32), *ACM Computing Reviews*, in press.

8. Bar-Hillel, Y., A. Kasher, and E. Shamir, *Measures of Syntactic Complexity*, Technical Report No. 13, Applied Logic Branch, Hebrew University, Jerusalem, 1963, to appear also in *Advances in Machine Translation* (A. D. Booth, ed.), North-Holland Publishing Co., Amsterdam.

9. Belnap, N. D., Jr., *An Analysis of Questions;* preliminary report, Doc. TM-1287, System Development Corp., Santa Monica, Calif., June 1963.

10. Bobrow, D. G., *Natural Language Input for a Computer Problem Solving System*, Ph.D. Thesis, MIT Project MAC, September 1964; summary in (11).

11. Bobrow, D. G., A question-answering system for high-school algebra word-problems, *Proceedings of Fall Joint Computer Conference 26*, 1964, pp. 591–614 [a summary of (10)].

12. Burck, G., and the editors of *Fortune, The Computer Age and its Potential for Management*, Harper and Row, New York, 1965.

13. Chomsky, N., Formal properties of grammars, in *Handbook of Mathematical Psychology* (R. D. Luce, R. R. Bush, E. Galanter, Eds.) Vol. 2, John Wiley and Sons, Inc., New York, 1963, pp. 323–418.

14. Cooper, W. S., Fact retrieval and deductive question-answering information retrieval systems, *J. ACM*, **11**, 2 (April 1964), pp. 117–137.

15. Cooper, W. S., Automatic fact retrieval, *Science Journal*, **1**, 4 (June 1965), pp. 81–86.

16. Kraft, D. H., A comparison of Keyword-in-Context (KWIC) indexing of titles with a subject heading classification system, Am. Doc., **15** (1964), pp. 48–52.

17. Darlington, J. L., *Translating Ordinary Language into Symbolic Logic*, MAC-M-149, Project MAC Memo, MIT, March 1964; abstract in *Mechanical Translation*, **7**, 2 (1963).

18. Doyle, L. B., The microstatistics of text, *Inform. Storage Retrieval*, **1**, 4 (1963), pp. 189–214. Also available as Doc. SP-1083, System Development Corp., Santa Monica, Calif., February 1963.

19. Fraenkel, A., and Y. Bar-Hillel, *Foundations of Set Theory*, North-Holland Publishing Co., Amsterdam, 1958.

20. Ginsburg, S., and J. Ullian, *Ambiguity in Context-Free Languages*, Doc. TM-738/005, System Development Corp., Santa Monica, Calif., January 1964.

21. Giuliano, V. E., Comments [to (43)], *Comm. ACM*, **8**, 1 (January 1965), pp. 69–70.

22. Green, B. F., Jr., A. K. Wolf, C. Chomsky, and K. Laughery, BASEBALL: An automatic question answerer, in *Computers and Thought* (E. A. Feigenbaum and J. Feldman, Eds.), McGraw-Hill Book Co., New York, 1963, pp. 207–216. Volume II of this Report appeared as Technical Report 306, Lincoln Laboratory, MIT, Lexington Mass., April 1963, and includes flow charts.

23. Gutenmakher, L. I., *Electronic Information-Logic Machines*, Interscience, New York, 1963.

24. Harrah, D., *Communication: A Logical Model*, The MIT Press, Cambridge, Mass., 1963.

25. Kasher, A., and D. Louvish, *Syntactic Simplification*, Technical Report No. 14, Applied Logic Branch, Hebrew University, Jerusalem, 1963.

26. Katz, J. J., and J. A. Fodor, The structure of a semantic theory, *Language*, **39** (April-June 1963), pp. 170–210; appeared also in *The Structure of Language*, Readings in the Philosophy of Langauge (J. A. Fodor and J. J. Katz, Eds.), Prentice-Hall, Inc., Englewood Cliffs, N.J., 1964, pp. 479–518.

26a. Katz, J. J., Semi-sentences in *The Structure of Language, Readings in the Philosophy of Language* (J. A. Fodor and J. J. Katz, Eds.), Prentice-Hall, Inc., Englewood Cliffs, N.J., 1964, pp. 400–416.

27. Katz, J. J., and P. M. Postal, *An Integrated Theory of Linguistic Descriptions,* The MIT Press, Cambridge, Mass., 1964.

28. Kellogg, C., The fact compiler: a system for the extraction, storage, and retrieval of information, *Proceedings of the Western Joint Computer Conference,* 1960, pp. 73–82.

29. Kirsch, R. A. Computer interpretation of English text and picture patterns. *IEEE Transactions on Electronic Computers,* **EC-13,** 4 (August 1964), pp. 363–376.

30. Kirsch, R. A., A. Cahn, C. Ray, and G. H. Urban, Experiments in processing pictorial information with a digital computer, *Proceedings of the Eastern Joint Computer Conference,* 1957, pp. 221–229.

31. Kleene, S. C., *Introduction to Metamathematics,* D. Van Nostrand, New York, 1952.

32. Lindsay, R. K., A program for parsing sentences and making inferences about kinship relations. *Symposium on simulation models: Methodology and applications to the behavioral sciences,* South-Western Publishing Co., Cincinnati, Ohio, 1963, pp. 111–138.

33. Machover, M., *Contextual Determinacy in Leśniewski's Grammar,* Technical Report No. 16, Applied Logic Branch, Hebrew University, Jerusalem, May 1964.

34. Parikh, R. J., *Language-generating Devices,* Quarterly Progress Report No. 60, Research Laboratory of Electronics, MIT, January 1961, pp. 199–212.

35. Quillian, R., *A Notation for Representing Conceptual Information: An application to semantics and mechanical English paraphrasing,* Doc. SP-13A95, System Development Corp., Santa Monica, Calif., October 1963.

36. Rankin, B. K., III, *A Programmable Grammar for a Fragment of English for use in an Information Retrieval System,* National Bureau of Standards, Report 7352, Department of Commerce, Washington, D.C., June 1961.

37. Raphael, B., *SIR: A Computer Program for Semantic Information Retrieval,* Ph.D. Thesis, MIT, Project MAC, June 1964; summary in (38).

38. Raphael, B., A computer program which "understands," *Proceedings of Fall Joint Computer Conference,* **26,** 1964, pp. 577–589; summary of (37).

39. Salton, G., A document retrieval system for man-machine interaction, *Proceedings of the ACM,* New York, 1964, L2.3-1/20.

40. Schlesinger, Y., *The Sentence Structure and the Reading Process,* Ph.D. Thesis, The Hebrew University of Jerusalem, 1964.

41. Simmons, R. F., *Answering English Questions by Computer: A Survey,* Doc. SP-1556, System Development Corp., Santa Monica, Calif., April 1964; cf. (43) (preceding article in this book of readings).

42. Simmons, R. F., *Synthex 1964: A Progress Report and a Research Plan,* Doc. TM-1807, System Development Corp., Santa Monica, Calif., May 1964.

43. Simmons, R. F., A slightly revised edition of (41), *Communications ACM,* 8, 1 (January 1965), pp. 53–69.

44. Simmons, R. F., Reply to Comments, *ibid.,* p. 70. [A reply to Giuliano (21).]

45. Simmons, R. F., and D. L. Londe, *Namer: A Pattern-Recognition System for Generating Sentences About Relations between Line Drawings,* Doc. TM-1798, System Development Corp., Santa Monica, Calif., June 1964; *Proc. ACM Twentieth Nation. Conf.,* August 1965, pp. 162–175.

45a. Slagle, J. R., *Experiments with a Deductive Question-Answering Program*, *Communications ACM*, **8**, 12 (December 1965), pp. 792–798.

46. Stone, J., R. F. Bales, Z. J. Namenwirth, and D. M. Ogilvie, The General Inquirer: A computer system for content analysis and retrieval based on the sentence as a unit of information, *Behavioral Science*, **7**, 4 (October 1962), pp. 484–498.

47. Thompson, F. B., *Semantic Counterpart of Formal Grammars*, TEMPO General Electric Co., Santa Barbara, Calif., 1963.

48. Travis, L. E., Analytic information retrieval, in *Natural Language and the Computer* (P. Garvin, Ed.), McGraw-Hill Book Co., New York, 1963, pp. 310–353.

49. Turing, A. M., Computing machines and intelligence, *Mind*, **59**, 236 (1950), pp. 433–460; appeared also in *Minds and Machines* (A. R. Anderson, Ed.), Prentice-Hall, Inc., Englewood Cliffs, N.J., 1964, pp. 4–30.

50. *Current Research and Development in Scientific Documentation*, No. 13, National Science Foundation, November 1964. Items: 2.11 (J. Sable); 2.17 II (H. P. Edmundson, J. L. Kuhns, C. A. Montgomery, and D. Swanson); 2.19 (P. Garvin); 2.65 (P. Baxendale); 2.67 (M. Kochen); 2.73 (J. W. Kuipers, R. F. Barnes, R. S. Glantz, and H. M. Ohlman); 2.81 (D. Hillman); 2.125 (L. M. C. J. Sicking); 2.127 I (H. Borko, L. B. Doyle, and R. E. Wyllys); 2.127 III (J. D. Ford, Jr., and C. H. Kellogg); 2.190 (J. W. Perry); 5.3.21 (J. Harlow and Q. A. Darmstadt); 5.3.30 (S. N. Jacobson and N. H. Hardwick).

Computerized Bibliographic Services for Biomedicine

by Leonard Karel, Charles J. Austin, and Martin M. Cummings

The recording of medical knowledge dates back to the third millennium B.C., when prescriptions of various drugs and other methods of dealing with diseases were written on Sumerian tablets and Egyptian papyri. Among the earliest evidence of logical classification of such records is the catalog of hieratical books graven on one of the walls of the ancient Egyptian library at Edfu (1).

Centuries elapsed before private collecting of books led to the establishment of public libraries, and before the ever-increasing volume of literature led to the establishment of specialized scientific and medical libraries. The National Library of Medicine, at present the largest medical library in the United States and one of the largest in the world devoted to the biomedical sciences, had its origin in 1836 with the formation of the Library of the Surgeon General's Office, United States Army.

Price has stated (2) that both the number of scientific periodicals and the number of papers in them have increased tenfold every half century, beginning with 1750, when there were about ten scientific journals in the world. The biomedical literature has followed this trend.

Bearing on this growth is the rapid increase throughout the world of persons involved in medical and health-related activities. Indeed, in the United States alone, the number of people engaged in health professions multiplied by a factor of 5.8 between 1900 and 1960 (3), while the total population multiplied by a factor of only 2.4 (4).

The phenomenal increase in the volume of biomedical literature and in the numbers of contributors and users has not, however, been paralleled by equivalent growth of medical libraries. This lack of parallel growth of medical libraries and of information storage and retrieval methods and facilities adequate for today's needs has led to serious inadequacies in the capability of libraries to catalog, index, store, and retrieve published literature for the use of scientists, physicians, and others (5, 6).

The computer has been seized upon as a new means of assisting and supplementing the traditional library approach to management of the published literature. At the National Library of Medicine the computer has been successfully used for retrieval of reference material, and this success portends an exciting future for the entire field of information retrieval.

History of Bibliographic Control

The first comprehensive index of medical journal literature was the *Index Medicus* published by the Library from 1879 to 1927. Replaced from 1927 to

SOURCE: *Science,* 148, May 7, 1965, pp. 766–772.

325

1956 by *Quarterly Cumulative Index Medicus,* published by the American Medical Association, *Index Medicus* reappeared as a monthly library publication in 1960, superseding the monthly *Current List of Medical Literature.*

The *Current List of Medical Literature* was prepared manually by typing citations on 7½- by 12½-centimeter cards, which were then mounted on a large panel for photographing. This laborious process was replaced in 1960 by a partially mechanized system. In this system special paper-tape typewriters were used to imprint citations on tabulating cards; these were then machine-sorted and automatically photographed, by a Listomatic camera, on rolls of film. The developed film was cut and assembled into pages for printing.

This partially mechanized system, although better than manual techniques for preparing *Index Medicus,* could not meet demands for quick retrieval of citations from the rapidly expanding biomedical literature. To provide better control of this literature (7), the National Library of Medicine in 1961 developed specifications for a computer-oriented information storage and retrieval system, which it called MEDLARS (Medical Literature Analysis and Retrieval System) (8). The objectives of this system were as follows.

1. To improve the quality of *Index Medicus* while increasing the number of journals indexed in it.

2. To reduce the time required for preparing the monthly editions of *Index Medicus.*

3. To provide for increased depth of indexing.

4. To provide for the production of compilations similar to *Index Medicus* in form and content but devoted to specialized subject fields.

5. To provide for prompt and efficient searching of a large computer store of information for citations to biomedical and biomedically related literature.

6. To reduce duplication of literature-screening activities carried on by academic and other institutions and organizations in the United States.

7. To provide for the incorporation of monographs and other nonjournal literature into MEDLARS (9).

The system design was completed in January 1962. The preparation of computer programs, installation of equipment, training of personnel, and detailed system testing took approximately 2 years. The new system went into operation in January 1964.

Description of the System

MEDLARS has three major subdivisions (see Fig. 1): (i) an input subsystem in which the skills of professional indexers are used in connection with the capabilities of a large-scale digital computer; (ii) a retrieval subsystem in which the capabilities of professional literature searchers are used in connection with computer manipulations; and (iii) a publication subsystem that converts retrieved citations, and descriptors characterizing these citations, into photopositive film.

INPUT SUBSYSTEM. Through the input subsystem, citations and other information are fed into MEDLARS. In the initial step toward storage of information, journals are analyzed by intensively trained literature analysts who assign to each article appropriate descriptors from the Library's controlled vocabulary, called "Medical Subject Headings."

After the journal articles have been indexed, Flexowriter typewriter operators prepare basic-unit records by converting information on the indexers' data sheets to codes on paper tape. The basic-unit record entering the computer consists of journal reference, article title, authors, and subject descriptors. Typewriter copy produced concurrently with the coded paper tape is checked for accuracy by a staff of proofreaders; then

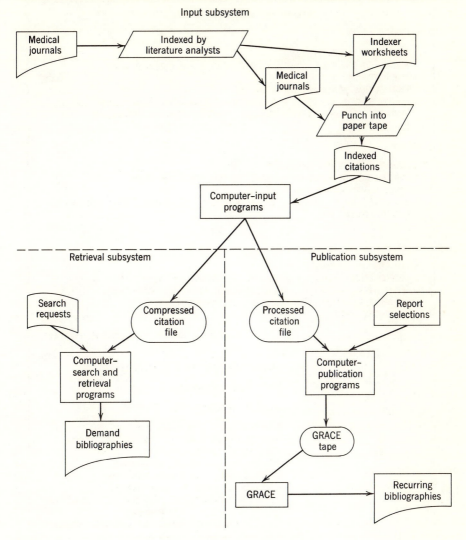

Fig. 1. MEDLARS flow chart.

the tapes are spliced in batches and fed into the computer.

Through the computer's input programs, the information on the paper tape is recorded on reels of magnetic tape, edited, and incorporated into two major data files—the Compressed Citation File and the Processed Citation File. The Compressed Citation File contains highly coded citations that can be retrieved as "demand bibliographies"—that is, bibli-

ographies intended not for publication but for individual use of the requester, and providing references on highly specific subjects (see Fig. 2). The Processed Citation File on the other hand, contains citations used in publishing *Index Medicus* and other "recurring bibliographies"—that is, bibliographies intended for serial publication and wide dissemination (see Figs. 3 and 4).

RETRIEVAL SUBSYSTEM. Through the

THERAPY OF CHROMOBLASTOMYCOSIS.

631366

ARIEVICH AM, VATOLINA VM
(RESULT OF THE TREATMENT OF CHROMOMYCOSIS PATIENTS WITH
AMPHOTERICIN B)   (RUS)
VESTN DERM VENER 38:30-2, JAN 64
*AMPHOTERICIN B, BITES AND STINGS, *CHROMOBLASTOMYCOSIS, DRUG
THERAPY, IODIDES, KNEE, REPTILES, THIGH, USSR (1), VITAMIN D
2, ZOONOSES

762521

GARDNER JT, PACE BF, FREEMAN RG
CHROMOBLASTOMYCOSIS IN TEXAS. REPORT OF FOUR CASES.
TEXAS J MED 60:913-7, NOV 64
AMPHOTERICIN B, *CHROMOBLASTOMYCOSIS, EPIDEMIOLOGY, PODOPHYLLUM,
RADIOTHERAPY, SU

                                                                        040470

25144

SOLOMON LM, BEERMAN
AMPHOTERICIN B AN   ELECTROCARDIOGRAPHIC, VENTILATORY AND
ARCH DERM CHICAG   HEMODYNAMIC CHANGES WITH CHRONIC LUNG
*AMPHOTERICIN B,   DISEASE AND PHLEBOTOMY.
INJECTIONS, INTRA

                            NATIONAL LIBRARY OF MEDICINE (MEDLARS)

                                                                        040470
                            BANTA HD, GREENFIELD JC JR, ESTES EH JR

                            LEFT AXIS DEVIATION

                            AMER J CARDIOL 14:330-8, SEP 64

                            AMYLOIDOSIS, CORONARY DISEASE,
                            *ELECTROCARDIOGRAPHY, FRIEDREICH'S ATAXIA,
                            GERIATRICS, HEART ANEURYSM, HEART
                            ENLARGEMENT, HEMOCHROMATOSIS,
                            HYPOKALEMIA, MUSCULAR DYSTROPHY,
                            MYOCARDIAL INFARCT, MYOCARDITIS,
                            MYOTONIA ATROPHICA, PATHOLOGY, PULMONARY
                                            CONTINUED
                            NATIONAL LIBRARY OF MEDICINE (MEDLARS)

Fig. 2. A demand bibliography produced by the computer printer.

retrieval subsystem, citations stored in the computer are recovered. Requests for bibliographic citations from physicians, scientists, librarians, and others are forwarded to a staff of specialists with extensive training in indexing and in the logic of computer searching. These search specialists analyze the requests, enumerate the relevant search elements, and formulate search statements linking these elements logically. Formulated statements designed to retrieve demand bibliographies are punched into paper tape and fed into the computer. Formulated requests for recurring bibliographies are punched into cards rather than paper tape. The retrieved citations, machine-edited and sorted, are recorded on magnetic tape and decoded into natural language prior to being printed, either on cards or on continuous tabulating paper, by the computer printer.

PUBLICATION SUBSYSTEM. The publication subsystem (see Fig. 1) provides recurring bibliographies by processing citations for eventual printing from photopositive film. The magnetic-tape files of retrieved citations are used for preparation of print copy by a computer-driven phototypesetter called GRACE, an acronym for Graphic Arts Composing Equipment. GRACE is also

used occasionally for preparing demand bibliographies.

Operating at a speed of about 300 characters per second, GRACE can use 226 different characters in preparing 23-centimeter-wide positive photographic film or paper. Character sets include a 6-point font of regular and bold-faced upper- and lower-case characters, a 10-point font of upper-case characters only, and a 14-point font of upper-case characters only. The exposed film is developed by an automatic film processor,

---

observed by difference spectrophotometry. Inada Y, et al. **Arch Biochem** 106:326–32, 20 Jul 64
Light-induced pH changes related phosphorylation by chloroplasts. Neumann J, et al.
Arch Biochem 107:109–19, Jul 64
Kinetics of the hydrolysis of benzoylglycine ethyl ester catalyzed by papain. Sluyterman LA.
Biochim Biophys Acta 85:305–15, 4 May 64
Effect of pH on extraction and activity of ox-kidney urate oxidase. Truscoe R, et al.
Biochim Biophys Acta 89:179–82, 8 Jul 64
A discussion of the pH dependence of the hydrogen-deuterium exchange of proteins. Hvidt A.
C R Lab Carlsberg 34:299–317, 1964
Intracellular pH of rat atrial muscle fibers measured by glass micropipette electrodes. Lavallee M.
Circ Res 15:185–93, Sep 64
Observations on pH and haemolytic complement. Ibe EC, et al. **Immunology** 7:586–94, Sep 64
Effect of environmental CO2 and pH on glycerol metabolism by rat liver in vitro. Longmore WJ, et al.
J Biol Chem 239:1700–4, Jun 64
Discrimination between alkali metal cations by yeast. I. Effect of pH on uptake. Armstrong WM, et al. **J Gen Physiol** 48:61–71, Sep 64
Relation of pH to preservative effectiveness. II. Neutral and basic media. Wickliffe B, et al.
J Pharm Sci 53:769–73, Jul 64
The validity of pH and Pco2 measurements in capillary samples in sick and healthy newborn infants. Gandy G, et al. **Pediatrics** 34:192–7, Aug 64
[Acid-base equilibrium in acute experimental carbon monoxide poisoning] Marchiaro G, et al.
Rass Med Industr 33:452–3, May-Aug 64   **(It)**

HYDROGEN PEROXIDE (D1, D3)

Generation of hydrogen peroxide in erythrocytes by hemolytic agents. Cohen G, et al.
Biochemistry (Wash) 3:895–900, Jul 64
Generation of hydrogen peroxide during the reaction of nitrate with oxyhemoglobin. Cohen G. et al.
Biochemistry (Wash) 3:901–3, Jul 64
Studies on the bioluminescence of Balanoglossus biminiensis extracts. 3. A kinetic comparison of luminescent and nonluminescent peroxidation reactions and a proposed mechanism for peroxidase action. Dure LS, et al. **J Biol Chem** 239:2351–9, Jul 64
Fluorometric study of antihistamenes. Jensen RE, et al. **J Pharm Sci** 53:835–7, Jul 64
Preferential localization of radioisotopes in malignant tissue by regional oxygenation. Finney JW, et al.
Nature (London) 202:1172–3, 20 Jun 64

rat liver] Durien-Trautmann O, et al.
C R Acad Sci (Paris) 259:2547–50, 12 Oct 64
(Fr)
[Enzymatic beta substitution of phosphoserine and cysteine by sulfite. Some remarks on the mechanism of beta substitution in the presence of pyridoxal phosphate enzymes] Fromageot P, et al.
J Biochem (Tokyo) 55:659–68, Jun 64   **(Fr)**

HYDRONEPHROSIS (C6)

Experimental renal erythrocytosis; role of the juxtaglomerular apparatus. Mitus WJ, et al.
Arch Path (Chicago) 78:658–64, Dec 64
The natural history of primary pelvic hydronephrosis. Roberts JB, et al. **Brit J Surg** 51:759–62, Oct 64
Multicystic and cystic dysplastic kidneys. Pathak IG, et al. **Brit J Urol** 36:318–31, Sep 64
Results of treatment of hydronephrosis. Balfour J, et al. **J Urol** 82:188–91, Sep 64
Solitary adenoma with hydronephrotic atrophy: xanthomatous papillary ademona. Deniz E, et al.
J Urol 92:263–6, Oct 64
The abdominal mass in infancy and childhood.
Urol Survey 14:183–91, Oct 64
[Plastic operation (Boarl-Küss) on the urinary bladder: technic, indications, results] Deuticke P, et al.
Urol Int 18:100–12, 1964   **(Ger)**
[Rare complication following vesicovaginal fistula surgery] Pogoreiko IP, et al.
Akush Ginek (Sofiia) 40:127,   May-Jun 64
(Rus)

HYDROPHTHALMOS (C11, C16)

[Tubular dysfunction and oculo-cerebral syndrome, Description of a new variety] Denys P, et al.
Bull Acad Roy Med Beig 4:485–511, 1964 **(Fr)**

HYDROXAMIC ACID (D2)

Selective modification of uridine and guanosine. Kochetkov NK, et al.
Biochim Biophys Acta 87:515–8, 22 Jul 64
Reactions catalyzed by amidases. Acetamidase. Jakoby WB, et al. **J Biol Chem** 239:1978–82, Jun 64

HYDROXIDES (D1, D8)

The solubility of heavy metal hydroxides in water, sewage and sewage sludge. I. The solubility of some metal hydroxides. Jenkins SH, et al.
Air Water Pollut 8:537–56, Oct 64
[On the effect of gamma-aluminum hydroxide and gamma-aluminum oxide on the antigenic activity of

---

Fig. 3. Part of a page of *Index Medicus* reprinted from film produced by GRACE.

ACETABULUM

Articular and fibrocartilage calcification in hyperparathyroidism: associated hyperuricemia. Vix VA. **Radiology** 83:468–71, Sep 64

ACHILLES TENDON

Triiodothyronine binding to red blood cells and Achilles tendon reflex as thyroid indices. Sabeh G, et al. **Amer J Med Sci** 248:253–9, Sep 64

Tendon repair using cohesive steel reinforcement. Myers HC, et al. **Amer Surg** 30:668–70, Oct 64

Tryptic peptides obtained from gelatins derived from normal and rheumatoid arthritic collagens. A preliminary study. Steven FS. **Ann Rheum Dis** 23:405–7, Sep 64

Achilles tendon areflexia in diabetic patients. An epidemiological study. Krosnick A. **JAMA** 190:1008–10, 14 Dec 64

[On the pathogenesis of hypercholesteremic xanthomatosis] Greiling H, et al. **Deutsch Med Wschr** 89:1887–91, 2 Oct 64 **(Ger)**

ALKAPTONURIA

[Alkaptonuria (observation on a 7-year-old boy)] Lopez-Linares M. **Acta Pediat Esp** 22:744–52, Oct 64 **(Sp)**

AMYLOIDOSIS

Multiple myeloma with paramyloidosis presenting as rheumatoid disease. Goldberg A, et al. **Amer J Med** 37:653–8, Oct 64

A case of Still's disease with amyloidosis demonstrated at the Postgraduate Medical School of London. **Brit Med J** 5421:1384–7, 28 Nov 64

ANKLE JOINT

[On the joints around the taius, with special reference to the relation between the capsula articularis and vagina tendinis] Arai K, et al. **J Jap Orthop Ass** 38:515–6, Sep 64 **(Jap)**

ANKYLOSIS

Audiometric manifestations of pre-clinical stapes fixation. Carhart R. **Ann Otol** 73:740–55, Sep 64

Experimental cervical myelopathy. I. Blood supply of the canine cervical spinal cord. Wilson CB, et al. **Neurology (Minneap)** 14:809–14, Sep 64

Non-articular rheumatism. Parry CB. **Practitioner** 193:288–98, Sep 64

A controlled study of carisoprodol and aspirin in periarthritis of the shoulder and cervical spondylosis. Redding JH. **Practitioner** 193:331–3, Sep 64

[Arthrolysis in posttraumatic stiffness of the elbow] Deburge A. **Presse Med** 72:2933, 21 Nov 64 **(Fr)**

[Apropos of cervical arthrosis] Dry J. **Progr Med (Paris)** 92:605, 10 Oct 64 **(Fr)**

ARACHNODACTYLY

A genetical view of cardiovascular disease. The Lewis A. Conner memorial lecture. McKusick VA. **Circulation** 30:326–57, Sep 64

Marfan's Syndrome. Bayliss VD, et al. **Indian Heart J** 16:142–54, Apr 64

An etiologic concept concerning the obscure myocardiopathies. James TN. **Progr Cardiov Dis** 7:43–64, Jul 64

[Case of Marfan syndrome associated with some dermatological disorders] Mukai T, et al. **Acta Derm (Kyoto)** 59:175–84, Aug 64 **(Jap)**

ARTHRITIS

Role of lymph nodes in adjuvant-induced arthritis in rats. Newbould BB. **Ann Rheum Dis** 23:392–6, Sep 64

Parenteral vs. oral folic acid antagonists. Auerbach R. **Arch Derm (Chicago)** 90:553–7, Dec 64

Use of high-definition films and immersion technic in early diagnosis of metabolic and systemic disorders. Walker BQ. **Cleveland Clin Quart** 31:227–30, Oct 64

Vitallium patelloplasty in patellar chondromalacia. Coretti JH, et al. **J Amer Osteopath Ass** 64:164–9, Oct 64

Physical therapy in the treatment of temporomandibular arthritis. Altman I. **J Amer Phys Ther Ass** 44:1091–2, Dec 64

Physical medicine in chronic arthritis. Bowie MA. **Mod Treatm** 1:1299–312. Sep 64

Surgical treatment of chronic arthritis. Marmor L. **Mod Treatm** 1:313–27, Sep 64

Electrocardiogram in cervical arthritis. Galli GA, et al. **Rheumatism** 20:98–102, Oct 64

Horace Pern (1872–1936). Rheumatologist and remarkable member of a remarkable family. (Pern H), Kelly M. **Rheumatism** 20:90–2, Oct 64

[Comparative clinical studies with paramethasone and prednisone] Mathies H, et al. **Arzneimittelforschung** 13:1058–63, Dec 63 **(Ger)**

[Isoenzymes of lactate dehydrogenase in clinical diagnosis] Hendrich F, et al. **Z Ges Inn Med** 19:351–4, 15 Apr 64 **(Ger)**

[Calcifying and ossifying arthropathies and paraarthropathies of the knee] Boffano M. **Ann Radiol Diagn (Bologna)** 37:93–150, 1964 (254 ref.) **(It)**

[On 2 cases of chondromalacia of the patella] Giordano L. **Friuli Med** 19:325–30, May–Jun 64 **(It)**

[Arthritis in humans and PPLO] Aria M, et al. **J Jap Orthop Ass** 38:691–2, Oct 64 **(Jap)**

[Histopathological study on experimental arthritis using the fluorescent antibody technic] Hashiguchi T. **J Jap Orthop Ass** 38:695–6, Oct 64 **(Jap)**

[Survey on the incidence of arthritis] Shichikawa K, et al. **J Jap Orthop Ass** 38:529–30, Sep 64 **(Jap)**

ARTHRITIS, INFECTIOUS

Hemophilus influenzae pyarthrosis in an adult. Goldstein E, et al. **Arch Intern Med (Chicago)** 114:647–50, Nov 64

Lactic dehydrogenase (LDH) and transaminase (GOT) activity of synovial fluid and serum in rheumatic disease states, with a note on synovial fluid LDH isozymes. Cohen AS. **Arthritis Rheum** 7:490–501, Oct 64

Complications of ACTH and corticosteroid therapy. Popov SE, et al. **Fed Proc [Transl Suppl]** 23:984–6. Sep–Oct 64

Infections in paregoric addicts. Oerther FJ, et al. **JAMA** 190:683–6, 16 Nov 64

Treatment of septic arthritis. Ward JR. **Mod Treatm** 1:1232–42, Sep 64

[Polyarthritis in rats induced by Mycoplasma arthritis. 3. Characteristics; role of "peri-pneumonia-like organisms"] Amor B. et al. **C R Soc Biol (Paris)** 158:1244–6, 1964 **(Fr)**

[Experimental polyarthritis in rats induced by Mycoplasma arthritis. IV. Immunological phenomena (animals subjected to active immunization)] Kahan A, et al. **C R Soc Biol (Paris)** 158:1320–2, 1964 **(Fr)**

[Use of dimethoxyphenyl peniccillin (Staphcillin) and methylphenylisoxazolyl peniccillin (Staphcillin V) in orthopedic surgery] Takayama T, et al. **J Antibiot [B] (Tokyo)** 17:193–201 Aug 64 **(Jap)**

ARTHRITIS, JUVENILE RHEUMATOID

A case of Still's disease with amyloidosis demonstrated at the Postgraduate Medical School of London. **Brit Med J** 5421:1384–7, 28 Nov 64

Sarcoidosis among children in Utah and Idaho. Beier Fr, et al. **J Pediat** 65:350–9, Sep 64

Management of arthritis in children. Kelley VC, et al. **Mod Treatm** 1:1270-87, Sep 64

[Considerations on a case of Wissler's syndrome

Fig. 4. Recurring bibliography (from the *Index of Rheumatology*) reprinted from film produced by GRACE (see text).

inspected, and cut into page-sized sheets (see Figs. 3 and 4).

Man-Machine Relationships

Because MEDLARS is a man-machine system, its success is directly dependent on the "intellectual input." Such input is provided by several kinds of specialists.

Specialists in medical subject headings are responsible for formulating the controlled vocabulary basic to consistent, efficient, and accurate analysis, indexing, and searching of biomedical literature. This controlled vocabulary, known as "Medical Subject Headings," is the dictionary to *Index Medicus* and its related publications. It is the key to retrieval of information for recurring and for demand bibliographies, and the base for most of the computer programs. Not only does it provide descriptors for indexing and for retrieving citations to the biomedical literature stored in the computer, it also provides descriptors for cataloging books and for preparing the public card catalog used at the National Library of Medicine and elsewhere.

The controlled-vocabulary list is developed from recommendations made by (i) trained professionals engaged in indexing and in searching the biomedical literature, (ii) users of *Index Medicus* and MEDLARS, and (iii) advisory panels composed of physicians, biomedical scientists, and other health specialists. Prior to its acceptance or rejection, a recommended medical subject heading is examined for potential usefulness, possible ambiguity, synonymity with existing controlled-vocabulary terms, and compatibility with subject headings in vocabularies of other organizations concerned with biomedical literature. Collaboration on development of subject headings is maintained with the American Medical Association, the American Dental Association, the American Rheumatism Association, and a number of other groups.

The 1965 edition of "Medical Subject Headings," published as part 2 of the January 1965 issue of *Index Medicus*, contains over 6300 subject headings, arranged in two sections: alphabetically with cross references, and in subject categories.

Despite the number of subject headings in the controlled vocabulary, there is still a deficiency of descriptors for categories such as psychiatry-psychology, public health, epidemiology, and environmental health, and these categories are currently being reexamined. Furthermore, because of increasing interdisciplinary research, demands are growing for development of more research-oriented descriptors; for development of descriptors in biophysics, biomathematics, veterinary medicine and the social and behavioral sciences, among others; and for greater hierarchical structuring among the individual categories of headings. Activities to meet these needs are now in progress.

Other specialists engaged in preparing input for the computer are the indexers. Using the "Medical Subject Headings" list as a guide for accuracy, consistency, and specificity, trained indexers assign to each journal article those medical headings which best describe its subject content and ideas.

The magnitude and significance of the indexers' task may be seen from the fact that 152,030 articles were indexed in 1964, and that the library's Indexing Section plans to index 300,000 articles annually by 1970. Worldwide surveys have shown that some 15,000 biomedical and related serial publications are published annually (10). Of these, 6000 serial publications, containing over 300,000 articles annually, are regarded as worthy of being indexed by the National Library of Medicine. The magnitude and significance of the indexers' task may be further seen from the various publications that are dependent on indexing—*Index Medicus, Bibliography of Medical Reviews,* and a number of specialized bibliographies.

Preparation of the basic publication, *Index Medicus,* is a demanding and difficult task. In 1961 an average monthly issue of *Index Medicus* had 450 pages and contained references to more than 10,000 articles. The January 1965 issue of *Index Medicus* had 691 pages, cited 14,665 articles, and, in addition, contained two special features—(i) the latest revision of "Medical Subject Headings" and (ii) the "List of Journals Indexed in *Index Medicus,*" giving the titles of the 2472 journals then indexed by the library. In 1961 the annual total of articles indexed was 132,154; in 1964 it was 152,030. In 1961, 12,661 journal issues were indexed; in 1964, the figure rose to 15,497.

Decisions on the inclusion of new journals or the omission of journals previously listed are made with the assistance of an advisory committee of medical librarians, physicians, and biomedical scientists. This committee also assists the library in establishing indexing policies.

Beginning with the March 1965 issue, *Index Medicus* contains a monthly "Bibliography of Medical Reviews." The March 1965 bibliography consists of selected articles indexed in the January, February, and March issues of *Index Medicus.* In subsequent months the bibliography will cite articles indexed in the current month's *Index Medicus.* As in the past, a *Bibliography of Medical Reviews* will be cumulated annually and published as a separate volume.

The annual *Bibliography of Medical Reviews* now being assembled will contain references selected from over 2400 journals regularly indexed in *Index Medicus* and from 539 journals not regularly indexed. Volume 10, a cumulation of review articles cited in 1964, contains references to 4270 articles taken from 2300 regularly indexed journals and 240 articles from other journals.

Still other specialists whose skills are used in connection with the computer are the searchers. After journal articles have been indexed and the citations have been fed into the computer, trained searchers formulate subject statements necessary for retrieving those citations that satisfy inquiries received from clinicians, scientists, teachers, and librarians.

References retrieved by computer search may be organized in various formats and printed. If desired, all subject headings assigned by an indexer to a given citation can be printed with the citation, thus providing a profile that aids the requester in judging the appropriateness of the citations retrieved (see Fig. 2).

Representative of recurring bibliographies are *Index Medicus* and *Bibliography of Medical Reviews,* both published by the Library; *Cerebrovascular Bibliography,* published by the National Institute of Neurological Diseases and Blindness and the National Heart Institute; and *Index of Rheumatology,* published by the American Rheumatism Association. Recurring bibliographies in various formative stages are "Index to Dental Literature" and bibliographies relative to fibrinolysis and thrombolysis, sudden death in infants and children, smoking and health, drug-induced abnormalities, and venereal diseases.

Of special interest is the *Index of Rheumatology.* As a result of cooperation between the American Rheumatism Association and the National Library of Medicine, this index is now being produced semimonthly by the library and published by the association (11). Expected to provide over 6000 citations annually from the periodicals now indexed by the library, the index is the first regular subscription bibliography, aside from the librarys' own publications, to be fully attributable to MEDLARS (see Fig. 4).

First Year's Experience

Of particular significance is the practical experience gained in the first year of MEDLARS' operation. Despite imperfections in the controlled-vocabulary list, need for improvements in indexing practices and techniques, and some retrieval difficulties imposed by these deficiencies, the results have been most heartening. Experience gained from more than 1300 searches made for physicians, scientists, teachers, librarians, and others has established the practicability of MEDLARS beyond question.

Appreciating that there is as yet no wholly satisfactory method of objectively evaluating the effectiveness of information storage and retrieval systems, the library has relied heavily on consumer reaction and appraisal. Evaluation of critical reports indicates that the percentage of missed entries is minimal; furthermore, the relevance of retrieved citations, as determined by the individual requesters' evaluation of demand bibliographies, appears to be satisfactory. New and more precise measurements of relevance are under study.

In some appraisals of demand bibliographies the inclusion of papers of inferior quality among the citations has been criticized. Since evaluation of literature for quality is not part of the indexing function of the library, this criticism cannot be met. Other criticisms relate to the librarys' present inability to store and retrieve references from monographs, books, abstracts, and other nonjournal publications. The library is attempting to acquire sufficient personnel to expand its coverage to include books and monographs in its automated system.

For the library to try to index all of the world's substantive biomedical literature in the depth required by specialized information centers seems impracticable. It is the library's intent, therefore, to avoid unnecessary duplication by supplying specialized information centers with relevant bibliographies on magnetic tapes. It is hoped that these centers will then analyze and refine the material in the light of their specialized requirements. Already, cooperative arrangements involving the library and several

universities have been made to test this concept.

Because MEDLARS was designed to serve three purposes—to provide demand bibliographies, recurring bibliographies, and high-speed printing—it is likely to prove more economical and more utilitarian than a system designed to serve a single function. Also, its location in a research library increases the efficiency of the system, since the library can provide original documents of photocopies of the articles required by the user, and traditional reference services are available to supplement the services of the computer system.

Research and Development

The library realizes that MEDLARS is only an initial response to the need for improved documentation technology directed toward better biomedical communication and modernization of library techniques. It is in this spirit that the following activities have been planned for implementation within the near future.

DECENTRALIZATION. In accordance with the library's legal responsibility for wide dissemination of scientific and technical information in medicine, a three-phase program to decentralize the MEDLARS search and retrieval capability was begun in late 1964. This program calls for production of compatible, duplicate tapes which would be made available to medical schools, research institutions, governmental organizations, and industry for use in their own computer facilities. These groups would then have the same search and retrieval capabilities as MEDLARS.

In the first phase of decentralization, the library has initiated two pilot studies, one at the University of California, Los Angeles, with computer equipment not compatible with that installed at the library, and the second at the University of Colorado, with compatible equipment. The University of California is reprogramming the library's Honeywell tapes for use on IBM computers and will test the concept of regionalization of services. It will also use the tapes to support the activities of a specialized brain research center. The contract with the University of Colorado provides for experimental use of MEDLARS, as in studies of selective dissemination of information.

The second phase will be the formation of a network of additional search centers in areas with large concentrations of scientific manpower. Interest in this part of the program is so high that requests for sharing in the MEDLARS' searching capability have already been received from more than 40 university medical centers, private corporations, and government agencies.

As an aid in the selection of additional search centers, the library has developed certain criteria: the service potential of the institution; its computer resources and consequent responsiveness to bibliographic demands generated by the automated system; its interest in conducting further research and development based on use of MEDLARS tapes; and its ability to provide services on a regional basis, such as distribution of specialized monthly bibliographies to physicians and scientists at local institutions.

The third phase of the decentralization program will be the provision of data tapes and program tapes, at cost, to interested institutions within the United States and abroad, and experimentation with the linkage of established centers in the United States through the use of data transmission equipment.

AUTOMATED ACQUISITIONS AND CATALOGING SYSTEM. The acquisition of new books by a library is comparable to the purchase-order and accounts-payable function of a private firm. This library function and the related cataloging of acquisitions are obvious candidates for automation. A systems analysis of these functions has been made by the National Library of Medicine, and an automated system has been designed to improve the capacity and efficiency of these processes through the use of available computer equipment. Computer programming to implement the first step of this new system is now under way. Mechanization of the cataloging operation will produce: (i) a rapid cataloging service that can be used by other libraries for their acquisitions and cataloging activities; (ii) a printed book catalog listing all new acquisitions in the National Library of Medicine each year, with a cumulative list published every 5 years; and (iii) incorporation into MEDLARS of citations to selected monographs.

ON-LINE INPUT. In an effort to improve the quality and extent of bibliographic input into MEDLARS, the library is exploring a system for direct communication between the indexer and the computer. Such a system would have the following characteristics.

1. Simultaneous, direct, immediate, edited indexer-to-computer input, with resulting elimination of clerical work now required for punching paper tape and elimination of errors generated by this clerical work.

2. Visual display of each data record at each indexer's station.

3. Entry of corrected input records, on magnetic tape, into the main computer files within 24 hours of indexing.

GRAPHIC STORAGE AND RETRIEVAL SYSTEM. Plans are now under way for development of a graphic-image storage and retrieval system that will permit rapid photocopy retrieval of the full text of documents in the library's collection. The library envisions a system that will tie the bibliographic capabilities of MEDLARS to the graphic capabilities of this new photocopy system.

Conclusion

By its development of improved media for dissemination of information, the National Library of Medicine is fostering a greater awareness and a better understanding of research and development efforts in behalf of public health and clinical medicine, and a more rapid translation of research into clinical application. The library's transformation from a passive repository of information to an active ally of the researcher, teacher, and clinician has led to increased use of medical library facilities and has stimulated thinking through better communication of published information. The library's success in using automation for bibliographic control of medical literature suggests that other disciplines that have not already developed automated techniques of literature-reference retrieval might profitably do so.

REFERENCES

1. Thompson, J. W., *Ancient Libraries* (Univ. of California Press, Berkeley, 1940), pp. 4–8.
2. deSolla Price, D. J., *Science Since Babylon* (Yale Univ. Press, New Haven, Conn., 1961), p. 97.
3. U.S. Public Health Service, *Health Manpower Source Book* (Government Printing Office, Washington, D.C., 1960), Section 18.
4. U.S. Bureau of the Census, *Historical Statistics of the United States* (Government Printing Office, Washington, D.C., 1960).
5. U.S. President's Commission on Heart Disease, Cancer and Stroke, *Report to the President: a National Program to Conquer Heart Disease, Cancer and Stroke* (Government Printing Office, Washington, D.C., 1964), Vol. 1; R. K. Cannan, *Fed. Proc.*, **23**, 1119 (1964); R. H. Orr, G. Abdian, C. P. Bourne, E. B. Coyl, A. A. Leeds, V. M. Pings, *ibid.*, p. 1133; R. H. Orr and A. A. Leeds, *ibid.*, p. 1310; R. H. Orr, G. Abdian, A. A. Leeds, *ibid.*, p. 1297.
6. Becker, J., *Amer. Library Assoc. Bull.*, **58**, 227 (1964).
7. Garrard, R. F., in *Information Retrieval Today*, W. Simonton, Ed. (Univ. of Minnesota Press, Minneapolis, 1963), p. 119.
8. U.S. Public Health Service, *The MEDLARS Story at the National Library of Medicine* (Government Printing Office, Washington, D.C., 1963).
9. Schiller, H., *Library J.*, **88**, 949 (1963).
10. Lazarow, A., statement before Subcommittee on Departments of Labor and Health, Education, and Welfare and Related Agencies, *Departments of Labor and Health, Education, and Welfare appropriations for 1965, Hearings before the House Committee on Appropriations, 88th Congress, 2nd Session* (Government Printing Office, Washington, D.C., 1964), p. 259.
11. Ruhl, M. J., and L. Sokoloff, *Arthritis Rheumat.*, **7**, 615 (1964).

Design Experiments in Automatic Information Retrieval[1]

by G. Salton, E. M. Keen, and M. Lesk

Introduction

Considerable attention has been paid in recent years to the organization of information centers. Various plans have been advanced for the establishment of partly mechanized information and library centers, and recommendations have been drawn up specifying the organization of a national document handling system (1, 2). In general, such plans stipulate use of a given equipment complex to store the information to be searched. Provision is normally made for introducing search requests from a variety of input stations, some of which may be situated far away from the central equipment, and users are often allowed to submit their requests asynchronously, and independently of each other.

Nearly all of those proposals are, moreover, based on a number of underlying assumptions, which though unproved and unaccompanied by supporting evidence, are nevertheless stated with forcefulness and considered to be axiomatic. The principal assumptions may be stated as follows:

1. A computer cannot perform the intellectual work required to analyze the content of a document, and information centers must therefore rely on a large staff of human subject experts to assign keywords to all items stored in the system.

2. The intellectual aids to be used as part of the manual analysis and indexing procedure, including dictionaries, thesauruses, and hierarchical subject arrangements are best prepared and maintained by committees of experts in the subject areas under consideration.

3. The users of the service, being unaware of system restrictions and operations, should not submit search requests directly to the system but must work through human intermediaries who analyze the query statement and prepare suitable search formulations for introduction into the program.

A system organization based on these principles leads to a service in which only the search operations themselves are mechanized (that is, the comparisons between analyzed information items and analyzed search requests), but most other operations are carried out semimanually or manually. It also results in an information system which suffers from several built-in weaknesses.

The first potential weakness is the scarcity and increasing unavailability of subject experts who are willing and able to perform a manual content analysis of the documents and search requests. As a result many existing nonconventional search systems are hampered by a difficult personnel problem which may be expected to grow more severe as time progresses. The second weakness is the inadequacy of the presently available

[1] This study was supported in part by the National Science Foundation under grants GN-360 and GN-495.

dictionaries and authority lists which are used to control the assignment of subject identifiers to the stored information. These dictionaries are often produced manually by committees appointed for this purpose, and the final product reflects no consistent point of view. The effectiveness of the resulting authority lists is therefore subject to question. The third weakness is the absence of meaningful user interaction with the system, so that individual user needs, and reactions by users to initial search efforts, cannot usefully be taken into account in order to improve the service.

The SMART document retrieval system which has been operating on an IBM 7094 for the past two years has been used extensively to test a large variety of automatic retrieval procedures, including fully automatic information analysis methods, automatic procedures for dictionary construction, and iterative search techniques based on user interaction with the system (3–6). The evaluation results indicate that presently held assumptions concerning the design of information systems may be erroneous, and point the way to alternative design criteria. Some of the experiments conducted with the SMART system are outlined briefly, and some of the results are described in the remainder of this study.

The SMART Experiments

SMART is a fully automatic document retrieval system operating on the IBM 7094. The system does not rely on manually assigned keywords or index terms for the identification of documents and search requests, nor does it use primarily the frequency of occurrence of certain words or phrases included in the document texts. Instead, the system goes beyond simple word-matching procedures by using a variety of intellectual aids in the form of synonym dictionaries, hierarchical arrangements of subject identifiers, statistical and syntactic phrase generating methods, and the like, in order to obtain the content identifications useful for the retrieval process.

Stored documents and search requests are then processed *without any prior manual analysis* by one of several hundred automatic content analysis methods, and those documents which most nearly match a given search request are identified. Specifically, a correlation coefficient is computed to indicate the degree of similarity between each document and each search request, and documents are then ranked in decreasing order of the correlation coefficient (3–5). A typical search request processed by the system is shown in Fig. 1. Three analyzed forms of this request, produced respectively by a word stem identification process (null thesaurus), a synonym dictionary look-up (regular thesaurus), and a phrase identification method (statistical phrases), are shown in Fig. 2. Finally a typical output product listing documents in decreasing correlation order with the request is shown in Fig. 3.

	PAGE 345
ENGLISH TEXT PROVIDED FOR DOCUMENT DIFFERENTL EQ	SEPT. 28, 1964

GIVE ALGORITHMS USEFUL FOR THE NUMERICAL SOLUTION OF	1
ORDINARY DIFFERENTIAL EQUATIONS AND PARTIAL DIFFERENTIAL	1
EQUATIONS ON DIGITAL COMPUTERS, EVALUATE THE VARIOUS	1
INTEGRATION PROCEDURES (TRY RUNGE-KUTTA, MILNE-S METHOD)	2
WITH RESPECT TO ACCURACY, STABILITY, AND SPEED.	2
	2

Fig. 1. Typical search request.

```
┌─────────────────────────────────────────────────────────────────────────────┐
│ OCCURRENCES OF CONCEPTS AND PHRASES IN DOCUMENTS          SEPTEMBER 28, 1964  │
│ DOCUMENT      CONCEPT, OCCURS                                        PAGE 17  │
│                                                                              │
│ DIFFERNTL EQ  ACCUR 12   ALGORI 12   COMPUT 12  DIFFER  24   DIGIT   12       │
│               EQU   24   EVALU  12   GIVE   12   INTEGR 12   METHOD 12  NULL  │
│               NUMER 12   ORDIN  12   PARTI  12   PROCED 12   RUNGE-  12  THESAURUS │
│               SOLUT 12   SPEED  12   STABIL 12   USE    12   VARIE   12       │
│                                                                              │
│ DIFFERENTL EQ 4EXACT 12  8ALGOR 12  13CALC 18  71EVAL  6   92DIGI  12         │
│               110AUT 12  143UTI 12  176SOL 12  179STD 12   181QUA 24  REGULAR │
│               269ELI  4  274DIF  36  356VEL 12  357YAW  4   384TEG 12  THESAURUS │
│               428STB  4  505APP 24                                           │
│                                                                              │
│ DIFFERNTL EQ  4EXACT 12  8ALGOR 12  13CALC 18  71EVAL  6   92DIGT  12         │
│               110AUT 12  143UTI 12  176SOL 12  179STD 12   181QUA 24  STATISTICAL │
│               269ELI  4  274DIF  36  356VEL 12  357YAW  4   375NUM 36  PHRASES │
│               379DIF 72  384TEG 12  428STB  4  505APP 24              LOOK-UP │
└─────────────────────────────────────────────────────────────────────────────┘
```

Fig. 2. Indexing products for "differential equations."

The system may be controlled by the user in that a search request can be processed first in a standard mode. The user can then analyze the output obtained and depending on the information returned to the system as a result of previous search operations, the request can be reprocessed under altered conditions. The new output can again be examined, and the search can be iterated until the right kind and amount of information is obtained (6, 7).

The SMART systems organization makes it possible to evaluate the effectiveness of the various processing methods by comparing the output obtained from a variety of different runs. This is achieved by processing the *same* search requests against the *same* document collections several times, while making selected changes in the analysis procedures between runs. By comparing the performance of the search requests under different processing conditions, it is then possible to determine the relative effectiveness of the various analysis methods.

The actual evaluation calculations are based on the standard *recall* and *precision* measures, where the recall is defined as the proportion of relevant matter re-

trieved, while precision is the proportion of retrieved material actually relevant. If a dual cut is made through the document collection to distinguish retrieved items from nonretrieved on the one hand, and relevant items from nonrelevant ones on the other, the two measures may be defined as follows:

$$R = \frac{\text{number of items retrieved and relevant}}{\text{total relevant in collection}},$$

and

$$P = \frac{\text{number of items retrieved and relevant}}{\text{total retrieved in collection}}$$

where R is the standard recall and P is the standard precision. The computation of these measures is straightforward only if exhaustive relevance judgments are available for each document with respect to each search request, and if the cutoff value distinguishing retrieved from nonretrieved material can be unambiguously determined (8–10).

In the evaluation work carried out with the SMART system, manually derived, exhaustive relevance judgments were used since the document collections

ANSWERS TO REQUESTS FOR DOCUMENTS   SEPTEMBER 28, 1964   PAGE 83
  ON SPECIFIED TOPICS

CURRENT REQUEST—*LIST DIFFERNTL EQ NUMERICAL DIGITAL SOLN
OF DIFFERENTIAL EQUATIONS

REQUEST   *LIST DIFFERNTL EQ NUMERICAL DIGITAL SOLN OF DIFFERENTIAL EQUATIONS
———

GIVE ALGORITHMS USEFUL FOR THE NUMERICAL SOLUTION OF ORDINARY
DIFFERENTIAL EQUATIONS AND PARTIAL DIFFERENTIAL EQUATIONS ON DIGITAL
COMPUTERS. EVALUATE THE VARIOUS INTEGRATION PROCEDURES (E.G. RUNGE-
KUTTA, MILNE-S METHOD) WITH RESPECT TO ACCURACY, STABILITY, AND SPEED.

ANSWER	CORRELATION	IDENTIFICATION
384STABILITY	0.6675	STABILITY OF NUMERICAL SOLUTION OF DIFFERENTIAL EQUATIONS W. E. MILNE AND R. R. REYNOLDS (OREGON STATE COLLEGE) J. ASSOC. FOR COMPUTING MACH. VOL 6 PP 196–203 (APRIL, 1959)

ANSWER	CORRELATION	IDENTIFICATION
360SIMULATIN	0.5758	SIMULATING SECOND-ORDER EQUATIONS D. G. CHADWICK (UTAH STATE UNIV.) ELECTRONICS VOL 32 P 64 (MARCH 6, 1959)

ANSWER	CORRELATION	IDENTIFICATION
200SOLUTION	0.5663	SOLUTION OF ALGEBRAIC AND TRANSCENDENTAL EQUA-TIONS ON AN AUTOMATIC DIGITAL COMPUTER G. N. LANCE (UNIV. OF SOUTHAMPTON) J. ASSOC. FOR COMPUTING MACH., VOL 6, PP 97–101, JAN., 1959

ANSWER	CORRELATION	IDENTIFICATION
392ON COMPUT	0.5508	ON COMPUTING RADIATION INTEGRALS R. C. HANSEN (HUGHES AIRCRAFT CO.), L. L. BAILIN (UNIV. OF SOUTHERN CALIFORNIA, AND R. W. RUTIS-HAUSER (LITTON INDUSTRIES, INC.) COMMUN. ASSOC FOR COMPUTING MACH. VOL 2 PP 28–31 (FEBRUARY, 1959)

Fig. 3. Typical retrieval results produced by the SMART system.

processed are all relatively small. More-over, the choice of a unique cut-off was avoided by computing the precision for various recall values, and exhibiting a plot showing recall against precision. Consider as an example, a typical search request QA5 processed against a collec-tion of 82 documents in the area of documentation. Three documents in the collection were judged relevant to the request, and the ranks assigned to these relevant documents (when the docu-ments are arranged in decreasing corre-lation order with the search request) are 1, 4, and 28, respectively, for the retrieval process illustrated in Fig. 4. By choosing successive cut-off values after the retrieval of 1, 5, 10, 15, 20, 25,

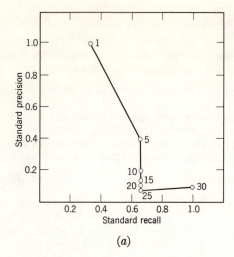

(a)

Request QA5   (Statistical Phrase Process)

Top 15 Documents				Relevant Documents		
Rank	No.	Correlation		Rank	No.	Correlation
1	X03	0.5264		1	03	0.5264
2	76	0.4817		4	21	0.4328
3	43	0.4776		28	72	0.2037
4	X21	0.4328				
5	45	0.4162				
6	79	0.4125				
7	05	0.3931			Normalized recall 0.8861	
8	37	0.3537				
9	56	0.3496				
10	10	0.3350				
11	27	0.3278				
12	12	0.3158			Normalized precision 0.7431	
13	59	0.3072				
14	40	0.3027				
15	33	0.3006				

(b)

Fig. 4. Evaluation results for Request QA5. (a) Recall-precision graph (cut off after 1, 5, 10, 15, 20, 25, and 30 documents). (b) Ranks and correlations of relevant documents.

and 30 documents, one obtains the following standard recall and standard precision values:

recall $\quad \dfrac{1}{3}, \dfrac{2}{3}, \dfrac{2}{3}, \dfrac{2}{3}, \dfrac{2}{3}, \dfrac{2}{3}, \dfrac{3}{3};$

precision $\quad \dfrac{1}{1}, \dfrac{2}{5}, \dfrac{2}{10}, \dfrac{2}{15}, \dfrac{2}{20}, \dfrac{2}{25}, \dfrac{3}{30}.$

The recall-precision graph of Fig. 4a results by plotting these seven recall-precision pairs.

Recall-precision graphs, such as that of Fig. 4a, have been criticized because a number of parameters are obscured when plotting recall against precision—for example, the size of the retrieved document set and the collection size (11). Such plots are, however, effective to summarize the performance of retrieval methods averaged over many search requests, and they can be used advantageously to select analysis methods which fit certain specific operating ranges. Thus, if it is desired to pick a procedure which favors the retrieval of *all* relevant material, then one must concentrate on the high recall region; similarly, if *only* relevant material is wanted, the high precision region is of importance. In general, it is possible to obtain high recall only at a substantial cost in precision, and vice versa (8–10).

In addition to the standard recall and standard precision measures, whose value depends on the size of the retrieved document set, it is also possible to use indicators which are independent of the retrieved set. In particular, since the SMART system produces ranked document output in decreasing order of correlation between documents and search requests, evaluation measures can be generated which are based on the ranks of the set of relevant documents, as determined by the automatic retrieval process, compared with the ranks of the relevant documents for an ideal system where all relevant items are retrieved before any nonrelevant one.

Two particularly attractive measures with this property are the normalized recall and normalized precision, which are defined as follows (7, 9):

$$R_{\text{norm}} = 1 - \frac{\sum\limits_{i=1}^{n} r_i - \sum\limits_{i=1}^{n} i}{n(N-n)},$$

$$P_{\text{norm}} = 1 - \frac{\sum\limits_{i=1}^{n} \log r_i - \sum\limits_{i=1}^{n} \log i}{\log \dfrac{N!}{(N-n)!\, n!}},$$

where n is the size of the relevant document set, N is the size of the total document collection, and r_i is the rank of the ith relevant document when the

documents are arranged in decreasing order of their correlation with the search request.

These measures range from 1 for a perfect system in which all relevant items are placed at the top of the retrieved list, to 0 for the worst case where all nonrelevant items are retrieved before any relevant one. Furthermore, when the normalized measures are used, the retrieval performance of a given system can be expressed by two numbers only, instead of requiring a complete recall-precision graph.

Both the normalized recall and the normalized precision measures reflect overall systems performance. A value of 1 for either implies a value of 1 for the other, contrary to the situation which obtains with the standard recall and precision measures. The two normalized measures differ, however, in the weights assigned to the relative positions of the relevant documents in the ordered list of retrieved documents. Specifically, the normalized precision measure assigns a much larger weight to the initial (low) document ranks than to the later ones, while the normalized recall measure assigns a uniform weight to all relevant documents (7). Both of the normalized measures are suitable for computation by automatic equipment, and can be used as evaluation parameters independently of the number of retrieved items (9, 10). For the sample request of Fig. 4, the normalized measures are given by the following equations (see Fig. 4b):

$$R_{\text{norm}} = 1 - \frac{(1-1)+(4-2)+(28-3)}{3(82-3)} = 0.8861;$$

and

$$P_{\text{norm}} = 1 - \frac{(\log 1 - \log 1) + (\log 4 - \log 2)}{\log \dfrac{82!}{(82-3)!\,3!}}$$

$$= 0.7431.$$

The following document collections have been used in experiments conducted with the SMART system:

1. Computer Science (IRE-3): a set of 780 abstracts of documents in the computer literature, published in 1959–1961, and used with 34 search requests.

2. Documentation (ADI): a set of 82 short papers, each an average 1380 words in length, presented at the 1963 Annual Meeting of the American Documentation Institute, and used with 35 search requests.

3. Aerodynamics (CRAN-1): a set of 200 abstracts of documents used by the second Aslib Cranfield Project (12), and used with 42 search requests.

It is seen that these collections belong to distinct subject areas, thus permitting the comparison of the various analysis and search procedures in several contexts. The ADI collection in documentation is of particular interest because full papers are available rather than only document abstracts. The Cranfield collection, on the other hand, is the only one which is also manually indexed by trained indexers, thus permitting a comparison of the standard keyword search procedures with the automatic text processing methods.

The evaluation results obtained with these collections are summarized in the next section.

Evaluation Results and Design Criteria

In attempting to generate useful criteria for the design of information systems, a number of obvious questions suggest themselves: First, can automatic text processing methods be used effectively to replace a manual content analysis? If so, what part or parts of a document should be incorporated in the automatic procedure? Is it necessary to provide vocabulary normalization methods to eliminate ambiguities caused by homographs and synonymous word

groups? Should such a normalization be handled by means of a specially constructed dictionary, or is it possible to replace thesauruses completely by statistical word association methods? What dictionaries can most effectively be used for vocabulary normalization? What should be the role of the user in formulating and controlling the search procedure? These and other questions are considered in the evaluation process described in the remainder of this section.

Language Normalization

In a manual system, where each information item is identified by a few carefully chosen keywords, the presence or absence of a given keyword becomes of crucial importance, since failure to provide a certain needed keyword may mean the difference between a retrievable item and one which is not. In an automatic text processing system, it is possible to generate for each item many different information identifiers, as seen in Fig. 2 for the request of Fig. 1; the importance of each individual identifier is then much reduced since a small number of poorly chosen terms are often offset by the much larger number of correct ones.

By the same token, if the natural language texts are to form the basis for an automatic assignment of information identifiers to documents, then the question of language normalization takes on an even greater importance than in many manual systems. Indeed, there will not then exist any human intermediaries who might resolve some of the ambiguities inherent in the natural language itself, or some of the inconsistencies introduced into written texts by the authors or writers responsible for the preparation of the documents.

A large number of experiments have therefore been conducted with the SMART system, using a variety of dictionaries for purposes of language normalization in each of the three subject fields under study. The performance of the following dictionaries is studied in particular:

1. *Suffix* "S" process, where words differing by the addition of a terminal "s" are recognized as equivalent (for example, the words "apple" and "apples" are assigned a common identifier, but not words "analyzer" and "analyzing").

2. The *word stem dictionary*, where all words which exhibit a common word stem are treated as equivalent; for example, "analysis," "analyzer," "analyst."

3. The *synonym dictionary*, or thesaurus, where a set of synonymous, or closely related terms are all placed into a common thesaurus class, thus ensuring that common identifiers are derived from all such terms; documents dealing with the "manufacture of transistor diodes" can then be retrieved in response to queries about the "production of solid state rectifiers."

4. The *statistical phrase dictionary* which makes it possible to recognize "phrases" consisting of the juxtaposition of several distinct concepts. Thus if a given document contains the notion of "program," as well as the notion of "language," it could be tagged with the phrase "programming language." The statistical phrase dictionary incorporated into the SMART system is manually constructed and contains a large variety of common noun phrases for each of the subject areas covered. A phrase identifier is assigned to a given document whenever all the specified phrase components co-occur in a given document.[2] Phrases may be particularly useful as a means of including in a document representation terms whose individual components are not always meaningful by themselves; for example, "computer" and "control" are reasonably nonspecific,

while "computer control" has a much more definite meaning in a computer science collection.

5. The *concept association method* in which concepts are grouped not by reference to a preconstructed dictionary, but by using statistical co-occurrence characteristics of the vocabulary under investigation. Thus, if two given terms co-occur in many of the documents of a collection, or in many sentences within a given document, a non-zero correlation coefficient can be computed as a function of the number of co-occurrences. If this coefficient is sufficiently high, the two terms can be grouped, and can be assigned jointly to documents and search requests. Associative methods are therefore comparable to thesaurus procedures, except that the word associations reflect strictly the vocabulary statistics of a given collection, whereas a thesaurus grouping may be expected to have a more general validity (14, 15).

Some of the language normalization tools used—for example, the thesaurus—are manually constructed word lists requiring considerable ingenuity to determine an appropriate arrangement for the included terms. Others are automatically derived, such as the stem dictionary and the concept association lists. In either case, not all dictionaries are equally useful for retrieval purposes. Experiments conducted with the SMART system lead to the following principles of dictionary construction (16):

1. Very rare terms which occur in a representative sample document collection with insufficient frequency should not be placed into separate categories in the dictionary, but should be combined if possible with other rare terms to form larger classes, since low-frequency categories provide few matches between stored items and the search requests.

2. Very common high-frequency terms should either be eliminated since they provide little discrimination, or should be placed into synonym classes of their

---

[2] More restrictive phrase generation methods can also be used by incorporating into the phrase generation process a syntactic recognition routine to check the syntactic compatibility between the phrase components before a phrase is actually accepted (13).

own, so that they cannot submerge other terms which would be grouped with them.

3. Terms which have no special significance in a given technical subject area (such as "begin," "indicate," "system," "automatic," etc.) should not be included.

4. Ambiguous terms, such as for example "base," should be coded only for those senses which are likely to occur in the subject area being considered.

5. Each group of related terms should account for approximately the same total frequency of occurrence of the corresponding words in the document collection; this ensures that each identifier has approximately equal chance of being assigned to a given item.

These principles can be embodied into semiautomatic programs for the construction of synonym dictionaries, using word frequency lists and concordances derived from a representative sample document collection (16).

The principal evaluation results obtained with the word normalization procedures are summarized in the output of Fig. 5, where normalized recall and precision figures are given, averaged over 34, 35, and 42 search requests for the IRE, ADI, and Cranfield collections, respectively. The following performance characteristics are derived from the output of Fig. 5:

1. The general trend of all performance curves is the same for all collections and for both normalized recall and normalized precision.

2. The differences in performance between the various dictionary procedures are smallest for the Cranfield collection in aerodynamics, most likely because the vocabulary used in that subject area is less ambiguous than the vocabulary used for the other collections. The dictionaries may then be expected to provide less help under these circumstances than would be the case for collections in a less technical subject area.

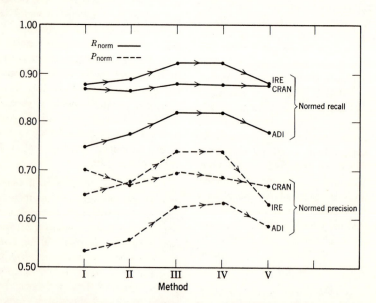

Fig. 5. Normalized recall and precision figures for various language normalization methods. *Dictionaries:* I, suffix "S"; II, stems; III, thesaurus; IV, statistical phrases; V, concept-concept association. *Collections:* IRE, 34 queries; ADI, 35 queries; CRAN, 42 queries. The arrows on the lines indicate direction of change, and the lines of the "graph" do not represent intermediate values.

3. The word stem dictionaries appear to be more powerful in providing language normalization than the suffix "s" process alone.

4. A further improvement in recall and precision is obtained when complete synonym classes are recognized by means of a thesaurus, over and above the word stem process. This is confirmed by the recall-precision plot of Fig. 6 for the ADI collection, where standard recall is plotted against standard precision, averaged over 35 search requests, for both the word stem and the thesaurus processes. The best performance curve is clearly the one which is closest to the point where both recall equals 1 (everything that is relevant has been retrieved) and precision equals 1 (nothing irrelevant has been retrieved). The curve representing the thesaurus process in Fig. 6 is obviously superior over the complete performance range.

5. The statistical phrase process is only slightly superior on the average to the standard thesaurus method. The improvement is largest for the ADI collection, where the vocabulary is least technical and most ambiguous.

6. The statistical word association method is superior to the word stem method, thus indicating that increases in retrieval effectiveness can be obtained over a simple word stem matching method by automatically constructed statistical procedures, without manually derived dictionaries. If a well-constructed thesaurus is, however, available, its performance will generally be superior to the purely statistical devices.

It should be noted that language normalization procedures can be applied in many different ways to improve the performance of a text processing and information retrieval system. Specifically, by suitably varying a number of parameters it is possible to recognize several different types of term associations, and once an association between terms has been recognized, it is possible to assign to it a smaller or a greater weight. Two main parameters that can be used in this connection are the cut-off value K in the

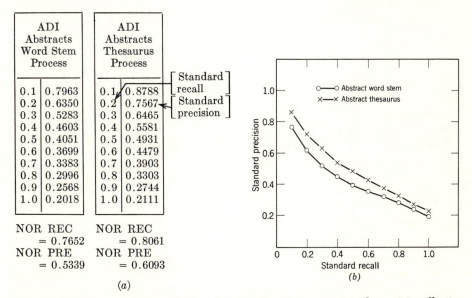

Fig. 6. Thesaurus evaluation results. (*a*) Recall and precision tables—ADI collection (averages over 35 search requests). (*b*) Recall-precision graph—ADI collection (averages over 35 search requests).

association coefficient below which an association between terms is not recognized, and the frequency of occurrence of the terms being correlated. When all terms are correlated, no matter how low their frequency in the document collection, a great many spurious associations may be found; on the other hand, some correct associations will not be observable under any stricter conditions. The spurious associations result initially in low precision, but the few important associations will eventually produce improved recall in the high recall region. This is reflected in the curve for the "null concon all" process (word-word associations performed for *all* word stems regardless of frequency) of Fig. 7.

Increasingly more restrictive association procedures, applied first only to words in the frequency range 3 to 50, and then in the frequency range 6 to 100, eliminate many spurious associations, but also some correct ones. This results in a smaller initial loss in precision, but also in a poorer recall performance for high values. The output of Fig. 7 then confirms the fact that more exhaustive indexing procedures which may supply a large number of additional information identifiers, such as, a statistical word association method applied to all words of a collection (regardless of frequency) are generally useful to improve recall at some expense in precision.

The experiment illustrated in Fig. 7 also indicates that dictionary performance will vary a great deal, depending on the type of collection, the number of included terms, the frequency range of the terms, and the characteristics of the texts used.

Document Length, Term Weights, and Manual Indexing

A principal difference between manual and automatic information analysis systems is the relative difficulty in manual systems of discriminating among keywords by weights assigned to reflect their relative importance. This results in the "all or nothing" situation where a given identifier is either present or not, and each identifier is considered to be equally important. In an automatic system, on the other hand, it is easy to assign weights to individual identifiers, as shown in Fig. 2. These weights can be derived in part by using the fre-

Null Concon		Normed Recall	Normed Precision
Frequency	K		
All	0.60	0.9233	0.7419
3–50	0.60	0.9379	0.7754
6–100	0.45	0.9463	0.7791

(a)

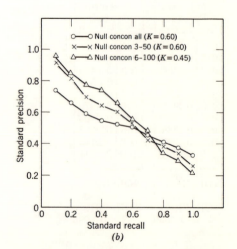

(b)

Fig. 7. Comparison of statistical word-word association strategies (IRE-2 collection, averaged over 17 search requests). (a) Normalized measures. (b) Standard recall-precision curve.

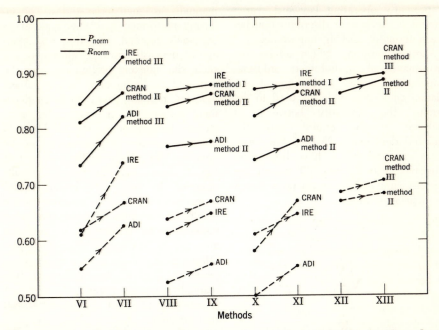

Fig. 8. Normalized recall and precision figures for variations in weight, length, and correlation method. *Methods:* document length—VI, titles only; VII, abstract (CRAN, IRE) or short text (ADI); weighting scheme—VIII, logical (no weights); IX, numerical weighting; matching function—X, overlap function; XI, cosine function; manual indexing—XII, abstract (automatic text process); XIII, indexing, manual. *Collections:* IRE, 34 queries; ADI, 35 queries; CRAN, 42 queries. The directed lines indicate direction of changes, not a "plot" of intermediate values as in a 'graph.'

quency of occurrence of the original text words, and in part as a function of the various dictionary mapping procedures. Thus, ambiguous terms which in a synonym dictionary correspond to many different concept classes, can be weighted less than unambiguous terms.

The relative usefulness of analyzing document sections of varying lengths, and of utilizing weighted terms is reflected in the output of Fig. 8 where normalized recall and precision values are shown averaged over 34, 35, and 42 search requests for the IRE, ADI, and Cranfield collections, respectively. The first section of Fig. 8 shows a comparison of a "title only" option, where only document titles are used in the analysis, with a "full abstract" or "full text" process. The dictionary methods used for the various retrieval experiments are

indicated on the graph of Fig. 8 by referring to the dictionary method previously used in Fig. 5. The graph of Fig. 8 makes clear that the title only process is inferior, compared with an abstract processing method, and that larger document excerpts than merely titles are needed, if adequate retrieval performance is to be obtained. This result is of particular interest because of the widespread advocacy of permuted title indexes (also known as KWIC indexes) for information search and retrieval purposes.

The second section of Fig. 8 reflects the improvement obtainable by using weighted word stems, compared with unweighted stems. It is clear from the figure that term weights are useful for retrieval purposes, and it can be inferred that one of the main drawbacks of presently operating keyword search systems is the lack of discrimination between terms of varying importance.

Another variation which affects the performance of an automatic information retrieval system is the type of correlation coefficient which is used to determine the similarity between an analyzed search request and the analyzed documents. Two of the correlation measures which have been used extensively with the SMART system, are the cosine and overlap correlations, which are defined as follows:

$$\cos_{qd} = \frac{\sum_{i=1}^{n} d_i q_i}{\sqrt{\sum_{i=1}^{n} (d_i)^2 - \sum_{i=1}^{n} (q_i)^2}},$$

and

$$\text{overlap}_{qd} = \frac{\sum_{i=1}^{n} \min(q_i, d_i)}{\min\left(\sum_{i=1}^{n} q_i, \sum_{i=1}^{n} d_i\right)},$$

where q and d are considered to be n-dimensional vectors of terms representing an analyzed query q and an analyzed document d, respectively, in a space of n terms assignable as information identifiers.

Both the cosine and the overlap functions range from 0 for no match to 1 for perfect identity between the respective vectors. The cosine correlation is more sensitive to document length, that is to the number of assigned terms, because of the factor in the denominator, and tends to produce greater variations in the correlations than the overlap measure.

The third part of Fig. 8 shows that in general the more sensitive cosine measure produces better results than the overlap coefficient. The differences in performance tend to be smallest for the IRE collection.

The Cranfield collection was available for purposes of experimentation both in the form of abstracts and in the form of

manually assigned index terms. The indexing performed by trained indexers is extremely detailed, consisting of an average of over 30 terms per document. As such, the indexing performance may be expected to be superior to the subject indexing normally used for large document collections. A meaningful comparison with standard manual keyword indexing systems may therefore not be possible. The output in the last part of Fig. 8 shows that the retrieval results obtained by using the manual index terms are only slightly superior to the results for the automatic text processing methods. The differences in performance are in fact smaller than those pertaining to any of the other methods compared in Fig. 8, thus indicating that manually assigned index terms may not be essential to obtain adequate retrieval performance.

As the collection sizes increase, the manual indexing procedure may be expected to decrease in effectiveness, because of the variabilities among indexers, and the difficulties of ensuring a uniform application of a given set of indexing rules to all documents. The computer process will, however, not decay as the collections grow larger, and one may anticipate for large collections of operational size an even smaller difference in performance, and a clearer advantage for the automatic process.

Real Time Information Retrieval

Most presently operating automatic information systems perform a single search operation for each search request, and the user of the system must submit a completely new request if he is dissatisfied with the initial response. This situation is not ideal, since it assumes that a single information analysis and search method will prove equally useful to all customers, and furthermore that all users have the same type of need and will thus be satisfied with the same type of answer. In actual practice, users have many different needs, some want-

Search type	Normalized Recall	Normalized Precision
Initial search	0.7601	0.5566
First iteration	0.8083	0.6967
Second iteration	0.8234	0.7481
Third iteration	0.8267	0.7554

(*a*)

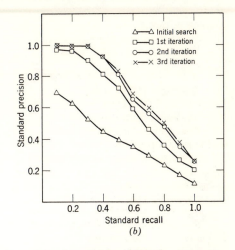

(*b*)

Fig. 9. Performance characteristics of iterative retrieval methods (ADI documentation collection—averages over 22 search requests). (*a*) Normalized measures. (*b*) Standard recall-precision curve.

ing very exhaustive answers, others being content with a single reference.

This situation is well recognized, and it is widely felt that the new computer time-sharing organizations, which permit a multiplicity of users to obtain access, more or less simultaneously, to a central equipment complex, can be used advantageously to provide individualized service to each customer according to his need. Accordingly, several iterative search methods have been simulated with the SMART programs (6, 7). In each case, a user first obtains some output in response to an initial query, and depending on what he learns from this output, he returns enough information to the system to permit a reprocessing of the original query under altered conditions.

The most effective procedure tried so far is the "relevance feedback" process, in which the user returns to the system a list of document numbers previously retrieved, together with information concerning the usefulness of each document for his search purpose. The system then automatically adjusts the original query by increasing the weight of query terms originally contained in documents

identified as relevant, and simultaneously decreasing the weight of query terms contained in the nonrelevant document set. This process can, of course, be repeated several times, and results each time in a modification of the query vector in the "direction" of the document set termed relevant, and away from the document set termed nonrelevant.

The results of three iterations performed with 22 search requests processed against the ADI collection are shown in Fig. 9. The first step of query modification is seen to result in a large-scale improvement in retrieval effectiveness, while the second and third iterations provide a smaller, but still noticeable increase in effectiveness.

Realistic tests of iterative search techniques can only be made in a real-time environment with adequate time-sharing equipment. The initial tests performed so far do, however, suggest that iterative search techniques appear to offer major promise for more effective search operations.

Conclusions

The principal conclusions resulting from the tests conducted with the

1. *Term Weights*
    Weighted word stems $\gg$ Logical stems
    Weighted synonym classes $\gg$ Logical synonym classes
2. *Document Length*
    Full summaries (2000 words) $>$ Abstracts (150 words)
    Abstracts (150 words) $\gg$ Titles only
3. *Synonym Recognition*
    Abstracts with thesaurus $\gg$ Abstracts null
    Summaries with thesaurus $>$ Summaries null
4. *Phrase Recognition*
    Synonym and phrase recognition $>$ Synonym recognition (thesaurus) only
5. *Syntactic analysis*
    Syntactic analysis with thesaurus $\gg$ Word stem match
    Syntactic analysis with thesaurus $>$ Synonym recognition
    Syntactic analysis with thesaurus $\sim$ Statistical phrase recognition
6. *Term-Term Associations*
    Stem-stem associations $>$ Simple word stems
    Concept-concept (thesaurus class) associations $\sim$ Synonym recognition
7. *Manual Indexing*
    Abstract stem matching $\sim$ Index term match
    Index term with thesaurus $>$ Abstracts with thesaurus

Fig. 10. Overall evaluation results (based on experiments with 3 collections in 3 topic areas). $\gg$ "much greater than"; $>$ "greater than"; $\sim$ "about equal to."

SMART system are summarized in Fig. 10. These results suggest that the designers of future information centers should investigate the use of automatic text analysis to replace the standard manual subject indexing. Among the techniques likely to be implemented in practice are the synonym recognition and phrase generation methods made possible by thesauruses and phrase dictionaries, and the statistical term-term association procedures. Document identifiers may be expected to be based on document abstracts, or longer document excerpts, and weights will be assigned to improve retrieval performance. A variety of additional techniques including expansion by subject hierarchies and automatic syntactic analyses may be used under special circumstances, but their general applicability is still unproved.

REFERENCES

1. Committee on Scientific and Technical Information (COSATI), Recommendations for National Document Handling Systems, Report PB 168267 distributed by National Clearinghouse, November 1965.
2. Rubinoff, M., ed., *Toward a National Information System*, Spartan Books, Washington, D.C., 1965.
3. Salton, G., A Document Retrieval System for Man-machine Interaction, Proceedings of the ACM 19th National Conference, Philadelphia, Pa., 1964.
4. Salton, G., and M. E. Lesk, The SMART Automatic Document Retrieval System —An Illustration, *Communications of the ACM*, 8, 6, June 1965.
5. Salton, G., Progress in Automatic Information Retrieval, *IEEE Spectrum*, 2, 8, August 1965.

6. Rocchio, J. J., and G. Salton, Information Search Optimization and Iterative Retrieval Techniques, Proceedings of the Fall Joint Computer Conference, Las Vegas, November 1965.

7. Rocchio, J. J., Document Retrieval Systems—Optimization and Evaluation, Doctoral Thesis, Report No. ISR-10 to the National Science Foundation, Computation Laboratory, Harvard University, Cambridge, Mass., April 1966.

8. Cleverdon, C. W., The Testing of Index Language Devices, *Aslib Proceedings*, **5**, 4, April 1963.

9. Salton, G., The Evaluation of Automatic Retrieval Procedures—Selected Test Results Using the SMART System, *American Documentation* **16**, 3, July 1965.

10. Salton, G., The Evaluation of Automatic Information Systems, *Proceedings of the 1965 International FID Congress*, Spartan Books, Washington, D.C., 1966.

11. Fairthorne, R. A., Basic Parameters of Retrieval Tests, 1964 ADI Annual Meeting, Philadelphia, October 1964.

12. Cleverdon, C. W., J. Mills, and M. Keen, *Factors Determining the Performance of Indexing Systems*, Vol. 1, *Design*, Cranfield, England 1966.

13. Salton, G., Automatic Phrase Matching, in *Readings in Automatic Language Processing*, D. Hays, ed., American Elsevier, New York, 1966.

14. Doyle, L. B., Indexing and Abstracting by Association, *American Documentation*, **13**, 4, October 1962.

15. Giuliano, V. E., and P. E. Jones, Linear Associative Information Retrieval, in *Vistas in Information Handling*, P. Howerton, ed., Spartan Books, Washington, D.C., 1963.

16. Salton, G., Information Dissemination and Automatic Information Systems, *Proceedings of the IEEE*, **54**, 12, December 1966.

Systems Technology for Information Retrieval[1]

by Manfred Kochen

1. Introduction

This article attempts to sketch an overall picture of the kind of a worthwhile, computer-based IR system that could be realized at this time. The judgment of what is worthwhile is evidently personal. It reflects the conviction that priorities should be assigned as follows: (1) tutorial information service based on synthesis and evaluation; (2) aids to bibliographic control; (3) current awareness; and (4) retrospective searching. All four services are important and should be provided by a good IR system.

Service 1 aims primarily to help a practitioner keep up in his understanding of topics that he needs to apply in everyday judgments and actions. Its typical user is a practicing doctor, ten years out of professional school, who wishes to *understand* the latest advances in toxicology rather than just be *informed* of the antidote for a particular poison or the engineer who wishes to understand the formulas and data that he uses rather than looking them up and routinely applying them.

Service 2 is intended mainly to help the librarian who is responsible for managing a document collection and maintaining it in a useful form. He is the intermediary between the IR system (library) and the user. He regards aids to bibliographic control—for example, cataloging, indexing, circulation control —as a way of amplifying *his* performance in the face of mounting arrearages.

Services 3 and 4 aim chiefly to help the information specialist. He is a professional searcher in an information center who extracts from library materials answers to questions posed by researchers at the frontiers of their specialties. His answers are fragments of knowledge—information—rather than a teachable, unified presentation. The professional searcher, like the librarian, is an intermediary between the IR system and the ultimate user. He regards aids to current awareness (for example, dissemination schemes and newsletters) and aids to retrospective search (for example, computer search of an index to produce a bibliography or computer search of text to extract a paragraph) as a way of amplifying *his* ability to meet his obligation.

It is, of course, possible to consider completely automating the roles of both the librarian and the searcher. However, this has not been shown to be either feasible or advantageous, and will not be considered here. Both roles may, of course, be filled by the ultimate user himself. A researcher may, for example, spend one quarter of his time doing his own literature searching and maintaining current awareness entirely on his own; he may even be his own librarian and rely almost entirely on his private collection of books, journals, reprints, and so on. He may not even be able to make effective use of a search specialist. It is highly questionable whether such a user could use an automated version of the search specialist more effectively,

[1] This paper was originally prepared for the Educom task-force on networks as background material for its conference in Boulder, Colorado, in July 1966.

as those who argue for direct user—IR system interaction would have to show.

2. Projection of an IR System: Tutorial Information Service Based on Evaluation and Synthesis

Figures 1 to 4 show, without detail, how services 1 to 4 can be provided. Consider Fig. 1a—a system for building up the files to be used in the tutorial information service. Suppose that the system contains a central processing unit like that of an IBM 7090 or 360, and a large auxiliary memory like an IBM Datacell. The process begins by loading the memory with references to documents. Suppose, for the sake of exposition, that these are documents that have been indexed and abstracted by the

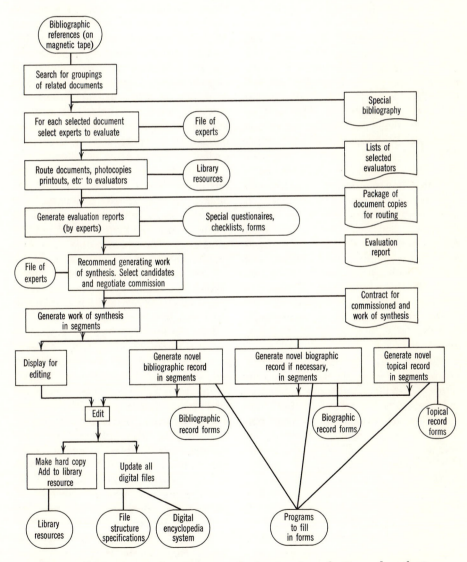

Fig. 1a. Construction and maintenance of subsystem 1: evaluation and synthesis.

dozen or so people at the Highway Research Information Service (2). About 5000 of these references—title, author, index terms with roles and links, and abstracts—have been stored on magnetic tape during 1965, with continuation at this rate. Before each such record from the tape is loaded into the Datacell, it is compared with all the records for all documents loaded so far to determine if it "belongs together" with one or more of these. If it does, an appropriate link (two pointers) is set up.

Deciding whether two or more documents "belong together" is a complicated problem. Criteria for "belonging together" include the presence of inconsistencies, of gaps, of needless redundancy, and above all, the likelihood that the several documents *together* add up to more than the same documents *separately*. Suppose that we could think of a document as a sentence generated by a special grammar. The grammar is such that *any* sentence it produces can refer to or be referenced by another such sentence, is attributable to an author (speaker), and does not deviate from conventionalized rules of well-formedness (rules of formation), logical and material truth, and relevance. Then, two sentences "belong together" if they are contradictory, logically coupled (for example, by equivalence or implication), or if they coimply a nontrivial third sentence.

Suppose that somehow a tentative grouping of documents that "belong together" is built up. Before references and groupings are stored in the Datacell, they are evaluated. At least one evaluator is assigned to prepare an evaluation report for each document. He is chosen on the basis of interest, availability, competence, and objectivity. He is to record his personal evaluation of some aspect of the document for a particular purpose. He is to do this by responding to a kind of modernized checklist or preformatted message, possibly by using a keyboard and a text-displaying cathode-ray tube. The preformatted messages used in recording evaluations are to represent the information that various people need in order to decide how deeply to delve into a document, if at all. Eventually, the evaluation report can be prepared much sooner, perhaps as a by-product of refereeing.

Using the evaluation reports, an editorial board decides if and when a tentative grouping of documents that "belong together" is worth acting on. If so, the board commissions a selected expert to produce a "work of synthesis." This can be a new scholarly research paper that resolves an inconsistency indicated by the group of documents, or it can be an original research paper that fills a gap, or it can be just a flag to authors and editors indicating that this is a crowded field in which there is already much redundancy. It might also be a survey/review paper, book, or tabulation.

For each new work created through this novel IR system, three types of secondary records are also generated. The first type is a bibliographic record. It includes data resulting from descriptive cataloging. The second type is a biographic record. It is essentially a dossier on the author. The third is a topical record. It contains units of an indexing/query language relevant for coupling to the contents of a document.

Like the form in which the evaluation report is stored, the three types of record as well as the work of synthesis itself are represented in novel forms. Digital information technology has greatly extended the options and media for storing, transmitting, displaying, processing, and creating representations of documented records. It is somewhat analogous to the way in which motion picture technology has enriched the media for man's expressive powers beyond still photography. How can these new opportunities be well-utilized?

Consider the form of the biographic record, for example. It is to be treated as consisting of elementary, undecomposable segments. Each such segment represents an item of information—the value of a variable—that is deemed significant for users of that kind of record. Record identification number is one segment; author's last name is another; so is city of birth, and so on. Many of these segments within one record must be interlinked, as author's last name is to author's first name. This can be done in a variety of ways: by a generalization of the idea of pointers; by the use of *n*-place relations; or by the use of what is known as "links" in information retrieval. There are also links from a minimal segment in one record to a minimal segment in another record, in the same file; links from a minimal segment in one record to segments in other files; links of a segment that is an aggregate of minimal segments to other such macrosegments.

The reason for storing documents in this segmented form is to make it possible to search the files with one or more segments specified and to retrieve one or more segments related to what is given in a known way. For example, suppose that "John E. Green," "Miami," and "1965" are given as search specifications (author, city of birth, and date of birth) and the pseudonym used by that author in 1943 is wanted. The three input segments may be adequate to specify a unique record identification number, and linked to that will also be the desired datum.

Whereas Fig. 1*a* sketches an arrangement that helps to maintain the system for the tutorial information service, Fig. 1*b* shows the procedure for providing the service. All the above-mentioned records, evaluation reports, and works of synthesis constitute a "digital encyclopedia system." Suppose, for example that a querist who is using it wants to know "the maximum temperature on the lunar surface." Linguistic analysis of the query could transform it into "find x such that x is the maximum temperature on the surface of the moon." Logical analysis

could further classify the query as incomplete, because it did not specify whether the maximum was to be taken over all points on the lunar surface, over all time, or both. Further logical-semantic analysis, using the topical record file (that is, some substantive understanding of physics), would quickly reveal that "temperature on a surface" is either meaningless or incomplete. It must be the temperature of a thing—of a rock or a spacesuit, for example. If the querist did not know or realize this, he might appreciate being tutorially informed or at least reminded.

If, indeed, several hundred temperature measurements have been reported, the querist might be well served, first, with an overview of the different purposes of the measurements, the different techniques used, and the general nature and classification of the results. He might then be able to reformulate a query based on this increased understanding. That query might be in form suitable for "conventional" retrospective searching. The increase in understanding gained up to the point of reformulating the original query might, however, be far more valuable than any specific fragment of information, even the final answer.

There are evident advantages to a system that helps to digest, to limit, and to master the bulk of retrieved information. Many people would welcome being kept up-to-date by competent and trusted sources. But the process of synthesis, with its selection, reelaboration, discarding and reevaluation of knowledge, could also be a source of anxiety about authoritarian control of the worst kind. These are not groundless fears, for there are real dangers of malfunction due to accident, mismanagement, seizure of control by irresponsible leaders, deliberate abuse or misuse, and so on. It is of critical importance to investigate the stability of the system under such disturbances, and to design sufficient safeguards and protective devices to

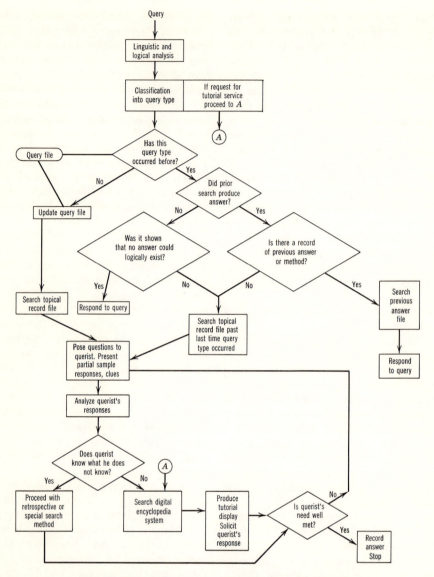

Fig. 1*b*. Use of subsystem 1: tutorial information service.

keep undesirable deviations under control.

3. Bibliographic Control and Current Awareness

Figure 2 sketches a procedure for creating a variety of files pertaining to the items collected by a library, so as to enable the library to control circulation, acquisitioning, inventory, access, and so on. The key problem is, of course, cataloging for better access. Access and aids to current awareness are important to the researcher at the frontier of his specialty in need of a well-defined fragment of knowledge. "Keeping up," the theme of the preceding section, is important to the average person who needs better understanding, to the practitioner, and to the specialist who must borrow from other specialties. The queries posed by such a person often reflect partial ignorance about what it is that he needs to know and what it is that he might yet learn. Sometimes he does not know precisely what questions to ask until he is halfway toward answers. Sometimes answers precede the questions. Frequently he is unaware of just what he does not know that, if he realized it was known, he would find of great interest. Often people who have queries of this kind are

too inhibited, pessimistic (actually realistic in terms of services that they have been conditioned to expect), or insecure about how to proceed to even try to pose them.

Most of the research effort in information retrieval has been expended on various ingenious schemes for automatic indexing, that is, subject cataloging. Some schemes are simple—they use a word or a phrase to index a textual document if the phrase occurs both in the text and in a subject authority list. Other schemes use a phrase to index a docu-

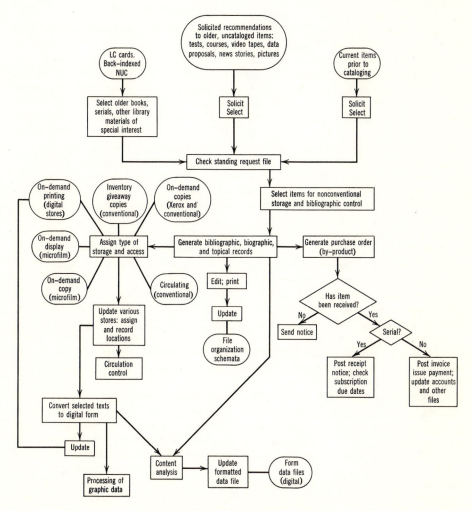

Fig. 2. Aids to bibliographic control.

ment if it is repeated in that document sufficiently often. A variant of this is to require a high enough frequency with which a potential index phrase co-occurs with selected other terms in sentences of the document. Still another scheme requires an index term both to satisfy a frequency criterion and also to be the subject of a sentence in an abstract of the document. Some schemes look for those phrases in a text for which the variance among documents in the same class is significantly less than the variance between documents of different classes. A variant of this scheme is to look for phrases for which the in-document repetition frequency contrasts sharply with the frequency of occurrence of that term in the general language.

There are many more such schemes (5). Many have been analyzed and some have been implemented on a small scale and found to produce more or less impressive results in comparison with conventional ways of indexing. There is no convincing evidence, however, that fully automatic, high-quality indexing on a scale large enough to be practical is feasible and advantageous. Useful aids to bibliographic control are more likely to emerge as by-products of the processes of document generation.

The time when new materials are added to a library—whether they have been cataloged previously, are being recataloged, or are cataloged for the first time—seems the most appropriate one for checking to see if the new items can meet any standing requests for documents on a topic. This means checking a description of the topic against descriptions of the newly arriving items, and notifying the originators of the standing request when there is a match. This method is used in selective dissemination procedures. Proper indexing is only one of the problems in making such schemes successful. Maintaining a current and good description of the standing requests is another. Comparing such descriptions without the rigidity of letter-by-letter matching is yet another. The idea that holds the greatest promise toward improvement of this service is to use all available clues about the originator of the standing request as well as about the authors, including responses to past notices of documents that are classified by type of author.

Computer aids for several of the boxes shown in Fig. 2, which represent processes, have been successfully implemented. Providing aids to current awareness, such as those sketched in Fig. 3, presents problems similar to those discussed above.

4. Retrospective Searching

Although they are assigned the lowest priority here, aids to this type of service have received the greatest emphasis. One of the simplest schemes for retrospective searching—based on coordinate indexing—is also useful to illustrate the kind of "systems arithmetic" that it is possible and valuable to do before deciding on any system. The systems analysis illustrated here shows how cost and universal availability of conveniently usable, sophisticated, yet little used private terminals can limit—perhaps fundamentally—the competitive advantages over systems that use modern technology over systems that do not.

Retrospective search requests can be usefully classified into 5 types: (a) Known-item search, (b) 24-hour–2-week search, (c) ½-hour–24-hour search, (d) search for data to be delivered in 5 minutes or more, (e) search for data to be delivered within 5 minutes (see Fig. 4). Strictly speaking, only (b) and (c) are called retrospective searching, in that a list of references to past documents is the desired response to such requests. A broader interpretation of the request would, however, include delivery of the documents—or at least more documents than are available in a traditional citation—in the desired response. If "search" is interpreted to include location of a needed docu-

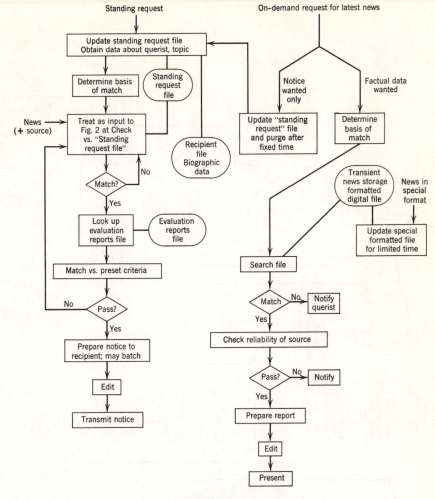

Fig. 3. Current awareness.

ment, then (*a*) is clearly retrospective searching, too.

Requests (*d*) and (*e*) have either documented data or a statement asking that the original request be revised or clarified as the desired response. The latter, however, is part of the desired response for (*a*), (*b*), and (*c*) as well. In no case should the response to (*d*) and (*e*) consist of undocumented data.

Typical queries illustrating (*a*) through (*e*), respectively, are:

(*a*) Do you have the book by Price with the diagram showing growth of literature? Response: Do you mean *Science Since Babylon* by de Solla Price?

(*b*) Produce a bibliography on the effect of radiation on the production of cancer in mice. Response: 20–100-item list of titles and authors; followed by delivery of a selected dozen or so.

(*c*) Is there a publication on the IBM photo-optical system I can refer to in the paper to be finished tomorrow? Response: News-story.

(*d*) What is the maximum temperature on the surface of the moon? Response: Do you want the mean free

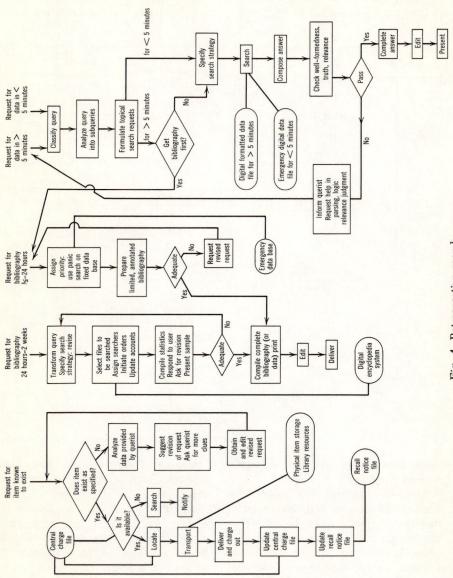

Fig. 4. Retrospective search.

path between collisions of molecules or the temperature of a particular object there?

(*e*) What is the antidote for cobalt poisoning, needed to rescue a recent victim? Response: Information adequate to effect rescue.

Retrospective literature searches are conducted by the Engineering Societies Library at $7/hour and by the Science and Technology Division of the Library of Congress at $8/hour, to name only two such services. At the ESL, for example, an annotated bibliography can be supplied in about two weeks at a cost of approximately $50 on the average. The full resources of this library, including a good subject catalog, but no machines, are used. If Cleverdon's results (1) were to generalize to the ESL service, the recall ratio would be between 0.7 and 0.9 and the relevance ratio about 0.2.

Can any of the numerous proposed computer-based retrospective search systems do significantly better in at least one aspect, such as quality, convenience, or cost? Convenience is often equated with the very short response times characteristic of on-demand service. Consider a "time-shared" system that is aimed at providing on-demand man-machine conversational service at stations remote from the central store and control. Suppose that it had to store the equivalent of the catalog plus indexes for a library, such as those used by ESL in its search service. Assume that the system has three parts: a central processor and multiplexor (CPU), a central store for the index, and N_T remote terminals.

Let U be the total number of users (subscribers) of this system, and suppose that each one poses, on the average, u queries/month. Thus, Uu queries/month must be serviced. If the N terminals are equally distributed among the U users, so that S users, with $S = U/N$, share a terminal, queues at a terminal may form or its use may have to be scheduled. One way to minimize queue-

ing is to assign to a user one primary terminal and a secondary terminal which is to be used if the primary one is busy, and so on. If the user's place of work is distant from these terminals, he should be able to sample its status by telephone. Still, he may wish to schedule his use.

Ideally, of course, each user should have his private terminal. At present this may be economical for touch-tone dataphones. One way to use these in on-demand retrospective searching is for the querist to key in numerical codes for subject headings that he looks up in a subject authority list. He uses this like a telephone book. Suppose that he seeks articles on the effect of alcohol on reaction time. He keys in, say, number 0021 for the predicate "effect of ——— on ———," followed by 0000, for "space," followed by 0123 for "alcohol," then 0000 for "space," then 6730 for "reaction time." Before he has had time to key in more items, he hears a pre-recorded message on the telephone: "You want documents on the effect of alcohol on reaction time? Press *Y* if yes, *N* if no."[1] He presses *Y*. The recording continues: "Press *H* if in humans, *D* if in dogs, *C* if in cats, *R* if in rats." He presses *H* and listens. "Press *T* if you are interested in the effects of alcohol on humans in tracking tasks, *R* if in picture recall, *W* if in heeding a warning signal, *D* if in signal detection, *N* if you don't care in what task."

At the other end there is a computer with an audio-response unit, such as the IBM 7770 & 7772 ($1200/month for 32 words), and other sophisticated devices for accessing complete prerecorded messages. It also has a magnetic disk on which an index is stored. Suppose, for the sake of this calculation, that the index is stored as a table. The table has as many entries as there are subject headings in the authority list, say *T*. The number that the querist looked up in his directory is the (dialable) address of a

[1] Suppose that the letters are coded from 1010 for *A* to 1035 for *Z*.

table entry. The entry consists of all the document identification numbers that have been posted under the subject heading corresponding to this entry. Let D denote the total number of documents in the library which are thus indexed. Each document identification number must consist of at least $\log_2 D$ bits, and more for error detection/correction purposes.

Although each user may have his private touch-tone dataphone [$1/month more than ordinary telephones, plus $25 for a (Modulator) subset, plus $9/month for local telephone line charges, or more for long distance, plus $3/month for a special card dialer], a diversity of more expensive terminals will be needed. Some of these are (very expensive) high-speed printers; others are ordinary typewriter terminals such as the IBM 1050, 2741, or teletypewriters.

Consider a general expression for the cost, C, of providing such aids to retrospective search. It is the sum of four major terms. The first is the cost of using the terminals and being on-line. The second is the cost of using high-speed large storage for the coded index (for example, magnetic disks). The third is the cost of using lesser-speed very large storage of information that can be displayed to the user in English rather than in code (for example, Datacells, microfilm, etc.). The fourth is the cost of using the central processing unit (CPU plus core memory). These give a lower limit on the cost per query, as compared with the $50 or so charged by the Engineering Societies Library.

1. The first term is the product of N_T, the number of terminals, and c_T, the cost, say in dollars/month, per terminal. If S users agree to share a query terminal, U/S query terminals are needed. The cost of renting a query terminal can vary from the $38/month for the touch-tone dataphones already mentioned, to $150/month for a simple teletypewriter, to about $500/month for more sophisticated teletypewriters or

display units with keyboard input, scope display, and some local buffering. Low-cost remote-control I/O terminals with keyboard and display vary in purchase price from about $4000/unit (for example, Sanders Model 720 or Bunker Ramo Teleregister Model 203 on the basis of 8 units) to $6000. To this cost must be added the cost of a control unit which varies from $3500 (for controlling 8 units) to $20,000 (for controlling 12 units). These devices vary in viewing area (from $5'' \times 7''$ to $6\frac{1}{2}'' \times 8\frac{1}{2}''$), in the number of characters that can be displayed (from 32 to 1196), in the character repertoire (from 50 to 64), and especially in the ability to produce vertical/horizontal line drawings.

Updating the files with incoming documents is at least as much of a problem as servicing requests for retrospective search. Let D' be the number of documents per month received by the library. Suppose that the terminals, like those used to service queries but at the more sophisticated end of the spectrum, are used to enter data about these new acquisitions. Suppose, further, that entering these data ties up the terminal for about $\frac{1}{2}$ hour/document. Assuming 22×8 work-hours/month, about 350 documents/month can be entered on one terminal, and $D'/350$ terminals, used solely for this purpose, would be needed. Thus

$$N_T = U/S + D'/350.$$

To estimate c_T, assume a cost of $250/month for the terminal alone, averaged over the various terminal types. To this should be added the service charge for being on-line, which varies from $5 to $30 per terminal hour, typically about $500/month for 25 hours of on-line use during the month. Experience with the existing time-sharing systems indicates that a querist would rarely get off the terminal before half an hour elapsed. Again, one terminal used full-time could accommodate about 350 queries, or uses, per month. If each of U querists posed u queries per month, and these were to arrive in a strict time order, then only $350/u$ querists could be serviced by one fully used terminal. Furthermore, with $S = 350/u$, one of the S querists may find a queue of as many as $S - 1$ other queries ahead of him, or, say, $(S - 1)/2$ on the average. Thus he could expect to wait $(S - 1)/2 \times \frac{1}{2}$ hours before his query gets attention. Once it does, he has the capability for on-line interaction with the system during the half hour while his query is being serviced on the terminal. However, queues for getting on a terminal are hardly tolerable.

To complete the estimation of c_T, the cost of a full-time skilled operator for the terminal as an intermediary between the querist and system should be assumed. Long-distance telephone charges (about \$25/hour, less for WATS) will be ignored here, as will be the services of subject experts to supervise updating and general overhead, which may be as high as 150 per cent of the total cost. A sum of \$350/month is estimated to cover all these costs.

Thus $c_T = \$1100/\text{month},$[2] if each terminal is used only 25 hours/month, that is, with $25/175$ or $\frac{1}{7}$ utilization. Telephone congestion theory suggests that it may be possible to accommodate about $\frac{1}{5}$ of all U users on terminals simultaneously (to avoid queueing even at peak loads). This would make $S = 5$. The number of queries per user per month, u, is probably quite small and variable. Realistic values for u might be around 1 query/user/month. This would suggest using only 2.5 hours/terminal/month, something that is not now offered commercially. A 25 hour/month terminal would have to be shared by $S = 50$ rather than five people, with a possible two-week wait for one of the 50 to get on with his monthly query.

The existing or forthcoming commercial time-sharing services will hardly be able to accommodate more than about 200 simultaneous users without unwelcome delays in response time. That is, U

could be about $5 \times 200 = 1000$. Quite possibly, if each terminal were to be used only 2.5 hours/month, shared by five rare users, then U may be increased. The cost of the terminal (\$250/month) may then be the dominant figure in c_T. It is likely, however, that the use of terminals for retrospective searching will be less than a few per cent of the total varied uses of the terminal and the time-sharing system. If, say, five people with retrospective search requests share a terminal that is used 25 hours/month with users of other services, they may have to wait on a queue. If they insist on on-demand service and have only one query/month each, they will want a 2.5 hours/month terminal, at, say, \$800/month.

2. The second term in the expression for C is the product of K, the number of characters or bytes which have to be in high-speed storage, and c_K, the cost of high-speed storage (\$/character or byte). It will be necessary to store the coded index in this way. This is a table with T entries, where T is the number of subject headings in the subject-authority list. Each entry contains as argument a code for the subject heading. This must be at least $\log_2 T$ bits long, including code identification and check bits. Each entry contains a list of on the average t coded document identification numbers indexed under that term. It is well known that $t = Dd/T$, where d is the average number of index terms per document. The latter varies from 1.6 subject headings per book cataloged by the Library of Congress to as much as 100 in special cases. A typical value for d may be 10. Each document identification number must be at least $\log_2 D$ bits long, plus code identification and check bits.

Taking $D = 2^{20}$ (about a million documents), $T = 2^{15}$ (about 32,000 subject headings) and allowing six bits for code identification and enough additional bits for single-error correction plus double-error detection, about $t \times 32 +$ 27 bits per entry should be allowed.

---

[2] $\$1100 = (250 + 500 + 350)$.

That is about $320 \times 32 + 27$ or about 1285 bytes/entry.[3] Altogether, about $10 \times 2^{22} \doteq 40 \times 10^6$ bytes of storage would be required for this index. The cost of this, estimated at $8000/month for 250 million bytes or characters of disk storage, or $32/million characters/month, is about $1300/month. Adding to this the cost of an audio-response unit would make it about $2500/month.

These costs would, of course, decrease if shared with other types of uses, but at a resulting loss of convenience measured by increased waiting times at various queues.

3. The third term in the expression for C is for the use of Datacells or their equivalent. A Datacell costs $2800/month. Each stores 418 million bytes with about $\frac{1}{2}$-second random access time. Up to eight Datacells can be controlled by one unit costing $700/month. How many Datacells are needed?

Suppose that, as before, $D = 2^{20}$, and that $D' = 2^{13}$ documents/month. That is, the library grows at 96,000 documents/year, about 9.6 per cent. Assume that a technology such as that of Datacells has an obsolescence period of five years, so that a five-year expansion should be planned for. Thus data about $2^{20} + 5 \times 96000 = 1.5$ million documents must be stored. The data to be stored about each document must spell out what is coded in the index table in order to facilitate communication with the user. Assume for each document about 200 characters' worth of data about the author, about 800 characters' for descriptive cataloging (title, collation, etc.), and about 500 characters' for subject cataloging. A Library of Congress Catalog card has, on the average, 440 characters, so that the 1500 characters assumed here can display nearly three times as much information as can be placed on such cards. Thus about $1.5 \times 10^6 \times 1500 = 2250$ million characters

(or bytes) need to be stored. This would require 6 Datacells at a cost of $17,500/month.

4. During the half hour on a terminal that is needed to enter or service a query, at most a few, say T_q, minutes on the Central Processor are needed. To see this, consider servicing a query. A typical query may require the looking up of ten coded subject headings in high-speed storage. For each, a list of about 320 document identification numbers are read out (taking a fraction of a second). These 320 lists are searched for numbers common to all of them. This will require about $(320)^2$ comparisons (6) if each list is unordered, less if it is ordered. Each comparison takes no more than, say, 100 microseconds, as a liberal upper limit. Thus no more than ten seconds are needed to do the searching. Updating the index requires sorting and merging. If done weekly, this may take at most an hour of CPU time or, say, $T_U = 4$ hours/month. Typical costs[4] of CPU time are $c_p = \$180$/hour or $3/minute. Thus no more than $4 \times 180 = \$720$/month is required for updating. Allowing $T_q = 1$ minute of CPU time/query adds $\$(Uu/60) \times 3$/month to this fourth term.

5. The total cost is:

$$C = [N_T c_T] + [Kc_K] + \left[\frac{(D + 5 \cdot 12D')}{400 \times 10^6} \right.$$
$$\left. \times I \times 2800 + 700 \right]$$
$$+ \left[\left(Uu \frac{T_q}{60} + T_u \right) c_p \right]$$
$$= \left[800 \left(\frac{U}{S} + \frac{D'}{350} \right) \right] + 2500$$
$$+ 17,500 + \left(\frac{Uu}{60} + 4 \right) \cdot 180.$$

If $S = 5$ and $u = 1$, and U is of the order of 1000, it is clear that the first term

---

[3] $t = \dfrac{2^{20} \times 10}{2^{15}} = 320$, 1 byte = 8 bits.

[4] At a University Computing Center. It is noteworthy that CPU costs are decreasing even as CPU speeds are increasing. Cost of human labor is increasing.

dominates. The second and fourth terms combined measure the cost of the central configuration, including CPU and high-speed memory. It is negligible in comparison with the other two terms.

If $u = 1$, then U is the number of queries per month to be processed. The cost per query is then, approximately $C/U \doteq 800(1/S + 8000/350 \cdot U) + 20{,}000/U + 180(1/60 + 4/U)$, with $D' = 8000$.

With $S = 5$ and $U = 1000$, the cost per query is approximately \$183. Compare this with the \$50 or so per query by conventional methods. Of course, conventional methods do not permit on-line querying, nor searches of the sophistication possible here, and they do deliver bibliographies within two weeks. If a request for retrospective searching could be met within two weeks, and if the average wait is $\frac{1}{2}((S - 1)/2)$ hours for access to a terminal used 25 hours/month, then two-week ($12\frac{1}{2}$ hour) access can be obtained with $S = 49$, at a cost per query $800(\frac{1}{49} + \frac{1}{44}) + 23 \doteq$ \$53/query.

To reduce the cost per query is to reduce the terminal cost, c_T, or to increase S, the number of users sharing a terminal.

Increasing S means possible delays in getting on the terminal. In a sophisticated service there would, presumably, be a variety of modes and priorities of terminal use, with users who pay more per query having to wait less than others to get on the terminal.

Decreasing c_p means giving up some of the display features of the terminal and foregoing the services of a trained operator. The minimal cost of such a terminal is probably that of a dataphone with audio responses as described earlier, with \$38/month for equipment rental plus, say, \$62/month for being on-line with such an instrument no more than 2.5 hours/month and shared by five users. When there are, say, 10,000 such users, the cost per query could go down to $100/5 + 23 \doteq$ \$43.

5. Technological Advances

Some examples of recent technological developments were introduced when we discussed feasibility and advantages—technical and economic—of a possible retrospective search system. These devices and their use in a system were described in a very sketchy manner, with numerous approximations. It is also important to realize that they are only a small sample of the equipment that is commercially available now and that is becoming available at a very rapid rate.

Processing units are already very fast, in the nanosecond range. In one nanosecond light travels about a foot, so that in a processing unit which is a foot long the travel time for a signal may be as much as the switching time. Nonetheless, trends towards integrated circuit technology and microminiaturization make it reasonable to anticipate CPU's at drastically lowered costs, perhaps one for every few terminals.

Current sort-merge programs for files of up to 25,000 variable length records exist for an IBM 7090 and require 30 minutes maximum. Faster programs that use blocking techniques are being developed. The estimate of an hour/week for updating an index on the newer machines, such as the IBM system 360, is surely a conservative upper limit.

Of the three parts of a system—the central processor, the large, slower auxiliary stores, and the terminals—the latter are most likely to be congested if utilized at a high rate. The CPU is most likely to be idle while there are queues to obtain access to the large shared stores. This suggests utilizing the fast CPU for processing tasks other than those of routine updating and servicing of queries. Preparation of concordances as aids to indexing is a possibility. For an average text of 3000 words, it now takes about five minutes of IBM 7090 time to prepare a concordance. A Permuted Title Index for 2000 to 3000 documents can be made in about 30 minutes. Syntactic analysis of sentences in documents to be indexed for file updating is another possibility.

In addition to large digital stores, such as the IBM Datacell and RCA's RACE, a number of devices are under development, for example, a trillion-bit file being developed by IBM for the Atomic Energy Commission in Livermore. Such very large memories would be applicable for storage of full text, graphic data, and special formatted files. The contents of the National Union Catalog, for example, would require storage of this capacity. So would the "Digital encyclopedia system" file shown at the bottom of Fig. 1a. The "Emergency digital data file" in Fig. 4 would require faster access time to probably not as large a data base, and disks (magnetic or photoscopic) may suffice. Core storage would probably be reserved for the housekeeping functions of the central processor. There would be no direct transmission into core except from auxiliary disk-type memories. The latter might be used mainly to let a limited amount of (expensive, fast) core memory act as if it were much larger by swapping program segments back and forth between core and disks (with return from core to disk via drum, for example). Disks would also be used to store a coded version of the index.

Beyond digital storage techniques, there are impressive developments in microform transport, copying, and recording technologies. The IBM 1350 photo-image system, for example, transports a 70×35 millimeter film chip through pneumatic tubes at 25 feet per second to a station where a chip image is created by contact with the microfilm in an aperture card. It can service about 1000 random requests for chips in one hour. Such stores are close to that end of a spectrum of information stores exemplified by Xerox copies and books/journals in conventionally printed form. Technologies for long-distance transmission of Xerox copies and slow-scan tele-

vision are also advancing impressively, but the kind of systems illustrated arithmetically in Section 4 may show that such techniques are not yet competitive with airmail transport of tapes or hard copies.

Whereas conventional voice-grade telephone lines permit transmission of about 2000 bits/second, at standard rates, experiments in transmission of digital data over a transatlantic cable have shown that 8000 bits/second can be reliably transmitted ($20,000/month for a leased line). If time-division communication systems replace current methods during the next decade, costs can be expected to decrease further. Important trade-off studies involving the use of high-capacity (and high-cost) channels for transmitting rarely requested, centrally stored data, as compared to duplicating (for example, on microfilm) much of the central store at each regional center, are required. The possibility of implementing a network of such regional centers—each one of them servicing, through concentrators, local computing centers—is one of the most important developments in systems technology. There as already a wealth of options among communication channels. The amount of traffic in digitally encoded messages is already nearly equal to the amount of voice traffic over telephone lines and is growing at a much faster rate. With Voice PCM (Pulse Code Modulation) the distinction between transmission of analog or digital signals may become very subtle. Table 1 gives a general view of what is commercially available in the communications industry.

Terminals have already been mentioned. Input of text via punched cards requires the labor of keypunching and verification, about 1 cent/word. Storage on magnetic tapes is economical for archival purposes; a reel of tape costs about $32 and can readily store 30,000 references (titles, authors, and other descriptive data and subject headings).

TABLE 1

Analog	Bandwidth	Digital	Kilobits per second
		TWX	100
Voice	4 KC	TELEX	100
		Dataphone	2.4
Telpak A	48 KC	Telpak A	18–20
Telpak B	100 KC	Telpak B	36–40
Telpak C	240 KC	Telpak C	100
Telpak D	1 MC	Telpak D	500
Half-Video	2 MC	T-1 carrier	1500 short-haul
Video	4 MC	T-2	6000
"Exotic"	up to 20 MC	T-4	220 000

A charge of about $5 is made for having an operator mount a reel of tape, however. It takes several minutes to search a reel of tape. Automatic character-reading devices exist now only for limited fonts. The IBM optical reader ($3,000/month), for example, reads 480 characters of a single font from about 400 documents/minute. Another commercially used reader, by Rabinow, can also read a single standard font at comparable speed, high reliability, and at a cost of $84,000; this firm is also delivering custom-made multifont readers, at considerably higher cost, to special customers. Voice-recognition devices are still very far from practical availability. On the display side, there are impressive advances in photocomposing technology. Current devices produce only 12 pages/hour and use about one minute of computer time per page. Devices that produce a multifont transparent master of high quality, including graphics, at 600 characters/second, and are driven by magnetic tape, are under development. So are sophisticated terminals permitting on-line editing. Facilities for producing copies of such masters at two to ten cents/page are now commercially available.

The quantity and quality of current accomplishments in information systems technology match the pace at which it is advancing. An attempt at completely cataloguing the state of the art would thus be obsolete before it is complete. The state of the art and growth in software is now nearly the same as that in hardware. Indeed, some software systems are beginning to look for hardware implementations of significant functions.

Modes of use—for example, standard operating procedures—and system design techniques are still in a primitive stage of development. Application areas have yet to be logically structured, and this article is a contribution toward structuring the area of information retrieval in its relation to systems technology.

A minimal system for retrospective search, such as that sketched in Fig. 4 and discussed in Section 4, is barely realizable at this time even with the impressive current state of information systems technology. The Central charge file, for example, should allow a person who knows of the existence of a certain paper but does not recall the exact title or even all details of the author's name to (*a*) ascertain the existence of this item in the library and (*b*) to determine its availability, within seconds or minutes at most. As many as half of all items cataloged in a library may be unavailable at one time, for one reason or another. To determine whether the library holds an ill-specified but existing item, the entire catalog would have to be available and would have to be searched with intelligence. Storing the catalog of a million-item library so as to allow user-machine conversation could be accomplished with a Datacell, as already indicated, but the response times will be in seconds. Delivering the wanted item can also be accomplished with recently announced technology, for example, the IBM photo image retrieval system.

Tying all the different technologies together into a total system requires special interfaces and considerable system-design and development work that is very costly and time-consuming. To implement a reasonably sophisticated retrospective search system in, say, three years would require a major, concerted effort—almost at the pace of a crash program. It is hard to imagine that retrospective searching could seem sufficiently worthwhile to generate this kind of urgency. Users may continue to complain about current inadequacies in retrospective search, but it is questionable whether they will enthusiastically invest in or buy an improved retrospective search service, if only that is offered. Even if improved current awareness services are also added, it is doubtful whether this will make much difference.

It is assumed here that a genuine latent need exists for an improved tutorial information service, such as that shown in Figs. 1a and b. The assumption that such service is worthwhile and could generate the sense of urgency needed to mobilize the needed resources for the realization of a system in a reasonable time period is based on the dramatic increase of interest on the part of universities (for example, EDUCOM) and new business enterprises generated by recent developments in closer man-machine coupling (for example, computer-based instruction and on-line debugging).

What would it take to demonstrate, by construction and operation of a significant prototype, that such a system is technically and socioeconomically feasible? An analysis such as was undertaken in Section 4 for a retrospective search system, is much more difficult in this case because there are as yet no good procedures for grouping documents that "belong together," and no good designs for a data structure such as that underlying the "Digital encyclopedia system" which allows storage and retrieval of record segments.

I. Technical feasibility
  A. Standard operating procedures and forms for management and users of a tutorial information service
    1. What information does a user need to decide how deeply to delve into a document, if at all? Answers to this are prerequisite to the design of a questionnaire or checklist for the evaluation report. The applicability of current techniques in survey design supports belief that useful answers can be obtained.
    2. What types of instruction does a user need as a function of how much he already understands? The impetus to research on such questions due to computer-based instruction is quite likely to produce partial answers. Such answers are critical for rational design of data structures to represent the works of synthesis, so as to allow a user to get as much or as little detail as he needs, and to decide when and where to plunge into deeper detail if a short synopsis of a topic is given. Similar questions also relate to design of data structures for representing bibliographic, biographic, and topical records.
    3. By what criteria can the extent to which a querist's need is met be determined?
    4. In a man-machine conversational mode, which functions in the processes of linguistic/logical query analysis, query classification, query reformulation, recog-

nition of query recurrence, judgments of relevance, etc., should be assigned to hardware, which to software, which to clerical-type people with standard operating procedures, which to other types of people?

5. What languages should be available for different kinds of users in which to formulate the questions, instructions, and responses to the system?

6. What procedures are there for guaranteeing the integrity of messages that are generated, stored, transmitted, processed, or displayed in the system? For preventing, detecting, or correcting errors? For safeguarding against accidental or deliberate invasion of privacy or confidentiality of sensitive data or mismanagement of the system?

B. Data bases

1. There are already a large number of significant collections of indexed documents on magnetic tape. MEDLARS has now over 15 reels of tapes with about 30,000 references (subject heading, title) per tape. NASA has a similarly large number. EURATOM has close to 100,000 references in *Nuclear Science Abstracts* on tape, and the collection amassed by Chemical Abstract Services is equally impressive. How can all these tapes, in their different formats and their great number and diversity, be used together, if a total, integrated search service were to be developed?

2. Vast quantities of text (and graphics) are printed by means of linotype machines or transmitted in digital codes over communication channels, making it feasible to process such data by digital computers. The full text of the *New York Times,* for ex-

ample, exists on (uncorrected) perforated paper tape. It is possible, although not simple, to read such tapes into disks or cores and perform content analyses on the text by computer.

C. Software

1. What are efficiently automated procedures for managing the on-line generation of evaluation reports, bibliographic, biographic, and topical records by many users "simultaneously"? Experience in the development of time-sharing systems should be applicable to this problem.

2. What are effective algorithms and programs for grouping related documents? What information should be supplied about each document to make possible decisions about whether two documents "belong together"?

3. What are good strategies and programs for loading data into a data structure (updating files) and searching data structures in response to various queries?

4. What are efficient procedures for parsing sentences in the one or several languages used in a conversational mode? For translating certain command sentences into actual operations? For transforming interrogative sentences into answer-searching routines?

D. Hardware

1. What interfaces must be provided to permit a variety of on-line terminals of differing sophistication to be tied into the same system?

2. On what basis should priorities be assigned to the development of the numerous competing technologies for very large memories? It is more a question of providing guidance for the idea- and technology-rich hardware development arts than searching for new technologies or develop-

ments that would meet the needs which are now not being met. This guidance will not come from a better understanding of needs to be met but, rather, from what can be put on the market that is sufficiently attractive in flexibility, convenience of use, reliability, and cost.

3. How can hardware be used to support software developments?

II. Socioeconomic feasibility

A. Generating and satisfying demand

1. How valuable is convenience in using a computer? Programmers with access to an on-line terminal for debugging can do in a few days to one week what it took them two to four weeks to complete by using the conventional facilities of a computing center (one to eight hours turnaround time). Students with ten hours of preprogrammed tutorial instruction in elementary statistics could pass the same examination with higher grades than students who studied the same topic in an one-semester college course. Problems that would otherwise not be programmed, topics otherwise not studied, questions otherwise not asked, would be undertaken if it were sufficiently "convenient" to do so. People who would otherwise not avail themselves of information systems technology would do so if it is sufficiently "convenient."

2. How much less is a ten-second response worth than an one-second response, assuming the same response? How does this relation vary with the types of queries to which the responses are relevant?

3. How does the accuracy and precision of a response relate to its value. A response to "What is the elevation of Boulder, Colorado?" asserting "Between 2,000 and 8,000 ft. above sea level" is accurate but imprecise; the response, "Between 6153 and 6159 ft. above sea level" is more precise but inaccurate. Which is more valuable?

4. What is the distribution of users over services of different value (that is, quality)? Relatively few users will pay a high price for very high-quality service and probably very few will pay anything for *very* low-quality service. How does quality of service rendered relate to convenience (that is, response time, simplicity of conversational language, adequate features for display and generation of information input, etc.), to precision, accuracy, and complexity of the question?

5. What is the frequency of use— in, say, queries per user per month—as a function of query type and the distribution of response quality over query types?

B. Costs and supply

1. How does the cost of supplying a terminal vary with the quantity purchased and the quality? What are the prime determinants of quality for different-purpose terminals? How much less costly is an input-only device than a device with input as well as printer or display output capability? How much more costly is a device permitting hard-copy production in addition to display?

2. How does the cost of a large memory vary with the total storage capacity, the mean and variance of the time to produce a response, and the serial readrate?

3. How do these costs vary with time, not assuming revolutionary technological advances?

4. What are the costs of software support as a function of system size, quality of service, and time

schedule of implementation? How are these costs changing with time?

5. What is a reasonable projection for availability of hardware and software as a function of time between order placement and delivery?

C. Organizational

1. How can the best minds capable of literature synthesis in a field of knowledge be motivated to contribute new works of synthesis in novel forms? What will compete with the prestige of leading professional publications, the royalties of a good publishing enterprise, the existing system of editors, referees, reviewers, promotion, and distribution?

2. How can top creative minds in a field of knowledge be motivated to submit objective, thoughtful, critical, and informative evaluation reports? How can this system improve on the existing procedures for evaluating literature both before and after publication?

3. What is the best way of managing an enterprise involving so many intimate man-machine partnerships? How should the management tasks be divided between machines and men?

4. What determines the inherent stability of a tutorial information system? Under what conditions will the system be able to control perturbations due to injection of *some* deviant inputs, some misuse or abuse? What can be done to allay inherent fears about authoritarian control, bias toward special interests, and stifling of full creativity and freedom of expression?

6. Conclusions

The preceding list of questions is a formidable one. Some of the questions are best answered by constructing a system with "quick-and-dirty" solutions to problems for which there is as yet no sound basis, and using the system to compile the needed empirical data upon which to build a rationale.

It can, of course, be argued that considerably more theoretical research is needed before any attempt at construction should be made. It might, for example, be required that an information-retrieval system must: mechanically recognize whether input strings are well-formed, whether they are questions or declarations; formally produce output strings in response to input strings which are not only well-formed but logically true and relevant. Then theoretical problems pertaining to structural ambiguity of sentences, for example, to the use of first-order predicate calculus (which is undecidable), would be considered fundamental. It is, of course, unrealistic to impose such requirements on an IR system which, if successfully implemented and managed, could still be an exciting enterprise and have significant social impact. Therefore, such theoretical questions were not included among those to be answered in showing the technical and socioeconomic feasibility of a tutorial information service.

It is true that there are deep theoretical problems underlying these questions. It is far from clear, however, that existing theoretical work can shed much light on them. The creation of a new theory suitable for the fundamental problems that are relevant to *real* rather than hypothesized systems will probably have to be preceded by a phase of empirical data gathering. We are, perhaps, in a stage comparable to that of the early life sciences, when naturalistic observations and classification of empirical data were a far more reputable activity than speculative theorizing, even if it was mathematically sophisticated and profound.

For these reasons, a well-managed and boldly conceived enterprise for a tutorical information system appears to be the most recommendable next major step. This does not, of course, reduce the current critical need for more and better high-level investigations into the mathematical and conceptual underpinnings of more rationally designed information-retrieval systems. Such research into basic problems is inevitably a slow process, and its progress and progress on IR systems technology can occur independently. The success of the proposed tutorial information system for a specific subject area depends almost entirely on entrepreneurial-mangerial genius in mobilizing the high-quality resources that could now be brought to bear on such a project.

REFERENCES

1. Cleverdon, C. W., "Report on the Testing and Analysis of an Investigation into the Comparative Efficiency of Indexing Systems," ASLIB Report, Coll. Aeronautics, Cranfield, Bucks Co., U.K., October 1962.
2. Irick, Paul, "Highway Research Information Service," *Traffic Engineering and Control,* October 1965, pp. 385–388; see also Irick, P. E., and W. N. Carey, Jr. The New Highway Research Information Service, *Highway Res. News,* No. 18, March 1965, pp. 5–15.
3. Kochen, M., *Some Problems in Information Science,* New York: Scarecrow Press, 1965.
4. Kochen, M., *Information Retrieval System Theory,* in preparation.
5. National Science Foundation, *Current Research and Development in Scientific Documentation,* No. 14, 1965.
6. Wong, E., "Time Estimation in Boolean Index Searching," *High-Speed Document Perusal,* final report on contract AF49(638)-1062 by M. Kochen to AFOSR, 5/1/62, pp. 69–81.

Name Index

Subject Index

Abstracting, 97, 131, 280, 351
Abstracts, use in indexing, 347
Abuse, in IR systems, 355
  see also Protection
Academicians, rule by, 15
  see also Encyclopedias; World brain
Acceptance, selective, 133
Acceptance rate, 4, 132, 142
  see also Evaluation; Relevance, ratio
Access, xi, 82, 99, 133, 213, 250, 356
  see also Hit-rate; Response time; Storage
Access time, requirements for, 109
Accessions, 97
  see also Acquisitioning
Accidents, in IR systems, 258, 355
  see also Protection
Accounting, in a library, 112, 334
Accuracy, of a retrieval system, 174, 178
  see also Evaluation; Hit-rate
Acquisitioning, 97, 334, 356
  see also Libraries
Action points, definition of, 128
  see also Business Intelligence System; Intelligence
Adaptive bioservo system, 217
Adaptive concept processing, 185
  see also Concepts
Adaptive library, 111, 202, 222
Administration, x
Administrative terminal system, 262
Administrator, information needs of, 40
Advanced Research Projects Agency (ARPA), 139, 253, 255
Aerodynamics, as test corpus for IR experiments, 342
Agriculture, national library of (NAL), 99, 122
Alerting service, 41, 154
Algebra, as topic for question-answering by machine, 284
Ambiguities, 218, 240, 295, 296, 331, 342
  mechanical resolution, 298
  semantic, 295
  syntactic, 295
AMNIPS (Adaptive Man-Machine Non-arithmetic Information Processing System), 142, 185, 194, 202, 203
  see also Relational data files

Analysis of variance, in IR, 176
  see also Clusters
Androidology, 241, 243
Answering, 310
  see also Questions
Archival material, 110
Arrearages, in libraries, 352
Articulateness, 52
Artifacts, 241
  see also Artificial intelligence
Artificial agent, 240, 241
  see also Artificial intelligence
Artificial intelligence, 206, 248, 292, 307
Artificial language, 295
  see also Interlingua; Programming languages
Assimilation of information, 51, 209, 210
Association of ideas, 32, 202
Associative indexing, 280
Associative information retrieval, 351
  see also AMNIPS
Associative memories, *see* AMNIPS; Memory; Storage
Associative processing, 103
Astronomy, as a topic for question-answering by machine, 277, 282
Attributes, 187, 266
  see also Concepts
Attrition of unassimilated information, 214
  see also Purging; Weeding
Audio-response unit, 361
Author citations, 111
  see also Citations
Authoritarian control, dangers of, 355
  see also World brain
Authoritative elite, 15
  see also World brain
Authority lists, 337
  see also Indexing; Subject, headings; Thesauri
Automata, 241
  theory, 289
  see also Androidology
Automatic abstracting, 131, 280
  see also Abstracting
Automatic content analysis, 337
Automatic index, 47

381